CROSSO
PICTUREE

Children's Literature and Culture
Jack Zipes, *Series Editor*

For a complete series list, please go to
routledge.com

CROSSOVER PICTUREBOOKS

A Genre for All Ages

SANDRA L. BECKETT

Routledge
Taylor & Francis Group
NEW YORK AND LONDON

First published 2012
by Routledge
711 Third Avenue, New York, NY 10017

Simultaneously published in the UK
by Routledge
2 Park Square, Milton Park, Abingdon, Oxon OX14 4RN

Routledge is an imprint of the Taylor & Francis Group, an informa business

First issued in paperback 2013

Typeset in Minion by IBT Global.

Library of Congress Cataloging in Publication Data
Beckett, Sandra L., 1953–
   Crossover picturebooks : a genre for all ages / Sandra Beckett.
     p. cm. — (Children's literature and culture ; 82)
   Includes bibliographical references and index.
  1. Picture books. 2. Picture books—Publishing. 3. Picture books—Bibliography. 4. Books and reading. I. Title.
  Z1033.P52B43 2011
  002—dc23
  2011022878

ISBN13: 978-0-415-73037-2 (pbk)
ISBN13: 978-0-415-87230-0 (hbk)
ISBN13: 978-0-203-15403-8 (ebk)

To Paul, Jordan, Jeremy, Jason, and Danielle
in loving appreciation of their support and encouragement

Contents

List of Figures

Series Editor's Foreword

Dedicated to furthering original research in children's literature and culture, the Children's Literature and Culture series includes monographs on individual authors and illustrators, historical examinations of different periods, literary analyses of genres, and comparative studies on literature and the mass media. The series is international in scope and is intended to encourage innovative research in children's literature with a focus on interdisciplinary methodology.

Children's literature and culture are understood in the broadest sense of the term children to encompass the period of childhood up through adolescence. Owing to the fact that the notion of childhood has changed so much since the origination of children's literature, this Routledge series is particularly concerned with transformations in children's culture and how they have affected the representation and socialization of children. While the emphasis of the series is on children's literature, all types of studies that deal with children's radio, film, television, and art are included in an endeavor to grasp the aesthetics and values of children's culture. Not only have there been momentous changes in children's culture in the last fifty years, but there have been radical shifts in the scholarship that deals with these changes. In this regard, the goal of the Children's Literature and Culture series is to enhance research in this field and, at the same time, point to new directions that bring together the best scholarly work throughout the world.

Jack Zipes

Acknowledgments

Many people and organizations have contributed in various ways to this study. Unfortunately, it is impossible to name them all. I am particularly indebted to the many authors and illustrators around the globe who have graciously discussed their work with me and generously granted permission for it to be reproduced in this book. Their names will become evident in the pages of *Crossover Picturebooks*. I would like to extend my collective thanks to the many friends and colleagues who have contributed in some way to this book, in particular Diane Bielicki, Nina Christensen, Corrado Federici, Yukiko Fukumoto, Vanessa Joosen, Lena Kåreland, Maria Nikolajeva, Junko Nishimura, Lissa Paul, Jean Perrot, Kimberley Reynolds, Rolf Romören, Zohar Shavit, Masaki Tomoko, Thomas van der Walt, Anne de Vries, and Jack Zipes. My deep gratitude goes to the staff at the International Youth Library in Munich and the International Institute for Children's Literature, Osaka, notably Jochen Weber and Yasuko Doi. I wish to thank Four Courts Press and Routledge for permission to reprint extracts of essays published in *Studies in Children's Literature 1500–2000* and *New Directions in Picturebook Research*, respectively. I should further like to acknowledge the generous financial support of the Social Sciences and Humanities Research Council of Canada, Brock University Chancellor's Chair for Research Excellence, the Humanities Research Centre at Brock University, and Brock University Experience Works. Very special thanks go to my research assistants, Darcy Berry, Assuntina Del Gobbo, and Carlene Thomas, who have enthusiastically shared my passion for crossover picturebooks.

Chapter One
Picturebooks as a Crossover Genre

There is no art for children, there is Art. There are no graphics for children, there are graphics. . . . There is no literature for children, there is literature.
—François Ruy-Vidal

Crossover Picturebooks: A Genre for All Ages is a follow-up to *Crossover Fiction: Global and Historical Perspectives*, which was published by Routledge in 2009. The earlier book deals generally with the phenomenon of crossover literature, and more specifically with novels and short fiction that cross from child to adult or adult to child audiences, while the present study focuses on picturebooks for all ages. The original intention was to include picturebooks in the first volume, but crossover literature is such an important and largely unexplored cultural phenomenon that a single book was insufficient to address all the genres that transcend age boundaries. Although crossover fiction is now widely recognized as a distinct literary form and marketing category by critics, publishers, booksellers, writers, and readers, the term "crossover" is still often used only to refer to children's and young adult novels read by adults. Picturebooks have not generally been seen as part of the crossover phenomenon, even though the trend of picturebooks for all ages pre-dated the landmark Harry Potter series. In September 1997, prior to the crossover hype, Judith Rosen published "Breaking the Age Barrier," one of the rare articles in English-speaking countries to deal not only with young adult fiction but also with picturebooks. The almost complete lack of attention paid to picturebooks within the discussion of crossover literature in most countries is particularly surprising since, more than any other genre, they can genuinely be books for all ages. This study seeks to address the neglect of a genre that deserves special attention within the widespread and ever expanding global trend of crossover literature.

1

Picturebooks are quite distinct from other narrative forms due to the complex interplay of text and image (or, perhaps more accurately, verbal and visual texts). In her insightful study *Radical Children's Literature*, Kimberley Reynolds attributes much of children's literature's ability to stimulate and nurture innovation to the fact that "many children's texts operate two semiotic systems simultaneously: the visual and the textual." Referring to picturebooks in particular in a 1990 article, David Lewis attributes their capacity for innovation to what he calls their "inescapably plural" nature.[1] This unique feature of picturebooks is what makes them one of the most exciting and innovative contemporary literary genres. It is often the experimental or "radical" nature of these picturebooks that gives them appeal with adults as well as children, as I discussed in a paper titled "Breaking Boundaries with Radical Picture Books" in 2002.[2] This is not an entirely new phenomenon, as Chapter 2 clearly demonstrates, but today's picturebooks repeatedly challenge the conventions, codes, and norms that traditionally governed the genre. Profound, often controversial content, some of which will be discussed in Chapter 5, and complex narrative strategies—hybrid genres, polyfocalization, metafictive discourse, intertextuality, parody, irony, and so forth—in both text and image provide narratives that are attracting an ever-increasing older audience of adolescents and adults to the genre. Several studies examine the so-called sophisticated techniques of contemporary picturebooks that are often referred to as "postmodernist," but without considering them in the context of the crossover phenomenon.[3] The innovative graphics and creative, often complex dialogue between text and image provide multiple levels of meaning and invite readings on different levels by all ages.

Picturebooks offer a unique opportunity for a collaborative or shared reading experience between children and adults, since they empower the two audiences more equally than other narrative forms. Carole Scott seems to place crossover picturebooks among the masterpieces of children's literature for this reason when she writes: "I believe that enduring works of children's literature are those with dual address that speak to both children and adults, and that picturebooks offer the greatest equality in the reading experience, since pre-literate children can engage in reading the pictures as the adult reads them the verbal text." As she and many other critics now point out, modern children often have better visual literacy skills than adults.[4] In addition to being more skilled at reading graphic details, they are often more receptive to untraditional visual and verbal narratives than adults. When the German edition of David Wiesner's *The Three Pigs* (2001) appeared in 2002, it provoked a controversial discussion about whether it was a book for children, for adults, or for all ages. Despite the age recommendation of four years and up, many critics found it difficult to believe that children could understand the 2002 Caldecott Medal-winning picturebook, which presents rather difficult philosophical ideas about reality and fiction.[5] However, Lawrence Sipe's 2008 case study convincingly demonstrates that young children can appreciate and even offer surprisingly sophisticated interpretations of this complex text.[6] Child-to-adult crossover literature is often equated with "dumbing down," but in actual fact, many crossover picturebooks offer challenging reading experiences for adults as well as children.

The picturebook has traditionally been seen as a children's genre. The critic Barbara Bader expressed this widespread view in 1976 when she wrote that a picturebook is "foremost an experience for a child" and Perry Nodelman echoes it in 1988 when he describes picturebooks as "books intended for young children."[7] A preliminary comment in a 1993 edition of *Papers* sums up the situation in the following words: "The picture book has, since its creation, been considered the prerogative of the young child. It will take much persuasion to destroy this image, despite the complexities which are quite clearly seen in today's picture books."[8] In the eyes of many contemporary authors and illustrators, the picturebook is a narrative form that can address any or all age groups. Authors and illustrators often deny and defy publishers' very age-specific categories of readers. Publishers themselves are questioning these borders and even creating series for all ages. The picturebook is, after all, merely a format. In 1997, Regina Hayes, president and publisher of Viking Children's Books, who has brought out a number of crossover picturebooks, used the fact that the picturebook is "just a format" to argue that there is no reason why its audience should be limited to children. Averse to the term "sophisticated picture books," she prefers to think of the works of the authors and illustrators she publishes, including J. otto Seibold, Jon Scieszka, Maira Kalman, and Istvan Banyai, as "'bridge books,' since they form a bridge between traditional picture books and longer works." The same year, the vice-president and associate publisher at Disney/Hyperion, Ken Geist, admitted he deliberately tries to place some crossover titles in a picturebook format.[9] Why should stories that fit into the thirty-two-page picturebook format automatically be released as children's books? The perception that picturebooks are essentially a genre for children is shifting more rapidly in some countries than others. In Norway, where the term *allalderslitteratur* (all-ages-literature) was coined in the 1980s, picturebooks are now widely considered under this rubrique as well. The crossover appeal of *Garmanns Sommer* (2006; English trans., *Garmann's Summer*), which was the first book from the Nordic countries to win the Bologna Ragazzi Award in 2007, is, according to the author-illustrator Stian Hole, "a characteristic trait in modern Scandinavian picture books, which are often labeled 'All-age books.'"[10]

Maurice Sendak, probably the world's best-known picturebook artist, has been claiming for years that "we have created an arbitrary division between adult and children's books that does not exist." Although he refers here to children's literature in general, using the example of Lewis Carroll, who "didn't set out to write for children," but rather to "writ[e] books," his own concern is picturebooks in particular: "What I write takes as much intense effort, as much creativity and dramatic sense as the so-called grown-up books."[11] When *Outside Over There* was released by Harper and Row in 1981 as a book for both children and adults, Sendak told Selma Lanes that he had "waited a long time to be taken out of kiddy-book land and allowed to join the artists of America."[12] Geraldine

DeLuca suggests, however, that "Sendak, in his quest for both audiences, may actually be leaving the child behind."[13] A number of critics expressed the view that Sendak's *We Are All in the Dumps with Jack and Guy*, published in 1993, is no longer a picturebook for children. Jane Doonan writes that it might seem that "only adults with a religious background, and with knowledge of the Holocaust, would be able to make anything of *Dumps* and that Sendak has produced a picture book for them rather than for children." This is not, however, the opinion of the critic, who continues: "It would be truer to say that he has created something that does not conform to generic expectations about picture books as children's literature only. *Dumps* shares with certain other modern picture books a quality that was formerly the preserve of folk and fairy tales: an open address."[14]

Sendak's views were shared by innovative publishers of the time and some children's publishing houses were founded with the express goal of producing picturebooks that abolish boundaries between children's literature and adult literature. One of the unsung pioneers was Robert Delpire, who was the first French publisher of Sendak's *Where the Wild Things Are*, published as *Max et les Maximonstres* in 1967. Delpire was at the origin of a graphic and thematic renewal of the picturebook that preceded the daring innovations of Harlin Quist and François Ruy-Vidal. The intended audience of the sophisticated children's books published by the controversial American publisher Harlin Quist has always been a subject of debate. His remarkable works were avant-garde when he began publishing in the 1960s and they remain so today. They featured some of Europe's most innovative young artists, including Nicole Claveloux, Étienne Delessert, and Henri Galeron, many of whom launched their careers with Harlin Quist. The unique and quirky look he brought to children's book publishing during the late 1960s left an indelible mark that is expressed in a *New York Times* statement printed on the back cover of one of the most famous Quist books, *The Geranium on the Windowsill Just Died but Teacher You Went Right On* (1971): "There are few publishers whose books are so distinctive that the mention of their names conjures up an immediate picture of a recognizable style. One such publisher is Harlin Quist." Despite the immediate attention and wide acclaim his books attracted everywhere sales in the United States did not match the enthusiasm. With the exception of a few bestselling titles like *The Geranium on the Windowsill Just Died*, which sold over half a million copies, they were bought primarily by a loyal following of adults. In North America today, they are remembered chiefly by a relatively small number of collectors who appreciate their innovation and striking artwork and design.

In 1968, a year after the creation of Harlin Quist Books, Quist established a partnership with François Ruy-Vidal that enabled him to publish and distribute his books in Europe as well as in the United States. During the six years he worked with Quist, Ruy-Vidal convinced great names of French literature, such as Eugene Ionesco and Marguerite Duras, to publish for children. His philosophy was to never work with children's authors and illustrators. Quist and Ruy-Vidal published the first of Ionesco's classic children's stories, *Conte numéro 1* (English trans., *Story Number 1*), in 1968, the same year that the four Contes pour enfants de moins de trois ans (Stories for children under the age of three) appeared in the author's memoir, *Présent passé, passé présent* (1968; English trans., *Present Past, Past Present*). In a *New York Times* article devoted to "Picture Books" in 1970, Barbara Novak, an influential theorist of American art, suggests that Ionesco's "radical innovation" pushed the children's book market further into "simple-mindedness and banality," producing books that are "an insult to any self-respecting age group." With regard to *Story Number 2* in particular, she writes: "It is the most natural thing in the world for Ionesco to write for children. The reversal of usual relationships, the fantasy, the credibility he donates to the incredible, along with the sheer delight in nonsense, all are more readily assimilable by children than by their elders." Novak sees Ionesco's tale, in which "reality becomes a matter of many alternative choices," proof of a counter trend of increasingly sophisticated picturebooks.[15] In *Radical Children's Literature*, Kimberley Reynolds uses the example of Ionesco's tales to show how "during the time when it was regarded as a mode suited only for the nursery, nonsense . . . anticipated and was called into the service of modernist movements in literature."[16] Children's literature provided the Theatre of the Absurd playwright with a genre in which he could pursue his aesthetic experiments with language and the absurd, and he introduces young readers to some rather complex notions in his deceptively simple stories. All the Harlin Quist books had a very European look and to this day they remain unique in American children's publishing.

Throughout the 1960s and 1970s, François Ruy-Vidal worked with several publishing houses, radically transforming the world of children's books by publishing authors and illustrators who were not specialized in children's literature. Critics often reproached him for creating books for adults rather than children, but Ruy-Vidal categorically refused to accept the specificity of children's literature. The theories he formulated more than forty years ago could constitute the credo of many crossover authors, illustrators, and publishers today:

> There is no art for children, there is Art. There are no graphics for children, there are graphics. There are no colours for children, there are colours. There is no literature for children, there is literature. Based on these four principles, we can say that a children's book is a good book when it is a good book for everyone.[17]

Ruy-Vidal was not merely echoing the vague, oft-expressed view of C. S. Lewis and many other authors: that a good children's book also appeals to adults. He was determined to avoid publishing books that were "formatted, targeted, utilitarian," so that he would be open to the more "authentic" projects proposed to him by authors and illustrators. Rejecting what he called the "false books" that abounded in children's publishing, his formula was to produce true books, that is, unique, creative works that take risks, have an emotional charge, and provoke reaction and reflection on the part of the reader. In addition to this precise notion of literature, Ruy-Vidal's goal was to "restore to children's book illustration . . .

its *lettres de noblesse* by ridding it of the stereotypes that traditionalist publishing was abusing,"[18] a goal he set out to achieve by engaging some of the most controversial young illustrators of the day, not only in the books he published with Harlin Quist but also in the many books he brought out later. Ruy-Vidal's groundbreaking children's books caused quite a stir in France in the 1960s and they continued to surprise and provoke in subsequent years.

Like his precursors Harlin Quist and François Ruy-Vidal, the French author and publisher Christian Bruel is known for his pioneering, visually sophisticated, and often provocative picturebooks whose ambivalent audience has been the subject of similar controversy. Between 1976 and 1996, Bruel directed the experimental publishing house Le Sourire qui mord (The biting smile), which had its origins in a collective of scholars, journalists, and artists created following the events of May 1968 with the aim of rethinking and renewing children's picturebooks. Their philosophy is hidden in the anagram of the publishing house's unusual name, "Le risque ou dormir" (Risk or sleep). It was founded with the express intention of breaking down the barrier between child and adult readers and eliminating the stereotypes and taboos in children's literature. Bruel objects to the idea of "livres pour enfants" (books for children), promoting instead stories that are accessible to children yet touch adults. "To make books for children is an error," he claimed in 1970, proposing instead that it is more appropriate "to make books that can be put into children's hands also." The publisher's views never changed. Two years before the disappearance of Le Sourire qui mord, the first page of the 1994 catalogue insists that a book is ultimately about "life," life that can sometimes be "crunched between baby teeth and wisdom teeth. . . ."

A number of avant-garde publishing houses were created with the intention of working especially with the image and graphic storytelling. Danielle Dastugue, who created Éditions du Rouergue in 1986, decided, in 1993, to develop a series of children's books largely dedicated to images and contemporary graphic expression. The catalyst for the new children's collection was the talented young artist Olivier Douzou, who came to her with the storyboard for his first book, *Jojo La Mache*, in 1993, and agreed to become the director. Determined to create unique books that would expand and renew the field of children's publishing, they published, for the most part, first-time illustrators from France as well as all over Europe, Latin America, Canada, and the United States. Critics generally agree that Rouergue's picturebooks are among the most innovative publications in French children's publishing in the 1990s. The publishing house has also gained an international reputation and a number of titles have been translated into several languages. The picturebooks published by Rouergue marked a rupture with earlier children's books, presenting a new relationship to childhood, an openness to new modes of expression, and a critical view of the world. Their innovative approach has been compared to that of the Sourire qui mord, which ceased to exist only three years after the creation of Rouergue.

The Spanish publishing house Media Vaca, established in Valencia in 1998 by Vicente Ferrer, shares a similar editorial philosophy, addressing sophisticated children's books to a crossover audience. Their series Libros para niños (children's books) targets "children of all ages" and beside the series title on the back cover is the recommendation "¡NO SÓLO para niños!" (NOT ONLY for children). If the "children's books" published by Media Vaca seem difficult, it is because Ferrer believes that children should never be given "boring" books; the publisher's catalogue accuses the creators of tedious children's books of thinking like tailors, that is, of believing that "children's books should be like children's suits: smaller by several sizes." Children don't have to understand everything in the books they read, insists Ferrer, who pointedly reminds us that adults don't comprehend everything either.[19] Media Vaca was created as an alternative to the highly conventional Spanish children's books of the 1990s, which Ferrer felt lacked complexity and multilayering. In his view, such books are created for a model of child that does not exist, that is, a child unable to feel things that she cannot explain or express in a rational manner. Media Vaca publishes complex books that do not invite rapid and comfortable reading but require effort and reflection. In their catalogue, the publisher justifies the appearance in the Libros para niños series in 2000 of *Los niños tontos* (Foolish children), written in 1956 by Ana María Matute, who stated that it is "not a book for children," but a book "about children." According to Ferrer, it was included in their catalogue because it is "a book about childhood, which is the most important part of anyone's life." The first page of the Media Vaca catalogue quotes an anonymous writer who left the following message on a wall in Valencia in 2002:

Life is as short
as the word life.
Childhood is as long
as the word childhood.

Javier Olivares illustrated Matute's stories "so that we 'grown-ups' may remember that it has not been long since we had a different life, and so that smaller persons may know that the things that they are thinking or that are happening to them have already been thought or lived through by others before them...."[20] These publishers all seek to offer picturebooks that bring the generations together. They acknowledge the continuum between children's and adults' understanding and experience and the continuity that connects readers of all ages.

Like the books in Media Vaca's Libros para niños series, many picturebooks announce their implied crossover audience in the paratext. Sometimes the book's author is responsible for the paratextual element (title, dedication, preface, afterword, etc.) that makes the crossover claim. The recommendation: "Ages: All" appears in small, discrete letters on the inside of the dust jacket of Jon Scieszka and Lane Smith's hugely successful *The Stinky Cheese Man and Other Fairly Stupid Tales*, published in 1992. As this is a picturebook that, like Wiesner's *Three Pigs*, lays bare the book and story making process, and self-consciously plays with paratexts, the author is obviously responsible for the age recommendation, as well as the words "Reinforced Binding" added below to convey the message that the book is sturdy enough to withstand the abuse of very young readers. It is not just in recent years that the paratext has played a crucial role in determining a crossover audience for a picturebook. In 1947, the German novelist and graphic artist Hans Leip gave the subtitle "Ein Bilderbuch nicht nur für Kinder/A Picture Book not only for Children" to *Das Zauberschiff/The Magic Ship*, a remarkable bilingual picturebook published for his four daughters. *A Visit to William Blake's Inn*, published in 1981 by the American author and illustrator Nancy Willard, also announces its intended dual audience in the subtitle "Poems for Innocent and Experienced Travelers," which refers transparently to Blake's *Songs of Innocence and of Experience*. Rather than

Figure 1.1 A Visit to William Blake's Inn by Nancy Willard, copyright © 1981, illustrated by Alice Provensen and Martin Provensen, reprinted by permission of Houghton Mifflin Harcourt, Inc.

leaving the author's subtitle to convey a more subtle message about dual audience, the publisher explicitly tells potential buyers on the dust jacket that this is a book for "readers of all ages." Sometimes publishers even take it upon themselves to alter paratextual matter to emphasize the book's crossover appeal. Although all Ionesco's children's stories are billed in his memoir as tales "for children under three years of age," *Story Number 4* became a tale "for children of any age," according to the front cover of the English edition illustrated by Jean-Michel Nicollet.

Often it is the publisher who specifies in the paratext that a particular picturebook is meant for a crossover audience. This is most frequently done in the blurb on the cover or dust jacket. It may also take the form of a publishers' note in the front matter, as in the case of the bestselling *The Geranium on the Windowsill Just Died but Teacher You Went Right On*. The author, Albert Cullum, dedicates it "to all those grownups who as children, died in the arms of compulsory education," while the publisher's note insists on the crossover audience addressed by both the author and illustrators (the twenty-eight different illustrators include Nicole Claveloux, Guy Billout, Henri Galeron, and Claude Lapointe):

They speak to children as from children;
they speak to adults as from adults.
They are adults speaking to adults
and to children from their own childhoods;
They tell of the hearts of children now . . .

On the back cover of the South African picturebook *Carnival of the Animals*, in which the writer and singer Philip de Vos and the illustrator Piet Grobler present whimsical creatures ranging from smoking tortoises in fishnet stockings who dream of doing the can-can to pianists (who, according to the author, belong with the beasts in the zoo), the publisher bills it as "a book for children of all ages (and for others who have remained young at heart)." When *Ein Tisch ist ein Tisch* (A table is a table), Peter Bichsel's sad story of a lonely, bored old man who invents his own language, was published in 1995 in picturebook format by the German publisher Suhrkamp with sophisticated graphics by Angela von Roehl, the publisher's insert stated that the picturebook was intended "for children, young people, and adults."[21] The blurb on the back cover of Tohby Riddle's *The Great Escape from City Zoo* (1997), which was shortlisted for both the Children's Book Council of Australia Picture Book of the Year Award and the NSW Premier's Literary Awards, rightly suggests that the book "soars straight and true right across age barriers. . . . " The marked increase in such recommendations in recent years may be the influence of marketing strategies being used for juvenile fiction, but they nonetheless have a well-established history dating back at least to the 1940s.

It is often pointed out that adults appreciate the artwork and the high aesthetic quality of many picturebooks. At the same time, the books examined in this study challenge and dispel the widespread assumption that young children are not interested in artistically sophisticated picturebooks. Many publishing houses founded with a crossover editorial philosophy set out to accomplish that goal with aesthetically beautiful picturebooks illustrated by talented artists and produced on high quality paper using the best possible printing techniques. The Japanese publisher Yasoo Takeuchi could be considered a pioneer in this domain, as he founded the Shiko-sha publishing house in Tokyo in 1949 with the conviction that a picturebook is "a work of art in itself, and is therefore not intended only for children." Shiko-sha has a reputation for artistic picturebooks printed on high quality paper. Their motto, as billed on their website, is: "Picture books for children from 0–99 years."[22] Many of Harlin Quist's books were large, lavish editions, which set a new standard of excellence in children's book publishing in the 1960s. In response to editorial constraints that dominated French children's book publishing, Nicole Maymat founded the publishing house Ipomée in 1973, in collaboration with the printer Dominique Beaufils. Maymat situates Ipomée, whose books are renowned for their aesthetic beauty, among other small publishing houses, such as Le Sourire qui mord, that were concerned with aesthetics of a non-commercial nature and wanted to offer readers "a different text/image relationship."[23] According to Maymat, they were resolved "to address sensitivities rather than age brackets." She repeatedly compares the risky position of those involved to that of funambulists (the funambulist is almost an iconic image of the publishing house), as they were trying to walk the tightrope of the so-called "border" between child readers and adult readers: "Alas! [she states] Books are classified in this manner and illustrated books 'are not intended for adults.' At least that's the way it was at the beginning of the 80s but the computer has not helped matters recently: a pigeonhole for each book, no more!"[24]

Ipomée was representative of a demanding aesthetic quality that was exceptional in the world of children's books. In her study *Une esthétique contemporaine de l'album de jeunesse* (A contemporary aesthetic of the children's picturebook), Jocelyne Béguery states that Ipomée's "aestheticizing choice" and their "preoccupation" with the book as a "beautiful object" led certain people to apply the term "bibliophilism" to their books, a term that the publisher categorically rejects.[25] Believing that all children have the right to "precious" books with high quality paper and printing, the small French publishing house Grandir, on the other hand, expressly uses the term "bibliophilism" to describe their goal: they wanted to introduce "bibliophilism for children" into the field of children's book publishing.[26] Founded by René Turc in 1978, Grandir produces high quality picturebooks of a very innovative nature. The name Grandir means "to grow up" and reflects an intention to provide books that take readers from childhood to adulthood. Some critics have questioned whether Grandir's books are really children's books, but Turc and his wife, both former teachers, have a great deal of respect for "the young reader's sensitivity and depth of judgment" and know, like Sendak, that the problem does

Figure 1.2 *L'histoire d'Héliacynthe* by Nicole Maymat, illustrated by Frédéric Clément, copyright © 1979 Ipomée, reprinted by permission of Nicole Maymat.

not lie with children. Turc explains: "It is adults who are in question here rather than children: they sometimes feel helpless when faced with Grandir's books, which are too different from what they usually see." According to the French publisher, bookstores and others weren't ready to distribute their "marginal books" in the early years.[27] It seems that the market was not ready for the avant-garde books of many of these publishers. In the latter half of the 1970s, the Quist books became smaller and less impressive, and in the 1980s the publisher was forced to branch out and add art monographs. For financial reasons, Ipomée was obliged to enter into association first with Albin Michel. Le Sourire qui mord was eventually forced to sign a distribution agreement with Gallimard and finally ceased to exist in 1996, although Christian Bruel lost no time in founding a new publishing house, Éditions Être (To be), which was launched the following year. In 2000, Rouergue found itself forced to join with Actes Sud, once again indicating the vulnerability of this unusual (some would say marginal) literature that rejects fashions, trends, conventions, and marketing demands.

Even today it is not easy for innovative publishers who refuse to make concessions with regard to aesthetic quality and generic expectations. The Danish author Oscar K., a pen name for Ole Dalgaard, claimed in 2008 that the "great artistic quality" of books falling into the crossover category is "a problem, because they can be difficult to fit into the framework generally laid out by adults for children's books."[28] In May 2010 after more than thirty-five years of publishing unusual, challenging picturebooks, Christian Bruel publicly announced the imminent closing of Éditions Être; the next day a group was set up on Facebook to try to save the distinctive publishing house. Many books by these avant-garde publishers, books that were reputed to be too difficult and inappropriate for children, have been reissued in recent years, often by small new publishing houses. Bruel's Éditions Être brought out new editions of many titles from Le Sourire qui mord catalogue and Ruy-Vidal likewise republished many titles from the 1970s and 1980s when he created Éditions des Lires, including Marguerite Duras's *Ah! Ernesto!* (2004) first published with Harlin Quist in 1971. *The Geranium on the Windowsill Just Died but Teacher You Went Right On* appeared in a new edition in 2000, its commentary on teachers and education—illustrative of Cullum's educational philosophy—apparently just as relevant in the new millennium. The substitution of new illustrations suggests, however, that the publisher considered the original illustrations still too avant-garde for the American public thirty years later. Some of these innovative works have been republished recently by large, well-established publishers, such as Gallimard Jeunesse or Seuil Jeunesse. Paul Cox's *Mon amour* (My love), first published by Le Sourire qui mord in 1992, was reissued by Seuil Jeunesse in 2003. In 2009, an omnibus edition of all four of Ionesco's children's stories was released by Gallimard Jeunesse, with illustrations by Étienne Delessert, to mark the centenary of the author's birth, but it did not appear in an English edition. A number of pioneering authors, illustrators, and publishers whose picturebooks had broken new ground in the 1960s and 1970s left the field of children's literature due to the constraints and conventions that continued to govern the genre, but have been drawn back by the exciting developments of the past couple of decades. Following a fifteen-year hiatus, Harlin Quist began publishing books again in the 1990s, reissuing some of his previous children's titles in addition to releasing new ones for European distribution. Ruy-Vidal returned to the French publishing scene with the creation of the publishing house Éditions Des Lires in 2003. After an absence of almost twenty-five years, Tomi Ungerer made his much-heralded comeback with *Flix* in 1998, winning the Hans Christian Andersen Award for illustration the same year. Contemporary crossover picturebooks owe much to the efforts of these pioneers who have been pushing back the boundaries of the genre for decades.

In the past, adults were generally seen only as co-readers or mediators of picturebooks, but now they are being recognized as readers in their own right. While this is not an entirely new phenomenon, adults now seem more willing to acknowledge the fact that they buy picturebooks for their own pleasure. Stian Hole goes even further, happily confessing: "When I was a boy, I read adult novels and poetry. As a grown-up, I read mostly children's stories."[29] The phenomenon of adults reading picturebooks seems to mark the ultimate transgression of the conventional age borders that have been arbitrarily created between children's books and adult books. In 1995, the critic Arne Marius Samuelsen drew the attention of the Norwegian public to the dual audience of picturebooks in a book titled *Billedboken: en glede og utfordring også for voksne* (The picturebook: A pleasure and challenge for adults too). Many adults have discovered the pleasure that Samuelsen discusses, seriously collecting picturebooks for their own use and enjoyment. A few publishers in the English-speaking countries were also acknowledging that fact in the 1990s. In 1997, Ken Geist of Disney/Hyperion, who "buys children's books for adults all the time," confessed his love for books like the nursery staple *Goodnight Moon* (1947) and the zany bestselling alphabet book *Chicka Chicka Boom Boom* (1989).[30]

Like other forms of children's books, the genre of picturebooks contains many classics that have always been much-loved by readers of all ages. Geist mentions *Goodnight Moon*, which was first published in 1947 and only gradually grew to be a bestseller, but is now a classic favourite with adults as well as children in North America. It was number eight on the *Publishers Weekly* Children's Hardcover Backlist in 2009 with sales of 653,140. Adults have always enjoyed William Steig's picturebooks, including the Caldecott Award-winning *Sylvester and the Magic Pebble* (1969) and the Newbery Honour Book *Doctor De Soto* (1982). One of the most notable examples of picturebook classics is Sendak's *Where the Wild Things Are*. The appeal of these picturebooks with adults may be due in large part to the nostalgia for books they loved as children; they, in turn, pass them on to their own children. Some picture-books could even be said to have a similar cult following to the children's novels, such as *Winnie-the-Pooh*, discussed in *Crossover Fiction*.[31]

Throughout the twentieth-century, there were picturebook series that captured the hearts of all ages. Since Jean de Brunhoff published *Histoire de Babar* (English trans., *The Story of Babar*) to immediate success in 1931, the Babar books have remained favourites with children and adults alike despite the harsh criticism they have faced in recent years. The Curious George books also fall into this category; they have been continuously reedited ever since Hans Augusto Rey and Margret Rey published the first title, *Curious George*, in 1941. The store Curious George Goes to WordsWorth in Cambridge, Massachusetts claims many of its customers are adults or college students and a large percentage of the fans who visit their website are also adults.[32] A number of more contemporary picturebook series have a faithful following of adults not only in their own countries, but also internationally. In 1985, the Swedish author-illustrator Sven Nordqvist published *Pannkakstårtan* (English trans., *Pancake Pie*), the first book in his hugely popular Pettson och Findus series, known in the United States as the Festus and Mercury series (although the original names are retained in some English translations). The books about the forgetful old farmer Pettson and his talented talking cat, Findus, charm readers of all ages thanks to the unique humour and quirky, richly detailed pictures. The series, which has nine books to date, has worldwide sales of over six million and has been translated into forty-four languages. Four years after Nordqvist launched his series, the Dutch author-illustrator Max Velthuijs published the first book in his famous Frog series, *Kikker is verliefd* (English trans., *Frog in Love*, 1989). As Toin Duijx states in her article about the winner of the 2004 Andersen Illustrator Award, "every child (and adult) in The Netherlands knows about the adventures of Frog."[33] He is very familiar to readers of all ages in other parts of the world as well. Published in more than fifty languages, the books about the loveable protagonist have captured the hearts of young and not-so-young around the globe. Picturebook series with crossover appeal are not limited to Western book markets. Hirokazu Miyazaki's Wani-kun (Little Crocodile) books about a loveable crocodile, which the Japanese author-illustrator began publishing in the 1980s, also found their way into the hearts of older readers in Japan and at least two have been published in English.[34] Miki Takahashi's unusual picturebook series about Kogeban (Burnt Bread)—a creation of the Japanese corporation San-X that has also inspired an anime series for television and diverse merchandise—offers an existential discussion of life seen through the eyes of a burnt loaf of red bean bread.

Some picturebooks are widely bought and read by readers of all ages because they constitute traditional gifts on certain special occasions in life, taking the place of a greeting card. Robert Munsch's tribute to mothers and their enduring love, *Love You Forever*, is a frequent Mother's Day gift. First published in 1986, it was number four on the 2001 *Publishers Weekly* "All-Time Bestselling Children's Books" list for paperbacks at almost seven million copies and also appeared on the hardcover list (number 128) with over a million copies.[35] The role reversal at the end of *Love You Forever* is not unlike that expressed in the French author-illustrator Grégoire Solotareff's *Toi grand et moi petit* (1996; You big and me small), which makes a very fitting Father's Day gift. It tells the story of the inseparable relationship between a little orphan elephant and the large lion who reluctantly adopts him, even after the elephant becomes much larger than the lion. Winner of the Deutscher Jugendliteraturpreis in 1997, *Toi grand et moi petit* is one of Solotareff's most popular books with adults as well as children. In the 1990s, the beloved Dr. Seuss (Theodor Seuss Geisel) published a number of trademark picturebooks that fall into this category. *Oh, the Places You'll Go!* (1990) has been finding its way onto bestseller lists every spring for more than two decades because it is such a customary gift for university and college graduates. In 2009, it was number twelve on the *Publishers Weekly* children's hardcover backlist with 455,725 copies. In 1997, Henry Holt senior editor Marc Aronson stated: "It's easy for adults to make the leap to picture books—28 or 32 beautiful pictures that cost less than an adult book. Picture books tend to have a compact emotional message, and adults tend to use them almost as a Hallmark card. . . ."[36] Not all picturebooks-cum-cards rely on emotional appeal, as witnessed by Dr Seuss's *Seuss-isms*, published in 1997. The collection of "wise and witty prescriptions for living" intended to guide young and old alike along the path of life makes a suitable cross-generational gift for a variety of occasions. The sequel, *Seuss-isms for Success* (1999), which focuses on survival in the business world, is reviewed on the Amazon.com site as "Just right for a recent MBA or graduate."[37] Having three sons with MBAs, we have more than one copy in the family.

A relatively small number of picturebooks attain overnight success with audiences of all ages. This is the case for a few celebrity picturebooks, notably Madonna's *The English Roses* (2003), which will be considered along with other crossover celebrity picturebooks in Chapter 6. It is highly doubtful, however, that many celebrity picturebooks will have the same long-term following as bestselling picturebooks by well-loved children's authors and illustrators. The second picturebook by Wolf Erlbruch, *Vom kleinen Maulwurf, der wissen wollte, wer ihm auf den Kopf gemacht hat* (1989; English trans., *The Story of the Little Mole Who Knew It Was None of His Business* and *The Story of the Little Mole Who Went in Search of Whodunit*), with text by Werner Holzwarth, was a phenomenal international success. By the year 2000, more than a million copies had been sold and it had been translated into at least eighteen languages. The book's tremendous appeal with a universal audience of readers of all ages was largely due to the humorous treatment of the scatological, Rabelaisian element. Erlbruch does not hesitate to depict explicitly the unmentionable bodily function of defecating that the author only alludes to in the text, and in so doing, echoes children's joy of transgressing. In 2007 it was made available to a new generation in a "plop-up edition." *The Story of the Little Mole Who Went in Search of Whodunit* is the ultimate bathroom book for all ages. Picturebooks may also become overnight bestsellers only within a specific country or language market. When Beltz & Gelberg published *Ottos Mops*, the most famous poem by the Austrian poet Ernst Jandl, as a picturebook with illustrations by the German illustrator Norman Junge in 2001, a year after the poet's death, it became an instant bestseller with adults and children alike in German-speaking countries. The success was undoubtedly due not only to the immense popularity of the dazzling masterpiece about the dog Mops and his master Otto, which is told using only the vowel "o," but also to the timing, as the death of the poet the previous year turned the book into a kind of homage to his memory.

Crossover picturebooks are multilevelled works that are suitable for all ages because they invite different forms of reading, depending on the age and experience of the reader. These multilayered books can be read over and over, providing new meaning with each reading. Children, adolescents, and adults read crossover picturebooks from their various perspectives, but they can all take equal pleasure in the reading experience. The disarmingly simple story of a book like *The Great Escape from City Zoo* can be enjoyed by very young children, but Tohby Riddle, who is a cartoonist for *The Sydney Morning Herald*, also successfully appeals to adults with his subtle popular culture references and his unique humour. Cartoonists often bring to picturebooks a genre of humour that appeals to young and old alike. The quirky pen-and-ink colour illustrations by Chris Riddell, who is also a political cartoonist for *The Observer*, add to the adult appeal of *Something Else* (1994) by the British author Kathryn Cave. The charming story about discrimination and tolerance, which the author wrote after listening to her then seven-year-old daughter on their way to school, won the first UNESCO Prize for Children's Literature in the Service of Tolerance (under 8s), but Cave claims on her website to write "for children of all ages" and a German bookseller told me it was a bestseller with readers of all ages in that country. Children enjoy the nonsense, reminiscent of Ogden Nash, in the playful verse of *Carnival of the Animals*, while adults will appreciate the darker undertones as well as the intertextual and cultural references (the entire book is inspired by the music of Camille Saint-Saëns). Stian Hole, who particularly likes the fact that adults and children often read picturebooks together, says that when he reads with his own children he appreciates "the small messages and humor in the story that is there for [him] as an adult reader."[38] Sophisticated intertextual allusions that cannot be decoded by children and seem to be there for the enjoyment of adults are a common trait of crossover picturebooks. Chapter 4 is devoted to the common practice of referencing the fine arts in contemporary picturebooks.

Even more so than other types of children's books, picturebooks that win major children's literature prizes are often those with strong adult appeal. This is not surprising since adults make up the jury for the majority of awards. Publishers with a crossover editorial policy have garnered a large share of these awards. Shiko-sha, for example, has won numerous international book prizes, including the Bratislava BIB Golden Apple Prize and the Bologna Children's Book Fair's Graphic Award. The relative newcomer Media Vaca, which publishes only three titles per year, has received several awards at the Bologna Book Fair; in 2002, they won the Bologna Ragazzi Award in both the fiction and non-fiction categories for Oliveiro Dumas's *El señor Korbes y otros cuentos de Grimm* (Mr. Korbes and other tales by the Brothers Grimm, 2001), which is intended, according to the publisher's catalogue, "to frighten and delight both young and old," and *Una temporada en Calcuta* (A season in Calcutta, 2001), by Lluïsot. Winning major international literary prizes is not a guarantee, unfortunately, that these outstanding books will be translated into English. Some are simply too unconventional for the Anglo-American markets. Even picturebooks by Wolf Erlbruch, winner of the Hans Christian Andersen Award in 2006, have never, or have only recently, been published in English (*Die fürchterlichen Fünf* [English trans., *The Fearsome Five*] appeared in English almost twenty years after its publication in German in 1990). This study examines a wide range of crossover picturebooks from around the world, many of which have never been published in English. It focuses on contemporary picturebooks, with emphasis on those published since 1990, although important earlier examples are also mentioned to provide a historical context. *Crossover Picturebooks: A Genre for All Ages* attempts to offer a global and cross-cultural perspective on a genre that plays an essential role in the crossover phenomenon. In many countries around the world, innovative works by picturebook artists challenge and dispel the widespread assumption that picturebooks are only for children.

Chapter Two
Artists' Books

The artist's book is a conquest of new territory.

—Henri Cueco

Some of the most innovative crossover picturebooks fall into the category of what have been termed "'artists' books' for children." Although artists' books have been called "the quintessential 20th-century artform,"[1] the definition and the term itself are still the subject of much debate. This study adopts the term "artists' books," as it has become the most widespread, but often "artist's" is written in the singular or even without the apostrophe. Numerous other labels are also used to refer to these books, including book art, bookworks, and book objects. Often artists' books are defined in terms of what they are not, and one website begins by categorically claiming: "They are not children's books."[2] In fact, some of the most innovative artists' books are intended for young readers. Unfortunately, they are, for the most part, not well-known, unobtainable, and overlooked by critics. In France, "les livres d'artiste pour enfants" have received some scholarly attention, for the most part thanks to Les Trois Ourses, an association founded by several librarians in 1988 to promote artists' books for children and make them available to French readers.[3] The French publishing house Éditions MeMo, which collaborates with Les Trois Ourses, specializes in artists' books for children from the past as well as the present. In Italy, Maurizio and Marzia Corraini, who began working with Bruno Munari in the 1970s, reedited titles which had previously been difficult to obtain, making them available not only in Italian, but also in English and French. In the English-speaking world, however, artists' books for children have been virtually ignored and, with very few exceptions, have received only passing mention by critics.[4] In his study of artists' books, Stephen Bury cites the "children's book" as an example of the genres into which the artist's exploration of the book extended, and his list of works includes Bruno Munari's *Prelibri* and *Andy Warhol's Children's Book*, while Johanna Drucker's seminal *The Century of Artists' Books*, first published in 1995, devotes a couple of sentences to Munari and mentions Dieter Roth's *Kinderbuch* (Children's book) in very brief terms.[5] Yet artists' books constitute one of the most influential and exciting areas of crossover literature.

The picturebooks examined in this chapter challenge not only the boundaries between adult books and children's books, but the boundaries of the book itself. Many of these innovative works question the conventional codex form, which dictates standard-size pages bound in a rigid sequence. Innovative experimentation with format and design has resulted in books that are also art objects and are sometimes referred to as "object-books" or "book-objects," the latter term being preferable since they remain first and foremost books. The Italian designer Bruno Munari uses the term "libro-oggetto" (book-object) to refer to several of his groundbreaking works and the Swiss artist Warja Lavater refers to the celebrated series of *imageries* that she began publishing in the 1960s as "livres-objets" (book-objects).[6] In book-objects, the narrative is told as much by the physical form as by the text and images. For these artists, the book is not merely a container for text and images, but a concrete, three-dimensional object. They explore every facet of the book and use all the resources of bookmaking, such as typography, paper, and binding, to tell the story.[7] Munari worked as a book designer before he began creating his own children's books in the 1940s. The Japanese artist and designer Katsumi Komagata spent a number of years working as a designer in the United States in the 1980s before founding his own publishing house, One Stroke, in Tokyo in 1990, in order to bring out his unconventional books. The works of these artists constitute a provocative reflection on the very structure of the book.

Although these books are sometimes designated as "'artists' books' for children," they appeal widely to adults as well. Indeed, some adults question their status as children's books. Disconcerted by their enigmatic, interactive nature, they feel that these books are unsuitable for young readers, even when they are addressed explicitly to that audience. Limited print runs and high production costs may result in a price tag that is prohibitive for most readers of any age, making them predominantly collectors' books. Not all artists' books are expensive, however, and artists who create books with a young audience in mind are generally particularly concerned with making them accessible to a wider public. However, even reasonably priced artists' books are often sold in art galleries and museum gift shops rather than children's book stores, while libraries are reluctant to lend them if they are fortunate enough to have them in their holdings. The fragile nature of many of these works often discourages adults (parents as well as librarians) from allowing them into the hands of children. Artists' books thus often have the paradoxical status of being children's books that are kept away from children at all costs. The new and exciting possibilities of these versatile books explain their appeal with young readers. Children enjoy the playful, interactive nature of these works, while adults admire the artist's ingenuity. Artists' books offer readers of all ages innovative and challenging books of exceptional aesthetic quality.

Early Experimentations

It is often pointed out that this art form did not really begin in earnest until the 1960s. However, a number of striking examples of artists' books for all ages were produced much earlier. At least one eighteenth-century artists' book has a crossover audience. Like most of the works by the British poet, painter, and engraver William Blake, *Songs of Innocence and of Experience* (1794) combines text and image using the technique he called illuminated printing. The introductory poem, which was first published in *Songs of Innocence* in 1789, states that all children could take pleasure in hearing the songs he had written. Over the past two centuries, children have indeed taken pleasure in Blake's poetry. Nancy Willard, who first read Blake's work at the age of seven, published the award-winning picturebook *A Visit to William Blake's Inn*, with illustrations by Alice and Martin Provensen, in 1981. The subtitle, "Poems for Innocent and Experienced Travelers," is a direct reference to the poet's work, and the author reminded me, in a letter dated March 21, 2000, that Blake wrote his happy songs "in a book that all may read," and that he also tells us that "every child may joy to hear" them. Willard's book of magical poems about life at an imaginary inn run by William Blake and staffed by dragons that "brew and bake" and angels that "wash and shake" the feather beds became the first book of poetry to win the coveted Newbery Medal. Like Blake's *Songs of Innocence and of Experience*, Willard's picturebook is intended for a crossover audience.[8]

At the end of the nineteenth-century and the beginning of the twentieth-century, the artists of the Vienna Secession and the Wiener Werkstätte (Vienna Workshops) completely rethought the children's book. The Vienna Workshops were founded with the intention of uniting the fine and applied arts to create beautifully designed objects of all kinds, including books. The members experimented with format, page layout, typography, and text–image relationship. The desire to communicate to children the cultural significance of beautiful books led to cheaply produced but high quality, artistically designed publications. The special character of children's book production at the time was largely due to individual publishers, such as Verlag der Wiener Werkstätte and Martin Gerlach & Co., as well as the Viennese art schools. These works demonstrated a wide range of the techniques possible in book art, including lithography, woodcuts, stencils, and so forth. Of particular note is the Gerlachs Jugendbücherei, which became famous well beyond Austria's borders. Between 1901 and 1920, thirty-four volumes were published in the famous series, each illustrated in colour by a different artist. *Die Nibelungen*, which was published in 1909 as volume 22, offers an excellent example of the trends of the Vienna Workshops. Carl Otto Czeschka, a prominent member of the Vienna Secession and a designer for the Vienna Workshops, is responsible for the illustrations and the design of the text, which was adapted from the ancient tale of knightly honour by Franz Keim. *Die Nibelungen* is a rather unassuming little book that gives readers no indication of the riches to be found between the rather plain covers. The sixty-seven-page book features eight double-page spreads printed in blue, red, black, and gold, as well as numerous small black-and-white vignettes, initials, and head and tail pieces. The text is written in gothic characters and all the pages, whether they contain text or illustrations, are framed by an ornamental border. This eye-catching frame highlights the small framed vignettes that are centred on a white background. An atmosphere of ritual and pageantry dominates the illustrations, which are reminiscent of the Byzantine imagery that characterizes the work of the Austrian artist Gustav Klimt. Czeschka's striking, abstract figures are solemn and ceremonial, while the decor is highly stylized. The decorative stylisation that was popular in applied arts at the time pervades the illustrations, where it is used for items as varied as wave foam, a ship's sails and figurehead, floor tiles, even horses and birds of prey. The geometric motifs and stylistic ornamentation of the bedclothes, draperies, clothing, armour, and weapons, as well as the use of the gold colour, evoke Klimt's "Golden Phase," so-named because paintings such as *Der Kuss* (The kiss, 1907–1908) contained gold leaf. *Die Nibelungen* is considered the best volume in the popular series and one of the finest examples of the Art Nouveau illustrated book.

The increasing interest of painters, sculptors, and designers in children's books at the beginning of the twentieth-century resulted in some very revolutionary picturebooks. 1919 saw the publication of one of the great forerunners of the contemporary picturebook, *Macao et Cosmage ou L'expérience du bonheur* (Macao and Cosmage or The experience of happiness), which was written and illustrated by the French painter and illustrator Edy Legrand. It was the first picturebook for children published by the Éditions de la Nouvelle Revue Française or NRF (the original name of the leading French publisher Gallimard), and it remains one of the most important books in the history of children's book illustration. *Macao et Cosmage* is the work of a painter at the beginning of his career; Legrand completed the book when he was only eighteen years of age. The artist would go on to become one of the most important illustrators of the twentieth-century, but his later work does not rival the brilliant daring, originality, and visual impact of *Macao et Cosmage*. Legrand's work marks a significant break from the romantic styles of illustrators such as Arthur Rackham, Edmund Dulac, and Kay Nielsen, who were popular in the early twentieth-century, the so-called "Golden Age of Illustration."

Macao et Cosmage contains fifty-four full-page engravings, vividly coloured by hand in the *pochoir* process. The book was revolutionary for a number of

Figure 2.1 Die Nibelungen, interpreted by Franz Keim, illustrated by Carl Otto Czeschka, Verlag Gerlach und Wiedling, 1909, Digital Image © The Museum of Modern Art/Licensed by SCALA/Art Resource, NY, reprinted by permission of The Museum of Modern Art.

reasons, most notably for the reversal of the conventional text–image relationship. The text is minimal (some pages are wordless) and the major role is attributed to the illustrations, which carry the narrative. In addition, the artistically handwritten text becomes a component of the image itself. Some pages consist of a single plate, while others are divided into two asymmetrical images. The page layout is further diversified by the fact that many of the images are framed by a solid, black, handpainted border, while others remain unframed. The author-illustrator experiments with typography: the placement of the text varies from page to page, and can be found within the frame, outside the frame, framed between two images, or actually framing the image itself.

Figure 2.2 Macao et Cosmage ou L'expérience du bonheur by Édy Legrand, La Nouvelle Revue Française, 1919.

A few of the illustrations seem to herald the graphic novel. A short foreword addressed to the child reader and signed familiarly "Your Friend, Edy-Legrand" insists on the importance of the images. Child readers are advised to look attentively because the author "only tell[s]" the story of Macao and Cosmage, whereas "the colours, the slightest objects, the smallest animals have a raison d'être" that they are intended "to discover" for themselves. *Macao et Cosmage* broke with standard publishing practices of the early twentieth-century. It is a large book with a square rather than rectangular format, which was highly unusual at the time. Unlike the carefully bound and costly books, with elegant tipped-in plates on fine paper, that were prevalent, Legrand's book had bold illustrations on course paper and it was quite inexpensive. It was an early attempt to make high quality books available to children of all economic backgrounds. While very fine copies of other prominent illustrators of the same period, such as Rackham and Dulac, are plentiful today, even a very good copy of *Macao et Cosmage* is quite rare.

It is not only the format of *Macao et Cosmage* that is innovative, but also the content. The author's highly critical attitude toward industrial and technological progress was unusual at the beginning of the twentieth-century. The anti-colonial perspective he adopts was also ahead of his time. The eponymous protagonists, a white man and a black woman, are portrayed and named on a striking doublespread that precedes the foreword and the title page. Their idyllic existence in harmony with nature is brought to an abrupt end when the uncharted paradisiacal island is discovered, and "an army of soldiers, colonists, civil servants, and scholars" arrives, bringing "blessed civilization." Eventually, Macao turns his back on the progress that was to have brought him happiness. The ending of the book seems quite bleak, especially to adult readers, but in the foreword the author offers the child addressee a glimmer of hope, saying that the story would be "sad" if he wasn't convinced that Macao and Cosmage "are happy today. . . . " The book has a very philosophical message that is encapsulated in the final line of the foreword: "The only mystery in life is penetrated when one knows where one's happiness lies." In the last unspoiled corner of the island (the image depicts two trees by a puddle-sized pond on a barren mountain), an elderly Macao finally "experiences happiness." The ultimate message is nonetheless pessimistic, as the last page of the book states: "Child! Macao was a wise man but the governor was right!" The relentless march of "civilization" and "progress" cannot be reversed. *Macao et Cosmage* played an instrumental role in establishing a new path for children's book illustration. However, because the author forbade the republication of *Macao et Cosmage* in 1947, it was not available again until 2000, when the French children's publisher Circonflexe offered a faithful reproduction targeted at ages six and up.

In the early years of the twentieth-century, there was a widespread search among avant-garde artists in many countries for innovative styles that would reflect the new age. European artists in particular sought to break down the traditional borders between non-visual art and visual art. The Russian avant-garde artist and designer El Lissitzky designed his first suprematist book, *About Two Squares*, while teaching in Vitebsk with Kazimir Malevitch. Published in Berlin in 1922, the children's book is a homage to Malevitch, whose *Black Square* initiated suprematism in 1913. The "grammar" of this art movement was based on simple geometric forms (notably the square and circle), which could communicate directly with everyone and be applied to all creative fields, including books. *About Two Squares* is at once a picturebook and a manifesto, in which Lissitzky offers a revolutionary rethinking of the children's book and the book in general, applying suprematism to the graphic arts. In "Our Book," published in 1926, he reflects on what the contemporary book should become in the new age. The traditional form of the book (jacket, spine, sequential numbered pages) must assume a new shape capable of expressing the times. In the young Soviet Union of 1926, he wrote: "The book is becoming the most monumental work of art. . . . By reading, our children are already acquiring a new plastic language; they are growing up with a different relationship to the world and to space, to shape and to color; they will surely also create another book." Lissitzky himself had already begun to create another book for the new era, a revolutionary book with a universal visual language that took into account "the semiliterate masses."[9] Paradoxically, this simplified, abstract narrative intended to ensure communication with everyone was considered by many to be elitist.

Lissitzky's avant-garde vision of book design and typography is best illustrated in *About Two Squares*, which presents a new way of arranging typography on the page and relating it to visual images. The letter and the word have a visual form like the image. In a large format book, Lissitzky tells his "suprematist tale" (he uses the Russian word "skaz" meaning "tale") in what the title page describes as "6 constructions," which resemble the artist's *Proun* compositions. The verso of the title page encourages the active participation of readers in an act of construction rather than of reading. The paradoxical directive "Don't read" at the top of the page is followed by a dynamic graphic line that zigzags down to the bottom left hand corner where "readers" are instructed to "Take—Paper Fold, Columns Colour, Blocks Build." The two flying squares from afar," one red and one black, descend upon the round red ball of the earth, where they discover "black alarming" chaos. The red square strikes a downward blow that shatters the chaotic black world of three-dimensional geometric shapes. The words that accompany this Construction also fall, contributing visually to the narrative. In the next illustration, a new, more orderly red world is reconstructed on a black square. In the final Construction, the red square hovers suspended over the transformed world while the much smaller black square exits the upper right hand corner. Lissitzky's children's book presents a clear social and political message that challenges the old social order and proposes a revolutionary transformation. His little tale is an allegory of a new society that young readers will help to build.

Lissitzky's dynamic images of geometrical forms being knocked down and rebuilt remind us of a child playing with building blocks, as Margaret Higonnet rightly points out. The innovative graphic design and typography are strikingly evident already in the title on the front cover, which, states Higonnet, "speaks like a child's rebus."[10] On a stark white background, the word *ПРО* (ABOUT) appears in small, slanted letters before a large black numerical "2" and the pictorial image of a red square. Lissitzky combines word, number, and pictorial image in a single visual language. A fine black line forms a large square that frames the title on the cover and each of the images in the book. Only the author-illustrator's name figures discretely at the bottom of the cover rather like an artist's signature on a painting (the two words of his name meet on a diagonal so that they share the "L"). Lissitzky bends all the rules of conventional typography in the brief fragments of text under the images, varying the type size and style, mixing upper and lower case, rotating letters, setting words on a diagonal, combining lines and words, and so forth.

The open ending on the last page, which is translated in the English version as "Here it ended, further," could be interpreted as an encouragement to the reader to continue the work of the two squares: "This is the end, continue." The transformation of society and humankind is a never-ending process. Lissitzky explicitly targets a crossover audience. On the second page, he dedicates the book "to all, to all children." The large white "P" that begins the Russian word for children (ribiatam) is set on a solid black rectangular background and tilted backward on the diagonal, as if poised to propel forward into the future. The book's creator also mentioned the intended audience in *Typographical Facts*: "In this tale of two squares I have set out to formulate an elementary idea, using elementary means, so that children may find it a stimulus to active play and grown-ups enjoy it as something to look at."[11] The square protagonists are introduced rather like the actors in a play. In "Our Book," Lissitzky refers to the triumph of cinema and the "new media which technology has placed at our disposal." *About Two Squares* is an attempt to give the book a "new effectiveness ... as a work of art" by mimicking the new media. "The action unrolls like a film. The words move within the fields of force of the figures as they act: these are squares."[12] Lissitzky's children's book was quite successful: the 3,000 copies of the book produced and sold in 1922 was a significant number for that time. In 1990, Artists Bookworks in the United Kingdom made this seminal book available to English-speaking readers by releasing a facsimile reprint with English translations printed on a transparent overlay to register over the original Russian. According to the website of the MIT Press, which published an edition the following year, Lissitzky's book "marked the beginning of a new graphic art and is among the most important publications in the history of the avant-garde in typography and graphic design." The revolutionary book, which attempts to address children in an abstract language, had a profound influence on other artists creating books for all ages.

Another very innovative children's book, *Die Scheuche: Märchen* (The Scarecrow: Fairy Tale), was published in Hannover, Germany in 1925 by Kurt Schwitters, one of the major figures of German Dadaism, famous for his Merz collages and assemblages. He was a friend and collaborator of Lissitzky, who published his 1923 manifesto, "Typographie der Typographie," (Typography of Typography) in Schwitters's *Merz* magazine. In spite of the revolutionary nature of Schwitters's children's books, they are not well-known.[13] The first two children's books he published in collaboration with the talented artist Kate Steinitz, *Hahnepeter* (Peter the Rooster, 1924) and *Die Märchen vom Paradies* (Paradise fairy tales, 1924), are more traditional than *Die Scheuche* despite the typographic experimentation (variations of type and size, a tilted layout of words, etc.). Schwitters and Steinitz hoped to create a whole series of "children's books of our times, yet timeless." De Stijl founder Theo van Doesburg, who had published a Dutch version of *About Two Squares*, suggested they make an "even more radical [picturebook], using nothing but typographical elements."[14] Schwitters was responsible for the text of *Die Scheuche*, but he collaborated closely with Van Doesburg and Steinitz as well as the talented typesetter Paul Vogt on the typography, layout, and design of the avant-garde book. The tale was brought out simultaneously as numbers 14–15 of *Merz* and by Apossverlag (an acronym for Active, Paradox, Oppose Sentimentality, and Sensitive), a pressmark created by Schwitters and Steinitz, as the latter was concerned that "the Merz label would prejudice teachers (not children) against these new fairy tales for our times."[15]

Die Scheuche was influenced by constructivism and De Stijl, two movements which had an important impact in Germany, particularly at the Bauhaus. Like Lissitzky, Schwitters experiments with new forms of typography and adapts his innovative ideas to a young audience. The Futurists had already combined various types and sizes of typefaces on the same page, but Schwitters takes this further, developing a revolutionary illustrative typography. He uses letters, words, sentences, and sounds as he would use any medium. Text is transformed into image in illustrations entirely composed of typographical elements. In keeping with Dada literature, *Die Scheuche* is a nonsense text, but Schwitters also borrows the conventions of the fairy tale, including the formulaic incipit, to tell the revisionist tale of a scarecrow who "once upon a time" was well dressed in a top hat, tux, cane, and beautiful scarf. It is an absurd, slapstick story in which the elegant Scarecrow is pecked and mocked by Monsieur le Coq and his hens, beaten and cursed by the farmer, and then stripped of his fancy garments by the ghosts of their former owners. The bodies of the flat characters are composed of very large capital letters, to which other typographical elements are added to form legs, feet, arms, etc. The eponymous protagonist is largely constituted of an "X," which represents his tux, while the Bauersmann (farmer) is a "B" that gives him a protruding belly. Paul Vogt willingly worked with these new typographical ideas, agreeing for example to cut the large "O" they needed for the body of Monsieur Le Coq. Nor did he refuse, as Steinitz says "every ordinary typesetter would have," to set "the big *B* slantwise" to allow the angry man to boot the useless Scarecrow.[16] This particularly dynamic page is one of the best known images from the book. The Scarecrow's top hat is made up of a black square and a straight line, his cane of two lines, and his beautiful lace scarf of curlicues and loops. These letter-characters are somewhat recognizable figures, especially Monsieur Le Coq.

The size of the letters and words as well as their organization on the page all help to carry the narrative. The hens peck in a circle around Monsieur Le Coq, as the farmer grabs the scarecrow's cane. As in Dada sound poems, the tone and emphasis of voice in which the words should be read is suggested, for example, the capitalization of "ACH" in the refrain-like line: "ACH so schöne Spitzenschal" (OH such a lovely lace scarf). In his quest for a new visual language, Schwitters creates a very rhythmic narrative that is at once graphic

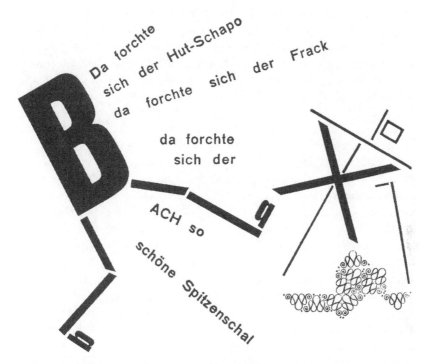

Figure 2.3   Die Scheuche: Märchen by Kurt Schwitters, Kate Steinitz, and Theo Van Doesburg, Apossverlag, 1925.

and sonorous. The artist's interest in theatre is evident in the dramatic page layout of the book. In the congested closing scene, the figures are all crowded toward the right side of the page "as if the characters in the drama were all exiting together at one side of the stage."[17] Like *Macao et Cosmage* and *About Two Squares*, *Die Scheuche* is not only revolutionary in form but also in content. The nonsensical revisionist tale can also be read as a political allegory, as both Margaret Higonnet and Jack Zipes point out.[18] The pretentious Scarecrow is brought low by the hungry birds and his belongings are returned to their rightful owners. The darkness brought on by the farmer's violence, when he grabs the cane from the scarecrow, is replaced by light when a youth takes possession of the cane. *Die Scheuche* was a very revolutionary work far ahead of its time, and it has only recently begun to receive serious critical attention. As in the case of Legrand's *Macao et Cosmage*, Schwitter's children's book is perhaps his most original work.

In 1937, the French writer Lise Deharme, one of the muses of surrealism, published *Le Cœur de pic* (The Heart of spades or The woodpecker's heart or The pick-axe heart, a play on words because spades in French is "pique," while "pic" means "woodpecker" as well as "pick"), a book of short poems for children, accompanied by twenty black-and-white still life photographs by Claude Cahun, a prominent figure of the Parisian avant-garde. Their project fascinated the surrealists André Breton, Man Ray, and Robert Desnos. *Le Cœur de pic* has the distinction of being the only book for children ever published by José Corti, one of France's most prestigious publishing houses. Its founder, José Corticchiato, published the work of his surrealist friends, including André Breton and Paul Éluard, who wrote the preface of *Le Cœur de pic*. Deharme's "thirty-two poems for children," which resemble nursery rhymes, are complemented exquisitely by Cahun's strange and disquieting photographs. Heterogeneous objects, such as flowers, leaves, branches, combs, bird's feathers, and feather pens compose striking, often surprising, little tableaux. As in all her work, Cahun uses photography to challenge the objectivity so often associated with this medium. The evocative atmosphere of these tableaux combines fantasy, mystery, humour, even cruelty. Ordinary objects are used to create a mysterious, strange world of the imagination. One of the photographs depicts three shoes on a set of wooden steps leading down into the darkness. Among them is a glass clog decorated with a white flower, evoking reminiscences of Cinderella's glass slipper. The accompanying text is equally enigmatic, beginning and ending with the same haunting lines: "three little shoes / my shirt burns me / three little shoes / climb up the stairs" (43). A tiny doll's hand, severed from its body, appears in a number of the symbolic photographs. Like many of the avant-garde children's books of the early twentieth-century, *Le Cœur de pic* is not well known, although it was republished in 2004 by Éditions MeMo. The French publisher recognizes the book as an object, one that is intended for all ages. They insist on their website that appreciating "a beautiful object" is not limited to a particular age group and therefore their books are intended to appeal to "young and old alike."[19] It is a belief and ambition shared by all the artists discussed in this chapter.

Breaking New Ground with Book-Objects

In the 1950s, Italian designers, notably Bruno Munari and Enzo Mari, began to use artistic and graphic language to create exceptional works for children, based on their observations of children's learning styles. The multi-talented Italian artist Bruno Munari, whom Picasso called "the new Leonardo," had a significant influence on the editorial world throughout much of the twentieth-century. A painter, sculptor, designer, maker of toys, and architect, Munari was also an illustrator and author for both children and adults. As a young artist in the 1930s, Munari was involved in the Futurist experiments with bookmaking and creating metal books from tin cans. He illustrated Tullio d'Albisola's verses in the second famous Litolatta book, *L'anguria lirica* (The lyric watermelon, 1934). Although the text–image relationship is rather conventional, the format of this book-object is revolutionary: from the pages to the binding it is entirely constructed from tin. Munari would never cease to explore and question the conventions of the codex (binding, standard-size pages, fixed sequence, etc.), in order to find new structures for the book.

Munari's interest in children's books began as a result of his personal relationship with his son, whose birth in 1940 inspired his first games and books for children. In 1942, Munari began working as a graphic designer with the Italian publisher Giorgio Einaudi, and in the 1970s he directed Einaudi's picturebook series Tanti bambini, in which his innovative L'Alfabetiere (first published in English in 1960 as ABC) was republished.[20] The daring innovation that defines all Munari's books is especially evident in those addressed to children. For this reason, his children's books have always drawn the attention of adults. The groundbreaking book Nella notte buia (English trans., In the Darkness of the Night), published in 1956, has taken on cult status and become a landmark in children's publishing, but its appeal is not limited to young readers. Corraini markets Munari's classic Nella nebbia di Milano (1968; English trans., The Circus in the Mist) as a book-object that actively involves the reader, whether "adult or child." A special place is devoted to Munari by Corraini, which bills itself as a publisher of "both 'artists' books and children's books."

Like Bruno Munari, Enzo Mari was one of the most provocative and influential Italian designers of the latter half of the twentieth-century. He was also a writer, artist, and art theorist, who, sometimes in collaboration with his wife, Iela, produced several very innovative children's books. Each of his creations is the result of careful analysis and research. Mari's theoretical ideas on aesthetics and perception, expressed in books such as Funzione della ricera estetica (Function of esthetic research, 1970), were demonstrated visually in his picturebooks. The designer had already shown his interest in children in 1957 when he created the Sedici animali (Sixteen animals) puzzle for the Italian company Danese, which was founded in Milan at the end of the 1950s, by Bruno Danese and Jacqueline Vodoz, in order to produce unique objects by artist-designers (these were exhibited in their showroom/gallery). Danese's meeting with Bruno Munari and Enzo Mari in 1958 led to the production of many innovative creations, which included books as well as games and other objects. Mari's puzzle is composed of sixteen wooden animals that fit into one another like a jigsaw puzzle. This puzzle-object functions as both a toy and a work of art and is appreciated by children as well as adults. A classic icon of twentieth-century design, it has gone through a number of re-editions. The most recent limited reissue sells for 341€, which means that it is most likely bought for the enjoyment of an entire family. When Enzo Mari addresses children, whether in toys, games, or books, his goal is to stimulate their imagination and their creativity; in so doing, he manages also to appeal to adults.[21]

As in Italy, designers and artists in other European countries were experimenting with the book as an object. The Swiss-German artist Dieter Roth (he later changed his name to Rot), who eventually settled in Iceland, is an extremely diverse artist well-known for his highly influential artists' books, some of which were produced for children. A poet as well as an artist, Roth chose the book as his medium of exploration and he became a pioneer of the modern artists' book. In the mid 1950s, he began deconstructing the formal qualities of conventional books (flat pages, traditional binding, fixed sequence, etc.) and proposing alternative structures. In *Bok* (Book, 1958), Roth cut holes in the pages and did away with the codex, permitting the reader to organize the pages in any order, while *Daily Mirror* (1961) was composed of the found material of a newspaper cut into 2 cm squares bound as a 150-page book. One of his best-known books is undoubtedly *Literaturwurst* (Literature sausage, 1961), which consisted of a sausage skin stuffed with ground up novels and mixed with spices and ingredients from sausage recipes. However, his first, and perhaps most remarkable books, are children's books; with them he began the exploration of alternative book structures that would mark all his work. His first children's book, titled simply *Kinderbuch* (Children's book), was conceived in 1954 for the son of the German dramatist and concrete poet Claus Bremer. Roth's playful approach to the book was suited to a young audience, but publishing houses were reluctant to take on such innovative books. Roth was unable to find a publisher either in Switzerland or in Denmark, where he moved in 1955, and the first copy of *Kinderbuch* was discarded. When he moved to Iceland in 1957, Roth, along with the writer Einer Bragi, established the publishing company, forlag ed., which provided him with a new independence and lack of restrictions that were conducive to his innovative book concepts. The first title published was *Kinderbuch*, a square book containing twenty-eight letterpress cardboard pages, with hand-cut and die-cut holes, that are folded in half and spiral-bound. The innovative book consists of op-art-like geometric shapes and patterns in various sizes and colours, and the perforations allow glimpses of patterns and colours from the pages beneath. The colours and shapes give the book a striking harmony and rhythm. Roth deconstructs the standard-size pages of the codex by varying the sizes of the pages. This children's book marked the beginning of Roth's production of artists' books. However, the previous year he had hand produced three copies of another children's book, titled *Bilderbuch* (Picturebook). It is another square picturebook, which consists of approximately twenty sheets of transparent colour foil with rectangular die-cut holes of various sizes in a spring-clip folder. Roth's two children's books were published together in 1976 in the collected works he edited with the Stuttgart editor Hansjörg Mayer. As in the case of *Bok*, the basic titles chosen by Roth for his children's books (*Kinderbuch* and *Bilderbuch*) reflect the fact that structural explorations of the book became the subject matter of the book itself. *Kinderbuch* remains one of the artist's best and most beautiful books.

The Swiss artist Warja Lavater has gained an international reputation with the innovative "imageries" or "folded stories" that she began publishing in the 1960s. She has referred to these mobile works as "radical" books and they seem to herald the trend that Eliza Dresang would describe forty years later in

Radical Change: Books for Youth in a Digital Age (1999). In actual fact, Lavater does not consider them to be books at all, but rather "book-objects" or even sculptures. These versatile books can be read as double-page spreads, either in a conventional manner from left to right or from back to front, or they can be hung and read from top to bottom, or they can stand, allowing all the pages to be viewed simultaneously. Lavater created the prototype of her first folded book, *Le Petit Chaperon rouge* (Little Red Riding Hood) in New York at the end of 1959, in a minuscule format no larger than a stamp. The first tale to be printed, however, was *William Tell*, a co-publication between the Museum of Modern Art (MoMA) in New York and the Swiss publisher Basilius Presse in 1962. *Le Petit Chaperon rouge: une imagerie d'après un conte de Charles Perrault* (Little Red Riding Hood: An imagery adapted from a tale by Charles Perrault) would be published by the French publisher Adrien Maeght in Paris in 1965, inaugurating a series of six tales by Charles Perrault (in actual fact, five by Perrault and the Grimms' *Snow White*) that are undoubtedly her best known works. The final tale in the series, *La Belle au bois dormant* (Sleeping Beauty), was published in 1982. All of Lavater's *imageries* are printed from original lithographs by the artist. Special editions of several of these tales were also made for the Museum of Modern Art in New York. Children quickly appropriated the expensive luxury books meant to be sold in museums to art lovers.

Katsumi Komagata describes his discovery of an "old-fashioned book-store" in Paris, where "some wonderful books" produced by an artist using lithographs were treated as "art objects" by the bookshop owner.[22] He is obviously referring to Lavater's books in the Librairie Maeght on rue du Bac. While the Japanese artist was working in the United States, he discovered Munari's books in the shop of the Museum of Modern Art in New York. Like Munari, Komagata began creating books for children when his first child was born. As he explains in the blurb of *Blue to Blue*, he hoped these books would expand children's imagination. They are nonetheless crossover works and the artist "expect[s] both adults and children to be flexible when they read [his] picture books."[23] The Form and Colours website designed to promote Komagata's books in the United Kingdom (they are not well known in the English-speaking world) markets them as "books for adults and children alike," which are "as much examples of book art for children as a delight for book lovers." Komagata's first books for children were the Little Eyes series, ten small wordless books published, in 1990, after the birth of his daughter, Aï. The title is an intentional play on words, as Aï is a homonym of "eye," but it also means "love" in Japanese. Perhaps the artist also had the homonym "I" in mind, in light of young children's preoccupation with their own person. The small books are made not only for "little eyes," but also for "little hands," so they are user-friendly and easy to handle for babies and toddlers. There is no binding; instead, a kind of paper case contains twelve cards, folded in three sections, which have to be opened, adding rhythm and movement to the act of reading because, as the artist reminds us, babies are constantly moving. Komagata considers it the "minimal book, the basis of the future book." The artist was strongly marked by the books of Munari, whom he calls "the pioneer" in the field of "three dimensional action books."[24] In turn, Munari expressed his admiration for Komagata's work in 1994. Like Munari, the Japanese artist explores new structural formats for the book and new ways of reading it. The Komagata exhibition organized to mark the centenary of Munari's birth clearly indicates that the Japanese artist is the heir to Munari's pedagogical thinking and his playful and creative approach to the book as a three-dimensional object.[25]

Book-Games

Book-objects that involve a significant element of play are sometimes referred to as book-games. Munari's early books for children fall into the category of what he calls the "libro-gioco." The books of the historic series he published in 1945, while he was a graphic designer for the publisher Mondadori, are all designated as "animati" (moveable books), and contain a variety of surprises, including flaps, inserts, and cut-outs. Although these devices later became commonplace in picturebooks, they were quite revolutionary at the time. Munari's remarkable books were created, as Komagata's would later be, with his own child in mind, as he had been unable to find anything he felt was suitable for his five-year-old son. In his view, the children's books available at the time were designed to appeal to the adults buying the books rather than the intended readers, so he tested his book projects on his son to ensure that they were effective.[26] Under the simple title I libri Munari, seven of the planned series of ten books were published by Mondadori. All the books in the series have the same rectangular dimensions, but the number of pages varies from eight to twenty-four. In many of the books, Munari offers an alternative to the standard-size pages of the conventional book, using pages of different sizes.

The first book in the series, *Mai contenti* (Never content), was published in English both as *What I'd Like to Be* (1953) and *The Elephant's Wish* (1959). Like humans, the animals in *Mai contenti* are dissatisfied with their lives and dream of being something else. The humorous illustration on the cover depicts a blue fish with large ox horns and a yellow bird as the pupil of its eye. Like several books in the series, *Mai contenti* can be turned into a guessing game. Each animal's fantasy is revealed when readers lift the flap of a camou-flaged insert positioned in the approximate area of the animal's mind. In this ironic, circular story, the elephant, "bored with being a big heavy animal," dreams he is a bird, but the bird is "bored with flying and singing," and wants to be a fish, the fish would like to be a lizard, the lizard dreams of being an ox, and the ox would like to be an elephant. The final line reminds the reader that "the elephant dreams too." Thus Munari brings readers full circle and they can begin the book again.

The cover of the third book takes the form of a door and the title, *Toc toc: Chi è? Apri la porta* (Knock, knock: Who's there? Open the door; English trans., *Who's There? Open the Door*), invites the reader to open the door. The reader enters the book to become the protagonist of the story. Munari felt it was fundamental that children's books should not have a protagonist: "In my books the protagonist is the child him/herself ... who opens the door in the book *Toc toc: Chi è? Apri la porta*, a book in which there are many characters ..., but where there is no protagonist."[27] A cut-out in the cover forms a peep hole through which a bird peers, as if deciding whether or not to let the reader in. The title's question is repeated throughout the book, and this questioning of readers is a common strategy in Munari's children's books. The book consists of six doublespreads of different coloured paper glued one inside the other in decreasing size, the largest constituting the cover. Page size helps to tell the story, as the pages constitute doors and objects that must be opened to continue the narrative.[28] They reveal ever smaller animals until all the pages, or portions of them, are visible simultaneously at the centrefold. On the first doublespread, the giraffe Lucia stands listening to a wooden crate from Verona (in the English translation, the animals are given common English names and the Italian cities are replaced by major European cities). Inside the crate, readers discover a zebra with a trunk from Lugano, which, in turn, contains a lion with a valise, and so forth. In the fourth book, *Il prestigiatore verde*, large flaps are also opened to reveal the magician Alfonso's surprises, but this time the flaps are not simply rectangular as they were in the previous book. On the first doublespread, the magician asks readers to guess what is inside a piece of furniture. A hexagonal flap opens to reveal the conjurer himself standing on a table. Surprise is an essential element of the playfulness of Munari's book-games.

The fifth book in the series, *Storie di tre uccellini* (A tale of three little birds; English trans., *Tic, Tac, and Toc*, 1957), is composed of three books within a book. This format allows Munari to expand the book's fixed structure by creating additional spaces within it. However, the format is intrinsically linked to the content. The mini-books tell the story of three birds who end up in a cage in the frame story of the larger book. On the cover, the yellow, red, and blue birds are depicted together behind bars that bleed off the page. Each mini-book bears its own title: "Storia di Ciò" (The Story of Ciò), "Storia de Cià," and "Storia de Cì." Cut-outs are also used to show a bird or part of a bird on the pages beneath. In the sixth book, *Il venditore di animali* (*Animals for sale*), page size again varies according to the progress of the narrative. On pages of ever decreasing size, the animal salesman tries unsuccessfully to sell a child ever smaller exotic beasts, including a flamingo, a porcupine, an armadillo, a bat, and a millipede, but the child is not interested because of their strange habits. In the end, all the pages are partially visible, as in *Who's There?* A sheet on the final endpaper opens to reveal the humorous ending: the child would like a roast turkey with French fries. The green string that had joined the salesman's hand to each of the animals now joins a chicken leg to a fork.

The last book to be published in 1945 was *Gigi cerca il suo berretto: dove mai l'avrà cacciato?* (English trans., *Jimmy Has Lost his Cap*), which uses a series of inserts with flaps to take the reader on a search for Gigi's lost cap. In 1997, Corraini brought out two previously unpublished titles in the series, *Il prestigiatore giallo* (English trans., *The Yellow Conjurer*) and *Buona notte a tutti* (English trans., *Goodnight Everyone*), which also contain pages of different sizes and/or inserts of varying sizes with flaps to lift. Under the flaps of *Goodnight Everyone*, readers discover creatures sleeping: a boy under a cover in bed, a fish behind a rock in an aquarium, and a cat under a pillow on the couch. Munari reserves two surprises at the end: hidden under a large flap, which looks identical to an umbrella hanging from the attic ceiling, is a sleeping bat, while the final small flap reveals a wide-awake moon. Munari's game-books have lost none of their popularity with the children and parents of the digital age. In 2010, a complete set of I libri Munari was listed on Bloomsbury Auctions in Rome for 4000–6000 €.[29]

In 1965, Enzo Mari published *Il gioco delle favole* (The fable game), an inventive children's "book-game" that is, in fact, a book to be endlessly constructed, deconstructed, and reconstructed. The book-game consists of six cards that can be interlocked. With the simple elegance so characteristic of his work, the artist represents forty-six simple animals borrowed from old and new fables (lion, fox, bear, wolf, etc.), as well as natural elements (sun, moon, trees, plants, etc.) and some objects (an apple, a boot, etc.) that could be found in classic fairy tales. One illustration portrays a crow sitting in a tree above a fox, immediately evoking La Fontaine's fable "Le corbeau et le renard" (The crow and the fox) or Aesop's version "Corvus et vulpes." Despite the simplicity of the animals, generally depicted in only one or two colours, they are very expressive thanks to small details, their poses, and even their colour. The artist does not necessarily use the appropriate colour: the previously-mentioned fox is a vivid red, as is a rabbit, while a bright yellow dog barks at a more traditionally coloured rooster. The cards can be put together in a multitude of combinations, stimulating creativity, storytelling, and imaginative play. Children can invent their own fables or entirely different kinds of narratives; the storytelling possibilities are endless. Since Corraini reissued *Il gioco delle favole*, it has had several reprintings. It is a timeless classic that is considered even today to be one of the most important and ingenious games designed for stimulating creativity.

The various strategies that Munari uses in his own game-books are shared with children, parents, and educators in *La favola delle favole* (The fairy tale of fairy tales, 1994), a large book-game that allows children to create "their own personal books to treasure and to read when they are great-grandparents." The paratext clearly indicates that Munari targets this book-game indirectly at a crossover audience of children and future adults. The fifty-seven large pages are held together by two fold back clips, making them completely interchangeable. A preface, signed by Munari, provides some game rules concerning the construction of the book as well as the story. He suggests the use of coloured sheets of paper as a background to drawings done on transparent paper or the creation of "special effects" with cut-outs from the coloured sheets, then provides the materials that children need to physically create their story. *La favola delle favole* gives readers of all ages new insights into Munari's creative process in general.

Komagata has also published book-games with three-dimensional cards to colour, titled simply *Workbooks: Red Series* and *Green-Yellow Series*. In 1999, a special issue of the Japanese magazine *Bessatsu Taikyo*, titled "Let's play with picture books," was devoted to unique picturebooks with a ludic element that often involves the format. Komagata's work was given special attention and a previously unpublished book, *Are you OK?*, was included in the magazine. It is perhaps not surprising that his card-style books in the Little Eyes series were labelled toys, which have a much higher tax rate than books, by a French customs officer when the artist sent them to Lyon for the "1, 2, 3 Komagata" exhibition in 1994. Munari describes the Little Eyes series as "a game for all ages."[30] The ten mini-books in the series are autonomous but combine to create one large book about the world around us. Inspired by Munari's *Prelibri*, they offer a similar encyclopedia for pre-school children. A different theme or concept is introduced in each of the ten books, which constitute as many visual games to accompany the child from birth. The first three books were created when Komagata's daughter was six months old and are designed specifically for babies, whereas the remaining books are intended for slightly older children. His daughter's development and responses to visual stimuli continued to inspire his later works. Komagata thus uses his artistic skills in the service of neurological and socio-cultural development.

Number 1 in the series is appropriately titled *First Look* (1990) and is designed especially for "babies from 3 months." For the first six books in the series, Komagata uses the same format: twelve double-folded cards in a cardboard case. Little eyes are presented with a variety of shapes and forms (circles, triangles, squares, etc.) in the first book, the only one entirely in black and white. By using cut-out shapes, Komagata playfully presents the concept of volume. Three of the books deal specifically with colours. Designed as a "second step for babies," number 2 is an introduction titled *Meet Colours*. Number 3 invites readers/viewers to *Play with Colours* by offering more complex and surprising interactions between forms and colours. Although the third book is described as "advanced for babies," the Forms and Colours website informs potential buyers that "this set is great fun for and actually very popular with design-conscious adults." Number 6 bears the interrogatory title: *What Colour?* and relates colour to its occurrence in nature (a black bird and red cherries decorate the cover). Number 4, *One for Many* (1991), examines the world of geometry using colourful forms in different configurations (on the first card a circle divides into two shapes), while number 5, titled *1 to 10*, looks at numbers.

In the tradition of Munari, Komagata combines essential themes and concepts with art and play. Whereas books 4–6 are categorized as "learning for children," the remaining books in the series are billed as "fun for children," and the emphasis is on the play element. All the previous books adopted the double-folded card format, but Komagata adopts new formats for the subsequent books. In number 7, a theme-oriented book titled *The Animals*, folds are used in a different manner to create surprising effects that delight readers. The folds in each of the eight cards get increasingly larger, so that the fold behind is partially visible and an image is formed (whale, elephant, chicken with an egg, cloud, etc.). When the card is unfolded, the image changes in surprising ways, presenting a scene with several animals. The thematic approach is continued in number 8, *Friends in Nature*. By showing the rain following the fine weather in nature, Komagata introduces the cyclic recurrence of natural laws that is a major theme in his work. This book consists of four booklets, in which the picture undergoes subtle changes from page to page, changes which suggest a mini-story.

The last two books in the Little Eyes series, *Walk & Look* and *Go Around* (1992), are the most playful. The format requires the child to move in order to "read" these books. Both books consist of four cards which use accordion folding, but in a slightly different manner. In both cases, the cards depict images (themes or subjects) that change depending on the direction from which they are viewed. However, the cards in number 9 are three-sided, with the accordion-folded images on only one side. This format makes the cards easy to stand up and since the double images only occur on the accordion-folded side, the reader is obliged to move only slightly to view the two images. The last book is more complex, as the cards have images on both sides of the accordion folding, thus creating four different scenes on each card, for example, the four seasons or the four stages in a penguin's life. The absence of the two straight sides makes standing the cards more of a challenge. As the title suggests, children are required to "go around" the card to "read" it. The accordion-folded images of the last book are contained in four, long narrow sleeves that constitute a kind of puzzle. When they are put side by side in the correct order, they form the image of a bee near a large flower on one side and on the other a small boy looking up at what is presumably the same bee above his head. In this series, Komagata begins with the simplicity of forms but shows the complexity of their relationships. Readers of all ages will find their certainties questioned and their perceptions modified. On one website, readers are warned that they are expensive: "At $375 for all ten, these may be the kids books you never let the kid touch,"[31] while a comment posted July 21, 2008 on Ohdeedoh.com, a website devoted to "home, design, and children," states: "The books aren't cheap, but they will surely be enjoyed and later cherished as works of art."

In 1996, Komogata published *Motion* in his Mini Book series, which also includes the books *Shape* and *Scene*. The books in this series take the form of a case containing twelve cards to be viewed on both sides. *Motion* is inspired by Book 2 of Munari's *Prelibri*, in which a stylized white man walks, jumps, and exercises. The simple image changes according to the viewer's angle. In *Motion*, the figure of a gymnast engages in similar movements around the square hole in the centre of the cards/pages that constitutes his body. Munari considered the reading of books like his *libri illeggibili* to be mental gymnastics. In these two books, reading literally becomes a form of gymnastics, as children move about the work viewing and often imitating the figure. The work's innovative creativity was acknowledged when it won special mention at the Bologna International Children's Book Fair in 2000.

Artists' books have played an important role in the development of the concept of ludopedagogy or education through play. Artists like Munari and Komagata realize that artists' books can be playful tools capable of stimulating children's creativity, learning, and development. Play is an essential element of all their books and inseparable from the act of reading. Late in his career, Munari developed workshops for children based on what he called "Giocare con l'arte" (Play with art), leading the first at the Brera museum in Milan in 1976. Mari and Komagata have also led creative workshops for children in several countries. At the Children's Workshop of the Centre Georges Pompidou in 1965, children who were given Warja Lavater's accordion fold book, *Le Petit Chaperon rouge* not only viewed it and played with it, but actually "play[ed] it like a musical instrument."[32] This invasion of museums, art galleries, and other bastions of high culture by children, for the purpose of creative play, is characteristic of the often irreverent appropriation of high culture by popular culture in contemporary society. Artists' books are finding their way out of museums and into the playground.

Wordless Books

In many artists' books, the narrative is carried more by the images than by the text, which is generally minimal or non-existent. A large number of books that fall into this category are wordless. In 1949, Munari began publishing the famous series of books he called "libri illeggibili" (unreadable books) because they contain no words to read. As an artist, Munari did not really believe they were "unreadable," but he warns readers who feel that only text can be "read" to expect a different language. His experimentations in these books were intended to discover if "it's possible to use the materials that make up a book (excluding the text) as a visual language. . . . Or can the book as object communicate something independently of the printed words?"[33] The importance of the *libri illeggibili* to Munari is evident from the fact that he would continue to produce them throughout his lifetime. He proposes an innovative type of communication that involves neither text nor image. These books tell visual stories by means of format, binding, colour, paper, transparencies, perforated or torn pages, and inserts. According to Munari, these visual stories "can only be understood by following the thread of the visual discourse"[34] A cotton thread literally carries the thread of the narrative in a number of these innovative books, but the thread never imposes a story, leaving readers free to construct their own narrative. The beginning and ending can occur anywhere in these versatile books. Munari's early *libri illeggibili* were handmade works in a single copy or very limited editions, but he later adapted his works for mass production. In 1984, Munari designed *Libro illeggibile MN 1* especially for Corraini. The popular book is currently in its seventh edition (each edition having had a print run of thousands) and sells for a mere 3.50€. Munari created this *libro illeggibile* in a small, square format that is meant for tiny hands. A piece of string or, in the case of the most recent edition, a piece of orange thread, binds together the thirty-two small pages of brightly coloured heavy paper cut in a variety of shapes. Like the *Libro illeggibile con pagine intercambiabili*, created in 1960, this book has "interchangeable pages." The conventional formal aspects of the book, such as the title page and colophon, are also missing from Munari's "unreadable" books. These book-objects can be displayed in a standing position, adding the dimension of the play of light and shadow on the coloured forms of the pages.

The "books without words" produced by Iela and Enzo Mari in the 1960s have become classics. The couple's graphic innovation revolutionized Italian children's literature. Enzo Mari has received much more critical attention than his wife, Iela, despite the fact that she published several picturebooks on her own in addition to those on which they collaborated. Their first books were conceived for their own children and, like those of Munari and Komagata, they were based on close observations of their young children. The first books they designed, *La mela e la farfalla*, translated into English as both *The Apple and the Moth* and *The Apple and the Butterfly*, and *L'uovo e la gallina* (English trans., *The Chicken and the Egg*, 1970), are wordless books which examine nature's circular life cycles. According to Enzo Mari, they conceived a series of six small, square books, in which the images were to clearly correspond to the represented object in appearance and scale. The apple, the butterfly, and the chicken are all on a scale of 1:1. Books were still conventionally rectangular, so the square format was quite unusual at the beginning of the 1960s. The absence of a cover and the spiral binding would allow readers to begin at any point, eliminating the traditional book's idea of a beginning and an ending in order to emphasize the theme of the eternal cycle. The *Apple and the Butterfly* was published by Bompiani in 1960, and, according to Iela Mari, the books *L'uovo e la gallina* and *Mangia che ti mangio* (English trans., *Eat and Be Eaten*) had already been planned for the same publisher.[35] Enzo Mari admits that *The Apple and the Moth* was a total failure because the small book was lost among the large, coloured covers of the fairy-tale volumes that adults favoured at the time. In order to present them to other publishers, the two picturebooks were given a more conventional, larger format with a hard cover that gave them a beginning and an ending.[36] Both books use striking visual graphics to tell circular stories of the cycle of birth, growth, and reproduction. Inside a red apple, an egg gives birth to a caterpillar which, in turn, burrows out and becomes a chrysalis and finally a butterfly in *The Apple and the Butterfly*. Then the whole cycle begins again. *The Chicken and the Egg* depicts a chicken laying an egg, the hatching of the egg, and the development of the chick, which, in turn, becomes a chicken. Unusual perspectives are offered: only the lower part of the body and legs of the chicken are visible as the egg is laid and one doublespread depicts the yellow and white interior of the egg on a shiny black background. These children's books demonstrate how Enzo Mari works with form in all his designs: everything superfluous is eliminated in a desire to achieve simplicity and to express the essence.

The picturebooks that Iela Mari published on her own share the same qualities as those created in collaboration with her husband. In her wordless picturebooks, the narrative is structured by changing forms and the cycles of nature. The first to be published, in 1967, was *Il palloncino rosso*, which appeared in English in 1969 as *The Magic Balloon* but was also published subsequently under the more accurate title *The Red Balloon*. In this surprising book, representational forms are continuously transformed from one page to the next in what Carla Poesio refers to as "a wordless poetic narrative."[37] A little boy inflates a red balloon, which takes off into the sky and attaches itself to a branch, where it becomes a red apple, until it falls to the ground and breaks apart, taking the shape of a large red butterfly, and then landing on a stem where it turns into a red flower. The hand of the same little boy picks up the flower which assumes the shape of an umbrella as storm clouds threaten. The final, striking illustration depicts the umbrella from above, so that readers glimpse only the boy's two little feet walking home. The metamorphosis loses some of its impact in the later, smaller edition of the book. The more extensive white space of the original edition highlights the fine line of the china ink and the transformations of the red object. *The Red Balloon* is easily understood by small children, but it is thought-provoking for adults as well. Iela Mari continues to explore the cycles of nature in *L'albero* (1972; English trans., *The Tree* and *The Tree and the Seasons*), in which the same scene is used to depict the silent beauty of the changing seasons. In *Eat and Be Eaten*, finally published in 1980, each spread depicts a predator pursuing its prey. With each page turn, the prey in turn becomes a predator. The Emme catalogue describes Mari's book as "a mortal Ring Around the Rosy of hunger and satiety. . . . " The last children's title she published, *Il paesaggio infinito* (The infinite landscape, 1988), consists of sixteen eye-catching cards—depicting animals in a shifting landscape—that can be mixed and matched to create an ever changing narrative. Although Iela and Enzo Mari's picturebooks have a limited range of colours, the details and precision of the drawing are outstanding. They reproduce with remarkable accuracy the pattern on a butterfly's wings, the blossom on an apple tree, or the rough texture of a chicken's foot. The simplicity of line and purity of form combined with the playfulness of the artists' images make their books unique and timeless. Their experimentations on communication through the image resulted in wordless picturebooks that stimulate the imagination of readers of all ages.

Warja Lavater also began experimenting with visual communication in the late 1950s. Like Munari, Lavater was influenced by the Bauhaus movement. At a very early stage, she felt that the combination of codes and signs linked to forms and colours could create a kind of new language that would no longer be verbal, but visual. The artist refers to the visual code of her *imageries* as "pictorial language" or "pictograms."[38] The only text is the legend on the flyleaf at the beginning, which explains the elementary code based on colours and forms. Guided by the symbols, readers construct their own version of the story. According to Lavater, her pictorial language has its origins in traffic signals, whose efficiency as a visual code had struck the artist during her first visit to New York. While this influence is evident in many of her works, it is most clearly demonstrated in *Die Rose und der Laubfrosch: eine Fabel* (The rose and the tree frog: a fable), a charming little story about traffic lights which Lavater wrote to prevent her two-and-a-half-year-old grandson from crossing the street on a red light. The fable, which the artist considers to be her only "children's book,"[39] was published in 1978 by a different editor from her other works.

Lavater's visual code remains the simplest and most effective in the first work that she conceived using this technique. In *Le Petit Chaperon rouge*, there are only eight icons and they are limited to dots (Little Red Riding Hood is symbolized by a red dot and the wolf by a black dot), with the exception of one rectangle and a squared "U" shape for the bed. Readers easily follow the movements of the little red protagonist as she moves from scene to scene. In later books, a proliferation of more elaborate icons results in a more complex visual code that is less easily decoded without referring closely to the legend. Even *William Tell*, which was published prior to *Le Petit Chaperon rouge* although it was created later, is already more complex. Some characters and motifs retain the earlier simplicity: William Tell is a blue dot, his son is a smaller blue dot, Gessler's hat is a red triangle, and the forest is once again a group of green dots. However, the Tyrant Gessler, the knights, and the soldiers are all represented by symbols that combine multiple shapes. The later Perrault tales are also more complicated. In *Blanche-Neige* (1974), Snow White is a black, white, and red dot that represents her three distinguishing physical features, the evil stepmother is a yellow dot with a black centre that symbolizes her black heart, and the dwarfs are red diamonds outlined in yellow as if they exude a golden aura.[40]

In *Le Petit Poucet* (1979), Little Thumbling's brothers are simple blue dots, but the protagonist is distinguished by a purple centre, which no doubt denotes his intelligence, and all are encircled by purple shapes symbolizing their bonnets. In contrast, Lavater did not deem it necessary to represent the distinctive headgear of Little Red Riding Hood in the earlier tale, even though it is an inherent part of her name. The symbols are even more diverse and complicated in *Cendrillon*, published in 1976. Cinderella is an elegant silver dot ringed with black and blue, and superposed with two matching blue ovals that represent her slippers. In the narrative itself, the icon is sometimes completely splattered with black to represent the cinders of the hearth. The elaborate nature of the visual language of this tale is well illustrated by the scene portraying Cinderella's arrival at the ball. In a colourful, fancy swirl of orange gown, the heroine enters the ballroom, where the prince, a richly decorated triangle with protruding swirls that evoke a moustache, is surrounded by his dot-guests and flanked by the two stepsisters, whose circular icons are now laden with gold ornaments. The king's small triangular

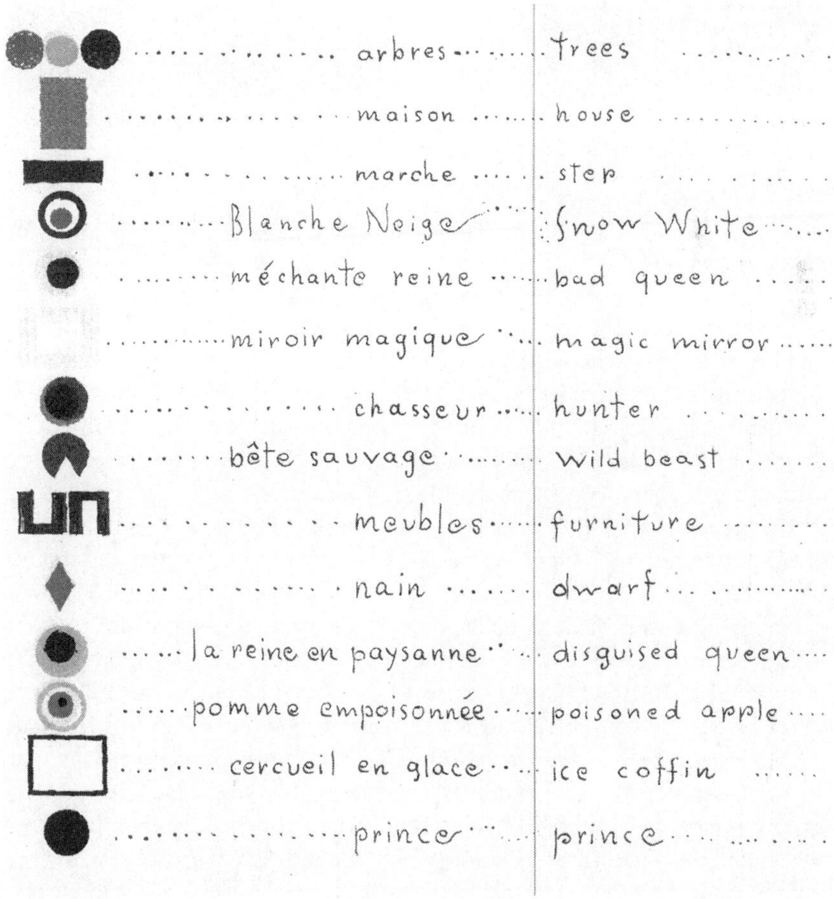

	arbres	trees
	maison	house
	marche	step
	Blanche Neige	Snow White
	méchante reine	bad queen
	miroir magique	magic mirror
	chasseur	hunter
	bête sauvage	wild beast
	meubles	furniture
	nain	dwarf
	la reine en paysanne	disguised queen
	pomme empoisonnée	poisoned apple
	cercueil en glace	ice coffin
	prince	prince

Figure 2.4   Blanche Neige: une imagerie d'après le conte by Warja Lavater, 1974, copyright © Warja Lavater/SODRAC (2011).

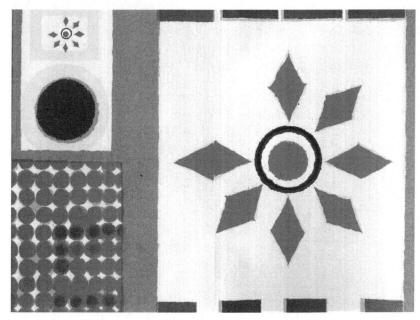

Figure 2.5   Blanche Neige: une imagerie d'après le conte by Warja Lavater, 1974, copyright © Warja Lavater/SODRAC (2011).

servants and soldiers stand at attention, while the fancy, gold-crowned dots of the king and queen occupy a podium, and the simple dots of the proletariat gather outside the line that represents the palace walls.

Lavater seemed to feel that her visual code was not entirely adequate to tell Perrault's least known tale. *La fable du hasard* (The fable of fate), based on Perrault's "Les souhaits ridicules" (The foolish wishes, 1968) as retold by the Brothers Grimm in "The Poor Man and the Rich Man," is the only book in the series that has any text beyond the legend. A handwritten foreword by the author appears on the first double-page spread. Even the narrative itself has some text, as the final two-page fold contains Perrault's moral, but the handwritten text is part of the image. The commas that separate the string of adjectives in the second line are replaced by a series of dots that trail down the page like cosmic dust and blend in with the other dots of the image. The text is necessitated in part by the much more complicated pictograms. The poor man and his wife are charmingly portrayed as two complementary green swirls outlined in yellow, which seem to hold hands, or rather tails. The rich man and his wife, on the other hand, are appropriately represented by two dissimilar, unequal, and detached vertical jagged lines. The amount of text is greatly increased in the legend, where detailed explanations are given along with the interpretation of the symbol. All of the icons, with the exception of those representing "serenity" and the descriptive "a good meal for each day," are accompanied by at least one line of explanatory text. The symbol for the saddle is followed by a text of six lines, which includes the rich man's second wish that sticks his wife on the saddle. His other wishes are given beside the symbols for horse and rain, the latter being one of the few self-explanatory symbols. The icon for the sun needs no commentary, but the artist includes a complex idea from the Grimms' tale: "it burns the hard of heart, but it shines for the pure of heart." Such abstract notions cannot easily be rendered visually, but the meaning of the penultimate double-page fold of the couple basking in the rays of a golden sun should be evident to most readers. The two swirls that represent the couple even seem to smile happily at each other (the pink shading around them gives them a rosy, blissful glow). The rather cluttered legend of this tale contrasts sharply with the simple legend of the first tale, and its heavy reliance on text makes this book less accessible to young children.

In some of Lavater's "Folded Stories," which will be discussed in a subsequent section, the artist includes a summary that covers the entire back of the concertina folding rather than complicating the legend. This is the case for two tales published in 1965: *Hans im Glück* (Lucky Jack, Folded Story 14, 1965) and *The Ugly Duckling* (Folded Story 15, 1965), where the tale is told briefly in three languages (German, English, and French) on three folds each. In these books, the legend is in black and white even though the pictorial narrative that follows is in colour. Although an "old woman" figures in the legend of both tales, Lavater does not retain the same symbol but varies it slightly. While the majority of the symbols are quite abstract, some are more figurative, notably the dog's teeth in *The Ugly Duckling*. A few of the symbols lie midway between, as in the case of the icon for the old woman, which resembles a female figure kneeling with rounded back, bowed head, and breasts. The ugly duckling is a thick vertical line with a rounded top, to which two curlicues are added as wings to represent the beautiful swan. Although the swan is quite stylized in the black-and-white legend, it is much more figurative in the narrative itself, which is rendered in colour. The grey stick with a touch of orange for the beak gradually changes colour and shape throughout the story. A great deal of thought obviously goes into even the most abstract symbols. While the mother duck is represented by an almost complete circle, the pretty ducklings are a neat half circle, and the wild ducks are an untamed version of the half circle with sides that curve up in an unruly manner.

Lavater manages to infuse her visual retellings with suspense, drama, and energy. The impression of movement is particularly striking in *La fable du hasard*, where the very first image draws viewers into a spiral as they follow a wandering Fortune, disguised as a poor beggar, first to the house of the discordant rich couple who turn him away, and then to the house of the harmonious poor couple who immediately bid him enter. A series of very dynamic double-folds depict the rich man jumping on his horse and riding after Fortune in ever larger loops that evocatively imitate the galloping horse, until he overtakes him and makes his three foolish wishes. The colourful, dramatic illustration of the bloody scene in which the huntsman arrives to rescue Little Red Riding Hood and her grandmother are reminiscent of a smouldering volcano about to erupt, whereas a similar scene in *Le Petit Poucet* evokes an actual eruption. In both cases, the human contents of the villain's stomach are released unharmed in a spectacular graphic display of dazzling colour and dynamic movement. As the artist herself writes in the foreword to *La fable du hasard*, these classic tales are retold in a "new language," a "visual language" that gives "complete freedom of interpretation" to the reader.

The French artist Jean Ache (pseudonym of Jean Huet) used a very similar visual code, which he called *abstraction narrative*, to recast several fairy tales in the 1970s. The geometrical shapes he employs to tell "Le Petit Chaperon Rouge" and "Cendrillon" in *Le monde des ronds et des carrés* (The world of circles and squares), published in Japan in 1975, are strikingly similar to those used by Lavater. He also includes a legend at the beginning of the tale in both Japanese and French. Little Red Riding Hood is once again a red (or slightly orange) dot or "circle," but the wolf is a black square. The wolf's symbol is somewhat complex, as it is divided into two triangular shapes by a jagged white line that represents its pointed teeth. Ache's geometric forms are not limited to squares and circles, as the volume's title suggests, and he also introduces into his narrative icons that do not appear in the legend. Ache's version of "Little Red Riding Hood" did not appear until ten years after Lavater's, but his "Cinderella" was published a year before hers. Further, he had already used the same visual code to retell "Le Petit Poucet" and "La Belle au bois dormant" in a collection of fables and tales titled *Des carrés et des ronds*, published in Paris in 1974. Although the visual codes used by the two artists are quite similar, the works themselves are very different. Ache's books have a very conventional picturebook format and the visual retelling is supported by a verbal narrative. The tale is told briefly on the verso in both Japanese and French, while the illustrations appear on the recto. The illustrations also have captions that echo an important line from the text on the facing page.

Bruno Munari's *libri illeggibili* were not his only wordless books. The *Prelibri*, which will be discussed in the next section, were also remarkable wordless books published with very young children in mind. As we have seen, they had a profound influence on Katsumi Komagata's Little Eyes series. The Japanese artist designed the ten small wordless books in order to communicate with the "little eyes" of his baby daughter. He describes these books as "tools of visual communication" designed to "promote . . . dialogue" between "adult and child."[41] Many of Komagata's other works are also wordless, and even when they have text it is minimal.

Material-Books

Artists who address a young audience immediately perceive that young children have a very sensorial and physical relationship with books. The act of "reading" can involve all the senses. For most of the artists considered in this chapter, the material and the feel of a book are as important as the content and the graphic element. Munari's experimentations with the *libro illeggibile* were intended to discover if it is possible to "communicate visually and tactilely" using only "the materials from which a book is made" (paper, format, binding, sequencing of pages, etc.). Munari points out that paper is conventionally used "to support the text and illustrations," rather than as a means of communication.[42] His use of different materials was even more audacious in his books intended for children. In 1980, when the artist was more than seventy, he presented his celebrated series *I prelibri* (The pre-books) at the Bologna Book Fair and published them with Danese. In 2002, Corraini reissued the books (still available at 120€) with a great deal of difficulty, as the materials used in 1980 were no longer available. The *Prelibri* are twelve small square books composed of a wide range of materials, including wood, paper, cardboard, plastic, and fabrics such as felt and fur. Even the bindings are constructed of a variety of materials, including twine, string, metal, and plastic. Packaged together in a case as a book of books, they have a very small format that allows them to fit easily into the hands of three-year-old children. Like the *libro illegibile*, readers can begin anywhere and go "forward or backward."[43] For that matter, they can also be read upside down by toddlers who cannot distinguish either the front from the back or the top from the bottom. As the title indicates, they are intended to be a child's very first books, introducing toddlers who do not yet read to the object known as the "book." For that reason, each one is titled simply *Libro* (Book), and numbered 1 to 12. Munari invites small children and their parents to experience books not just with their eyes, but with all their senses. The simple narrative in these multisensory books is visual, tactile, and even auditory, as in the case of Book 9, whose wooden pages provide an acoustic dimension as the pages are turned.[44]

The use of diverse materials and inserts creates delightful visual and tactile surprises for the young reader of the *Prelibri*. A red thread runs through Book 1, a button and a hole are found in the middle of fabric pages in Book 8, and a fur tail is hidden between the pages of Book 12. The red thread that runs through Book 1 demonstrates that the artist's techniques are similar whether he is creating books for toddlers or for adults. Adult readers will immediately be reminded of some of Munari's *libri illeggibili*. The *Prelibri* are the result of many years of experimentation with the book as an object. In Munari's view, all books are objects and surprise should be an integral element of every book. It was the lesson he hoped to teach young children with his *Prelibri*.

Munari began his experimentations with materials in children's books early in his career. In 1940, he conceived the "book-game" *Il merlo ha perso il becco* (English trans., *The Blackbird Has Lost Its Beak*), a visual interpretation of a popular Italian children's song. The work was not published, however, until 1987, by Danese. In 2001, it was reissued by Corraini in a bilingual Italian and English edition. The book is accompanied by a musical cassette which contains, in addition to "Il merlo ha perso il becco," three other songs about birds in three different languages. Although it is categorized as a "book-game," it is being dealt with in this section because Munari uses the technique of serigraphy, that is, silk-screen printing on transparent plastic sheets. This process allows the construction and deconstruction of the blackbird, following the words and rhythm of the popular song. The words of the song are printed in a white block on each recto. On the first page, the blackbird's beak appears alone on the recto. When the plastic page is turned, the beak is, of course, now visible on the verso, while an eye appears on the recto. The next verso depicts the beak and the eye (to which a tiny black pupil has been added). The rectos continue to add body parts (a wing and one leg, the other leg, tail, head, body, etc.), until the entire blackbird is represented on the last verso. In Munari's free interpretation of the popular song, the blackbird even loses some of its internal organs. The transparency of the pages allows the artist to create a three dimensional effect: when the lungs are superimposed on the body, the red of the heart on the page below can be seen before it is actually added. Since the book can also be read from back to front, readers can reverse the game and deconstruct the blackbird. In his preface, Giovanni Belgrano points out that Munari's book has assumed new meaning in light of today's ecological problems: the blackbird that gradually loses all its body parts can be seen to represent nature under threat. Book printing conventions are challenged in Munari's innovative book. A transcription of the music by Davide Mosconi appears on the copyright page. Paratextual information (a preface as well as publisher's details) is printed on a single sheet of yellow paper, while Danese's name and logo at the top is folded to form a tag for the plastic bag in which the book and cassette are packaged. This so-called "book-game" is thus packaged more like a toy than a book.

Munari and other artists have achieved a variety of interesting effects through the use of semi-transparent or translucent paper rather than clear plastic sheets. Those that also include cut-outs will be examined in the next section. Katsumi Komagata's *Found It!*, a bilingual book published in both Japanese and English in 2002, is entirely composed of heavy, translucent pages that are painted on every other doublespread, so that on the alternating doublespreads readers see only a muted mirror image or echo of what is clearly perceived on the other side. When the illustration of a grasshopper is seen through the paper from the next doublespread, the reversed grasshopper is now superposed on a leaf on the verso. The use of translucent paper makes it possible for the artist to create layered sequences that give the book dimensionality. The degree of translucence in *Found It!* allows each sheet to be read over several others, resulting in an ever-shifting spatial composition. Komagata uses the translucent paper to create the surprise element that is so important in all his work, a lesson he learned from Munari. *Found It!* is structured entirely around the final, climactic surprise: a four-leaf clover that is completely hidden by a yellow butterfly of exactly the same shape on the previous page. The yellow butterfly seems to transform into the green four-leaf clover. The triumphant words "found it!" on the last page of the otherwise wordless story reveal that the entire narrative has been a quest for the elusive four-leaf clover. In addition to the visual possibilities offered by its translucency, the heavy, smooth paper provides an unusual tactile sensation. Komagata also uses the paper to question publishing conventions. *Found It!* has a heavy paper dust jacket that can be removed to reveal a plain white paper cover with absolutely no text on either the covers or spine.

While Munari and Komagata use semi-transparent pages to create realistic effects of daylight, water, fog, mist, and so forth, Lavater employs translucent paper or transparencies in some of her books to represent a spiritual or supernatural dimension. *Le miracle des roses* (The miracle of the roses, 1986), based on the legend of Saint Roseline, tells the story of a pious young woman in the Middle Ages who secretly fed the poor with food from her father's castle. The miracle occurs one January day when she unexpectedly runs into her father with her apron full of bread. When she opens her arms, she discovers, much to her amazement, that her apron is full of roses. The thirty-nine-page *imagerie* can also be read with a transparency that adds haloes of light or architectural details to the illustrations. In the 1990s, Lavater began a new series of "imageries en transparence" (imageries in transparency) adapted from Japanese folktales. As in *Le miracle des roses*, the legend appears in four languages, and a summary of the traditional tale is also given in each of the languages except Japanese.

The series was inaugurated in 1991 with *Ourasima*, the tale of a poor young fisherman who is rewarded with a magic shrine that grants his every wish for releasing a fish which is, in fact, the daughter of the King of All Seas. In these books created in the final years of her career, Lavater has a very developed sense of the overall composition of the book-object. Unlike her earlier works, the artist uses the entire book to tell the visual narrative. *Ourasima* and the other Japanese tales have the same format as the Perrault tales, also published by Adrien Maeght, but the back side of the concertina folding is no longer left blank. Lavater had used the back side of some of her earlier tales, such as *Hans im Glück* and *The Ugly Duckling*, but only to offer a verbal telling of the story. In *Ourasima*, one doublefold is dedicated to the brief verbal text, but the remaining folds of the back offer a pictorial representation of the sea that is the tale's setting. On a few folds, the reverse side even seems to reflect events taking place on the front side. For example, in the stylized sea of blue and white wavy lines on the third doublefold, readers see the princess (a white circle outlined in blue) being caught in the large green fish net that the young fisherman (a green diamond) casts out over a pale blue sea from his small boat. On the back of the same fold, a white dot in the blue sea corresponds to the luminous fish-princess that Ourasima releases. Lavater works with the translucence of the paper to add a mysterious luminosity to the tale's supernatural elements. Readers can only appreciate the story fully by playing with the light shining through the folds. The strange radiance of the fish caught in Ourasima's net indicates the true identity of the magical princess.

The blurb suggests that Lavater's abstract imagery reaches a new level of perfection with *Ourasima* due to simpler and more expressive coding. However, even the basic geometric forms, such as the diamond of Ourasima or the circle of the princess, are made more complex by the addition of little string-like appendages that become arms to cast a net or to hand over a shrine. Some symbols are less abstract and resemble the actual object, as in the case of the fisherman's net or the turtle that carries Ourasima to the underwater kingdom. After the protagonist's return, the folds become quite busy, as the symbols are multiplied to represent the villagers whose wishes Ourasima grants, the delicacies with which they are showered, and the guards who pry open the shrine when they realize it can produce gold (the one condition imposed by the princess was that the shrine must remain closed). In a whirl of colour and supernatural energy, the King of All Seas buries everything and everyone in sand. The final, harmonious fold shows only rolling sand dunes against a dark blue that matches the deep blue of the sea on the reverse side of the folds, and the figure of Ourasima, who has floated to the top of the gold-coloured sand. At the end of the tale, Ourasima has undergone a strange transformation: the diamond shape of the poor fisherman, who alone survived the sand's devastation, is no longer solid green but has become a luminous white. Harmony has once again been restored to the universe.

Ourasima was followed by *Tanabata* (1994), inspired by a Japanese legend about the star-crossed lovers the Weaving Princess Orihime (Vega), daughter of the Sky King, and the cow herd Hikoboshi (Altair), who are separated by the Milky Way and allowed to meet only once a year on the seventh day of the seventh lunar month, a festival that is still celebrated in Japan. In this book, the translucent paper aptly evokes the light of these heavenly bodies. In 1997, Lavater published *Kaguyahime*, based on the oldest Japanese folktale, "The Tale of the Bamboo Cutter." When a peasant discovers a beautiful little girl, Kaguyahime (Princesse Lumineuse), in a mysterious, shining stalk of bamboo in a bamboo forest, he adopts her. She grows up to become an extraordinarily beautiful young woman who imposes impossible tasks on her many suitors. The radiantly beautiful young woman turns out to be a moon princess, who must return to her own people. As in the other Japanese tales, the translucent paper of this *imagerie* allows the artist to give the pictorial narrative a luminous, otherworldly quality.

Munari uses fabrics in some of his *Prelibri*, but a number of artists create books entirely of fabric. Today many fabric books are created for very young children, but they are generally mass-produced books of very little interest. When her son was born, the French artist Louise-Marie Cumont began creating wordless fabric books as well as what she terms "tapis de lecture" (reading rugs), deconstructed books in which the pages are all visible at once. *L'homme au carré* (The squared man, 1992) is a small fabric book with a requisite square format. The sand-coloured border around the white pages creates the effect of a window through which readers peer. This book uses the same technique as Istvan Banyai's *Zoom*, but in reverse, recreating the effect of a camera lens gradually zooming in and bringing the reader ever closer to the small red square seen in the distance on the first page. The tiny red square turns out to be the body of a stylized human figure, which comes closer and closer until, in the final image, the red square fills the frame completely. Cumont's book immediately evokes the red square in Lissitzky's *About Two Squares* and the artist admits that her small red square seems to be a reference to Malevitch, although it is not of a revolutionary nature. She is particularly interested in Malevitch's reflection on the human figure in painting, which allowed him to turn the human face into a black square on a white background. Cumont, who adopted the "warm" medium of fabric on the birth of her son, stresses its close link to humanity because it is "the first material" to come between the mother's body and that of the child, a kind of "second skin." Fabric has "a memory" and "lives like a language," according to Cumont, whose "palette" is made up of fabrics from Europe and Asia that coexist in her books regardless of the period or country. [45] The themes of her books are taken from the repertoire of important existential questions, as well as everyday situations. On the linen pages of *Les voitures* (The automobiles), created in 1995, scenes from the "real" life of adults on the rectos are mirrored on the versos by scenes from the imaginary life of children, for example, a man pushes a red car on the recto, while a boy plays with his red toy car on the verso. Cumont is not offering one narrative for children and another for adults, however, but a story that brings the two together.

The Greek artist Ianna Andréadis also creates fabric books. *Le petit livre des couleurs* (The little book of colours, 1997) is a small square book in which the different sized pieces of fabric compose tableaux that change as the pages are turned. Although Andréadis uses fabric rather than construction paper, the structure of the book is reminiscent of Munari's *Libro illegibile MN 1*. Fabric books by artists are generally unique pieces or produced in very small numbers. Fifty numbered copies of *Le petit livre des couleurs* were produced, while the twelve-page book of Andréadis's *Villes* (Cities, 2003) was limited to twenty copies. Cumont creates her works on request. The fabric books by both Andréadis and Cumont are distributed by Les Trois Ourses in Paris. Artists' fabric books tend to be rather expensive books. While the price of Cumont's *L'homme au carré* is only available on request, *Les voitures* sells for 1,000 €. Andreadis's books are somewhat more modest in price, ranging from 80–170 €. These artists explore the use of fabric materials to communicate both visually and tactilely in new ways.

Cut-Out Books

Material also plays a fundamental role in cut-out books, but the material used is almost exclusively paper, and paper-cutting techniques help to tell the story. In Munari's groundbreaking book *Nella notte buia* (1956; English trans., *In the Darkness of the Night*), the narrative is carried more by the different types of paper and the perforations, inserts, and flaps than by the text, which is minimal. The book was produced thanks to Giuseppe Muggini, a printer and editor in Milan, who supervised its hand printing on carefully selected paper. *In the Darkness of the Night* was the result of Munari's experiments with the *libri illeggibili* and the desire to communicate with different types of paper. The pages are composed of three very different papers, each marking an abrupt change in the narrative and thus dividing it into distinct chapters of sixteen pages each. In the company of a young cat, the reader is plunged into the dark night by the initial pages of black construction paper, on which silhouettes of characters and objects are printed in blue. On the first recto, the cat looks beyond the right hand edge of the page and onto the next page, as if he were peering around a corner. This curious detail goes unnoticed by many adults, according to Munari, who claims that "children are extraordinarily observant, and often notice things that grownups do not."[46] The dark night is penetrated by a golden glow visible through a small, round hole that perforates each of the black pages toward the top. In the first chapter, the vague narrative focuses on the mysterious star-like light that men in top hats (reminiscent of circus acrobats) attempt to reach by precariously assembling ladders one on top of the other. On the final black page, they tumble to the ground, losing their top hats, without having identified the source of the light that shines through from the underlying page.

The second chapter is told on semi-transparent pages that render the light of a new day. Blades of green grass, as well as various diurnal insects, have been printed on the rectos of the translucent pages, while the versos offer the muted mirror image of the same scene. Komagata was obviously strongly influenced by these pages when he created *Found It!* The reader/viewer perceives the images of several translucent pages simultaneously, creating a sense of three-dimensional space. The source of the yellow light that pierces the darkness turns out to be the light of a firefly, which Munari humorously depicts as a lantern attached to the underside of the insect. Readers-viewers follow the firefly into the meadow, where the insect seeks a place to sleep during the daylight hours. Several ants eventually lead readers into the third part of the book, which is composed of pages of grey-beige recycled wrapping paper—full of impurities—that represents the earth. Ragged-edged holes of varying sizes and shapes perforate these pages to effectively evoke a cave. Readers are invited to crawl through the cave and each hole offers new discoveries printed in black: stalactites and stalagmites, prehistoric rock art painted on the walls/pages, and the remains of an antediluvian animal which, according to the narrator's humorous claim, died after eating "a fossilized fish." The artist's picture of the prehistoric animal shows a large museum-quality fish fossil lying in the area of the stomach. These pages also include inserts which offer further discoveries. Munari's sense of humour is once again evident when the reader lifts the flap of a pirate chest to find, not treasure, but items which seem to belong in a garbage pail: an old boot, a fish skeleton, a bone, and so forth. An underground river is evoked by the insertion of four small translucent white pages painted with green fish. In the cave, readers do not know if it is day or night, but when they reach the exit, black sky can be seen through the final hole.

A small sheet of yellow paper glued to the endpaper (it is actually an insert with information on the author) can be glimpsed through the holes in the last black page, creating the fireflies that once again illuminate the night sky. The cat sits on the back endpaper ready to begin its nightly prowl, bringing the story full circle and portraying in a striking manner the cyclic rhythm of night and day. As we shall see in the next chapter, the cyclic pattern found in so many artists' books is a widely used strategy in contemporary wordless picturebooks. According to the author, this remarkable book was originally turned down by several publishers because it "did not have any text."[47] Valentino Bompiani pronounced it "cute," one of Munari's usual strange creations, but he refused to take it on, adding: "But this is not a book, where is the text?"[48] In actual fact, the book is not entirely wordless. Several different voices narrate parts of the story: the cat's voice is heard in speech bubbles in the first chapter, while a first person plural voice encourages readers to follow the firefly into the meadow or wonders how long they have been in the mysterious cave.

The techniques used to draw readers into Munari's classic *Nella nebbia di Milano* (In the fog of Milan, 1968; English trans., *The Circus in the Mist*) resemble those of *In the Darkness of the Night*. Between heavy grey-brown endpapers, readers journey through the milky opacity of Milan's fog, which is evoked very effectively by translucent white pages on which figures and objects are printed in black, except for the few, sometimes muted, green lights. In his reflections on the *libro illeggibile* in *Da cosa nasce cosa*, Munari cites the example of a quire of the shiny paper used by architects and engineers, which "has a sense of fog about it: turning those pages is like entering fog," and he points out that he used this effect in *Nella nebbia di Milano*.[49] Through the fog, readers gradually begin to glimpse the colourful, exciting world of the circus, created on bright-coloured craft paper with clever cutouts. Every page in the circus section contains holes or partial holes, except the page depicting a close-up of a sad-looking lion in a cage (perhaps a hole would have allowed him to escape). In six superposed pages, increasingly smaller holes are cut to form an ever-changing variety of circular objects, including a target, a railway sign, a gong, and the moon. Readers eventually leave the vivid pages of the circus to head home through the park in the fog of further translucent pages. Munari uses this picturebook as an example of the child-reader as protagonist in his work: "In my books the protagonist is the child himself who looks at, who enters into the fog."[50] The semi-transparent pages in *Nella nebbia di Milano* allow Munari to create very ingenious details. The text that accompanies the bird printed on the first page tells readers "birds fly a little in the fog," but when the page is turned, the same bird seen from the reverse side is less distinct and flies in the opposite direction, as the text tells us they "quickly return." The majority of the translucent pages are printed on both front and back, creating very interesting possibilities beyond the simple, reversed mirror image effect and the changes due to the underlying pages. Whereas the tree on the final page is painted on the recto, the bird and the bush are painted on the verso, giving the latter a muted, misty effect when viewed from the recto, but a sharper appearance from the verso, as if the fog has shifted, improving visibility. This technique allows Munari to add humorous little surprises. For example, the people on the bus, who are seen from the back on the recto on which they are painted, become more ghost-like when the page is turned, an effect that is heightened by the addition of black eyes that pierce the fog and stare eerily at the reader.

Komagata has also engaged in very innovative experimentations with paper, which plays an essential role in all his works. The word "paper" even finds its way into the title of his famous Paper Picture Book Series (1994), which, according to the author's blurb in *Blue to Blue*, resulted from his "fortunate encounter with a paper company." The sumptuous books in the series are made "especially for lovers of paper" and are marketed on the One Stroke website as being suitable "for interior design," as well as for children. Paradoxically, these books are not in the holdings of the International Institute for Children's Literature, Osaka because of the potential risk of paper cuts. The quality of the paper is truly outstanding and the effects are breath-taking. The paper of each page is different, offering a wide variety of colours and textures which are largely responsible for carrying the narrative (the text is minimal). Komagata's skillful use of paper texture to assist the narrative is perhaps best illustrated by a scene in which small salmon follow a black whale northward through an icy, frozen sea strikingly evoked by shiny, textured white paper. The importance of colour in the three books is obvious from the choice of titles. Although each cover is a solid colour, a cut-out allows readers a glimpse of the range of colours and shades of the graduated pages inside. The three round holes cut diagonally in the cover of *Yellow to Red* reveal most of the graduated coloured pages of the book, which, as the title suggests, range in colour from yellow to red. The beautiful array of papers and colours can be fully appreciated when the cover is opened. In *Green to Green*, four square cut-outs form a window into the book, where the reader catches a glimpse of the graduated green and salmon pages cut to form a mountain against a blue sky. The single hole in the cover of *Blue to Blue*, the final book in the series, resembles a porthole through which the reader views the sea, formed by graduated pages cut in wave shapes and superposed with a translucent full page that creates the effect of mist or fog.

Only two or three pages in the entire book are full pages. The blue and white paper chosen for the final full page in both *Green to Green* and *Blue to Blue* creates the blue sky with wispy white clouds that forms the backdrop of all the other pages. The remaining pages in the books have all been reduced by some form of cutting. Even the few full pages generally have cut-outs. The paper cutting techniques used in the last book of the series are particularly masterful. All the graduated pages between the first and last full pages are cut to form waves, creating a turbulent sea in various shades of blue and a little, foamy white. *Blue to Blue* tells the story of the life cycle of salmon. The baby salmon that hatch from the eggs at the beginning of the story are represented by small cut-outs in the blue paper and their eyes are formed by tiny red dots on the page underneath. The cut-outs become larger as the salmon grow. Eventually they are no longer represented by a single hole cut in the paper, but by more elaborate cuts, while the eye is now a hole cut in the paper rather than a dot drawn on the page beneath. Some illustrations are formed by a complex superposition of multiple intricately cut pages, as in the case of the growing salmon swimming over rocks and through drifting seaweed. This scene is created by a small brown page cut to represent the rocky sea bed superposed on a green page cut to depict seaweed, behind which a blue page with cut-outs of the growing salmon is only partially visible against the waves of the sea and the sky above. When the small brown and green pages are turned, the two visible salmon become an entire school of fish.

All the books in the series contain die-cut shapes of animals (in a wide range of coloured paper) which can be viewed against the recto or the verso. The chick protagonist of *Yellow to Red*, who wakes up alone one morning, encounters several different species of birds in its search for its mother. When readers of *Green to Green* open the book, they immediately discover the cut-out of the head of a black cat, who stares up at a window cut in the first full page to match exactly the window in the cover. Through the eyes of a cat indoors peering out, readers now glimpse the same scene that was visible through the window in the cover. Komagata's domesticated cat protagonist jumps through the window and discovers the wild animals of the field, forest, and mountain (squirrel, monkey, lizard, etc.). Toward the beginning of *Blue to Blue*, the back half of a large, grey salmon swims into the gutter, the numerous cuts in the tail creating the effect of movement as it lays its eggs in the river. To the delight of readers, the front half of the salmon suddenly swims out of the gutter toward the end of the book. Sometimes a double or triple insert increases the viewing possibilities. When the salmon go in search of the parents they do not know, they encounter a swan with her ducklings, which leads them to wonder where their moms and dads are. The white swan and her two brown ducklings are

おやをしらない サケのこどもたち。
はくちょうの おやこに あいました。
じぶんたちの おやは どこだろう？

Figure 2.6 *Blue to Blue* by Katsumi Komagata, copyright © 1994 Katsumi Komagata, reprinted by permission of Katsumi Komagata.

separate cut-outs which offer several viewing possibilities: the ducklings can be viewed on the verso opposite their mother, they can appear nestled against their mother on the recto, or they can disappear behind her when the mother is viewed on the verso under the baby salmon.

Like Munari, Komagata uses paper to evoke the cyclic passage of time. Whereas *Nella notte buia* spans a twenty-four hour period from night to night, *Yellow to Red* takes us from dawn to dawn. As the sun travels from east to west, the colours shift from yellow to red. However, hidden beneath what appeared to be the final red page is an entirely unexpected blue page that was not announced in the title. Separating the red and blue pages is an owl that can be viewed against the setting sun or the night sky. Komagata reserves yet another surprise when the reader turns the blue page to discover a final yellow page, representing the dawn of a new day. Between the two pages are the chick's parents, who can be viewed separately or together, either crowing at nightfall with the hen in the foreground or at daybreak with the rooster in the foreground. Thus readers are brought full circle and the cycle of another day begins, as the chick awakes to the crowing of its parents. *Blue to Blue* offers another of the cyclical stories for which Komagata has a definite predilection: readers follow the salmon until they are fully grown and have returned to the river where they were born in order to spawn. "Now they know what parents are," writes the author humorously. Komagata's books are intended to be shared by parents and children.

Figure 2.7   Blue to Blue by Katsumi Komagata, copyright © 1994 Katsumi Komagata, reprinted by permission of Katsumi Komagata.

Komagata uses the same techniques in two books published in 2004, *Sound Carried by the Wind* and *A Place Where Stars Rest*. The Japanese edition of both books is available with an English or German translation. Although the text of many of Komagata's books is made available in other languages on a separate sheet of paper, *A Place Where Stars Rest* was published in French in 2004, under the title *L'endroit où dorment les étoiles*, by Les Trois Ourses, who promote and distribute Komagata's books in France. The book was commissioned by the city of Grenoble as a gift to each baby born in the city in 2004 and, like other such books, is designed to appeal to the new parents as well. Both *Sound Carried by the Wind* and *A Place Where Stars Rest* share with the Paper Picture Book Series the same format, cover style, textured papers, paper cutting techniques, and die-cut shapes. In every respect, they look like they belong to the series. They have the same elegantly textured cover, one in green and one in white. A musical note is cut into the cover of *Sound Carried by the Wind*, suggesting that the sounds carried by the wind are, in fact, a form of music. This book offers a lyrical story about the sounds that the wind carries through the sky and the forest, over the hills and rivers: chirps, moos, oinks, and quacks, whose owners are present as cut-out shapes inserted between the pages. This is one of the rare books in which Komagata actually includes the picture of a child, although the black silhouette shape listening to the sounds is only a shadowy figure. A star-shaped hole adorns the cover of *A Place Where Stars Rest*, providing a glimpse of several pages of white paper. This book is composed entirely of white paper of different shades, weights, and textures, with the exception of one black page that represents the night sky. The text appears in red on the white pages, but on the black page, dazzling silver text matches the stars themselves. The shapes of various plants and animals alluded to metaphorically are also cut out of white paper (e. g., a sheep when readers are told that the stars are too numerous to count). As in the Paper Picture Book Series, the pages are all graduated, and the tops of several are rounded, evoking the dome of the sky. The small page painted with fish, which Komagata inserts toward the end of the book, is reminiscent of the small translucent pages printed with fish in Munari's *Nella notte buia*. Perhaps Komagata intended it as a homage to the predecessor for whom he has such great admiration.

Komagata's elaborate paper-cutting techniques become increasingly complex in each book in the Paper Picture Book Series, but he goes even further in *Boku, Umareru-yo!* (I'm gonna be born), published a year later, in 1995. Like *Blue to Blue, Boku, Umareru-yo!* deals with birth, but this time it is the birth of a human baby. The heavy cardboard cover of the square book was doubled for the front cover so that an orange piece of paper could be inserted behind the cut-out of a foetus. The Japanese title of the book curves its way around the foetus on the orange paper that shows through the hole. In this very unusual book inspired by his four-year-old daughter's account of her memories of the time she had spent in the womb, Komagata evokes birth from the point of view of the baby. Two very distinct narrative voices tell a poetic story of creation and birth from the perspective of the foetus/baby. Although the voice that begins the story seems to be that of an anonymous third-person narrator, it is, in fact, that of the foetus, who switches to the first person as it becomes more developed. This voice adopts a cosmological vocabulary to describe the miracle of human creation as the foetus has personally experienced it. The innumerable "stars" in "mommy's belly" are sperm; only one of the thousands of stars manages to reach "the large planet from another world." This star and planet create new life and a "new star" begins to grow. In an entirely different tone, an anonymous narrative voice intervenes to provide medical explanations of the foetus/baby's observations from an adult perspective, for example, "at two months, with a size of four cm, the foetus begins to resemble a human being." This voice is distinguished from the other by the use of a smaller font size. Sometimes the adult comments are also quite poetic. The amniotic fluid is likened to the sea of our origins, and the voice describes the "vertiginous eternity" of "this sea of life." The foetus's reaction is entirely physical, as she thinks how "pleasant" it is to "float in the warm water."

The umbilical cord, so crucial to the developing baby, plays a major role in Komagata's book. When the baby says she hears "mommy's soft voice," the adult narrator explains that the umbilical cord makes these exchanges possible. It is via the umbilical cord that the baby informs her mother that she is ready to be born (by means of a hormone explains the second, more scientific and didactic voice). The book is composed of a combination of very heavy paper and lighter, somewhat translucent pages, all in warm shades of yellow, orange, pink, and red, which evoke the warmth of the womb. The orange tones predominate because Komagata believes "the baby in the uterus perceives an orange glow."[51] On a sheet of translucent paper, the baby about to be born peers into the birth canal, created by a series of graduated holes cut into the pages of heavy craft paper. The last hole is cut to form the umbilical cord which can stretch out to reflect the narrative. As she feels herself being pushed and "detached" from mommy, the baby comments on the lengthening of the umbilical cord that "attached" her to her mother. Komagata wanted the umbilical cord to be cut into the book in such a way that it would lengthen. Rather than removing the paper from the last hole, it is cut to form the umbilical cord which extends when readers open the doublespread. This created a difficult technical challenge for the printer, who had to ensure that the cord would not get tangled in the machinery.

Figure 2.8 Boku, Umareru-yo! by Katsumi Komagata, copyright © 1995 Katsumi Komagata, reprinted by permission of Katsumi Komagata.

Holes are used very cleverly throughout several of Komagata's books. Like his book about birth, *Namida* (Tears, 2000) was also directly inspired by the artist's daughter, in this case the inexplicable sadness she sometimes experienced. The shapes of an eye and that of a tear are cut out of the front cover. As in *Boku, Umareru-yo!* the front cover has been folded under (but not glued this time) to create another eye-catching effect. In the underflap, a round circle has been cut out to form the pupil of the eye, which is painted in blue on the title page, so that the eye is formed by the superposition of three different layers of paper. The tear that is the protagonist of the charming story infiltrates the pages of the entire book in the form of a tear-shaped hole cut out of the centre of every page. The only visual sign that the tear falls from a child's eye are the two small red slippers on the first page above the large tear. The tear falls toward her black dog, which is illustrated in the next recto holding one of the slippers in his mouth, as if expressing his love for the crying child. The artist plays with perspective throughout the book. On the next recto, one slipper has been enlarged many times, so that the tear that has fallen on the ground seems miniscule in comparison (its small size is emphasized by the tiny ant that has crawled into the scene). Later in the book, a close-up of the same dog shows the tear falling from his eye and landing, on the following doublespread, at the feet of the same child (the dog has drunk her tear from a puddle). Toward the end, the tear even falls from the eye of the ant, which is now gigantic in the striking close-up. The tear is thus shared by the child, the dog, and the ant, but it also becomes part of nature. The child's tear is absorbed into the ground where it nourishes the roots of a tree; it falls as dew on a leaf to quench the thirst of a butterfly or an ant, or as a raindrop from dark clouds in a storm; eventually it makes its way to the sea and then into a tap that is undoubtedly in the child's home. The artist suggests that a child's tears are part of nature's life cycle, nourishing plants and animals, in a process that somehow seems to ease the child's sorrow. *Namida* is a simple, yet powerful, narrative that touches readers of all ages.

At the request of the French artist Sophie Curtil, who conceived the series Livres artistiques tactiles (Artistic tactile books), Komagata began creating a series of "tactile books" in 2002, in which cut-outs play an essential role. These books are a co-publication of One Stroke, Les Trois Ourses, and Les Doigts qui rêvent (Dreaming fingers), a small French publishing house dedicated to producing high quality picturebooks for visually impaired children. Komagata's books have increasingly appealed to the sense of touch, not only due to the different paper textures, but also to the cut-outs, which readers are encouraged to manipulate. The creation of a "tactile series" thus seems a logical step in the artist's evolution. The title of the second book in the series, *Leaves*, appears in English, as it does for many of Komagata's books, but also in Braille. The only text is a short, introductory, haiku-like text in Braille and English. The cover has the characteristic cut-out design, this time of a leaf. The leaves that are the subject of the book take the form of inserts cut out of very textured white paper and superposed on pages of coloured craft paper. The entire narrative is told by the inserts and the paper. It is once again the story of a life cycle, this time of leaves. The only text, other than the title, is a short introduction that explains the cyclic pattern of life without referring specifically to leaves. The concluding line could be applied to most of Komagata's books: "And so the cycle goes on, forever. . . ." Between the page of text and the blank facing page is a small, unidentifiable insert of textured paper, which becomes a longer insert between the next opening, and by the third opening becomes identifiable as a twig because a small leaf has begun to unfurl. The one leaf grows larger, then a second appears, and eventually the twig bears many leaves. Between the subsequent doublespreads, the artist inserts leaves of various species of trees. In the final pages, a large single leaf is depicted with ever more holes and missing chunks until all that is left is the original twig. *Leaves* invites readers of all ages, those who are visually impaired and those who are not, to explore the evolving shapes and textures of tactile images that evoke the natural world.

Book-Sculptures

Artists' books are very often three-dimensional objects. Alberto Mondadori, whose father's publishing house had brought out Munari's first children's books a few years earlier, claimed that the artist's *libri illeggibili* initiated "a new language" analogous to that of cinema and music. He predicted that, in the future, these books would "constitute a new genre."[52] This "new genre" is also akin to sculpture. In a close reading of Munari's unreadable book, *Libro illeggibile MN1*, the Moravian-born sculptor Milos Cvach, who now lives in France, rightly points out that he can also treat it like "a sculpture" animated by the ever-changing light. Cvach's own artists' book *Dans tous les sens* (This way and that, 2007) is described as a "livre-sculpture" (book-sculpture) and "the heir of the *libri illeggibili*." In the tradition of Munari's books, the narrative is told by means of colours, forms, and cut-outs. The heavy paper and the metal rings of the binding allow the book to stand easily. Like *MN1*, *Dans tous les sens* can be viewed as "a small coloured sculpture."[53] As the title suggests, it can be read in any direction, including upside down. *Dans tous les sens* is Cvach's fifth "artist's book for old and young alike."[54] As we have seen, Komagata considers Munari to be "the pioneer" in the field of "three dimensional action books." Like his predecessor, Komagata uses a variety of techniques to draw readers into a three-dimensional world constructed in paper. His very first books, the Little Eyes series, which make use of folds and cut-outs, are at once book-games and book-sculptures. Many of the artist's books are works of paper architecture that draw on the traditional Japanese art of origami.

In the early 1990s, Komagata used paper-cutting techniques to create what he called "the spiral format book." It is a form of folded book that can be read sequentially by following the folds of the work, or as an opened work of a single large sheet on the floor or on the wall. When it is unfolded, it loses its sculptural quality to take on more of a graphic presence. Komagata created these spiral books in an attempt to change the established pattern of reading to which the artist is expected to adhere. Many artists question the conventional linear reading process, whether it be the horizontal left-to-right movement of Western books or the vertical right-to-left movement of Eastern books. In Komagata's case, he hoped to change "the one-way movement" that the Japanese artist is forced to observe when "the texts are typeset vertically" and readers use their "right hand to turn the pages and follow the story that goes from right to left."[55] In the spiral book series, one large square sheet of paper is cut and folded, then pierced with a hole, leaving numerous holes when it is unfolded. Readers of Komagata's spiral books must continually turn the book to follow the wordless story. It is now a widespread strategy in contemporary picturebooks to oblige the reader to turn the book in various directions to read the narrative (Sara Fanelli's 1994 picturebook *Button*, which follows the journey of a red button lost from a man's overcoat, is an excellent example). Komagata also breaks with the conventional linear narrative pattern, because readers can enter the story of the spiral books at any point. Through the holes in the first book, *Tsuchi no naka ni wa* (Adventures underground, 1993), readers follow a woodlouse (aka wood bug, armadillo bug, roll up bug) that has numerous encounters underground. Although readers may choose to begin elsewhere, the story starts on the title page, where the bug protagonist heads toward the hole that has been pierced through the folds at varying angles. The holes do not line up perfectly to create a single hole through the book from the cover, as in *Namida*, but form an attractive gradation of the layers visible from the cover. This is a wordless book, but it nonetheless contains typographic symbols in the form of question marks and one exclamation mark. Komagata uses the same strategy in the other books of the spiral series. A question mark at the beginning of the story indicates not only the bug's curiosity concerning the hole, but that of the reader as well. A tail enticingly draws the bug and the reader down the hole, and only on the other side can its owner be identified as a lizard. As the bug continues its journey in the underground tunnels, followed closely by the reader, it encounters a squirrel, an ant hill, a snake, a centipede, a bear, and finally another woodlouse. At one point in his adventure, an exclamation mark indicates his surprise when he comes across a very large bug all curled up. The much smaller protagonist beats a hasty retreat.

The subsequent volumes of the spiral book series are constructed around the same concept. In *Umi no bōken* (Adventure in the sea, 1993), readers follow a fish through the hole and into the depths of the sea. As in the case of the lizard's tail in the previous book, octopus tentacles can be seen extending beyond one hole, but the fish (and probably most young readers) does not identify the creature until it swims through the hole. The fish is visibly frightened, but so, too, is the octopus, and both exit the hole, the octopus in the lead. Again the use of the question mark heightens the suspense at one hole. In this book, Komagata multiplies the exclamation marks. One punctuates the surprise of suddenly coming upon a starfish, a lobster, crabs, and clams after passing through a single hole. The use of the exclamation mark is particularly expressive in the scene that depicts another large, open-mouthed fish coming toward the little protagonist or later when an eel chases the fish around in a circle. The presence of another exclamation mark may lead young readers to interpret his last encounter as yet another predatory scene when two large spotted fish come toward the little fish with their mouths open. However, these two spotted fish resemble the protagonist and their toothless, open mouths appear to be smiling. The fact that all three fish leave the last hole together seems to confirm that the protagonist has joined up with its parents. The story follows a pattern very similar to *Yellow to Red*, reuniting the young animal protagonist with its parents at the end. In the final book of the spiral series, readers follow a bird that encounters various animals as it flies through the woods to the field in *Mori ni nohara ni* (Through the forest to the field, 1993). Each of the spiral books is contained within an attractive cardboard case, whose colour (red, blue, and green respectively) is in keeping with the subject. The protagonist is depicted heading toward the hole that also pierces the case. The spiral books constitute intriguing book-sculptures which can also be unfolded to lie flat, offering a very different simultaneous reading.

Komagata uses a similar cutting and folding technique in two book-sculptures published under the title *Pata Pata*, Japanese for the sound made when pages are turned. Published in 1995, *Snake* is a wordless book constructed from a single sheet of paper that has been cut and folded to form the shape of the titular snake. The paper is white on one side and yellow on the other, creating a multi-coloured reptile on which spots have also been painted in various colours. Holes have been cut the entire length of its body, reminiscent of the holes in the spiral books, although these are irregularly spaced and of varying sizes. The snake's head constitutes a very unconventional "cover," while the colophon occurs on the last triangular fold that forms the tail. The eye is a round hole and the mouth is a triangular cut that reveals part of a blue dot, as if the snake is in the process of swallowing something. *Snake* is a colourful book-sculpture with which young children will also want to play. The other title in the series, *Soraga Aoito Umimo Aoi* (Sea is blue when sky is blue), which was published the same year as *Snake*, is also a book-sculpture cut out of a single sheet of paper. This book has a more pedagogical intention, however, as it deals with basic science questions concerning the colours of light.

Komagata's first book in the tactile series, *Plis et plans* (Folds and planes, 2003), has a rectangular, horizontal format in keeping with the subject matter. The title indicates the importance of folds in this book, which presents geometric forms (circle, square, triangle) through the use of cuts and folds in the paper. As the reader turns the pages and lifts the folds, the forms change. In this mobile narrative, abstract forms are transformed into their opposites:

the small becomes large and the single becomes multiple. Readers are invited to invent mini-narratives in the folds of the book. *Plis et plans* ends where it begins and can be read in either direction. In a brief introduction in Japanese, French, and Braille, Komagata addresses children in a haiku-like form to describe, in very enigmatic, poetic terms, the transformations that take place in the book which begins and ends "slowly slowly," while an afterword helps adults understand the artist's intention. The book becomes a tactile, three-dimensional object, whose form is constantly shifting in a very dynamic manner. It is, in essence, an ever-changing moveable sculpture. Komagata's innovative books allow readers to experience the space of the page in an entirely new manner.

Komagata adopts a new format in *Little Tree*, published in 2008 in a trilingual edition: Japanese, English, and French. It is, in fact, an artist's pop-up book, whose intricately cut pop-ups make it Komagata's most expensive book to date. Composed of coloured and textured heavy paper, the book has exquisite pop-ups on every doublespread. When the page is turned, a tree pops up on the centrefold. The artist once again tells the story of a life cycle, here in direct relationship to the changing seasons and the passing years. It takes the theme of *Leaves* one step further and tells the life story of a tree. The tiny unrecognizable seedling that emerges from the snow on the first doublespread gradually grows; leaves appear in spring; the green leaves turn to yellow and then red in autumn against warm, rust-coloured pages; the stark branches of the bare tree are silhouetted against the barren, grey background of winter. The seasons and the years pass. The doublespread that evokes the passage of many springs presents a tree covered in pink foliage standing on pink paper, evoking cherry blossom season in Japan. In this book, even light plays a role in telling the story. Komagata draws shadows on a few of the pages to draw readers' attention to the real shadows cast by the light, shadows which are constantly changing. The life cycle of the tree is linked to that of the birds that nest in its branches and to the man who is buried at its base. The tree, too, dies and when children return to catch cicadas and the elderly want to rest beneath it, the tree is gone, leaving only memories on an empty doublespread. The final doublespread brings us full circle, as a seedling sprouts in a scene that duplicates the first opening. *Little Tree* is a very poetic and ingeniously crafted book, which received special mention in the Fiction category of the Bologna Ragazzi Award at the Bologna Children's Book Fair 2010. Komagata's innovative experimentation with the book as a three-dimensional object has continued Munari's legacy and produced new spatial forms of artists' books.

Accordion Books

Book artists frequently experiment with the accordion book, which is composed of one continuous strip of paper folded accordion style and generally enclosed between two hard covers. These books are also called concertina books or leporello. Accordion books are a variation on the codex, in which the continuous flow of paper, unlike a scroll, is folded into page-like units so that it can function as a book with openings or as a single unfolded unit. However, they are also a form of book-sculpture. Folding books have a long tradition in Asia, notably in China and in Japan, where they were still popular in the Meiji period at the end of the nineteenth-century. They were also used in the Americas for the Mayan and Aztec codices, which were folded books of long strips of bark or animal skins. Komagata uses a variety of folding techniques in his Little Eyes series. In *Walk and Look*, for example, cards are folded accordion style and mounted between covers. As viewers "walk" around these books and "look" at them from different angles, the image and its meaning shift. Warja Lavater was inspired by the prefabricated folded books used by calligraphers in New York's Chinatown, which, in addition to the "doublepages" of standard books, provide "non-interrupted flowing tales."[56] The artist has used this format to tell a number of Japanese tales.

Although Lavater conceived her first *imagerie* in 1959, she did not publish her first book until 1962. The preceding year, Enzo Mari used the sixteen animals of his wooden puzzle to create the limited edition wordless accordion book *L'altalena*, which was first published by Danese in 1961, and reissued by Corraini in 2001. In it, the artist explores the concepts of weight, shape, quantity, and balance. The title appears on the wordless book in four languages: the words "L'Altalena," "See-Saw," "Balançoire," and "Die Wippe" are stacked one above the other on the end of a red see-saw, much as the animals themselves will be on the inside pages. Although the images obviously depict a see-saw, and that word appears in English on the cover of the original edition, Corraini oddly gives the title of the book in English on their website as "The Swing." The sequential images are narrated on one continuous folded sheet of light, high quality paper. The pages unfold between two soft green covers on which the text and image appear in vivid red. Unlike the majority of Lavater's accordion books, *L'altalena* does not stand easily due to the very light paper, the soft cover, and the large format (17 x 24 cm).

Mari's design principles are immediately recognizable in *L'altalena*. Although the cover is brightly coloured, the inside pages are white with dark, monochromatic images in only grey-black and brown. The artist's love of simple archetypal shapes is evident in the stylized animals of *L'altalena*. Mari thus demonstrates his tenet that "the shapes of toys must be based on archetypal images, and these images must be realized with the highest possible quality and not in the style of 'children's drawings.'"[57] The see-saw is depicted at the bottom of each doublespread as a simple, brown line balanced on a brown circle. The empty, perfectly balanced see-saw is the only image on the stark white background of the otherwise empty first doublespread. On the subsequent folds, the see-saw teeters back and forth as one animal after another is added, ranging from a duck and a bird to a camel and an elephant.

The grey-black bodies of the animals are silhouetted strikingly against the white background, sometimes fitting tightly together, at other times leaving negative white spaces between them that form interesting and eye-catching shapes. The animals are textured by the use of the technique of xylography or wood engraving, the oldest of the graphic arts. Finally, all sixteen animals have been piled on the see-saw, as many as six high, with seven on the heavy side and nine on the other. At that point, readers see the first sign of trouble, as the bird loses its balance. On the following doublefold, all the animals have been tossed into the air. When the see-saw teeters to the other side, however, the animals assume a new order, fitting even more tightly together than previously. The five animals remaining on the left side are now stacked in an almost completely reverse order. The final double fold is even more surprising. All the animals now fit snuggly together, as they do in Enzo's puzzle, in the centre of a perfectly balanced see-saw. Enzo's truly remarkable work can be a book, a game, or a decorative strip to hang up. Design and illustration meet in this delightful book for young and old alike.

Almost all of Warja Lavater's works are accordion books. In France, her books were called "Imageries," whereas in Switzerland and Germany they were marketed as "Folded Stories," highlighting the format rather than the visual code. The Swiss artist herself refers to these unusual books as sculptures. She stresses the mobility and versatility of their unique format. The signs can be followed by viewing the doublefolds in a conventional manner from left to right. In the majority of Western accordion books, the story unfolds in that direction. However, the artist points out that it is also possible to go backwards "with much more continuity than in the classic book."[58] Although these books can be read as doublespreads, either from left to right or back to front, they can also stand, allowing all the pages to be viewed simultaneously. The fluid format of accordion books often necessitates the creation of slipcases. The Museum of Modern Art in New York had a little blue slipcase made for *William Tell*, whereas Adrien Maeght chose plexiglass cases to contain the Perrault series. Eventually, a colourful cardboard case beautifully illustrated by the artist was designed so that the entire set of six tales in their transparent cases could be sold as a boxed set. The unique boxed set is currently commanding prices in excess of 1,000 € on the rare book market.

In Switzerland, Lavater's first book, *Wilhelm Tell*, was published as "Folded Story 1" by Basilius Presse in 1962. All of her subsequent accordion books published in that country became part of the series of "Folded Stories," which includes a total of nineteen volumes. The technique of concertina folding offers dramatic possibilities that Lavater uses very skilfully in conjunction with form, colour, and proportion. The action unfolds in a very cinematographic manner; zoom effects are achieved by increasing or decreasing the size of the coloured symbols. Suspense builds in *Le Petit Chaperon Rouge* as the black dot which represents the wolf moves through the green dot forest toward the little red dot. When the viewer unfolds the doublespread depicting the encounter, the black dot is suddenly huge and menacing in relationship to the little red dot. The black dot-wolf becomes even larger on the two-page folds that represent the climactic scenes in which he eats first the blue dot grandmother and then the little red riding hood dot. With basic geometric forms, Lavater skillfully interprets the archetypal motifs of the familiar traditional tales. In her rendition of the story of Snow White, the motif of the magic mirror, represented by a simple yellow rectangle, is particularly masterful. The folded format of the book allows a striking juxtaposition of the two doublespreads in which the queen consults her mirror. In a later juxtaposition that extends over four folds, the queen witnesses in the mirror the scene taking place in the forest, as the prince's kiss literally projects the poisoned apple from Snow White's throat. The treatment of the motif of the glass slipper in *Cendrillon* is both effective and humorous. Amusing scenes represent each of the stepsisters trying on the slipper while Cinderella sits on the sidelines in the hearth with the matching slipper, which is virtually invisible because it is represented on a much smaller scale and covered in ash. The following scene is situated entirely within the hearth. A resplendent Cinderella—almost the only figure not covered in ash—now takes centre stage to try on the slipper in front of the prince, whose proportions are humorously reduced so that he is no larger than the slipper.

Several of Lavater's Folded Stories published in the 1960s have an even smaller format than her Perrault tales. *Die Party*, Folded Story 4 (1962), was published the same year as her first book, *William Tell*. However, it is not a retelling of a traditional tale, but an original story told in black and white, as are several of her other early tales. On the first doublespread, which serves as a form of title page, the artist has handwritten in India ink a much more enlightening variation on the title: *Die vier temperamente: Sanguiniker, Choleriker, Phlegmatiker, Melancholiker oder Party bei*. The title is given only in German, but no translation is necessary, and the colophon gives the title simply as *Party*. The title is punctuated by two pictorial symbols that draw readers onward. The second double fold consists of the legend, which is presented in a very different manner from the majority of her works. A square with a heavy black frame is divided into four smaller squares by dotted lines and within each square a temperament is written in German. It is linked by an equal sign to a second similar square, in which four black symbols correspond to the temperaments. Some of the temperaments in the first square are described by several adjectives beginning with "s," three of which are given in German and one in English. The sanguine temperament is described as "stark" (stout) and "schnell" (swift), the choleric as "schwach" (slight), and the phlegmatic as "slow." The simple corresponding symbols will recur in subsequent works: a spiral (sanguine), a zigzag (choleric), a circle (phlegmatic), and a wavy, upside-down "V" (melancholic). Two of the five additional symbols under the squares are decoded in German, two in English, and the fifth is the internationally used French word "buffet." In an attempt to reach as universal an audience as possible, the artist provides a thoughtful multilingual legend without resorting, as she will in later books, to giving the entire legend in several languages.

Folded Story 5, *La promenade en ville* (The walk in the city), was also published in 1962. Like *Die Party*, it is entirely in black and white, with the exception of the green and red traffic lights, but this time the title and legend occur only in French. Even the publication details are given in French, although it was brought out by Basilius Presse. The French language probably seemed the logical choice for a narrative about a young lady walking her dog. Lavater is continually experimenting with variations on her ingenious pictorial code. In this case, the legend leads directly into the story. Four of the elements in the brief key are accompanied by the usual abstract symbols, but the handwritten script of the first two, "une demoiselle" and "son petit chien," simply continue as solid and broken meandering lines which trace the promenade of the young lady and her dog across the folds of the book. The two paths rarely run parallel, but twist, turn, and crisscross along the folds. One can easily imagine the dog curiously sniffing at litter in the street, stopping to urinate at a pole or a tree, encircling a garbage pail curiously, and so forth, as he and his owner make their way through town. The legend suggests that the promenade will not be without incident, as it also includes another dog, an enemy, and a gentleman. Not surprisingly, the remaining elements are red and green traffic lights, which add the only colour to the otherwise black-and-white book (even the covers are devoid of colour: the front cover is white and the back cover is a dark grey that borders on black).

A similar format was used a few years later for *Re . . . Re . . . Revolution Re . . .*, Folded Story 12 (1965), and *Conform . . . . ismus . . . . ity . . . . isme*, Folded Story 17 (1966), which almost seem to form a diptych presenting contrasting concepts. The titles of these books again suggest the artist's predilection for abstract notions that can be expressed by a single universally understood word. The stutter-like repetition of "re" in the title evokes all the connotations of the prefix "re": "afresh," "anew," "one more." Revolution has been a recurring phenomenon throughout the history of humankind. On the cover of the later book, the word "Conform" appears by itself on a line and the suffixes are listed below in a row. Unlike *Die Party* and *La promenade en ville*, the legend of *Revolution* is found on a sheet that folds out of the cover and is given in three languages. It is the simplest of Lavater's legends, as it is limited to three very basic symbols representing the powerful man, the powerless man, and the revolutionary. The colophon neatly printed at the bottom of the verso contrasts with the handwritten scrawl in black ink that reproduces the title across the first doublefold, where the visual narrative begins around the word "revolution" on the lower right hand corner of the recto, drawing the reader onward. The artist also adds a single colour to the black-and-white visual narrative, oddly not red as one might expect in light of the subject, but green, perhaps a more positive, less violent and bloody slant on revolution. In *Conform*

.... *ismus* .... *ity* .... *isme*, Lavater returns to black and white. In this case, she seems to have felt the visual narrative is self-explanatory because there is no legend or summary.

Lavater experiments with folded books in a variety of sizes and shapes. In 1965, she adopted a very narrow, vertical format for Folded Story 11, whose lengthy, highly descriptive title leaves little doubt about the subject: *Walk, Dont Walk, Walk, Attendez, Gehe, Dont Walk, Passez, Warte, Walk, Dont.* Like the later children's book *Die Rose und der Laubfrosch*, also a tall, narrow book, *Walk, Dont Walk* is about traffic lights, a subject that seems to impose such a format. A legend is unnecessary in this book, as the visual language is less abstract and more figurative. Stylized, stick-like human figures with spidery limbs, vaguely reminiscent of the human figures in prehistoric rock art, move across the lower half of the splatter-painted folds. Like a choreographed dance, pedestrians walk, stop, wait, and walk, obeying the green and red circles that represent traffic lights. The variations in the shades of blue used for the human figures seem to reflect their pace. Individual pale blue figures begin walking slowly across the first fold, but their number quickly increases, as does their speed, until the crowd of figures becomes a dark blue blur that stops abruptly at a red light. Under the red light, a gap in the flow of figures marks the street, and on the other side the pale blue figures begin the cycle again. At one red light, the space between the figures on the two sides of the street contains squiggly, disjointed red lines that seem to fly through the air. A tiny eye (the only one in the book) confirms that the red lines, from which drops of red paint/blood fall, constitute the body parts of an accident victim who has crossed on a red light. Although *Walk, Dont Walk* can be read as conventional doublespreads, the narrowness of this book lends itself to considering more than one doublefold at a time. This work constitutes a particularly coherent and striking visual narrative when it is completely unfolded and viewed as an ensemble.

Lavater's final Folded Story (number 19), *Das Feuer und seine Höhlen* (The Fire and its caves), which was published in 1967, has a larger format than the other books in the series. Like *Walk, Dont Walk*, it is more figurative, using similar spidery stick figures. The story, which begins in the manner of a fairy tale: "Once upon a time there was a man," traces various states in the history of humankind from the discovery of fire to the quest of the artist. The allegorical tale is told briefly in three languages on a flap that folds out at the front. It is one of Lavater's most complex tales, but, as in the much simpler *Walk, Dont Walk*, the figurative nature of the pictograms makes a legend unnecessary. Although the familiar legend is eliminated, words are added to the pictorial narrative in a new way. At the top of alternating doublespread folds, the artist includes German titles or keywords that she feels require no translation: "Matriarchat," "Patriarchat," "Magie," "Mystik," "Kosmologie," and "Psychiatrie." On these doublefolds, the caves are depicted as partial circles, becoming ever larger until a completed circle represents cosmology. The final image could be a metaphorical reflection on the artist's role. From the final cave of psychiatry, which is once again a half circle like the initial cave in which man put fire, "the creative one will break lose not to find fire but light," writes Lavater in the verbal summary. The brief authorial text concludes with a line that reappears in other Folded Stories, encouraging readers to reflect on the relevance of these tales: "and if this were not an 'imagerie' it could be a true story. . . ." The tall, stylized, black human figures, vaguely reminiscent of *Walk, Dont Walk*, stand out strikingly against the fire-like orange background of the caves, creating very eye-catching graphic images. The central figure of the matriarch, who presides over the fire and seems to be telling a story, is distinguished from the seated figures listening on both sides of her: round pink circles with red dots are appended as breasts to mark her sex. Around the patriarch stand warriors with spears, whereas the magician is surrounded by figures in an ecstatic trance, and the mystic/preacher leads a more sedate group of worshipers. There are no human figures in the complete circle representing cosmology, and the "creative one" who breaks loose from the last cave does not take a human form but rather that of coloured cosmic dust rising into the sky.

The philosophical reflections on humankind that Lavater presents in a more figurative manner in *Walk Dont Walk* and *Das Feuer* are pursued in her more abstract visual code in *Homo Sapiens?* Folded Story 13, published in 1965. The use of the Latin scientific name for humankind makes the title of this folded story universal. Three languages again figure in the legend, but Lavater continues to strive toward a common language. Sometimes a single word suffices ("Sensation," "Ambition," "Tradition," "Emotion") or a word or its root is given with additional suffixes ("Clima . . . t . . . e"); in other cases two words are necessary ("Opinion . . . Meinung"). The attempt to simplify seems sometimes to complicate, as in the case of "Vanit . . . y . . . é," to which the lengthy German suffix is added below: ". . . eitelkeit." Unlike previous stories, *Homo Sapiens?* begins with text, which is hand printed in lines that are curved or on various angles. According to Lavater, the lives and emotions of homo sapiens are dictated by "mass production," and the fact that she gives this term only in English seems to lay the blame with the Anglo-American world. The question formulated in the centre of the doublefold, which asks whether homo sapiens remain "homo sapiens. Sapiens? Sapiens?" clearly indicates the meaning of the question mark in the title. This folded story is an ironic questioning of the appropriateness of the Latin term meaning "knowing man" or "wise man" for the human race in light of what it has become. In the bottom right hand corner of the first doublefold, inviting readers to follow, is a symbol that was not included in the legend: a somewhat derisory squiggly line portraying "homo sapiens."

La mélodie de Turdidi (The melody of Turdidi, 1971), an original tale in which Lavater takes up the unlikely subject of birdsong, was published simultaneously in Paris (in French) and New York (in Spanish and English). The tale is told on a fold following the legend and colophon. The multiple readings to which Lavater's pictorial narratives lend themselves are clearly demonstrated by the interpretation given to this story by Johanna Drucker in *The Century of Artists' Books*. She sees it as "a coming of age story" in which "a youngster in a musical family" finds "his own voice." She points out, as I have done with regard to the birds that eat the trail of bread left by Little Thumbling, that Turdidi resembles "a baby Pac-man though he was invented long before."[59] Turdidi looks even more like a blackbird, however. His symbol, a black circle with a red and white dot for an eye and a pie-shaped wedge cut out of the top, resembles a blackbird's head with its upturned beak open in song. Furthermore, the brief verbal summary informs readers that the "young singer" Turdidi belongs to the Turdidae family of "great singers." Turdidae is the zoological name for the thrushes (blackbirds, bluebirds, robins, etc.) whose family includes some of the most renowned songbirds in the world; their vocalizations are considered to be among the most beautiful on earth. Many identical young birds are grouped in two orderly rows around the much larger teacher, but Turdidi, whose eye colour distinguishes him from the others, stands apart singing in an entirely different direction. The melody that issues from the wide mouth of the teacher forms a beautiful, but highly structured design of different sized blue dots, while the melody from Turdidi's unique voice is represented as golden yellow dots of varying sizes which burst from him with spontaneous exuberance. Lavater often uses her pictorial language to express passions and emotions, and *La mélodie de Turdidi* is no exception. The artist tells the story of the singer's rapid rise to stardom and his immediate return to obscurity when jealous birds sabotage his night of glory.

In this modern tale, Lavater introduces the world of show business, in the form of film, television, antennas, projectors, lights, microphones, amplifiers, plugs, and electrical cords. Although these elements are all represented by simple visual signs, they almost all resemble the actual objects, so that some scenes are less abstract than in other books. One of the most striking images in the book shows Turdidi singing his heart out in what is recognizably a television recording studio, surrounded by the paraphernalia of the business. Grey dot-sparrows sit listening in the many antennae intended to capture and broadcast the young singer's voice. Sitting on the stage are two pigeon-journalists (after the word "pigeons" in the legend, Lavater adds the word "journalistes" in parentheses), symbolized very effectively by grey ovals with fluorescent green or pink shading that is very close to the colour of real pigeons. Turdidi's golden melody, which floats across the top of this aesthetically pleasing doublefold rendered largely in grey, black, and white, pervades the entire stage and encloses Turdidi in a yellow bubble in the next colourful doublefold. The subsequent spread cleverly repeats Turdidi's image on thirty tiny television screens that light up the darkness of the page. In front of each television, a viewing audience of anywhere from one to ten small birds sits enthralled by the performance (young readers may turn the doublefold into a counting exercise). The artist uses proportion and colour to create almost a visual translation of the musical term "crescendo." The dark page illuminated by the thirty tiny images of Turdidi on television screens is immediately followed by a vividly coloured image of the singer live on the stage, now so large that only half of the little bird is visible on the doublefold, making the sparrows in the audience look miniscule. Within the speakers on the stage, the symbol for Turdidi's melody is enlarged many times suggesting the amplification of the little bird's song. In one particularly beautiful doublefold, arcs of coloured light from the projectors beam across the stage in every direction, creating a dazzling display of colour that transforms the little black bird. As the performance, the colour, and the excitement all reach a crescendo, the three jealous birds cut the electrical wires and the following doublespread is plunged into darkness (Turdidi's eye is the only spot of colour in the otherwise black and grey artwork). The prominent presence of antennae on skyscraper roofs in a dark, drab spread representing the city in winter seems to mock the lonely, despairing bird whose song had once been broadcast over those same antennae.

Lavater's story has a fairy-tale happy ending, however. A single page turn (or unfolding) transforms the drab winter into a colourful spring scene, in which Turdidi discovers many young birds all singing his song. Once again, the melody seems to be carried over the waves of the many antennae. In the explosion of colour and melody in the final scene, Turdidi has now assumed the role of teacher and master, but his methods are obviously very different from those used by his predecessor. The birds are not singing with a single voice that echoes the master, but each retains its uniqueness, as music explodes in all directions. It is rare that Lavater includes text in her images, but on a doublefold that depicts an overview of the theatre, the star's name is billed across the top and along the side.

Lavater was extremely excited about the possibilities offered by the "leporello," which she described in 1991 as "a book that can be transformed into sculpture, standing on the ground, or hung, unfolded, on the wall." Naming a number of types of "book-objects" with which she has experimented, Lavater mentions the "livre-debout."[60] Although all her *imageries* could theoretically be categorized as "standing books," she uses the term to refer specifically to a book that is meant to stand in a circle. *Leidenschaft und Vernunft* (Passion and reason) was published by Basilius Presse as a "Steh . . . auf Buch" (Stand . . . up book) in 1963 and reissued in French, German, and English by Adrien Maeght under the title *Passion et raison* as "un livre . . . debout" (a standing book) in 1985. Inspired by philosophy, the book consists of abstract illustrations of chaos, disorder, civilization, ideology, moral, culture, ethics, and essence. Passion is symbolized by a chaotic red line and reason by an orderly blue square. The artist depicts the shifting interaction of the two forces, until a third entity is created: a red square representing "essence." In 1988, Lavater created another *imagerie* inspired by philosophy: *Ergo* is a reflection on René Descartes's argument "Je pense donc je suis," which became a foundational element of Western philosophy. Warja Lavater devoted her entire career to exploring the possibilities of the accordion book.

Mural Books

Lavater explains that Japanese folded books give you "non-interrupted flowing tales, from left to right or from top downwards."[61] Although the story flows from left to right in the majority of Lavater's works several of her books unfold from top to bottom. These books all have a much larger format than the series of Perrault tales. The same year that she published *Le Petit Chaperon rouge* in Paris, two fairy tales were published in the mural format in Switzerland, the Grimms' *Hans im Gluck* as Folded Story 14 and Hans Christian Andersen's *The Ugly Duckling* as Folded Story 15. The colophon informs readers—in German, English, and French—that these "Folded Stories" can be used "both as books and as wall decoration." This information, which is repeated on the back "cover," is superfluous as both books have a string hook taped to the back on the fold with the legend (the legend is upside down when the book is hung). This paratextual element also states that Lavater's "Folded Stories" provide an experience that stimulates the imagination of "both children and adults." *Ramalalup* (Folded Story 18, 1967), a philosophical tale about opposites (Ramala and Lup) who come to share the same wisdom, also has a vertical format, but, unlike the previous books, there is no hook to hang it. This book is unique in that the text has all been confined to the two covers: the legend appears on the front cover with the title and author's name, while the back cover contains the colophon and the summary of the tale. Both the textual and paratextual aspects of the book have thus been relegated to its exterior, leaving the interior entirely devoted to the visual narrative. *Moon Ballad*, published in New York in 1973, is an "imagery" adapted from the Grimms' "Sleeping Beauty," but it is a highly original retelling. The metal hook that allows the book to be hung clearly indicates that *Moon Ballad* falls into the category of what Lavater calls a "mural book."[62] Not only does Lavater impose a vertical rather than horizontal reading, but she tells the story from bottom to top, much to the surprise of readers who will undoubtedly start at the top (the hook end) when they first pick up the book. *Spectacle*, published in 1990, is described as a "pictoson mural," as she combines symbols and sounds in this depiction of the evolution of vowels and consonants, as symbols become letters. The format is much larger than her other works (175 x 30 cm), creating a long, vertical panorama, in eleven plates of soft cardboard, that can be hung by a hook. The legend and the explanation of the story are given in multiple languages on the back. A number of Lavater's *imageries*, notably the Perrault tales, have also been sold by Adrien Maeght mounted on wood as murals.

In 1995, the French editor Nicole Maymat brought out a series of books titled "livres-fresques" (fresco-books) with the children's publisher Seuil

Jeunesse. Although it was not their intention to produce artists' books, according to Maymat, the large-format accordion books are all exquisitely illustrated by artists and glued by hand. The folds of the heavy paper open up to form a long "fresco," which can be displayed hanging on a wall or as a "standing book." The poetic and philosophical texts, all poems, have the beauty and high quality that characterized all the books published by Maymat's own publishing house, Ipomée. The relatively short texts gave the artists a great deal of freedom to experiment with the folded format. In all of the books, the text of the poem is artistically integrated into the illustrations and becomes an integral part of the artwork. The books are contained in a coloured cardboard slipcase, which has a rectangular cut-out—a kind of window into the book—through which the title and part of the cover illustration can be seen. The first book, *Le secret du rêve*, is inspired by the poem "The Secret of Dreaming" by the Australian Jim Poulter and illustrated by the French author and illustrator Claire Forgeot, who, since 1994, has devoted herself entirely to her painting. Inspired by Aboriginal Australians, who believe that "the Land is sacred/and man must be its Caretaker," Poulter tells their creation story through a Dreaming of the Spirit of Life. The Secret of Dreaming was passed along through the elements and the species until it finally reached Man, who understood that he must protect the Dreaming of all living creatures. The magnificent artwork for this book, which was created on old wooden stair steps, portrays the different stages of the Dream's transmission. The original version of the poem as well as the French translation are printed on the back of Forgeot's "fresco," so it can be read on both sides, like a number of Lavater's folded books. The French version of the poem is also integrated into the ten illustrated panels of the recto.

The second book in the "livres-fresques" series was *L'orange bleue* (The blue orange), written by the Moroccan poet Abdellatif Laâbi and illustrated by the Italian-born artist Laura Rosano (both now live in France). The book is a poetic homage to the titular "blue orange" that is our planet earth. On heavy black paper, Rosano created collages that combine torn paper, white cut-outs, and photographs (of children, food, etc.). The striking mosaic-like technique used throughout was actually created with tiny pieces of paper from chocolate bars that the artist painstakingly glued by hand. Intricately cut white paper was used to create a decorative border or architectural details which, along with the mosaics, give the book a Moorish feel. Animals were created by paper folding techniques in white rice paper. Text and image are inseparable: the round "O" of "Orange" in the title becomes an aerial view of the earth, composed of Rosano's delicate mosaics. Most of the text is handwritten in white cursive script on the black background, but there are a number of very artistic typographical experiments. In large upper case black letters cut out of white paper and glued on, the word "SILENCE" screams its mute message on the first doublefold. On the following opening, the word "EARTH" is spelled out in six languages in letters cut from a variety of earth-coloured paper that explode vertically from a large brightly coloured vessel of torn paper, like a volcano erupting during the earth's birth. Sometimes ribbon-like white lines weave their way through the illustrations separating the lines of text or linking words. On a striking doublefold of a large tree, the final letters of the words "infini" (infinite) and "rêves" (dreams) are linked across the gutter by the wavy white line into which they have been integrated and thus pulled out of their context in the poem and given new meaning. The words that formulate the poet's aspirations for a new world flow as if from a fountain, in curved lines which are accentuated by multicoloured mosaic-like curved lines. On the reverse side of the concertina folding, the poem is written from right to left, in both Arabic and English. The third book in the series, *La maison des mots* (The house of words, 1998), is based on a Brazilian poem by Rachel Uziel and illustrated by the Brazilian illustrator Angela Lago. The idea for the poem was inspired by Uziel's five-year-old daughter Aurylia, who declared one morning: "People are the house of words." Lago has interpreted Aurylia's words literally in her illustrations. In all languages and colours, people are born from words and reach out their hands to dance around full of tenderness. The original Brazilian text again appears on the recto of the folded fresco. Unfortunately, the superb Livres-fresques series could not be continued due to the high production costs.

Object-Books

Artists have also experimented with books as spatial objects of very large dimensions, which are categorized here as object-books rather than book-objects. Some object-books even become spaces in which to read, play, or perform. These artists' books are at once a book, a game, and an object to use. A number of very interesting examples are to be found in the world of Italian design. Both Enzo Mari and Bruno Munari were interested in all aspects of the child's world, and, in addition to books, designed games, toys, furniture, and other objects for children. In 1967, Danese published Enzo Mari's *Il posto dei giochi* (The place of games), a three-metre folding, corrugated cardboard sheet in ten panels, with abstract images and cut-outs intended to stimulate children's imaginations. Although he originally conceived a less expensive product, he was forced to "decorate" it or it would not have appeared. Resembling an oversize accordion book, it is at once a room screen and a playground that can be transformed into a fortress, a wall, a bridge, a hiding place, and a multitude of other things. *Il posto dei giochi* was faithfully re-produced by Corraini in 2008.[63] The previous year, Corraini organized an exhibition at the Casina di Raffaello (the children's activity centre in the Villa Borghese in Rome), where Mari's *The Fable Game* was enlarged to child-size proportions. As with the original book-game, children could rearrange and reinvent it, but now they could not only play with it, but play in it. It could be turned into a small labyrinth, a theatre backdrop, a space in which to read, or whatever else their imagination devised.

Munari takes the concept of the book as object to another dimension with his *Libro letto* (1993), formed from the homograph/homophone *letto*, which means both "read" and "bed." The book is composed of large differently coloured pieces of padded fabric in the form of soft sheets to be used as pages or a comfortable bed. It is a square, large-format book that can be transformed into a bed by detaching the coloured, soft padded fabric pages and joining them end to end with the zippers. In the design magazine *Domus*, Munari describes it as a "habitable book."[64] As well as being laid flat like a bed, it can be folded up and transformed into a tent or a hut. The short phrases of text printed on the border that runs along two edges of the "pages" constitute a story regardless of whether they have been joined to form a book or a bed. The story changes with each construction. Children can bring to the book-bed any book they choose, or they can simply dream, inspired by the text on the edge of their bed. Munari gives the bedtime story new meaning with *Libro letto*. Munari's work inspired Katsumi Komagata to create similar object-books, based on his own books. The child can enter the book in a large scale fabric replica of his book *Snake*, created in 1997, which has holes through which the child can crawl. It is somewhat ironic that the artist retains the title *Pata Pata*, evoking the sound that pages make when turned, for the large soft book that is virtually soundless. Like those of Munari's *Libro letto*, the "pages" of *Pata Pata* can be separated into individual squares. Two works in Komagata's Mini Book Series, *Shape* and *Motion*, also inspired a series of cushions which can be used to create a labyrinth by combining forms and colours. Munari and Komagata offer children "books" in which they can invent and re-invent stories.

Crossing Boundaries with Artists' Books

Artists' books transcend the traditional form of the book and allow readers to experience its space in new ways. Many of the books examined in this chapter are innovative not only in form but also in content, introducing philosophical topics and complex concepts with extreme simplicity. Readers of all ages are led to question their assumptions and beliefs, and often forced to recognize that their view of the world is flawed or partial. Often these unique books did not sell well in their day, as many of their creators were far ahead of their time. Artists' books offer readers of all ages innovative, challenging books of exceptional aesthetic quality, but the artists who create them often have to overcome major obstacles. Komagata raises the problem of the perception of "three dimensional action books" by the public, which tends to be suspicious of books that seem to rely on format to appeal to children, often classifying them in the "temporary goods category."[65] When Komagata exhibited at the second Artists' Book Fair in New York, he felt that the attention his books drew was due to the public's curiosity as to whether or not an artist can maintain the quality of his art in works that address children. The unconventional format can even lead to a questioning of their status as books. As we have seen, the books Komagata sent to Lyon for an exhibition in 1994 were labelled as toys by a French custom's officer, who, it is true, may simply have been anxious to collect the higher tax. Such innovative books often do not fit into conventional book marketing systems. To illustrate that his books do not conform to the Japanese distribution system, Komagata points to works like *Snake* that have no spine on which to put the title. The fluidity of accordion books, such as Lavater's, may necessitate special packaging in slipcases. Book stores and libraries often have difficulty shelving artists' books due to the unusual formats.

Artists' books expand the boundaries of the conventional book in the directions of objects, games, toys, sculpture, murals, music, and so forth. The unique works of artists such as Bruno Munari, Iela and Enzo Mari, Warja Lavater, and Katsumi Komagata also transcend geographical, cultural, and age boundaries. Artists' books, especially those that are wordless, lend themselves particularly well to border crossings, which may take place either before or after their publication. In Lavater's first books, the legend appeared in only a single language,[66] but early on it was expanded to include several languages, generally English, French, German, and Japanese, although the legend of *Spectacle* is translated into eight languages. Enzo Mari gave the title of his wordless accordion book *L'altalena* in four languages. The titles of Komagata's books are often given in English as well as Japanese. This is true of wordless books (*Snake, Found It!*), as well as books with text which are otherwise entirely in Japanese (*Yellow to Red, Green to Green*, etc.). Short preliminary texts are often given in several languages, as in Munari's *Prelibri*, wordless except for an introductory text in four languages. When Komagata's books contain text, it is available in other languages, notably English and German, on a separate sheet of paper inserted in the book. One of his most recent books, *Little Tree*, is completely trilingual (in Japanese, English, and French). Even when artists' books contain text, the narrative is carried largely by colour, form, paper, image, and so forth, so that readers can enjoy the book without necessarily understanding the words.

Artists' books appeal to young and old alike, transcending the arbitrary boundaries that attempt to divide readers into specific age categories. Lavater admits her initial astonishment when people began telling her their children liked and even understood the luxury edition of *Le Petit Chaperon rouge*, but she now proudly claims that the "pictorial language" of her *imageries* appeals to all ages.[67] Many of her titles, including the most complex and philosophical, can be found in the collection of the International Youth Library in Munich. Initially, Komagata could not believe that Munari's *Prelibri* had been produced for children, but successive readings changed his mind and he looked forward to the day when he could "play together with [his] own children using

[Munari's] books." In 1999, the Japanese artist stated that Munari's books were now "old and worn out, but still [a] treasure" that he intended to give his daughter as a wedding gift.[68] Many of these artists began creating books for a young audience after the birth of their own children, but they include adults in their target audience. Their books encourage communication and playful interaction between adults and children. Because artists' books often have interesting three-dimensional formats that appeal to a variety of senses, they can have immense appeal even for young toddlers. They level the playing field, empowering children and adults more equally. The reader/viewer is invited to become author/storyteller and each reading can produce a new version of the story. A profound complicity exists between artist and reader. The innovative picturebooks of these artists have a universal language that appeals to all ages and cultures.

Many of these innovative books are considered true art objects and they are frequently marketed to adults and art collectors in museum shops and art galleries. Some are even published by museums or art galleries. Both Munari and Lavater have had books published by the Museum of Modern Art in New York. A number of books are put out by publishers who specialize in "artists' books" or who are at the same time art galleries. Lavater's Parisian publisher, Adrien Maeght, specializes in books that are treated as art objects. Corraini, with whom Munari collaborated toward the end of his career, is a contemporary art gallery as well as a publishing house that brings out "both artists' books and children's books."[69] Artists' books may be unique works or issued in very limited editions, as in the case of Dieter Roth's children's books. We have also seen that some works, notably certain fabric books, are produced by hand on request only. Production costs are usually high and mass-producing such books is extremely difficult. While many of these books may seem to be luxury books for an elite adult audience of book art enthusiasts, they are intended to be shared with children.[70] Indeed, most were designed first and foremost for young readers.

Artists' books have often been associated with a number of other arts, including film, theatre, choreography, and music. It has been pointed out that Munari's books introduce a new language closely related to movies and music. Not only do the colours and forms give his books harmony and rhythm, but some of the materials also give them an acoustic dimension. The book–music relationship takes on another dimension in Hervé Di Rosa's wordless accordion book *Jungle* (1991), which is accompanied by a CD with the music Michel Redolfi conceived as a forest of sounds to correspond with the fourteen panels of the artist's Brazilian jungle fresco. The mobility of the format and the "fluid unfolding" of the images in Lavater's accordion books led the artist herself to compare them with theatre, choreography, and film.[71] Lavater's *imageries* based on the Perrault tales actually inspired an award-winning series of six digital image movies marketed for a general audience. The films are accompanied with music by the composer Pierre Charvet, who, using sound synthesis software, composed specific sounds which correspond to the geometrical "codes" of Lavater's work. The *Imageries* obtained the Pixel-INA award in the Art category, the European award of Media Invest Club, and the mention "best sound track" at the "Imagina 1995" exhibition. In his book *About Two Squares*, El Lissitzky sought to imitate the new technological media, which, in the 1920s, was film.[72] Artists' books have much in common with digital media due to their interactive nature. For some critics, Lavater's book-objects published in the 1960s represented "a twenty year advance in computer icons and menus."[73] We have already seen that a number of her characters bear a striking resemblance to Pac-Man in the popular video game developed later. Elisabeth Lortic suggests that the multiple entry points of Komagata's spiral books resemble CD ROM's and may even have prepared the way for them.[74] It is not surprising that a number of these avant-garde books have inspired works in other media. Lavater's *imageries* based on the Perrault tales were also the object of an interactive CD-ROM project. Komagata insists that what he calls "three-dimensional action books" are essential because they express the pleasurable and unique experience of the high-tech age.[75]

According to Henri Cueco, a French artist and poet who has published for children, artists' books open new horizons for the book: "The artist's book is a conquest of new territory."[76] Artists' books have had a very significant influence on contemporary picturebooks. The innovative works of Bruno Munari, Enzo and Iela Mari, and Warja Lavater, among others, attracted other artists to children's books. Over the past few decades, artists from many fields have enriched the world of children's books. As we have already seen, numerous artists are also illustrators, and picturebooks are being recognized as an art form in their own right. The French artist and illustrator Paul Cox created *Le livre le plus long du monde* (The longest book in the world) as a "quadrichronie in homage to Bruno Munari." In the manner of the original version of Enzo and Iela Mari's *The Apple and the Moth*, *Le livre le plus long du monde* has no cover or title page. Four silkscreen printed images present a very simple narrative, using only minimal colours and shapes. Cox tells a never-ending story that goes from sunrise to nightfall and begins again. Within a large circle divided horizontally into two to create a horizon, the small half or full circle of the sun moves through the sky until night falls. The book's spiral binding allows readers to begin at any point. Like the work of the illustrator to whom the book is dedicated, the simple poetic visual narrative is appreciated by adults as well as children. *Le livre le plus long du monde* was published in 2002 by Les Trois Ourses, which specializes in artists' books. The same year Seuil Jeunesse published Cox's *Cependant . . .* (Meanwhile . . .), a lengthy, 116-page visual narrative bearing the apparently equally paradoxical subtitle "le livre le plus court du monde" (the shortest book in the world). The images on the thick cardboard pages of *Cependant . . .* offer a snapshot of the diverse activities taking place around the globe at the same moment. In the space of a single second, readers travel through twenty-four hours, passing from day to night.

A clock indicates the time every five pages, as readers travel from meridian to meridian, encircling the planet. The illustrations depict adventures, catastrophes, and events from daily life. People are milking a cow, riding an elephant, climbing a mountain, travelling through the snow on a sled, sunbathing, being born, getting married, undergoing an operation, playing football, working in a chain gang, experiencing a tornado, and so forth. Unusual associations can be made between apparently unrelated images, for example, the umbilical cord attached to a newborn baby is echoed in the cable that attaches an astronaut to his spaceship. The simple, square images are composed of coloured dots (in the primary colours) that resemble the pixels of digital images. Like *Le livre le plus long du monde*, *Cependant* . . . is a spiral-bound book that allows readers to begin at any point. Both books can also be read in either direction. The General Council of the Val de Marne bought *Cependant* . . . in order to offer a copy to all the children born in that department in 2003. Cox believes that when confronted with innovative and unusual books, children, no less than adults, are aware of their newness and the emancipatory energy that they convey.[77] Cox's books illustrate extremely well the ambivalent nature of the border between artists' books and picturebooks. Contemporary picturebooks seem to defy all the boundaries. Katsumi Komagata questions the need to categorize artists' books or books of any kind. Expressing his discontent with the term "*shikake-ehon*" or "mobile books," the Japanese artist states categorically: "books are books, that's all."[78]

Chapter Three
Wordless Picturebooks

A wordless book offers a different kind of experience from one with text.... Each viewer reads the book in his or her own way.

             —David Wiesner

A significant number of the artists' books discussed in the previous chapter are wordless books that could also have been examined in this chapter, including all of Warja Lavater's accordion books and Iela and Enzo Mari's picturebooks, as well as many works by Bruno Munari and Katsumi Komagata. With the exception of a few relatively rare artists' books often published for bibliophiles, the majority of wordless picturebooks prior to 1970 tend to be educational books with an explicit pedagogical purpose. An early French example, published by Nathan in 1902, bears the descriptive title *Trente histoires en images sans paroles à raconter par les petits* (Thirty stories in images without words for children to tell). Most wordless books of this type present sequences of images intended to introduce children to narrative by inviting them to formulate what is happening in a series of events. Jacqueline Danset-Léger rightly points out that the aesthetic element is sacrificed to meaning in these wordless books, which she feels later influenced books published in the highly regarded Père Castor series created by Paul Faucher, in 1931, for Flammarion.[1] This influence can be seen notably in the "histoires en images" books, such as the well-known Dutch-born illustrator Gerda Muller's *Histoires en 4 images* (Stories in 4 images, 1967), in which a short narrative is told in four equal-sized, wordless, horizontal panels per page. A number of critics point out that these early wordless picturebooks are generally presented as books from which the text has been removed with the expectation that it will be restored by readers, who are encouraged to verbalize the story.[2] In some cases, a pre-existing text is actually eliminated. In *How Picturebooks Work*, Maria Nikolajeva and Carole Scott mention a Russian picturebook, titled *Picture Stories* (1958), in which the short verses by Daniil Kharms and other poets were removed in some Russian editions of the book because the visual narrative of Nikolai Radlov's illustrations is sufficiently clear on its own.[3]

In a 1975 French study devoted to the image in children's books, Marion Durand and Gérard Bertrand choose to refer to wordless "mini-récits" (ministories) as stories "*à parler*" (to talk) rather than "*sans paroles*" (without words). Traditionally these books were targeted at pre-readers, but Durand and Bertrand insist on the fact that they were intended to encourage very young children to talk.[4] The picturebooks *What? When? Where? Who?*, published in 1984 by the Dutch-born Leo Lionni, who lived primarily in Italy once he became a children's author and illustrator, are all subtitled "Pictures to Talk About." As Sophie Van der Linden points out, such books are educational aids that require mediation and stimulate exchange between children and adults. She cites the example of the picturebooks in Casterman's series Ma vie en images (My life in images), whose goal is to "further the child–adult relationship."[5] Wordless picturebooks of an educational nature have little or no interest for adults except in their role as mediators. In recent decades, however, wordless picturebooks have not only shed this educational function, but, in many cases, have developed into highly sophisticated books that appeal equally to children and adults. Thanks largely to the innovative books of artists such as Bruno Munari, Iela Mari, and Warja Lavater, the wordless picturebook became a favourite medium for artistic and graphic experimentation from the 1960s on.

The passage "from pedagogical material to graphic narration" took place in France about 1970 with the appearance of wordless narrative picturebooks "coming from Italy," according to Isabelle Nières-Chevrel. Unlike the baby concept books of earlier decades, the aim of these books "was no longer listing ... but telling."[6] Of course, that does not mean that there were no wordless picturebooks prior to that date. One of Tomi Ungerer's early children's books, *Snail, Where Are You?*, which was published in the United States in 1962, appears on a number of wordless picturebook lists, although it is not entirely without text. The question formulated in the title is repeated on each doublespread, where readers/viewers must find the snail(s) that hide in a wide variety of disguises (for example, as a tuba or the eyes of an owl). Like many wordless picturebooks, it is a concept book for young children. In the hands of gifted picturebook artists, even the *imagier* was turned into an aesthetic wordless picturebook that could be appreciated by adults as well as children. The very first children's book by the popular French children's author and illustrator Claude Ponti was *L'Album d'Adèle* (Adèle's picturebook), a wordless picturebook created for his baby daughter Adèle and published by Gallimard in 1986. All of Ponti's picturebooks have crossover appeal largely because he always works "with the essential idea in mind that children are human beings 'in process.'"[7] Although *L'Album d'Adèle* opens in the tradition of the *imagier*, presenting all kinds of toys and everyday objects to be recognized and named, as well as the cute little chicks that have become Ponti's trademark, it gradually escapes from the restrictive codes and conventions of the genre. Sophie van der Linden rightly sees this innovative book as a powerful "defence in favour of the plastic image," in which the latter no longer merely serves the text.[8]

Over the past thirty years, wordless picturebooks have gradually established themselves as a distinct genre or sub-genre within the realm of children's books. Since the late 1990s, there has been a marked surge in the number of wordless picturebooks being produced; they seem to have become a contemporary publishing trend in many countries. A new generation of artists is exploring the exciting possibilities offered when pictures are the only narrative medium of the book. Some author-illustrators specialize in this type of book. A number of young illustrators are adopting the genre from the outset of their careers. The Swiss author-illustrator Katja Kamm, who won the Deutscher Jugendliteraturpreis with her first picturebook in 2003, launched her career with two much acclaimed wordless picturebooks. Design plays a major role in the works of this illustrator, who plays cleverly with our viewing habits. By changing the solid background colours from one spread to the next in her first picturebook, *Unsichtbar* (2002; English trans., *Invisible*), elements are visible or disappear, creating witty unexpected mishaps: a boy loses his pants; a girl stumbles across an invisible dog that pees on her ball; a cyclist rides into an invisible tree. Kamm's second picturebook, *Das runde Rot* (The round red, 2003), is a humorous yet thoughtful book about figurative representation that is reminiscent of Iela Mari's *The Red Balloon*, as it tells the journey of a red round form that continues to change function: apple, spare wheel, record, lollipop, yo-yo (the latter flies away and finds its way back into the girl's arms). The award-winning Belgian author-illustrator Anne Brouillard has been producing wordless picturebooks since 1990, when she published her first picturebook, *Trois chats* (Three cats). In 1993, she won both the Premio Graphico at the Bologna Children's Book Fair and the Golden Apple at the Biennial of Illustration Bratislava (BIB) for another wordless picturebook, *Le sourire du loup* (The wolf's smile, 1992). Her research on the narrative possibilities of illustrations has led to very sophisticated picturebooks that appeal strongly to adults. According to the French critic Isabelle Nières-Chevrel, Brouillard's *L'orage* (The storm, 1998) constitutes "one of the finest examples of a narrative carried entirely by the image."[9] Despite the awards and recognition Brouillard has received for her work, which now includes more than thirty picturebooks, the Belgian illustrator has not had the success she deserves with readers and she remains virtually unknown in the English-speaking world. Although wordless picturebooks should cross cultural borders with particular ease since the only translation required relates to the paratext, they do not seem to fare any better than other foreign picturebooks in penetrating English-language markets. On the other hand, wordless picturebooks by well-known English-speaking illustrators have no difficulty finding their way into international markets. David Wiesner, for example, has been published in more than a dozen languages.

David Wiesner's passion for wordless storytelling found its ideal medium in picturebooks, and he has become one of the world's most beloved and highly acclaimed picturebook artists. He won his first Caldecott Medal for the almost wordless picturebook *Tuesday* and his third for the wordless picturebook *Flotsam*. Wiesner's website is titled "The Art of Visual Storytelling," and his career has been devoted to exploring and developing that art. Some picturebook artists, such as Shaun Tan and Arnal Ballester, have taken the art of graphic storytelling to new heights in highly innovative, lengthy wordless books which challenge current definitions of the picturebook and masterfully demonstrate the remarkable versatility of the genre. A number of publishers also give special attention to wordless picturebooks, even creating series devoted entirely to the genre. The current popularity of wordless picturebooks can be explained in part by their appeal with readers of all ages. The creators of wordless picturebooks can reach a very broad readership, while their publishers can hope to sell in a wide market.

Many wordless picturebooks are true artists' books, as are many picturebooks in general. The fact that a chapter of this book is devoted to artists' books is certainly not meant to imply that illustrators are not artists. The term picturebook artist is often used throughout this study, especially when referring to author-illustrators and the creators of wordless picturebooks. Picturebook authors and illustrators in general have often been denied artist status. In a tongue-in-cheek commentary on the oft-heard expression "That's Not Art, That's Illustration," the influential American illustrator Brad Holland wrote:

> Almost everybody is an artist these days. Rock and Roll singers are artists. So are movie directors, performance artists, make-up artists, tattoo artists, con artists and rap artists. Movie stars are artists. . . . The only people left in America who seem not to be artists are illustrators.[10]

While it is true that "some wordless books leave readers feeling shortchanged," as a reviewer of *Flotsam* states,[11] that is certainly not the case with Wiesner's bestselling picturebook or with any of the other crossover picturebooks included in this chapter. In the works of these illustrators, visual storytelling is truly an art.

Pictorial Narratives in the Tradition of Japanese Scroll Painting

The famous "Journey" books by the Japanese author-illustrator Mitsumasa Anno are wordless picturebooks with undisputed crossover appeal. The first book, titled simply *Tabi no ehon* (My journey), won the prestigious Golden Apple Award of the Bratislava International Biennale in 1977, and over the next couple of years it was published in many Western countries (the English edition appeared in 1978 under the title *Anno's Journey*). Anno's books offer a fascinating interplay of Western and Asian aesthetic codes. In *Anno's Journey*, the Japanese artist records his travels through northern Europe in 1963 and 1975, and recognizes his debt toward Western culture. The book is a wordless panorama of exquisitely detailed watercolour-and-ink paintings that present a profusion of details drawn from European history, legend, folklore, literature, art, music, and popular culture. At the same time, his wordless "Journey" books are strongly rooted in Japanese culture. These books have been described as technical masterpieces in which the lack of margins, in the words of the blurb in the English edition of *Anno's Journey*, allows the "stories without words [to] unfold from page to page, in the tradition of Japanese scroll painting."

The one narrative thread running throughout Anno's book, bringing readers full circle, is the recurring figure of the silent, solitary traveller in a boat or on horseback who appears on each doublespread. *Anno's Journey* is a poetic meditation on art and life masterfully rendered in pictorial form. From the bird's eye view of the artist-philosopher, readers/viewers witness life in all its stages and manifestations: a wedding, a move, and a burial; children at play, adults at work, people of all ages engaged in the gamut of human activity (strolling, drinking, fighting, eating, bathing, painting, praying). The book's appeal with adults is undoubtedly due in part to this philosophical dimension. However, children are also capable of appreciating such depth of philosophical reflection. The creators of wordless picturebooks understand that readers of all ages experience metaphysical concerns and they do not hesitate to address them in books accessible to very young children.

The intricacy and minute detail of Anno's complex pictures with their many cultural allusions fascinate readers of all ages. Children have no difficulty recognizing famous storybook characters such as Little Red Riding Hood and the wolf, Pinocchio, and the Pied Piper of Hamelin, as well as more recent popular culture figures like the characters from *Sesame Street*. Many references are beyond the decoding abilities of most children, however, and seem to be intended for the informed adult reader, for example the dog from Aesop's fable "The Dog and the Shadow," Beethoven sitting at a window, and details from numerous paintings. Child readers may be disadvantaged by their limited cultural heritage, but this is compensated, at least in part, by an "ability to perceive and sift visual detail [that] often outdistances that of the adult."[12] They will, for example, appreciate the witty anachronism that results when the artist adds his signature and the year 1976 to a medieval building with large towers and Gothic windows.

A publisher's insert in the English version provides a list of "things to look for," including references to art, literature, and music. This rather heavy-handed checklist may encourage some children to treat the book as a treasure hunt in which the goal becomes the discovery of as many allusions as possible, but other readers will see these references in the same light as all the other details in Anno's rich world. As Leonard Marcus observes, "the hunt or puzzle element plays a larger and perhaps more intrusive role" in the sequels, *Anno's Italy*, *Anno's Britain*, and *Anno's U.S.A.* (and more recently in *Tabi no ehon V* [*Anno's Spain*] and *Tabi no ehon VI*).[13] The later books no longer share the vague, somewhat mysterious atmosphere and timeless, "mythic" dimension that makes *Anno's Journey* a much more introspective journey for his readers, although all constitute a journey through time and space. The many recognizable sites and associated characters in the subsequent more historical books invite readers to engage in a more structured game of identification. Marcus fittingly describes the new role given to the reader as that of the sight-seer rather than the adventurer, while his journey now resembles "a tourist's itinerary."[14] Marcus is particularly critical of *Anno's U.S.A.*, which was based on the artist's travels throughout the United States in 1983. However, Anno brings an innovative approach to his version of American history, telling it in reverse—from West to East and from the twentieth-century to the seventeeth. Western readers wishing to have historical events presented chronologically would have to read it from back to front, in keeping with the Japanese tradition. While the first "Journey" book no doubt has more crossover appeal than its sequels, all of Anno's experimental work has attracted the attention and admiration of adults.

Mural-Style Wordless Picturebooks

Whereas *Anno's Journey* evokes Japanese scroll painting in a conventional book format, other author-illustrators have experimented with various forms of folded spreads to create mural-style books. The Swiss author and illustrator Jörg Müller, who won the Hans Christian Andersen award in 1994, a decade after Mitsumasa Anno, gained immediate acclaim with his first book, *Alle Jahre wieder saust der Presslufthammer nieder oder Die Veränderung der Landschaft* (Every year the pneumatic hammer rushes down, or, The changing landscape, 1973), which received the Deutscher Jugendliteraturpreis (German Youth Literature Award) in 1974. The poetic, rhyming German title was lost in the English translation, titled simply *The Changing Countryside*. This picturebook is actually an unbound series of seven fold-out spreads intended to be viewed successively. The large format of each spread, wordless except for a date, immerses viewers in a landscape that evolves from one spread to the next, as urbanization and industrialization encroach on an idyllic countryside, and the palette shifts from gold and green to grey. Each picture is executed from the same perspective, allowing viewers to easily witness the changes that take place over a period of two decades. On the first peaceful spread, dated "Wednesday, May 6, 1953," a small, Victorian house stands in the rolling meadows of the German countryside, as cows graze and a farmer ploughs his field. A train dominates the background of in the 1956 spread, while a bulldozer fells a stand of old trees to make way for storage tanks in the 1959 image. In 1963, there is still a pond on which boys skate, but construction vehicles work behind them, and smokestacks spoil the view of the mountains. The house is demolished by a wrecking ball in 1969. In the final spread, there is no longer any trace of the house, fields, trees, or pond; a four-lane highway runs through the centre of the spread, surrounded by high-rises, factories, and a department store. The almost wordless murals portray the landscape as a helpless victim that suffers silently from so-called progress. Müller's powerful picturebook, which is still in print in both German and English, is a moving testimony of the destruction of the environment brought about by urbanization. It will evoke for adult readers the changes they have witnessed in their own communities, while providing children, who may not yet have lived long enough to experience such destruction, with an unforgettable visual demonstration.

Anima, the first children's book by the French author and illustrator Katy Couprie, assumes an accordion format, unfolding to create a long mural or "fresco," the term preferred by the artist. All of Couprie's unique books are true works of art. She claims to make "livres de peinture" (books of painting), works that are "very linked to the object book."[15] Couprie's use of the term "objet livre," so close to Warja Lavater's inverted term "livre-objet," evokes the latter's "imageries," which were forerunners of picturebooks like *Anima*. Couprie's picturebook falls more precisely into the category of what Lavater refers to as a "mural book." Unfolded, it could be used as a frieze in a child's bedroom or playroom. Although the book seems to consist of one long folded sheet of paper, closer inspection reveals that the doublespreads are carefully glued together to create that impression, as they are in Lavater's *imageries*. As with many accordion books, *Anima* is contained in a slipcase, in this instance a cardboard case bearing the beautiful cover image of the book itself.

Couprie did drawings for *Anima* in Africa and later organized the succession of animals according to the folds of the book. Page after page unfolds to reveal a tangled mass of African animals dashing, bounding, leaping, flying, and riding in the same direction, apparently fleeing some unseen danger. The scene evokes reminiscences of the untold story of Noah's Ark, that of the animals who were not embarked on the ark but left behind to face the impending flood. The artist points out that despite the animals' distorted proportions, the book contains only "real" animals because she wanted a "true bestiary." Couprie's bestiary is nonetheless quite unique, "a bestiary in which the animals are together without eating each other, the predators mixed with the potential victims," a bestiary that allows the artist "to thwart . . . creation." *Anima* is, in fact, a very philosophical bestiary. Although Couprie confesses her choice of animals was firstly "affective" (she mentions in particular her love of marsupials and elephants), the selection also reflects aesthetic and philosophical considerations. The mesmerizing spiral formed by the distinctive banded black-and-white tail of a ring-tailed lemur captures the reader's attention on the first page. The artist has a predilection for the spiral, a figure that is present everywhere in nature, whereas she dislikes straight lines, which are not natural and are foreign to her instinctive style of painting. Throughout the book, the tails of numerous other animals (iguana, rodent, possum, lizard) take the form of eye-catching spirals. From the first page, this visual journey is marked by the spiral's spiritual significance as an ancient symbol of inner journey and initiation.

The long spiral tail on the fold of the first doublespread draws the reader's eye onto the facing page, where its owner is perched on the partially visible head of a camel, staring directly and intently at the reader. The choice of the lemur can be explained by the characteristic wide-eyed stare that it shares with its primate cousins, monkeys and apes, a stare that often startles and unsettles viewers. The fact that the lemur must turn its head to look at the viewer (due to the limited movement of their eyes in the socket) increases the mesmerizing effect of the hypnotic stare. Couprie uses a similar strategy for the spread that is reproduced on the cover. Whereas the other animals face forward, a raccoon in the foreground turns its head toward viewers and fixes them with its intent gaze. From the beginning readers are captivated; on the second doublespread they are swept up in the frenzied movement of a vast host of wild animals that carries them inexorably toward the right. Multiple animals of the same species increase this sense of movement, notably on the second doublespread, where the first of four racing giraffes is only completed on the next spread, propelling the reader forward with the animals.

Elephants have a special place in *Anima*, where they occupy an entire doublespread and then literally sprawl onto the next spread. The artist points out that the elephants are the only animals that do not look at readers at all. The elephants' role in *Anima* is that of "old stone . . . monument, rock," but they are nonetheless ultimately caught up in the frenzy of the other animals. An elephant that seems to have lost its footing and sprawls backward is one of only two animals in the entire book that are not facing toward the right. The other is a pelican positioned on the centrefold of the final doublespread, where it occupies the head of the herd. Turned toward the stampeding animals, the stationary pelican seems to bring the last elephant to a screeching halt, thus forcing the entire moving mass to a sudden stop in the middle of the final doublespread, which is left half empty. All the animals end up bumping into the monumental elephants. According to the artist, the only animal that is in open opposition to the rest is the pelican, who has stepped back to adopt "a philosophic attitude." The intriguing title (the copyright page provides a dictionary definition of "animal" and its etymology from "*anima*, souffle, vie" [*anima*, breath, life]) seems to announce the book's philosophic slant. The artist's observations on the animals suggest the reflective nature of this extraordinary bestiary. The large white space on the first page, which evokes the lull before the storm, is complemented by a large blank space on the page where the pelican brings the stampede to a standstill. The emptiness and stillness that precede and follow the frenzied movement create a striking and aesthetic symmetry between the opening and closing pages. The completely blank doublespread at the end of the book not only restores the calm after the tumultuous stampede, but it seems to provide a meditative space in which readers can, like the pelican, engage in their own philosophic reflections.

The technique of dry pastels allows Couprie to blur the colours, increasing the sense of chaotic movement in *Anima*. Her palette consists predominantly of red, yellow, and brown ochre hues, the earth tones of Africa. However, the artist's choice of animals was largely "tactile," that is, a choice of "materials." She describes the largely instinctive "plastic organization" of the work that is dictated, for example, by movement or feel, as in the desire to juxtapose feathers and furs. The paper used in the book is identical to that of the original artwork, giving the same feel, delicacy, resonance of light, and warmth of colour. Its texture helps to create the impression of long hair, thick fur, soft feathers, slimy skins, and shiny scales. Prior to the publication of *Anima* by Le Sourire qui mord in 1991, Couprie had no idea that her aesthetic choices would result in a rather expensive book. While the artist feels a book should be available to all, she is unwilling to make compromises. For that reason, there are a rather limited number of publishers with whom Couprie feels she can work. These are small publishers who, like Le Sourire qui mord, share a truly collaborative relationship with their authors and illustrators, and are willing to take the risk that a book will not be easy to sell. Within the range of artistic fields, Couprie feels that children's books provide the only really interesting sphere, in which it is still possible to work with a maximum of creative liberty and a minimum of compromise.

The wordless picturebook *Hvad mon der sker?* (Wonder what will happen?), published in 1997 by the prolific and highly original Danish author and illustrator Dorte Karrebæk, is literally a mural in book format. The wordless picturebook would seem to be the ideal genre for an artist who claims that "pictures [are her] language."[16] The artwork for *Hvad mon der sker?* was originally created as a twenty-six-metre painting for the children's area of the Louisiana Museum of Modern Art in Denmark, which is renowned for its special exhibitions of innovative contemporary art. Karrebæk was invited to create a work on an underwater theme to be displayed for three months. Since the two other artists, who had been given the themes of heaven and earth, were creating large works in the centre of the room, she decided to create a work that would go completely around the walls. As it was impossible to get a twenty-six-metre long sheet of paper, the work had to be completed on two sheets. Readers of Couprie's freize-like work follow a moving horde of realistic African animals as they race from left to right across the folds, whereas readers of Karrebæk's long narrow band-like work seem to be carried by the current, along with a little yellow fish, past fantastic underwater creatures that often swim in the same direction, but sometimes move counter to the current and sometimes remain stationary. At the end of the exhibition, Karrebæk had the rolled-up mural under her arm during a visit to her publisher, Gyldendal, who, on seeing the painting unrolled on the floor, immediately wanted to do the book. In order to create the broadside format picturebook, the long mural had to be cut into many pieces, and the man responsible for this insisted the artist be there to give her permission at each cut. The pieces were subsequently put back together and the work was given to a Danish children's museum.

The genesis of *Hvad mon der sker?* demonstrates the artist's spontaneous, intuitive manner of working. Karrebæk began by drawing a little yellow fish with feet and every morning she painted "what was happening" that day, hence the title of the book. However, it was not until the artist arrived at the end of the very long sheet of paper that she found an answer to the question, an answer inspired by the philosophical works of P. D. Ouspensky and G. I. Gurdjieff, who claim that the most interesting time in life is the period prior to birth when we go from fish-like creature to human being. It is not surprising that readers do not realize until the very end that the strange world of *Hvad mon der sker?* is that of the womb. The little fish's progress through a precarious, phantasmagorical underwater world full of bizarre, often monstrous creatures, traces the adventures of a human foetus until birth. The human embryo has often been compared to a fish with gills and that is what it literally becomes in Karrebæk's remarkable work. Propelled through the water by a small propeller-like appendage on its head, the comical little yellow fish resembles a child's bath toy. On the final doublespread, the little fish is rescued by a red-haired angel who, in a surprising sequence of four scenes, detaches the propeller (a long arrow indicates its trajectory toward the sea bottom) and unzips and removes the yellow fish skin to reveal a human baby. Karrebæk's depiction of birth is witty and fantastical, rather than realistic. On the final page, the tongue of the angel/midwife is stuck out to show the effort required to push the baby through a crevice in what appears to be enormous female buttocks to the mother waiting to catch the crying baby at the other end. The tiny baby assists by pulling its way along an umbilical cord that is attached to a cup hook on the inside.

Karrebæk's work is infused with energy, enthusiasm, and exuberance. Her characters are portrayed in a caricatural style and her entire visual world is characterized by a fantastic, grotesque element that is well demonstrated by *Hvad mon der sker?* The mysterious underwater world is full of strange aquatic and amphibious creatures, many of which are part-human, part-animal hybrid beings. Anthropomorphic fish wear glasses, watch television, and live in shell houses with windows and even flags. While many of the fish-like creatures have human limbs, many of the humans possess webbed feet and hands. Some of the bizarre creatures are decidedly Bosch-like, but the surprising colours are generally cheerful and bright, and humour is never absent. Large predatory fish have long, red-painted finger nails and wear high heels or other assorted footwear. Most of the female figures are playful, red-haired mermaids, some of whom also have webbed hands. Clever, witty touches make the fantastic creatures unique, for example, the mermaid whose long red braid ends in several fish hooks baited with worms or the male mermaid who rides a large snail coach along the seabed.

The grotesque takes on a more burlesque note in a scene depicting a motley group of creatures dancing, playing musical instruments, and engaged in acrobatic stunts, much to the delight of the little yellow fish. An eel in yellow heels sticks its head out of the coral to listen to the music, while an ugly fish who is obviously no music lover plugs its ears with human hands. This cheerful, energetic scene, which puts a smile on the little fish's face, is one of the only non-threatening scenes in the entire book, but immediately thereafter the sea suddenly becomes once again dark and frightening, as if we have descended into the blackest depths of the ocean. These dark scenes are particularly reminiscent of Bosch. One long-beaked creature with huge feet seems to have swum or flown directly out of a Bosch painting into Karrebæk's book. The artist uses different techniques to portray the creatures according to the needs of the narrative. Bright, vivid creatures rendered in oil suddenly lose their colour in the blackness (one ugly creature is bright green on one side of the fold and dark blue-black on the other). The little yellow fish stands out vividly, as the only touch of bright colour in the dark waters. To create the glowing, phosphorescent creatures that inhabit the black depths, the artist switches to pastels. The grotesque monsters that still try to catch the fish-baby after it has been rescued by the angel are rendered in delicate line drawings on a monochromatic background, as if have lost their material reality.

Many of the comic details are of a sexual nature, which should not be surprising in a book about pregnancy and birth. The pertinent theme of anatomy is treated with the illustrator's characteristic wit. Despite the very strange nature of Karrebæk's aquatic world of the womb, human anatomy receives special attention. One very provocative scene depicts a dragon-like sea creature pumping oxygen into a fish bowl containing a nude human couple. The couple's sexual organs (the male's dangling penis and the nipples of the woman's drooping breasts) are highlighted in red. From their glass bowl abode, equipped with table and toilet, the male makes an obscene gesture at the little yellow fish who stares in with a puzzled look (evidently the man does not appreciate being the object of prying eyes). The huge green eyes that peer cross-eyed into the glass bowl behind the couple are no doubt those of the curious monster who seems to be keeping them as pets. Two dark doublespreads swarm with little worm-like creatures that look decidedly like sperm. On another humorous doublespread, a schoolmarm mermaid with sagging breasts and a cane teaches male and female mermaids and a number of other sea creatures a class on anatomy, using a chart that shows skeletons of a man, a fish, and a mermaid. Breasts are a recurring motif throughout the book. In a close-up of a mermaid queen with long, flowing red hair and a curvaceous behind, which is nude except for a thong attached to her scaled tail, the reader's eye is drawn toward her bare breast by the gaze of a lascivious fish below licking its chops. The mermaid queen holds the little yellow fish in her hand, having rescued

Figure 3.1 Hvad mon der sker? by Dorte Karrebæk, copyright © 1997 Dorte Karrebæk, reprinted by permission of Dorte Karrebæk.

him from a vicious-looking female fish with long, streaming red hair, long red finger nails, long legs in red heels, and large breasts with prominent nipples. On the same spread, the little yellow fish, who has narrowly avoided being eaten, peers curiously into the crack of her backside.

Later the little yellow fish smiles contentedly in the arms of a golden-haired mermaid with bare breasts. The final scene depicts a human mother, with long, flowing red hair reminiscent of the mermaids', putting the baby to her swelled breast on the back endpaper. By depicting the mother on the endpapers against a stark white background, her outside world is clearly separated from the strange inner world of the womb.

While some of the female figures encountered in the underwater world are beautiful, gentle, kindly, and endowed with maternal instincts (the angel and several mermaids), most are extremely grotesque, vicious-looking, and predatory. Swimming in the opposite direction to the mermaid queen is a completely nude frog-like hag with long, streaming hair and sagging breasts. Another very ugly feminine creature has a long anteater-like snout that ends in a plunger. A bare-breasted siren figurehead on the prow of a ship displays shark-like teeth as she attempts to gobble the little yellow fish. Her gaping mouth mirrors that of so many other sea creatures in this watery world, where almost every creature is eating, looking for something to eat, being eaten, or attempting to escape being eaten. Interestingly, all the human figures in this underwater world are male (with the exception of the angel) and they seem to be all in danger of being eaten. Many of the sea creatures adopt human eating habits: a fish in red heels sits at a table eating with trident forks; a lizard-like creature with breasts and heels holds a knife and a fish in human hands; a male shellfish with human limbs puts lemon on a fish; a lobster uses his one human hand to salt the fish he holds in a huge claw; and a red devil-like creature with a trident fork and a huge knife attacks a can of sardines. The net from which the little yellow fish escapes the lengthy fish food chain at the end of the book seems to lead to fish heaven because an angel, who looks remarkably like the red-haired mermaids, has her arms out ready to catch the little fish and comfort it.

Karrebæk's profound, yet humorous books are very successful with children. Her work has repeatedly been praised for its childlike view of the world. Whereas adults tend to find her fantastic, often grotesque, visual world utterly absurd, children consider it quite natural. The illustrator explains this dual reception of her books in the following manner:

> What I draw is the way children experience things, something adults do not see at all. . . . The older we grow the more adept we become at processing impressions and experiences. We adults do not perceive with our eyes or our reason, but with our thoughts. Children experience the world in a far more immediate way.[17]

Very small children like the book more than their mothers, according to the artist, who suggests this is perhaps because they remember being in their mother's womb.[18] Karrebæk's unconventional children's books, which have played a major role in the development of Danish picturebooks, often make adults feel very uncomfortable. The illustrator feels fortunate that some Danish publishers are willing to bring out such unconventional books even when they know they will not sell easily.

Wordless Picturebooks by Avant-Garde Publishers

Both Katy Couprie and Dorte Karrebæk acknowledge their debt to publishers who are willing to risk taking on unconventional books. Karrebæk mentions editors such as Susanne Vebel at Alma and Anne Mørch Hansen at Høst og Søn, who have brought out some of her more recent, controversial books. These editors are content in the knowledge that some children will appreciate these remarkable picturebooks. In a few European countries, such as Denmark, even major publishers like Gyldendal seem willing to go out on a limb to produce innovative books by exciting picturebook artists, as in the case of Karrebæk's *Hvad mon der sker?* However, in many countries where large corporations now dominate the publishing market, notably in the United States and Britain, it is generally only the smaller publishing houses that are willing to ignore commercial dictates. It is not surprising that a significant number of wordless picturebooks have been brought out by small publishers with a reputation for innovative and provocative books.

The wordless picturebook *Number 24*, by the French artist Guy Billout, was published during the height of the Quist books and was named one of the ten best children's books of 1973 by the *New York Times*. Quist approached the young artist about doing a book, and although it was to be his first book, Billout claims to have been granted, for the first time ever, "total freedom." He knew immediately that "it was going to be a wordless story," but he points out that he had "no sense at all of addressing [him]self to a young audience."[19] In an unconventional square format, *Number 24* presents a rather surreal series of pictures of colliding vehicles viewed while a man awaits the arrival of the Number 24 bus. As the tiny figure of the businessman waits beneath the bus sign, each approaching unmanned vehicle is hit by a larger one in absurdly surreal situations: a locomotive steams into a car, knights on horseback charge a tank, a huge ship destroys a skiff coasting down the road, a truck barrels into a cable car, and so on until the Number 24 bus arrives, the first vehicle to have an operator. The book's visual wit has crossover appeal and is evident from the cover illustration, which indicates that the bus will also be hit by another bus. However, nothing in the internal pages suggests the collision depicted on the cover. The wary businessman looks cautiously behind the bus from both sides before he climbs on, and the final page, like the first, resembles an empty stage with only the bus sign and the walls that hid from view all the large vehicles. Viewers of all ages are conscious of the tension created between the violent, chaotic content of the illustrations and their soft, careful lines and cool, subdued tones (the only vivid touch of colour in the predominantly grey spreads is the small yellow sign bearing the number "24"). In 2006, one critic wrote that *Number 24* "belongs to a mostly vanished breed of book: visual entertainment for children and adults—its abstract message and skillful construction just as pleasurable for each age group."[20] However, in the contemporary picturebook scene, such books are by no means a "vanishing breed," quite the contrary.

Couprie's *Anima* was only one of numerous wordless picturebooks brought out by Le Sourire qui mord between 1976 and 1996. Two particularly innovative books appeared in the series Grands petits livres (Large little books) in 1986, *Vous oubliez votre cheval* (You are forgetting your horse) and *Rouge, bien rouge* (Red, very red). As the series' title seems to imply, these "little" picturebooks are, in fact, complex, crossover works that tackle difficult themes, such as illness, sexuality, violence, and the subconscious. The author-publisher is concerned by the fact that many children's books ignore complete chunks of the reality experienced by children. Both books consist of ambiguous and disparate pictures that are probably even more disconcerting for adults than for children.

In *Vous oubliez votre cheval*, conceived by Bruel and illustrated by Pierre Wachs, the illustrations on the recto are single coloured plates, while those on the verso are in black and white and often present more than one image in interesting page layouts. Although it does not seem to be simply a case of distinguishing between reality and the dream world, the black-and-white images tend to be more traditional and realistic, while the coloured images are quite surrealistic, the stuff of dreams and the subconscious. Since Le Sourire qui mord's books were intended to provide springboards for dreams and rely heavily on symbolism, it is not surprising that they are strongly influenced by the traditional tale. I have discussed elsewhere the intriguing doublespread that alludes directly to the story of Little Red Riding Hood. While these are perhaps the least disconcerting of the paired images in the book, even they remain quite ambiguous and puzzling.[21] The following doublespread immediately evokes another fairy tale, *The Frog Prince*, because the black-and-white verso portrays a prince in medieval garb standing by a pond. However, two small framed insets in the upper right corner depict much more perplexing pictures. The upper image of a frog perched on a celestial orb, perhaps the moon, is directly linked to the larger image because the prince's gaze is fixed on the frog and the same night sky constitutes the background of both images. The meteorological map of Europe and half of Africa in the lower inset is much more enigmatic. Does the map announce rain to fill fairy-tale and/or real frogs' ponds or perhaps an Old Testament-style plague of frogs? In the colour plate on the opposite page, a globe, which also depicts Europe and, more prominently, Africa, sits on the bottom of a very deep, almost empty, tiled pool, while a contemporary boy holding a firehouse climbs an extension ladder in pursuit of the large green frog perched at the top. Observant readers will notice that a puddle beside the globe takes the shape of the African continent, while a much smaller puddle constitutes the island of Madagascar. Perhaps plagues of frogs are no longer limited to ancient Africa, but have spread to contemporary Europe.

The tale of Goldilocks finds its way into the first doublespread of *Vous oubliez votre cheval*, which focuses on the bear as a cultural icon. The black-and-white page is split into two horizontal images, but bear tracks traverse them both from bottom to top. In the upper frame, the bear tracks separate Goldilocks eating porridge, in front of a table with three chairs, from a muzzled dancing bear whose head is turned in her direction. On the lower half of the divided page, a female explorer or hunter sits dozing in an armchair on a polar bear rug. Apparently she is dreaming of the bear constellations, as Ursa Major (the Great Bear) and Ursa Minor (the Little Bear) are depicted in round framed insets in the upper corners of the image. The round images seem to replicate for readers the view of the sky that the sleeping woman probably observed through the lenses of the binoculars that now lie on the bear rug. The perplexing coloured image on the recto shows a large brown bear stepping off a surface into space in the direction of a tiny island on which sits a telescope, continuing the optical instrument motif from the facing page. However, the stars and crescent moons on the blue background constitute a uniform pattern that also includes bees, suggesting that we are perhaps looking at wallpaper in a child's bedroom. The impression that we are in a nursery is heightened by the presence of a little pink stuffed bear, a book, a small pillow, and several baby bottles, some of which seem to float in space. It is also possible that the background is not wallpaper, but rather a bedspread or a carpet, on which the baby bottles would then be lying. The little pink bear (Ursa Minor) contrasts sharply with the big, real-looking bear (Ursa Major), which looks strikingly like the dancing bear from the facing page, now liberated and seeking its fortune in the stars. Despite the connections that can be made to the black-and-white facing page, the surreal image on the recto remains ambiguous and baffling. The intertextual references in these particular doublespreads may provide readers with the thread of a mini-narrative, albeit one that remains fragmented and enigmatic, but it is unlikely that even the most competent readers will be able to make any associations from one doublespread to the next. Even the rather odd title remains mystifying as the reader closes the book.

Conceived by Christian Bruel and Didier Jouault, *Rouge, bien rouge* is illustrated by Nicole Claveloux, who was one of the main illustrators for Harlin Quist before joining Le Sourire qui mord's stable of illustrators. Her unique, irreverent style has always appealed to adults as well as children. *Rouge, bien rouge* is slightly less baffling than *Vous oubliez votre cheval*, because the colour red gives coherence to the book. The blurb on the back cover reveals that red is the "password" that gives readers access to the images of *Rouge, bien rouge*, although the publisher's catalogue warns readers that red is an "appealing," but also a "secret, always ambivalent" colour.[22] The chubby Little Red Riding Hood on the cover is intended to provide a key to unlock the enigmatic pictures. With the exception of the colour, however, there seems to be very little, if any, connection between the intriguing illustrations. An observant reader will notice that blood is a recurring motif, not surprising in a book about red perhaps, but somewhat unexpected in a picturebook addressed to young children. Claveloux adopts a very quirky approach to injury and illness, which are, after all, common childhood experiences. In one plate, a child with red measles seems to take pleasure in the fact that everything in his bedroom—furniture, turtle, doll, stuffed elephant, book, roller skates—is equally covered in red spots, apparently having caught the contagious disease.

The most interesting spreads confront children and grown-ups. Their worlds seem strangely separate; often the child is an outsider peering into or surreptitiously entering the domain of adults. The head of a young boy is partially visible in the corner of a mirror over a bathroom sink into which blood red nail polish is dripping. His fearful gaze at the slightly ajar door suggests that he is guilty of transgressing household boundaries. A little red-head with pigtails has abandoned her clown-like doll and, with a look of intense concentration, applies iodine or mercurochrome to the red hand of a fierce-looking native chief in war paint who, incongruously, sleeps peacefully in a soft bed on the floor, entirely oblivious to the child's presence. A similar bottle of red antiseptic recurs in a plate that shows a nurse preparing to treat an adult patient, while a small boy in a Lone Ranger costume watches with a pained grimace. The patient's finger has apparently been stung by the large, menacing insect isolated on the completely white background of the facing page. Viewers are positioned in such a way that they see little more than the hands of the nurse and patient; instead their attention is drawn to the reaction of the child who can barely see over the table and whose presence seems to go unnoticed by the grownups. The theme of bites and blood is continued on the following doublespread, a melodramatic scene in which a vampire couple tiptoe through a house, unaware that they are being spied upon by two children from the darkness of a slightly ajar door. While the older boy watches with surprise and curiosity, the younger boy's face clearly expresses fear, their reactions reflecting their age difference. Readers are left to decide whether the couple are vampires furtively seeking fresh blood or actors in their stage costumes stealthily returning from an evening performance so as not to waken the children. The latter interpretation is suggested by a poster on the wall that features a smiling couple on a stage in front of the backdrop of a castle, apparently preparing to take a bow at the end of a performance.

The majority of the doublespreads in *Rouge, bien rouge* depict only children, but when more than one child is present, there seems to be an emphasis on age difference. In one scene, three children—perhaps siblings as two have the same red hair—are portrayed, in descending order of size, in the process of painting tattoo-like red pictures on each other. While the two youngest,

Figure 3.2   Rouge, bien rouge by Christian Bruel and Didier Jouault, illustrated by Nicole Claveloux, copyright © 1986 Le Sourire qui mord, reprinted by permission of Christian Bruel.

both boys, are attempting to erase part of their drawing on the child in front, apparently dissatisfied with their artistic endeavours, the oldest, a prim-looking girl with her nose held haughtily in the air and her braided pigtails tied neatly on top of her head, seems to be quite pleased with her drawing on the back on the smallest child: a smiling mermaid with flowing hair and large breasts. The youngest child seems quite oblivious to the provocative nature of the art he sports almost the entire length of his body. The art reflects the interest of the artist and not the wearer of the art. The youngest has drawn what appears to be a Dracula on the back of the older boy's upper leg, while the older boy has drawn a skull and crossbones on the back of the girl's arm. It is not clear who drew the picture on the belly of the puzzled stuffed Panda bear on the bottom of the facing page. The motif of painting recurs in a subsequent subversive doublespread, in which a small boy has added red house paint from a large pail, depicted on the verso, to his paint set and uses it to paint a red dog on a glass door. Through the glass door, viewers glimpse a reddish-coloured dog disappearing down the steps. The feces that the real dog has left on the doorstep have inspired the boy's artwork, as his red dog is in a squatting position directly over them. Such subversive children's art can only take place in the absence of adults.

In some of Claveloux's illustrations, conventional roles are turned upside down. In a spread depicting three children about the same age as the body artists, the oldest, a girl who looks much too young to be a babysitter, spanks the bare red bottom of a boy, whose painful grimace on an equally red face is directed at the viewers, while the youngest, a toddler, looks on as he talks on an old-fashioned telephone. The older girl seems to have enthusiastically appropriated the role of an adult she has seen administering this form of corporal punishment (perhaps the owner of the boxing trophy sitting on the mantel). On one spread a group of screaming adults are crouched on the ground around a rooster, intent upon a betting game, while on another a group of shouting children—including a baby being supported under the arms by two toddlers—are engaged in a street manifestation. Claveloux's representation of children and adults blurs the borders between the two.

The illustrations of *Rouge, bien rouge* contain more echoes and recurring motifs than those of *Vous oubliez votre cheval*. The younger of the hidden boys in the vampire scene looks decidedly like the small boy in the Lone Ranger costume on the preceding page. The stage curtain in the poster of the same spread evokes the blood-red curtain from which Little Red Riding Hood peers, a curtain whose folds reveal other frightening images from children's nightmares: a wolf, a devil, and a dwarf or elf. The latter, in turn, seems to announce the dwarf/elf carrying presents in the small framed image on the last page of the book. Attentive readers will notice possible connections throughout the book, but they do not seem to throw any light on the enigmatic images and they certainly do not help readers construct a coherent narrative. For most readers, they will probably go entirely unnoticed. Le Sourire qui mord's wordless picturebooks live up to the general goals of the publishing house: emphasizing dreams and the imagination, refusing stereotypes and taboos, and abolishing the borders between children and adult.

One of the first books published by Christian Bruel's new publishing house Être was the wordless picturebook *Petits Chaperons Loups* (Little Riding Hood Wolves, 1997), conceived by Bruel and illustrated by Claveloux.[23] The second title in the series Vis-à-Vis, an original concept that presents "two books in one" (blurb), *Petits Chaperons Loups* opens up to reveal two books side by side, one devoted to Little Red Riding Hood and the other to the Wolf. Each doublespread of the two books consists of a colour illustration on one side and a small pen-and-ink drawing on the other, both on stark white backgrounds. The pages of the two books can be turned separately or simultaneously, in order or randomly; readers can focus on the doublespreads of one book, the juxtaposed colour illustrations of the two books, or the two juxtaposed doublespreads. With the exception of the first illustrations depicting Little Red Riding Hood disguised as the wolf and the wolf in a riding hood, which serve as inside covers for the two books, there is no clear relationship between the facing colour illustrations, although the connection between the large colour pictures and the small black-and-white vignettes of each book is somewhat more evident. Readers are expected to play a very active role in creating the narrative in this highly interactive book, which provides an excellent example of the digital-age books that Eliza Dresang describes in *Radical Change: Books for Youth in a Digital Age*. Dresang points out that radical books often address a dual audience, but she also states that books with interactive, non-sequential qualities appeal "strongly to contemporary children but not always to contemporary adults."[24] While the format may appeal especially to young readers, the sexual innuendo in some of Claveloux's illustrations (for example, the lascivious wolf at a pinball machine displaying a sexy Riding Hood in a slinky red dress who is reminiscent of Tex Avery's Red Hot Riding Hood) seems intended particularly for adults, although even young children will appreciate the image of Little Red Riding Hood bending over her basket revealing her underpants. Readers of all ages will discover new connections and meanings with each reading of Bruel and Claveloux's innovative wordless picturebook.

Olivier Douzou, the innovative young director of Éditions du Rouergue, gradually began to write as he drew and to add text to his books when he found the image was unable to express an idea, seeking to eliminate the border between the two narrative modes and to make text and image entirely complementary. However, he was initially committed primarily to illustration and it continues to have a predominant role in his picturebooks, several of which are wordless. In *Esquimau* (1996), one of his most popular picturebooks, the story begins on the initial doublespreads that contain the publication details: an Eskimo walks across the snow from his igloo carrying a long flat stick on the copyright page, he marks an X in the snow on the spread that serves as title page, and he begins digging in the snow with his stick on the doublespreads that bear the name of the author-illustrator and that of the publisher. At the point where the story normally opens, the Eskimo has laid down his stick and is about to begin ice fishing as a penguin wanders into the vast white landscape. More penguins continue to arrive and suddenly a huge crack opens up in the ice sending everything—Eskimo, penguins, and igloo—flying into the air as if after a violent explosion. The humorous scene depicts the penguins somersaulting through the air and the igloo separated into ringed layers like lifesavers as its numerous contents catapult into the air: armchair, electric stove, refrigerator, bathtub, television, telephone, and a cuckoo clock that houses a penguin rather than a cuckoo. The Eskimo and one penguin end up adrift on an iceberg that gets continuously smaller as they float further south, with the Eskimo using his stick first as a paddle and then as a mast. On one doublespread, the passage of time is indicated very effectively by eight squares in alternating colours of yellow and blue, with either a sun or a moon. The surprising ending is a gag that seems to have dictated the entire book. When the stranded pair finally reaches land, their iceberg is a tiny block of ice on the stick that the Eskimo carries ashore. The last doublespread bears a single word in huge letters, as the eponymous protagonist shouts the word "Eskimo" as if he is peddling a giant Eskimo Pie ice cream bar on the beach.

Like Olivier Douzou, the Japanese author and illustrator Kota Taniuchi privileges pictures over text, the latter having a very minimal role in any of his picturebooks. Taniuchi was quickly recognized as one of the talented young artists of his generation when he was the first Japanese winner of the Bologna Children's Book Fair Premio Grafico in 1971 for his third book *Natsu no asa* (Mornings in summer, 1970; English trans., *Boy on a Hilltop* and *Up on a Hilltop*). The importance he attributes to visual storytelling is demonstrated especially well in *Nichiyobi* (Sunday, 1997), an almost wordless picturebook that contains only four lines of text. Like many of his picturebooks, Nichiyobi is published by Shiko-sha, as Taniuchi shares the crossover notion of the picturebook of its founder, Yasoo Takeuchi. Japanese picturebook artists have a particular talent for wordless picturebooks, as we have already seen in the case of Mitsumasa Anno. According to Okiko Miyake and Tomoko Masaki, characteristic features of Japanese picturebook art, such as simplicity and omission, "try to convey something words cannot do, making readers themselves fill in the gaps."[25] Taniuchi insists in the 2003 interview on his website (from which subsequent quotations by him are also taken) that his purpose is not "to teach children through picturebooks," but rather to have them "discover for themselves through the images." In his eyes, it is important "to see things before naming them," so he feels that the ideal audience for his picturebooks are children who do not yet know how to read since "they know how to look and thus to imagine." He adds, however, that "adults should conserve this child's view." His words echo those of Dorte Karrebæk and many other picturebook artists. It is noteworthy that the French edition of *Nichiyobi* received the Prix Espace Enfants 1998 for "the book that each child should be able to offer to his parents."[26]

Nichiyobi can be read on two very different levels. On one hand, Taniuchi tells an extremely simple story about a Sunday morning when the toys seem to come to life in a sleeping household: three wooden dolls ride around the interior of a house on a toy train. The initial still-life-like images of the table bear signs that the family has, despite their absence, already had breakfast: broken shells in egg cups, coffee in a pot, and open jam jars. Taniuchi creates an imaginary world in a very real décor. As the train progresses around the house, the dolls seem to climb aboard without the assistance of a human hand, until three dolls are enjoying the Sunday morning train ride. Toward the end of the book, they appear to have descended from the train on their own and they now sit by a bed, along with a yellow toy truck. In the final spread the dolls have been placed in the back of the yellow truck, which is now being manipulated by a boy with blurred features. Taniuchi's paratextual reflections on the last page of the book reveal that the toys are there for adults moreso even than for children. The artist explains: "I don't know why, but children, abandoning their toys, often take great pleasure in entertaining themselves with all kinds of objects of everyday life. . . . When they grow up, they are more interested in real toys, miniature cars and dolls for example. When we become adults, we prefer what is authentic. We are no longer satisfied with copies . . . because it is good form to believe in the 'virtues of authenticity.'" *Nichiyobi* nostalgically evokes childhood and the time of unbridled imagination.

On another level, *Nichiyobi* is a study in the aesthetics of traditional Japanese art: simplicity, purity, harmony, and a sense of absence (the concept of negative space or *ma*). Since 1970, Taniuchi has lived largely in Europe, especially France, but the perspective in his art is Japanese rather than Western. In an uncluttered space, minimal objects are organized in sophisticated compositions. Sometimes only a partial view of objects or compositions is presented and the angle from which they are viewed shifts constantly. The first illustration is a single spread depicting a smiling green doll standing by a teapot, an egg cup, and a mug on a shiny surface. When the page is turned, the initial composition appears in the centre of the doublespread because the perspective has receded to reveal more of the table. The viewpoint continues to shift: viewers see the side of the table from below as the train reaches the edge, they are on eye level with the train as it flies across the page in its downward trajectory, and they view it from above when it reaches the floor. A close-up of a geometrical design on the floor turns out to be part of a rug on which a cat sleeps (stretched across an entire doublespread), oblivious of the passing train. Thanks to the illustrator's understanding of *ma*, a key element of artistic composition, the space around and between the subjects in *Nichiyobi* forms beautiful, artistic shapes that the eye lingers over. In this space, Taniuchi also makes very artistic use of shadows and reflections. An unseen light source causes the train and the dolls to cast long shadows over the centre of one doublespread as the train crosses the gutter. In the first spread, the green

Figure 3.3   Nichiyobi by Kota Taniuchi, copyright © 1997 Shiko-sha, reprinted by permission of Kota Taniuchi and Shiko-sha.

doll's image is reflected on the table as if in a mirror. Jane Doonan examines the manner in which the artist uses the domestic objects to create "a display of the degree to which light is reflected off different surfaces in lustres ranging from highest polish to matt."[27] These reflective objects include wood, porcelain, metal, egg shell, glass, fabric, and fur. The different effects are obtained largely by the texture of the high-quality paper, but also by the density of the oil paint. Through ordinary objects of everyday life, which are endowed with symbolic meanings, Taniuchi manages to portray a transcendent serenity, beauty, and mystery. According to the artist, a picturebook offers "a privileged space" in which to express feelings, impressions, and a particular atmosphere. In his mind, the essential difference between a painting and a picturebook is "the space that [he] has to express a feeling." As a picturebook artist, his objective is not "to tell stories, but to create a world in which each person can immerse him or herself and invent his or her own story."

The first book in Media Vaca's Libros para niños series was a wordless book by Arnal Ballester bearing the descriptive Catalan title *No tinc paraules* (I have no words, 1998). Ferrer and Ballester had ongoing conversations about the status of the child reader and the role of the image in Spanish children's books. They questioned the widespread belief that children should always read works created specifically for them, feeling that this "underestimates their skills and ability" and is at odds with the fact that "the child lives within an adult world and not in a ghetto."[28] They also lamented the fact that images were considered necessary only for people of a low cultural level, including children, and that visual language was therefore seen to be without complexity. In their reflections on the misunderstanding of the role of the image in children's books, Ferrer and Ballester noted an absence of stories that were entirely visual. When Ferrer decided to create the publishing house, he asked the well-known illustrator for a work to launch the children's collection and, not surprisingly, Ballester proposed a wordless story. The aim was to create a seemingly simple story, related solely in images and capable of provoking multiple interpretations and appealing to both children and adults.

Many critics would probably hesitate to refer to this work as a picturebook due to its exceptional length: 120 pages. The unusual book is described on the illustrator's website as "a narrative in images," and the story is told by means of approximately fifty red, black, and white framed images on a red background. The images are printed only on the recto, the verso is left entirely blank. While the majority of the framed illustrations are single, rectangular images that cover most of the page (except for a white margin around the frame), a few pages have smaller, square images. The narrative begins and ends with the same vignette, which represents a small section of map, bringing the protagonist and the reader full circle, a characteristic that is shared by a surprising number of wordless picturebooks. The image gets progressively larger until it covers almost the entire page, creating a sense of movement as readers are drawn into the story. In a similar manner, the images become progressively smaller at the end, as protagonist and readers return to the starting point. There are also a couple of sequences narrated in smaller images with lighter backgrounds on pages punctuated at the bottom by a repeated icon in a tiny red square. These pages may represent the protagonist's thoughts, as opposed to events. The Media Vaca catalogue rightly refers to Ballester's knowledge of and clever use of "visual grammar." His strange protagonist, a rather stereotypical Black man in red overalls, is reminiscent of a pantomime character or a Charlie Chaplin-like silent film actor. Ballester's book offers an exercise in mime storytelling. As Tomie DePaola reminds readers in an introductory note to his wordless picturebook *Sing, Pierrot, Sing: A Picture Book in Mime* (1983), "the words, as in all mime, are in the eyes of the listener." Readers follow the protagonist's ramblings across a map, which is drawn with the care of a draughtsman and marked with street names in a strange language as well as icons, until he reaches a port where the real adventure begins.

Figure 3.4   No tinc paraules by Arnal Ballester, copyright © 1998 Arnal Ballester and Media Vaca, reprinted by permission of Arnal Ballester and Media Vaca.

As in Bruno Munari's *Nella nebbia di Milano*, Ballester's narrative is focused on a surprising trip to the circus. At the port, the Black protagonist enthusiastically hails the arrival of a large ship, which turns out to be carrying a cargo of circus animals (giraffe, lion, tiger, elephant) and performers (clowns, trapeze artists, tightrope walkers, acrobats, magicians, musicians). The ship seems to replace the conventional circus tent, and the protagonist wanders among the various performers during their acts, causing problems and mishaps due to his ignorance and misunderstanding. His antics and clumsiness add a comic element that is appreciated by children as well as adults. A very carnivalesque, even burlesque atmosphere pervades the intriguing pictures. In one scene, a tightrope walker carrying car race signs assumes the role of a matador with a bull charging across the high wire. Some of the humour verges on the slapstick. The protagonist loses his heart literally to a woman in a Flamenco outfit who fires a canon through his chest. A dotted line links the round hole in his chest to a floating heart, which another woman tries to catch in a butterfly net. In the subsequent spread, a doctor takes the pulse of the dazed protagonist whose arms now resemble those of a rubber man. Strikingly absent from this circus are spectators, other than the protagonist himself, but he does not behave like a spectator, intruding among the performers and more often than not occupying centre stage.

Ballester animates his mute pictures by borrowing a number of techniques from comics and cartoons, including dust clouds, force marks, speech and thought balloons, and light bulbs. The protagonist's meanderings are humorously reflected in those of several ducks. The duck motif is introduced on the opening endpapers, where a lone duck follows a white trail on a red background toward the right to enter the book, while the final endpapers continue the trail (now revealed to be a smoke trail) to the smokestacks of the boat in the bottom right hand corner, obviously the duck's final destination. The ducks' wanderings are traced by broken lines or, when the pace is speeded up in the canon scene, by smoke trails. The artist adapts the conventional graphic symbols of comics to a wordless picturebook: speech balloons are pictorial or contain unspecified language. The light bulb as a graphic symbol for the birth of an idea is exaggerated and used in a parodic vein. When the protagonist reaches the port on the map, a huge, very bright light bulb bursts out of the water. In the next spread, the large ship steams into port, while the light bulb sinks on the horizon like a large sun. At the end of the story, the light bulb seems to sink back into the water as the ship sails out of the port and the protagonist returns to his starting point. Ballester's parodic use of these conventional graphic symbols is evident in another spread, where three light bulbs appear above the protagonist's head. One light bulb, brightly lit and contained within a white bubble, is used in the traditional sense, while the two others appear in black bubbles crossed out with an X, thus comically indicating the bad ideas that preceded the protagonist's good idea.

As is often done in comics, Ballester uses a clock to represent time in his narrative, but it is a very unusual clock. Throughout the narrative, the protagonist carries a large clock on a long string as if it was a balloon. He rarely lets go of the long string, which is responsible for some of the mishaps at the circus. The first time visible to the reader in the third illustration is 5:49, while the clock indicates 5:55 on the following page. As the reader follows the protagonist, the passage of time is marked by the clock. Initially, only minutes have passed between views of the clock, but as the narrative progresses, the time lapse is often much greater. The ship arrives in the port shortly after 6:00 and the circus is well underway by 6:42. Sometimes only the string is visible, so readers are unable to tell the time. From about 12:00 until 5:41, readers do not see the clock's face and events become somewhat timeless. This timelessness is increased by the fact that the hour is not followed by am or pm. One senses that it must be night, although the light bulb sun on the horizon at the beginning and end could be setting or rising. While swinging on a trapeze with a skimpily clad artist, the protagonist suddenly looks at the clock (it is 5:41), and his eyes remain fixed on the clock throughout the next spreads as he hurries from the circus and once again runs through the streets on the map. As the clock marks 6:00, twelve hours—almost to the minute—after the protagonist's adventure began, he lets go of the string and then disappears from view.

Ballester's enigmatic story is puzzling for readers of all ages, who will try, often unsuccessfully, to grasp a narrative thread in the sequence of ambiguous, even deliberately misleading images. Publishing this highly unconventional wordless book to launch the new publishing house was a daring move on Ferrer's part. *No tinc paraules* was well received by readers of all ages and earned international acclaim, including being named Best Children's Book by the Caracas Banco del Libro as well as the Montreuil Salon du Livre in France. In Spain, however, the book's launch met with disconcerted silence on the part of critics. In private conversations with the illustrator, some critics accused him of having created a book for adults rather than children. It took approximately ten years before Spanish critics began to acknowledge the innovative and influential nature of Ballester's book. The presentation of the series launched with *No tinc paraules* insists on the fact that a good book can accompany us throughout life: "There is nothing strange about starting to read at age seven and reali[sing] that one is still holding the same book in one's hands at age seventy-seven" (7). This is a view shared by all the publishers examined in this section.

Visual Journeys in Cinematic Picturebooks

Arnal Ballester's *No tinc paraules* is a visual narrative that borrows very heavily from mime and silent film. Although very different in style, the same can be said of *Clown*, the only wordless picturebook by the British children's author and illustrator Quentin Blake. Published in 1995, three years before Ballester's book, *Clown* was aptly described in an Amazon. co.uk review as "a silent film between book covers." Originally, the story was to have contained text, but Blake decided that because it was about a clown, he should "tell the story in mime."[29] When he eliminated the words, Blake realized that he would have to add more pictures, and some pages have sequences of several small images (as many as six per page). Readers of all ages have always appreciated Blake's expressive cartoon-style illustrations, which he draws with a Waverley pen. His predilection for this scratch nib pen, which was invented in the nineteenth-century to do copper plate handwriting, is due to its ability to depict the artist's feelings about his characters and their actions.

The narrative follows the adventures of a clown who is thrown into the trash with other toys and then goes on a mission to try to rescue the unwanted stuffed animals. Although *Clown* may share some of the characteristics of film, in the illustrator's eyes, there is one notable difference. While discussing *Clown* during interviews for Teachers' TV, Blake distinguishes between illustration and animation: "One of the things that is different in an illustrated book from an animated film is that you *choose* a moment. In an animated film a moment would happen very quickly, whereas something you can only do in illustration is to have that split second you can keep and go back to."[30] One particularly striking example in *Clown* is the full spread in which the protagonist remains suspensefully suspended in the air after being thrown out of a window. Although he was not initially conscious of the symbolism, Blake admitted during the making of the Teachers' TV programme that the book deals with those who are excluded from society, the homeless and the disadvantaged. The nameless eponymous hero "can be any of us," according to Blake; he becomes a kind of Everyman. The exuberant protagonist encounters people of all ages, ranging from spoiled children to unfeeling adults, but it is a little girl who finally agrees to help. Blake, who was appointed the United Kingdom's first Children's Laureate, maintains that a children's book can be a place where adults and children meet on equal terms. This is certainly true of his wordless picturebook, which can be read on several levels and was equally well received by critics and children. *Clown* won major children's literature awards chosen by adults, notably the 1996 Bologna Ragazzi Award, but it also won the 1996 Nestlé Smarties Book Prize (Bronze Award, 0–5 years category), which is selected by children.

Blake admits that some adults found *Clown* disconcerting because of the absence of text. During his interviews with Teachers' TV, the illustrator reflects on the advantages of wordless books: "Of course one of the advantages of a book with no words is that you have to talk about whether you've understood it or not. You have to discuss, even only with yourself what is actually happening, what do those gestures mean, what is happening next?" It is the question Dorte Karrebæk asks viewers in the title of her wordless picturebook. This interaction with the wordless book is contrasted with an adult's reading of a book from beginning to end, without every "meeting" the book and engaging with it. "Whereas with *Clown* because there are no words, you have to meet it, you have to know that you've been involved in it," Blake states. While this type of reading is necessary in the case of wordless books, he insists that all books should be read in this manner. Blake's reflections on *Clown* offer an apology of wordless picturebooks and a lesson in reading them.

The Hungarian-born picturebook artist Istvan Banyai offers a unique cinematic view of the world in his wordless picturebooks. Each of them could be referred to in the terms used by one critic to describe his second book:

"a visual journey, a cinematic picture book without words."[31] Before gaining an international reputation as an innovative children's illustrator, Banyai had established himself as a renowned commercial illustrator and animator in the United States in the 1980s and this work marks his children's books. Many of the sophisticated images in his picturebooks could easily serve as magazine covers. Although Banyai continues to produce commercial illustrations for publications such as the *Atlantic Monthly*, *The New Yorker*, *Time*, *Playboy*, and *Rolling Stone*, as well as cover art for recording companies and animated short films, his "unique philosophical and iconoclastic vision" has earned him an international reputation as a gifted artist that transcends the "the status of commercial illustrator."[32] He is commended for his originality, as well as his sense of design and composition. His art is very much in tune with pop culture and appeals particularly to a hip urban audience that includes children as well as adults (the illustrations in his wordless picturebooks include the latest technology trends, for example, what may be the first representation of an iPod). The playful, serendipitous nature of his art ensures its appeal with kids. On the jacket of *Minus Equals Plus*, Banyai describes his art as "an organic combination of turn-of-the-century Viennese retro, interjected with American pop, some European absurdity added for flavor, served on a cartoon-style color palette . . . no social realism added." The distinctive, flat, boldly coloured drawings appeal to comic book and film fans of all ages and the succession of detailed graphics resembles animation cels. The use of perspective and visual special effects also bears the mark of an animator. The world is presented from unusual points of view in mind-bending visual journeys that invite readers to reflect on visual perception and on illusion and reality.

Like the other picturebook artists in this section, Banyai makes extensive use of cinematographic techniques, such as zoom shots, angle shots, point of view shots, tracking shots, pan, and back lighting. Banyai's first picturebook, *Zoom*, published in 1995, recreates the effect of a camera lens gradually zooming out, frame by frame, with each page turn. It is also possible to experience the effect of zooming in by reading the book from back to front. In Banyai's strange landscapes, things are never as they appear. The first image is a close-up of a rooster's comb, but it is only identifiable when the page is turned to reveal the upper body of a rooster. Even when readers think they know what they are seeing, one page turn is generally sufficient to dispel that confidence. Banyai heightens the effect of his surprising images by alternating the full-colour illustrations on the recto with a solid black verso. As we zoom out, the successive images reveal that children are watching the rooster through a window in a house on a farm, which turns out to be a toy farm set with which a girl is playing. On turning the page, readers often discover that the previous image presented a world within a world. As the perspective continues to recede, the toy farm is on a catalogue cover read by a boy on a cruise ship, which is actually depicted on a poster on the side of a city bus, while the bus itself is an image on a television screen being watched by a native American in the desert. Several page turns later, readers discover that the native American is on a postage stamp on a letter being delivered to a tribal chief in the Solomon Islands. The island becomes smaller and smaller as the plane flies off, and when the plane disappears, the earth is a globe and finally a tiny white dot on the recto of a black doublespread that represents the vast blackness of space.

Astute readers will quickly begin to look for hints of what is to come on the next page. Older readers will perhaps link the concept of Banyai's book with Charles and Ray Eames's 1977 landmark documentary film *The Powers of Ten*, an adaptation of the 1957 book *Cosmic View* by Kees Boeke. The short documentary film explores the relative scale of the universe, in factors of ten, in an effort to make science and technology more interesting and accessible to the public. Viewers are taken on a voyage from a picnic in Chicago to the edge of the Universe, zooming out to cover ten times as much space every ten seconds. Within minutes, the entire earth can be seen, as it is in *Zoom*. Like viewers of *The Powers of Ten*, Banyai's readers find themselves behind the lens of an imaginary movie camera zooming out. Although less scientific, *Zoom* offers a similar philosophical adventure. Banyai's first wordless journey was hailed as one of the best children's books of the year by the *New York Times* and *Publishers Weekly*, and also won a National Children's Choice Award, which is selected by children. Both children and adults were enthralled by this crossover picturebook which Banyai dedicates to his wife and son. *Publishers Weekly* pronounces the sequel to *Zoom* a book "for all ages," but so, too, is *Zoom* and the illustrator's other picturebooks.[33]

Banyai's picturebooks are all marked by their conceptual originality, but they become increasingly complex. For many, *Zoom* remains Banyai's best book, in part because his subsequent books are unable to surprise readers to the same extent. As the title suggests, Banyai's next picturebook, *Re-Zoom*, also published in 1995, is a companion or follow-up to the earlier book. Banyai adopts the same layout and cinematic technique as *Zoom* to once again challenge assumptions about appearances. In order to maintain the element of surprise for readers who are familiar with *Zoom* and may expect the sequence of illustrations to expand to infinity in the same manner, Banyai does not limit his play in *Re-Zoom* to spatial relations, but also adds the dimension of time. A prehistoric cave painting turns out to be a design on the wristwatch of a young man doing a rubbing of carved hieroglyphs in an Egyptian tomb, which is actually inside the Luxor Obelisk in the Place de la Concorde in Paris, which, in turn, appears on an 1836 poster on a modern movie set. The movie set is in a tropical rainforest in India, which is drawn on a trunk in a boat in a painting in an artist's studio on an island near Mt. Fuji. In a witty, intratextual allusion to his picturebook, Banyai depicts the Japanese fan decorated with Mt. Fuji on a publicity billboard with the phone number "1(800)RE-ZOOM," and then has the billboard appear in a wordless book read by a boy in a subway car. Modern and traditional images are cleverly blended, as in the picture of a woman in traditional Japanese dress wearing a walkman. There are numerous references to cinema and the other arts. The humour that results from the incongruous juxtaposition of cultural markers may go over the heads of young readers. A black-and-white Alfred Hitchcock and a blue bodhisattva are mounted on an elephant in India, while Einstein and a rather glum Picasso ride the New York City subway. The ending of *Re-Zoom*, which leaves readers in a subway tunnel as the train's red tail lights disappear into the darkness, is less powerful than the outer-space journey in *Zoom*.

As will be clearly demonstrated by subsequent examples, wordless picturebooks often present dream narratives, taking readers on a journey through a dreamscape that blends reality and fantasy. Banyai's third picturebook, *REM* (1997), presents the dream world experienced during rapid eye movement sleep. Readers follow a series of ever-changing images, which, from one page to the next, transform into other apparently unrelated images. A pair of eyes becomes a drop of water which transmogrifies into a small blue man who grows into a tall magician. A snowman transforms into a princess and she kisses a frog who turns out to be a prince, and they join the other characters on a bus. It is only toward the end of the book, when the perspective recedes to show a bedroom (the bus has stopped at two large bare feet), that readers discover they have been experiencing a boy's dreams. Attentive readers will notice that the book the boy has fallen asleep over is open at the scene of the frog becoming the prince. The other mystifying objects that inhabited his dreams are to be found in the real-life objects that surround him, although the boy himself seems unaware of the connections. When the boy goes to the bathroom, his bedroom is reflected in the mirror above the sink and again in the water in the basin. As he brushes his teeth, the content of his dream whirls down the sink drain. The mirror reflects the much emptier bedroom, but a familiar blue doll sits beside the tap and a life-size version of the red bulldog watches him.

Banyai's last wordless picturebook, *The Other Side*, was published in 2005. Although the title helps the reader understand how the book functions, it is more challenging than his previous books. The recto and verso of each page present a scene viewed from one side and then the other. Like his previous books, *The Other Side* is full of clever twists and each page turn generally reserves an unexpected surprise. Readers will undoubtedly try to find a narrative thread, as several scenes are subtly interconnected. The first page provides diagrams showing how to make a paper airplane, while the two subsequent images depict an interior view of an apartment window through which a paper plane can be seen, followed by an exterior view of a boy at an adjacent window releasing a fleet of paper planes. The following page depicts a jet flying over a city on one side and on the other a view of the passengers inside, one of whom is reading a magazine. The beach scene on the magazine cover provides the content of the next set of images. The final images take us back to the beginning, showing an inside view of the apartment where the boy makes his paper airplanes and then an exterior view showing the girl and boy at their respective windows. Following the last recto-verso pair of images, Banyai adds a characteristic surprise: a final image presents another exterior view of the apartment building (the two children are still visible through their windows), but this time at night, thus creating a new set of paired images. The boy and the girl and some of the items from their respective rooms recur throughout the book, so that there are considerably more links between the paired images of *The Other Side* than, for example, in Bruel and Wach's *Vous oubliez votre cheval*. Readers will still have difficulty constructing a narrative, but the recurring motifs, images, and striking digital colours provide an intriguing and graphically stunning book. While Banyai's latest book is the most demanding, his wordless picturebooks are all intriguing, thought-provoking exercises in visual imagination. Their sly humour appeals to adults as well as children. The artist offers a truly global view, moving easily from the United States to Europe to Asia in his illustrations. At the same time, readers never know exactly where the scenes are set, so that his visual journeys have universal appeal for readers of all ages.

From Wordless Picturebook to Film

The cinematic quality of some wordless picturebooks has led to a film adaptation. The French author, illustrator, and graphic designer Sara, who is also scriptwriter for television cartoons, acknowledges the influence of the cinema on her work and its importance in the conception of her picturebooks, many of which are wordless.[34] Her passion for cinema as well as photography is evident in her picturebooks, which often have the dark, mysterious atmosphere of the film noir. The torn paper technique that Sara favours makes her books immediately recognizable and it quickly became her trademark. While other illustrators, such as Leo Lionni, have used the technique from time to time, Sara is one of the few artists, along with Eric Carle, to use it systematically. Torn paper has become a language with its own "grammar" for Sara. The different papers, which are always of very high quality, allow the artist to create striking contrasts. Sara distinguishes between a painting and a picturebook in much the same way as Kota Taniuchi. She contrasts an oil painting, in which she is able to "seize an intense moment" with a picturebook, which consists of a succession of images spread over time in order to "seize the slightest feeling." Sara's skill with torn paper is such that she is able to express subtle nuances of feelings and moods. She speaks of "the uncertainty of the tear" that allows her to privilege emotion and the unconscious.

Each of Sara's picturebooks creates a distinctive, evocative atmosphere. Her best-known work is the wordless picturebook *À quai* (Alongside the quay), published by Seuil Jeunesse in 2005. The book required the same form of editing as cinematic art, so it led quite naturally to a short animated film, produced in 2004. The film accompanies the book in the form of a DVD at the beginnning, but it was also shown at numerous film festivals. Like the book, the film is wordless and created exclusively from torn paper, but it offers another version of the story. *À quai* is an enigmatic story about a port, a captain, a woman in red, and a yellow dog (the shadow of Sara's dog, Gange, who died in 2002, haunts many of her picturebooks). Sara's palette is generally warm, but at the same time black has a very strong presence. Her bold, striking figures against a dark background are unforgettable, from the little, yellow dog to the sensual, mysterious woman in red. Solitude and encounters are recurrent themes and, like so many of her books, *À quai*, presents an atmospheric story about friendship and compassion between people who lead a hard life.

The wordless picturebook is the ideal medium for this silent, secretive artist who is wary of words. In a society that privileges verbiage and the written text, according to the illustrator, her picturebooks are an apology of silence, the unspoken, and non-verbal communication, all of which favour reflective thought and meditation. The artist uses the technique of torn paper because it allows her to communicate "feelings and emotions directly." The degree of subtlety and complexity with which Sara is able to render these stories in her chosen medium is remarkable. Sara considers her role to be that of a "metteur en scène" (producer) and refers to her readers as "spectateurs" (spectators). "What I present is a shadow theatre in which the spectator, the reader is also the author." Because readers see only "silhouettes," they are obliged to get involved. As Sara puts it, the reader/spectator is "the author of his or her *regard*" and must "listen to his or her feelings, moods, and emotions to enter into these wordless picturebooks."

Sara's works are published as children's books, but they are not exclusively for a young audience. Her confidence in the competence of young readers is evident in all her work, which makes no concessions based on age, either in the aesthetics or the subject matter. The images, although figurative, are so minimalist that they verge on the abstract. Sara redoes her images until she achieves an extreme purity and simplicity, but they are far from simplistic and clear cut. She uses visual imagery to reflect on difficult, often profound subjects, such as love, solitude, liberty, rebellion, and the quest for an ideal. Some of her subjects may resonate more with adults than children, as in the case of *À quai*, which presents the nocturnal meeting on a quay of a captain, torn between his desire for freedom on the open seas and his need for love, with a sensual, voluptuous woman in red. The work is complex because Sara includes three points of view on the meeting of the dog, the sailor, and the woman in red; in addition to the wordless narrative and the film, the illustrator includes a fictional letter written by the woman in red to the reader. Sara deplores the fact that publishers categorize books according to age, preferring to refer instead to "shared universes." On her website, the artist offers details about her private life "pour petits et grands curieux," that is, for inquisitive readers of all ages.[35]

A much earlier example of a very cinematic wordless picturebook being turned into a movie is *The Snowman*, which is the best-known work of the British author and illustrator Raymond Briggs. Published in 1978, the charming tale about a little boy whose snowman comes to life at midnight was turned into a twenty-six-minute animated film by Dianne Jackson four years later. The film, which was nominated for the Academy Award for Animated Short Film in 1983, became an immediate success when it was aired on Christmas Eve 1982. As both an animated film and a musical, *The Snowman* has become a part of British and international Christmas popular culture. Like the book, the film is wordless, with the exception of the song "Walking in the Air," which is performed when the boy and the snowman take flight. Howard Blake wrote the music and lyrics of the song and also composed and conducted the complete orchestral score for the film with his orchestra, the Sinfonia of London. Told in Briggs's signature picture strip style, *The Snowman* consists of 175 skillfully composed frames in the soft, muted colours of the snowy air in winter. The layout varies constantly, with pages containing up to twelve frames. Like a number of other wordless picturebooks, it tells the story of a fantastic nocturnal journey that brings the child back to his bed before morning. The page depicting the boy flying off to the snowman's wintry northern world is the first full plate in the book, and it is followed by two doublespreads that highlight the magical journey. The boy awakens the next morning to find the snowman has melted, and the viewer is left to wonder if the night's adventure was a dream. This is nonetheless belied when the boy discovers he still has the scarf with a snowman pattern given to him by Father Christmas. Chris Van Allsburg's *The Polar Express* evokes reminiscences of Briggs's much earlier Christmas favourite; both works achieved critical and popular success with a very diverse audience.

Like Chris Van Allsburg and Istvan Banyai, David Wiesner invites viewers of all ages to look at the world through new eyes. His books have often been described as cinematic, in large part due to the fact that they convey the sequence of events or thoughts that precede and follow each picture. The artist admits that he has always been fascinated by and curious about what comes before and after the captured image. Some of his books, most notably *Flotsam*, use cinematographic techniques to draw viewers into the story. When the wordless picturebook *Flotsam* won the 2007 Caldecott Medal, Wiesner became only the second person in the award's long history to have won three times. The cinematic nature of *Flotsam* was recognized in 2006 when Houghton Mifflin/Clarion Books participated in the first-ever Picture Book Video Awards, a program created and organized by The Book Standard/VNU Business Media. Students and graduates from top film and animation schools in the United States competed to created a sixty-second "trailer" for *Flotsam*.[36] In *Flotsam*, as in all his books, Wiesner takes the ordinary and makes it extraordinary. The story begins with a small boy beachcombing on an apparently ordinary trip to the beach, but, in fact, the innovative visual storyteller invites both children and adults on a mysterious, imaginary journey under the sea. The illustrations of *Flotsam* could be shots intended for a film; like Van Allsburg, Wiesner uses ingenious perspectives. With zooms and low-angle shots, the viewer approaches the protagonist until the moment of his fabulous discovery on the seashore. In this book, photography is also the subject matter, as the item washed up on the shore is an old-fashioned, barnacle-encrusted underwater camera which would seem to be part of the wreckage from a sunken ship. The camera contains a roll of film, which, when developed, reveals previously unseen magical images from the sea bottom. The dreamlike images include moving cities, an octopus in a lounge chair, a clockwork fish, and so forth. In the camera's photos, the real world is intermingled with the surreal, as in so much of Wiesner's work. The camera has not only travelled through the depths of the ocean, but also through the past, because the last photo, the most wondrous of all, is a photo within a photo: a girl holds a photo of a boy holding a photo, and so on, in a visual timeline of children from around the world. Assisted by his magnifying glass and microscope, the boy enlarges the embedded photos to reveal children from various geographic locations and ever earlier historical periods. The protagonist takes a picture of himself holding the previous photos and returns the camera to the ocean, but readers follow it until, with the help of several underwater creatures, it is discovered by another child in this neverending story. Like Banyai, Wiesner's graphic storytelling offers a mind-bending journey of the imagination.

Wordless Picturebook Series

A number of publishers have created collections that specialize in wordless picturebooks. Several of Sara's picturebooks, including *Dans la gueule du loup* (In the wolf's jaws, 1990), were published in the series La langue au chat, which she herself directed at the now defunct French publishing house Épigones from 1990 to 1995. The title of the series is taken from the French expression "donner sa langue au chat," which means literally "to give one's tongue to the cat" and figuratively "to give up trying to find the answer." Although the meaning is not the same, it evokes the English idiom "the cat got your tongue." The expression makes a particularly pertinent title for a series created with the objective of publishing wordless books that "let the images speak."

The most remarkable wordless picturebook series to date is undoubtedly Histoire sans paroles (Story without words), which was created by Autrement Jeunesse in 2004 while Sandrine Mini was an editor with the publishing house (by September 2010, eighteen titles were available in Autrement's innovative series). Although the tag line under the series name explains that these books are "pour lire avant de savoir lire" (To read before knowing how to read), they are also intended for older readers, as the publisher's catalogue and the open-ended age recommendation (three years of age and up) indicate. The publisher insists that although they do not contain a single word, the books are none-theless intended to be "read." In a broadside format, each book "tells a story using pictures." One of the first books, *Mon lion* (My lion), published in 2005 by the Belgian-born French illustrator Mandana Sadat, received a great deal of acclaim. The touching story about an encounter between a lion and a child, and their ensuing friendship was awarded the France Télévision prize in 2005 and chosen by the Mexican program "Biblioteca Escolar y de Aula" in 2006. When the attacking lion sees the little boy's tear, he carries him safely home, fighting off another lion and enduring the spears of the villagers. In the final pages, Sadat evokes the dreams of the new friends. The lion's dream of return-ing to the boy's village is confined to a small bubble, while the boy's dream of the lion extends across an entire doublespread and includes all the animals he observed at the waterhole from the safety of the lion's back. The absence of text seems to have facilitated cross-cultural collaboration, as a number of books in the Histoire sans paroles series are by illustrators from other coun-tries. In 2007, the well-known Brazilian artist Fernando Vilela published the picturebook *Le chemin* in the series. Although the title translates literally as simply "The path" or "The way," the publisher offers a much more descriptive English translation: "The way to the princess." Vilela borrows the codes of traditional medieval romance to tell the story of a knight who conquers dan-gerous creatures with his spear in order to rescue a beautiful princess. Every page turn brings an exciting new adventure to test the knight's courage. At the same time, Vilela rejects the stereotypes of the grand narrative, offering a very original take on the traditional genre, one which appeals to all ages.

A number of titles in the Histoire sans paroles series are debut books by exciting new illustrators. *Le songe* (The dream, 2009) is the first book by the French illustrator Édith Cadot. In a palette of warm earth tones, Cadot tells the story of a young Native American who, mesmerized by the flames of the campfire, enters into a state of dreaming and makes an initiatory journey. He seems to follow horses that escape from the flames of the fire and, in a wide range of landscapes, including the desert, a canyon, a mountain, the sea, and the plains, he undergoes a series of trials. The gigantic animals he encounters were announced by the tall shadows of animal shapes around the fire at the beginning of the story. The protagonist is chased by a herd of bison, swims with enormous fish at the bottom of the sea, and must pass enormous ghost animals in the plains. At last, he seems to find the object of his quest, a herd of marvelous, multi-coloured horses, which then metamorphose back into the flames of the fire. On the back endpapers, the young man is depicted back at his camp among the other dreaming members of his tribe. Without the title, it would only be as the reader closes the book that the initiatory nature of his journey would be revealed.

The Histoire sans paroles series also includes books by established illus-trators with international reputations. One of the most recent titles is *Eau glacée* (Ice water) by the American illustrator Arthur Geisert, who published his first book, *Pa's Balloon and Other Pig Tales*, in 1984. Geisert's crossover appeal is demonstrated by the manner in which he began his career in children's books. His first big break came at a Boston Print Makers member show, where an adult editor from Houghton Mifflin asked to see more of his work and passed it along to the children's editor. *Eau glacée* features Geisert's now legendary pig characters and the detailed engravings that make all his picturebooks immediately recognizable. It tells the story of the inventive pigs' ingenious solution to the water shortage problem on a very hot, dry little island. On a balloon-cum-sailing vessel, the pigs travel to the North Pole to tow back an iceberg that they equip with a sail. The illustrations are in colour except for two striking engravings midway. On the verso, the dark silhouettes of the two strange vessels appear in a round frame, as if they are being viewed through a telescope, while the facing page depicts a close-up of the pigs dark silhouettes dancing on the iceberg near a bonfire that constitutes the only touch of colour on the entire doublespread. Back on their island, the pigs combine work with play, industriously refilling the reservoir with giant ice cubes on which they frolic. The final spread mirrors an earlier scene in which the pigs sit around a table studying a globe and devising a plan, but now their water jug is filled with ice water and cool air blows in the door from the primitive air conditioning they have rigged up outside with a block of ice and a fan. Geisert's ingenious pigs and his intricate etchings are a hit with all ages, so *Eau glacé* adds a crossover title that is certain to attract attention to Autrement's wordless series.

Autrement came up with a clever, unique strategy to increase the wordlessness of the Histoire sans paroles series. The books are presented in a cardboard slip cover—open at both ends—bearing the conventional publication details: title, illustrator, series, publisher, ISBN number, and so forth. When the slip cover is removed, even the front and back covers of the book are wordless. The books published in this innovative series truly offer a "story without words."

Paratext in Wordless Picturebooks

Autrement's Histoire sans paroles series seeks to reduce to a minimum even the editorial paratext, including the details normally provided on the covers.[37] Generally the books in this series contain no paratextual elements whatsoever. Many wordless picturebooks do, however, contain some paratext, and in that case it plays a particularly important role as it is generally the only linguistic element. It has sometimes been said that wordless picturebooks are never completely without text due to the presence of the title. In the eyes of theoreticians such as Gérard Genette, however, the title is an element of the paratext rather than an integral part of the text. In the case of the picturebook genre, so-called paratextual components such as endpapers, title page, and even covers increasingly become an essential part of the text, as many authors and illustrators utilize every aspect of the book to tell the story. If the title is considered a paratextual element, it is certainly the most important and the most intimately linked to the text itself. Since it is the only text in completely wordless narratives, the title often offers an invaluable decoding tool for readers. In some cases, it may provide the only key to unlocking the story, while in less ambiguous narratives, it may merely corroborate the reader's interpretation of the pictures.

In *Va faire un tour* (Go for a walk, 1995) by the Belgian illustrator Kitty Crowther, winner of the prestigious Astrid Lindgren Memorial Award in 2010, the title expresses in words the message that is explicitly clear in the first illustration of an angry mother glowering at a dejected-looking child as she points toward the kitchen door: "Go for a walk!" Crowther's mother and child are whimsical, imaginative creatures drawn in very simple lines. The chastised protagonist obeys and glumly makes a trip around the whole world with her hands behind her back and her eyes cast down the entire way. A wordless map of the world on the endpapers traces the itinerary of the little creature whose familiar figure can be seen off South America walking across the Atlantic Ocean. The story is told in a series of small, rectangular vignettes (one or two per spread) in muted colours and striking black lines, and these are framed on the expansive white space of the page. One spread remains entirely blank as the protagonist walks under the ice in the Arctic. For Crowther, who is fascinated by the line because it can express so many different things, drawing is a form of writing. If emotion is present, as in *Va faire un tour*, the illustrator continues page after page (57 pages in this case), following the rhythm of her hand and unaware of what is coming next. Without ever once changing her stance or raising her downcast eyes to look around her, the glum little protagonist walks around the world, through oceans and lakes, across deserts and ice fields, through forests and cities, until she returns back home. The first vignette on the final page sets up a striking contrast with the opening vignette: pointing toward the dinner table rather than the door, the mother smiles down at the child, who is transformed by her happy smile and wide-eyed expression. The last frame shows mother and child eating contentedly at the table, but the conventional happy ending has a twist. The front-page story of the newspaper, which is depicted prominently in the foreground of the last vignette, features the protagonist. The photo captures a crestfallen Nessie staring after a disappearing figure that readers immediately recognize as the protagonist. Early in her trip, she had walked through Loch Ness and right past the monster whose initial delight at the appearance of a new playmate had turned to dejection when she continued walking out of the loch, apparently oblivious to both the monster and the photographer hiding in the grass. In the final frame, the knowing smile and the complicit look of the protagonist as she stares directly at the reader, whose eye, in turn, is riveted on the news story, suggests that perhaps the sullen protagonist took in more than we think on her walk around the world.

In some wordless picturebooks, the title sheds absolutely no light on the visual narrative. The title of Dorte Karrebæk's *Hvad mon der sker?* merely puts into words the question that formulates naturally in viewers' minds. The question mark takes the form of a red worm, whose eyes stare back at the title in a questioning, perplexed manner that reflects the reaction of readers themselves. In the case of Elise Fagerli's *Ulvehunger* (Wolfhunger, 1995), the book's title may provide astute readers with their first clue that this version of "Little Red Riding Hood" deviates radically from the familiar Grimm version. Although the word immediately evokes the hunger of the wolf that gobbles up Little Red Riding Hood and her grandmother, the word *ulvehunger* actually has a double meaning in Norwegian. As in French, being as hungry as a wolf or having a "wolfhunger" is a common expression for being very hungry. Most Norwegian readers are likely to presume, however, that the expression refers to the hunger of the infamous wolf, whereas Fagerli presents a Little Red Riding Hood who is far hungrier. Although few readers will realize it until they have read the surprising story, the ambiguous title contains in a nutshell the essence of Fagerli's remarkable book.

An author-illustrator may use the title or subtitle to categorize a picturebook in the wordless genre. The subtitle of *The Entertainer* (1992), by the American writer and illustrator Michael Willhoite, is "A Story in Pictures." In black-and-white line art, Wilhoite's narrative tells the story of a little boy who is discovered juggling in the park, becomes a famous entertainer, and eventually gives up fame and fortune, as well as unhappiness and loneliness, to go back to juggling in the park. Wilhoite's "story in pictures" offers a lesson that can be appreciated by readers of all ages.

Publishers' inserts in wordless picturebooks often provide information intended to orient and assist young readers. In Mitsumasa Anno's *Mori no ehon* (1979), published in English as *Anno's Animals*, paratextual information on the last page provides clues to help readers find the animals that are cleverly hidden on each page. The paratextual information often changes from edition to edition and country to country. The publisher's insert that provides a list of "things to look for" in the English version of Anno's *Tabi no ehon* (*Anno's Journey*) was not included in the original Japanese edition. Similarly, the publisher's insert on the dust jacket of the English edition of Tord Nygren's *The Red Thread* seeks to assist young readers in decoding the enigmatic work by providing a lengthy "Can you find" list that includes the names of storybook characters, artists, and their subjects. Warning readers that Nygren's "fantastical tableaus are a bricolage of allusions to "history, art, and children's literature," the insert seeks to reduce the strangeness of his visual world by drawing attention to the "familiar elements" which readers can try to find as they follow the red thread. Although these paratexts are addressed to children, it is quite possible that adults have more need of assistance than children.

When the paratext is provided by the book's author or illustrator, it generally has a greater significance for readers. Even a dedication may have a direct bearing on the narrative. Kitty Crowther links her dedication, "For Maximilien," in *Va faire un tour* directly to the narrative with a small line drawing of the protagonist. On the facing page, the dedicatory text explains the origin of the story:

To You,
who one day
cursed
the entire earth
because
nothing
was going
as you wanted.

Many authorial paratexts take the form of a preface or afterword. The wordless picturebook *Mélisande*, published in 1960, contains a foreword by the well-known children's author Margery Sharp, who conceived the book. Despite the reputation of Sharp and the illustrator Roy McKie in the field of children's literature, *Mélisande* is not only for children. The seriousness is taken out of opera in this "pictorial memoir" of an opera-singing dog told in black-and-white cartoon-style illustrations. Sharp's brief foreword sets the tone for the wordless narrative:

To speak with any assumption of intimacy concerning the great artist known as Mélisande is, alas, impossible. A most loyal and unselfish comrade—a "perfect pet" in the rehearsal room—she nonetheless hedged every private thought and emotion with delicate reticence which none would fail to respect and beyond which only a cad would attempt to pry. Many of her relations are still living—it is known she was one of a numerous family—but they too have preserved the same dignified and, (may one say it?), rare discretion. What follows is thus no more than a brief sketch of the great diva's dazzling, all-too-brief public career.

The reticence of the dog protagonist as well as that of her surviving family members explains why a wordless narrative is the appropriate medium in which to tell this rags to riches tale of a canine's rise to fame and fortune.

The Middle Passage: White Ships/Black Cargo (1995), by the American artist Tom Feelings, chronicles the horrific story of the transatlantic journey of enslaved Africans to the Americas entirely in pictures, except for a foreword by the artist and a brief introduction by historian John Henrik Clarke. The latter provides a concise account of the slave trade that Feelings renders so powerfully in monochromatic black-and-white illustrations on large over-sized pages. The visual narrative opens with a peaceful doublespread evoking life in their African homeland, but almost immediately the artist begins depicting the atrocities of these pages of history: burnt villages, rape, whipping, branding, crowded holds—a host of dehumanizing conditions. The suffering is palpable and the screams coming from the captives' open mouths are almost audible. In the foreword, Feelings discusses the genesis and genre of *The Middle Passage*, which he began writing in 1974 and only completed twenty years later. *The Middle Passage* is often categorized as an adult book, but Feelings' choice of the picturebook, which is generally considered a children's genre, has resulted in an ambivalent status and a crossover audience. It received the Coretta Scott King Award, which acknowledges outstanding African American children's authors and illustrators, but reviewers and critics have acknowledged its appeal for both young and adult audiences. Feelings's narrative provokes a powerful reaction in readers of all ages. In the foreword, Feelings, best known for his children's book celebrating African creativity, *Soul Looks Back in Wonder* (1993), explains why he chose to tell the painful story in a picturebook. His reading on the subject of slavery convinced him that the language of the Western world is "so infused with direct and indirect racism that it would be difficult, if not impossible, using this language in my book, to project anything black as positive." He felt, as he puts it in the foreword: "the more words I read, that I should try to tell this story with as few words as possible, if any." When he decided to attempt "to tell the story through art alone," he envisaged an audience of Africans of all ages: "I believed strongly that with a picture book any African in this world could pick up and see and feel what happened to us on those ships."[38] In Feelings's mind, a picturebook is not only for children. The artist, who referred to himself as a storyteller in picture form, links the picturebook genre to storytelling, "an ancient African oral tradition through which the values and history of a people are passed on to the young." In the foreword, he elaborates: "Illustrated books are a natural extension of this African oral tradition. Telling stories through art is both an ancient and modern functional art form that enables an artist to communicate on a large scale to people young and old."

Kota Taniuchi's postscript to *Nichiyobi* provides the raison d'être of the picturebook: "This book is a memory of childhood, of the time of imagination." His reflections on the very different role of toys in the lives of children and adults provided the inspiration for the almost wordless crossover picturebook. Despite the fact that Taniuchi's text is preceded by a small portrait of the illustrator, it constitutes a kind of brief epilogue rather than an autobiographical note. Its position opposite the last page of the story gives it a closer relationship to the text than most notes by or about the author, which are normally separated from the text by one or more pages. Due to its prominent position, readers are unlikely to overlook Taniuchi's paratextual note.

When paratexts such as prefaces and afterwords are not written by the author or illustrator they tend to be even more removed from the text. In the case of Ballester's *No tinc paraules*, the afterword by Dolores Fuzilli is separated from the last page of the narrative by three blank pages. Fuzilli's text is essentially a reflection on how to read a wordless book, and the reader might well question the place of any paratext in a book that announces in the title that it "has no words." Like Crowther's dedication to *Va faire un tour*, however, Fuzilli's afterword is directly linked to the narrative by a small vignette at the top of the page. In the same colours and style as the text's illustrations, Ballester portrays the mouth of a Black figure, presumably the protagonist. From the open mouth protrudes a long, black tongue, suggesting the act of speech, but the small bird on the tip of the tongue seems to replace the words. Ballester's image, like Fuzilli's afterword, is a commentary on wordless picturebooks. Ultimately almost every book has some words, in the form of paratext, so it would be more accurate to speak of "wordless narratives" than "wordless picturebooks."

Almost Wordless Picturebooks

Even the visual narrative in many wordless picturebooks is not entirely without text. Words may appear as part of the décor. This is the case in a number of books already examined. In Banyai's *Re-Zoom*, the telephone number on the billboard incorporates the picturebook's title in a clever self-referential allusion. Words appear on magazines, signs, and posters in *The Other Side*, which also contains comic-book style onomatopoeias ("Bang" and "Honk Honk") and a word balloon. The balloon issues from a penguin crossing the road and the words are obviously a playful allusion to the book's title: "Look out before you go to the other side!" The only words in Kitty Crowther's *Va faire un tour* appear on the newspaper in the final frame. In the case of Bertrand Dubois's *Sens interdit* (No entry), published by Éditions du Rouergue in 1998, even the title on the cover is part of the image, a "No entry" street sign.

Maps, blueprints, and charts bearing words that are often at least partially legible are found in the detailed illustrations of a number of picturebook artists known for their technical mastery. *Free Fall* (1988), which was the first title both conceived and illustrated by David Wiesner, features a leatherbound atlas that inspires the dreams of a young boy. The first page depicts the boy in bed clutching the atlas over which he has fallen asleep, while the last page shows him waking from his fantastic dream. The frame situation for the surreal journey is similar to Van Allsburg's *Ben's Dream* as well as Banyai's *REM*. As in *Ben's Dream*, the boy's bedtime reading is the source of the surreal dream sequence. On the verso of the first doublespread, the atlas is open on the bed, while, on the recto, a loose page blows over a landscape as the boy's green checked bedspread is transformed into an aerial view of checkerboard fields on the earth below. In a similar manner to *REM*, objects depicted in the boy's room on the closing page (toy dinosaurs, chess pieces, books, croissant, salt shaker, leaf pattern on the wallpaper) appear transformed in the surreal dreamscape. The map lands in a giant chess game being played by mortal pieces before blowing past a medieval castle into a forest where an enormous dragon hides among trees that become giant books, one of which seems to contain the map. The boy, a miniature dragon, and other figures become characters in the pages of the giant books, entering and escaping from their pages. Then suddenly, the boy, like Alice, becomes gargantuan and towers over the tiny chess characters. Allusions not only to *Alice in Wonderland*, but also to other classics such as *Gulliver's Travels*, *The Wizard of Oz*, and *The Water-Babies* add further layers to the boy's medieval romance-style quest for an elusive map. Old and modern motifs are blended: mounted on a pig, the boy leads a caravan along an abyss—into which the map falls—toward the illuminated skyscrapers of a modern city. In the next doublespread, the map is in pieces, as are the buildings, and they all fall through space, reminiscent of the pack of cards flying down on Alice before she awakens from her strange dream. The doves at the window and the goldfish in the bowl by the boy's bed explain the final scenes, where the boy rides on leaf-swans over a green checkered quilt-seascape with jumping fish. *Free Fall*, like a number of later wordless picturebooks, explores the haunting alternative reality of dreams and their association with the everyday waking world.

Wiesner's *Sector 7* (1999) also contains a map (of Sector 7) with text, as well as a globe (with only numbers) and numerous blueprints. The floating cloud factory that the protagonist visits with his cumulonimbus cloud friend resembles a Victorian design for a submarine, a kind of Grand Central Station in the sky (complete with "Arrivals" and "Departures" boards). There officious grownups give the clouds their boring assignments on blueprints until the boy, a talented artist, creates new blueprints of fantastic aquatic animal shapes. It is noteworthy that the adults' tedious blueprints contain text while the boy's exciting new blueprints consist entirely of images. Wiesner's detailed watercolours include words not only on the blueprints and map, but also on the signs on the Empire State Building and at the Sector 7 Cloud Dispatch Centre. In some cases, words are visible but illegible on the blueprints, as well as on the dispatcher's clipboard or the sheet of foolscap the boy's teacher is reading in the elevator of the Empire State Building. Another author-illustrator who includes blueprints in some of his books is Arthur Geisert. In *Lights Out* (2005), the plans for the protagonist's elaborate contraption are tacked up on the wall of his bedroom. The illustrator's meticulous etchings are often reminiscent of Victorian-era diagrams and blueprints.

Barbara Lehman's fascination with maps was at the origin of *The Red Book* (2004), a wordless picturebook about a wordless picturebook, which was a 2005 Caldecott Honor Book. Unlike the maps in most wordless picturebooks, however, hers are without text. The only words in the book are on street signs or fragmented on the side of a truck. The front flap introduces readers to the concept of mise en abyme on which the book is structured: "This book is about a book. A magical red book without any words—just like the one in your hands right now." As in the case of Michael Ende's *The Neverending*

Story, Lehman's book is packaged to imitate its fictional counterpart. The Swedish illustrator Tord Nygren uses a similar technique in his wordless picturebook *Den röden tråden* (1987; *The Red Thread*), although the self-reflexive allusions appear on only two doublespreads and do not constitute the subject of the book. In one spread, a boy reads *The Red Thread* in bed as his room is invaded by storybook characters from the books on his shelves, and in the facing spread the book lies open on the floor at the last doublespread. Lehman's wordless picturebook tells a more coherent, but still somewhat complex story about a little girl who finds a red book in a snow bank on her way to school. The square illustrations, in watercolour, gouache, and ink, are framed in black and have thick white borders, creating the effect of a page within a page. A single square framed image sometimes occupies the entire page, while at other times four small square images share the page. A series of square illustrations depict first a map, then an island, a beach, and a boy, who, in the facing illustration, finds a red book buried in the sand. A similar sequence of city scenes eventually zooms in on the girl. In this metafictional work, the characters' actions shape the course of their own stories in the book within the book. It is only in the pages of the book within the book that readers discover the girl in the city and the boy on the beach meet up. The circular pattern encountered in so many wordless picturebooks is more complex in Lehman's visual narrative, in which readers are left to imagine what will happen when another child picks up the magical red book that the girl drops as balloons carry her off to the boy's island. The ending is not unlike Wiesner's *Flotsam*, in which another child finds the magical camera. Citing Banyai's *Zoom*, one reviewer of Lehman's book claims that unlike many "wordless picture books [that] often seem to be the province of fine artists indulging in high-concept braggadocio," *The Red Book* has definite "child appeal," along with an ability to touch adults.[39]

The only text in a number of picturebooks is a short prologue at the beginning, which is generally limited to a single page. Nicole Claveloux's *Dedans les gens* (Inside people, 1993), which was published in Le Sourire qui mord's innovative small format series Petite collection, is described as a picturebook "sans texte ou presque" (without text or almost) on the Livres au Trésor website. The indefinite terminology reflects uncertainty as to whether the eight short lines of text at the beginning should be considered an inherent part of the narrative. The preliminary text is clearly integrated into the narrative by the facing image of the young actor, an image that is partially repeated on the recto of the next doublespread. The text, written in the form of a poem, is a prologue that introduces a play of sorts. Claveloux sets the stage literally for the story of a baby/actor, who moves forward in the Theatre of the World followed by all his "forgotten roles." We are the sum of our past roles, suggests Claveloux. The text quotes the protagonist, who believes he is "improvising," but the anonymous third-person narrator informs readers that in actual fact "old figures" meddle in his acting.

The pages that follow portray the young actor leading a parade of haunting, Bosch-like creatures. While one side of the doublespread depicts the procession like a long frieze bordered by white on the top and bottom, the facing page presents one or more small images on a white background. The alternation of the layout from one page to the next increases the sense of movement. Most often, the small image is a vignette, sometimes two, reproducing a detail from the fresco, although not necessarily a detail from the facing page. In a few instances, it is a pencil sketch of one of the characters, the most striking being a preliminary sketch of the protagonist on graph paper. The last small image, along the bottom of page 52, represents the first five characters of the procession now walking in the opposite direction, as if they have come full circle. The narrative ends with five illustrations that gradually zoom in on the half-hidden face of a frog-like creature until viewers see only a couple of light green spots on an otherwise black page from which even the white margin has disappeared. Claveloux's prologue, in combination with the title, establishes the universal nature of this philosophical visual narrative, in which the baby/actor represents Everyman on life's journey.

Dorte Karrebæk made her breakthrough in 1989 with an almost wordless picturebook *Der er et hul i himlen* (There is a hole in the sky), which won the Danish Ministry of Culture's Award for Illustrators in 1990. The only text in *Der er et hul i himlen* is a very brief prologue that states: "On days when the sky is covered in mist, the sun takes a holiday, and where it usually shines there's a hole in the sky." The story actually begins on the dust jacket, where a little girl peeks out at readers through a hole in the sky. Through the hole, the little girl jumps into a world of daydreams in a book that is subtitled "A Salute to the Dreamer." The protagonist's daydreams concern the everyday events in the daily routine of any child: playing, eating, dressing and undressing, bathing, listening to a bedtime story, and falling asleep. Juxtaposed with these daily rituals seen through the eyes of a child is the adult's realistic view of the same events. The succession of "free associations" that constitute the magical images of the child's daydreams occupy most of the page, while the adult's interpretation is presented as "a chronological, causal progression" in a sequence of small panels—not unlike a strip cartoon—whose position changes from one spread to the next. Kirsten Bystrup suggests that this wordless cartoon strip functions almost like a "text."[40] It constitutes a second pictorial narrative from an entirely different point of view, creating, as Maria Nikolajeva puts it, "a tension between the external and the internal visual space."[41] Karrabæk reminds adults that what they consider monotonous routine can be full of wonder and magic for a child. The dreamlike atmosphere of *Der er et hul i himlen* is characteristic of all of Karrebæk's picturebooks, even when the stories are firmly rooted in reality. *Der er et hul i himlen* marks a turning point in the illustrator's work, introducing her distinctive style of "using the pictures to tell the story," even when her picturebooks contain text. The artist claims that this narrative style of illustration results from the fact that when she was young she was too shy to express herself except through her drawings. When you are unable to say it, you turn to illustration, "a silent language."[42]

Arthur Geisert has published a number of almost wordless picturebooks, including *Oink* (1991) and *Oink Oink* (1993), in which the only word, repeated throughout, is "Oink." They are undoubtedly the noisiest almost wordless picturebooks of all time, as the word "Oink" is repeated up to seventeen times in some of the illustrations of the sow and her eight piglets. With a single word, Geisert manages to express a wide range of emotions, including joy, fear, and anger. *Lights Out*, published in 2005, contains one page of introductory text, which poses the conundrum faced by the protagonist: how to obey his parents' 8:00 pm lights-out rule but still have time to fall asleep before the room is dark. The initial page containing the text constitutes a kind of half-title page, as the words "Lights Out" appear at the top in a large font. The visual narrative shows the complicated kinetic processes that allow the inventive protagonist to resolve his dilemma. The predominance of image over text in Geisert's picturebooks is explained by his choice of medium. The etching process that Geisert uses in all his books is complex and time-consuming so he always completes the drawings before the text. For the wordless and almost wordless books, like *Lights Out*, Geisert admits that many revisions of the art are required to get the action to work smoothly and believably.

In some picturebooks, a text by another author constitutes a prologue that is nonetheless an integral part of the narrative. The only page of text in Elise Fagerli's *Ulvehunger* (Wolfhunger, 1995) relates word for word the admonitory scene from the Grimms' "Rotkäppchen," as it appears in a 1990 Norwegian translation. Fagerli thus creates the expectation that her dramatic woodcuts, in black and white with touches of red, will take up the story where the text leaves off and continue the well-known classic tale. The suspension points at the end of the text reinforce this expectation, as does her first illustration of the mother wagging her finger at her daughter as she hands her the basket. The paratext, on the other hand, hints strongly at a deviation from the Grimms' tale. The blurb on the back cover asks: "What really happened out in the woods the day Little Red Riding Hood met the Wolf?" and adds: "Read *Ulvehunger*—maybe you'll be surprised!" Although Fagerli's wordless picturebook takes the Grimm's text as its starting point, it is a parodic visual retelling in which the heroine eats both the wolf and her grandmother. In addition to the Grimm extract, the book contains one word, "RAP" (belch), integrated into the final image like a comic speech bubble to indicate the gargantuan burp that Little Red Riding Hood emits in front of her dumbfounded mother.

A sophisticated poem by Hubert Michel about a starfish that dreams of becoming a celestial star, appears opposite the title page in the otherwise wordless picturebook *La belle étoile* (2001; English trans., *Little Star*) by the Burkina Fassoborn French illustrator Antonin Louchard. In soft colours applied with visible brushstrokes, Louchard tells the touching story of a red starfish that is washed up on a beach, worn in a little girl's hair, snatched by a seagull that leaves it high in the night sky, before falling back to earth, where it splashes into the ocean and finds its way back to its original position on the ocean floor. Louchard's illustrations clearly convey the action, while creating a dreamy atmosphere in keeping with the poem. The gull flies so high into the sky that the earth can be seen as a globe far below. The little star stands out as the only red star visible in the night sky and then it falls back to earth, across a doublespread, as a shooting star with a long golden tail. At the end of the book, the little star sits once again on the ocean bottom next to the anchor of a sailboat near a lighthouse, in exactly the same place as at the beginning of the story, but night has replaced day, indicating the passage of time. Grown-ups and children alike find subject for reflection in the allegorical journey of the little starfish.

Some picturebooks contain a single line of text in their visual narrative. Mandana Sadat includes one line of text in the picturebook *De l'autre côté de l'arbre* (On the other side of the tree). The illustrations for the book were selected in Bologna in 1996 while Sadat was still a student of decorative arts, and they became her first picturebook, published by Grandir in 1997. The four words of the traditional fairytale incipit: "iiil était une fois . . ." (ooonce upon a time . . .) are integrated into the image, where they issue diagonally out of the mouth of a conventional-looking fairy-tale witch, who is, in fact, a storytelling witch. The familiar formula, which the witch stresses by drawing out the first vowel, marks the beginning of a story within the story, which will also be told entirely in pictures. The power of tales, encapsulated in these four words, brings together the storyteller and the young girl who wanders into the forest at the beginning of the book.

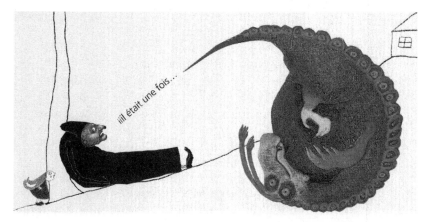

Figure 3.5 De l'autre côté de l'arbre by Mandana Sadat, copyright © 1997 Grandir, reprinted by permission of Mandana Sadat and Grandir.

Whereas the few words of text in *De l'autre côté de l'arbre* appear midway through the book, the two words in Peter Schössow's German picturebook *Meehr!!* (1999) are pronounced by the adult protagonist on the last page. The grown man who stands on a sand hill enjoying a gusty wind on the cover reappears on the first doublespread, now startled looking and windblown, staring after his hat, which has been carried off, along with countless other objects, by the gale-force wind. He and his dog run after the hat, then he is carried off his feet and turned head over heels, he flies with the birds and planes over the sea and the land, eventually landing heels over head on the beach by the house on stilts from which he had departed. The final single spread shows the smiling man standing on a crate in the wind saying "Noch mal!!" (Again!!). Like a child, he wants to repeat the experience, which was at first unsettling, but ultimately exhilarating.

Some of Sara's picturebooks contain text, but it is always brief and she still "let[s] the images tell the story." The text is only "a guide that suggests an approach to the reader, that of 'letting the images speak for themselves.'" Sometimes Sara writes a text that adopts the viewpoint of one of the book's characters and "talks about his or her way of living the events," as in *À quai*, where the woman in red's letter to the reader provides another point of view. When she adds text, it is often at the request of a publisher concerned that a wordless picturebook is more difficult to sell. Sara explains the function of text in her books in the following words: "In this case, the text is a handrail to hang on to in order to descend the stairs that lead to one's deeper emotions."[43] In her view, the text is a kind of psychoanalytical tool that allows readers to access their innermost feelings. One of Sara's most remarkable near-wordless picturebooks is *Révolution*, which was published by Nicole Maymat for Seuil Jeunesse in 2003. Along with *À quai*, it was awarded the Golden Apple at the 20th Biennial of illustrations in Bratislava in 2005. Sara's familiar torn-paper technique is particularly striking in the red, black, and white illustrations of this oversize book on high quality paper. The story begins and ends with a page of bright red paper that highlights the subject in a strikingly silent manner (according to Maymat, the colour red belongs to Sara). With one exception, the few words of text are all exclamations that underscore the emotions of the characters. Two initial wordless doublespreads of revolutionaries ascending a hill carrying a large flag with the image of a red lion on a black background are followed by a close-up with the first word, the simple exclamation "Ooooh!" The page turn explains the revolutionaries' surprised dismay, as two large black tanks turn their guns toward the men. The words "The tanks!" are unnecessary, but serve to punctuate the men's horror. The single word "Prisoner!" stands out on the stark white background of a doublespread that is largely blank except for a black space in which the imprisoned flag-bearer's head and hands are visible. The words "Good bye! little flag!" on the next doublespread depicting the lone flag on the hill express the prisoner's desolation. Wordless spreads of the prison camp precede a close-up of the prisoner, whose brows are knitted in thought, and one word encapsulates his thoughts: "Escape. . . ." The rest of the book is wordless, except for the exclamation that expresses the amazement of the guards: "Yes! it was a lion!" The red lion descends from the flag, enters the prison camp, and carries the prisoner off on his back as the guards fire at them. It is perhaps significant that the few words in this powerful visual narrative accompany the pages that condemn violence, oppression, imprisonment, and concentration camps, whereas the final pages that offer a message of hope and liberty are without words. In all of Sara's books, the text is always at the service of the image.

The text in almost wordless picturebooks often has the purpose of establishing the time. Without integrating a clock, a calendar, or a similar device, precise time and the passage of time is difficult to represent in a wordless picturebook. In Kitty Crowther's *Va faire un tour*, a wall clock in the first frame indicates 6:30, while the grandfather clock in the last frame marks 7:00, indicating that the little protagonist has made her world tour in the space of half an hour, the time it takes her mother to prepare dinner. In Geisert's *Lights Out*, an alarm clock in the protagonist's bedroom repeatedly shows the time from 7:30 on the first page to 8:30 on the final page, where he is seen fast asleep in bed through his window (32). Willhoite adopts a different approach in *The Entertainer*, where the passage of time is effectively conveyed by round insets of a tree branch that mark the changing seasons (bare in winter, budding in the spring, and in full foliage in summer).

In Kota Taniuchi's *Nichiyobi*, which contains four lines of text (two on the first and two on the last pages of the book), the first line establishes the time, almost like a stage direction at the beginning of a play: "Sunday, 9 o'clock." The final line of text—"Et maintenant, en voiture!" (And now, all aboard!), which accompanies the last illustration of the dolls in the yellow truck, reinforces the circularity of the visual narrative, as the dolls prepare to set out on another journey, this time by truck. The days of the week are written in a flowing line of text on the final page, beginning and ending with Sunday. The intention is not to teach the days of the week, as in a concept book, but rather to give Sunday, which is in red and appears twice, a special status. Perhaps Taniuchi is suggesting that Sundays have a special magic or that they are particularly cherished by the boy with the blurred features manipulating the truck or children in general or, for that matter, adults and children alike. The opening line of text in *Nichiyobi* establishes the day and time of the events, while the final line seems to suggest that these events are repeated Sunday after Sunday. The use of text in *Nichiyobi* clearly indicates the circular pattern characteristic of so many wordless or almost wordless picturebooks.

The text in David Wiesner's Caldecott Medal-winning *Tuesday* (1991) is limited to a few words—set against a white background—which give the time. Wiesner's story opens in a very similar manner to Taniuchi's, by establishing the day of the week and the time: "Tuesday evening, around eight." However, the story actually begins slightly earlier, on an illustrated page that precedes the copyright and title pages. The page is divided into three vertical panels that depict the initial moments of the strange phenomenon as experienced by the frogs themselves: in the first frame three frogs sleep peacefully, while in the second one startled frog rises into the air on its lily pad, as the two others open their eyes in amazement, and finally a second frog excitedly rises above the pond as the first waves down at him from above. The page layout is varied constantly, as is the angle and viewpoint, as Wiesner takes readers above or below the action, head on or behind it, up close or far away. As if manipulating a camera, Wiesner zooms in and out, pans, and offers unusual angles. The large, landscape format resembles a movie screen. The first illustration after the title page presents a series of three horizontal panels that gradually zoom in on a turtle witnessing the surprising spectacle, while readers are taken even closer in the following doublespread depicting the frogs flying low over the terrified turtle. A striking doublespread shows a panoramic landscape shot in which dark birds perched on telephone wires are silhouetted against a night sky full of hundreds of flying frogs on lily pads, while three superposed vertical framed panels depict close-ups of frogs riding their lily pads like flying saucers (in the third a frightened, squawking bird is pursued by a grinning frog). Wiesner captures the sheer delight of the frogs at this startling opportunity. Another doublespread offers a wide, cinematographic scene, viewed from the flying frogs' perspective, of the houses, lawns, and trees below as they invade the city. The cover illustration of *Tuesday* adds another temporal precision: the hands of a large town clock indicate almost 9:00 and alert readers will notice that two frogs are partially visible in the bottom corners.

Unlike Taniuchi, Wiesner adds further temporal precisions that clearly mark the passage of time. The time "11:21 P.M.," which appears on the stark white background of a verso, is echoed on the clock on the facing illustration. There a man gazes unbelievingly out the corner of his eyes at frogs waving at him through the window. The legacy of cartoons and comics is evident in the illustrations of *Tuesday*. Frogs fly through the laundry on a clothesline and come out transformed into super-hero frogs with capes. Narrow panels inset on a doublespread showing the exterior view of quiet houses depict frogs entering a house by the window or the fireplace. An old woman sleeps in an armchair, oblivious to the frogs who swarm around her, watching television, manipulating the remote, and admiring her landscape paintings, while her cat observes warily from a dark doorway. The next time update, "4:38 A.M.," marks the approach of dawn. At daybreak the frogs lose their ability to fly and fall back to earth, as their lily pads land in trees, on roofs, and on chimneys. The sun is rising as the frogs make their way back to the pond. The last inset of the doublespread depicts a disgruntled bullfrog strumming his fingers deject-edly on a lily pad and another gazing longingly up at the sky. In a much more explicit manner than in *Nichiyobi*, the final line of text in *Tuesday* indicates that a variation on these extraordinary events occurs the same day the following week: "Next Tuesday, 7:58 P.M." The precision, "7:58 P.M." rather than "around eight," seems to establish the authenticity of the improbable events. The following Tuesday at the same time, it will be the pigs' turn to fly in this open-ended story that could continue forever. The paratextual information on the dust jacket, apparently written by the author, offers a tongue-in-cheek authentication of the strange narrative: "The events recorded here are verified by an undisclosed source to have happened somewhere, U.S.A., on Tuesday. All those in doubt are reminded that there is always another TUESDAY." Paradoxically, time and place remain vague in *Tuesday*, as in *Nichiyobi*, even though all the text, including the title, provides temporal details. The almost wordless picturebooks of both Wiesner and Taniuchi encourage readers of all ages to use their imagination.

The remaining almost wordless books in this section have minimal text throughout most of the narrative. This is often in the form of brief captions. Twenty years after *Number 24*, Guy Billout published *Journey: Travel Diary of a Daydreamer* (1993) with the innovative American publisher The Creative Company. Like *Number 24*, *Journey* has detailed graphic illustrations in muted tones, but it is not entirely wordless. Brief captions accompany the illustrations which tell the story of a long, unusual journey that transcends temporal and spatial laws. On the verso, a cryptic caption accompanies a picture of a boy gazing out a train window, from which we glimpse only a small portion of a scene that is depicted in its entirety on the recto, where surreal, fantastic details are added. The modern world is juxtaposed with historical and even pre-historical elements. The captions mention month and location, weather conditions, or the scenery, in a spidery text that highlights the story's dreamlike quality. One caption bears the vague temporal caption "December, or maybe it was August," along with a view of a modern railroad bridge, while the recto depicts a tyrannosaurus and a triceratops leaping across it. The illustration opposite the caption "August 13, a blue moon" depicts a surreal scene of wolves entering a medieval castle property by crawling under a moat as if it were a carpet. Billout's "sophisticated visual puzzles" have been compared to those of David Macaulay's *Black and White*, but one reviewer pronounces them "more perplexing than provocative." The cryptic, hermetic text does little to enlighten readers and there is no apparent coherence to the strange illustrations. Readers are left to decide if Billout is representing a boy's daydreams, a surreal vision of history or life, or a metaphorical vision of "the artist's journey through life."[44] The latter interpretation is supported by the substitution, toward the end of the book, of a white-haired older man wearing the same suit as the young boy. On "January 30, midnight," the white-haired man takes his suitcase down from the rack, but the empty train car is accompanied by the date "March 11." The man seems to have aged further by the last illustration, as he now has a cane. With his suitcase, he stands looking out over the Atlantic, watching the train disappear into the distant horizon beside train tracks that end abruptly at the edge of the cliff beside him, as if to indicate that this is the end of the line for the protagonist. As in *Tuesday*, the use of date and time captions does not add to the reality of the story, but heightens its strangeness.

Billout also uses captions in *Something's Not Quite Right* (2002), another almost wordless collection of surreal images, which, in this case, are not connected by any narrative thread whatsoever. The book was first published, under the title *Il y a quelque chose qui cloche*, by Harlin Quist in 1998. The composition of the picturebook is somewhat reminiscent of *The Mysteries of Harris Burdick* (1984), although Chris Van Allsburg's introduction to the portfolio version of the book provides a frame story for his enigmatic black-and-white drawings, which are accompanied not only by a title, but also a brief caption. For example, the picture of a nun sitting in a chair floating in a cathedral is labeled "THE SEVEN CHAIRS: The fifth one ended up in France." In both books, readers are left to imagine stories for each of the mysterious pictures and captions. Like *The Mysteries of Harris Burdick*, *Something's Not Quite Right* was reviewed as a book for all ages. The publisher's blurb is careful to point out that the oversized book, which consists of thirty-three large paintings bordered in white, is the work of an "artist" and "not an illustrator," no doubt in the hope of increasing sales among adults. The paintings, which are very European in flavour, present autonomous scenes from nature or architecture. In this book, the captions are limited to a single word, which nonetheless involves some clever wordplay reminiscent of David Macaulay. Billout's minimal text encourages readers to linger over the pictures, reflecting on the relationship between the word and the image. Readers will immediately see that "something's not quite right" in the cover illustration of an ocean liner traveling over a huge gorge, although the "not quite right" element is not blatantly obvious. It reminds us of Van Allsburg's gigantic ocean liner crashing its way into a Venetian canal. Without the caption "Handicap," perhaps readers would not notice that the golfer's lost ball is lodged in the gullet of the ostrich standing incongruously on the golf course. The back cover copy informs readers that "the smallest detail can make the greatest difference," and encourages them to solve the "tiny mystery" on each page. Readers must look closely at the illustration titled "Mimetism" to notice that one of the pigeons in the foreground has wheels in place of feet, while the Boeing 747 about to touch down on the nearby runway is missing the front wheels of its landing gear.

Billout's pictures contain the unexpected, in the form of anomalies, incongruities, and paradoxes. Each page reserves unusual surprises for readers of all ages as the artist juxtaposes items in a very surreal manner. Absurd climactic and geographical situations are a common theme. A page labeled "Dune" depicts a smooth white mountain, against a clear blue sky, being climbed on one side by a figure in a white robe and on the other by a person in a parka. The clever visual trick allows the same dune to suggest desert sand and drifted snow. The caption "Ice Age" introduces a plate in which New York's Flatiron Building, like the prow of a ship, cuts its way through ice, while a penguin waddles across the foreground. In an illustration titled "Canyon," the same building is perched on the edge of an abyss at the former intersection of Broadway and Fifth Avenue. The succinct captions under-score the irony or paradox inherent in the illustration. All the bridges that cross the Seine River are severed so that Paris's Île de la Cité floats free in "Secession," while in "Skyscraper" a pointed church steeple scratches a blue line across the surface of the full moon. The captions add to the sophisti-cated wit of Billout's images. The caption "Attack" gives new meaning to the fanciful illustration of a solitary man in a field of snow looking up in shock at an equestrian statue, while his hat lies on the ground near a snowball that seems to have been fired from the canon aimed at his head. The adult appeal of this book is not surprising, as the sophisticated stand-alone images were originally done for *The Atlantic* magazine.

Ann Jonas's almost wordless picturebook *Round Trip* was seen as a very exciting experimentation in graphic design when it was published in 1983, and it was a *New York Times* Best Illustrated Book of the Year, as well as an ALA Notable Book. Like Banyai's picturebooks, *Round Trip* is a visual adventure in observation. The striking black-and-white illustrations are, in fact, optical illusions in the nature of M. C. Escher's works. Jonas's book is a perfect mar-riage of format and content because the story announced in the title is literally a round trip. The journey begins at home as the sun rises and takes readers to the city, where they are told to turn the book upside down and return home. On the return journey, readers see different sights, ending up back home under a moonlit sky. The blurb on the back cover gives away the illustrator's stratagem, but many readers will figure it out from the cover, where the title and author's name appear a second time upside down, as in a mirror image. Jonas's masterful black-and-white illustrations work equally well when viewed upside down. The sun shining on the pond in their neighbourhood in the morning becomes their moonlit street on the return trip, while a bridge, with water running under it and cars driving over it, turns into a fence bordered by telephone poles under a starlit sky when turned upside down. Jonas uses the same technique in the aptly titled picturebook *Reflections* (1987), although this time the illustrations are in full colour. A child's day begins at dawn in bed in a small seaside town and ends back at home in bed as the sun goes down. When turned upside down, sailboats become kites, a ferry turns into a restaurant, and a boatyard is transformed into a campground. *Round Trip* and *Reflections* are not entirely wordless, but they contain very little text and the text is of virtually no interest. In *Round Trip*, the text is placed on oppo-site sides of the doublespread for each direction of the journey, whereas in *Reflections*, both lines of text appear on the same page. When pages with text in *Round Trip* are turned upside down, the words go virtually unnoticed and the illustration becomes essentially wordless. Only the first/last page has text when read both directions, opening and closing the journey. The discreetness of the text in *Round Trip* is increased by the fact that it is artfully integrated into the illustrations, appearing in white on black for the initial journey and black on white for the return.

A few years after *No tinc paraules*, Media Vaca published another very audacious book in their children's series, a book that was not without words, on the contrary, it contained 80,000 words, as indicated by the title, *Mis primeras 80.000 palabras* (My first 80,000 words, 2002). On the cover, the title is contained within the open mouth of the rather grotesque head of a screaming toddler. While it is not wordless, the book's 80,000 words are expressed in images.[45] Two hundred and thirty-one of the most prestigious illustrators and graphic artists from approximately twenty countries (including Olivier Douzou and Nicole Claveloux) were asked to choose their favourite word in their native tongue and illustrate it for this 224-page book edited by Ferrer himself. Many of the words and/or illustrations are quite surprising in a book targeted at children. Among the words included are *amoque* (defined as a sudden attack of murderous fury, a form of homicidal madness observed in Malaysia), *asesino* (assassin), *femme fatale*, *nishthurta* (the transliteration of a Hindi word used to describe a cruel act that causes pain and suffering), and *putréfaction*. Some of the illustrations are no less disturbing. Like all the books published in Media Vaca's children's series, *Mis primeras 80.000 palabras* is intended for readers of all ages.

In the picturebooks examined in this section, words have not been entirely excluded. Rather than detracting from the image, the few words in these picturebooks enhance the image. The image carries the narrative and the text is essentially a support. It highlights, punctuates, or situates the visual narrative of almost wordless picturebooks, often serving a function of mise en scène or stage direction.

Wordless Dream Sequences

A striking number of wordless picturebooks present visual journeys, either realistic or imaginary.[46] Like Banyai's *REM* or Wiesner's *Free Fall*, many constitute journeys into a surreal dreamscape. Nicholas Heidelbach's *Ein Buch für Bruno* (A book for Bruno, 1997) depicts the flights of fancy of two children who, from the everyday world of their living room, swing into and out of a fantasy world as they dive into a book adventure. This multilayered wordless picturebook, which has been considered suitable for both adults and children, constitutes an exploration of the meaning of the act of reading. Barbara Lehman's *The Red Book* was followed by two more wordless picturebooks which also recount magical journeys. In *Rainstorm*, a lonely boy in a gray manor house on a rainy day finds an old key that unlocks a trunk, in which a ladder leads down into a tunnel and eventually back up a winding staircase to a sunny island lighthouse, while in *Trainstop*, the train on which a little girl is travelling is stopped in a tunnel by Lilliputian people who need her assistance.

In the latter, the girl's train trip then continues as if the whole adventure was merely a daydream. Some picturebook artists use wordless spreads to evoke only the dream sequences.[47]

In these wordless picturebooks, the lengthy dream sequence is preceded and followed by images rooted in reality which are accompanied by text. The absence of text in the central pages slows the pace as readers linger over the pictures. The effect is that of changing real time to dream time, when everything seems to move much more slowly. The lack of text also reflects the speechlessness and silence that characterize many dreams. Chris Van Allsburg used this strategy in the 1980s in *Ben's Dream* (1982). The text is limited to the opening and closing pages; between pages 6 and 30 the narrative is entirely visual. The text on the first three pages sets the scene for the dream sequence that follows. When dark rain clouds put an end to Ben and Margaret's plans to play baseball, the two friends go home to study for a geography test on great landmarks of the world, but Ben is lulled to sleep by the steady rhythm of the rain on the window during the exceptionally heavy downpour.

The wordless sequence begins with Ben suddenly "awakening" with a start to discover that his house is adrift on an immense sea. His journey around the world on a floating house takes him past the remarkable monuments pictured in his geography book, only they are all partially submerged. The house floats by the Statue of Liberty and Big Ben, under the Eiffel Tower, past the Leaning Tower of Pisa, the crumbling columns of the Parthenon, the head of the Sphinx, the spires of the Taj Mahal, and the Great Wall of China. While children will seek to identify the different landmarks, adults will admire the artistry with which the illustrator integrates Ben's modest small-town home into these famous sites in hatched pen-and-ink line drawings. Van Allsburg uses the striking angles and unusual perspectives that characterize all his works: readers are placed behind the Statue of Liberty, above Big Ben, inside the Eiffel Tower, and beside Ben on his front porch when they pass Sphinx. As the house passes Mount Rushmore, the eyes of the stone presidents rotate to stare directly at Ben, and George Washington opens his mouth slightly to pronounce the words: "Ben, wake up." These words, the only text in the dream sequence, appear in a comics speech bubble. In fact, it is not the former president waking Ben, but Margaret yelling at the window. As the story returns to the real world, where the storm has passed, the text resumes. Observant readers will notice small details in the illustrations which provide clues to another level of meaning within the story. The ending reserves one of Van Allsburg's characteristic twists, which is accessible to all ages. It turns out that the small figure looking out the window of another floating house near the Sphinx was Margaret, who had the identical dream when she also fell asleep studying geography. Van Allsburg excels at evoking a dreamworld between reality and fantasy. As in all of his books, readers of *Ben's Dream* are left to determine exactly where the two worlds meet.

The Danish author and illustrator Søren Jessen uses the technique of framing wordless pages between pages with text in order to explore the extraordinary world of the child's imagination in his picturebooks. In this case, the lack of text seems to reflect the protagonist's speechless amazement at the wonders discovered on his fantastic journey. Jessen's first book, a picturebook, appeared in 1990, and the much-acclaimed author-illustrator has since published books for all age groups: children, young adults, and adults. Like Wiesner, Jessen has a gift for portraying the unusual with a remarkable down-to-earth quality. As in *Tuesday* and *Free Fall*, the border between fantasy and reality is questioned. However, like Karrebæk's *Der er et hul i himlen*, Jessen's picturebooks juxtapose the differing perspectives of a child and an adult. Jessen uses the text–image relationship to underscore the contrast between the two viewpoints in *Faldt du?* (Did you fall? 1999), which won the Danish Ministry of Culture's Award for Illustrators in 2000. The central wordless section is preceded by four pages with text and followed by another two. On the pages with text, the images are framed with wavering black brush strokes and large white margins, while the colours are predominantly black, white, and grey. A boy in a batman suit walks along the street with his father and then falls while traversing a crosswalk (known in some countries as a zebra crossing). The few lines of simple text at the beginning inform readers that one day Rasmus accidentally stepped between the white lines of the crossing: "And then he fell." Jessen describes *Faldt du?* in the following manner: "A story about a boy who falls, but it's not an ordinary fall—it's the fall of all falls. But his father doesn't realize that at all. To him it was just another ordinary fall."[48] The illustration which precedes the wordless sequence introduces a fantastic element and prepares the surreal sequence, as the boy seems to slip between two white lines of the crosswalk.

The wordless pages adopt a distinctly different visual language: the frames disappear in the vividly coloured, full-bleed doublespreads rendered in powerful brushstrokes. In nine fantastic doublespreads, the little boy, with his Batman cape spread out above him, falls and falls and falls, sometimes head over heels, through an imaginary world of surreal images often inspired by Magritte and especially Dali. The space through which Rasmus falls is filled with very strange sights: skyscrapers on rocks, penguins with propellers, elephants wearing flippers, a crocodile with dragonfly wings, and an elephant with camel-like legs. Gnomes paint black stripes on zebra, an obvious allusion to the crosswalk that is still visible far above the falling boy. The final wordless doublespread shows the boy diving toward the crosswalk and, when the page is turned, he is lying on the crosswalk, still in a diving position. The text on the final two pages consists only of the father's very matter-of-fact words: "'Oops,' said Rasmus's Dad. / 'Did you fall?'" Although the father comforts the boy, he is completely unaware of the traumatic nature of his son's fantastic fall. The minimal text highlights the gulf between the father's and son's view of the event. The child's perspective prevails, not only by the number and power of the wordless spreads, but also because the realistic opening and closing pages are themselves framed by endpapers that depict the white lines of the crosswalk on a blue background, as they appear in the dreamlike sequence.

Like *Faldt-du?* Jessen's picturebook *Gaven* (The gift), published in 2007, is also "a story about the very different ways grownups and children perceive the world," which makes it, according to the author-illustrator, "truly a book for adults as well as kids."[49] The opening and closing pages, in which a father brings a present home to his son and later returns to see how he likes it, are accompanied by brief text, but the majority of the book is wordless. The "present," the best Frode had ever received, is not the fancy new television but the cardboard box in which it came. When his father closes the door behind him, Frode flies out through the window and over the roofs of the town in the box-cum-spaceship. The pages devoted to the boy's magical journey are wordless. The illustrations on the pages with text are once again framed by large white margins, while the fantastic journey is depicted on colourful, full-bleed doublespreads. However, in this book there is a transition between the two styles, as the first textless page retains the framed image but depicts the boy in the box breaking out of the image into the white margins. The following doublespread remains somewhat anchored in reality; rendered in muted colours (mostly grey, black, and white), the boy flies over a realistic city. The completely white backdrop of the sky, against which the city is painted, contrasts strikingly with the subsequent doublespreads, which are covered entirely with acrylics that are applied with bold brush strokes. The first of these doublespreads artfully evokes the transition from reality to the fantastic world of the boy's imagination because it shifts gradually from monochromatic, cool greys to warm, vivid colours. The final page also evokes a transitionary state between two worlds. Although there is one line of text, it is distinctive because the line is curved rather than straight. The frame is once again absent, the background is white, and the image bleeds to the lower edge. These are all signs that the boy sitting in the box waiting for something strange to happen is on the verge of another wonderful adventure.

The wordless pages that portray the fantastic world of Frode's imagination are reminiscent of *Faldt-du?*, again containing numerous references to the paintings of Magritte and Dali. The surreal world is inhabited by a crocodile with a squirrel-like tail, a fish carrying a bone, the legendary Nessie, blue card-playing hens, flying pigs, tortoises carrying candles or bearing numbers on their backs, and pink elephants with a penchant for fishing. Tall naked trunks topped with Christmas trees tower above skyscrapers; trees grow on meteors in outer space; a tree in leaf bears one giant orange, while a leafless tree bears one giant apple core. Observant readers will notice that, in the manner of *REM*, items in Frode's bedroom are integrated into the surreal dreamscape. While some items are clearly visible, including a

Figure 3.6   Gaven by Søren Jessen, copyright © 2007 Søren Jessen and Gyldendal, reprinted by permission of Søren Jessen and Gyldendal.

toy fish, a miniature ladder, a small lighthouse, a ball, numbers hanging on the wall, a picture of an air balloon, and several stuffed animals (a tortoise, a blue hen, and a dog), others, such as a toy tree and an apple core, appear only in the shadows. Jessen's strange fantasy world is at once whimsical, intriguing, and menacing. The constant shift in moods is reminiscent of Lewis Carroll's *Alice*. Smiling, Frode flies across a cheery golden evening sky; alarmed, he dangles in the blackness of outer space, where gravity loss has caused the box to turn upside down; terrified, he falls from the box and plunges from the blackness of space past threatening rain clouds to the golden sky below. In the illustrations, the box is carefully marked with black arrows and the words "OP" (UP) and "NED" (DOWN), to ensure the right side is kept up. These instructions are enlarged to constitute the book's endpapers ("UP" at the front and "DOWN" at the back). This explains the arrows that find their way into Frode's imaginary world. Like Wiesner, Jessen excels at presenting the fantastic world of a child's imagination. In the almost wordless picturebooks of Van Allsburg, Wiesner, and Jessen, the portrayal of the fantastic is not in opposition to reality but another side of it, another way of seeing.

From Picturebooks with Text to Wordless Picturebooks

A number of wordless picturebooks were originally conceived as books with text, but the author-illustrator ultimately chose to tell the story exclusively through the pictures. *L'orage* (The storm, 1998), the best-known picturebook by the Belgian author-illustrator Anne Brouillard, is one such book. Like David Wiesner, Brouillard specializes in wordless picturebooks. Her first picturebook, *Trois chats* (Three cats), published in 1990, was wordless. In 1993, she won both the Premio Graphico at the Bologna Children's Book Fair and the Golden Apple at the Biennial of Illustration Bratislava (BIB) for another wordless picturebook, *Le sourire du loup* (The wolf's smile). According to the French critic Isabelle Nières-Chevrel, Brouillard's *L'orage* is her most "ambitious" wordless picturebook and constitutes "one of the finest examples of a narrative carried entirely by the image."[50] Despite the awards and recognition Brouillard has received for her work, which now includes more than thirty picturebooks, the Belgian illustrator has not had the success she deserves with readers and remains virtually unknown in the English-speaking world. This can be explained in part by the fact that her poetic picturebooks are very challenging and make no concessions to readers. They are inspired by the illustrator's memories and experiences, and the subject matter is often of a very anecdotal nature.

Rather than grand adventures, her narratives feature the trivial events of everyday life. Brouillard lives in close contact with the elements and considers them an integral part of her life. For her, "events" such as "changes in light, the passage of the seasons, the fall of night, the onset of snow or a storm" are "true picturebook subjects." She cites the examples of *Il va neiger* (It's going to snow, 1994) and *L'orage*. Her poetic visual narratives constitute "strolls from one place to another to tell both the passage of time and the weather."[51] A title such as *Promenade au bord de l'eau* (Walk on the water's edge, 1996) comes to mind, but the illustrator also describes *L'orage* as "a walk in a space and a time."[52] In *L'orage*, the action is essentially limited to a cat entering a house and two strollers being caught in the rain. In Brouillard's picturebooks, characters are not clearly defined; they are vague figures, reflections, shadows. As one would expect, the illustrator has a predilection for painting landscapes. With her medium of choice—egg tempera—she creates atmospheric and sensual scenes that are often set in the countryside. *Voyage*, a wordless picturebook published in 1994, is inspired by a landscape observed through a train window. *L'orage* presents a series of inside and outside views of a house in the country as a storm approaches, breaks out, and gradually subsides. Isabelle Nières-Chevrel rightly describes it as a "meteorological narrative."[53]

Images are of paramount importance for Brouillard; even in her books with text, the images carry the story. Her first books, such as *Trois chats* and *Le sourire du loup*, were "born in text," and she admits that was "a spontaneous way of writing" at the beginning of her career. According to Brouillard, the situation was slightly different with *L'orage*, which was also originally conceived with text. She wrote fragments of the text but never completed a definitive version, sensing early on that the images would be overshadowed by the text. "In our culture, text takes precedence over image," says

Brouillard, who believes that when a book contains both, the image is not considered as "a full-fledged narrative."[54] The illustrator therefore made a deliberate choice to eliminate the text in order "to intensify the evocative aspect, the atmosphere, the sensations," and to ensure that readers experience the storm physically. In her atmospheric illustrations, she manages to evoke not only subtle changes in light and shadow, but sounds and smells. The artist is convinced that readers can perceive sound—that of water, footsteps, or a lost conversation—in images.

Brouillard's desire to tell the story exclusively in pictures led to a very detailed study of every aspect of the images: size, background, framing, layout, sequencing, viewpoint, and so forth, as she is conscious that even the most subtle change in the layout can be highly significant. As Sophie Van der Linden has stated, Brouillard's books demonstrate clearly that wordless picturebooks require a great mastery of the internal functioning of the picturebook.[55] Many wordless picturebook artists find that they require more images or frames in order to close narrative gaps. When Brouillard decided to eliminate the text in *L'orage*, she felt the necessity to add more images notably at the beginning, to fill gaps "particularly in the representation of the space." The places are the same, she points out, but the light and the viewpoint change. Brouillard actually built a model in order to better visualize and depict the space in *L'orage*. As Isabelle Nières-Chevrel points out, Brouillard "imagines a camera eye moving around in a three-dimensional space" that includes the inside of a house and an outside landscape.[56] One of the French doors depicted in the first doublespread is open, inviting readers to enter. In the following image, which is framed by a large white margin, readers find themselves in the room seen through the French doors of the previous picture. The facing full-bleed illustration draws readers into the adjacent room, where a black cat can be seen through a window. In the next illustration, framed once again by a white margin, readers join the cat outside, where its gaze carries ours toward the sky. The sky itself, however, is depicted on the facing full-page spread. These scenes are followed by an atmospheric, full-bleed doublespread showing an exterior view of the house, behind which dark clouds loom menacingly against the blue sky. Small recurring details allow readers/viewers to orient themselves in the space created by Brouillard, but only if they remain very attentive: a red bowl, a glass bottle, a red coffee pot, a potted plant, and so forth.

According to Brouillard, the size of the images and the light that emanates from them creates the rhythm and the ambiance of her books. In the early pages that precede the storm, the visual narrative unfolds slowly on warmly-lit double and single spreads. As the storm approaches, the pace picks up in two doublespreads, which each have sequences of four framed half-page images on a white background. This change in the layout allows the illustrator to present two successive events on each of the single spreads, while at the same time showing two simultaneous events in two different spaces on the doublespread.[57] Brouillard's picturebook demonstrates how pictorial narrative can present simultaneity in a manner that is impossible for verbal narrative. The two doublespreads convey a series of almost simultaneous events. In the first, a potted plant is overturned, the saucer under it breaks, and the noise wakens the sleeping cat on the piano bench, while the second evokes the meeting of the two cats: the black intruder and the gold resident who has taken refuge under a chair. Between these two sequences, one full-page spread portrays heavy rain streaming down a window. As the storm's fury continues to build, the rhythm accelerates further in a series of three small, dark vignettes, whose increasing size seems to reflect the building storm and culminates in the dark, facing full-bleed spread where lightening appears to strike the house. After the storm, the smaller images give way to the larger, more peaceful images that characterized the beginning. Brouillard creates a wonderful sense of symmetry in *L'orage*, which begins and ends at the same point. Numerous details contribute to the symmetry. While the black cat outside the window announces the storm by looking intently up at the darkening sky, the gold cat inside heralds the sun's return by staring out the window at a blue sky. The facing full-spread of the tree-lined blue sky with white clouds mirrors the earlier image of a very similar patch of sky with dark clouds overtaking the white. The final image is a sunnier variation on the first doublespread, in which attentive readers will notice subtle, but significant differences. Through the doors on the right, readers now see two cats sleeping peacefully (the black cat has replaced the gold one on the piano bench) and in the oval mirror between the doors, the vague figures of the two strollers are reflected.

The various spaces depicted in Brouillard's books do not fit together in an obvious manner and the sequence of images can only be understood by taking into consideration changes in lighting, colour, scale, and framing, and by paying close attention to details. The attentive, perceptive reader will sense that the recurring motifs need to be linked and pieced together. Isabelle Nières-Chevrel describes the decoding work required of the reader of *L'orage*, who must rely on "all the clues to construct—sometimes in a state of uncertainty—spatial, temporal, and causal relations that are not explained by a verbal narrator."[58] Brouillard likens some of her books to "silent film," in which there is no "commentary," except that made by viewers themselves. The coherence of the graphic narration in Brouillard's silent stories, as in many wordless picturebooks, depends to a great extent on cinematic techniques. Furthermore, the large, full-bleed doublespreads resemble a movie screen. Nières-Chevrel rightly compares the shifting viewpoint of the "visual narrator" of *L'orage* to that of "the eye of a camera," which is constantly varying "its framing and angles of vision."[59] Brouillard uses a variety of shots, including long, medium, and close-up, to capture the spatial dimension. Because wordless picturebooks like *L'orage* require so much work on the part of the illustrator, Brouillard believes that the

Figure 3.7 *L'orage* by Anne Brouillard, copyright © 1997 Grandir, reprinted by permission of Grandir.

reader must also make an effort to reconstruct time and space in order to enter her universe. Her sophisticated picturebooks are for discerning readers who are willing to stroll slowly through the images of a book, engaging with them, and constructing the story as they go.

The Australian author-illustrator Shaun Tan also makes great demands on the readers of his wordless book *The Arrival*, which was published to great acclaim in 2006. Like Arnal Ballester's *No tinc paraules*, *The Arrival* is difficult to categorize. At 130 pages, it is generally considered too long to be classified as a picturebook. The lengthy wordless book has often been called a graphic novel without words. Even for Tan, who is known for his innovative and sophisticated picturebooks, *The Arrival* is a daring experimentation that explores entirely new territory. The book traces the journey of an immigrant arriving in a strange new land and presents everything through his eyes. The author-illustrator, whose own parents had immigrated, did some research into Australian migrant communities, especially Chinese, thinking that the subject had potential for an illustrated story, but he had no idea what kind of story. Completing *The Arrival* took Tan five years, and a couple of those years were spent "developing multiple drafts of the story at different lengths." He admits it was "originally intended to be a fairly simple thirty-two-page picturebook called *My Suitcase* . . ., with about sixteen paintings and some words, so quite conventional." Tan describes the evolution of the project that eventually led to *The Arrival*: "It was not a satisfactory treatment of the material, and I kept expanding it while breaking each page into more and more panels; then dropping all text and shifting to a more photo-realistic style." There is a realistic silent film quality to *The Arrival* which is heightened by the many small frames that borrow the sequencing of comics. Tan admits that the size made it "a very burdensome and sometimes depressing project" and that "sustaining the continuity of objects, lighting effects and so on" was a struggle.[60] In his meticulously drawn images, Tan manages to tell a very complex narrative, with intertwining stories, flashbacks, memories, dreams, and a full range of subtle emotions and perceptions. The remarkable book, which won the NSW Premier's Literary Awards Book of the Year 2007 and the Children's Book of the Year Award from the Children's Book Council of Australia in 2007 as well as Best Comic Book for the French version at the Angoulême International Comics Festival in 2008, opened new paths for the picturebook genre, and notably crossover picturebooks.

Reading Wordless Picturebooks

As Anne Brouillard's and Shaun Tan's works clearly demonstrate, reading wordless picturebooks can be very challenging for readers of all ages. In many books, a protagonist or a recurring figure is a valuable guide for readers/viewers of a visual narrative. The colour red constitutes a marker in a surprising number of works. In Ballester's *No tinc paraules*, readers follow the Black man dressed in red overalls and clutching the string of his strange balloon-like clock, much as they follow Mitsumasa Anno's solitary rider throughout his journey in *Tabi no ehon*. The black lines and shading of the detailed monochrome illustrations in Japanese artist Daihachi Ohta's wordless picturebook *Kasa* (Umbrella, 1975) are relieved only by the bright red umbrella belonging to the little girl whom readers follow throughout the narrative. In *Rouge, bien rouge*, it is Little Red Riding Hood and the colour red itself that are supposed to provide the thread that links the enigmatic images. In the Swedish picturebook *Den röden tråden* (1987; English trans., *The Red Thread*), by author-illustrator Tord Nygren, readers follow a red thread as it winds its way from the beginning of the book to the end, where it crosses the cover to begin anew. The thread occasionally crosses the pages in a fairly straight line but more often it meanders haphazardly through the images. It evokes the real red cotton thread that Bruno Munari uses to carry the thread of the narrative in several of his wordless *libri illeggibile*. Similarly, in Nygren's picturebook, which is a sophisticated, self-conscious reflection on narrative, the thread is a common metaphor for "narrative progression."[61]

Readers' narrative expectations are questioned, and perhaps even ridiculed, by the disparate and ambiguous pictures of Nygren's visual narrative. The author-illustrator presents his readers with different types of narrative as they follow the red thread. One doublespread offers a very comprehensible, if unusual, love story in a sequence of fifteen tiny pictures. The chronological visual narrative recounts a man's quest to find the woman of his dreams. Despite the strange journey accomplished by bee, umbrella, dragonfly, snail, grasshopper, and owl, it is a straightforward story with the conventional happy ending: the man holds his beloved in his arms in the final scene. The other doublespreads, however, present a much more complex and enigmatic form of narrative with an endless possibility of meanings. Without the enigmatic red thread, readers could be content to enjoy the intriguing pictures of a magician, a puppeteer, a Pierrot tightrope walker on a red thread attached to the moon, and so forth, but its presence encourages readers to try to make connections between the apparently unrelated spreads. This urge is heightened by the discovery of figures that recur in subsequent spreads. Scott suggests that *The Red Thread* stimulates "a significantly different reading experience for child and adult," the child reader being content to follow the thread from page to page, while the older reader "is driven to struggle with finding meaning, logic, and progression that the thread provokes." In her mind, adult readers will find more to interpret than child readers, but Nygren suggests that "the child's view is straighter, simpler, less neurotic, and more serene."[62] Perhaps the child who deliberately turns his back to the red thread/tightrope, which mesmerizes the adults, and gazes instead directly at the reader represents for Nygren the ideal child reader of this wordless picturebook and the genre in general. In *The Red Thread*, Nygren seems to present a lesson in reading wordless picturebooks. On the back endpapers, a green witch sweeps the last words from the page into a heap of single letters on the floor. Nygren literally sweeps words out of the picturebook, where they have become useless refuse.

As *The Red Thread* illustrates so eloquently, wordless picturebooks provide a different narrative experience from books with text. David Wiesner, who is a master of the genre, pointed this out in his Caldecott Medal acceptance speech for *Tuesday*: "A wordless book offers a different kind of experience from one with text, for both the author and the reader. There is no author's voice telling the story. Each viewer reads the book in his or her own way. The reader is an integral part of the storytelling process."[63] Readers/viewers of these picturebooks fill the wordless spaces with their own imagined storylines, thus assuming the active role of storyteller. Children are undoubtedly more comfortable in this role than many adults since they are often far more adept at reading visual images. However, some children still feel that this role belongs to an "author" rather than to the reader. After reading Shaun Tan's *The Arrival* in a pilot project involving two wordless picturebooks, a Congolese boy asked the leaders if they could "now . . . have the book with words," so they could "see if they had got the story right."[64] Wordless picturebooks create a certain equality between readers of all ages. Without the guidance of a verbal text, each reader/viewer interprets the pictorial narrative differently. In fact, each reader can create a different story on every reading, as Søren Jessen likes to point out.[65] Although even the sophisticated narrative of a picturebook like *The Arrival* can perhaps be comprehended on a rather basic level on the first reading, repeated viewings deepen the reader's understanding of the story, adding new information. Sophie Van der Linden suggests that when the eye is "freed" from the text, it seems to "exercise more subtly its discovery of the image and engage in a true reading of its codes."[66] Wordless picturebooks can inspire an infinite number of narratives. Wiesner sees the "interactive" nature of wordless picturebooks, which are read in a different manner by each reader and thus provide "limitless possibilities," as the essential advantage of "visual storytelling."[67] This feature of wordless picturebooks also explains much of their crossover appeal because readers/viewers bring their own personal experience and knowledge to the reading of the visual images and the construction of the narrative.

While wordless picturebooks have established themselves as an important genre, they do not correspond to the picturebook's traditional norms of a shared "reading" experience and are therefore often considered rather disconcerting by publishers and adult mediators. Publishers have even requested, as in Sara's case, that the illustrator add words to a wordless picturebook. Sophie Van der Linden states that parents and booksellers in France are disconcerted by wordless picturebooks despite the "publishing revival" that they have experienced there in recent years.[68] The works examined in this chapter show that the recent interest in wordless picturebooks is a widespread phenomenon. Many wordless picturebooks are among the greatest successes in the vibrant field of contemporary children's picture-books. Multilayered wordless picturebooks, such as those examined in this paper, reach across borders, those of culture as well as of age. In today's globalized and digitized world, wordless picturebooks will undoubtedly continue to become, along with graphic novels, an ever more important and successful sector of the international book market.

Chapter Four
Picturebooks with Allusions to the Fine Arts

You don't have to know everything about art history . . . to enjoy these stories.
—Stian Hole

A facet of contemporary picturebooks that has particular appeal with a crossover audience is the often highly sophisticated referencing of fine art.[1] Many picturebook artists obviously share the Danish author-illustrator Sören Jessen's view that "fine art is a great inspiration for illustrations."[2] A large number of illustrators are formally trained in the fine arts, so it is natural that they are influenced by the artists and artworks they have studied. Many illustrators admit that they initially intended to become artists. The Australian picturebook artist Tohby Riddle went to art school immediately after high school and was moving toward a career as a painter. 2000 Hans Christian Andersen award winner Anthony Browne, who was trained at Leeds College of Art, originally wanted to be a painter, but a need to earn an income took him in a different direction and today he is one of the world's best-known picturebook artists.[3] Many of today's illustrators borrow the visual grammar of well-known, and even some not so well-known, artists, and some are master recyclers of the canonical works of our artistic heritage. In *A Theory of Parody: The Teachings of Twentieth-Century Art Forms*, Linda Hutcheon argues quite convincingly that parody, in the very broad sense of any revisiting or recontextualizing of previous works of art (what is often referred to by the more neutral term "allusion"), is a characteristic shared by all the arts in the postmodern world, but she does not mention picturebooks.[4] Allusions to the fine arts and metadiscourse on art are a significant and widespread phenomenon in contemporary picturebooks that appeal to a crossover audience. Indeed, John Stephens claims "citation of high culture art works is endemic in contemporary picturebooks throughout the world."[5] Although some of these citations are textual, the vast majority are visual.

The Scavenging of Styles

Many picturebooks contain allusions to the stylistic conventions of an entire genre or to the style of a school, period, or movement. This applies, of course, not only to Western art, but also to art from other traditions. Niki Daly's illustrations for *The Dancer* (1996), the story of a young girl who travels to the mystical Tsodilo Hills in search of the rain maiden during a severe drought, are inspired by San rock paintings in the Kalahari. Contemporary Japanese illustrators are often inspired by traditional Japanese scroll painting. Mitsumasa Anno's "Journey" books are in the tradition of venerable Japanese artists such as Kibi, the eighth-century envoy to China, and the Zen Buddhist painter Sesshū Tōyō, who journeyed to China in the fifteenth-century. People and activities crowd Kibi's scroll painting, which tells stories in picture form, while Sesshū's renowned *Landscape of the Four Seasons* is a very long scroll of evolving landscapes and changing seasons. As in the case of his revered predecessors, Anno's journeys and observations greatly contributed to the formulation of his artistic style and philosophy. The picturebook artist Daihachi Ohta draws on traditional Japanese art in the pen-and-brush illustrations of *Tamamushi no zushi no monogatari* (The tale of Tamamushi Shrine, literally The tale of a Little Shrine of Iridescence, 1980), which is set in the ancient town of Nara. Written by Takeji Hiratsuka, the old tale of a sculptor who makes a very beautiful altar decorated with the iridescent wings of an insect, won the third Japan Picture Book Award. As in Anno's picturebooks, small figures of all ages and social classes are engaged in a multitude of activities in spaces that are flattened out so that there is no set viewpoint. In *The Magic Horse of Han Gan* (2006), winner of the Deutscher Jugendliteraturpreis in 2005, the Chinese-born author-illustrator Jiang Hong Chen, who now lives in France, imitates the style of the eighth-century Chinese painter Han Gan, to tell the story of the renowned painter who had to tether his horses because they were so lifelike they might otherwise run away. Chen's illustrations, dominated by a palette of browns, blacks, and reds, are painted directly on silk in the traditional Tang style of Han Gan and his master Wang Wei. Frédéric Clément appropriates the colours, motifs, and techniques of Middle Eastern art in both *Le collier* (The necklace, 1992), an oriental tale by Christiane Baroche, and *Mille et une nuits: Histoire du portefaix avec les jeunes filles* (2002), his remarkable interpretation of the story "The Porter and the Three Ladies of Baghdad" from the *Thousand and One Nights*. The distinctive blues in Clément's palette are those of the Middle East, what is widely known as "Islamic blue," or what his publisher Nicole Maymat describes as his "Sidi-Bou-Saïd blues." The tale embedded in *Le collier* is distinguished from the frame story by the fragments of Moorish architecture and the Arabic characters inserted in the text. In *Mille et une nuits*, the illustrations are painted on shards of oriental ceramic, pieces of old wood, stones, bones, nuts, and even the artist's own tools, with the painstakingly minute detail of the great tradition of Middle Eastern miniaturists.

In the majority of picturebooks examined in this chapter, the artistic allusions are to Western art. That is even the case in some of the Asian picturebooks discussed. The first doublespread in Jean Claverie's rendition of Charles Perrault's *Riquet à la houppe* (Ricky with the Tuft), published in France in 1988, introduces the viewer into a classic "Artist's Studio" scene. It evokes the general atmosphere of traditional Dutch paintings from the period of Rembrandt and Jan Vermeer of Delft through details such as the clothing (large white collars and tall black hats), the artist's red beret and palette reminiscent of self-portraits by Rembrandt, and the subtle play with a hidden light source that throws Riquet's shadow on the curtain. Claverie's soft pastel watercolours effectively evoke the richness of the oils of the Dutch masters. The previous plate, in which Riquet and the plump wet nurse whose breast he suckles are bathed in the light streaming in a large Renaissance window, evokes strong reminiscences of Vermeer's masterly treatment and use of light from a window in domestic interior scenes of ordinary life. In light of the subject, the painting that immediately comes to mind is the aptly titled *The Milkmaid*. In the "Artist's Studio" spread, a group of adults are gathered around a portrait of the young Riquet: in the foreground Claverie depicts a woman playing a musical instrument, a large dog, the artist, and a second seated man who bears a striking resemblance to the artist, but holds a pen and paper rather than a palette. Like many artists, Claverie often playfully represents himself in his pictures. Here the artist and his scribe lookalike seem to constitute a double self-portrait that cleverly alludes to the dual role of many picturebook creators who, like Claverie himself, are at once author and illustrator. In this parody of the common "Artist's Studio" theme, the adults' eyes are all riveted on the child prodigy who has become the centre of attention, a witty reminder that picturebook illustrators have placed high art in the service of the child.[6]

Picturebook artists often engage in what several critics have referred to as the "scavenging" of styles.[7] The illustrations of an entire book may evoke a specific artistic movement. The Swiss-born author-illustrator Armin Greder's *Die Insel* (2002; English trans., *The Island*), is hauntingly told, with charcoal illustrations, in the somber European expressionist tradition. Allusions to Edvard Munch's *The Scream* draw on the artist's bleak themes of despair and melancholy to reinforce the chilling themes of Greder's narrative about an outsider who is a victim of the fear, hatred, and violence of xenophobia. The melancholic atmosphere of the Norwegian author-illustrator Stian Hole's *Garmann's Summer*, with its effective use of light and shadow to create mood, was inspired by his "favourite painter," Edward Hopper.[8] The abstract forms of the unusual characters in *Hando Kjendo: Søndag* (Hando and Kjendo on Sunday, 1999), by Tore Renberg and Kim Hiorthøy, are inspired by the raw art of the COBRA art group. The two friends, who discover strange wonders as they walk on an uneventful Sunday, are complete opposites: Hando, tall, thin, and green, with short arms, cries when he talks, while Kjendo, short, fat, and red, with long arms, laughs when he talks. The Irish illustrator Niamh Sharkey went through "a Klee phase" when she was illustrating Richard Walker's retelling of *Jack and the Beanstalk* (1999) and this influence is evident in the backdrops and colours of her quirky interpretation, which is also somewhat reminiscent of Lane Smith.[9] The German author-illustrator Melanie Kemmler adopts a surrealistic style in her picturebook *Der hölzerne Mann* (The wooden man, 2003), which was nominated for the Deutscher Jugendliteraturpreis in 2004. Although the book, with its extremely easy text in the tradition of the cumulative tale "This is the House that Jack Built," is targeted at very young children, the deceptively simple illustrations are full of surrealistic details that only attentive adult readers will discover. In fact, only cultured readers familiar with art history are likely to recognize the reminiscences of the surrealist painter and sculptor Giorgio de Chirico. Kemmler's fantasy town evokes the strange oneiric cityscapes of the Greek-born Italian artist's *pittura metafisica* period, with which it shares the solemn and rather mute colours, long perspectives, deep shadows, flat light, geometrically-shaped buildings, absence of people, and eery atmosphere. Wooden figures and toys replace the mannequins and statues in the barren streets of Kemmler's dreamlike landscape.

Illustrators scavenge styles both consciously and unconsciously. The actor with the baby face in Nicole Claveloux's wordless picturebook *Dedans les gens* advances across the Theatre of the World followed by all his "forgotten roles" in the guise of bizarre, haunting creatures that seem to have issued from Hieronymus Bosch's paintings. While there are no obvious, specific references, the colours, composition, mood, and notably the strange, hybrid creatures, which blend traits of humans, animals, and inanimate objects, are reminiscent of Bosch. Human

Figure 4.1   Dedans les gens by Nicole Claveloux, copyright © 1993 Le Sourire qui mord, reprinted by permission of Christian Bruel.

bodies have an egg head or the head of a bird or monkey, while even stranger human-like figures have a milk pitcher, light bulb, clock, or beaker in place of a head. Several grotesque robed creatures have an assortment of large animal skulls for heads. Three very bizarre figures have heads of strange, interconnected glass vessels containing fluids, giving them the appearance of a walking alchemy laboratory. Claveloux's choice of style emphasizes the striking contrast between the baby-faced actor and the grotesque creatures that are his former selves. Claveloux's artistic "scavenging" seems to be quite deliberate. Children will probably not recognize the appropriated style in *Dedans les gens*, but they will experience the same sense of strangeness that viewers feel when they contemplate one of Bosch's fantastic paintings. On the other hand, even French children seem able to identify the Matisse influence that marks Katy Couprie's work, including her wordless picturebook *Anima*. She points out that images are not created from a vacuum: "They are resurgences, images that one has 'eaten,' digested. They are part of a personal patrimony. . . ." As an exchange student at The School of the Art Institute of Chicago, Couprie went every single week for an entire year to see the Matisse paintings in the museum's permanent collection. The images of those paintings return in spite of the artist, without any conscious choice on her part.[10] This opinion is shared by François Ruy-Vidal, who states that graphic artists, like authors, create, "probably unconsciously," from a long cultural heritage to which they bring their originality. In his own case, he admits to being influenced by Albrecht Dürer and Hieronymus Bosch. The publisher cites a number of the great illustrators with whom he has worked, pointing out the influence of Breughel and Bosch on Eugène Delessert, and Breughel and Dürer on Alain Letort. More specifically, Ruy-Vidal describes how the nightmarish scenes of Francisco Goya permeate Denis Pouppeville's illustrations for Gilbert Lascault's *5 + 1 histoires en forme de trèfle* (5 + 1 clover-shaped stories, 2003), one of the first books published by his new publishing house Des Lires. The publisher argues that "even if the reader does not have this culture and does not recognize the cultural winks, it nourishes him or her all the same, even the children!"[11]

Some illustrators tend to adopt a single style throughout their entire oeuvre. Anthony Browne's manifest penchant for surrealism has made it a distinctive feature of his own style. Chris Van Allsburg's surrealist tendencies are more subtle, but he admits: "If all artists were forced to wear a badge, I'd probably wear the badge of surrealism. I don't mean something as extreme as Salvador Dali's melting clocks, but a gentle surrealism with certain unsettling provocative elements."[12] Although Van Allsburg does not generally refer directly to specific works of art, the detailed surrealist images of books like *The Mysteries of Harris Burdick*, (1984), *Ben's Dream* (1982), *Just a Dream* (1990), and *The Z Was Zapped: A Play in Twenty-Six Acts* (1987), with their playful blend of the ordinary and the extraordinary, are strongly reminiscent of René Magritte.[13] Likewise, Alain Gauthier's surrealism is generally quite vague, although François Ruy-Vidal believes he is fascinated by the work of the Belgian surrealist artist Paul Delvaux, who had a predilection for train stations (trains are a recurring motif in Gauthier's work).[14] Occasionally his illustrations contain direct allusions to specific works, however. The first illustration in *Les papillons de Pimpanicaille: Comptines et formulettes d'ici, de là-bas et d'ailleurs* (Pimpanicaille's butterflies: nursery rhymes and children's catchwords from here, there and everywhere), published by Ruy-Vidal in 1980, is a dreamy, probably subconscious reworking of Magritte's *Man in the Bowler Hat*, in which the man now faces viewers, while two small girls sit on his shoulders pointing up at either the man himself or the ship that is sinking in the watery brim of his hat.

Other versatile picturebook makers mimic a wide variety of styles, depending on the mood or atmosphere they wish to create. Maurice Sendak, "a frank and enthusiastic scavenger," in the words of Barbara Bader,[15] borrows styles ranging from nineteenth-century engravings to romanticism to cartoons. Wolf Erlbruch's work has been compared to Japanese woodcut art, the metaphysical world of De Chirico, the surrealism of Max Ernst, and the stylistic diversity of Pablo Picasso. The Irish illustrator P. J. Lynch, who is strongly influenced by Arthur Rackham, references the work of Pre-Raphaelite artists to present the subject of love, while his dramatic use of the chiaroscuro technique is reminiscent of the artists Caravaggio and Georges de la Tour. David Wiesner's picturebooks have resonances of Italian Renaissance artists, such as Raphael and Da Vinci, as well as Escher and Sendak. Another enthusiastic scavenger is the Alsatian picturebook artist Tomi Ungerer. His images for *Allumette*, which deals with the serious themes of poverty, war, and oppression, are evocative of German painters from the period between the two world wars, such as Otto Dix, while the rowdy, densely-populated crowd scenes and carnivalesque situations of *The Beast of Monsieur Racine* (1971), which is dedicated to Sendak, are reminiscent of Pieter Brueghel the Elder. The work of the Slovak illustrator Dusan Kállay, winner of the Hans Christian Andersen award in 1988, also contains references to various painting traditions, which he has absorbed and reworked in an entirely personal manner. There are reminiscences of surrealists such as Max Ernst, but also of Brueghel and Bosch, notably in the carefully controlled chaos of his compositions.

While the choice of artistic styles is immediately obvious in some cases, in others the selection may reflect rather sophisticated intentions or simply personal taste, or they may be entirely arbitrary. Vladimir Radunsky chooses a highly unlikely style for his picturebook *The Mighty Asparagus* (2004), which has its origins in the traditional Russian folktale *The Turnip*. The lavish illustrations by the Russian-born author-illustrator, who now divides his time between New York and Rome, are inspired by Italian Renaissance paintings. Into this incongruous setting, Radunsky humorously plants his "humongous, stupendous, splendid, catastrophic vegetable." In contrast, the influence of Italian Renaissance painting in Tomie DePaola's *Jingle, the Christmas Clown* (1992) seems a logical choice. The journey of "*Il Circo Piccolo*—The Little

Circus" across the countryside to a small Italian village is depicted as a procession vaguely in the style of Benozzo Gozzoli's fifteenth-century fresco *Procession of the Magi* in the Magi Chapel of Palazzo Medici-Riccardi in Florence. The festive, vibrant processions of the Renaissance painter, which are crowded with figures, many of which are animals, offer a pertinent model for this circus arriving in a poor village just before Christmas. Paul O. Zelinsky's adoption of the style of Italian Renaissance art in his Caldecott Medal-winning version of *Rapunzel* (1997), or even in his earlier Caldecott Honor Book *Rumpelstiltskin* (1986), seems to provide the perfect setting. The same can be said of the impressionistic quality of the delicate illustrations that evoke Sleeping Beauty's dreams in *Songes de la Belle au bois dormant* (Dreams of Sleeping Beauty, 1996), by the French author-illustrator Frédéric Clément. Speaking of the illustrators of fairy tales in particular, Perry Nodelman observes that they "frequently choose styles that evoke periods of history not particularly related to the tales but that they perceive to share the values they find in the tales."[16] The same observation can be made with regard to the illustrators of many picturebooks.

Certain artistic movements are more popular with illustrators than others, impressionism and surrealism being among the favourites. The avant-garde illustrators of the 1970s were particularly drawn to the surrealists. Patrick Couratin's *Shhh!*, published by Harlin Quist in 1974, is inspired by the work of Magritte. The choice of surrealist aesthetics is not surprising in light of the fundamental relationship between surrealism and childhood. Anthony Browne repeatedly claims that children naturally see things in a surreal manner: "I believe children see through surrealist eyes: they are seeing the world for the first time. When they see an everyday object for the first time, it can be exciting and mysterious and new."[17] The illustrator compares children more specifically to surrealist painters on the Walker Books website: "All children are surrealists in a sense. . . . One of the things the surrealists were trying to do was to paint familiar things as if they were seeing them for the first time. Children are, of course, actually seeing them for the first time." Browne turns to his own personal experience, pointing to his obsession with art from ages seventeen to twenty-one: "In art, I loved the pre-Raphaelites and Rembrandt first. Then I discovered Salvador Dali and it was like finding something I already knew."[18] On the Walker Books website, however, the illustrator claims his fascination with surrealism dates from his discovery of Dali and Magritte at the age of eleven, and he adds: "when I see my childhood drawings I realise that they are not very different from the illustrations that I do now." The wit and visual playfulness of Browne's style reflects that of the surrealist movement. Elaine Williams rightly states: "From his lifelong attraction to surrealism he has absorbed the wit and visual playfulness of the movement, but also the darker sense of a world where nothing can be taken for granted, where the ground shifts constantly."[19] Surrealism became a vehicle for addressing the problems and uncertainties experienced by young people. When a charge of copyright infringement forced Browne to replace the allusions to Magritte's works in *Willy the Dreamer* (1997), he opted for those of Van Gogh, shifting from surrealism to impressionism.

Some illustrators cleverly blend two or more styles in the same book. Shaun Tan acknowledges that *The Lost Thing* owes much to the urban landscapes of the artists Jeffrey Smart, Edward Hopper, and John Brack, to whom he apologizes in the book. Many of the delicate miniaturist paintings in Clément's *Mille et une nuits* depict female nudes, some of which are reminiscent of nineteenth-century paintings of harems such as Ingrès's *La Grande Odalisque*. Numerous examples of the blending of styles can be found in the visual retellings of folk and fairy tales. In P. J. Lynch's *East o' the Sun and West o' the Moon* (1991), the portrayal of the heroine in the gloomy thick wood bears the mark of Rackham, while the portrait of the couple embracing evokes the Pre-Raphaelites and the play with light and shadow in the scene in which the girl finally sees the face of her lover in the candlelight evokes De la Tour. The Russian husband-and-wife team Andrej Dugin and Olga Dugina blend the styles of Pieter Brueghel the Elder, Albrecht Dürer, and Hieronymous Bosch, among others, in their visual retelling of the folk tale *Die Drachenfedern* (English trans., *Dragon Feathers*), which Arnica Esterl retold in German in 1993. The artists themselves provide the models for two of the characters: the rich innkeeper bears a striking resemblance to Brueghel, while the poor, handsome woodcutter's son, who loves the innkeeper's daughter, is modelled after Dürer's 1493 *Self-Portrait at 22*. Readers of all ages can appreciate the general atmosphere of the realistic masterpieces of the Renaissance and the eerie, fantastic Bosch-like creatures (two such creatures appear in the bottom right-hand corner of the cover, but even the imposing dragon on the cover is a hybrid creature with the wings of a bird, the hooves of a goat, and claws that resemble human hands). However, only readers with knowledge of art history will decode many of the illustrators' allusions to past masters, for example, Dürer's characteristic signature, which is carved upside down into a rock on the second opening. As Tina Hanlon rightly points out, "at different stages of . . . individual development, [such pictorial narratives] may be enjoyed for their beauty and imagination, admired for their realistic details, or analysed in depth by older readers intrigued by the layers of literary and artistic intertextuality."[20]

The wide range of styles evoked in Tord Nygren's *The Red Thread* includes impressionism, surrealism, cubism, and naïve art. The scope of the artistic allusions is suggested in the publisher's insert of the dust jacket, where a list of references includes an eclectic array of artists and art subjects. Mitsumasa Anno's books are described by Perry Nodelman as a "charming blend of the American primitive and the Japanese traditional, of Hokusai and Grandma Moses."[21] Similar statements could be made with regard to Daihachi Ohta, whose work is greatly admired by Anno. Ohta's style varies according to his subject matter, and his work is known especially for its harmonious blending of traditional and modern elements. Anno's magical tale *Kageboshi* (1976; English trans., *In Shadowland*), inspired by Andersen's *Little Match Girl*, juxtaposes Western-style watercolour-and-ink paintings, which represent the "real" world, with black-and-white pictures executed in oriental paper cut technique (each one cut from a single piece of paper), which symbolise the world of shadows. In the Japanese picturebook *Wani-kun no mukashi-banashi* (Little Crocodile's fairy tale, 1994), Hirokazu Miyazaki blends styles in a rather sophisticated manner to evoke two narrative levels. The illustrations accompanying the embedded story that Little Crocodile is reading, titled *The Legend of the Dragon*, are surrounded by a double black frame and are the style of nineteenth-century copperplate engravings, which contrast strikingly with the watercolour pastels of the rest of the book. In one doublespread, Miyazaki combines the two styles in a single illustration that releases the fire-breathing dragon from the frame so that he seems to invade the "real" world of Little Crocodile (or rather the protagonist appears to enter the dragon's story because the green decorated letter that begins each page of the embedded narrative now appears on the recto above Little Crocodile). Perhaps the most striking example of the blending of artistic styles is to be found in Anthony Browne's *Voices in the Park* (1998), in which four simian characters, two adults and two children, recount their visit to the park, showing just how different perceptions of the same events can be. While the story told by each character is very simple, the polyphony of voices speaking in the first person creates a complex, multi-layered work. As the story moves from one voice to another, atmosphere, feelings, even landscapes change, due largely to Browne's adoption of a different artistic style to portray the perspective of each character.

When Kelek was asked to do an edition of Perrault's tales for Hatier, the French illustrator was initially reluctant, not wanting to attempt what had already been done so many times in the past. She ultimately decided "to travel down the ages on the iconographic level," using "classical painting," as a brief afterword explains. Each plate in the collection is inspired by the work of a different artist. The cover illustration of "Puss in Boots" appropriates the painting *The Fortune Teller*, a genre piece that exists in two versions by the Italian Baroque master Caravaggio. While Puss adopts the stance and clothing of the foppishly-dressed boy in the original, Kelek seems to suggest that he also embodies the fortune teller who reads his palm. The title of the original painting is an apt description of the cat that not only foresees but also brings about the good fortune of the miller's youngest son. Kelek's plate for "La Peau d'âne" (Donkeyskin) is inspired by Diego Velázquez's painting *The Infanta Dona Margarita de Austria*, to which the illustrator adds the donkeyskin and the fairy godmother. Other paintings are quoted more faithfully in the frames on the wall behind the protagonist, but the largest and most prominent is attributed to Kelek (the first two letters of her name appear on the gold frame). Kelek transplants *Le Petit Chaperon rouge* into the Venetian Renaissance interior of Vittore Carpaccio's *The Birth of the Virgin*, substituting the wolf for Christ's grandmother in the large bed. Her interpretation of the dramatic bed scene is actually a complicated superposition of two Carpaccio bedroom scenes, as elements from *The Dream of St. Ursula* are also integrated. In addition, a detail is taken from *Dormitio Virginis* (*The Death of the Virgin*) so that Kelek's illustration is a masterful montage of elements from three different paintings by the Venetian master.[22]

Within a single fairy tale, Kelek may allude to more than one artist. For the beautiful heroine of "La Belle au bois dormant" (Sleeping Beauty), Kelek borrows the woman from Titian's most famous Venus, *The Venus of Urbino*, which marks the end of the painter's Renaissance period and the beginning of his mannerist tendencies. The illustrator necessarily closes the young woman's eyes, which gaze frankly at the viewer in the original, and she also veils Titian's sensual, nude Venus with a layer of thin white gauze. The dog that sleeps at the bottom of the bed in the Italian painting is now curled up in the fold of one of the sleeping woman's arms, perhaps a witty allusion to the affectionate indulgence lavished upon dogs by the French. The image of purity and innocence that seems to emanate from the sleeping child-woman, heightened by the visible sky and the pink and blue tints reflected on her flesh, is nonetheless questioned. The grotesque bronze animal head with open jaws, which replaces the scroll and flower design in the background of the original, suggests the violence of the secret desires of the sleeping woman. These are manifest in the preceding plate, which depicts an Ophelia-like figure in a long, white gown, but wearing an incongruous, heavy gold crown and surrounded by baroque monsters which, in the words of Jean Perrot, "seem to have issued as much from the world of Hieronymus Bosch as that of Goya or the Italian mannerists." In the nightmarish dream, the fairy-tale heroine is surrounded by the monsters of desire: a Sphinx glances back at her knowingly, a horned, long-tailed monster sits with its back turned, and an enormous chimera turns toward the reader. As Perrot rightly points out, "the frenzy of passions still threatens the innocent woman."[23] Kelek also sometimes blends styles in a single plate. In one illustration for "Le Chat botté" (Puss in Boots), she mimics Gustave Doré's famous nineteenth-century engraving closely, but the cat, whose hat, cape, and boots are now a vivid red colour, is standing on fantastic, Bosch-like creatures. Using a playfully parodic mode that is subtle and sophisticated, Kelek refers to numerous past masters representing a wide range of aesthetic movements in her edition of Perrault's *Contes*.

Illustrators may refer to the characteristic manner of the entire oeuvre of a particular artist. In his early books such as *Topsy-Turvies: Pictures to Stretch the Imagination* (1968) and *Upside-Downers: More Pictures to Stretch the Imagination* (1969), Mitsumasa Anno drew his inspiration from the illusionist works of M. C. Escher, which he discovered in 1961. The last spread of *Topsy-Turvies*, which is a variation on Escher's visual play with perspective and impossible spaces, is reminiscent of the lithograph

Waterfall. The play with perspective and logic in Anno's books, as in the Dutch artist's works, intrigues viewers of all ages. Although Anthony Browne uses the general iconic conventions of surrealism, he most often adopts the manner of Magritte. Allusions to Dali are also present, but they are much less common. Browne's works frequently quote and requote specific Magritte paintings. In fact, the Belgian surrealist artist has accompanied Browne throughout his career. In his very first picturebook, *Through the Magic Mirror* (1976), which evokes reminiscences of Lewis Carroll's *Alice*, Browne uses the surreal images of Magritte to create an imaginary, alternate world for the bored protagonist. There are several references to the trappings of the man in the bowler hat, who is found in multiple paintings by Magritte, including *Golconda* and *Decalcomania*. He reappears in the picturebook *Look What I've Got* (1980), walking in the background of a park scene, as well as in *Zoo* (1992), as a small figure at the back of a crowd scene. One illustration in *Voices in the Park* includes bowler hat lampposts, trees, and clouds, not to mention the one in the shadow on the ground that humorously turns Charles's mother into "The Woman in the Bowler Hat." The obsessive recurrence of the bowler hat shape in this illustration symbolizes the mother's controlling presence in the life of her son, who is literally in her shadow. Familiar Magritte motifs such as bowler hats, pipes, lampposts, mirrors, windows, easels, eyes, apples, and stylized trees trimmed in unusual shapes haunt Browne's oeuvre.

All Sören Jessen's picturebooks contains surrealist elements, some of which are direct references to Magritte, Dali, and Ernst, among others. They create the strange atmosphere of his picturebook *En fuldmånenat* (A full moons night, 1995), in which a small boy floats through the air trying to catch a teddy bear that has escaped from his bedroom. There are running mouths, free floating noses, and a flock of flying eyes, which come together in one of the final illustrations to form faces, as well as many other surrealist motifs familiar to anyone who knows Dali's work, including flying fish and a burning signpost. In an e-mail dated June 15, 2009, the illustrator admitted that the long-legged elephant trekking through the snowy mountains with a tower on its back in *Faldt du?*, as well as the burning chair in the spread with the two blue card-playing hens in *Gaven*, are "conscious references" to Dali (the iconic elephant on long, spindly legs that is a recurring image in Dali's work first appeared in the 1944 painting *Dream Caused by the Flight of a Bee Around a Pomegranate a Second before Awakening*). Many other allusions in Jessen's picturebooks seem, on the contrary, to be quite conscious. In *Faldt-du?* a flaming television, a burning match, a soft television screen, and a winged clock are reminiscent of Dali, while an airborn armchair, a floating window, items floating on rocks, and green apples (a recurrent motif) are reminders of Magritte. With the exception of a Daliesque flaming water spout, the surrealist allusions in the more recent picturebook *Gaven* are predominantly drawn from Magritte and include an umbrella, a pyramid, and an open window with white clouds in a blue sky. The hybrid creature in the last

Figure 4.2   En fuldmånenat by Søren Jessen, copyright © 1995 Apostrof, reprinted by permission of Søren Jessen.

spread of the surrealist sequence seems to be a parody of Magritte's painting *Collective Invention*, which depicts the reverse of a mermaid, a creature with the head and upper body of a fish and the belly and legs of a woman. Jessen reverses the image again, portraying a creature with the body of a man and the tail of a fish, but he also adds a bird's head. Although there are identifiable allusions to specific paintings in Jessen's picturebooks, they are generally to a detail of a painting rather than to an entire work. As the illustrator himself puts it, he is "not as direct in [his] references to art as for instance Anthony Browne," preferring "to play it more subtle." Readers who want to identify all the allusions have to work much harder, but the illustrator does not intend them to do so. The surrealist elements are used in order to create a certain atmosphere. In *En fuldmånenat* (A full moon night), for example, he wanted "to make a book with a nightlife feel to it."[24] As in the works of the artists to whom he pays homage, Jessen's strange fantasy world is both intriguing and menacing for viewers, effectively evoking the enigmatic and unsettling atmosphere of dreams.

Within the impressionist movement, the Dutch painter Vincent Van Gogh, who is really a post-impressionist artist, is certainly a favourite with picturebook illustrators. They are often inspired in a broad way by the sunny canvases of his later period. However, even when illustrators borrow the colours and style of Van Gogh's work in a very general manner throughout an entire picturebook, they often refer specifically to one painting. *Bedroom at Arles*, one of his best known paintings, seems to hold special appeal. It is one of the Van Gogh paintings that find their way into Willy's studio in *Willy the Dreamer* when Browne is forced to find substitutes for the Magritte works. In the French picturebook *Mathieu* (1998), published the year after *Willy the Dreamer*, the popular picturebook artist Grégoire Solotareff borrows Vincent's bedroom for the friend of his mouse protagonist. Mathieu's friend just happens to be called Vincent and in his bedroom the two mice play cards in the familiar, solid bed. Solotareff mimics *Bedroom at Arles* with a great degree of faithfulness: the solid wooden bed with the red spread and two pillows, the table in the corner with the blue basin and pitcher, the two wooden chairs, the green-framed window, the clothes hooks behind the bed, the same number of paintings on the wall, and so forth. Van Gogh actually painted three versions of this scene, but the first painting is considered his best, largely due to its vivid colours. Solotareff gives the room an even brighter, cheerier look, by using a more vivid yellow. He also simplifies the picture slightly by eliminating a few objects so that the room has a slightly less cluttered look. The most notable transformation in Solotareff's illustrations is the two mice sitting in the bed. However, attentive readers will also notice that the two portraits on the wall above the bed are now portraits of mice. Solotareff seems to have a special fascination with this painting. The following year, he published a picturebook titled *La Chambre de Vincent* (Vincent's bedroom, 1999), which tells the story of two mice, Mitsou and Kim, who visit Vincent's bedroom. Like Vincent, they are artists, and the kind painter leaves his paints and brushes for their use. They can't imagine that the mouse trap under the bed was left by Vincent, unless he has become "completely mad." The illustration on the cover depicts the two mice sitting on the end of the familiar bed and the inside illustrations show several views of Van Gogh's room, as well as a number of his paintings.[25] In a Swiss picturebook titled *Kunst aufräumen* (2002; English trans., *Tidying Up Art*, 2003), which playfully deconstructs and reconstructs the works of famous artists in an attempt to make them more orderly, Ursus Wehrli seems to prepare for a spring cleaning in Van Gogh's room, piling the furniture and other objects on the bed. However, the illustrator also seems to adopt a child's view of cleaning a bedroom by hiding a number of objects under the bed. The original and Wehrli's "tidied up" version of Van Gogh's *Bedroom at Arles* appear on the cover of this highly original book which neatly reconfigures nineteen canonical masterpieces from Pieter Brueghel to Paul Klee.

Another artist whose manner is often appropriated by picturebook artists is Henri Rousseau, undoubtedly because the primitive, instinctive, childlike quality of his naïve art is seen to have particular appeal for children. Illustrators often borrow Le Douanier's "exotic landscapes" in a general manner when the text evokes the jungle. In one of several Rousseau-like jungle landscapes in *The Red Thread*, Tord Nygren incorporates the manner of a second artist: in an opening in the dense foliage, Van Gogh can be seen painting in the yellow cornfield. Nygren has introduced the artist himself into this parody of *Wheatfield with Crows*. A huge Van Gogh sun replaces the large red disk that adorns the centre of several of Rousseau's canvases. The eccentric bird that mimics the shape and colour of flowers in Rousseau's *Exotic Landscape* is wittily replaced by an actual blue flower. The tropical bird from *Exotic Landscape* has taken flight and wings its way over the cornfield where Van Gogh paints his crows, so that the bird, as well as the sun motif, link the two artists superimposed in Nygren's illustration. The intertextual play in *The Red Thread* is quite sophisticated and sometimes perplexing even for critics. Carole Scott puzzles over the juxtaposition of Van Gogh painting and Linnaeus lecturing two children on botany amid a field of giant plants.[26] Linnaeus's presence can only be explained if the reader recognizes the allusion to Rousseau, who drew inspiration from illustrations in botanical books.

The landscape ukiyo-e painting of Katsushika Hokusai inspires the general atmosphere of numerous contemporary Japanese picturebook artists. Hokusai's most famous works are the ukiyo-e series of colour woodblock prints *Thirty-Six Views of Mount Fuji*, which depict the iconic mountain in different seasons and weather conditions from a variety of locations. In the manner of the nineteenth-century prints, a number of picturebook artists offer different views of the famous mountain in their illustrations. In Kazuyoshi Iino's parodical tale *Negi-bouzu no Asatarou* (The adventures of a Leek-Boy, Asataro, 1999), a leek-boy uproots literally, leaving home and setting out to fight for justice in traditional Japan. The landscapes offer several views of Mount Fuji depicted in different colours, but only one evokes a specific Hokusai print. In beautiful pastels, Iino paints a red, snow-covered peak which, despite the soft colours of his palette, evokes *South Wind, Clear Sky*, also known as *Red Fuji*. In Rintaro Uchida and Shigeo Nishimura's *Gatagoto Gatagoto* (Rumbling train, 1999), which won the Japan Picture Book Award, readers are suddenly transported into the world of traditional Japanese painting toward the end of the story, as the train passes out of a cityscape into a landscape reminiscent of Hokusai's prints. Nishimura offers different views of the famous mountain in the background of two doublespreads. In the illustration that abruptly transfers readers from the contemporary period to a more traditional Japan, the snow-covered red mountain that forms a back drop to the passing train once again mimics the iconic print known as *Red Fuji*. The famous series of prints have

Figure 4.3   *Gatagoto Gatagoto* by Shigeo Nishimura, copyright © 1999 Doshinsha, reprinted by permission of Doshinsha.

even inspired Western illustrators. Nicole Claveloux's *Vaguement* (Vaguely, 1990), with its play on the French word for "wave" (*vague*), consists of a succession of lyrical visual and verbal variations on the subject of waves inspired by Hokusai's celebrated series. The first woodblock in the series and the artist's most famous work is *The Great Wave off Kanagawa*, which depicts an enormous wave threatening ships with the ever-present Mount Fuji in the background.

While Iino's reminiscences of Hokusai are quite vague, Nishimura adds details from specific paintings that only cultured readers will identify. The trees, the litter being carried by two men, and notably the distinctive figure on horseback, whose head is hidden by a large hat, are inspired by Hokusai's *Hodogaya on the Tokaido*. Although Nishimura does not respect all the details of colouring, composition, and perspective, the source is unmistakable. The bundle carried by the figure on the right of the original print has been replaced by a grotesque red mask, announcing the final carnivalesque doublespread, in which contemporary Japanese dressed in traditional costumes get off the train. The Hokusai-style trees are still in the background, but the lively, colourful atmosphere contrasts starkly with the tranquil setting of the nineteenth-century print. Huge animals invade the space in a fantastic, burlesque manner. It seems that the train's destination was a spring festival. Contemporary details, such as cameras, knapsacks, and suitcases, clash with the traditional attire of kimonos and samurai warrior dress. The distant view of Mount Fuji on the following page is suggestive of *Shichiri Beach in Sagami Province*, but it also contains details reminiscent of other paintings. The traditional building in the foreground and the kite high in the sky remind us of *A Sketch of the Mitsui Shop in Suruga in Edo*. Whereas the original painting shows a man dropping something from the roof, Nishimura humorously depicts a large black bird that has dropped a fish. The illustrator adds a man in a topknot looking through a telescope at either Mount Fuji or the drama of the two birds and the fish. The orange-coloured sun over Mount Fuji, as well as the bridge and the river evoke the painting *Sunset Across the Ryogoku Bridge from the Bank of the Sumida River at Onmayagashi*. Mount Fuji is a popular subject in Japanese art due to its cultural and religious significance, but in picturebooks, it often becomes an iconic backdrop for very humorous and playful stories.

Tadao Yoguchi takes a novel, modern approach to classical Japanese art in *Active ukiyoe—Classical Japanese Pictures Revisited* (2005), which "revisits" a number of well-known artworks with the aid of a transparency divided into tiny black squares (contained in an envelope at the back of the book). A small reproduction of the painting appears on the verso under a few lines of text, while the full-page reproduction on the recto is a somewhat blurred, distorted version intended to be viewed through the transparency. Moving the transparency over the picture creates the effect of changing movement, light, or colour, changes which illustrate the text. For example, the plum blossoms in

Suzuki Harunobu's *Plum Blossoms at Night* shine in the darkness. With regard to Eishousai Chouki's *Firefly Viewing*, the author writes: "Firefly viewing isn't a one-way affair. They too enjoy their own flickering glow, reflected in your eyes." The transparency not only causes the fireflies to shimmer in the night, but also creates the impression that the lady's fan is moving. In the case of Katsushika Hokusai's *A Fine Breezy Day*, the iconic mountain is dyed red by the morning sun. The clever effects produced by the transparency fascinate adults as well as children.

The intertextual referencing of art in some picturebooks is limited to an iconic face, sometimes that of an artist rather than a subject. Fam Ekman's picturebooks almost always contain some references to canonical art, often of a rather subtle nature. In the case of *Jente i bitar* (Girl in pieces, 1992), it was the author, Sissel Bjugn, who suggested that Ekman use the Mexican artist Frida Kahlo as her inspiration for the protagonist, Deborah. It does not seem to be a reference to one particular self-portrait of the artist, but she is nonetheless immediately recognizable. The author's choice of Frida Kahlo had a very personal side, as Bjugn herself had broken her neck at the age of twenty-three. Her intention, however, was to have fun with a famous face in a children's picturebook, and she wanted "a Jewish face" (Frida Kahlo claimed to be part Jewish).[27] The protagonist bears the name of the Biblical prophetess who led the Israelites at a time of oppression, because she herself is a prophet in this story about forgiveness. When the little girl breaks her parents' vase, which she was cleaning as punishment for another misdeed, she feels so guilty that she ends up breaking into pieces and has to be glued back together again. *Jente i bitar* won the Brage Prize the first year the prestigious Norwegian literary prize was awarded, one of only two picturebooks to have claimed the honour to date.

Some illustrators use recognizable general themes from high art, such as familiar religious motifs. Maurice Sendak introduces the motifs of the Deposition, the Pietà, and the Resurrection into his picturebook *We Are All in the Dumps with Jack and Guy* (1993). The "Poor Little Kid" transcends death in a series reminiscent of many religious paintings by great masters. Peter Neumeyer examines the doublespread in which the kid is taken down from the moon as in a Renaissance Deposition.[28] The range of artistic "scavenging" in contemporary picturebooks is truly remarkable.

Art Fantasy

Illustrators commonly use the style of one or more artists to illustrate fictional works inspired by the life or works of those artists. This includes the new genre of art books that the children's author W. Nikola-Lisa refers to as "art fantasy," which he defines as "fantasies that bring to life past masters (and their works) in new, exciting—even surprising—contexts."[29] Some art fantasies remain rooted in everyday experience while others are situated in an entirely imaginary world. *El cuadro más bonito del mundo* (The most beautiful painting in the world, 2001), by Miquel Obiols and Roger Olmos, is a metaphorical story about Joan Miró's art. The artist equips himself with a new whip and dresses like an animal tamer in order to try to tame the five wild spots of colour he keeps prisoner in his studio, but their escape takes him on a journey in search of them. Olmos's colourful illustrations complement Obiols's poetic and surrealistic text in this imaginative homage to the Catalan painter. *El sueño de Dalí* (Dali's dream, 2003), published two years later by Carlos Arbat, is another surreal story in which Dali dreams of constructing a house for Gala from his dreams. Gala's house of dreams takes the form of the Dali museum in Figueres, Catalonia, with the distinctive gigantic eggs sitting on the edge of the roof. The illustrations are full of motifs and details from Dali's work: his signature soft watches, the *Lobster Telephone*, and a portrait of Mae West. The miniature circus of mobilist Alexander Calder comes to life in a very playful manner in *Roarr: Calder's Circus* (1991), written by Maria Kalman with photographs by Donatella Brun. The creative typography allows the irreverent text to follow the figures, curving between the "Flying Flippolinis" and following the swaying movement of the derriere of the belly dancer Fanny.

A number of picturebooks tell the story of an animal, either belonging to an artist or depicted in a painting. *Le cheval de Léonard de Vinci* (Leonardo da Vinci's horse, 1997), by Michel Piquemal and Daniel Maja, tells the story of Fino, who could have been as famous an inventor as his illustrious master. Miguel Ángel Fernández-Pacheco won the Premio Nacional de Literatura Infantil 2001 (National Children's Literature Award 2001) for *La verdadera historia del perro Salomón* (The true story of the dog Salomon, 2000), the story of the dog that appears in Diego Velásquez's *Las Meninas*. In the imaginative story, the servant of the Spanish Golden Age writer Francisco de Quevedo, a contemporary of Velásquez, is enamoured of a lady of the court and has himself transformed into a Great Dane in order to be close to his beloved. When the fairy forgets the magic words to break the spell, he is forced to remain a dog for much longer than anticipated. The tale of the dog/lover is one of the love stories that six courtiers from the painting tell the Infanta so that she won't be bored as she poses for Velásquez. Javier Serrano was awarded second prize in the Nacional de Ilustración 2001 for the illustrations he did for the book, which also won the International Prize for Illustration of the Fundación Santa María 2000.

Fiction and fact are often intertwined in a child-centred story that presents an artist through the eyes of a fictional child protagonist. A popular example from the 1970s is Christina Björk and Lena Anderson's *Linnea in Monet's Garden* (1978), in which a young girl travels to Paris to visit Claude Monet's home in Giverny. In *Looking for Vincent* (1992), Thea Dubelaar and Ruud Bruijn tell the story of Van Gogh's life as seen through the eyes of a young boy whose aunt has fallen in love with the dead painter. Michael Garland's *Dinner at Magritte's* (1995), in which a bored young boy visits his neighbours, René and Georgette Magritte, and is invited to stay to dinner with their guest Salvador Dalí, includes numerous visual and textual allusions to Magritte's works, as well as a Daliesque soft clock. Attentive readers will notice that the front page of the father's newspaper in the first plate contains a Magritte citation announcing the dinner party scene, in which the artist at the head of the table is rendered as *The Son of Man*. While many of these books are devoted to a single artist, others evoke a wide range of artists from different periods. In Richard Kidd's *Almost Famous Daisy* (1996), the young protagonist travels around the world painting in the settings of famous artworks while the artists themselves (Van Gogh, Monet, Chagall, Gauguin, and Pollock) paint the same scenes.

Many child-centred art fantasies involve a visit to a museum. In James Mayhew's *Katie's Picture Show* (1989), the protagonist jumps into several paintings and has an adventure in each of them while visiting the gallery with her grandmother. In *Lulu and the Flying Babies* (1991), by the British newspaper cartoonist Posy Simmonds, a little girl who does not want to visit the pictures in the museum is carried by two winged cherubs through the galleries and into the worlds depicted in the works of art. Jacqueline Preisse Weitzman and Robin Preisse Glasser's *You Can't Take a Balloon Into the Metropolitan Museum* (1998) was the first in a series of books in which famous paintings and sculptures that a little girl visits in a museum or gallery with her grandmother are reworked in the illustrations of the celebrated New York sights her balloon drifts through when she is obliged to leave it outside. Young readers may not immediately pick up on the fact that the balloon's adventures reflect works viewed in the museum, but by the second and third book in the series, they know what to expect. Although some are a little forced, many urban scenes echo the works in clever and amusing ways. While several of the zany characters wreak havoc onstage at the opera, the girl and her grandmother view the rather chaotic painting *Autumn Rhythm* by Jackson Pollock. Generally the paintings in museums are reproduced quite faithfully in these books. Gabrielle Vincent's popular series about a bear named Ernest and a mouse named Célestine includes one titled *Ernest et Célestine au musée* (Ernest and Celestine at the museum, 1985), in which the little mouse gets lost in an unnamed museum that is obviously the Louvre. When a little girl wants to show her baby elephant friend the city's art in Marie-Christine Hugonot and Maïté Laboudigue's *Un éléphant, ça trompe énormément* (An elephant eludes enormously, 1993),[30] the museum is one of several places in which the baby elephant, whose name is Pompon, manages to hide by disguising himself as a Pompon sculpture. The French sculptor François Pompon was a forerunner of modern sculpture famous for his stylized animal figures, and the elephant Pompon humorously mimics *The White Bear*, a huge marble sculpture also known as *The Polar Bear in Stride* that is found at the Musée d'Orsay in Paris.

In an art gallery, the elephant replaces the horse in *Man on a Horse*, by the Russian artist Wassily Kandinsky.

A number of art fantasies involve a child entering the worlds depicted in paintings, as in the case of *Lulu and the Flying Babies*. Bjørn Sortland and Lars Elling published *Raudt, blått og litt gult* (English trans., *Anna's Art Adventure*) in Norway in 1993. On a visit to the museum where her uncle works as a guide, a little girl has to go to the bathroom and she goes from painting to painting asking where the toilets are. Rembrandt can't help as he hasn't "been to the bathroom in more than three hundred years," but he remembers that Duchamp flouted tradition and "exhibited a disgusting little toilet and called it art." After finding and putting on a mysterious red dress and a straw hat, the protagonist wanders into a series of masterpieces. The origin of the mysterious dress and hat becomes clear when she ends up as a model for Munch's *Girls on a Pier*, in which the central girl in a red dress and yellow hat has become decidedly shorter, causing the dress to trail behind her. She wanders through Van Gogh's yellow fields, rides through a blue sky on a pipe that is "definitely not a pipe," is rescued from the sky by Chagall, who seems to take her for an angel, offers her green apple to Cézanne for one of his still lifes, and is splattered with blue paint by Pollock whom she assists with a painting. When she finally finds Duchamp's toilet, it turns out to be a useless dusty, old urinal in the attic. She removes the mysterious red robe responsible for her adventure when she sees the time on a Dali melting clock and returns to her uncle to ask where the washrooms are. Elling's illustrations mimic the targeted artists in a variety of different ways. Rembrandt's self-portrait is merely quoted, as Louise has not yet donned the magic dress. Mondrian's painting is reproduced faithfully except for the inclusion of the small figure of Louise and a couple of crows that have flown in from Van Gogh's painting on the next spread. The artist may be included in his modified painting, as is Van Gogh in *Wheatfield with Crows*. Sometimes only a detail from a painting is worked into Louise's encounter with the artist, for example, the superposition of the head from *Dora Maar Seated* on the model walking with Picasso. Elling is content to give a mere reference to a motif from a painting in the spread of Andy Warhol selling cans of Campbell's soup on the beach. The references in *Anna's Art Adventure* are sometimes over children's heads. The scene involving Magritte's pipe does not even mention the name of the artist. However, two pages of notes on the artists and their works are presented at the end of Sortland and Elling's book. Quite a number of the books mentioned thus far contain brief biographical notes on the artists at the back, but many of the best art fantasies avoid such heavy-handed didacticism. The books that generally have adult appeal are those that do not explicitly draw attention to the allusions or explain them to readers.

When Sortland's protagonist finds the mysterious red dress on the floor in the museum, she can't imagine who would have undressed there and she wonders if another little girl has had an urgent need to go to the bathroom.

Louise looks around but doesn't see anyone walking around stark naked. Sortland seems to be alluding to an earlier Norwegian picturebook in the same art fantasy genre, Fam Ekman's *Hva skal vi gjøre med Lille Jill?* (What are we going to do with Little Jill?), published in 1976. Unlike most books in the genre, *Lille Jill*, which was made into an animated film in 1987, has black-and-white illustrations. Ekman portrays the loneliness of a child and the experience of feeling very small in a big adult world. The parents, who don't seem to take much notice of their daughter, are nonetheless worried about the fact that she sits alone in a chair in her room, so they hang a painting of a little girl on the wall. Jill enters into conversation with the girl, who confides she would like a horse. While searching for a horse for the little girl, Jill takes shelter in a museum during a rainstorm, and there the paintings come to life, as they often do in "art fantasies." In the museum, which is a combination of two well-known museums in Oslo (the exterior is modeled after the Vigeland museum and the inside after the Nationalgalleriet), the first work of art to catch Jill's eye is a statue of a woman's nude torso. On a doublespread, Ekman humorously juxtaposes two images of the statue which, in this case, is her own creation: in the first, Little Jill stares up at the statue and in the second she has shed her clothing and is posing nude on the pedestal imitating the stance of the statue. In the following illustration, a museum guard examines the abandoned clothing without noticing the new living nude statue in the background. Jill continues through the galleries of the museum, entering a number of paintings. In the first two cases, the naked girl is depicted on the verso studying the framed painting, while on the recto she has been integrated into an unframed rendition of the original. The paintings are not very well-known, but it is not important that readers recognize them. According to Ekman, the first is *Breakfast* by the Norwegian painter Gustav Wentzel, and the naked white body of Jill occupies the empty chair at the table in the otherwise dark painting. In Edvard Munch's *The Day After*, Jill is sitting on the bed beside the hung-over woman who has managed to sit up but is clutching her head. The third painting, which covers much of the doublespread, is a compromise between the two techniques: framed only by the dots of Pierre Bonnard's pointillist style, Little Jill sits in the painting with her feet hanging out. When she finally comes upon a sculpture of a knight on horseback, the old knight is delighted to help her because he has been sitting on the horse for 509 years. Little Jill escapes into the painting with the other little girl and they ride off together on the horse. In the final doublespread, which is almost identical to the first, attentive readers will notice that not only is Little Jill no longer curled up in the corner of the huge armchair, but the little girl has disappeared from the bench in the painting. Ekman's picturebooks have wide adult appeal and have often been described as *allalderslitteratur* (all-ages-literature) since the term was coined in Norway to refer to crossover literature in the 1980s. In Norway, they have also become collectors' items for adult art connoisseurs, although Ekman insists on the importance of "the connection with the child inside."[31]

The artistic allusion is sometimes so subtle that it may go unnoticed. In Fred Bernard and François Roca's *La Comédie des ogres* (The ogres' comedy, 2002), which received the Goncourt Jeunesse prize in 2002, the referencing is largely limited to the names of the members of the ogre family: the father Goya, the wife Cézanne, and their son Vermeer. Although the publishers' blurb states that the ogre family is "a little artistic," there is no indication of any artistic talent in the narrative and this book would hardly qualify as an art fantasy. The description may refer to the fact that, as has often been the case with artists, the ogres are outcasts who live a marginal life on the fringes of society. Certainly, Bernard did not choose the ogres' names arbitrarily, at least in the case of the parents. Paul Cezanne was described as an ogre, due to his monstrosity and clumsiness, while Francisco Goya's *Saturn Devouring his Son*, which hung in the painter's dining room, is a disturbing portrait of the god Saturn consuming one of his children. The colours of Roca's palette are reminiscent of those used by Goya.

While the artistic allusion in *La Comédie des ogres* is quite limited, some art fantasy picturebooks contain extensive, sophisticated artistic metadiscourse. Miles Hyman appropriates Van Gogh's palette to illustrate Jean-Luc Fromental's fanciful story about a pig that loses an ear and becomes a famous artist in *Le cochon à l'oreille coupée* (The pig with the cut ear, 1994). In the manner of the Van Gogh-like figure in the straw hat painting in a field on one doublespread, the pig artist can be seen painting at an easel set up in the barnyard. Apparently the "porcine prodigy" himself does not paint in the style of Van Gogh, however, as his paintings displayed at the Café Bohême include a *Goret et Guitare* (Piglet and guitar) à la Picasso, a *Truie au bain* (Sow in a tub) à la Degas, and a *Ceci n'est pas une saucisse* (This is not a sausage) à la Magritte. The full page of challenging text superposed in a frame on the verso of each doublespread makes this a book for older children. Tomie dePaola's *Bonjour, Mr. Satie* (1991) presents the adventures of a worldly-wise, traveling cat, Mr. Satie, whose artist friends include Pablo, who painted his portrait during his blue period. Whereas dePaola's rendition of Mr. Satie's portrait is a humorous parody, not of Picasso's *Portrait of Erik Satie*, but of *The Old Guitarist*, the controversial new paintings that Mr. Satie is asked to compare with those of Henri [Matisse] in Gertrude's Salon in Paris are reproduced fairly faithfully. Unable to declare one style of painting superior to another, the cat art connoisseur pronounces both artists winners. The surnames of Mr. Satie's famous friends who frequent Gertrude Stein's salon are listed on the back flap, but they will have little interest for most young readers. This encounter of famous personalities of 1920s Paris is aimed at a rather sophisticated audience able to understand the witty tongue-in-cheek humour. A few of the visual puns, such as the image of Satie as Picasso's *Blue Nude*, may even go over the heads of adults.

The same year that dePaola published *Bonjour, Mr. Satie*, Rigo (Martín Martínez Navarro) and Ricardo Alcántara released *El caballo acróbata* (The horse acrobat, 1991) in Spain. They borrow the colourful horse from the bottom left hand corner of Marc Chagall's *Song of Songs III* to tell the story of Colorin, a violin-playing horse who leaves his farm to join the circus. There he is discovered by a famous artist, who remains unnamed in the text but is transparently identified in the subtitle, "A fantasy with Marc Chagall." In the narrative itself, a sign over the entrance to the circus tent prominently displays the name "Cha-gall." All the illustrations are inspired by the work of the Russian-French artist, whose exuberant and poetic blending of shapes and colours takes its inspiration from Eastern European Jewish folk culture. Rigo's pictures are full of Chagall's characteristic motifs and symbols, such as fiddlers, roosters, fish, flowers, trees, lovers, circus performers, windows, the little houses of Vitebsk, and, of course, horses. In "Cha-gall's" circus tent, which is crowded with vaguely familiar figures from Chagall paintings, Colorin discovers "the world of his dreams." A single Chagall painting is rendered faithfully on the final page of the narrative. Inspired by his new animal model, Chagall has just put the final touches on the large canvas *Song of Songs III*, which sits on an easel next to the artist holding his palette and brushes. The humorous implication is that Chagall is appropriating Rigo's colourful visual world, in which Colorin pre-existed. This is underscored by the mise en abyme, in the cover illustration, of a minute Chagall at the circus painting Colorin as he appears in the centre of the cover with Rigo's signature immediately below. An afterword provides a biography of the artist, but unlike most paratextual elements of this nature, it is beautifully framed with further Chagall-style motifs by Rigo.

The early 1990s were rich years for picturebooks inspired by famous artists and one of the best crossover picturebooks in this category is *Pish, Posh, Said Hieronymus Bosch*, written by Nancy Willard and illustrated by Leo, Diane, and Lee Dillon. The text, which was also published without the pictures in a fantasy anthology for adults, is a highly imaginative poem about the poor housekeeper who is being driven to distraction by the odd creatures that come to life under the brush of one of the world's most eccentric painters. As the copyright page of the picturebook indicates, the text type was hand-lettered by the illustrators, and the sepia colour used gives the feel of old manuscripts. According to the note on the author at the end of the book, Willard's fascination with Bosch dates from her university years, but her text does not contain specific references to the artist's works. The note on Bosch, which also appears at the end of the book, explains that "Bosch's creatures served primarily as a departure point and a source of inspiration." Willard's fantastic images evoke vague reminiscences of the painter: "a pear-headed priest," "witches' familiars," "a two-headed bat," "a mole in a habit," "a thistledown rabbit," "a three-legged dish," or "a head wearing claws." The most precise allusion is the "pickle-winged fish" on which the housekeeper rides back to her relieved master. It recalls, in a comic mode, Bosch's strange flying fish, especially the winged fish mounted by a fat man and a lady in *The Temptation of St. Anthony* triptych, although *The Garden of Earthly Delights* also has similar flying creatures. The playful, exuberant mood of *Pish, Posh, Said Hieronymus Bosch* is very different, however, from the dark, pessimistic tone of the Bosch paintings that inspired Willard and the Dillons.

The reminiscences of Bosch in the text are complemented and enhanced by the visual interpretation of Leo and Diane Dillon, whose playful look at the artist's bizarre, often grotesque creatures is the result of a longstanding admiration for Bosch. Their portrayal of the eponymous protagonist resembles self-portraits of the historic Bosch. In the corner of the cover illustration of Bosch painting is the faithfully reproduced canvas of *The Wayfarer,* which is only partially visible and may therefore go unnoticed by many readers. In addition to the creatures mentioned in Willard's text, the Dillons evoke many others that reference the artist's works more directly. In the foreground of the cover illustration, a little smiling monk, undoubtedly St. Anthony himself, and a strange creature (with a green winged fish body) whose bird head capped with a funnel mimics "the devil's messenger" from the left panel of *The Temptation of St. Anthony* triptych, watch with rapt admiration as the master who created them paints a picture that remains invisible to the viewer. While the smiling artist paints contentedly in the foreground, his housekeeper fights off a kitchen full of strange creatures in the background of the illustration. While the Dillons's illustrations do not contain the myriad details of Bosch's teeming paintings, they nonetheless succeed in creating the general effect of crowding (this is particularly evident in the celebratory dinner scene on the back cover, where the entire frame is crammed with the household's bizarre creatures gathered around the happy couple). A heavy, ornate frame, whose strange creatures seem to have escaped from the paintings, was fashioned by the Dillon's son, Lee, to contain each illustration. The effect is that of looking into a mirror in Bosch's mad household. The reflected scenes resemble as many framed paintings that include the artist himself. The mirrored scenes are reminiscent of the mise en abyme that André Gide so appreciated in the works of Memling and Quentin Metzys. They could almost be the invisible canvases on which Bosch is working in several of the illustrations. *Pish, Posh, Said Hieronymus Bosch* is a truly exceptional title among the scores of art fantasy books published over the past couple of decades. Although *Pish, Posh, Said Hieronymous Bosch* contains a biographical note on Bosch, it is not distinguished from those on Willard and the Dillons, and therefore does not assume the same didactical purpose as in some of the previous books. Like Willard's *A Visit to William Blake's Inn,* this book is meant for readers of all ages. It is, after all, dedicated to two children, as well as "to wives and housekeepers and mothers everywhere," to which Willard added in my personal copy "and for Sandra, who is all of these and a scholar-teacher as well." In my copy, she also identified the hybrid creature drawn on the dedication page as

St. Nicholas, "the patron saint of scholars and children." This is indeed a book for everyone.

Direct Allusions to Specific Works of Art

We have already seen in the section devoted to art fantasies that many picture-books include allusions to specific works of art or parts of them. These may or may not be combined with more general allusions to an artistic movement or an individual artist's style. An illustrator may simply integrate a single well-known motif or figure from an artist's work. In the South African picture-book *Hier is ek* (1996; English trans., *Here I Am*), one of Piet Grobler's African landscapes includes two Daliesque soft watches, one hanging over the branch of a tree and the other lying on the decorated frame around the illustration in the manner of *The Persistence of Memory* (12). Wolf Erlbruch's rendition of the first woman in *De schepping* (In the beginning, 2003) will evoke reminis-cences of Sandro Botticelli's *The Birth of Venus*, as her arms cover her breast and her pubic area in a very similar gesture. The allusion is made obvious by her long hair floating on the wind. In Botticelli's painting, the soft breath of the winged Zephyrs who have blown Venus over the Egean waves to shore causes some of her golden tresses to stream out in the same direction, but in Erlbruch's humorous rendition, it is the effect of the disquieting gale-force wind created by God.

Many picturebooks contain only a single spread that references a specific painting. It may simply serve as an inside joke for knowing readers, but often there is an additional function. Sometimes it serves as mise-en-scène for the story. The American-born Canadian author and illustrator Dayal Kaur Khalsa often included allusions to famous works of art in her pictures. The cover of *I Want a Dog* (1987) is an easily recognizable reworking of George-Pierre Seurat's *Sunday Afternoon on the Island of La Grande Jatte*, to which more dogs have been added. Some of the people in the original have also been replaced by dogs. Seurat's park thus becomes a paradise for dog walkers, in which dogless little May sits with her substitute roller skates on a leash. The French author-illustra-tor Bruno Heitz opens *Renaud le corbeau* (Renaud the crow, 1995), an unusual picturebook midway between a medieval romance and a comic book, with a very recognizable version of Van Gogh's *Wheatfield with Crows*, allowing the crow chronicler to distinguish the "décor" of common crows from that of the heroic Renaud, set against the golden background of palaces. The reference may comment on the events or characters. Gerard Failly's illustrations for the 1978 edition of Eugene Ionesco's *Conte numéro 2* makes the connection to the sur-realists explicit in the last image of Josette's mother, depicted as two eyes and a sexy mouth hanging in frames on the wallpaper, a direct reference to Salvador Dali's *Mae West*. It may also be a sly comment on the mother's sexuality. In *The Balloon Tree* (1984), the Canadian author-illustrator Phoebe Gilman models the evil archduke and the princess's little dog after Arnolfini and the dog in Jan van Eyck's famous portrait of Arnolfini and his wife. In some cases, the allusions reflect a character's state of mind. In Anthony Browne's *The Tunnel*, the terrifying image of Rose's petrified brother is a reference to Magritte's *The Song of the Violet*, in which two figures of men have turned to stone. Erica Hately rightly describes this Magrittian citation as "an index of interiority," arguing that "the frozen boy could represent Rose's feelings of alienation from her brother or the boy's own feelings of social isolation."[32]

Female characters in the story are often associated with female figures from well-known paintings who exemplify grace and beauty. Once again, the allusion may serve chiefly as a humorous wink at knowing readers or it may have a more profound significance. The delicate portrait of Beauty in Étienne Delessert's version of Madame d'Aulnoy's *Beauty and the Beast*, published by Creative Education in 1983, is modeled after Flora, the goddess of spring, in Sandro Botticelli's *Primavera*, one of the most famous masterpieces of Florentine art. In the painting by the Early Italian Renaissance artist, Flora scatters flowers in the garden of Venus. Delessert does not reproduce the figure faithfully: only her face and neckline are partially visible and her features are slightly caricatural. Much of her figure is hidden behind what appears to be a beautiful, multi-coloured piece of stained glass that frames a single rose. Yet Beauty's model is immediately recognisable to adult readers. A closer inspection reveals that a few details are reproduced quite accurately. Delessert replicates several of the flowers that decorate her neckline and those in her blonde hair, particularly the four on the right side below the level of her eyebrows, where he crops the image. Surrounded by flowers in a spring-like setting, Beauty dreams of a single rose as her father's ship sails away in the background. Delessert's choice of the *Primavera* for this particular scene is inspired. The painting exemplifies beauty and grace, the qualities of Madame d'Aulnoy's fairy-tale heroine, while at the same time encompassing the tale's essential flower motif. Fam Ekman provides an entirely different take on Botticelli's *The Birth of Venus* in *Dagbok forsvunnet* (The missing diary, 1995). In this whimsical story, a statue comes stiffly down off its base to go in search of her stolen diary full of secrets (in the first illustration a caricatural rendition of the Statue of Liberty stands in a Scandinavian city holding a large pencil rather than a torch in her raised arm and clutching her diary to her bosom in the other). In her search, the statue questions various people, including "a scantily clad person missing a tooth." The illustration depicts a caricatural Venus whose hands no longer cover her private parts because she has just lost a tooth (force marks trace the movement of the tooth falling to the ground). Her lips have parted to reveal the gap in her teeth and her right hand has just gone to her mouth, while her face registers her shock and consternation at this unexpected event.

Sometimes the reworked painting is used to establish a particular mood or atmosphere. A revisioning of Magritte's surrealist painting *Time Transfixed* is used by two illustrators to reflect changes in the life of their child protagonist. Browne reworks the painting in *The Visitors Who Came to Stay* (1984) to suggest the strangeness in Katy's life when her single father's girlfriend, Mary, and her son pay a visit. The British author and illustrator Colin Thompson uses the same painting in *Looking for Atlantis* (1993), in which the boy protagonist has lost his grandfather. The train no longer protrudes from the fireplace, into which the boy is peering, but has whooshed across the gutter of the doublespread to enter a brick tunnel in the bookcase in the next room; the boy is portrayed in both rooms simultaneously. The surrealist painting is in keeping with the strange atmosphere of Thompson's split illustrations, in which the "everyday" world dominates the upper part of the doublespread while the lower section reveals a hidden world under the floor. Thompson also uses reminiscences of Bosch to develop the mysterious atmosphere that pervades the book. The boy sits dejectedly staring out to sea, apparently unaware of the mysteries around him. The strange island in the background is borrowed from Bosch's *The Garden of Earthly Delights*, while the man zooming past the island on a flying fish evokes the man mounted on a flying fish and holding what looks like a fishing pole in *The Temptation of St. Anthony* triptych. One of the first surreal images in Soren Jessen's *Gaven* is a large tree with lighted windows and a clock in the trunk, which closely mimics Magritte's *The Voice of Blood*, although instead of an illuminated house there are only rows of lit windows and the round sphere above has been replaced by a clock. The same haunting image appears prominently on three doublespreads, most notably at the beginning and end of Frode's fantastic journey. Jessen's tree grows on a large building with rows of windows that mirror those in the trunk. The tree's roots are growing over the building, as nature encroaches on the city. Attentive readers will note the progression of this invasion in the final scene before the boy returns to his room because small trees have already sprouted from the roots that now extend onto a neighbouring building.

Jean Claverie often adapts the visual grammar of the French baroque painter Georges de la Tour, who illuminated his nocturnes with a candle or a lamp, setting up a strong play between light and shadow. Like La Tour, Claverie uses a variety of light sources to illuminate his characters and create similar light and dark contrasts that take on symbolic meaning. The technique is sometimes used to create an atmosphere of meditation and self-reflection. In *Musée Blues* (Museum blues, 1986), written by Susie Morgenstern, Claverie parodies La Tour's masterpiece *Magdalen with the Smoking Flame*. The subject of the humorous story is art: parents continually drag a young boy to museums and other places of learning until he revolts and creates his own museum. In one of the illustrations, the protagonist reads in the candlelight with a skull on his knees, as does the subject of La Tour's painting. In both cases, the skull is a symbol of mortality and the inevitability of death. Claverie's more delicate treatment of the light is partly due to the medium, as he works in watercolours, but Jean Perrot attributes it also to the fact that he likes to reproduce the soft blue light of the television screen, that of the "modern" image.[33]

Sometimes the text and illustrations of an entire book are inspired by a single painting. That is the case for Dorte Karrebæk's *Den sorte bog: om de syv dødssynder* (The black book: on the seven deadly sins, 2007), a lengthy picture-book of 72 pages, which has its origins in Bosch's *The Seven Deadly Sins*. The illustrator admits that she has always been influenced by Bosch and that she can lose herself completely in front of this particular painting at the Prado in Madrid (the Danish illustrator now resides in Spain). She considers it a book for both children and adults, but she admits that it does not sell well despite the very positive reception by critics and the press, because reviewers say they would never show it to children. The story begins when a boy finds a small black notebook, whose strange contents are at once cruel and fascinating. A brief, but highly instructive introduction seems to have been written by an author who intended the book to be found and read by another. It contains a description of his years of experimentations with insects: "I have isolated seven character-istics, which are prevalent in the world we live in, and grafted them into seven different species that I closely describe on the following pages." The seven char-acteristics are, of course, the seven deadly sins. After reading the notebook, the boy sets out on a scientific expedition, armed with the book and a wooden box in which he will pin the various specimens collected. Detailed observations are

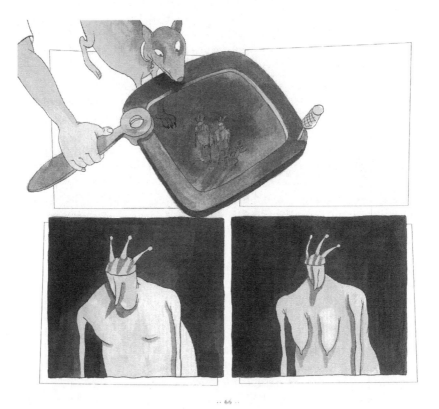

Figure 4.4   Den sorte bog: om de syv dødssynder by Dorte Karrebæk, copy-right © 2007 Dorte Karrebæk and Forlaget Alma, reprinted by permission of Dorte Karrebæk.

accompanied by cartoon-style drawings of the grotesque creatures that have been endowed with the very worst human traits.

The Flemish publisher De Eenhoorn created a series of highly original picturebooks which bring paintings to life by providing the backstory. One of the famous paintings by Pieter Brueghel the Elder inspired the first book in the series, *Dulle Griet* (aka Mad Meg), published in 2005 by the author Geert De Kockere and the illustrator Carll Cneut. The illustrator revisits the Flemish painting, reproduced on the back cover, in which the legendary figure of Mad Meg, wearing an apron, a soldier's breastplate, and a helmet, dashes across a landscape, hair streaming, toward the mouth of hell brandishing a long, lethal sword in one hand and assorted loot in the other. At the beginning of the story, Griet is presented as an adorable child, a little girl like any other (her nickname then was Little Marguerite), but as she grows older she transforms into Marguerite the Fury and then finally Mad Meg. The first doublespread, which depicts the young girl fulfilling her desire to throw people off the top of a tower out of curiosity, sets the tone for a very gruesome journey into hell with Mad Meg. In the end, she literally plunges into hell and asks the Devil for his hand in marriage. On one doublespread, Cneut's caricatural rendition of Mad Meg adopts the same stance as her model to stride through a reproduction of a major portion of the painting. It is the point at which Meg hesitates momentarily before entering the large open mouth that she recognizes as the devil's mouth, the gate to hell. As Meg approaches the monstrous head from Brueghel's painting, the smell of decomposing flesh pervades the air and continues to worsen. Cneut's reworking is quite sophisticated, as he even includes reminders that Breughel's original work was influenced by Bosch, for example, the fish that devours and is devoured, a reminder of one of the deadly sins, Gluttony. The determined Meg kicks out of her way the little devils that laugh hysterically as they stick their enormous forks into human flesh and roast it over the fire for amusement. She forces her way aggressively through a throng of frightening creatures that become increasingly monstrous and inhuman. Like Karrebæk, Cneut portrays grotesque creatures that symbolize a dehumanized humanity. The unusual black front cover of *Dulle Griet*, like that of *Den sorte bog*, announces the blackness of the subject matter and immediately creates an atmosphere of grimness. Cneut's highly-textured illustrations, which are overlaid with an antique patina, effectively evoke Brueghel's paintings, and the red that some have begun to call "Cneut red" is perhaps borrowed from the Flemish painter's palette. The village scenes in the opening spreads and the final illustration are reminiscent of more joyous Brueghel paintings. Many of the illustrations are crowded with figures in the manner characteristic of Brueghel's style and they spill off the pages. Cneut explains: "My illustrations continue into the invisible. My readers have the freedom to complete them in their heads. This often confuses adults, but never the children."[34] De Kockere and Cneut's backstory to the famous painting *Dulle Griet* challenges the boundaries of the picturebook.

Geert De Kockere also wrote the text for the second book in the series, *Voorspel van een gebroken liefde* (Prelude to a broken love, 2007), this time illustrated in coloured woodcuts by Isabelle Vandenabeele. Their inspiration for this picturebook is the 1928 painting of the same title by the Flemish expressionist painter Edgard Tytgat, which represents a man comforting a woman as her leg is amputated. This unusual picturebook portrays a man and woman walking toward "de grote dag" (the big day), which has been interpreted as their wedding day, as they think about love and each other. The narrator explains that their "love is no coup de foudre, but something that had grown gradually. As violets grow." In the beginning, the couple shares the same ideas about the future, but as they continue to walk, their thoughts and feelings begin to drift apart. The man thinks about happiness and is absorbed in his dreams and expectations, while the woman thinks about obligations and feels more and more oppressed and suffocated by love. In the end, the woman cuts loose, bringing a definitive end to the prelude. De Kockere and Vandenabeele's narrative about love, dreams, and reality attempts to unravel the mystery of a painting that still mystifies specialists.

While some picturebooks allude to only a single artwork, others include references to a wide range of paintings and sculptures. On a reproduction of a painting superposed on the front endpapers of *The Mighty Asparagus*, Vladimir Radunsky thanks and apologizes to numerous painters, including Piero della Francesa, Giovani Bellini, Perugino, Fra Angelico, Andrea Mantegna, and Pietro and Ambrogio Lorenzetti. The detailed copyright particulars are printed, probably with deliberate irony, on the reproduction of another painting on the back endpapers. The number and detail of Radunsky's references in a book for relatively young children may seem surprising, but the illustrator explains his intentions in the following manner: "This book was inspired by my travels in Italy where I see so many glorious Renaissance paintings. I always think what a pity it is that so many children in America may never see these paintings, or will see them when they are already grown-ups, or that this art will be offered to them in such a boring manner that it won't touch them. *The Mighty Asparagus* is my attempt to introduce children to a few pieces from the collection of classics in this, I hope amusing, way."[35] A few paintings and details of paintings are reproduced faithfully in the illustrations. The prosperous Renaissance town setting that provides the backdrop for the story is borrowed from Ambrogio Lorenzetti's aptly named fresco *Allegory of Good Government: Effects of Good Government on the City*. A large detail from the painting constitutes the background of the first spread, in which the king stares across the gutter at the "amazing" thing growing in his own backyard. In the background of another spread, a smaller version of the same scene is viewed from the base of the mighty asparagus. Almost the entire painting seems to appear on a subsequent doublespread but much of it is hidden under a layer of paint that traces the path taken by the falling asparagus that now lies in the foreground of the illustration. The illustrator not only appropriates the subjects, but also the techniques of the old masters. In order "to repaint the faces and figures borrowed from the classical paintings to turn them into

[the] grotesque personages" required for the story, Radunsky needed to use "a more or less classical technique of tempera." The king and queen are caricatural versions of the *Portrait of Federico da Montefeltro* and the *Portrait of Battista Sforza*. The parodic portrait of the Queen as Battista Sforza on the back cover is quite faithful except for her oversize mouth and her bug eye that stares sideways at the reader. Further, what was originally a tempera on panel painting now resembles a photo on paper that has been cut by hand to leave a very uneven white border.

There is nothing arbitrary in Radunsky's choice of paintings. The king, who, after managing to fell the mighty asparagus (with a lot of help), feels he must be "a wise and brave king after all," is humorously modelled after a Renaissance man nicknamed "the Light of Italy" and known for imposing justice and stability on his tiny state. The king's "remarkably wise" advisers, who make such profound statements as: "Amazing! What a mighty asparagus!" are the subjects of Andrea Mantegna's *The Court of Mantua*, closely reproduced with two exceptions: the eyes of Ludovico Gonzaga, which immediately catch the reader's eye, are again bug-like, and they no longer turn toward the man with whom he is conferring but upward toward the mighty asparagus that now grows beside the tree beyond the arches. The various onlookers include the mother and child from Masaccio's fresco *The Distribution of Alms and the Death of Ananias*. Among the individuals and groups who make pronouncements on the felling of the mighty asparagus along its great length on the pull-out page toward the end are the reclining lady in green from Ambrogio Lorenzetti's *Allegory of Good Government* and Giovanni Bellini's *Portrait of the Doge Leonardo Loredan*. The minstrels singing "The Ballad of the Mighty Asparagus" on the final page are borrowed from Piero della Francesca's *Nativity*. With consummate skill, Radunsky tells his story using characters and settings from an amazing variety of Italian Renaissance paintings and frescoes.

Allusions to the works of canonical Western artists figure prominently in the profusion of minute cultural icons that make up Mitsumasa Anno's "Journey" books. He uses artistic allusions systematically in the series, but not always with equal success. For the Japanese illustrator, life and art are not separate realms, but inextricably intertwined. In the first "Journey" book, *Tabi no ehon*, inspired by his initial trip to Europe, the many figures from paintings that the solitary, enigmatic little traveller on horseback encounters are mostly from French artworks. The list of "things to look for" in the publisher's insert begins with "details from paintings by Courbet, Millet, Renoir, Seurat and others." As to be expected, Anno's second "Journey" book, published in English as *Anno's Italy*, contains numerous references to famous paintings and sculptures by great Italian masters. The three Muses from Botticelli's *Primavera* join in a street procession, Fra Angelico's *The Annunciation* and Leonardo da Vinci's *The Last Supper* are set in the Italian countryside, and the Venus de Milo is being offered for sale along with pop art portraits of Sophia Loren in the shadow of Michelangelo's *Pietà* in a teeming Renaissance square. The statue of David that stands at the entrance to the Palazzo Vecchio may be the copy that overlooks the Piazza della Signoria or Anno may have replaced it with the original that is housed in the Gallery of the Academy of Fine Arts. Anno's artistic allusions nonetheless move freely through both time and space. He does not hesitate to include Cézanne's *Card Players* sitting at a table outside a farmhouse in the Italian countryside. The afterword of *Anno's Britain* (1981) informs readers that Anno's traveller encounters "idyllic pastoral landscapes from paintings by Constable and Gainsborough," but these are quite difficult to identify as the illustrator has a predilection for the countryside and his own illustrations are largely pastoral.

In the "Afterword" of *Anno's U.S.A.* (1983), the author-illustrator insists on the fact that he wants his readers "to work to discover for themselves" as many references as possible, but it is nonetheless this "Journey" book that provides them with the most detailed list of artistic allusions, including titles of specific paintings: "George Caleb Bingham's *Fur Traders Descending the Missouri*, Grant Wood's *American Gothic*, Edward Hicks's *The Peaceable Kingdom*, and famous paintings by Winslow Homer, James McNeill Whistler, Andrew Wyeth, Tasha Tudor and many more." The artist seems to have felt that even armed with the titles, only "the sharp-eyed (and sharp-witted) viewer" would be capable of identifying them. While Anno's journey through Spain was often inspired by artists (the cover illustration reflects his visit to the ancient town of Toledo, where El Greco lived), few details of paintings are worked into the illustrations. On one spread, he quotes a series of paintings faithfully within frames and then, on the same spread, he plays with motifs and subjects from those paintings. The proximity of the quotation and the parodic reworking helps readers to get the joke. Picasso's *Guernica* is the only unframed painting and this is because a barefoot Picasso stands with a paintbrush in front of it, still completing the work. Near him, a child copies a detail from the painting. The star and the curved line in the Miró painting are reflected in the star a girl carries on a stick, while a man attempts to mimic the stance of the grimacing deformed figure in Dali's *Soft Construction with Boiled Beans*. Goya's *The Nude Maja* and *The Clothed Maya* are depicted side by side. One of the most effective reworkings is that of Goya's *The Straw Mannequin*. Women holding a sheet reflect those in the framed painting above them. The mannequin, which is absent from the painting has been thrown high into the air in such a manner that it completes both the painting and the parodic scene below. Only one of the paintings is parodied in a separate spread. Goya's painting of a cart pulled by a man, followed by a woman, and accompanied by a dog is recognizable enough that Anno draws his version in the streets of the following cityscape.

Although Anno's quotations are not generally parodic, they sometimes have a highly ludic function. In the first book, a nude bather in a tub, reminiscent of Edgar Degas's *The Tub* or one of Pierre-Auguste Renoir's bathers, is hidden from view to all but the reader by a wall, against which Anno wittily places a ladder that a man is just starting to scale. Readers are left to imagine the outcome. The recontextualization of elements from specific paintings is often quite sophisticated. Another page cleverly combines scenes from Seurat's two monumental masterpieces: his *Bathers at Asnières* are positioned close to the figures from the foreground of *A Sunday Afternoon on the Island of La Grande Jatte*, which he began the following year in the pointillist style. Sitting in the field between the two groupings is the artist doing one of the preparatory studies for *La Grande Jatte*. In a doublespread depicting daily life on a large farm, the women from Millet's *The Gleaners* can be seen gathering grain in one of the fields close to a dense forest where Little Red Riding Hood is gathering flowers. The reader may not immediately notice that Anno's illustration also includes the cart loaded with hay and the two large haystacks from the background of Millet's painting, because, although they remain in the same position, the bird's eye view greatly alters the perspective and therefore the proportions. The rider approaches the scene from the left, like a mirror image of the man on horseback that can be seen in the distant right background of Millet's painting. The entire scene is reminiscent of the vicinity of the village of Barbizon near the Forest of Fontainebleau, where the painters of the Barbizon school worked. It was Millet in particular who documented the daily activities of farm labourers, and Anno, too, takes pleasure in recording the rustic life of simple folk. In the final doublespread, which seems to continue the plains of Barbizon, the peaceful scene contrasts with the teeming life that spills over most pages and the eye is immediately drawn to the two figures bowed in prayer from Millet's *The Angelus*. Anno is particularly fond of this icon, which recurs unexpectedly fifteen years later in the delicate, rosy-hued watercolour spread that closes *Anno's Magic Seeds* (1994). In the multi-layered tale and mathematical tour de force about Jack and his magical seeds, Anno borrows Millet's icon to depict Jack and his wife, with their heads bowed, praying for a good crop after planting the seeds. The presence of a new element, Jack's son, who, hat in hand, stares up at the sky, does not make the scene any less recognizable.

While Tord Nygren's *The Red Thread* contains general allusions to the style of a variety of artists, as in the case of the typical De Chirico arched building on a public square no longer deserted but now filled with people, the illustrator also incorporates many specific artistic references into the fantastical tableaus. In the very disparate-looking crowd on the opening doublespread, the easily recognizable Mona Lisa (her creator stands on the other side) should alert young readers to the presence of other familiar figures from paintings, although they will certainly not decode them all. Against a backdrop reminiscent of a Vasarely painting, Mona Lisa is joined by Jan van Eyck's Giovanni Arnolfini, one of Rousseau's *Football Players*, one of Renoir's *Two Little Circus Girls*, Modigliani's *Leopold Zborowski* and a woman in a blue dress who resembles *Elvira*, as well as a number of figures from Picasso's works, including his young son Paulo in Harlequin costume, *Child with a Dove*, and *Igor Stravinsky*. They all stand around a large egg that is about to hatch, an allusion to Constantin Brancusi's egg-shaped sculpture *The Newborn*. Another illustration depicts Picasso's *Three Musicians*,

Figure 4.5   Den röda tråden by Tord Nygren, copyright © 1987 Raben and Sjögren, 1987, reprinted by permission of Tord Nygren.

looking decidedly less cubist, playing under a tree while a Pierrot entertains a group of children.

The motley group of children and adults that Nygren appropriates from canonical paintings in *The Red Thread* is engrossed in watching the egg hatch. The egg itself may be a multi-layered artistic allusion that also references another Swedish picturebook. In 1978, the author-illustrator Lennart Hellsing published *Ägget* (The egg, 1978), in which an egg dreams about what it will become when it grows up, one of the many possibilities being to become an "art egg." The Swedish word "konstägg" can actually mean either an "artificial" egg or an egg that is an art object, and young Swedish readers will probably grasp the transparent play on words. The illustration by Fibben Hald shows the interior of a museum, undoubtedly the old Stockholm Museum of Modern Art, where several people are standing around Constantin Brancusi's *The Newborn*. In order to help young readers decode the parody, an egghead is reading about the white marble sculpture in a catalogue on which the name Brancusi is clearly written. In Hellsing's book, the artistic allusion is limited to one illustration and one particular moment in the narrative, when the egg protagonist fantasizes about an artistic future.

A similar situation occurs in *Willy the Dreamer*, in which Anthony Browne's chimpanzee protagonist dreams that he is a painter. In Browne's case, however, even though this is the only episode that is directly related to the topic of art, artistic allusions occur throughout the book, as they do in all his works. Even Willy's dream of becoming "a famous writer" contains allusions to art, notably Magritte, as if writing and art are inseparable, as indeed they seem to be for Browne and many picturebook artists. This scene is a wonderful parody of characters and scenes from Carroll's *Alice* books, while at the same time cleverly alluding to Browne's own version of *Alice's Adventures in Wonderland* (1988). Children of all ages will enjoy the humour of the transformation of Carroll's characters into simians, but they are unlikely to recognize the parodic treatment of Sir John Tenniel's illustration of the Cheshire cat or Magritte's *Ceci n'est pas une pipe*, also known as *The Treachery of Images*. A label "This is not a hat" appears on the Mad Hatter's top hat, but since the rim is a banana this really is not a hat. It is noteworthy that Willy writes his version of *Alice* with a pen that is "not a pen" but a banana. Browne's entire oeuvre is a complex interweaving of his own books with other works of art, film, and literature.

The most popular art icon in children's books is Leonardo da Vinci's *Mona Lisa*. This is not surprising since it is, as Donald Sassoon points out in his 2001 history of the *Mona Lisa*, "the world's most famous painting,"[36] and therefore probably the most easily recognized by young readers. Frédéric Clément's allusion to the *Mona Lisa* in *Magasin Zinzin, ou, Aux Merveilles d'Alys* (1995; English trans., *The Merchant of Marvels and the Peddler of Dreams*) is limited to her smile and part of her nose, but the tiny detail is nonetheless sufficient to allow recognition of the renowned painting. As Linda Hutcheon suggests in *A Theory of Parody*, Leonardo's masterpiece undoubtedly tops the list of the most parodied works in the visual arts,[37] and picturebooks are no exception. Illustrators who parody the *Mona Lisa* follow in a long tradition of artists who have had fun with the enigmatic lady: the French artist Arthur Sapeck (Eugène Bataille) gave her a pipe, Marcel Duchamp added a moustache and a goatee, and Andy Warhol multiplied her in his *Thirty Are Better Than One*. Illustrators often follow Bataille's and Duchamp's lead, adding a single, incongruous detail to an otherwise faithful imitation. Clément adds a beauty mark, which is one of the many items in the strange collection of wonders in the bags, boxes, trunks, and suitcases of the eccentric peddler Frédéric Tic Tic. The Swiss author-illustrator Béatrice Poncelet adds bright pink lipstick, as well as some touches of blue, pink, and yellow eye shadow around her right eye in . . . *Et la gelée, framboise ou cassis?* (. . . And the jelly, raspberry or blackcurrant? 2001). A crescent moon replaces her smile in Henri Meunier's *Ronde de nuit* (2002) when the protagonist visits the museum while walking the moon. In a decidedly more irreverent treatment, Dick King-Smith replaces Mona Lisa's nose with a pig's snout in *Triffic Pig Book* (1991). The endpaper of his book offers three "famous pigtures," which all receive a similar makeover: a Van Gogh self-portrait, a "Pigcasso" portrait of Dora Maar, and a portrait of Henri VIII after Hans Holbein the Younger. The American illustrator Holly Hobbie's rendition of the Mona Lisa in *Toot and Puddle* (1997) has some facial hair, but the most notable difference is the folded hands protruding out of the frame. Although the painting still hangs in a museum in Paris, it is surrounded by porcine sculptures, and it is one of these works of art, rather than the Mona Lisa, that Toot is admiring from his perch on a museum chair. The humour is heightened by the facing page, which depicts Puddle painting a self-portrait (in Van Gogh colours) and finally posing next to the completed painting, his proud smile mirroring the grin of the self-portrait, which in turn reflects that of the Mona Lisa.

Sometimes the humour stems from the recontextualization of the famous icon. "Mona" sits at a computer in a newspaper office in one of Pef's illustrations for *La guerra delle campane* (The war of the bells, 1982; French trans., *Scoop!*), a picturebook based on a short story by Gianni Rodari (her name appears on a piece of equipment at her desk). Despite the fact that Mona Lisa is rendered in black and white (the three doublespreads in the book that depict the interior of the newspaper offices are in black and white, while the imaginative news stories invented by a young journalist who prefers to present the news in a positive fashion are portrayed in colour), Pef retains a certain play of light and shadow on her face. In the bottom right hand corner of the illustration, the iconic portrait faces the opposite direction, staring at the viewer out of the other corner of her eyes, while her left hand now rests on her right, but in the same characteristic, folded position, which turns her into a rather lazy secretary in the new context. Her smile seems to reflect her amusement as she listens to her boss reprimanding the young journalist whose unconventional attitude toward journalism prefers to "desensationalize" the news.

Allusions to individual works of art tend quite often to be parodic or to constitute a pastiche of the original. In *Here I Am*, Ann Walton's whimsical, fantastic story of a grandmother who journeys, by means of an assortment of wild animals, from South Africa to the Netherlands to visit her new grandchild, Piet Grobler's jungle scene is a witty reworking of Rousseau's *The Dream*, in which the nude Yadwigha lounging on a sofa is replaced by Gran scantily clad à la Jane in a leopardskin. The old lady retains the same pose but her hand is slightly raised pointing at a gorilla that has been added in the upper right corner. The gorilla seems to have swung in from one of the Douanier's other jungle paintings—which often include simians[38]—to provide the grandmother's next means of transportation. Grobler cleverly reworks small details of Rousseau's painting, as in the case of the orange-coloured serpent, attracted by the snake charmer in the original, that is extended across the entire illustration and onto the next page. The resulting humour is appreciated even by readers who do not decode the subtleties of the parody.

It is not surprising that Anthony Browne was attracted to the forerunner of the surrealists, whose paintings draw us compellingly into his dreams. Browne's reworking of the same Rousseau painting in *Willy the Dreamer* is particularly appropriate since the artist was depicting Yadwigha's dream. Browne's playful treatment of the snake motif superposes details from another painting producing a witty *bricolage*. The snake twined around the trunk, holding a banana in its mouth, echoes parodically the serpent that proffers the apple in Rousseau's earlier *Eve*. Another snake slides down one of the ladders discreetly worked into the foliage in an obvious allusion to the game of *Snakes and Ladders*. Children's games and fine art are given equal status in Browne's illustrations. He replaces the wild cats, retained in Grobler's illustration, by a house cat—perhaps foreshadowing the Cheshire cat-ape in the next dream sequence. The sofa is now bright pink and occupied by a rather conventional family watching television, which evokes vague reminiscences of the opening scene of *The Simpsons*. Browne targets adult readers in a second cultural reference that links the couch scene to psychotherapy: the man sitting at the end staring intently at Willy the dreamer is unmistakably Sigmund Freud. Although some of the most overt references in picturebooks are based on individual works of art, these may still be multileveled and quite complex.

Not all illustrations that appear to parody a painting were intended to be interpreted in that manner. Shaun Tan admits that his illustration of the landing in *The Rabbits* (1998) could almost be read as "a satirical parody" of Australian naturalist painter E. Phillip Fox's *Landing of Captain Cook at Botany Bay, 1770*, but says that was not really his intention. On his website, Tan discusses at some length the source painting for his illustration "They came by water," which appears on the book's cover. *The Rabbits*, written by John Marsden, is a very simple, but dark, story about colonization: rabbits invade Australia and destroy the civilization of the native armadillo-like creatures. It is an allegory of the colonization of Australia by Europeans as well as the infestation of rabbits brought by the Europeans. Fox depicts the historical first landing of Cook and his crew in Australia, at Botany Bay in 1770; a sailor behind Captain Cook holds the large red flag with which they will claim the land for England. "Everything about the source painting by E. Phillips Fox contains a familiar ideology, all about progress and destiny, the planting of flags and the arrival of legitimate historical narrative," says Tan.[39] In his illustration, viewers are invited to read these same ideas "in a less recognisable and more challenging form." According to Tan, his illustration "borrows rather than alludes, evoking a certain 19th century European way of framing moments of historical significance, where key figures are actors on the world's stage, supernaturally well composed, monumental and mythical." The four central figures striding ashore in Fox's painting are retained as rabbits in identical stances. The commanding central figure of Captain Cook becomes the equally authoritative figure of the Captain of the rabbits. The rabbits wear similar clothing and carry the same accoutrements (flag and gun).

The second-in-command points his left arm at the armadillos on a distant hill that replace the two Aborigines of the original painting, while the soldier who points a gun at the Aborigines in Fox's painting is mirrored by a rabbit figure in the same position pointing a gun at the armadillos. As in the original, a fourth figure plants the large red flag. Tan points to the parallels between the illustration and the intertext: "There are similar lighting and atmospheric effects at work, although quite exaggerated, and the use of oils on canvas with thin yellow glazes emulates the technique used in paintings of the period." However, Tan reworks Fox's painting in his own inimitable style. Valleau rightly points out that the angular lines of the exaggerated rabbits emphasize their menacing and hostile nature, while the exaggeration of the ship (the large, curved bow) suggests "the overpowering effect the rabbits have on Australia."[40] Whereas Captain Cook's ship is anchored in the background and therefore appears quite small in the original, the captain of the rabbits' boat is closer to shore and seems to take on enormous proportions, dominating the entire illustration. Tan himself describes the scene in the following terms: "The ship leaps forth like a skyscraper or knife, echoed by scalpel-like shadows and pointed feet, collars and guns, the lighting is more theatrical than ever." Fox's positive, optimistic portrayal of colonization has been cleverly subverted to suggest a postcolonial message of its negative effects. However, the illustrator's intention is not to use Fox's painting for ideological or didactic purposes: "I wanted to introduce a surreal dreamlike quality, ambiguous in terms of mixed awe and dread, exaggerated but not caricatured or didactic. Most of all, I wanted to produce an image that was enigmatic and thought-provoking." Tan has certainly succeeded in doing so in this spread which haunts readers long after they have closed the book.

Parodic Play with Framed Paintings

When the artistic allusion is contained within a frame and hangs on a wall, young readers will often sense that they are being called upon to make what Umberto Eco calls an "inferential walk" outside the text, even if they do not have the competence to identify the artwork and decode the parody. Illustrators who use what René Payant refers to as *citation* (quotation) in painting[41] seldom choose the cited artwork randomly. Unlike the representation of other objects in a room (a vase on a table or a cushion on a chair), paintings evoke a multitude of intertextual associations dependent upon the viewer's experience. Often a single painting, either faithfully reproduced or humorously reworked, is added as a kind of visual joke that may only be appreciated by adults. Many such allusions are found in picturebooks that do not fall into the crossover category, where they provide a source of amusement for adult co-readers. In Tony Ross's "Le Petit Chaperon rouge" (1978), for example, the reproduction of the painting commonly known as *Whistler's Mother* hangs above the wolf disguised as granny. It highlights the fact that the wolf, which has just leaped out of bed to switch off the light after glimpsing his reflection in the mirror, does not look the least like an old lady. In the Norwegian picturebook *Fy Fabian* (Darn Fabian, 2001), the paintings that the illustrator Hilde Gammman hangs on the walls reflect the young cat-like protagonist's state of mind. Tranquil, conventional landscapes with familiar images, such as an elk in the sunset, adorn the walls of his home, where he feels secure with his parents whose long tails mirror his own. At school, a painting of the Mona Lisa hangs on the wall beside the teacher, who smiles reassuringly on the frightening first day. As he sits at a table drawing with the other children, none of whom have tails, Fabian's sense of difference and insecurity is emphasized by Picasso's distorted portrait of Maya with green hair (*Maya with a Doll*) and more especially by Van Gogh's self-portrait with a bandaged ear. This painting is particularly symbolic because the protagonist will attempt to cut off his tail. In the office of the doctor that Fabian visits after his self-mutilation, a reproduction of Edvard Munch's *The Scream* hangs directly above his head, reflecting his troubled state of mind.

The Japanese-born author and illustrator Satoshi Kitamura admits that his award-winning picturebook *Me and My Cat?* (1999) contains numerous allusions to artworks that go unnoticed. In addition to the names of Nicholas's cat (Leonardo) and "the next-door-neighbor cat" (Gioconda), several illustrations depict a painting in its entirety or in part to punctuate events taking place in the narrative. The paintings are reproduced in simple lines, but colours, composition, and even details are faithfully retained. After waking up one morning in the body of his cat, Nicholas tells himself not to panic and forces himself to consider the situation in an armchair, where he immediately falls asleep below a Japanese painting of a sleeping samurai. Leonardo, in Nicholas's body, does not like the protagonist and attacks him under a painting of Raphael's *St. George and the Dragon*. The painting, which hangs askew in a room that has been turned into a war zone by the angry cat-boy, is not fully depicted, but is still easily identifiable. The figure of the blonde princess who prays mystically in the background of Raphael's painting is echoed humorously by that of Nicholas's mystified, blonde mother, who witnesses her son fighting the cat from the same position in the background of Kitamura's illustration. In the following illustration, the worried mother holds her son, or rather "Leonardo-in-[Nicholas's]-shape," under her arm, in a parodic imitation of the *Madonna and Child* painting on the wall in the background. Another *Madonna and Child* is mimicked after the doctor's visit, as the mother holds her supposed son "tight in her arms." As in the previous scene, the mother's red and blue clothes and blonde hair echo those of the Madonna, but the formerly frenetic mother now sits quietly, albeit "still very upset," and still surrounded by chaotic clutter. A crooked painting of Raphael's *Deposition of Christ*, which was painted for a mother in memory of her son, hangs over the scene in which Nicholas-Leonardo is sprawled between his mother and the doctor. Kitamura's illustration may actually parody Michelangelo's *Pietà*, as the sculptor accused Raphael of plagiarism and having learned everything about art from him, which would make this a highly complex reference that most readers will indeed miss.

Often the visual joke includes a reworked detail in the painting itself. Browne also incorporates a framed version of *Whistler's Mother* into an illustration of *Gorilla* (1983), winner of the 1984 Kate Greenaway Award. Hanging on the wall behind the gorilla that has put on the father's hat and coat to take Hannah to the zoo is the familiar painting, but the subject's face has become that of a gorilla, just as the gorilla is being substituted for the girl's busy father in the story. Directly opposite the gorilla hang another hat and coat of Hannah's absent father, this time a grey hat and black coat, which may evoke vague reminiscences of the faceless subject of Magritte's painting *The Son of Man*. In crossover picturebooks, clever references of this nature are quite frequent. An example that even some children will appreciate is the humorous rendition of one of Monet's famous paintings of the bridge over the water lily pond at Giverny in Colin Thompson's *Looking for Atlantis*. Attentive readers will notice that a cartoon-like frog now sits on the bridge while one of the realistic fish that seem to have escaped from the aquarium and are swimming freely about the room has swum into the painting.

One of the paintings most commonly cited in this manner is the *Mona Lisa*, which is sometimes reproduced within a simple frame, sometimes in a very elaborate gold frame. It is the painting Ernest studies on the cover of *Ernest et Célestine au musée* while a bored Célestine tries to pull him away. In many cases, the painting is reworked slightly to create a visual joke. One of Jim Harris's illustrations for Susan Lowell's *The Three Javelinas* (1992), depicts the backsides of the eponymous porcine protagonists peering out their window at the coyote they have tricked, while the eyes of an amused Mona Lisa, whose enigmatic smile is almost a complicit smirk, glances sideways at them out of her frame. A smaller version of the comical illustration is repeated on the back cover of this witty Southwestern retelling of "The Three Pigs." Harris seems to have a predilection for Leonardo's iconic painting, no doubt due to its familiarity with very young readers. One of his illustrations for Mike Artell's *Petite Rouge: A Cajun Red Riding Hood* (2001) also contains a revisioned *Mona Lisa*. This time the reworking is more extensive, as he replaces Leonardo's model with a goose, in keeping with this version's main characters (Petite Rouge and her grandmother are geese). Mona Lisa seems to smile benevolently at Petite Rouge, Grand-mère, and the cat TeJean, who are rolling around on the floor in laughter after tricking Claude the gator. In both retellings, the painting punctuates the moment at which the protagonists get the best of their villainous opponent. Harris thus provides two possible explanations for Mona Lisa's enigmatic smile, both involving the witnessing of the downfall of a fairy-tale villain. In *Gorilla*, Anthony Browne gives the *Mona Lisa* a gorilla face in the painting that hangs on the wall as Hannah goes upstairs the night before her birthday with gorillas on her mind. Maurice Sendak's rendition of the *Mona Lisa* in *Higglety Pigglety Pop!* (1967) relies almost solely on recontextualization for its humorous effect. In this tribute to Sendak's dearly departed dog Jennie, the Sealyham terrier sitting on a chair at the table bears a surprising resemblance to the subject of the painting hanging above its head. In particular, the dog's mouth seems to reflect Mona Lisa's famous enigmatic smile. In a different manner, Dayal Kaur Khalsa recontextualizes the *Mona Lisa* in *Green Cat* (2002), which is a humorous retelling of the folktale *The Crowded Room*. The famous painting is one of the many eclectic items with which the Green Cat fills the room of two squabbling siblings in order to teach them an exaggerated lesson.

The *Mona Lisa* is not the only painting that Jim Harris hangs on the walls of his illustrations. While several are faithful reproductions of existing paintings, others are reworked in the manner of his Mona Lisas. *Petite Rouge* contains another parodic painting. When Petite Rouge, her grandmother, and the cat have laughed themselves out under the watchful eye of Mona Lisa, they all take a nap. With TeJean in her lap, Grand-mère sleeps in her big rocking chair in front of a parodic rendition of Grant Wood's *American Gothic*. The famous painting of a stern-looking country couple posed in front of a white house is one of the most familiar images in twentieth-century American art. By replacing the human figures with geese, Harris offers yet another comical treatment of one of the most parodied artworks in American popular culture. The small white house in the Carpenter Gothic architectural style is reproduced faithfully, as are the pitchfork and the couple's distinctive clothing (colonial print apron and overalls), but the woman's long neck is graced by a goose's head and the man's spectacles rest on a goose's beak. Despite the painting's popularity, many children will not recognize it, but they can still appreciate the comic effect of the portrait of the grandmother and the apparently deceased husband who is ever absent from the tale.

The Swedish-born Norwegian illustrator Fam Ekman often hangs simple reproductions of recognizable paintings on the walls in her illustrations, no doubt because in her childhood home in Stockholm, they had "a lot of strange and exciting paintings on the walls, that certainly meant a good deal to [her]."[42] A painting of a man in a bowler hat hangs on the wall in *Da solen gikk ned* (When the sun went down, 2002), where an earlier scene had depicted a man in a bowler hat peering out a window at five dour men in bowler hats holding up green apples as if they were about to throw them at the reader. In her parodic recasting of the tale of Little Red Riding Hood, *Rødhatten og Ulven* (Red Hat and the wolf, 1985), Fam Ekman hangs three simply drawn, but easily recognizable, paintings on the wall of the sparsely decorated living room. Reproduced in black and white, the paintings now reflect the tile floor, while the missing colour has been applied to the walls. The fact that all the paintings are French reminds readers that the original literary version was Perrault's, although Ekman's story, like so many retellings outside the French-speaking world, is more closely modelled on the Grimms' version. The paintings seem carefully chosen for their subject matter, although only a cultured elite may realize that they constitute a mise en abyme of themes in Ekman's narrative. Picasso's painting of Marie-Thérèse asleep in a chair, titled *The Dream*, reveals the fresh, naive sensuality and erotic appeal of a budding young woman, and it is thus that Little Red Riding Hood has often been represented by male authors and illustrators. Perhaps Ekman is even suggesting that Picasso, who painted *The Dream* at the little château of Boisgeloup, was a wolf who seduced the naive, young Marie-Thérèse. Chagall's painting, *I and the Village*, in which the green head of a youth and the whitish head of a cow stare fixedly at each other, reflects the subject of Ekman's retelling, in which a naive young boy named Little Red Hat encounters the wolf when he goes to the city (this painting dates from Chagall's first trip to Paris). Degas's pastel *The Tub* announces the scene in which the wolf surprises the grandmother taking a bath in an old-fashioned tub filled to the top, a comical contrast with the original's young bather whose body is entirely exposed to the viewer. Unlike the other spreads in the book, the two plates of the grandmother in the tub are in black and white, as is Ekman's reproduction of Degas's pastel. While this helps to draw attention to the parody, only adult readers are likely to make the association.

The pertinence of the citations in *Rødhatten og ulven* would suggest that they were deliberately chosen, but Ekman admitted, in an e-mail dated January 19, 2001, that the selection of these particular paintings had been based largely on the fact that they would be "fun to draw" and would lend themselves well to her simplified manner of "re-doing" them. However, she did find the theory about the tub scene in particular "very interesting" and admitted that what she "thinks" does not necessarily reflect what she is doing "unconsciously." When illustrators pay homage to specific artists and art works, it is not always in the visibly intentional manner of Anthony Browne.

Like Ekman's paintings in *Rødhatten og ulven*, those hanging on the walls in Browne's *The Big Baby* generally quote specific works fairly accurately, but one is deliberately and playfully misquoted. In both cases, the allusions have a parodic function and constitute a playful mise en abyme of events and themes in the story. The paintings reproduced faithfully are entirely dependent upon recontextualization for their parodic effect. Munch's *The Sick Child* hangs above Mr. Young who, when he feels the least bit ill, becomes, in his wife's terms, "a Big Baby." Unlike many of his better-known expressionist paintings, the one of Munch's sick sister remains anchored in reality, as does the scene it mirrors below of John's father sick in bed. In contrast, Dali's famous painting *Sleep*, which depicts a large face sleeping propped up on crutches, is used to reflect the surreal situation that results when Mr. Young drinks a whole bottle of "Elixa de Yoof" tonic in his obsessive desire for eternal youth, and awakes to find a baby's body attached to his disproportionate, adult-sized head. The last painting is much less well known, but the manner in which Browne misquotes it assures that it will catch the attention of viewers of all ages. When

John's father calls Mrs. Young into the bedroom later to tell her about his "TERRIBLE dream," it is no longer the Munch that hangs over the bed but a playful reworking of John Henry Fuseli's romantic work titled *The Nightmare*, in which John's baby-father has replaced the little, grinning demon which sits on the sleeping woman in the original (the substitution of a dragon's head for the luminescent horse's head is no doubt simply because children will consider it more nightmarish). In *Piggybook* (1986), Browne reworks Gainsborough's *Robert Andrews and His Wife* in a similarly playful and simple manner. Once again, the composition respects the original, but Robert Andrews now has a pig's head and only the blank form of his wife's contour remains on the bench. Children do not have to recognize the painting to deduce that the absent feminine figure represents Mrs. Piggot, who has finally walked out on her chauvinist pig husband and sons.[43] When the artistic allusion takes the form of a more or less recognizable painting hanging on a wall, the frame acts as a marker signalling the presence of Art and preparing the reader for a potential parody.

Multi-Level Parodies

Some picturebooks, notably those by Anthony Browne, contain sophisticated, multi-level parodies that are at once intertextual and intratextual. In his modern fairy tale *The Tunnel*, Browne mimics Walter Crane's famous illustration of the encounter of Little Red Riding Hood with the wolf from his 1875 toybook *Little Red Riding Hood*. The anthropomorphized wolf dressed in peasant clothes and leaning on a twisted walking stick is integrated into the bark of an enormous tree that dominates the entire doublespread in which Rose flees through the forest. Browne creates an eery, nightmarish atmosphere with one of the surrealist details that are the signature of his work: a large branch is supported by a crutch reminiscent of the one that props up the face in Dali's *Sleep*, which would appear four years later in *The Big Baby*. By surrealistically mimicking Crane's well-known nineteenth-century illustration, the contemporary picturebook artist offers a very masterful blending of styles. While young readers will certainly make out the wolf in the tree, the allusion seems to be addressed particularly to cultured adult viewers able to recognize it as Crane's work. Attentive young readers may nonetheless recognize the parodic intent since Browne carefully adds an intermediary level to the intertextual referencing. A framed print of Crane's famous illustration hangs conspicuously on Rose's bedroom wall, one of several allusions to the story of Little Red Riding Hood to be found in the first spread of *The Tunnel*.

This technique is not reserved only for lesser known art works. Munch's famous expressionist painting *The Scream* was familiar to many young people even before the image became a popular culture icon thanks to the 1996 thriller *Scream*. Miles Hyman nonetheless ensures that children decode the parodic intention in his illustration of a screaming woman in the 1994 picturebook *Le Cochon à l'oreille coupée* (The pig with the cut ear). A partial view of Munch's painting is depicted in the upper left-hand corner of the same doublespread. The scream that issues from the fat lady "squeezed into a fuchsia suit" when she sees a pig in the museum interrupts the latter's contemplation, not of *The Scream*, but of "an elongated woman by Modigliani." A similar reference in Browne's *Voices in the Park* is less transparent and more complex. The mouth of a woman (or rather a female simian) is wide open as she screams. It is only in a later illustration, which provides a close-up of the newspaper the gorilla is reading on the park bench, that we notice the reproduction of *The Scream* on the front page. If readers turn back to the original illustration, they will notice that the trees are echoing the scream in the background.

In *Piggybook*, the parodic allusion that Browne reworks subsequently is more easily identifiable as it is contained within a frame. The portrait hanging in the Piggots' living room at the beginning of the book is an immediately recognizable rendition of Franz Hals's *The Laughing Cavalier*, but when this scene "*en rose*" is repeated toward the end of the book "*en bleu*" (this reflects the evolution of the work of the Dutch master, whose colours were bright in the earlier works and sober in the later ones), the laughing cavalier has been replaced by a pig in the same dignified pose, while Mr. Piggot and his sons have been transformed into "real" pigs rooting around on the floor for scraps in a highly undignified manner. "The Laughing Pig" portrait is a parody "in the second degree" (to borrow Gérard Genette's terminology in *Palimpsestes: la littérature au second degré*), because it mimics Browne's earlier version of *The Laughing Cavalier*, itself an ironic recontextualization of the Hals's masterpiece. Browne's double-coded parody provides a second level accessible to the many readers—adults as well as children—who will not recognize the Dutch master's most famous painting.

Browne uses a similar strategy in *Willy the Dreamer*. In the first illustration, Willy dreams in a pink armchair beneath a faithful quotation of Magritte's *Castle in the Pyrenees*, but on the last page the huge rock floating above the sea has taken on Willy's features. As in *Piggybook*, the second picture offers a kind of surrealistic parody, not only of Magritte's painting but also of Browne's own illustration (the carpet has become grass, the lines of the armchair are visible through the protagonist, a Willy pattern has replaced the flowers on the wallpaper, etc.). The semi-transparent Willy that Browne now depicts in the armchair evokes reminiscences of Magritte's *This Is Not a Pipe*. He seems to be suggesting that "this is not a chimp," but Jane Doonan feels that the protagonist's wink saves him from the fate of a Sherlock Holmes, who is killed by his creator.[44] The cover illustrations add further layers to the parody. On the front cover, Willy floats in an armchair that has partially turned to stone and the seascape below, where a full-scale boat in a bottle floats on the water, is now full of iconic bananas (a banana lighthouse, banana sailboats, banana fish). On the back cover, Willy, still dreaming, flies off into the sunset on his rock-armchair. Multi-level parodies involving citations of canonical art provide layers of complexity for readers of all ages. Young readers may only decode the intratextual allusion to a painting depicted in the same book by the illustrator, without realizing that it is a citation of the work of another artist. For more competent readers, with greater decoding skills, these crossover picturebooks offer a richer and more sophisticated intertextual reading experience.

Artists' Studios and Museums

Often illustrators are not content to quote or misquote one or more isolated paintings, but extend the parody to an entire collection of artworks. When Willy dreams that he is a painter in *Willy the Dreamer*, he is depicted in an artist's studio surrounded by parodic citations of several of Magritte's most famous paintings, each bearing Browne's characteristic signature. This page is, as Erica Hateley rightly puts it, "a culmination" of the illustrator's Magrittian references: "The visual changes that theoretically render these paintings as parodic are all consistent with Browne's use of bananas and chimps through-out his works, particularly in those books where Willy appears."[45] A close look at Magritte's famous pipe reveals that it is actually a banana. Bananas replace the apple that dissimulates the face in *The Son of Man*, the enormous nose in *The Philosopher's Lamp*, and the bread in *The Golden Legend*. Although Browne retains the shape of the apple in *The Postcard*, it has nonetheless taken on the colour of a banana, suggesting another work, *This Is Not an Apple*. Magritte's reworking of the Venus de Milo, *The Flying Statue*, receives the head of a gorilla in Browne's recasting, which evokes yet another Magritte citation. Willy the painter adopts the same stance as the artist who stands painting a real-looking, one-armed nude in *Attempting the Impossible*. On the top left, Browne playfully reproduces the painting titled *Not to Be Reproduced*, adding chimpanzee-like ears to the reflection Willy contemplates in the mirror. Nor is Browne content to reproduce the painting only once, but develops it into another of his clever multi-level parodies. When Willy dreams of fierce monsters toward the end of the book, the reflection with the oversized ears has now stepped backward out of the mirror and looks at an even more frightening image, not of the back of his head, as in the original, but a frontal view of a monstrous whiskered and fanged creature whose banana ears give the hairy head the look of a Viking in a horned warrior helmet. The book reproduced from the original painting is still sitting on the mantelpiece, but the title is now clearly legible. Attentive readers will note that the book actually has two titles, both suggestive of dual personalities: *Beauty and the Beast*, according to the spine, and *Dr. Jekyll and Mr. Hyde*, according to the front cover.

Gilles Bachelet's *Mon chat le plus bête du monde* (English trans., *My Cat, the Silliest Cat in the World*), published in France in 2004, evokes reminiscences of Browne's *Willy the Dreamer*. In Bachelet's comical story, the narrator is a painter and the protagonist is his pet/subject, a feline who looks decidedly like an elephant. Just as Browne devotes a plate to the artworks of Willy the painter, Bachelet dedicates an entire page to pastiches of famous paintings that present the narrator's elephant/cat: Botticelli, Manet, Picasso, Magritte, Dali, Chagall, Cézanne, and Matisse. The numerous artistic references amuse adult readers of *Mon chat le plus bête du monde*, just as they do adult readers of *Willy the Dreamer*. In another illustration that depicts the narrator painting a portrait of his cat/elephant, several books sit on a table, none of which have been chosen randomly. One book is by Jean de Brunhoff, the creator of *Babar*, while another is devoted to Magritte. The artist's name automatically brings to mind his most famous painting *Ceci n'est pas une pipe*, aka *The Treachery of Images*, undoubtedly a comment on this cat that is not a cat, but an elephant. *Mon chat le plus bête du monde* won the Prix Baobab de l'Album at the Salon du Livre de jeunesse de Montreuil in the award's second year of existence in 2004.

The "strange landscape" where a vulnerable-looking Willy finds himself in another illustration of *Willy the Dreamer* is the vast desert-like expanse of Dali's most famous painting *The Persistence of Memory*, which a plague of bananas has rendered even stranger. The artist's characteristic limpid clocks have been replaced with bananas, with one exception: the clock that melts on a banana has perhaps been retained to ensure recognition of the Dali reference. The rocky cliff in the background has been zoomorphized to represent the profile of a sleeping gorilla. Into the familiar landscape, Browne introduces motifs from other famous works by Dali: the subject of *Sleep* is now a sleeping banana, the "burning giraffe" is a flaming banana, and hanging from one of Dali's open drawers is a banana peel. For the nightmarish plate in which Willy can't run, Browne borrows the setting of De Chirico's *The Uncertainty of the Poet*: the hauntingly empty arcaded square, the distant train under a cloud of smoke, the abrupt shadows, and the banana tree in the foreground (which some viewers unfamiliar with the painting will mistake for a parodic addition). Illustrators often borrow the settings of famous paintings. Older readers may know the originals, adding intertextual meaning, whereas for young readers it merely creates a particular, desired atmosphere. The illustrator replaces De Chirico's torso with Willy and, in the background, adds the dark figure and long shadow of Buster Nose pursuing the frozen protagonist. Even the title page of *Willy the Dreamer* contains a Magritte reference, a reworking of one of the artist's *Key to Dreams* series, in which, as in the original, only a single label ("banana") actually corresponds to the object. Magritte's original has been described as "a school reading primer gone wrong," explaining the tremendous appeal of this particular image with young readers.[46]

In the sequel to *Willy the Dreamer*, *Willy's Pictures* (2000), the chimpanzee protagonist is an artist who reworks his favourite pictures. Willy does not have an artist's studio like the one he dreamed about in the previous book, but he is depicted working at a desk surrounded by his artist's tools. In the first plate, Willy is painting his version of Botticelli's *Birth of Venus*, while a reproduction of the original sits on the desk beside him. In Willy's rendition, titled "The Birthday Suit," the goddess on the shell has been replaced by a gorilla whose hands hide its private parts. Simian Zephyrs now blow the goddess to shore, while the cloak is being offered to Venus, not by one of the Horae, but by Willy, whose arms are in the same position as he proffers the advice: "Quick, cover yourself up!" A blushing Willy runs from the women's changing room in a reworked version of Jean-Auguste-Dominique Ingres's *The Turkish Bath*, now humorously filled with lolling female gorillas who, except for the central figure with her back to the viewer, have been modestly "covered up" by Browne. In Seurat's *Sunday Afternoon on the Island of the Grande Jatte*, all the humans have predictably been replaced by simians, but young viewers will not overlook the fact that the pet monkey on a leash in the foreground has undergone the opposite transformation and is now a human on all fours. Willy's collection of pictures also includes a simian Mona Lisa, whose pose, serenity, and gaze capture those of Leonardo's despite the gorilla features. Even the *sfumato* background is scrupulously retained, but with a surrealist touch, as it is possible to make out body parts and animal heads in the indistinct shapes. Browne does, however, add one particularly humorous touch to "the mysterious smile," curling Mona Lisa's lips to suggest that she has no teeth. Attentive readers will notice the upper dentures sitting on the ledge beside her. The enigmatic smile of this Mona Lisa is either the result of taking out her dentures or wearing only a half set. In addition, she holds a toy Willy maternally in her folded arms.

Willy is not the only familiar character to feature in these reworked paintings; young readers familiar with Browne's work will immediately recognize the protagonist's nemesis Buster Nose. In front of the shuttered shops of Edward Hopper's *Early Sunday Morning*, Willy is depicted taking his tormentor Buster Nose for a walk on a leash. Browne turns Jan van Eyck's *The Arnolfini Marriage* into "My Nightmare," by replacing the Arnolfini couple with Buster and Millie Nose, while Willy issues a Munch-like scream in the foreground of the painting, a position originally occupied by a dog. Perhaps the cleverest touch is the reworking of the mise en abyme in the painting: the convex mirror at the back that reflects the couple, as well as the artist in the original—so admired by André Gide—is replaced by a television set that also reflects the couple and the artist, in this case Willy. Willy replaces the straw-stuffed mannequin that four women toss in a blanket in Goya's *The Straw Mannequin*, while the women themselves have become brightly-dressed gorillas.

Several of the reworked paintings in *Willy's Pictures* focus on the theme of the artist and his creation. Willy is substituted for one of the peasant women in Millet's *The Gleaners*, who become "The Kind Women" helping him paint the grass, while croissants and loaves of bread replace the hay stacks in the background. The illustration titled "Coming to Life" apes, with amazing likeness, Michelangelo's *The Creation of Man* from the ceiling fresco in the

Sistine Chapel. Browne manages to capture the pose and muscular physique of Michelangelo's Adam in his gorilla rendition of the first man. Only the hand that reaches out to god appears to be human, while God's hand has been replaced by Willy's chimp hand holding a paintbrush. The artist is, after all, the creator who gives life to his gorilla-man. Willy's "Nearly a Self-Portrait" mimics Frida Kahlo's *Self-Portrait with Monkeys*, which Browne likes because "she seems to be showing a similarity between herself and the monkeys." In Browne's rendition, the resemblance between the artist and the monkeys is truly striking! The illustrator also replaces the monkey peering from the foliage in the background with the head of Diego Rivera. The final image once again depicts Willy's desk, but the artist is absent and a chimpanzee mask lies on the desk, while Willy's sweater hangs over the chair as Browne himself walks out. The true artist is the subject of Willy's portrait on the cover, Anthony Browne himself.

Whereas Browne presents an artist's studio full of parodic citations of works by the same artist in *Willy the Dreamer* and an artist's collection of paintings in *Willy's Pictures*, the French author-illustrator Yvan Pommaux creates a large private collection of eclectic art works in *John Chatterton détective*, which won the Deutscher Jugendliteraturpreis in 1995. This retelling of "Little Red Riding Hood" is the first in a series of picturebooks featuring a cat detective who solves mysteries based on well-known fairy tales. A doublespread depicts Little Red Riding Hood being held hostage by an obsessed art collector-wolf to obtain from her mother the one painting he needs to complete his "wolf collection," "Le loup bleu sur fond blanc" (Blue wolf on a white background). As in Browne's books, an animal is substituted for the human subjects in the portraits and sculptures reproduced in the wolf's art collection. The coveted painting, "Le loup bleu sur fond blanc," which John Chatterton inherits for solving the case of the missing girl in red, is highly reminiscent of Keith Haring's *Barking Dog*, but Pommaux told me it is the work of a friend who is influenced by Haring. The wolf's passionate interest in this particular piece is no doubt due to the fact that he himself dresses entirely in blue. The unifying theme of the wolf's eclectic collection is the lupine subject. As I have pointed out elsewhere, this is not just a case of a wolf collecting portraits of wolves as a human collects portraits of humans.[47] This wolf seems to have a narcissistic obsession with his own image and his collection of wolf paintings constitutes as many mirror images of the collector himself.

The wolf's eclectic art collection will amuse children, but only cultured adult viewers will be able to decode the parodied works. Although the originals are not depicted with the same degree of faithfulness as Browne's, it is nonetheless possible to label many of the artworks borrowed from the Western tradition: a wolf poses, sword at his side, in a Van Dyck-style portrait, next to a wolf lounging in a setting reminiscent of Watteau or Fragonard. A wolf's head pronouncing the word "loup" parodies Magritte's word-images, many of which includes the names of animals. Hals's *The*

Figure 4.7   John Chatterton détective by Yvan Pommaux, copyright © 1993 L'École des loisirs, reprinted by permission of Yvan Pommaux.

Laughing Cavalier is a scowling wolf, while Giacometti's *Walking Man II* has become a "Walking Wolf II," whose purposeful stride mimics not only the well-known sculpture, but also the stance of the wolf himself as he talks on his cell phone. The sculpture of a realistic howling wolf, positioned so that it seems to be engaged in conversation with the wolf talking on the cell phone, is reminiscent of Antoine-Louis Barye's lifelike animal sculptures. In the opposite corner, a Dadaist sculpture is displayed next to a small analytical cubist painting. A wrapped and tied wolf's head parodies Christo's wrapped objects, particularly *Packed Horse*. The ominous-looking black sculpture in the foreground is not unlike Alexander Calder's large stabiles made out of heavy metal, one of which is aptly titled *The Black Beast*. A wire sculpture at the far right transparently parodies the American sculptor's earlier wire animals, but, ironically, it resembles his *Sow* more closely than the she-wolf in *Romulus and Remus*, a possible allusion to another fairy tale in which the wolf plays a prominent role. Pommaux admitted, rather surprisingly, that he hadn't given the references any thought when he drew the wolf's art gallery. He later realized he should have because the wolf collection fascinates adult readers. In fact, it provoked so much interest from adults that, with the collaboration of his wife and daughter, he actually created a "musée du loup" which has toured libraries extensively.[48]

An animal is also substituted for the human subjects in the portraits and sculptures in the museum that Fam Ekman depicts in *Kattens Skrekk* (The cat's terror, 1992), the story of a cat with an obsessive fear of dogs. In this cat's world, dogs are to be found everywhere, even "in the museum," which has a canine curator. The cat peers fearfully in the exit of a room full of artworks with canine subjects. Ekman's museum collection, like Pommaux's private collection, quotes specific works of art. The presence of the iconic *Mona Lisa*, humorously adorned with dog ears, is certain to catch the attention of even the youngest readers, alerting them to the parodic intent in the citations. Ekman's selection of artworks seems to be less fortuitous than Pommaux's. The inclusion of the canine version of Gianlorenzo Bernini's life-size marble sculpture of *David*, the young shepherd who fearlessly slew the giant Goliath, is not revealed until later in the book. The only work of art in the museum with a human subject is Munch's *The Scream*, which is given a prominent position in the centre foreground below the terrified cat, on a partition that separates it from the other works. As the most famous example of the expressionist movement, art "born out of anxiety,"[49] *The Scream* appropriately evokes the cat's anguish. One might wonder why Ekman did not turn the screaming figure into a cat by adding ears and whiskers, but she was perhaps afraid that the painting would no longer be recognizable or that the cat would be mistaken for another dog. In an e-mail to me, she admitted having trouble seeing the ears on the *Mona Lisa*.[50] Next to the fearful face of the cat in the doorway are citations of Kasimir Malevich's *Black Square* and *Black Circle*. In the same manner

Figure 4.8 Kattens Skrekk by Fam Ekman, copyright © 1992 Fam Ekman and J. W. Cappelens Forlag a.s, reprinted by permission of Fam Ekman and Cappelen Damm.

that the "pure feeling" of Malevitch's early Suprematist works is expressed in black and white, "the cold, paralyzing intensity of the . . . feelings" of the terrified cat peering in the doorway is communicated visually by Ekman in stark black-and-white wood engravings. [51] It is as if Malevitch's black-and-white technique is applied to all the referenced artworks to make the cat's fear more tangible.

The Australian picturebook artist Tohby Riddle depicts the four animal protagonists of *The Great Escape from City Zoo* (1997), a flamingo, elephant, anteater, and tortoise, in a museum wearing the comical disguises (uniforms of human professions) that the runaways believe will allow them to fit in. On the walls behind them are three paintings, two of which are surrealist works particularly in keeping with Riddle's fantastic narrative. In addition to a Vasarely, Riddle depicts De Chirico's *Mystery and Melancholy of a Street* and, most notably Magritte's *Ceci n'est pas une pipe*. These puzzled animals in their incongruous disguises are not what they seem to be either; they are certainly not art lovers. Young readers are more apt to recognize the illustrator's parodic intention when artistic allusions are set in an artist's studio, an art gallery, or a museum.

Into a Dream World

References to art are used to shift from "reality" into a dream world in a number of the picturebooks already mentioned, including Anthony Browne's *Through the Magic Mirror* and *Willy the Dreamer*. In Fam Ekman's *Kattens Skrekk* (1992), the black-and-white illustrations contrast strikingly with the coloured pictures of the cat's dream embedded in the middle of the story, where the illustrator appropriates three of Rousseau's best-known paintings. For the sequence in which the cat dreams that he is a shepherd bitten by a large dog while asleep in the desert, Ekman parodies *The Sleeping Gypsy*. The position of the feline has been playfully inverted by superimposing the cat protagonist's head on the sleeping gypsy who is now a wide awake shepherd. The parody is continued in a second illustration that suggests the ambiguity inherent in the Norwegian title *Kattens Skrekk* which, like *katteskrekk*, could mean "being afraid of cats," as well as "what cats are afraid of." Instead of reacting with fear, as readers anticipate, the cat, fully awake and upright, uses the shepherd's staff, conveniently provided by the original artist, to beat the crying dog for disturbing his peaceful sleep. The substitution of a shepherd for the gypsy in the original will remind some readers of the dog-*David* sculpture in the museum. In his dream the cat is cast in the role of the fearless young conqueror of Goliath. A parodic rendition of *Portrait of a Woman* accompanies the next sequence, in which the cat protagonist, occupying the same position as the tiny cat in the original, tells his mother what happened, while the dog, a new element, stands shamefacedly on the other side. The angry mother cat's striking yellow hat is borrowed from the painting parodied in the following plate, where she punishes the dog by having him hitched to *Old Junier's Cart* to take them and all their relatives on a ride through a particularly hilly region of Sweden. The original painting was a cat's nightmare, as it contained three dogs, but Ekman nonetheless retains only the black dog that Rousseau insisted on painting under the cart in spite of suggestions that it was too large; she playfully makes it even larger to replace the mare hitched to the cart. Ekman's reworkings of Rousseau's celebrated paintings constitute humorous illustrations that appeal to very young readers, but the witty, sophisticated artistic references can only be fully appreciated by savvy adult art lovers.

The very same year that Ekman published *Kattens Skrekk*, on the other side of the Atlantic the American author-illustrator Dav Pilkey published a book about cats that uses artistic allusions in a strikingly similar manner. Like Ekman's book, Pilkey's *When Cats Dream* (1992) begins and ends in black and white, evoking the world as cats see it when they are awake, and uses colour in the central illustrations to evoke cats' dreams. In a black and white "softwarm lap," which turns out to be that of Whistler's Mother from the stark, ascetic canvas pertinently titled *Arrangement in Grey and Black No. 1: Portrait of the Artist's Mother*, Pilkey's cat falls asleep and the world becomes increasingly strange and more vividly coloured, as the cat moves into fantastic, Chagall-like dreamscapes. A series of ever more colourful and distorted versions of Whistler's painting marks the transition from the waking world to the world of dreams. In the final image, a green glow lights up the grinning face of Whistler's Mother, who kicks off her shoes and dons sunglasses as she basks in the rays of a large, bright yellow, crescent moon that seems to invade the room. One of the coloured doublespreads borrows Chagall's palette, his geometrical forms, and several motifs from *I and the Village*, but the familiar elements are transposed: the magical blossoming branch in the lower triangle of a circular form now illuminates the inside of the house on the right, the head of the cat in the foreground mimics the cow's, the house from which the cat has just escaped is added to the row of houses on the hill in the background, and a tiny Whistler's Mother can be seen still sitting in her chair inside. The final doublespread is a bricolage of motifs from different paintings: the cat and window from Chagall's *Paris Through the Window* join a feline version of one of his violinists.

To evoke cats dreaming in the jungle, Pilkey shifts temporarily to Rousseau's primitive visual world, in which large, predatory cats are often depicted. Not surprisingly, Pilkey takes inspiration from the aptly named painting *The Dream*, in the centre of which two large, wide-eyed cats gaze through the abundant undergrowth at the viewer. In the illustrator's rendition, two cats still peer through the grass at the reader but they are housecats after smaller prey (mice, birds, and fish) and they have been separated: on the right is a fearful-looking black and white cat, while on the left is a larger and fiercer-looking orange and black-striped cat in a predatory pose. Pilkey retains several other details from the painting, including the white-edged grass, the huge pink flowers, and the pale sun in a turquoise sky. The story's open ending has the cat falling asleep in a monochromatic Mona Lisa's arms, presumably to resume its colourful dreams. Ekman and Pilkey use artistic allusions very masterfully to shift their narratives from the "real" world into a fantastic dream world. Very young readers will be conscious of the striking change in atmosphere, while more cultured readers will have access to further layers of meaning.

Jochen Weber of the International Youth Library in Munich rightly wonders if a picturebook like Melanie Kemmler's *Der hölzerne Mann* is a book for small children, a book for experienced adults camouflaged as a book for small children, or both. Better yet, he proposes, perhaps it is simply a picturebook, unconcerned by the question of audience.[52] Yet the question of audience is inevitably raised in discussions of picturebooks containing artistic allusions. Like other forms of intertextuality, references to artworks would seem to be inaccessible to most children in light of their limited cultural heritage. According to Pierre Bourdieu, "a work of art has meaning and interest only for someone who possesses the cultural competence, that is, the code, into which it is encoded." In a similar vein, the American art critic and philosophy professor Arthur Danto states: "To see something as art requires something the eye cannot descry—an atmosphere of artistic theory, a knowledge of the history of art: an artworld."[53] It has been suggested that allusions to the visual arts in picturebooks address the adults who mediate children's books, including parents, librarians, and educators. Some critics feel that they are directed at an elite audience whose opinion carries weight, notably reviewers and critics, in the hope of winning acclaim from the children's book establishment.[54] Certainly some references are present for the entertainment of adults, either in their role of co-readers or as readers of picturebooks in their own right. Stian Hole admits: "I always like to send some postcards to the adult readers, since I appreciate humour when I read picture books with my children."[55] Although most of the picturebooks discussed in this chapter contain only a small amount of simple text and can therefore be appreciated on one level by very young children, many of the more subtle references may go over the heads of even adult readers. Shortly after the French edition of Browne's *Willy the Dreamer* was published, a salesperson at Chantelivre, a large children's book store in Paris, told me that she and her colleagues had not yet been able to decode all of the allusions in the illustrations. The extraordinary success of Browne's picturebooks is due to a large extent to their ability to appeal to readers at opposite ends of the sophistication spectrum.

Anthony Browne is now amused by the stinging criticism of one of his publisher's representatives, who claimed that he was "on an ego trip because the books weren't for children, like the Mr Men" books. His references are often considered too sophisticated for the conventional children's book market, which is why, as Julia Eccleshare points out, "Browne's books have played a central role in the move towards picture books for older children."[56] They have also been influential in the move toward crossover picturebooks. Many of the picturebooks examined in this chapter seem to assume a great deal of art history knowledge on the part of the reader, yet recognizing the artistic allusions is not a prerequisite for enjoying the book. The creators of these picturebooks offer their audience an array of reading experiences that range from the simple entertainment of discovering intertextual references and visual jokes through to decoding complex layers of meaning. Some of the visual jokes and puns are presented as minute details which young readers are quick to identify. Very young children can appreciate the banana and simian motifs that run through Browne's books. Older readers will recognize the general style and graphic vocabulary being mimicked. More sophisticated readers will identify references to specific paintings. With each revisit, readers of all ages will make new discoveries.

It is a mistake to presume, however, that adult readers necessarily decode the artistic allusions or even that they perceive more than child readers. Although John Stephens claims that "the dialogic relationship with Magritte and Dali" established in *Willy the Dreamer* would most likely pass unnoticed by a very young child, he nonetheless rightly points out that the child reader is often quicker to notice the complex intertextual and intratextual references which characterise Browne's work.[57] These picturebook artists obviously make certain assumptions about their audience's ability to take pleasure in intertextual allusions to artworks. Browne himself is convinced that children enjoy his visual games and notice many visual jokes better than adults. He feels, however, that they are encouraged to lose this skill as they get older. Many illustrators consider young readers more competent at reading visual images than adults. After expressing her fondness for artists whose works convey a distinctive pleasure and emotion (she cites Matisse, Dubuffet, Klee, and Picasso), Katy Couprie says that in her books she wants to create her own personal images without any rigid, preconceived idea of what children are or are not capable of appreciating or understanding. In her view, children constitute a more receptive audience for her images than adults: "If there are any people able to appreciate all the images, it is definitely children. It is adults who have problems with my images."[58] Stian Hole agrees and his remarks serve as a caution to all adults and especially to children's literature scholars:

> . . . I don't have the key to know precisely how children of different ages interpret the images and the text. Children and adults will always bring different baggage to the book. I believe some children probably read some of these "hidden messages" differently from grown-ups, but that doesn't necessarily mean that they are wrong or that they "miss" something. On the contrary, I often find it liberating how children are more open and straightforward in their confrontation with images and literature than adults. Children are not afraid of what they don't understand.[59]

While some allusions to artworks may be adult-oriented, these picturebooks are also meant for children. Picturebook artists embrace strategies that facilitate the decoding of artistic allusions and ensure the complicity of their young readers. They often choose paintings that have become popular icons in children's literature, such as the *Mona Lisa* or *The Scream*. When less known paintings are referenced, the paratextual matter may provide some assistance in recognizing the allusions. In Kelek's version of Perrault's *Contes*, an afterword subtly comes to the aid of readers by providing clues for decoding two of the references. It informs readers that the illustrator "puts *mère-grand* in the bed of a Carpaccio" and "for Beauty borrows from Titian the pose of Venus," but it does not identify the specific paintings. Even in the case of Titian, the indication remains vague, as the artist painted multiple Venuses. Despite the impressionist style of Hirokazu Miyazaki's illustrations for *Wani-kun no e-nikki* (Little Crocodile's illustrated diary, 1991), few adult readers would realize that the protagonist painting on a home-made boat is inspired by Manet's painting *Monet Working on His Boat in Argenteuil* without the assistance of the blurb on the back flap of the dust jacket. The painting is not named, but the blurb steers readers in the right direction: "Painting on boats suited the Impressionists. I guess Little Crocodile imagined himself being a 'Manet' when he painted." A visual clue

Figure 4.9 Wani-kun no e-nikki by Hirokazu Miyazaki, copyright © 1991 BL Publishing, reprinted by permission of BL Publishing.

is added in the form of an illustration on the back flap: the picture of Little Crocodile holding an umbrella over his head as he paints raindrops in the rain pokes fun at the advocates of painting *en plein air*, which was particularly popular with the impressionists. In Miyazawa's Little Crocodile story, as in Kelek's *Contes*, readers who peruse the paratext are encouraged to make an "inferential walk" through the works of a specific artist.

The substitution of animals for the human subjects of well-known works is another common strategy in picturebooks, as readers who do not have the competence to understand the significance of the allusion or even to identify the original artwork, will at least recognize the intent to parody and appreciate the humorous and playful treatment of pre-existing pieces of art. Illustrators may also have recourse to repetition, multiplying the allusions to the same painting or detail in order to ensure eventual decoding. Browne is not the only illustrator to engage in the repeated reference to a particular work of art within his oeuvre. The recurrence of Millet's *The Gleaners* in Mitsumasa Anno's books has already been mentioned. Such self-referentiality is perhaps a tongue-in-cheek attempt to appropriate definitively these iconic paintings. Several years before publishing *Anno's Magic Seeds*, the artist admitted during an interview: "I await the day when today's children will be adults. They will go to see the paintings in the Louvre and will say: 'Millet did that after Mr. Anno!'"[60] That is no doubt what the Magritte estate fears will happen when Browne's readers eventually encounter the surrealist painter's works in museums.

Whereas some readers bring to a picturebook their knowledge of the artworks being quoted, other readers will later approach these artworks using the picturebook as their point of reference. Without insisting, as Anno does, on the appropriation of a pre-existing work of art, Vladimir Radunsky also reflects on the future reaction of his young readers when they encounter the Renaissance paintings he quotes in *The Mighty Asparagus*: "Perhaps someday when the children see the originals of these paintings, they will remember where they saw them first and will treat them as old friends."[61] For some young readers, the normal intertextual process is reversed and they learn to recognize artworks through the illustrations of picturebook artists. These picturebooks prepare children to meet the world's artistic traditions and help them to build a cultural repertoire, while at the same time fostering "a sense of what is valuable in the culture's past."[62] In a sense these illustrators are also connecting their own work to that of a canonical cultural heritage.

In some cases, picturebook artists are now referencing the fine arts through the work of another contemporary illustrator. Sören Jessen includes a very obvious allusion to Anthony Browne in *Gaven*. On one of the surrealistic central spreads, a simian sits in a banana boat fishing, having baited his line with a banana. A huge banana has been stabbed on the end of a gigantic Magritte-like fork that stands upright in the boat like a strange mast, evoking reminiscences of surrealist paintings. A similar-looking fork is featured in Magritte's

The Portrait and the Spanish surrealist Joan Miró depicts the twisted tines of a fork stabbing a potato in *Still Life with Old Shoe*. The double-coded allusion to surrealist art and to Browne is evident even before the attentive reader sees the initials AB (Anthony Browne) on the front of the wooden boat. The initials have a second meaning that can only be decoded by Danish speakers, as AB are also the first letters in the Danish three-letter word for monkey (*abe*).[63] Although there is no explicit reference to Browne in *The Great Escape*, it is quite possible that Riddle's quotation of *Ceci n'est pas une pipe* alludes more to the British illustrator, who has made it a popular icon in children's literature, than to Magritte. Certainly most child readers are far more apt to associate it with Browne than with the surrealist artist.

Some picturebooks with this type of referencing are intended to educate the reader about artists or art movements. However, the majority of picturebooks which fall into the crossover category use artistic allusion primarily to serve the fictional narrative by establishing a setting or mood, or by adding information about the characters or events. While they could be put to a pedagogical purpose by mediators, that is generally not the author-illustrator's intention. Browne explains why he introduces artworks into his picturebooks: "I like the idea of trying to make 'Art,' with a capital A, more accessible to children. I believe we undervalue the visual as a society. Too often I see children's education mean that they grow out of pictures—away from picturebooks into words—as though that's part of the development of a child's education; the development of a child into an adult." While adult mediators can use such works to introduce children to the artists, artworks, and movements that inspired the picturebook artist, Browne downplays the pedagogical aspect: "I want children to realize that fine art doesn't have to be serious and heavy or even part of the education process. We can just lose ourselves and see ourselves in a painting that was painted 500 years ago."[64] The fact that subsequent works, namely *Willy's Pictures* and *The Shape Game* (2003), include information about the paintings quoted suggests a more pedagogical intention, although this could simply be a strategy to avoid further copyright problems. However, as *The Shape Game* was the result of a project developed by the Tate in partnership with the Institute of Education, it is not surprising that the book would have a pedagogical dimension.

While *The Mighty Asparagus* serves as an introduction to art history for children, many of the references will be recognized only by adults familiar with Renaissance painting. Reviewers generally agree with Radunsky's editor, who has pointed to the crossover appeal of the book due to the playful yet sophisticated artistic allusions. Some of the jokes seem to target an adult audience. In Radunsky's case, the crossover appeal actually stems from a pedagogical intent. When asked if he expected adults to read *The Mighty Asparagus* as readily as children, Radunsky replied: "Although my main readers are children and my main concern is to make my books funny, interesting and understandable first of all for them, I purposely use language, terms and images which would help a child make a step up into the adult world. Without pursuing any pedagogical purpose directly, I nevertheless see this approach as the main goal of children's books."[65]

In some cases, references to artworks are the illustrator's homage to an artist and his work. Anthony Browne's entire oeuvre seems to constitute a homage to Magritte, at least up until the artist's estate decided to take action against the illustrator's persistent unacknowledged use of his works.[66] During an interview in 2000, Browne told Julia Eccleshare that the Magritte estate had recently sued him for his "fake reproductions" of the artist's work in *Willy the Dreamer.* Browne's reaction suggests that he himself saw his referencing of Magritte in the light of a homage: "I thought that I was encouraging children to look at Magritte's pictures, but I had to take out all references to him for the new edition."[67] Further, the dust jacket of *Willy the Dreamer* states explicitly that Browne's pictures "pay homage to great painters." The illustrator was forced to recreate his award-winning picturebook for the new edition: "I had to repaint a lot of paintings in *Willy the Dreamer,* painting out all the direct references, not only to Magritte but also to de Chirico and Dali."[68] Numerous plates were altered, but most notably the illustration of Willy as a painter. With the exception of Magritte's *Attempting the Impossible,* the six paintings in this plate are all borrowed from Van Gogh in subsequent editions (perhaps reworking a painting within a frame causes more concern on the part of copyright holders). The illustrator admits having experienced a range of emotions, including anger, lack of confidence, and depression, because, as he puts it: "I was doing what painters have been doing throughout the ages, but it made no difference." Browne felt the situation was extremely ironic since Magritte himself had done the same thing in his day. After the problems with the Magritte estate, Browne told Eccleshare in 2000 that he did not intend to abandon his artistic allusions; his future picturebooks would continue to be inspired by the great masters but he would be "more discreet" about how he used their work.[69] However, the ramifications of the Magritte case only became evident when the publication of *Willy's Pictures* was in progress. A dismayed Browne was forced once again to rework a book when Walker approached the estates of Chagall, Picasso, Munch, Grant Wood, and Otto Dix, and was refused permission to use their paintings in this way. The first painting Browne wanted to include was Grant Wood's *American Gothic.* He had actually gone to the Chicago Art Institute on a trip to the United States to visit an exhibition dedicated "to the painting and its influence—showing all the different ways it had been referred to in film and advertising."[70] Despite the extensive intertextual history of *American Gothic,* even the Wood's estate refused the request. The Hopper estate was the only one to give permission, so *Early Sunday Morning* was retained along with older works not under copyright. The copyright page of *Willy's Pictures* acknowledges Browne's sources in a playful, informal manner. A picture of Willy carrying his portfolio is accompanied by a note that reads: "This book is dedicated to all the great artists who have inspired me to paint."

On the same page, readers are encouraged to refer to the original paintings reproduced in the back of the book in a second note that issues directly from Willy's mouth: "Look out for their pictures at the back of this book." It was undoubtedly Browne's commercial success and his international acclaim and influential status within the world of children's literature that mobilized the Magritte estate. It will be a great loss to children's literature if copyright issues cramp the style of illustrators who wish to use artistic allusion or even make it a hallmark of their style.

It is possible that some illustrators are simply engaged in a personal, often complex dialogue with certain artists and do not care in the least if it goes over the heads of all their viewers. Kelek's recycling of past masters is highly sophisticated and even cultured viewers quite interested in the fine arts may be at a loss to identify some of them. Kelek told me she does not expect readers to decode the references; they are there for the few people who recognize them and especially for the artist herself. As she pointed out, the pictures "work without the references."[71] Many illustrators agree with Kelek that artistic references do not have to be recognized in order for the work to be appreciated. Stian Hole does not expect children to pick up the many references and quotations in *Garmann's Summer* and he hopes that is not necessary to their enjoyment of the book. Acknowledging that some of the references "fly right over the heads of children," he adds: "you don't have to know everything about art history, music or Italian films to enjoy these stories."[72] Sören Jessen says that it is not important to him whether the reader recognizes the surrealist allusions in his work; he just wants "to make intriguing, mysterious, interesting pictures that capture the reader."[73] Despite the rather detailed referencing of Fox's painting in *The Rabbits*, Shaun Tan states: "Whether the source is recognisable is irrelevant: what does matter is the resonance." Tan rightly reminds us that ultimately "it's up to the reader to draw whatever meaning they wish."[74] Picturebooks with allusions to the fine arts are not targeted only at a culturally astute audience. Readers do not have to be familiar with the artistic references to appreciate the narrative. It is important to remember that illustrators and authors who reference or recreate preexisting pieces of art in their own works do so to enhance a new and original work of art. However, familiarity with the artistic style or artwork quoted adds further intertextual meaning. The more cultural background the reader brings to the picturebook, the more resonance it will have, as with any reading experience.

When the Venus de Milo is depicted as an elephant, *Whistler's Mother* as an ape, *The Laughing Cavalier* as a pig, or the *Mona Lisa* as a dog or a goose, high art loses its sacrosanct aura and is made to look pretentious and ludicrous. The effect is highly entertaining for readers of all ages, but these allusions may also constitute a form of playful revenge against the world of high art. Some picturebook artists are perhaps getting back at "fine artists" who do "real art" and are paid as much for one painting as an illustrator might obtain for the entire print-run of a successful book. (The Magritte estate may feel that at least one picturebook artist is making more on one picturebook than major artists do on a single painting.) Speaking of the "small art" of children's books, Allan Ahlberg seems to state rather too insistently that Janet "doesn't have any wish to frame pictures to hang on a gallery wall," but he admits that some of their friends in the same work might like to do so and consider that "a higher achievement."[75] In *The Great Escape from City Zoo*, Tohby Riddle's depiction of the four disguised runaway animals in the museum certainly seems to poke fun at high art. The four animals standing in front of Magritte's *Ceci n'est pas une pipe*, taking no notice whatsoever of the paintings, are not four people appreciating fine art in a museum; without the necessary cultural codes, they have no idea what they are supposed to be doing there. Browne also seems to ridicule high art in *Voices in the Park*, where a gloomy *Laughing Cavalier* and a crying *Mona Lisa* are displayed for sale in a garbage-littered street beside a panhandling Santa. The illustrator frees these miserable-looking figures from their frames in a subsequent plate which shows them dancing merrily in the street. Allusions to canonical art may constitute an invitation to give picturebook illustrations the same status as the artworks they appropriate and to view them as "Art with a capital A," to borrow Browne's words. Some illustrators would contend quite rightly that picturebook art can be more influential than fine art. Tohby Riddle ultimately became a picturebook artist rather than a painter because he wanted his ideas to reach a large public. As the Australian illustrator explains, "the book gets reproduced in the thousands and maybe hundreds of thousands and can quite quickly be distributed around the country."[76] Picturebooks by some of the most successful children's authors and illustrators have an even greater global impact, reaching readers of all ages around the world. Those which include the referencing of art have gained particular appeal with a wide crossover audience.

Chapter Five
Picturebooks with Cross-Generational Themes

... des histoires entre dent de lait et dent de sagesse

—Le Sourire qui mord

They talk about ... everything that belongs to a more accurate description of the world shared by children and adults.

—Oscar K ., *Danish Literary Magazine*

Many picturebooks deal with what are often considered "adult" themes, but, in fact, are cross-generational topics of interest to readers of all ages. The preceding chapters have already provided a number of noteworthy examples. More mature subject matter is not new to children's literature. Nursery rhymes and fairy tales, the staples of the children's nursery, are full of dark and disturbing themes, events, and images. In her paintings for *Nursery Rhymes* (1990), Paula Rego demonstrates clearly that these beloved works are actually colourful stories about madness, cruelty, and sex. Nursery rhymes commented upon society and politics; they were a means of disseminating important news and messages. Although there is a great deal of debate surrounding the origins and historical meanings of nursery rhymes, "Ring Around the Rosy" ("Ring a Ring o' Roses") is claimed to be about the deadly Bubonic Plague, "Baa Baa Black Sheep" has been linked to the slave trade, and "Mary, Mary, Quite Contrary" is purported to be about Bloody Mary and instruments of torture. Even without looking beyond the literal meaning of the words, "Hush-a-Bye, Baby" has a baby and its cradle falling out of a tree. Maurice Sendak borrows two nursery rhymes as the text of *We Are All in the Dumps with Jack and Guy* (1993) to spread an important message among contemporary readers. The tales of the Brothers Grimm, which for a time were relegated to the children's library, contain a repertoire of shocking and terrifying stories: Donkeyskin is a victim of incest, Hansel and Gretel of child abandonment and attempted cannibalism, and Snow White of attempted murder, while Cinderella's cruel stepsisters have their eyes pecked out by birds and Snow White's stepmother dances in red-hot iron shoes until she drops dead. The moral of Perrault's "Little Red Riding Hood" makes it clear that the little girl who is eaten, after undressing and climbing into bed with a wolf, is a victim of rape. Hans Christian Andersen's fairy tales also contain dark themes: an ugly duckling is the victim of discrimination and intolerance, a little girl has to have her red-shoed dancing feet cut off by an axe, and a poor little match girl freezes to death in the street. In Heinrich Hoffman's *Struwwelpeter,* a thumb-sucking boy has his thumbs cut off with giant scissors, a girl is burned to death playing with matches, a child who refuses to eat his soup wastes away and dies, and a boy who ventures out in a storm is carried off presumably to his death. Alice has many terrifying adventures in Wonderland, and both Alice books are overshadowed by repeated references to death, as is *Peter Pan.* All these stories, with their grim, often gruesome themes, have been deemed appropriate fare for children.

Widespread assumptions about the limited ability of children to deal with certain topics led to an unwritten code of proscribed subjects and to censorship or auto-censorship in children's literature. In many cultures, children's literary experiences have been limited by these concerns, depriving them of fictional opportunities to explore dark, painful, or simply complex subjects which touch them personally. Even in countries where the boundaries around children's literature are not so rigid and children's reading has not been censured to the same degree, notably the Scandinavian countries, some authors and illustrators have expressed concern. In 2008, the Danish author Oscar K., who now lives with his wife Dorte Karrebæk in Spain, voiced his fear that there is once again an attempt to keep "an often harsh reality out of children's books." He questions the motivation, asking: "for whose sake—children or adults?" He rightly points out that "children very often intuit and understand more than we care to believe."[1] Like his wife, Oscar K. maintains that to take children seriously is to present them with raw and undiluted reality. Without going as far as Oscar K., the English children's author and illustrator Edward Ardizzone acknowledges the need to present the real world to children:

> I think we are possibly inclined, in a child's reading, to shelter him too much from the harder facts of life. Sorrow, failure, poverty, and possibly even death, if handled poetically, can surely all be introduced without hurt. After all, books for children are in a sense an introduction to the life that lies ahead of them. If no hint of the hard world comes into these books, then I am not sure that we are playing fair.

Ardizzone points to nursery rhymes, which consist of "the very stuff of life itself," and to fairy tales like those of Andersen, which introduce children "to the poetry of the emotions, with the implication that children can enjoy sadness and the pleasure of tears at some sad tale as well as grownups."[2] Many authors and illustrators feel that it is our duty to tell children some terrible truths, which may cause horror and distress. They contend that children need to experience this painful learning in order to avoid repeating the mistakes of past generations.

Picturebook artists such as Maurice Sendak, Tomi Ungerer, and Wolf Erlbruch continue in the tradition of the Brothers Grimm, which explains their huge success with readers of all ages. According to Sendak, the tales collected by the Grimms appeal to all ages because they are "about the pure essence of life—incest, murder, insane mothers, love, sex."[3] Sendak was largely responsible for reintroducing subjects from the dark, disturbing side of childhood where monsters lurk. Published in 1963, *Where the Wild Things Are* won the Caldecott Medal and became not only a picturebook classic, but one of the most important picturebooks of the twentieth-century. Over the next two decades, Sendak would complete his ever darker trilogy with *In the Night Kitchen* (1970) and *Outside Over There* (1981), which were both Caldecott Honour Books. Critics have often pondered the profound and terrifying symbolism that Sendak manages to introduce into his children's picturebooks. As the first of these innovative books, *Where the Wild Things Are* caused the greatest controversy, even though it was the least disturbing. According to the author, it reflects his personal feelings as a child and constitutes "a children's level of seeing things." He comments on the very different response of adult and child readers to *Where the Wild Things Are*: "Adults find the book fearful; however, they misinterpret childhood. Children find the book silly, fun to read, and fun to look at. This, I feel, shows the gulf between childhood and adulthood."[4] The year before the release of *Where the Wild Things Are*, Tomi Ungerer had published *The Three Robbers* (1962). The publication of these two groundbreaking titles, both of which are far removed from the cute, safe, nursery world of cuddly stuffed toys, changed children's storybooks forever. Although Ungerer's irreverent picturebooks have been the mainstay of children's libraries around the world for almost five decades, until Phaidon Press began reissuing his books (beginning with *The Three Robbers*) in 2009, they had been out of print for years in English, much to the dismay of the many adults raised on books by the so-called bad boy of children's literature. After an absence of almost twenty-five years from the children's book field, during which he wrote adult books often of a darkly erotic nature, Ungerer made his much-heralded comeback with *Flix* in 1998, winning the Hans Christian Andersen Award for illustration the same year.

Like Ungerer, the avant-garde French publisher François Ruy-Vidal, who had his beginnings in the late 1960s after meeting Harlin Quist, recently came back to children's books after a long absence. In his view, adults prefer to offer children "intentional literature" by "psychopedagogues" rather than "Literature" by artists and writers, who are distrusted and thought to speak "the language of the devil." He accuses psychopedagogy of breaking children's lives into very specific stages and "pre-chewing" everything for them, with the result that children think that adults take them "for idiots." From the outset of his career, Ruy-Vidal favoured literature that took risks by authors such as Eugene Ionesco, Michel Tournier, and Pierre Gripari, authors "who were not afraid of words" or "what they conveyed," and by avant-garde illustrators such as Étienne Delessert and Nicole Claveloux. His views were shared by other creators and publishers of the 1960s and 1970s. Albert Cullum was a trailblazer in American education whose bestselling *The Geranium On The Window Sill Just Died but Teacher You Went Right On*, published in 1971, sold over half a million copies and became Harlin Quist's best-known book. Cullum understood that children want to be treated with respect and offered challenging books. A child in his second Quist picturebook, *You Think Just Because You're Big You're Right* (1976), offers a portrait of a librarian who reads them "stupid books" with a "dumb smile on her face." In a confirmation of Ruy-Vidal's statement, the child comments: "She must think we don't know anything— / that we're all a bunch of babies!" (34).

Sendak is an ardent advocate of children's right to be taken seriously despite adults' concerns. Accused of being a storyteller who tells children "inappropriate things," he claims to have learned from his father, who believed that any good story was suitable for kids. In Sendak's view, his father was "the perfect children's writer . . . because he told us what we really wanted to hear—all the details—sometimes gruesome, sometimes hilarious, and sometimes bewildering." One of the world's most famous picturebook artists holds a very different view from those who aim to protect so-called childhood innocence. "[Picturebook artists] understand that children know a lot more than people give them credit for [he states]. Children are willing to deal with many dubious subjects that grownups think they shouldn't know about." Like Oscar K., Sendak insists that "the anxiety comes from the adults who feel that the book has to conform to some set ritual of ideas about childhood, and unless this conforming takes place, they are ill at ease." He feels only children's authors and illustrators are expected "to protect the children," who remain otherwise "unprotected": "No one protects them from life, and all we're trying to do in a serious work is to tell them about life."[5] Critics such as Kimberley Reynolds have convincingly demonstrated how important it is to offer children fictional opportunities to explore dark and painful subjects that they themselves may be experiencing. As she rightly puts it: "Adults do not have the monopoly on powerful negative emotions or suffering."[6]

Today, many authors, illustrators, and publishers would maintain that there is no such thing as "adult" topics. Like children's fiction in general, picturebooks have freed themselves from the rigid moral codes and taboos that long governed children's literature. They now deal with a wide range of topics that are often quite contentious and very far from the standard fare of children's picturebooks.

Stages of Life and Family Relationships

The avant-garde publishers of the 1960s and 1970s were particularly interested in presenting all stages of life in their picturebooks, recognizing that human development is a continuum in which these so-called stages overlap. This is also a recurrent theme in contemporary picturebooks that fall into the crossover category. In 1966 and 1967, Harlin Quist published a series of picturebooks, written by Geraldine Richelson and illustrated by John E. Johnson, that focus directly on various life stages: *What Is a Baby?* (1966), *What Is a Child?* (1966), and *What Is a Grownup?* (1967). The second title was translated into French by François Ruy-Vidal (under the title *Qu'est-ce qu'un enfant?*) and published by Harlin Quist in Paris in 1968. In 1998, it was re-edited in both English and French, with humorous new illustrations by Nicole Claveloux. In thirty years, the text had not aged in the least (references here are to the 1998 French edition unless otherwise specified). Although this particular book focuses on the child, it does so through the eyes of parents, who never cease to marvel at their offspring. The book constitutes a kind of catalogue of the contradictory characteristics that make up a child. After asking if a child is a gift or a walking disaster, the textual and visual narratives go on to examine some of the "thousand and one things" (the original English edition says "a million and one things") that a child is, both "good things and bad things, sad things and fun things": a huge assortment of clothes that are always too small, a collection of illnesses and injuries, hair that needs combing (the children have only a couple of unruly hairs each), shoes that need lacing, mud on the rug, bedtime stories, endless good night kisses, a stray dog, a force "in perpetual motion," an adventurer, a sorrow, a kiss, "a . . . puzzle, a riddle, a mystery." The parents appear in only a few of the illustrations, as slightly larger versions of Claveloux's homely, chubby little girl and boy protagonists. The anonymous narrator who reflects on the nature of children asks, in the words of the original English edition, if a child is "a miniature grown-up who hasn't grown up yet."

The idea of the seeds of the grown-up already being present in the child is developed in Nikolaus Heidelbach's *Tout-petits déjà* (Tiny tots already, 1994), published by Le Sourire qui mord in 1994. In a very humorous mode, the German author-illustrator shows that while they are still very young, children are already preparing to become grown-ups. The panoply of children preparing for highly unusual professions includes Karine Prudence, who makes guardian angels, and Roseline Suave, who juggles objects whose total weight exceeds her own body weight. Among the portraits, Heidelbach includes a sly intratextual allusion to *La chambre du poisson* (The room of the fish), a picturebook he published the previous year about Albert Fafner, a lonely boy home alone with his imagination. In *Tout-petits déjà*, readers meet the imaginative boy as a baby who refuses to speak to journalists because he prefers to sleep and gather force to grow up.

Some picturebooks adopt a more metaphorical approach to deal with the stages of life and parent–child relationships. Quentin Blake's *Zagazoo* (1998) is a comic fable about life's ages from childhood to adulthood. When a "happy couple" receives a brightly-wrapped package containing a cute little pink creature identified by a label as "Zagazoo," they spend "happy days" throwing their new toy from one to the other. Soon, however, the new addition starts undergoing a series of transformations that are depicted literally as seen through the eyes of the parents: Zagazoo becomes, in turn, a screeching baby vulture, a clumsy little elephant, a mud-wallowing warthog, and a fire-breathing dragon. At the onset of adolescence, he turns into a hairy creature, but eventually he becomes a well-groomed and well-mannered young man who falls in love. When the young couple announces their marriage plans to Zagazoo's parents, the perspective shifts and the parents, seen through the eyes of the young people, have changed into a pair of pelicans. Blake's whimsical tale about the phases of life probably appeals more to adults than children. In a very different mode, Anne Brouillard deals with pending birth in her wordless picturebook *La famille foulque* (The coot family, 2007). The preparations for the coming birth in the titular family of coots are mirrored in the life of a human couple making their nest in a home opposite the same public gardens. Readers observe the bustling activity in the lives of parents, both animals and humans, during the cycle of the seasons from one spring to the next. In a sequential manner reminiscent of film, the same scene is presented at different times of the day throughout the year, as the two families observe each other in the park. As in all of Brouillard's subtle picturebooks, the passage of time and the changing light play a fundamental role in the narrative.

Family relationships, especially those between parents and children, are a common theme in children's literature, but some picturebooks focus heavily on the parents, increasing their adult appeal. Christian Bruel teamed up with the humorist Pef to create *Premières nouvelles* (First news, 1988), a highly original picturebook about the morning ritual of a family that is portrayed not as necessarily dysfunctional but rather as frighteningly typical in today's fast paced society. The story consists of two parallel narratives: Pef's black-and-white drawings of the domestic scene are set against a background of radio reports. The news on the radio between 7 and 8 a.m., which appears in italics across the bottom of the pages, constitutes the only text. The first opening of the dog sleeping in a quiet room represents the calm before the storm, which is announced by the crackling and buzzing onomatopoeia issuing from the radio sitting prominently on a table in the foreground. The one hour of programming includes the traffic report, weather, international and national news, financial report, breaks for publicity and music (indicated by lines of suspension points), society news, trivial events, sports, and cultural events, all of which humorously reflect the chaotic domestic scene unfolding in Pef's drawings. The first character to be introduced is the unshaven, irritable father in boxers who stands at the toaster in a cluttered kitchen. As the 7:00 news begins with a traffic report that focuses on traffic jams, the father eyes one in his own kitchen, where toy vehicles are strewn across the floor and a police car seems to make its way to a huge accident scene. As the father breakfasts, his partner showers while his oldest son, who looks strikingly like the father but is clearly not the son of the black woman, awaits his turn at the open shower door. The showering, complete with clouds of steam, is accompanied by a weather report announcing rain and morning fog. The announcement in the international news that an extension of localized conflicts in the world will probably replace the receding risk of star wars between the United States and the Soviet Union echoes the impending domestic conflicts in this household, as the oldest son kisses the mother (the hearts suggest that these are not filial kisses) and one of the younger sons waits impatiently outside the bathroom door with his legs crossed. The conflicts erupt on the next doublespread, where a lineup of irate kids wait to brush their teeth as their father shaves and then the latter angrily witnesses the mother giving money to the oldest son. The ellipses that link the text from one doublespread to the next and mark gaps in the broadcast result in some very funny juxtapositions. The item about a scientific study of parental types mentions only "modest repressives" or "liberated tending toward enlightened" (the mother showering while the oldest son waits at the open door and the father screaming angrily at everyone suggests that these parents do not fall into either of those categories), but the announcer's words are interrupted by the page break at the point he is about to give one more category. The broadcast continues after the page turn with the words "faits divers," which is the term used for minor news items such as accidents, murders, etc., but here it seems to qualify this couple's parental type: at that very moment the young black son is being viciously tripped by an older white half-brother. The six family members push and shove their way out the door just as the radio announces the record established by fifty wrestlers who all managed to get into one minibus, and as they race down the stairs, the two youngest members in the lead, we are given the race results. In typical Pef-style, the final page reserves a surprise that casts the entire story in a new light: two homeless men sit on the ground around the same radio, which is also a cassette player, and are about to replay the entertaining tape. The framing scene clearly indicates that *Premières nouvelles* is not intended only for children.

Some picturebooks direct attention almost exclusively on the parents. In *L'heure des parents* (The parents' hour, 1999), by Christian Bruel and Nicole Claveloux, Camille, the young lion cub-protagonist of their earlier book *Mon grand album de bébé* (My large baby album, 1989), imagines other parents as he waits to be picked up from school. Each doublespread offers different parental models taken from the animal world: nuclear family, single-parent family, communal family (a colony of beavers), and homosexual parents (two superb male lions in bathing trunks, as well as two deadly female panthers). There is no indication, however, that the lion cub's imaginings reflect any unhappiness with his own parents. Many contemporary picturebook artists reveal a darker, more disturbing side to family life. In *Papa, Maman*, Nikolaus Heidelbach sets out to demystify the role of parents. Like *Tout-petits déjà*, this picturebook was published by Le Sourire qui mord in 1994, and attempts to bring children and adults closer together. This time, however, Heidelbach focuses on parents. The book is presented as two different stories, with the one devoted to fathers beginning on the front cover and the one about mothers on the back cover. The transposition of the story to the animal world creates some rather incongruous and absurd images, but behind the humorous, light-hearted tone Heidelbach attacks preconceived ideas and clichés that convey the idea of a perfect and infallible parental model, an ideal to which few, if any, parents conform. In keeping with Le Sourire qui mord's editorial policy, conventional stereotypes are turned upside down. A father broods and gives birth, assuming responsibility for child care, while mothers are portrayed abandoning their children (leaving them in the nest of other animals or even eating them). Oscar K. and Dorte Karrebæk offer a similar portrayal in a burlesque mode in their series De tre (The three), in which the love-sick dog Carlo suddenly becomes a single father of five when the mother decides she would rather be a beauty queen. These authors are not afraid to show what some children know all too well: parents also have their faults and they can even behave cruelly toward their own children.

Albert Cullum's *You Think Just Because You're Big You're Right* (1976), which like *The Geranium on the Window Sill Just Died but Teacher You Went Right On* is illustrated by numerous illustrators, offers some scathing portraits of parents, as seen through the eyes of their children. While the author and illustrators adopt a child's perspective, according to the publisher's note the book addresses both adults who "have forgotten how powerless and ineffective a small child can feel" and children who "cannot imagine that the adults in their world were ever children like themselves—children surrounded by adults who perversely ignore some of their deepest concerns and deal out tragedy and elation seemingly at whim." The cover illustration by Patrick Couratin and Henri Galeron depicts a stern adult wagging the finger of his right hand, in a lecturing manner, at the lilliputian girl he holds disgustingly between two fingers of his left hand. The powerless, insect-sized girl nonetheless spunkily sticks out her tongue and thumbs her nose at the powerful giant. Among the "big" people whose authoritarian insensitivity and lack of understanding is portrayed with stark bluntness, parents are particularly targeted. In one poem, a child overhears her mother telling the doorman, on her birthday, that "she gave birth / to eleven years of trouble." Readers of all ages are moved by the girl's painful question: "Well, if she didn't want me, / why did she have me?" (12). In another poem, parents punish a boy for reading a "disgusting" magazine that he found in their bedroom. Henri Galeron's biting illustration underscores the mother's hypocrisy: the two-faced, lecturing mother is depicted with her two cheeks puffed up grotesquely to resemble a woman's bare buttocks. In these unhealthy child–adult relationships, it is the small child and not the grown-up that represents the voice of reason. One boy assures his obsessively over-protective mother: "I'll *always* be *your* baby. It's just that I don't want always to be *a* baby!" (36). Claude Lapointe's eerie illustration depicts the boy and his mother as if frozen in time by the blue light from a television screen in a dark, empty room, while a partially open door in the background allows a glimpse of the sunny, bright-coloured outside world that the boy is not permitted to experience. The uncanny ability of the author and illustrators of *You Think Just Because You're Big You're Right* to view the world from a child's perspective allows them to serve as go-betweens or "interpreters" between children and adults.

Dorte Karrebæk often deals with the complex family relationships in contemporary society. One of the author's favourite books is *Stamtræet* (The family tree, 1989), written by her daughter, Sussi Karrebæk, for a school assignment that consisted of making her own family tree. The illustrator confesses she was shocked as she saw the tree "being filled in with the complex relationships so typical of children of the 1970s." She realizes, however, that "such a mess isn't necessarily messy in the minds of children," and this is the message of *Stamtræet*. Showing the complicated family relationships of modern children by means of "an old-fashioned family tree" seemed particularly right to the illustrator.[7] She gives a modern twist to the motif by depicting the protagonist, twelve-year-old Minna Mogensen, as a tree, her feet constituting roots and her arms branches. The child thus becomes the nucleus of her own life story, as well as that of her family. Karrebæk evokes the child's world with humour, but her portrayal is always infused with profound empathy. She recognizes that childhood is "a serious matter," and that, although adults often "look upon children's lives with indulgence and laughter," children themselves take their lives very seriously. Her understanding of children and their imagination is due in part to the fact that she was obliged to take jobs in kindergartens and a crisis centre before being able to devote herself entirely to children's books. These years in social work continue to provide Karrebæk with material for her books.[8]

In *Stamtræet*, the young protagonist untangles the threads of her family history in the pages of her journal, but the story focuses on the father figure. She has had "Dads" in the form of the various men with whom her mother has lived, but she has never known her own father until she meets him by chance as an adolescent. In one of the poems in *You Think Just Because You're Big You're Right*, a young child reflects on the various women in her father's life. Wondering if "this one'll be [her] new mother," the child just wishes her father would "pick one." Catherine Loeb's evocative illustration depicts the child's head in the foreground while a wide variety of women walk in and out of multiple doors in a large room. The woman who walks out the central doorway is obviously the mother of the child, who asks herself in the last line: "I wonder why she went away . . . " (58). For older readers, the question is answered by all the women coming and going in the house. In another poem, a boy is locked out of his own home by his mother, who, as older readers will realize, is having an affair. The boy himself does not seem to understand the significance of the locked door and pulled shades, even when a strange man comes out and "almost step[s] on [him]" (54). Henri Galeron's illustration depicts a tiny vulnerable child running from the lover's giant foot which is about to crush him. These picturebooks adopt a child's perspective to address the manner in which adult relationships affect children, but their message sometimes seems intended more for adults than young readers.

Christian Bruel, Anne Bozellec, and Anne Galland tackle the theme of separation and divorce from the point of view of the child in *Lison et l'eau dormante* (Lison and the still water), published by Le Sourire qui mord in 1978. They denounce the idea that children are unable to understand and should be protected from the truth of a dying relationship. When her parents' marriage deteriorates, an eight-year-old takes refuge in her imagination, but her confusion, distress, and sense of helplessness continue to grow. In her dream world, she is a princess who learns that her royal parents refuse to divorce because of her young age. After failing in her attempt to give them her consent, she dives into a pond on the castle property, in what appears to be an attempted suicide. The story ends on an optimistic note, as Lison's mother, sitting at her bedside, finally sees her daughter's unhappiness and decides to leave her husband. In this case, the child's suffering comes, not from her parents' separation, but from their silence and their attempt to protect her from the truth. Bruel has always insisted that the child is a complete human being, at once perceptive and sensitive, who is aware of and affected by subtle changes in family relationships.

Some picturebooks challenge our often idealized view of childhood by reversing parent–child roles. In Karrebæk's *Pigen der var go' til mange ting* (The girl who was good at many things, 1996), which received the Danish Ministry of Culture's Award for Children's Literature, a girl is forced to look after her self-absorbed, immature, messy parents, as if they were the children and she the adult. This is a much more obvious condemnation of parents who neglect their children than, for example, the passive mother who leaves Ida to look after the baby in Sendak's *Outside Over There*. Through an innovative use of frames, Karrebæk reveals "the tensions in the dysfunctional family," as Carole Scott has clearly demonstrated.[9] The dejected-looking little girl within the small framed picture in the centre of the first spread steps out of the inner frame in the next illustration, as she assumes responsibility for herself and her parents. Subsequently, the small framed pictures within the pictures depict the parents, who are generally either arguing or sleeping after a night of drinking. According to the narrator, the parents spend their time "playing," and are only good at "staying up at night, and sleeping late in the morning." In the outer frame, the girl is portrayed doing the household chores or trying to ignore the parents' fighting and drunkenness. The self-taught girl, who has no time for school, tries unsuccessfully to educate her parents, adopting an indulgent rather than an authoritarian pedagogical approach. The illustration accompanying her proposal that they hold a costume party to celebrate the future changes is the first to abandon the picture within the picture and show the family together: the parents are holding hands and staring into each other's eyes rather than fighting, but they are still completely oblivious of their daughter at the end of the table. The fitting cat and dog masks that the parents wear to the party cannot be removed afterward. Forced to acknowledge her parents will never change, the girl decides to forget about her childhood and sets about growing up as fast as she can. The accelerated process is rendered very effectively by superposing three images of the growing girl wearing the same dress and a matching hair bow that gets progressively smaller as she gets ever taller. On the caricatural features of her characters, Karrebæk depicts feelings, moods, and emotions with exceptional skill. The expressive faces of the growing girl change from a resigned to a sad to a very defiant look: with her hand resting protectively on the shoulder of her younger, more vulnerable self, the oldest stares aggressively at the viewer. In an ironically understated way, the narrator says: "All children leave home sooner or later. The girl left sooner." The simple, childlike logic with which the uncompromising, disturbing story is told mitigates its tragic overtones and manages to give it a subtle humour. The ending is entirely optimistic as the girl, who has grown too tall for the confining, squared room, strides out eagerly through a large square cut into the roof and out into a world of light and promise. As the girl walks out of the book on the final page, the narrator reassures readers who may be concerned about her future: "And I can tell you, that the girl who was good at many things was good at finding a good place to stay, too."

Scandinavian picturebook artists often present the neglect many children experience in modern family life. The Swedish husband-wife team, poet and musician Thomas Tidholm and illustrator Anna-Clara Tidholm portray two half sisters who spend afternoons home alone after school in *Snälla barn* (Nice children, 2007). In this realistic look at life in a modern step family, the children are the liaison between the two absent parents, who relay their messages by cell phone. One day, both parents are late and the two girls have to manage on their own until their father/stepfather finally comes home. Readers are not told why the mother is still absent and there is an overwhelming feeling that this family is on the verge of break-up. Many adults found the book too painful and depressing, although children apparently identify with the young protagonists who spend lonely afternoons with the new technologies that replace absent parents. The naïve style that results from Anna-Clara Tidholm's choice of crayons and coloured pencils, rather than her usual watercolours, also explains the affinity children feel for the world she portrays.

Five years before *Snälla barn*, the Norwegian poet Gro Dahle and her husband, the author-illustrator Svein Nyhus, had used the same adjective, "nice," as the title of another picturebook that depicts a child ignored by her parents. *Snill* was widely acclaimed and well received by both children and adults. It won the 2002 Brageprisen (Brage Prize), the most prestigious Norwegian literary award. Nyhus believes the book has been sold to more adult women than young girls, sometimes as a gift to boost a friend's self-confidence.[10] Like the English word "nice," *snill* is a common, rather slippery term that can mean good, kind, or good-natured. Parents want their children to be "snill," generally meaning obedient and well-behaved, conforming to conventions and traditions. The irony or double-meaning of the ambiguous title is immediately obvious for the adult reader, but not for children. Dahle questions the role that girls are expected to play in society, that of being quiet, tidy, neat, smiling, pleasant, and so forth. She focuses on the "perfect" girl who is always well-behaved, never causes problems, and thus is often completely ignored, and encourages such girls to dare to be themselves. The protagonist of *Snill* is a little girl by the name of Lussi, who is initially depicted as a quiet, well-behaved child. The different types of paper that Nyhus integrates into his mixed media illustrations have a symbolic role, as they do in the work of Wolf Erlbruch. In the initial illustration, the studious little girl is bent over her school books working diligently at her homework against a background of paper from a school exercise book. The most disturbing illustration depicts a disproportionately tiny Lussi sitting in a living room of lined paper on a graph paper sofa between the very large, distorted figures of her father and mother, whose noses are buried in a newspaper and a book respectively. With her hands folded neatly in her lap, the silent, "well brought-up" little girl stares out at the reader with a false, bright smile. Small visual details contribute to the narrative. For example, an electric cord that is conspicuously unplugged in the foreground of the picture symbolizes the disconnection of this family. As Åse Marie Ommundsen rightly points out, this illustration "is asking (the adult reader) what is important in life."[11] Nyhus's experimental, yet easily accessible style is "characterized by sophisticated simplification," which explains its appeal with adults and children alike.[12]

Lussi is so quiet that she gradually disappears. Her parents and others can no longer see or hear her, and readers have more and more difficulty finding her in the illustrations. The tiny figure of Lussi with her hand in the air behind her classmates is unnoticed by her teacher, who towers over the students in front of a blackboard composed of blue accounting paper with columns of endless numbers. Eventually, the little girl disappears into the wall. When her absence is finally noticed, parents, teacher, classmates, headmaster, police chief, Lord Mayor, and firemen all look for her. Attentive readers will discern her faint figure in the wallpaper, in the outside wall of her house, or in a clock, where her falsely smiling face stares out from the centre of the face. It is only when Lussi begins to scream that her anger liberates her from the wall. A striking illustration depicts the little girl in a black rage, while people fearfully hide, run, and cover their ears. Other little girls and eventually Lussi's great-grandmother also step out of the wall. The theme of the invisible child is not new to children's literature; Ommundsen points to the example of Tove Jansson's *Det osynliga barnet* (literal English trans., The invisible child), published in 1963. The Norwegian critic also mentions the intertextual allusions to texts where females disappear into the wall, citing Charlotte Perkins Gilman's *The Yellow Wallpaper* (1899) and Patrice Kindl's *The Woman in the Wall* (1997).[13] The small, neat, quiet, well-behaved girl of the beginning is depicted on the last page as a dirty, untidy girl of normal size with her finger in her nose. Both the author and the illustrator play with the clichés that are used so unthinkingly by adults. Readers are urged to question accepted ideas about child behaviour and to examine their own child–parent relationships. This picturebook has been criticized by some for encouraging children to misbehave and rebel, but it seems directed especially at adults, questioning their idea of the ideal child. Bent Haller and Dorte Karrebæk make the same point in *Ispigen* (The Ice Girl, 2001), published the year before *Snill*: while the text describes the adults' approval of two obedient girls, the illustrations "ironically show them being led on a leash on all fours, begging like a dog, and crouching covered with a frog's skin."[14] Like Dorte Karrabæk and Oscar K., the Norwegian husband and wife team often collaborates on experimental, multilayered picturebooks for children and adults that deal playfully and ironically with very serious questions.

Dysfunctional families are frequently portrayed in the picturebooks of the French author-illustrator Claude Ponti. *Okilélé* (2002) deals with the rejection of a child by his parents and siblings. The unusual title is taken from what the infant understands to be his name when he misunderstands the words that express his family's reaction to him: "Oh! Qu'il est laid!" (Oh, how ugly he is! [7]). Although it is not mentioned in the text, the rejection of the new family member is evident from the first spread. One of the siblings is so disgusted that it actually vomits toads and snakes, a sly allusion to Perrault's tale "The Fairies." Everything the child does to try to improve the situation has the reverse effect: the mask he constructs to hide his offending face makes him look worse and the ropes he uses to connect his family for better communication end up in a confused tangle. The sad, unwanted child takes refuge under the kitchen sink to cry for hours. Ponti does not hesitate to include physical, verbal, and psychological violence in his picturebooks. He depicts the rage of the two, ferocious-looking parents towering over a pitiful, pleading little Okilélé, before the father walls him in under the sink. The father is shown laying the last bricks while the large, pleading eyes of his son peer out piteously from behind the wall. The accompanying text tells readers bluntly that "they didn't want to see him any more" and he could stay in his hole "until the End of Ends" (19). Ponti mitigates the harsh events through humour and fantasy. Okilélé's friend, Martin Réveil, has also been the victim of the family's violence: in a large speech balloon he tells the protagonist how he was hit every morning until he was completely "broken" (15). The fact that Martin Réveil is an animated alarm clock undermines the seriousness of the topic. Further, the practical Okilélé has turned his refuge/prison into an elaborate, comfortable living space with a back door, so he simply decides to leave home. After a fantastic journey, he returns to find his family's home in ruins and a stream of tears running through it. At the end of the stream of tears, perhaps an allusion to *Alice in Wonderland*, the protagonist discovers his family crying because nothing has gone right since Okilélé's departure. Ponti also provides young readers with a reassuring, happy ending: the unwanted child is reintegrated into the family and they rebuild their home together.

Animals are often substituted for humans to explore the subject of family relationships in a light-hearted, humorous tone. The group portrait of a dog clan, which opens *Min familie* (My family, 2004) by Oscar K. and Dorte Karrebæk, may appear to be a typical, albeit somewhat grotesque portrait of a large, harmonious family. The subsequent solo portraits of the family members reveal, however, that appearances are deceptive. In reality, this family is a strange assortment of tangled, troubled, and changing relationships, which reflect those of so many contemporary families. The authoritarian dog-father has both his wife and his girlfriend beside him, while the grandfather's ex-wife and her lover are also part of the family. Although the many illegitimate children in the group portrait are not unusual in a dog family, the latter is intended to be metaphorical. There is even a little human child, who ran away from his dog dealer parents. Tomi Ungerer also uses highly expressive and individualized dog as well as cat characters to explore family relationships and race relations in *Flix*. In this witty, playful look at racism and prejudice, a cat couple gives birth to a dog, a "genetic mishap" that is traced to a great-grandmother's secret marriage to a pug. His cat parents bring Flix up to speak cat (which he speaks with a dog accent), climb trees, and eat fried mice, but his basset hound godfather exposes the pup to his canine heritage, giving him swimming lessons and teaching him to speak dog (which he speaks with a slight "cattish accent"). At first ostracized, he eventually wins the respect of both communities and pursues a career in politics, campaigning to end cat–dog segregation. While some of the characteristic playful and humorous touches in the illustrations will be understood by all ages—for example, the no dogs allowed sign in an upscale Cattown restaurant, the rat-crossing sign in Cattown that urges drivers to speed up, or the St. Bernard statue in the church in Dog City—others, such as the monument to Laika (the first animal to orbit the earth) in Dog City, will only be fully appreciated by older readers. The story comes full circle, as Flix marries a French exchange student poodle and they give birth to a kitten.

A number of picturebooks dealing with parent–child relationships focus on the difficulty parents have in letting go as their children grow up. Christian Bruel and Anne Bozellec do so in a highly original manner in *Jérémie du bord de mer* (Jeremy from the seaside, 1984), the fantastic story of an eight-year-old boy who is afraid of the dark. One night, to the boy's great delight, he discovers a baby girl in bed with him and decides to raise her secretly. However, the little girl grows up at an accelerated rate: the first evening she is already three, within two days she is seven, and shortly she is sixteen. As she becomes more and more independent and begins to go out at night, Jeremy experiences the anguish of a parent who is surpassed by his child. After her painful departure one night, he comes to understand and be proud of his "daughter." The book was given a new look in 2007 when Bruel reissued it in an edition that combines or superposes drawings by Bozellec and photographs by Apy, effectively blurring the boundaries between reality and the imagination. A young male kitten's first night out on his own is seen through the eyes of his anxious parents in *Une nuit, un chat* . . . (One night, a cat . . ., 1994), by the French author-illustrator Yvan Pommaux. Adult readers will smile as they identify with their feline counterparts: "All cat parents await with dread . . . the night when their child goes out alone for the first time." In his inimitable trademark style, which borrows heavily from comics, Pommaux tells the story in a combination of third-person narration and first-person speech and thought balloons. The anthropomorphic feline characters are surprisingly human. The worried parents imagine a series of horrible misadventures, which culminate with their son Groucho being devoured by an enormous sewer rat known to be a kitten-eater. Preventing a kitten's first solo outing is dishonorable in the cat world, so the mother suggests her husband secretly follow Groucho. Although the unseen father intervenes twice to prevent a potential disaster, from the darkness he watches proudly as his clever son saves himself and his newfound girlfriend, Kitty, from the dreaded sewer rat. Strongly influenced by cinematographic techniques, Pommaux often seems to be wielding a camera rather than a brush. The story closes, as do many early films, with a circular framed close-up of the characters, as Groucho announces his intention of going out the next night. The consternation on the mother's face contrasts with the mischievous half-smile of her strikingly similar son, who has just assured her that nothing serious had happened on his outing (the father knows otherwise but does not share the knowledge with his anxious wife).

In several picturebooks, the father–son relationship is expressed in terms of a walk. In *L'amour qu'on porte* (The love we carry, 2007), a moving story by the French author Jo Hoestlandt and the Spanish illustrator Carmen Segovia, a father and son's regular Sunday walk through the forest to a cliff from which they watch the sunset, becomes a metaphor of their evolving relationship over the years. The narrator recounts these long walks with his father at essential stages in his life: childhood, adolescence, and adulthood. As a young child, the boy's father takes his hand and ends up carrying him on his shoulders; as an adolescent, the boy impatiently waits for his breathless father; as a young man, he prefers the company of a young girl to that of his father (her love proves to be fleeting). The book ends, as it began, with the traditional walk: the son still wears a red jacket and they still witness the same beautiful sunset, but time has passed. Urbanization has encroached on the forest and factories now dot the horizon, while the characters themselves have aged. A detail in Segovia's illustrations underscores this passage of time: the family photograph that depicts two tall figures towering over a tiny figure in red at the beginning of the story is replaced toward the end by one in which the figure in red is at least a head taller than the other two. The roles are now reversed: it is the son who proposes the walk, gives a hand to his stumbling father, and ends up carrying the exhausted old man. Now it is the father who asks if he isn't too heavy and the son who says: "What you carry with love is never too heavy." This tender story of the enduring love that binds parents and children throughout life is reminiscent of Robert Munsch's *Love You Forever* (1986), but fulfills even more the claim in the blurb of the latter that it is "a book that both children and adults will enjoy—over and over again."

In the case of Wolf Erlbruch's *Nachts* (At night, 1999), the walk around town that a little boy imposes on his sleepy father in the middle of the night, demonstrates the difference between child and adult attitudes and perspectives. Though they walk hand in hand (the two characters are cut out of the same 1940s German paper), father and son see the nocturnal world through entirely different eyes. Anxious to get it over with and go back to bed, the father walks along with his eyes barely open, continually pointing out that everyone is sleeping and there is nothing to see in the dark. Fons, on the other hand, sees a host of fantastic creatures and amazing sights all around them: a gorilla wearing a hat holds Fons's hand, a polar bear gives him a ride, and a large dog-bridge evokes the Magritte-inspired man-bridge in Patrick Couratin's *Shhh! Nachts* was originally written, under the title *'s Nachts*, for Children's Book Week in the Netherlands, which ensures a broad readership as tens of thousands of copies of the commissioned book are given away. Erlbruch deliberately created the book for a Dutch audience (both child and adult), which explains the presence of the sea and the large surreal fish pushing a giant strawberry in a pram. Additional strange sights also seem specifically targeted at the Dutch reader, including a tulip-headed creature roller skating and a rat poling a small, canal type boat. Back home, the father reiterates that there is nothing to see at night, but Fons is staring at the red and white ball that Alice had thrown to him as she passed through a large hoop held in the air by the White Rabbit. Readers are left to wonder if the fantastic sights that colour the night really existed or if they were figments of Fons's imagination. However, as is often the case in children's fantasy, the child is left with a real memento as "proof" of the fantastic events. The technical drawings and mathematical notations that Erlbruch routinely integrates into in his mixed media illustrations are particularly appropriate in this picturebook. These symbols of the rational, adult world are paradoxically deconstructed and reconstructed to create a fantasy world in which adults no longer believe. Similarly, some of the many images of moons in the book are cut from a French company's plans for a railroad in China. In *Nachts*, the worlds of the child and the adult are depicted simultaneously, explaining the book's appeal with both audiences. It offers an eloquent commentary on "the difference between children and adults." Konrad Heidkamp, the children's book editor of *Die Zeit*, rightly sees this as one of Erlbruch's greatest strengths: "He paints the child into the adult world and the adult into the world of children. The two worlds exist alongside one another, and neither has priority over the other. Children and adults smile across at each other with tenderness, affection and perhaps a little irritation. And that's absolutely not the same as seeing eye-to-eye."[15]

Love Stories

Michel Tournier, one of France's most successful crossover authors, claims that children are not interested in the theme of love. It seems that many picturebook artists do not share his opinion. When Wolfdietrich Schnurre's parable for adults, "Die Prinzessin," was published with illustrations by Rotraut Susanne Berner as the picturebook *Die Prinzessin kommt um vier*, the subtitle "Eine Liebegeschichte" (A love story) was deliberately added to increase children's accessibility to the whimsical, unsentimental love story between a bachelor and a lonely female hyena who claims to be an enchanted princess.[16] Tournier himself has written about love in his children's books. In fact, the award-winning picturebook he considers his best work, *Pierrot ou les secrets de la nuit* ("Pierrot, or the Secrets of the Night"), is, according to the author, a "lesson in love."[17] In this simple love story based on the classic love triangle, the author places three characters from the Italian *commedia dell'arte* in a French village setting, where Pierrot becomes a baker, Columbine a laundress, and Harlequin a house-painter. Although *Pierrot* was initially released for children in 1979, it has subsequently been published for adults as well. Tournier places the simple tale at the pinnacle of his art precisely because it appeals to readers at both ends of the spectrum, young children as well as cultured adults.

The love triangle is approached from a very different angle in *Un amour de triangle* (A love triangle, 2001), the first picturebook project of the French author-illustrator Anne Bertier. It is not, insists the author, "a work on geometry," but "a pure poetic fantasy." In this very unusual love story, triangles fall in love. The highly poetic text is full of clever wordplay, beginning with the title itself. Initially, Bertier adopted the fresh colours of spring, which is traditionally a time for lovers, but all the publishers she approached backed away from the project due to the technical difficulty of printing such a book. Many years later, Bertier came back to the project and redid the illustrations in black and white. The result was a more clearly "readable" and more powerful book, according to the author, who points out that it evokes the Tangram, an ancient Chinese puzzle consisting of seven geometrical pieces. The book was published in 2001 by Grandir in French as well as in Occitan, which was the language of the influential lyric poetry of the medieval troubadours. This poetry leaves its mark on Bertier's romantic love story, in which a medieval king and queen, who take the form of two triangles, love each other madly. Their entire world is composed of triangles: the castle, the jousting knights, and the nightingale in the tree (the nightingale is a common motif in Occitan poetry). Even the sexual act is described in geometrical terms: one beautiful starry night, the royal couple made "a multitude of geometric figures" and shortly thereafter "an adorable little triangle" was born. Bertier succeeds in her goal of making the text, illustrations, and graphic design into a coherent ensemble that includes even the typography (the letters are arranged in the shape of triangles). The parents' arguments over which side of the family the princess takes after, her father's isosceles triangles or her mother's right-angled triangles, saddens the little princess, who, in fact, is composed of equilateral triangles and is bored with life in a triangular world.

Bertier's story is also a fairy tale: the princess's fairy godmother appears and grants her wish to see life "from another angle." The artist claims her starting point for the book was precisely the idea of "seeing life from a different angle." Thanks to a mathematical, rather than a magical formula, Gertrude undergoes a transformation that makes her "all round." In her new shape, she is so radiant that a prince soon asks for her hand in marriage and the couple love each other even more madly than Gertrude's parents. *Un amour de triangle* is a playful poetic fantasy for readers aged seven to seventy-seven. The author fervently hopes that all her picturebooks address an audience of both adults and children.[18] *Mon Loup* (My Wolf), published in 1995, is also a love story for young and old alike, inspired by the inseparable couple of Little Red Riding Hood and the wolf.[19] The simple black-and-white illustrations and concise, poetic text make both these whimsical love stories accessible to very young children.

Love is a common theme in the books published by Ipomée, whose audience, like that of Grandir's books, has been questioned by adults. In 1986, Ipomée published one of the most remarkable love stories in picturebook format, *Le colporteur d'images* (The image peddler, 1986) by Anne Quesemand and Laurent Berman. At the beginning of what is described as a "ballad in 14 scenes," the two-person cast is presented like the characters in a

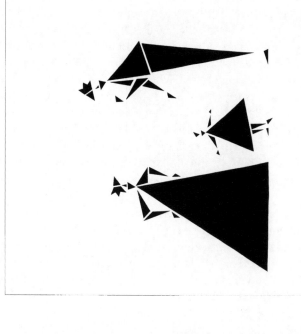

Ses

parents

l' adoraient.

«Elle me ressemble»,

disait le roi , «elle est du côté

des triangles isocèles». «C'est tout

à fait mon portrait» disait la reine,

«elle est du côté des triangles rectangles».

Le

roi

et la reine

tiraient chacun de leurs côtés.

Cela rendit triste la petite princesse.

Figure 5.1 Un amour de triangle by Anne Bertier, copyright © 2001 Anne Bertier and Grandir, reprinted by permission of Anne Bertier and Grandir.

play, which is set in Paris, the city of love. A brief prologue informs readers that the game of hide and seek that they are about to witness is "a true Love story." Two strangers meet briefly by chance one Sunday and then spend most of the story trying to find each other again. The protagonists, "the Woman" and "the Man," are known only as Mademoiselle A. and Monsieur M., the names that they give each other since they do not know the other's name. In the typographical tradition of Kurt Schwitters's *Die Scheuche*, text is transformed into image in a narrative that is composed almost entirely of typographical elements. The protagonists themselves are depicted as very fancy calligraphy letters: Mademoiselle A. is represented by an "A" in which one diagonal line ends with a foot in a high heel and the cross bar terminates on the left with a gloved hand, while the "M" that portrays the Merchant wears men's shoes. Readers follow the two characters through a city of letters in search of the elusive "other," until they finally meet in a nightclub, where the entertainment is a band of musical instruments composed of letters. After summoning up his courage, Monsieur M. approaches Mademoiselle A. who is sitting elegantly at a table having a drink, gallantly removes his hat, and bows slightly as he asks her to dance. In the white light cast by a spotlight on an otherwise black doublespread, the couple dances a seductive tango and gets to know one another. The rather ambiguous ending to this allegorical love story does not seem to be a happy one. The final doublespread depicts the hangover, solitude, and garbage of the day after, and the text, which is written in ever smaller characters on the diagonal up the recto of the spread states: "In the morning, the lovers are peddlers of magic loves." In French, each line of the text cleverly contains the combined letters "MA" or "AM," ironically linking intimately the lovers who seem to have gone their separate ways. As in Bertier's picturebook, the rather sophisticated wordplay in *Colporteur d'images* may not be understood by young readers.

Love stories in a minor mode are not entirely uncommon in picturebooks. *L'Heure Vide* (The empty hour, 2000), by Anne Herbauts, is a whimsical story that explains the twilight hour or "empty hour" between day and night. The Belgian author-illustrator, for whom writing is telling the indecipherable, the absence, the blanks, is often considered to be inaccessible to children. That hour that separates day from night is personified by L'Heure Vide, a strange, tall figure on stilts who combines light and darkness and is therefore rejected by both the Sun King and the Queen of the Night. One day, he learns about a beautiful princess who lives "on the other side." Although he falls deeply in love with the Princess of Dawn, the taciturn fellow never tells her of his love. Disguised as a heron he returns every night to see the Princess, but he never speaks to her, merely clutching against his heart an empty notebook in which he has placed a white rose that symbolizes his love. There is a sweet sadness about Herbaut's simple tale of unavowed love, but it is not troubling because the characters are only anthropomorphic personifications and therefore remain distant from the reader.

The protagonist of Henri Meunier's *Ronde de nuit* (2002) bears a resemblance to Herbauts's *L'Heure Vide*, as he is a strange, solitary man with an equally unlikely love. His nocturnal profession—he is a "montreur de lune" (moon leader), that is, he walks the moon like other people walk their dog except that the walk takes them all the way around the earth—makes his life difficult because he is in love with Zelda, who pulls the blue, moth-eaten veil of the night and whose contract therefore requires her to pass a good hour before him. A humorous scene shows the little man, who is a tenth Zelda's size, clinging to the veil of the night as she bends down to kiss him. Although Zelda returns his love, the two lovers can rarely be together. Meunier depicts the little man sitting in a tree cuddling the crescent moon in his arms like a stuffed toy as he interrupts his walk to sit and dream about his beloved Zelda. The phases of the moon are explained in terms of his love. Moonless nights are those when the protagonist is so sad about not seeing Zelda that he and the moon just watch the night go by without moving, waiting for her return. He waits for the day to pass and night to return so that he can see his beautiful Zelda. The days that he can spend loving Zelda, with the moon at their side at dusk like a pet, are the evenings when the moon is visible before nightfall. *Ronde de nuit* illustrates Meunier's vision of a picturebook text, which must "captivate, move, and surprise readers of very different ages." The French author-illustrator explains: "A picturebook is read by children as well as adults. I try therefore to address the two publics equally. Of course, the references, the culture, and the sensibility of the two audiences are quite different."[20] The ability to address a crossover audience is at once a challenge and a condition of the picturebook's success for the author of *Ronde de nuit*.

Ryoji Arai, who won the Astrid Lindgren Award for illustration in 2005, presents an even more unusual love story than Meunier or Herbauts in the award-winning Japanese picturebook *Mori no ehon* (1999; English title, *A Forest Picture-Book*). Arai illustrates a text by the poet Hiroshi Osada in this unique picturebook, which won the Kodansha Award for Picture Books in 2000. The story is presented as a kind of treasure hunt, in which a voice invites readers into the forest: "What you most prize is in the forest. What you most treasure is there." Walking through the forest in the company of a butterfly, a disembodied voice asks: "What are you longing for?" Readers wonder if the answer lies in the various sites in Arai's simple, colourful illustrations: a lake, a field of flowers, freshly-baked buns. They ask the invisible voice the same question and receive a poetic answer: "I long to hold the one I love by the hand, to look into my beloved's eyes." Only then do readers see the lovers: two small houses close to each other, one wearing a ribbon on its roof. The narrow road that joins them has two hands meeting in the middle. Arai's quirky presentation of love is at once poetic and humorous. The evocative, ambiguous nature of the story allows many different interpretations. A bilingual Japanese-English edition was produced by the Angel Foundation in 1999 with the intention, according to their website, of bringing "a message of Angels" to "young children as well as to their young parents." Arai's inimitable style, with its simple forms and vibrant colours, has a spontaneity that appeals to all ages and he has produced books for both children and adults.

David Macaulay's books, whether on technology, architecture, or fictional themes, are all considered to be picturebooks for a crossover audience. His characteristic detailed drawings of architecture are the vehicle for a very subtle love story in *Rome Antics* (1997), which opens with the release, in the Italian hills, of an errant homing pigeon that follows an old road—the via Appia—to Rome. At the city wall, the pigeon, apparently prey to the charm of the eternal city (or perhaps it is the romance in the air), has "a most unprofessional thought" (9): rejecting "standard pigeon procedure," which involves taking the direct route (that is, flying as the crow flies), the maverick pigeon takes "the scenic route" through Rome (11), an itinerary that is marked on a map of Rome "as the pigeon flies" at the end of the book (75). The pigeon's antics allow Macaulay to present some of Rome's unique architecture from very unusual, often dizzying perspectives. In the black-and-white drawings, readers follow the red, thread-like line of the pigeon's erratic, twisting trail through, over, under, and around some of Rome's most interesting sights. The title of the book is a play on words, as the antics of the pigeon are all in the service of romance, although this fact is not clear until the final two doublespreads. The pigeon finally enters an attic flat, where an artist removes a strip of paper from the bird's leg and, along with readers, reads the single word, "Yes," as the bright-eyed pigeon looks on in apparent understanding (72). The anonymous artist is a self-portrait of the author-illustrator, who, next to a shelf full of books on Rome, is working at a large easel on the last scene of the book. Only then does the reader understand the significance of the fact that the pigeon was released by a young woman at the beginning of the story.

The love theme in Macaulay's picturebook is so subtle that it may be missed by some young readers. It certainly can't be overlooked in *De bus naar Hawaii* (The bus to Hawaii, 2003) by the Flemish author and poet André Sollie, which tells a fanciful love story about an unlikely couple of opposites—big Guus and little Tine—who are deeply in love. As one would expect from the poet Sollie, *De bus naar Hawaii* is an extremely poetic text. In her immediately recognizable soft pastel illustrations outlined in black, the Flemish illustrator Ingrid Godon depicts Guus holding his tiny beloved in his arms like a baby or a doll on the cover. Stereotypes are reversed, as Guss cleans, washes, and cooks, while Tine does crossword puzzles and eats cakes on the couch. Their happiness would be perfect except for two things: Tine would like to be bigger, while Guus longs for the heat of Hawaii. This absurd story is a fairy tale with a twist. One morning, Tine's wish comes true, but not quite in the way she had intended: a dwarf-like Guus awakes terrified in bed beside a sleeping giant and flees; Tine sets out to look for him and takes the next bus to Hawaii, unbeknownst to her taking Guus along in her suitcase. This unusual couple will love each other forever, wherever they are and whatever their size. In the tag line to his review for *Die Zeit*, Jens Thiele describes the picturebook as "a love story for every size and every age."[21] Like many of Sollie's works, this crossover picturebook is published by Querido, which plays a very important role in the phenomenon of literature for all ages in Dutch-speaking countries. In 2000, Querido had published the picturebook *Wachten op matroos* (English trans., *Hello, Sailor*, 2002), a discrete homosexual love story by Sollie and Godon. The lighthouse keeper Matt scans the sea every day for the return of his friend, named simply Sailor, refusing to believe, as do his friends Rose and Felix, that he is never coming back. In the controversy during the implementation of the Equality Act in Britain in 2006, *Hello, Sailor* was one of the books cited in newspaper articles as being "forced upon schools" in order to include books with homosexual characters in school curricula.[22] In the Netherlands, the picturebook was received very positively and was awarded the prestigious Golden Slate Pencil in 2001.

Ooh-La-La (Max in Love) appeared in 1991 in the popular Max series by the Israeli-born American author-illustrator Maira Kalman. It tells the story of a New York millionaire poet-dog named Max Stravinsky who fulfills his dream of going to Paris, "that romantic, extravagant city of dreams." Spring is in the air and everyone except Max seems to be in love, that is, until he meets Crêpes Suzette, "the divine dalmatian" who plays the piano in a nightclub and whose "hotty spotty body" inspires love at first sight. The whimsical book is full of visual and literary jokes for young and old alike: the hunchback on top of Notre Dame, a man's hat labeled "this is not a hat," and the Parisian lady wearing the strategically placed bananas of Josephine Baker's infamous banana dance at the Folies Bergères. Some of the references and subtexts included by this artist who has done covers for *The New Yorker* are clearly intended for adults. An Amazon.com editorial review by Karin Snelson says the book is for "all ages, but perhaps especially for adults with stars in their eyes or Paris in their hearts." While older readers who know Paris will undoubtedly most appreciate Kalman's impressionist account of Max's stay in the romantic city, children will also be captivated by the quirky sense of humour and playful, musical text that appropriates French words and place names: "I am Fritz from the Ritz / which I quit in a snit / when the chef in a fit / threw escargot on my chapeau." Readers of all ages will be charmed by the happily ever after ending to the double love story of Max and Crêpes Suzette and Mimi and Jacques.

Two years before *Ooh-La-La (Max in Love)*, Max Velthuijs published *Frog in Love* (1989), which has become a book that adults give people they love around the world. *Frog in Love* received international acclaim and is the best-known title in his famous Frog series (Frog started out as a secondary character in the Klein-Mannetje [Little Man] series but evolved into the well-loved protagonist of his own series). According to Anne de Vries, the Chairperson of the jury that awarded Velthuijs a Silver Slate Pencil for this book in 1990, the author said that he was especially happy to receive the award because the book had been refused by his original publisher, Nord Sud Verlag, who thought that the theme was not suitable for youngsters.[23] As a result, the book was brought out by Andersen Press. Velthuijs, who is one the Netherlands' most famous picturebook artists, refused to draw boundaries between children and adults or children's books and adult books. His reply to those concerned about whether a topic was suitable or not for a young audience was the following: "Children are just people. They are somewhat smaller than we are but otherwise exactly the same. They deal with the same problems: sadness, pain, loneliness but also joy and happiness. So, why should we make problems about what is suitable for children? We are children ourselves."[24] The simple characters and situations make his books accessible to very young children, yet their universal truth charms adults as well. Always innocent and child-like, poor Frog doesn't know what is wrong with him when he experiences mixed emotions and cannot eat or sleep. The more worldly-wise Hare is the one who interprets Frog's symptoms and tells him he is in love. Velthuijs paints a charming picture of the lovesick Frog, who leaves gifts for Duck but can't pluck up the courage to talk to her and who injures himself trying to set a world high jump record to earn her love. The pragmatic Piglet tells him: "A frog can't be in love with a duck. You're green and she's white." Velthuijs's love story shows us otherwise: "A frog and a duck . . . / Green and white" can love each other dearly because "love knows no boundaries." Velthuijs's penultimate illustration shows Frog romantically rowing Duck in a blue rowboat on the river, while the final textless illustration depicts the two lovers hugging each other tenderly. In the tradition of the fable and fairy tale, Velthuijs's Frog books deal with universal themes, such as love, that concern readers of all ages.

In *Mon amour* (My love), Paul Cox tells a quirky love story about a man (his dress and the setting indicate he is Egyptian) who has everything he needs to be happy until the day he falls in love. In the second image, the man's red fez or tarboosh and his shoulders can be seen peering over bushes in the background at a nude woman bathing in the oasis. From his angle, he can only see the woman from the back, but readers have a full frontal view of her bare breasts. Like Frog, the protagonist tries to impress her, but, unlike Duck, the woman does not even glance at him. *Mon amour* was first published in 1992 by Le Sourire qui mord, whose books generally present more "adult" topics, but it was reissued by Seuil Jeunesse in 2003. The unusual book has a very small format and the pages are numbered in a very unconventional manner: each doublespread is assigned a single page number, so that the final verso in the seventy-page book bears the number thirty-five. The rectos depict thirty-five simple, four-colour illustrations surrounded by a double blue frame that creates the effect of a television screen. The starting point of the book was the illustrator's desire to explore the style of images that he had been using for some time in his art for magazines, small linocuts, in a less hurried manner in the context of a book.[25] Using minimalist means, Cox cleverly parodies the romantic novel in *Mon amour*. Readers are left to fill the gap between the images and the succinct text, which resembles the intertitles in silent movies. The text appears on the verso in pencil, generally printed in upper and/ or lower case but, on one page, written in script, as if to reflect the increased sophistication of the man's "new attempt at seduction": he grows a beard and buys a pair of fashionable boots. Adults will appreciate Cox's ironical love story, identifying with the love-sick man and smiling sympathetically at his failed attempts to impress his beloved. The protagonist experiences the full gamut of emotions experienced by those whose love is unrequited: melancholy, despair, jealousy, desire. However, the book also has definite child appeal thanks to the small format, the simple illustrations, and the humour. France's Ministry of National Education acknowledged the book's appeal with children when they included it in the new programs created in 2002 for Cycle 3 (elementary students ages 8–11). There is a slapstick element to Cox's humour that is reminiscent of cartoons. When the man climbs a pyramid, a gust of wind sends him toppling down the other side on his head; when he climbs a palm tree, he falls into crocodile-infested water. Cox's very brief text adds to the comical effect. Often a single word is sufficient to comment on the image, for example, "CROCODILE." The narrator's subsequent observation: "The feat ends miserably," points out the obvious, as the terrified man flees with the huge crocodile hot on his heels. The following image offers another view of the chase: his beloved sits staring dreamily out a window that faces in an entirely different direction. The man's emotions are expressed in a single word: "LARMES" accompanies the image of the man crying on a rock, "TRISTESSE" that of him walking in the rain, and "JALOUSIE" a picture of him spying on her with another man from behind the trunk of a palm tree. Toward the end of the story, a series of doublespreads containing only one word speeds up the rhythm as the adventure builds to a climax: "RÊVE" (he "dreams" they are together), "RÉFLEXION" (his "reflection" is depicted by three images of him pacing in a circle traced on the ground with the direction indicated by green arrows), and, on the penultimate doublespread, "ENFIN!" ("finally" he receives a kiss). The last doublespread reserves a surprise for protagonist and readers alike: the man is left staring in shock at a large green frog. Paul Cox's love story is ultimately a parodic rendition of the classic tale "The Frog Prince." The surprise ending gives new meaning to the exotic décor, which seems to be a sly allusion to the plague of frogs in the time of Moses.

Yvan Pommaux deals with love in its various stages in his picturebooks, often using anthropomorphic animals. Young love is broached in *Une nuit, un chat*, where Groucho meets Kitty on his first solo outing at night. Another young cat, Julot, falls madly in love with the kitten Lili in *Libérez Lili* (Free Lili, 1999). It is the love, and especially the quarrels, of an established couple that constitute the subject of his popular series of six picturebooks about an anthropomorphic crow couple named Corbillo and Corbelle. Older readers will appreciate the linguistic play in their names, which are derived from the French word for crow, "corbeau." The word "beau," which means "beautiful," is feminized ("belle") to form the female protagonist's name. The author explains that all the books in the series function in the same manner: a minor disagreement leads to ever more serious misunderstandings. Jealousy structures the story, which is punctuated by the angry outbursts of the male crow. Much of the humour stems from the repetition, as readers anticipate his characteristic fits of anger. Pommaux claims that he simply wanted to entertain children, but he admits that many adults buy these books, especially *Disputes et chapeaux* (Quarrels and hats, 1991). Adults tell the author that they find "many echoes of the crises that shake up today's couples" in these simple stories. The question of whether or not one can "talk about everything in a publication addressed to children" preoccupies Pommaux, who believes that it is indeed possible "to talk about everything, but not any old way." Like Sendak and so many other authors, Pommaux uses the example of fairy tales, which he has reworked very cleverly in his John Chatterton picturebook series. He points out that fairy tales deal with "the most serious and the most intimate problems": "They talk about murder, jealousy, violence, sex, without ever traumatizing children, but reassuring them on the contrary, forming them."[26] Pommaux presents the ups and downs of love relationships with realism. In *La pie voleuse* (The thieving magpie, 1984), the thief Pia attempts unsuccessfully to seduce Corbillo. In *Le théâtre de Corbelle et Corbillo* (The theatre of Corbelle and Corbillo, 1991), Corbelle plays the lead role in a play opposite Corbillo's old rival, Corbek. Their love scene provokes Corbillo's jealousy, exactly as the conniving, egotistic director had intended when he distributed the roles. Corbelle goes looking for Corbillo at the pond where he proposed in order to say she understands his jealousy, but instead of taking her in his wings and making up, Corbillo loses his temper and stubbornly refuses to acknowledge his jealousy. As always, the quarrel escalates and Corbelle goes back determined to put everything she has into the love scene, which she had thus far been playing badly. In the series, a little bird often observes and comments on the action or tries to advise Corbillo. This time he decides to leave everything to destiny rather than to say anything to Corbillo, who always behaves like a fool. When reconciliation seems hopeless, love suddenly overcomes all; each of the stories ends with the couple making up. When Corbillo finally shows up at the theatre, he and Corbelle fly into each other's arms, rewriting the love scene, while the duel that ensues between the Black Pirate (Corbillo) and the Count (Corbek) is very real. The director takes all the credit when the actors' improvisation turns the play into a huge success. Pommaux uses format to great effect in his picturebooks. The oblong format that allows him to mimic the big screen of the cinema is exchanged here for a vertical format that better duplicates a theatre stage.

All Pommaux's picturebooks borrow heavily from the comic book, but the Corbelle and Corbillo series constitutes a truly hybrid genre. The books in the series have been referred to as "albums-bandes dessinées" (picturebook-comics). The publisher actually classifies *Le théâtre de Corbelle et Corbillo* as a "bande dessinée" on the front cover. This designation disappears in the later book, *Disputes and chapeaux*, which shows the strong influence of film as well as comics. As the title suggests, this book tells the story of a lovers' tiff over a hat. When Corbelle finds the hat that Corbillo gave her on the day he proposed by the pond, he denies having given her that particular hat, gets the location of his proposal and a number of other facts wrong, and then refuses to admit he is wrong in an angry outburst during which he says he should never have proposed to her wherever it was. When the miserable Corbillo goes to the city where Corbelle has sought refuge with a friend, a huge party is underway and she is apparently having a wonderful time without him. Throughout the quarrel and the attempt to make up with Corbelle, Corbillo is advised by Robin, who seems to understand women better than the volatile Corbillo. Robin urges him to be patient and nice, but Corbillo once again explodes and throws the hat box containing his peace offering (a beautiful new hat for Corbelle) at his rival before flying off. The protagonist has had enough of the know-it-all Robin, who has not ceased lecturing him, and lands by the pond where he proposed to Corbelle to reminisce on his former happiness and his current solitude. In the end, the instincts of the hot-headed Corbillo turn out to be more effectual than Robin's rational advice because on returning home, the forlorn crow finds

Figure 5.2   Disputes et chapeaux by Yvan Pommaux, copyright © 1991 L'École des loisirs, reprinted by permission of Yvan Pommaux.

Corbelle lying seductively on a branch wearing her new hat. As Corbelle and Corbillo embrace happily, Robin, who lives next door, confesses his bafflement at their reconciliation. The final page is a rear view of the two lovers sitting wing in wing in the tree watching the sun set in the circular frame Pommaux often borrows from the end of old movies (even the word "END" appears at the bottom of the page). Pommaux is strongly influenced by the cinema, especially from the 1940s and 1950s era. The oblong shape of the book creates a wide screen effect that the illustrator uses very effectively to create large panoramic shots, as in the dark cityscape showing Corbillo and Robin first arriving in the city and the textless spreads of the discarded hat being carried away on the water of the pond and the party that is reminiscent of jazz club scenes from Humphrey Bogart-era movies.

Through two of her familiar, somewhat unisex, baby characters, Nicole Claveloux presents a drama of a rather adult nature in *Quel genre de bisous?* (What kind of kisses?), published by Le Sourire qui mord in 1990 and reissued by Être in 1998. The small format (the same as *Dedans les gens*) and the black-and-white illustrations give the four-act comedy the look of a comic strip. In Claveloux's humorous cover illustration of the two chubby babies in sleepers, one can already imagine them as adults: the suspicious baby in glasses leans away from the smiling baby's advances and formulates the titular question. One baby, loving and tender, wants to cuddle and kiss, while the other, a sour-faced, grumpy, distrustful baby, reasons, argues, philosophizes, and rejects the advances of the first. The second wants more information: why? what kind? When the first baby declares her love, the other begins a long, cold, rational, yet confused discourse. In the final act, the

Figure 5.3 Quel genre de bisous? by Nicole Claveloux, copyright © 1990 Le Sourire qui mord, reprinted by permission of Christian Bruel.

rejected baby stands with a suitcase and her back turned, as the second, who congratulates himself on cleverly getting rid of his importunately affectionate companion, explains patronizingly that life is complicated, with its obstacles, wounds, and deprivations. In a surprising coup de théâtre, the first baby hands the suitcase to the second, and wishes him "bon voyage." The story ends with a moral of a decidedly adult tone: "Some baggage never leaves. . . . " Readers of all ages can nonetheless appreciate this human drama and may recognize people they know in the two types that Claveloux portrays as toddlers.

Some picturebooks that present the physical love between parents seem targeted more at adults than children. The French husband and wife team, Jean Claverie and Michelle Nikly, did a triptych of large picturebooks on "The Art of . . . "for the publisher Albin Michel, which includes one on the art of kisses, *L'Art des bises* (1993). Although it offers elements for all ages, this is primarily a book for adults. The title page depicts a young boy studying a page in an anatomy book that shows the muscle involved in kissing and the label to which the small boy points, the "orbiculaire des lèvres" (the orbicularis oris muscle in the lips) is printed out in a child-like hand beside the book. As the title page clearly indicates, this is a pseudo-technical book on the "correct usage" of kisses. The first kiss discussed is "the original kiss" which generally takes place, explains the anonymous narrator, "between a gentleman and a lady who are going to become, a few months later . . . , a father and a mother." Claverie's first full-page spread shows the young couple, modelled after the author and illustrator themselves, in bed kissing. Like a pictorial diary, the illustration is dated January 20 at 23:30, while a small sketch on the facing page under the text of the couple feeling the pregnant woman's abdomen is dated August 10. Despite the playful manner in which parents' lovemaking is introduced into some picturebooks, they still seem more geared toward an adult audience. In *Qu'est-ce que vous faites là?* (What are you doing there?, 1993), by the Québécois author-illustrator Dominique Jolin, two children who think they are grownup and can look after themselves get into all kinds of trouble on a day their mother is particularly busy, but they discover that adults can also get into mischief. The children are awakened in the night by the noise their mother and Jules are making. Peering into the bedroom where their mother and Jules have obviously been making love, the children ask what they are doing (the dialogue is in speech balloons). While the embarrassed mother answers "Nothing . . . ," Jules replies: "We're playing!" and the story ends with all four engaged in a pillow fight. In the Israeli picturebook *A Lion in the Night* (2004), written by Meir Shalev and illustrated by Yossi Abolafia, a small boy also hears noises in the night, but he imagines that it is a lion. The lion turns out to be his father and mother (they are portrayed wearing a lion costume), whose lovemaking is the source of the alarming nocturnal noises. The humorous endpapers are covered with rough sketches of lions behaving like humans; one of the drawings depicts a male lion gallantly presenting a flower to a coy lioness. *A Lion in the Night* has huge appeal with adults, as do many of the other picturebooks by this Israeli author who also writes for adults.

Nudity and Sexuality

Nudity, even that of children, has frequently proven to be problematic in picturebooks, particularly in English-speaking countries. In Sendak's *In the Night Kitchen* (1970), Mickey falls "out of his clothes" and lands in a bowl of cake batter on his bare backside. The toddler protagonist spends much of the rest of the story naked. The nudity certainly didn't offend children, many of whom like nothing better than to run around naked, but it caused an uproar among adults, at least in the United States. The frontal view of his small penis and testicles particularly offended some critics, who felt obligated to remove the book from library shelves or to draw pants or diapers on young Mickey, or otherwise white out, black out, or cover up the offending genitalia. It is surprising enough that the book proved so controversial on its release more than forty years ago, but even today it continues to appear on lists of banned or challenged books. Sendak claims his intention was not to be controversial, but merely to avoid the "mess" of batter-soaked clothing. In addition to the nudity, some critics see disturbing sexual innuendo in the story's milky fluids and large, supposedly phallic milk bottle, interpreting it as a subversive tale of masturbation. For John Cech, the trip into the night kitchen is "a plunge into everything that is usually repressed in children's books: death, the body, sexuality, the dynamics of the unconscious, and the work of the soul."[27] Despite the controversial nature of the book, it has become a well-loved picturebook classic.

In *You Think Just Because You're Big You're Right*, published six years later, Albert Cullum criticizes adults' inability or refusal to discuss sexuality with children. Masturbation is the subject of one poem, in which a boy wonders why his know-it-all, "tough" father was so embarrassed when he caught him "doing it," since he is convinced his dad did it too. "Dads ought to know about things like that . . .," concludes the boy. Guy Billout's symbolic illustration depicts a smiling boy, who has dropped one of his boxing gloves to masturbate, while the legs of his prone father bleed off the page. Even the sight of animals mating embarrasses adults in the company of their children, according to Cullum. The rather vague words of a poem in which a little boy wonders why his mother is so mad about dogs "just playing" (46) are accompanied by Billout's child-like illustration of a mother impatiently dragging along her son, as he looks back at two tiny dogs mating in the street. In a poem dealing with children's curiosity about the opposite sex, Tina Mercie's provocative illustration portrays only the legs and feet of a small girl and boy: the girl's underpants are down around her ankles and the boy is holding his pants at knee level. Cullum's poem expresses the children's innocent curiosity and the inappropriate reaction of adults, who lay guilt and punish without listening or explaining: "They said we're bad. / They said we did a dirty thing." The children don't understand why they are forbidden to play together ever again: "We weren't doing anything bad. / We just wanted to see" (10). Children are curious about sex but are often not given the facts. Harlin Quist's innovative illustrators often defied the taboo concerning nudity in children's literature.

In the English-speaking markets, attitudes toward nudity in picturebooks seem to have changed little since the publication of Sendak's and Cullum's books in the 1960s. In 2007, the U.S. publisher Boyd Mills Press asked Rotraut Susanne Berner, one of Germany's best-known and most successful author-illustrators, to remove potentially offensive images of naked figures from one of her books for the U.S. edition. The most objectionable illustration depicted a cartoonish portrait of a nude hanging on the wall and a tiny, seven-milli-meter-high sculpture of a naked man with an almost invisible penis standing on a pedestal in an art gallery. Berner refused to accept any self-censorship although she was willing to consider having the publisher black out the offending images. "If you're going to censor something, then the reader should be aware of it," she stated. Both the author and the German public felt the request was absurd. "Micropenis excites US publishing house" was the headline in the German online edition of *Der Spiegel* magazine.[28] The wordless picture-books in Berner's Wimmel series, which follows the everyday life of children and adults through the four seasons, have won international acclaim and are bestsellers in many countries from Japan to the Faroe Islands. According to Berner, no other country had raised objections to the nude art that prevented the books from appearing in the United States. Censoring the nude in an art gallery setting does seem ludicrous. More than thirty years earlier, the numer-ous tiny nude pictures of Josette's father in Nicole Claveloux's provocative images for the French edition of Eugene Ionesco's *Conte numéro 4* (Story num-ber 4), published in 1976, was a profile of him hiding behind the living room door with his "micropenis" clearly visible. Claveloux's image is deliberately provocative: the nude father casts a devil-like shadow on the wall. There is another picture of Josette's father sitting buck naked on a potty. Not surpris-ingly, these illustrations were never used for an English edition of Ionesco's story. The penis is the entire subject of the French picturebook *À quoi sert le zizi des garçons?* (What's a boy's willy for? 2002), written by François Braud. In the knowledge that such topics have strong appeal to children, many of the books published by Éditions du Rouergue deal with transgressive subjects and taboos. As the use of the childish term "zizi" in the title announces, the sub-ject is treated in a funny, child-like manner. Maud Lenglet's colourful illustra-tions of boys' penises engaged in peeing contests and other innocent feats look like they were drawn by a child. When the know-it-all girl, who has spent the night secretly studying male anatomy under the blankets, announces to the boy at the end of the story that a boy's willy is "for making babies," the poor boy on the last page stands staring with consternation into his pants. It is only on the back cover that it occurs to the boy to counter by asking what a girl's "choupette" is for.

Nudity and sexuality do not have the same taboo status in many European countries that they do in the English-speaking markets. Countless examples can be found in picturebooks published over the past few decades. One of Alain Gauthier's illustrations for *Les Papillons de Pimpanicaille* (Pampanicaille's butterflies), the collection of nursery rhymes assembled by François Ruy-Vidal in 1981, illustrates a counting rhyme about a child being spanked by a father. The nursery rhyme uses the figurative expression "taper comme un boeuf" for hitting hard, so Gauthier depicts a man in a suit with the head of an ox spanking the bare bottom of a full-grown girl. The illustrator makes it obvious that both the victim and victimizer are greatly enjoying the experience. In the illustration that shows Max at work in the Swedish picturebook *Titta Max grav!* (Look, Max's Grave! 1991), the grammatically incorrect phrase "Max looks papers" is accompanied by a picture of Max sitting at his desk staring, not at the papers he and his blonde secretary are holding, but above them at her revealing cleavage. In Bart Moeyaert and Wolf Erlbruch's *De schepping*, the scene in which God creates woman takes on mild sexual nuances. In Moeyaert's text, God points to the woman, who, the narrator says proudly, is "beautiful and naked like me." Erlbruch's illustration shows God gesturing toward the woman with a thumbs up gesture that is echoed suggestively by the dog's erect tale, while, with the other hand, God gives the narrator a shove in her direction. The illustrator has cleverly placed God's hand in such a way that what appears to be a small penis could also be a finger, although it is pointed while the fingers of his other hand are rounded. The modesty with which the woman covers her pubic area and one breast with her hands is dictated by the Botticelli reference. Erlbruch alludes directly to the couple's lovemaking in the following doublespread, where the man eyes the woman with a smirk and a gleam in his eye as they stare over the headboard of their bed the next morning.

In some picturebooks, the entire story may revolve around a rather risqué theme, as it does in *Renaud le corbeau* (Renaud the crow, 1995) by the French author-illustrator Bruno Heitz. This unusual picturebook blends medieval romance with a comic book style to tell the humorous, less than heroic, story of a crow who makes his living as the royal spy. From his hiding place on the chandeliers, in the bed hangings, or under tables, the Machiavellian bird spies on the household and reports the intrigues (always of a sexual nature) to his master, the king, with the result that some courtiers find themselves in the oubliettes and some ladies in the scullery. His career as a spy begins when he intercepts the message that a carrier pigeon is secretly delivering to the princess's beloved and callously takes it to her father, who imprisons her in the tower. When the conniving crow narrowly avoids the spit for unwittingly allowing the handsome prince to rescue the princess, he accidentally stumbles into the rustic love nest of the couple he had so cruelly parted and expects to meet his end. Instead, "the two simpletons" adopt him as their pet bird. The scheming crow is not moved by the couple's kindness to repent, but remains true to his nature. In his role as domestic pet, Renaud the crow still hopes one day to be able to use his "viper's tongue." "Alas!" writes the chronicler, "The wife was faithful . . . the husband hardworking." The somewhat ribald tone that characterizes much medieval literature is retained throughout this medieval romance, which, despite the malevolent protagonist, has a happy ever after fairy-tale ending.

Tournier does not hesitate to "eroticize" the children's tale and describes *Pierrot ou les secrets de la nuit* as a "hymn to physical contact." The sensuality of this "lesson in love" was daring for the 1970s and even today remains rather rare in the children's literature of most countries.[29] The erotic suggestiveness of the ending particularly shocked many adult readers. When Harlequin arrives at Pierrot's bakery, thus creating a kind of *ménage à trois*, the former rivals watch with fascination as Columbine greedily separates the breasts of her life-sized brioche effigy and avidly plunges her nose and her tongue into "the mellow gold of the cleavage," before inviting them to join her in a kind of sensual Communion: "You too, my beloved, taste, eat the good Columbine! Eat me!" (32). Tournier's provocative statement, derived from Freud's theories, that "children's works must be eroticized, perhaps even in a more intense manner than books for adults," naturally scandalized some adult mediators.[30] Tournier regrets that he could not find a publisher abroad for *Pierrot*, a fact that he attributes to his refusal to avoid sex and other subjects that are considered taboo in children's literature. The author has bitterly denounced the censorship of conservative adults that prevents his texts from reaching a wide juvenile audience. He agrees with the critic who tells him that he writes "children's books that should not be put into all hands," but the author himself qualifies the statement by adding: "Not to be put into the hands of all adults."[31]

Violence

When Steffan Larsen asked if children's literature could get any worse, he was referring to Oscar K. and Dorte Karrebæk's series De tre (The three), which the Danish reviewer accuses of dealing with "ultra-violence," among other things.[32] Their hilarious series about two dogs, Carlo and Simba, and a rescued cat by the name of Gerda Røvlund, is certainly politically incorrect and it does include a great deal of violence, but it does so in such an absurd manner that it cannot possibly be taken seriously. In volume two, for example, Carlo is bitten in half by a giant dog and Gerda plays surgeon, operating as the blood flows profusely. In the third volume, Gerda makes dinner out of the dogs' pet. The burlesque antics of these twisted characters entertain adults and children alike. Perhaps the Danish author and illustrator get away with the extreme violence in part because they use animal characters rather than humans. It seems a burlesque approach to violence and the use of animal protagonists are not enough to get a picturebook published in English-speaking countries, however. Geoffrey Sainsbury wrote *Patavant et Patarrière* (2001) in 1937, under the title "Forelegs and Hindlegs." The story had its origins in a book project his sister had sent him, a sad story of a mare and her foal that he felt children would not appreciate. That led him to wonder if he himself would be able to write a children's story. The result was the comical story of Frankie, a very curious English foal who is cut in two by a train, and whose two halves, Forelegs and Hindlegs, lead separate lives until they miraculously find each other. Sainsbury's son-in-law, John Willett, finally illustrated the text in 1952, but British publishers of the time felt this piece of English nonsense was inappropriate for children. It was thanks to the French artist Gilles Mahé, who introduced the story to Éditions MeMo, that it was finally published in 2001 for readers six and up. It is telling that the British author's story has still not appeared in English.

Violence is particularly frowned upon in books for very young children. However, it is not absent from alphabet books intended for the youngest of all, as Chris Van Allsburg's *The Z Was Zapped* demonstrates. Joseph Stanton points out that "the brutal way that many of the letters are destroyed or threatened hardly fits with conventional ideas concerning what is appropriate for small children."[33] In addition to natural calamities, such as the avalanche that bombards the A and the lightning strike on the Z, the B is badly bitten, the C is cut to ribbons, the D is drowned, the F is flattened by an enormous foot, the K is kidnapped by gloved hands, the P is pecked by a malevolent bird, and the Q is quartered by a knife suspended in midair. Of course, violence enacted on inanimate objects, such as letters of the alphabet, is not as traumatic as that inflicted on living creatures. Eugene Ionesco did not shy away from violence in his tales for children under the age of three. In his memoir *Present Past Past Present*, each of his four children's stories was subtitled "Tale for Children Less Than Three Years Old" and the subtitle was retained when the first two tales were published in picturebook format. When *Conte numéro 3* was published with illustrations by Philippe Corentin, the subtitle was changed to "For children over three years of age" to target it at an older audience. It has been suggested that the violence in the text is the reason for this change. Throughout the story, there are repeated warnings that Josette could fall out of the airplane and be injured. However, the line that undoubtedly causes the most consternation is the following threat made by Josette's father: "If the butcher kills any more calves, I'm going to kill the butcher. . . ." The facing illustration depicts the butcher, in the form of a bull, standing in the shop door wearing an apron full of knives. A platter bears a human head, while hanging on the wall is a chart of the human body showing the best cuts of meat.

Humour is a common technique for making violence more palatable for younger readers as well as the adults who censor children's books. Most of the authors and illustrators considered in this section are not concerned with conventions and taboos, however, so humour is simply seen as the best vehicle for their story. François Ruy-Vidal uses humour in *Le Bistouri de Mlle Dard* (Miss Dard's bistoury), published in 1979, to present a warning tale in the tradition of Heinrich Hoffman's popular collection of moral tales, *Der Struwwelpeter*, that will not be traumatic for readers of any age. Older readers will immediately decode the intertextual reference to the German children's classic, which has often been criticized for its violence. Hoffman's humoristic intent was evident in the original title, *Lustige Geschichten und drollige Bilder mit 15 schön kolorierten Tafeln für Kinder von 3–6 Jahren* (Funny stories and whimsical pictures with 15 beautifully coloured panels for children aged 3 to 6), and the book was translated into English, under the title *Slovenly Peter*, by the great American humorist Mark Twain. Ruy-Vidal's story, in which the parents of a little boy who sucks his thumb threaten to have the man with the scissors come, is a direct allusion to the nightmarish story "Die Geschichte vom Daumenlutscher" (English trans., "The Story of Little Suck-a-Thumb"), in which an itinerant tailor uses giant scissors to cut off the thumbs of a little boy whose mother has warned him not to suck them. In Ruy-Vidal's rendition, the parents, a marquis and marquise, smoke, and the implication is that the little boy is just imitating his parents and perhaps they are the ones who should be punished. Like Dr. Hoffman's earlier work, Ruy-Vidal's moral tale is appreciated by both children and adults. The crossover audience for *Le Bistouri de Mlle Dard* includes doctors, according to the author, who claims a pediatrician in charge of one of the hospitals in Paris recommends the book to all his surgeons before they operate on a child.[34]

Violence against one's own child is a particularly difficult subject for a picturebook. Claude Ponti cushions parental abuse in humour in his picturebook *Okilélé*. Valérie Dayre and Wolf Erlbruch use the filter of fairy tale to present the ultimate form of parental violence against a child, cannibalism, in *L'Ogresse en pleurs* (The ogress in tears, 1986).[35] Dayre, who had previously been known for her screenplays, adult novels, and her work for the theatre, opens the story with the fairy-tale incipit, but continues in an unexpected manner that rivals the most horrific of fairy tales: "Once upon a time there was a woman so evil that she dreamed of eating a child." Erlbruch's ominous portrayal of a large, ugly, masculine-looking woman with an enormous chin and glassy eyes is suitably terrifying, and the narrator tells readers that her many vile deeds are so terrible that they can't even be mentioned here. Yet, the most terrible of all will be the subject of the story: the devouring of a child, not just any child but her own child. The grotesque woman who prowls the countryside with sinister resolve, scrutinizing all the children in her search for the most appetizing, is fastidious and finds them too small, too fat, too smart, or, in the case of a little black boy, missing a limb. Parents eventually become suspicious and hide their children indoors, leaving the eerie, surreal landscape completely deserted. Having visibly lost a great deal of weight, the starving ogress returns home, where she discovers the perfect child. Several days pass before she realizes she has eaten her own child. Erlbruch's decision not to represent the horrific scene has nothing to do with protecting young readers; he does so to highlight the horror and violence of the author's three shocking words: "Elle le croqua" (She ate him). The preceding doublespread depicts the ogress first catching sight of the cute, well-dressed little child standing by a plant on the table playing a bandonium, while a small, clothed monkey watches from his perch on the back of a chair. The three fatal words appear in a block at the bottom of an almost empty verso. Erlbruch zooms in so that the tiny monkey of the preceding page now fills the entire recto, where he eloquently expresses the horror of the shocking scene he alone has witnessed. His yellow eyes almost pop out of his head, his mouth is open wide in a terrified scream, and he beats his drum frenetically. Between the monkey on the recto and the single magnified leaf of the philodendron plant on the verso is the glaring, blank, empty space that the child had occupied only a moment before. This dramatic climax is not the end of the tale. The ogress continues to roam the countryside, now seeking a child to love, not to eat. The ogress insists on that fact, because, as the narrator points out, words can be misleading (the French expression "à croquer" has the figurative meaning of "to look good enough to eat"). Dayre's text is full of wordplay that is difficult to translate into English and perhaps reduces some of the anguish for young French readers while Erlbruch's cosmic imagery distances viewers and helps them cope with the horrifying events of what is, in Horst Künnemann's words, "an existential catastrophe" and "a drama of cosmic proportions."[36] In an article titled "How Much Cruelty Can a Children's Picturebook Stand?" Künnemann points out that admiring critics who added it to their collection "would not read it to their own children," and that despite the sales of more than 1.3 million copies of *The Story of the Little Mole*, the German edition of *L'ogresse en pleurs* was printed in only 15,000 copies.[37]

Self-harm has been the subject of very few picturebooks and is, as Kimberley Reynolds points out in *Radical Children's Literature*, "a relatively recent trend" in children's literature in general.[38] In 1996, Gregie de Maeyer and the sculptor Koen Vanmechelen tackled the difficult topic in conjunction with bullying in the daring Dutch picturebook *Juul* (Jules). The eponymous protagonist is a rather ugly puppet-like wooden sculpture that was constructed from rough pieces of wood by Vanmechelen. Bullied and tormented by peers whose absence makes them all the more disturbing, Juul is driven to inflict self-harm in order to rid himself of the body parts they ridicule: he cuts off his red hair, tears off his large "elephant" ears, pushes his cross eyes out of their sockets, and removes his stuttering tongue. By lying down on the railroad tracks, he manages to amputate his bow legs and ends up in a wheel chair. When his tormentors smear feces on the wheels of his chair, he plunges his hands in scalding water and burns them. With each act of self-harm his appearance becomes ever stranger, giving rise to further bullying. Paradoxically, Juul inflicts on himself the physical handicaps which often give rise to mockery and rejection. Finally, his entire body lies in pieces, the result of a complete self-destruction/deconstruction. None of his acts of self-harm alleviate the feelings of anger or hatred that he directs at himself. Toward the end of the story, this powerful, depressing portrayal of bullying and self-harm moves, as Reynolds also points out, into a "more optimistic, more didactic register," when a little girl shows Juul kindness and concern.[39] She puts what remains of Juul in her doll buggy and takes him home. Unlike the teasing voices that have surrounded him until now, the girl speaks gently to him. She puts a pencil in his mouth and gives him a piece of paper so that he can tell his story. "I had curls . . . / Red curls," begins Juul, who goes on to recount how he was teased and called "Copper wire!" and "Red shit!" Juul's willingness to talk about what happened suggests that the process of healing has begun. There is hope at the end that the girl's kindness and concern can dispel the self-loathing induced by so much rejection and that Juul will gain a new acceptance of himself. Through the use of a puppet, Maeyer and Vanmechelen are able to show violent self-mutilation and explore this disturbing subject in a picturebook. They offer a haunting depiction of the effects of rejection, mockery, and bullying that touches readers of all ages.

Gro Dahle and Svein Nyhus tackle the subject of violence in several of their picturebooks. *Bak Mumme bor Moni* (Behind Mumme lives Moni, 2000) is a powerful story about the dark side that children and adults alike carry within them. An ordinary little boy named Mumme is haunted by a monster who rides an enormous sixteen-legged black horse, breathes smoke like a dragon, and can quickly grow into a giant. The fact that the violent Moni is Mumme's alter ego and personifies the boy's rage will be clear to many young readers because Nyhus depicts the "monster" in the same green and white checkered coveralls as the protagonist. The poetic text and evocative illustrations convey very effectively the boy's emotions and troubled thoughts. The "long corridor" inside Mumme's head is depicted literally in a striking image of the child's head filled with doors, all closed except for one, from which Moni seems to be escaping, while the child stares perplexedly at the reader. With profound sensitivity, Dahle acknowledges the dark side of the subconscious that children are often left to confront on their own. Parents tend to be afraid of books like *Bak Mumme bor Moni*, convinced that they are too dark and dangerous, but Dahle's poetic text and Nyhus's symbolic, expressive illustrations deal with these frightening emotions in a positive, hopeful manner. *Bak Mumme bor Moni*, which was nominated for the prestigious Brageprisen 2000, was widely read by adults as well. As Agnes-Margrethe Bjorvand points out in an article devoted to one of Dahle and Nyhus's picturebooks, "in the Nordic countries, picturebooks no longer represent a genre exclusively directed at small children."[40]

A number of daring and innovative picturebooks tackle the difficult subject of domestic violence. The second poem in *You Think Just Because You're Big You're Right* concerns fighting parents who "say all the words / they tell me never to say." Jean-Michel Nicollet's bold, aggressive illustration on the facing page depicts the "mean, real mean words" the parents exchange as bullets issuing from guns that protrude from the angry parents' open mouths. It portrays eloquently the terrifying effect that such domestic verbal violence has on a small child, who, in this case, wishes she or he was at school instead of at home. Dahle and Nyhus deal with the even more challenging theme of domestic physical violence in *Sinna Mann* (Angry man, 2003). Nyhus explained the interesting genesis of the unusual picturebook in an e-mail dated July 3, 2010. The family counsellor Øivind Aschjem used the picturebook *Bak Mumme bor Moni* as a "conversation piece" in his therapy for violent men and, more broadly, in the treatment of abusers, victims, and witnesses to domestic violence. He found that discussing a children's picturebook was a useful, non-threatening way for men to talk about their own feelings and behaviour. After approximately a year of using *Bak Mumme bor Moni*, Aschjem contacted Dahle and Nyhus to "order" a book more directly focused on domestic violence. The result was *Sinna Mann*, which is described on the illustrator's website as "a therapeutic picture book for children (and adults)." An animated film based on the book was released in 2009 as part of Norway's Save the Children campaign against domestic violence.

In this powerful picturebook, a young boy witnesses the transformation of his Daddy into Angry Man who becomes a kind of violent monster, just as Mumme did in the earlier work. Dahle and Nyhus adopt a very sober style to tell their story of a hot-tempered man who becomes violent with both his wife and son. As in all Dahle's picturebooks, the language is very poetic and full of evocative metaphors. Although the young child does not understand what is happening, he senses that his father is not himself but possessed by an evil monster. An early sketch for the cover of the book depicted a monstrous, angular red figure towering over a tiny little boy between his legs. Perhaps the most chilling aspect of the illustration is the fact that the little boy imitates his father's stance and body language, showing the manner in which parents' behaviour patterns that of their children. In the final version, however, the illustrator toned down the image significantly, eliminating the frightening adult figure completely and focusing instead on the little boy who witnesses the violence and whose forlorn face is depicted against a vague, icy-looking background. In the illustrations within the book, however, the caricatural father is proportionately much bigger than the mother and son, often filling a large part of the doublespread. Nyhus's illustrations of a father who grows menacingly and becomes bright red with anger suggest effectively the oppressive fear in which the boy and his mother live.

Figure 5.4 Sinna Mann by Gro Dahle, illustrated by Svein Nyhus, copyright © 2003 J. W. Cappelens Forlag a.s, reprinted by permission of Svein Nyhus and Cappelen Damm.

From the beginning of the book, both the text and the images highlight his red hands, and notably his red knuckles. As Daddy transforms into Angry Man, his body becomes increasingly larger, while his head grows smaller to indicate his loss of reason and control. At the same time, the red colour increases until Angry Man becomes entirely red. His huge figure fills two-thirds of the doublespread as he towers menacingly over the mother he is about to grab with a grotesquely large open hand (the knuckles are conspicuously highlighted in red and the other hand is clenched in a fist). In the bottom right corner of the doublespread under the text, a tiny Boj is depicted huddled up in a foetal-like position in his bed with his hands over his ears in an attempt to shut out the horror. Although his father is not depicted beating the mother, Boj's troubled thoughts leave no doubt about the actual events: "Angry Man breaking through bricks and walls and mommy." A wall is one of the metaphors, along with a stop sign, that the boy uses on the previous page to refer to Mommy when she "grows big" and protects Boj from his father. The reader senses that it is not the "striking and striking and striking" of the living-room clock that reaches the boy's conscious so hauntingly. Angry Man has become so large in the following scene that his figure cannot be contained within the doublespread. The monstrous figure with long, gorilla arms who bends over the tiny doll-like figure of the mother that he holds in one huge hand, is, as Bjorvand has mentioned, reminiscent of the film *King Kong*.[41] The mother who became large to protect her son now becomes very small and vulnerable as she takes the brunt of her husband's violence, adding to the boy's feeling of guilt: "Little Mommy is so small. Sorry, Mommy, I'm sorry. I'm sorry, little Mommy. Angry Man is bigger than the house, bigger than a mountain, bigger than everything." Curled into an even tighter ball, the boy attempts to escape the horror in an inner dream world. Eventually the boy is able to talk about it and then to write about it, so that the father can receive the help he needs and the family can begin to heal.

The illustrator admits *Sinna Mann* was not a bestseller when it was released in 2003, because, as he puts it, "who wants to buy a children's book about a boy witnessing his father beating his mother?" Following the debate which surrounded the book in Norwegian newspapers, however, it has received a great deal of attention in Norway as well as Sweden, and it was reissued in 2008 and again in 2010.[42] Interestingly, it was translated into Chinese in 2005, four years before the Swedish translation. The story has universal relevance thanks to the caricatural characters who are named only Daddy, Mommy, and Boj (in the English translation the illustrator sent me the word "Boy" was accidentally substituted on one occasion for Boj, suggesting the origin of the unusual name). While the story is fictional, Dahle researched the subject extensively and includes quotes from men, women, and children who have experienced domestic violence. The fairy-tale-like episode in which the boy writes a letter to the King to tell him about his father is actually based on a true story that was revealed in March 2009 at the premiere of the film attended by King Harald V. During a therapy session with a small group of children, Aschjem had told them that it was important to tell someone about the problem, and a girl in the group had suggested they write a letter to the King. When they did so, Harald V invited them to visit him at the royal castle in Oslo, where he shook their hands, told them how brave they were, and assured them that they were not responsible. In the book, the large father figure of the King towers over a tiny Daddy who kneels before the larger Boj to beg his forgiveness. The ending remains open. The father is removed from the home, but the boy will be able to visit him. There is some hope that Boj's father will be able to return to his family after psychiatric treatment, although it is only hinted at in the happy images of the final page.

The subject of rape has been broached, generally indirectly, in picturebook retellings of "Little Red Riding Hood," but it has rarely been tackled directly in picturebooks. Piero Ventura and his son, the illustrator Marco Ventura, tell the story of the rape of a twelve-year-old girl in the Italian picturebook *Anna dei porci* (Anna of the pigs, 1987), which received the Silver Medal at the Society of Illustrators show in New York in 1998. Although the Venturas distance the story in time, portraying a medieval peasant girl, they initially present her as a very real-looking little girl. The striking, photo-like full-page spread of Anna and two of her pigs at the beginning of the book contrasts sharply with the soft, delicate illustrations throughout the rest of the book. The peasant girl in the rough clothing stands with her arms crossed and her bare feet planted firmly on the ground as she stares boldly into the eyes of the reader. The distinctive realistic style of this illustration is explained by its position on the facing page of a foreword by Cyrille Koupernik, which brings this tale of rape into the real world by encouraging adults to read it to children because "the big bad wolf" still prowls about. Koupernik makes it clear that this simple, poetic tale is intended to be a modern cautionary tale. Ventura's story is told initially in ballad form on two doublespreads illustrated by details from the subsequent illustrations, which are followed by a musical transcription. The subsequent narrative is essentially visual, with only a few words of text on doublespreads that depict tiny figures on wide, sweeping landscapes, in the manner of the Renaissance masters. The text takes the form of short notations that resemble journal entries. The doublespread dated March 23, on which Anna witnesses a camp of soldiers from her hiding spot among the branches at sunset, is followed by a series of wordless spreads that evoke her rape by the soldiers. The final spread in the wordless sequence shows Anna lying on the ground, as the last soldier to rape her walks away (only his leg is visible bleeding off the page to the left). The heartache is not over for the little orphan girl, who returns to her village the next day to find only a burned-out, empty shell. The once happy, easy-going girl seeks refuge among the animals in the hills and the forest, where she gradually rediscovers the simple joy of being alive. At the end of October, the little girl watching a flock of ducks flying south is visibly pregnant, and just before midnight on Christmas Eve she gives birth in the snow. The birth is associated with the Nativity; not only is Anna's child born on Christmas Eve, but a mysterious old man on horseback, who is likened to "a king from the Orient," comes to pay homage under a bright star. The poet seems to see him through Anna's eyes when he describes the old man as a "knight on his white horse," because he looks more like a patriarch and his horse is pale brown in the illustration. The author provides a hopeful, open ending to the story as Anna and the baby ride into the dawn of a new day and a new life mounted behind the kindly old man. The final lines of the ballad address Anna directly to reassure her that "the cruel fable" is over and a new life is beginning. Some critics have found the book's message too ambiguous, but the father and son team no doubt wanted to present a multilayered narrative for readers of various ages. The events are left largely to the reader's imagination in the prose narrative, but the ballad provides older children with more details, while the even more explicit preface is intended for adult mediators.

Death: The Ultimate Taboo

Death is part of the human condition, no matter what our age. Yet there is a reluctance to deal with death in picturebooks, especially in the English-speaking market. Meg Rosoff, who herself has written about death for young readers in *How I Live Now*, calls Wolf Erlbruch's *Ente, Tod und Tulpe* (2007; English trans., *Duck, Death and the Tulip*) a "tale that breaks the ultimate taboo." In an article on the book, she reflects on "who its audience might be—not small children, surely, for the topic is dangerous and inappropriate, likely to inspire nightmares. Unless the opposite is true, and taboo subjects create more fears than they assuage?"[43] Rosoff does not answer her own question, preferring to defer to readers, but she seems to agree with Erlbruch and many other contemporary authors that the subject can be dealt with effectively in picturebooks targeted at young children. The German publisher's website states that *Duck, Death and the Tulip* "will intrigue, haunt and enchant children, teenagers and adults," but the product description on Amazon.co.uk omits "children," as if afraid to market this picturebook for its chief audience. Very young children are often quite curious, sometimes even obsessed, by the idea of death. Books such as Erlbruch's speak eloquently and simply to their questions.

Among the strategies adopted to make the subject more palatable for publishers, mediators, and readers alike the most common are humour and distancing through the use of animal characters. In some picturebooks, vague hints of death merely provide darker undertones to an otherwise nonsensical story. When morning dispels the tortoise's can-can dreams in the *Carnival of the Animals*, ". . . once again / he plods along. / He plods along, he plods along / until his tortoise days are gone." When De Vos does take on death more directly in his nonsense verse, he does so by talking about fossils: "People say when you're a fossil / you are well and truly DEAD." The poet reminds readers that fossils once lived and had their chance at singing and dancing and he concludes on an unusually serious note: "Life is short for man and beast / so / while you can—/ Enjoy the feast!" Piet Grobler's humorous illustration, framed by fossil-like fish skeletons, depicts a dinosaur and an amphibian-fish dancing among the crosses and stones of a cemetery.

Many picturebooks do not hesitate to make death the central subject. Helme Heine led the way back in the 1970s with his first picturebook, *Elefanteneinmaleins* (Elephant multiplication table), which was published to wide acclaim in 1976 and selected for the honour list of the Graphic Prize at the Bologna Children's Book Fair the following year. It is a small picturebook about a very big subject: death and the meaning of life. The story is supremely simple: an elephant's droppings begin at one per day when he is little and increase by one with every year of life until the age of fifty, when they begin to decrease until, at the age of one hundred, there is no more lump. The narrator describes the old elephant's reaction in the following manner: "Now he thought of nothing at all. Not of grasses and leaves, and not of adding and subtracting. He was overjoyed. After one hundred elephant years, he had grasped the number zero." In *Elefanteneinmaleins*, Helme explores the concept of death in simple mathematical terms that nonetheless have a

Figure 5.5   Carnival of the Animals by Philip de Vos, illustrated by Piet Grobler, copyright © 1998 Piet Grobler, reprinted by permission of Piet Grobler.

profound philosophical meaning. Max Velthuijs also deals with the theme of death in the most basic terms in *Kikker en het vogeltje* (*Frog and the Birdsong*, 1991), one his most popular and acclaimed books. In 1992, he became the first person to receive both the Golden Slate-Pencil and a Silver Brush for this simple story about death and the importance of celebrating the joy of being alive. When Frog finds a blackbird lying motionless in the grass, Hare informs them it is dead. As Frog does not understand the concept of death, Hare, the intellectual who always offers philosophical reflections or thoughtful words of wisdom, tries to explain what it means. The friends give the bird a burial, complete with flowers, a stone on the grave, and a eulogy of sorts by Hare who acknowledges the bird's sweet singing and its well-earned rest. Their response to death is touchingly human. They are all very moved and walk away in silence, but suddenly Frog proposes a game. Life goes on. At the end of the day, as they roll happily in the grass, Frog declares that life is beautiful and as they walk happily home, they hear a blackbird singing beautifully. As in many picturebooks about death, this story is also a celebration of life. In *Frog and the Birdsong*, Velthjuis adds death to the basic existential themes that he manages to explore in a simple, humorous manner suitable for the very young. Both Velthjuis and Heine offer philosophical tales for children that appeal to readers at both ends of the spectrum.

In almost all his picturebooks, Olivier Douzou deals with serious themes and the big questions in life, issues that are not generally tackled in children's books, but he always does so in an extremely simple manner accessible to very young children. His first book for Éditions du Rouergue was *Jojo La Mache* (1993), a metaphorical story about death. The title is a play on words that substitutes "mache" (mâche means chews) for "vache" (cow); it is the story of an old cow who has been chewing for a very long time. One day, the cow begins losing her distinguishing traits: one night her horns disappear, the next her tail, at dawn on the following day her udders, then her spots. In a square field in the square book, Douzou depicts a rudimentary, square-bodied cow whose various body parts are detached right from the beginning. Jojo is extremely upset after each disappearance because a cow without these things is no longer a cow. The cow's consternation and the search for her body parts are at once funny and sad. The wordplay in the simple text increases the humour for readers of all ages. For example, the word "mamelle" (udder) is replaced by the rhyming word "gamelle" (mess tin or billy-can). One morning there is no sign of the cow, who has completely disappeared from the illustration. The voice of the narrator, probably a small child, informs readers that they looked everywhere. Even very young readers will notice, however, that spread by spread her body parts become part of nature. Jojo will always be there because her various body parts can be found in the night sky or the breaking day: her horns in the crescent moon, her tail in a shooting star, her udders in the rising sun, and her spots in the clouds. The whimsical story that begins as a comic mystery and then shifts into a sad mode has a consolatory ending.

Two years after the release of *Jojo la Mache*, Christian Bruel offered a philosophical reflection on death through the eyes of a field full of cows who react to the death of the legendary cow Zorro in *Rien n'est trop beau pour les amies de Zorro* (Nothing is too good for Zorro's friends, 1995). The simple illustrations by the Algerian-born illustrator Zaven Paré are reminiscent of rock paintings and highlight the fact that death has been the source of such reflections since the beginning of time. The cows who participate in this discussion bear allegorical names such as Valiant, Mischievous, Boastful, Naïve, Passionate, Mournful, and The Dark One. The enigmatic text recounts their reactions to Zorro's death and their desire to understand the notion of death. Although readers never know how Zorro died, it is likely he was taken to the abattoir. The cows know very little about the "other" they have lost, but they are grievously distressed by this bereavement as it forces them to reflect on their own mortality. The cows' reactions to death mirror those of human beings in a tenderly comical manner. They are unable to find the "words" to express their "grief" (39). One cow imagines Zorro and his mate together forever, but the down-to-earth Archivist states that nothing lasts. Another cow rejects the use of the euphemism "disparu" ("disappeared" in the sense of "departed"), insisting that Zorro is "dead" (35). Yet another describes their first encounter with death in existential terms:

The end makes us foolish, packed flank against flank . . .
. . . each with his death. And unable to do anything (30–31).

Their prise de conscience is evoked by the infinite blue space of a doublespread that bears only the thought-provoking words: "Never more. Forever" (32–33). This nothingness is captured even more strikingly on the following completely blank white page that contains only a page number. Despite its small format and minimalist illustrations, this is a very demanding book that is thought-provoking for adults as well as children.

At least one picturebook artist manages to make a dead person the protagonist of very humorous, even burlesque story. In the inimitable style that has earned him a faithful following among young and not-so-young Japanese and international readers, Taro Gomi deals with the subject of death in *Gaikotsu-san* (Mr. Skeleton, 1982). The first of his simple, colourful watercolour illustrations depicts the unusual protagonist, Mr. Skeleton, lying on his bed staring up at the reader with dark, orbit eyes. Much of the charm of this unusual book lies in the narration. On the opening spread, an anonymous voice asks readers: "You think he sleeps with his eyes open, don't you?" and then immediately answers his own question: "No. It's just that those aren't his eyes but holes" (7). The dialogue that the anonymous voice begins with Mr. Skeleton after posing a number of rhetorical questions directly to the reader suggests it represents the protagonist's conscience or intellectual guide. Readers learn that the protagonist is unable to sleep because he has the feeling he has forgotten something. He seems to have no memory or ability to think for himself (he is dead, after all). The humorous illustrations show the skeleton sitting up in bed, sitting pensively in a chair by a burning candle, and then wandering reflectively through the city. As he watches a woman hang her laundry on the line, he wonders if he has forgotten to do his laundry, but the voice reminds him a skeleton has no need of clothes. Each time the voice sets him straight, the skeleton repeats the same line: "It's true. You're right." (9) It wasn't a doctor's appointment because a skeleton can't be sick or a barber's appointment because he has no hair or the need to eat because he has no stomach. In some instances, his state of being dead is underscored. He didn't forget to mail a letter because he mailed his last letter a very long time ago when he was "still alive" (17) and he didn't miss meeting someone because the last time anyone waited for him was ages ago when he was "still alive" (25). In front of the mirror in the public washroom of a large store, Mr. Skeleton suddenly remembers the important thing he has forgotten and he runs home to brush his teeth. The story ends, as it began, with the anonymous voice telling readers again that he is not sleeping with his eyes open. The unexpected ending seems to turn Gomi's whimsical story about a skeleton into a playful reminder to young readers to brush their teeth before going to bed.

The Swedish author Barbro Lindgren, who has been breaking new ground in books for children of all ages since the 1960s, is perhaps the first author to present the subject of death overtly in a picturebook for toddlers. Although many books in the popular Max series by Lindgren and the illustrator Eva Eriksson have appeared in English as the Sam books, *Titta Max grav!* (Look, Max's grave! 1991) is not one of them. It has been considered both a children's book for adults and a small adult book for children. Like all the preceding Max books, it is written in baby talk and includes grammatically incorrect sentences of three to five words. *Titta Max grav!* is a self-reflexive parody of the series that follows the one-year-old protagonist of the previous books throughout his entire life, offering scenes from various stages of the life cycle. The story opens with Max as a baby in his bassinet offering his soother to the dog and goes on to depict him going to school, starting work in a bank, falling in love, having a family, being divorced, in a nursing home, and finally in his grave with his mourning family and friends lined up to pay their last respects in the book's only double-page image. Perhaps the author killed off her protagonist because she was tired of writing the popular Max books. Maria Nikolajeva and Carole Scott suggest that the book "may also address parents who are sick and tired of reading Max books to their children, as well as young parents who listened to Max books as children."[44] Max is not the only one who ages and dies, so, too, does his dog, who is omnipresent throughout the story. At one point Max ties wheels on the dog and eventually uses him as a footstool. In one scene, accompanied by the words "Max lady tired of Max," the wife holds the wheeled dog up disgustingly by the leash and says, in a small speech balloon: "It has been dead for years." When Max himself is old, he takes the dog to the natural history museum. In the penultimate illustration, the elderly, immobile Max, who

Figure 5.6 Titta Max grav! by Barbro Lindgren, illustrated by Eva Eriksson, copyright © 1991, Eriksson and Lindgren, reprinted by permission of Barbro Lindren and Eva Eriksson.

appears to watch television from his wheelchair, is hooked up to an intravenous which may or may not still be keeping him alive. A few words of English from the television show comment on the scene and remind us of Max's dog, because they reveal that the show is one of the most famous Monty Python sketches: "This parrot is dead. No, it's not. It's just resting." *Titta Max grav!* is especially appreciated by readers who are familiar with the series, many of whom will be relieved to see Max dead and gone.

Without being the main subject of the book, the theme of death naturally finds its way into *Garmann's Summer*, Stian Hole's story of a six-year-old Norwegian boy's anxious thoughts toward the end of the last summer before he starts school. The striking mixed-media collages of the remarkable picturebook focus on the boy's imaginings and convey effectively his anxious feelings. Hole has successfully created the desired "feeling of autumnal melancholy throughout the book, through colour and mood."[45] In the Nordic landscape, signs of autumn are all around, not only in nature, but also in the annual visit of his elderly aunts, who "arrive by boat from another time." Readers see his aunts as Garmann imagines them, that is, shrinking so that "soon they won't be able to see over the grass" (the illustration depicts only the head and shoulders of the three old ladies whose bodies disappear into the ground). Hole links a child's fear of starting school with grownup fears and the introspective boy reflects on life's transitions, especially aging and dying. His worries about not having lost his first baby tooth are linked to his aunts' dentures, which appear in a collage. Garmann thoughtfully offers his skateboard to an aunt who says that she will soon need a walker, and the old lady is depicted smiling gleefully as she does a board grab during a dexterous aerial in the clouds. When Garmann asks one of the aunts whether she is going to die soon, she replies "probably," adding that she will "put on lipstick and fly through the constellations." The boy imagines a colourful, winged Aunt Borghild, with a huge realistic head on a small body, flying serenely through the heavens in the company of a variety of other winged creatures. Garmann is still scared at the end of the story, but his aunts' fears of aging and dying help him to accept his own fear. Hole's story does not attempt to assure readers that there is no need to be afraid, whether of school or death, but rather to accept one's fear. Although some critics feel the literary tone, emotional complexity, and sophisticated graphic images (a unique painterly use of digital collage) are beyond young readers, Hole himself believes that "you don't have to explain everything" to children and cautions that they should not be underestimated.[46] Many Nordic picturebook artists share his opinion.

Thomas and Anna-Clara Tidholm repeatedly tackle dark and difficult subjects in their picturebooks. Their best-known book is undoubtedly *Resan till Ugri-La-Brek* (Journey to Ugri-La-Brek, 1987), which was awarded the Deutscher Jugendliteraturpreis in 1992 and has been adapted for the theatre several times. It tells the story of two children's encounter with death in the form of a search for their "lost" grandfather. The text that accompanies the image of the small figures of the children standing in their grandfather's empty apartment states that "Grandfather has been kidnapped" and "is now in another country," having left his glasses behind.[47] Older readers will immediately understand the true meaning of his disappearance. The children's parents refuse to tell them the whereabouts of their grandfather: "And Mom doesn't want to say anything / and Dad knows nothing." Often parents do not know how to talk to children about death or they are unable to confront it themselves. On one level, the story is quite straightforward: the children find their grandfather in the little village of Ugri-La Brek and give him his glasses; he assures them that he is fine and no longer needs his glasses; and they return home. However, this simple story can be read on a mythological or symbolic level by more sophisticated readers. The children's journey across a dark river to "the other side of the World," where there is "nothing / just nothing and nothing," evokes the crossing of the mythological River Styx to the Underworld. During their visit, the text hints that it is an inner journey: "Myran believes that she is maybe dreaming." Time also takes on a mythical dimension: "They travel for a thousand years, and they become a thousand years old." This aging is a sign of their new knowledge. The fact that they find their grandfather's apartment already occupied by "someone else's grandfather" on their return suggests that the journey to the other side has lasted some time, even though the parents are still having their afternoon coffee on the balcony, as they had been earlier when they had called from "far, far away, where you cannot hear it," that it was time to go to bed. The whole voyage seems to have taken place during their play in the yard, play that allows them to come to terms with death. The grandfather's death is presented from the child's perspective: he is depicted in a setting not unlike his apartment but darker, as if the children cannot imagine his new existence otherwise. Anna-Clara Tidholm uses her characteristic naïve, childlike style with which children immediately identify. The fact that the grandfather is probably dead is never mentioned verbally or visually, and the story does not have to be interpreted in that manner. Readers who are ready to deal with the reality of death will make the association and share the protagonists' new understanding. To the earlier lines about the parents' refusal to talk about it, which are repeated at the end of the story, the author now adds: "But Hinken and Myran know / They say nothing." Perhaps the children have dealt with their grief more effectively than their parents. Maria Nikolajeva and Carole Scott take issue with the view expressed by Ulla Rhedin, picturebook critic for the Swedish daily *Dagens Nyheter*, that the Tidholms "do not merely address children and adults on different levels, but rather address the adult coreader alone, using the child as a pretext." As they clearly demonstrate, this complex story offers layers for diverse readers.[48] The Tidholms' books deal with "existential problems at children's level in a way that is both poetic and philosophical and which appeals both to children and adults."[49]

The French author-illustrator and humorist Philippe Dumas also takes issue with the avoidance of the subject of death in *Ce changement-là* (That change), a book he published in 1981 after the death of his own father. Like Christian Bruel, Dumas rejects the euphemisms society uses in an attempt to avoid the truth: his father hadn't gone on a voyage, he hadn't merely left them, and he hadn't disappeared; he had died. The author contends that death is not something to avoid and hush up, but that it is essential to talk about it in order to be able to live better. He asks the fundamental questions that preoccupy readers of all ages: What does it mean to die? How does it happen? What comes after? To talk about death is to accept that it is part of life, no less than birth, childhood, adolescence, parenthood, grandparenthood, illness, and so forth. Dumas published *Ce changement-là* in the belief that talking about it banishes the fear of death.

Dealing with the death of a child is more difficult than the more accepted death of an elderly person. Using animal rather than human protagonists can make the subject less painful. The Japanese picturebook artist Keizaburo Tejima tells the story of a child's death in a family of swans in *Oohakuchou no sora* (1983; English trans., *Swan Sky*). A sick young swan is unable to join a flock of wild swans preparing to leave a half-frozen lake to fly north to their summer nesting grounds. After delaying their departure, the young swan's family eventually flies off sorrowfully, but ends up returning to stay with her until she dies. The sad story is told in haunting black woodcuts touched with muted colours of bluish grey, gold, and orange. Like many picturebooks that deal with death, it is also a story of acceptance and new life. The sadness is mitigated by dawn breaking over clouds that take the shape of a swan with outstretched wings and by the onset of a new day and a new season. In Asian literature, moreso than in Western literature, death is seen as a natural stage of the life cycle. The horror of Hiroshima is the inspiration for the French author-illustrator Martine Delerm's tender and sensitive portrayal of the death of a child in *Origami* (1990), which received the Prix Enfance du Monde 1992. The story is based on the true story of the death of twelve-year-old Sadako Sasaki of radiation sickness in 1957. In order to remember Sadako and to work towards peace, her friends created the Club of a thousand cranes, whose members fold paper cranes in memory of the deceased child. In Delerm's story, one of the protagonist's friends encourages the very ill Sadako to continue folding paper cranes, telling her that folding a thousand origami will cure her. Following the girl's death, the children continue to fold origami. The text is very poetic and the illustrations, which are in the delicate pastel colours characteristic of Delerm's work, are tender and serene. The picturebooks by Delerm and Tejima help both children and adults come to terms with the death of a child.

A few picturebooks actually portray death as a character in the story. Among the many books by Ipomée that are haunted by the theme of death,[50] the most striking image is presented in Anne Quesemand's *La*

Mort-Marraine (Godmother death, 1987), a variation on the popular tale collected by the Brothers Grimm about a child who is taken away by Death (not to the usual end but rather to be raised) when Death is surprisingly asked to be a godparent. Laura Berman's initial eye-catching black-and-white illustration represents the vulnerable baby in the arms of a skeleton that looks at him tenderly from its hollow eye sockets. An equally moving illustration depicts Death's bony hand on the shoulder of the boy studying by candlelight. These remarkable images present a striking contrast with the conventional visual depictions of Death. The most memorable portrayal of Death, however, is the titular character of Erlbruch's *Duck, Death and the Tulip*. Death is a recurring theme in the books of Wolf Erlbruch, who, like Sendak and Ungerer, has always drawn subjects from the darker, more uncomfortable side of childhood. The fact that the book by the internationally renowned illustrator was not brought out in English by an American or British publisher, but rather by the small New Zealand-based Gecko Press is indicative of the reluctance to deal with this difficult topic in children's picturebooks. Erlbruch evokes the fear that death inspires through the simple image of a duck who has the feeling she is being followed and discovers her stalker is Death: "Duck was scared stiff, and who could blame her?" writes the anonymous narrator. Erlbruch does not present the terrifying traditional image of the black grim reaper, but rather a smiling figure with a flat skull head and dressed in a beige, checked robe, brown mittens, and slippers. The figure will already be familiar to readers of Erlbruch's *La grande question* (2003; English trans., *The Big Question*), in which Death appears in a more clown-like yellow polka dot robe to give its viewpoint on the meaning of life: "You are here to love life." Although the skull-headed character is unexpected in a children's book about a duck (only the duck appears on the cover), there is something rather cute about the figure that helps readers of all ages confront the unpleasant subject. Over the ensuing weeks, Death is a constant presence that Duck comes not only to accept but even to befriend. Death is charmingly portrayed with human weaknesses and emotions. When Death catches a chill in the pond, Duck offers to warm him. The narrator's comment that "nobody had ever offered to do that for Death" suggests that Death is moved by this unexpected show of kindness, and a touching illustration portrays him smiling contentedly as Duck lies on top of him. Readers may wonder if the sleeping Duck is dead and Duck's own first thought when she wakes up is that she is "not dead." The favour will be repaid one cool night when Duck feels the cold for the first time and asks Death if he will warm her. The facing illustration is a touching picture of Death and Duck holding hands/wings and staring deeply into each other's eyes/eye cavities.

Erlbruch even broaches the topic of Death from a philosophical point of view in his picturebook. The two protagonists reflect on the afterlife and Duck recounts the various views held by her fellow ducks. Human philosophical and religious beliefs, which Death calls "amazing stories," are thus transposed into the world of ducks: the belief that you become an angel or that you will be roasted in a place deep in the earth "if you haven't been good." Duck is not without a certain resemblance to the graph paper duck in Erlbruch's *The Big Question*, the only character to have no idea why we are on this earth. Death's apparent lack of knowledge about what happens after death surprises Duck, but readers sense he simply does not feel that philosophical or religious views are important. Life and death are simple truths. In the top of a tree, which becomes a metaphor for the wide perspective Duck is now adopting (she sees her world, that of the pond, as it will be after her death), the two engage in a simple, metaphysical discussion of death. Erlbruch depicts Duck's and Death's heads above the foliage of the tree engaged in a dialogue like two philosophers. On the white space of the facing page, a black raven flies by, an omen of Duck's looming death. Like Duck, Erlbruch's readers will find talking about death easy in the presence of this not unkindly Death. When Duck can't bring herself to speak of her own death, Death finishes the sentence for her. Like the book's author, Death "wasn't coy about the subject." Duck's death is depicted in a very gentle manner: as snowflakes fall, Duck stops breathing and lies completely still. While most illustrations are on a stark white background, an extremely effective use of negative space in a book about death, the spread that depicts Duck's death presents an infinite blue background with flakes of snow gently falling and Death staring down at her with what appears to be compassion or tenderness.

Death's actions, as depicted by Erlbruch, are even more reassuring than his appearance. Death strokes Duck's ruffled feathers into place before carrying her to the river where he gently places her on the water for her final journey, a scene that evokes vague reminiscences of ancient funeral rites. The titular tulip is never mentioned in the text, but it plays a very important role in the visual narrative and it is the final image left with readers on the back cover. Perhaps it is largely the tulip that Death carries in the first doublespread that makes him less frightening. Readers see the incongruous red tulip behind Death's back, but it is not visible from Duck's position on the facing page. In the ensuing pages, Death usually has one or both of his mitten-clad hands behind his back, continuing to hide the tulip from Duck's view, although it is often, but not always, visible to readers. The tulip is conspicuously absent for several pages, but reappears lying beside Duck on the page depicting her death. Death watches Duck's body float off into the distance until she is lost to sight, "feeling almost a little moved," but tells himself "that's life." Death is inevitable, a fact of life. The final page is a picture of Death walking contemplatively while a fox chases a hare around him. Life goes on and Death will no doubt begin now to follow either the fox or the hare. Erlbruch explores the profound question of death with extreme simplicity in *Duck, Death and the Tulip*, which is one of the most remarkable picturebooks dealing with this difficult subject. Indeed, one reviewer pronounces it "one of the best books about death I've ever seen, for any age."[51]

Kitty Crowther depicts death as a child in *La visite de Petite Mort* (Little Death's visit, 2004). Through Petite Mort, the author seeks to demystify death and to reassure children. Although the grim reaper's sickle is retained, the curious little figure in black is not intimidating thanks to her smile, her nun-like appearance, and the company of a smiling little girl in a white dress. Death is not only personified but given admirable human qualities. The story begins by informing readers that, unbeknownst to people, "Death is a charming little person." Death thus becomes not only reassuringly human, but a child with whom young readers can identify. Petite Mort arrives gently and timidly to accompany the dying, but their reaction is always negative: they never speak to her, they're afraid, they're cold, and when she builds a fire to warm them they believe they are in hell. The unexpected reaction of the little girl Elsewise, who welcomes her smilingly, is not unlike Duck's offer to warm Death. Elsewise eventually explains to a mystified Petite Mort that she had been ill and always in pain before her arrival. Nowhere in Crowther's story are the dead depicted as really dead: Elsewise and Petite Mort become good friends and play together; when Elsewise has to leave the realm of the dead for another life, she returns as an angel so that she can forever be at her friend's side. Not only is Elsewise's reaction to death reassuring for children, but the ending gives her a vocation of making death easier for others. Now the two friends go hand in hand to accompany the dying and people are no longer afraid. Like Tejima's *Swan Sky* and Delerm's *Origami*, *La visite de Petite Mort* provides an opportunity to discuss the death of a child.

Four years before *La visite de Petite Mort*, Crowther had dealt with the topic of death in *Moi et Rien* (Me and Nothing, 2000), which focuses on the grieving that follows the death of a loved one. The first-person text, which is written in courier font as if it had been typed on an old-fashioned typewriter, resembles the notations in a diary, while the simple, caricatural drawings evoke those of a child. Narrated by a young girl named Lila, the unusual story begins:

Here, there is nothing.
Yes, there's me. Nothing and me. . . .

The strange words are not disturbing because they are followed immediately by a picture of a smiling Lila, wearing her father's jacket and the boots her mother "always told her to wear" so she wouldn't catch cold. The use of the past tense offers the first clue that the girl has recently lost her mother. The pictures on the following page are labelled, as if the little girl herself had drawn them in her journal: the first, labelled "Nothing and me," depicts the smiling heroine with her arm around her invisible friend, while the second, labelled "Nothing," portrays a character that is a cross between a scarecrow and a snow man. Although others cannot see her friend—she admits the other children find her strange—Nothing is a full-fledged character in the story. Gradually it becomes obvious, at least to older readers, that Rien conceals an absence in Lila's life. Not only has her mother died recently, but her father has not recovered from the death and is never there for the little girl. A picture of the father pacing is accompanied by the words "Dad has cares," but the words "and me too" follow immediately with a drawing of the little girl pacing in an exact imitation of the father's body language. The simple words and images convey poignantly the little girl's pain.

The mother's death is never explicitly mentioned in Crowther's text, but a "before" is associated with flowers with extraordinary names that her mother grew in the now abandoned garden. This happy past is evoked when the little girl takes Nothing to the forbidden shed where her father used to grow the seedlings for her mother's garden. Nothing represents the dead mother's absence and evolves throughout the story: from a painful nothing to a nothing that is full of good memories. Nothing shows Lila that "everything" can come from "nothing" by planting a small seed that grows into a large tree before our very eyes. In a scene reminiscent of Duck and Death in the tree top, Lila and Nothing climb the tall tree, from which they have a wide perspective that includes the castle where Lila's father works as a gardener. There the little girl is able to talk about him to her friend. A small black-and-white drawing at the bottom of the page adopts a light hearted note to show her father running into the unexpected tree on his way home, but the blow does not bring him to his senses. Pained by her father's continued neglect (at the table her father sits behind a newspaper ignoring her), the little girl wishes she, too, was dead. Nothing encourages her to plant seeds, but the despairing little girl tells him to go away because he doesn't understand anything. The appearance of a blue-throat seems to be a sign from her mother, as the bird is associated with her favourite flowers, so Lila plants them at the beginning of autumn. Through the cold winter, in the absence of Nothing, Lila accomplishes the necessary mourning. When the little girl finds a lilac bush (her name is a homonym of the French word for lilac) in the garden in the spring, she attributes it to Nothing, who reappears and is warmly welcomed. Nothing now represents the happy memories of her mother, whose absence Lila is finally able to accept. The flowers bring healing for the grieving father, who once again assumes his parental role, and life resumes. Crowther reserves a surprising, fantastic ending to the story: when the father finally gives Lila a gift her mother made for her before her death, in the box is a doll-size Nothing, a miniature replica of her imaginary friend. In a multilayered story that deals with both a child's and an adult's reaction to the loss of a loved one, Crowther offers levels for readers of all ages.

Whereas Crowther focuses on a child's reaction to her mother's death, *Michael Rosen's Sad Book* (2004) concerns an adult's grief and depression at the death of a child. It is a highly personal story, as the protagonist and narrator is the author Michael Rosen himself, whose teenage son Eddie died unexpectedly of meningitis in 1999. The fact that it is not a fiction, but a real story concerning the death of a boy known to many of Rosen's readers as a character in several earlier books makes this a particularly difficult picturebook. The author wrote it as a reply to children who asked him about his son and who accepted matter-of-factly that he was dead.[52] The emotions of sadness, loneliness, anger, even despair, are portrayed by Rosen's understated words and Quentin Blake's watercolour-and-ink illustrations. The mood is set by the front cover, which, in black lines and gloomy shades of grey, depicts Rosen and his dog walking in a dismal, trash-littered landscape under an overcast, grey sky. Blake uses this grey and black palette throughout the book when sadness pervades and shifts to brighter colours of yellow and red when memories of happier times break through. The simple text and pictures allow even very young children to understand the moods and emotions experienced by Rosen. The emptiness that Crowther evokes in *Moi et Rien* is expressed very simply in Blake's photo gallery, where an empty picture frame follows the pictures of Eddie as a baby, a boy, and a teen. Rosen's story assures readers that these emotions and the behaviour they trigger (he confesses the "bad things" he does) are common in the face of death. Although the *Sad Book* provides a glimmer of hope in the good memories that sometimes surface, unlike Crowther's *Moi et Rien* it does not end on a happy, optimistic note. Rosen is obviously still suffering painfully from the loss of his son at the end of the story. Blake's final illustration depicts the author's grey figure sitting writing dejectedly in front of a framed photograph by the light of a single candle on what appears to be his son's birthday. Some readers may feel it is a book for adults grieving the loss of a child but, as Kimberley Reynolds points out in her excellent analysis of the picturebook, the *Sad Book* can help children understand adult grief and depression. She rightly acknowledges its accessibility to readers of all ages: "Readers of whatever age who have suffered from depression themselves will recognize its symptoms and the strategies Rosen uses to manage it—not least telling others about what he is feeling. . . ."[53] On his website, Rosen expresses his hope that it will help "anyone who's been sad about anything at all." Rosen and Blake assist readers of all ages to confront a subject that is very painful and generally avoided in children's literature.

A personal story of grief and bereavement is told within the context of a well-known historical event that took the lives of hundreds of people in Olivier Douzou and Charlotte Mollet's *Navratil* (2000). A preface by Mollet, which constitutes an integral part of the story, explains the remarkable genesis of the book she illustrated. She accidentally made the acquaintance of the last French survivor of the Titanic when the key she dropped from her third-floor apartment opened the door into the memories of an extraordinary elderly gentleman of Czechoslovakian origin, by the name of Navratil. The unusual name, which means "he who will return," seemed to announce the destiny of the young boy who was to leave France at four years of age with his younger brother, his father, and "the luggage of those who leave forever." The story is narrated in the first person by the elderly Navratil, whose father had decided "to put . . . an ocean" between them and their mother, who had no knowledge of their secret departure. Douzou's text is integrated into Mollet's innovative illustrations, which blend engravings, fragments of literature and songs, and historical documents about the disaster, to create a multilayered narrative that fascinates and moves readers of all ages. The paper used in Mollet's collages contributes to the narrative. In two of the spreads, the sea around the Titanic is formed by fragments of Homer's *Iliade* and *Odyssee* (in Greek), demonstrating visually how the historical voyage of the Titanic has joined other legendary and mythical journeys in the collective consciousness. Mollet brings sound to a wordless spread that depicts jazz musicians playing and people dancing before the collision with the iceberg by using a musical score as the background of the dramatic scene. Another musical score is partially visible in the dark blue sea as the ship goes down with the band still playing. Douzou's simple text, accessible to very young children, is nevertheless extremely poetic. Navratil describes the rent that left "a scar in the history of the world" when the Titanic was ripped open that night by "a giant ice cube" from the Arctic.

In this small square book, Mollet evokes the drowning of the Titanic's victims in simple, yet powerful, framed engravings. The verso of one striking doublespread depicts the enormous, iceberg hidden ominously under the surface of the dark purple sea just prior to impact. In a small framed square on the recto, which seems to float like a giant ice cube submersed below the surface, a couple huddles together with their arms around each other as the water rises in the confined space. On the page following the loading of women and children onto lifeboats, the words "The others went down, souls and bodies" appear on a stark white background, while a small rectangular engraving of a few tiny, dark silhouettes on a deck or looking out windows sinks into a sea of words from a French novel. On the same sea of words on the facing page, a small square engraving offers a close-up of one of these featureless, anonymous souls. The square is divided into four frames that resemble the successive frames of a film, in which the body is shown falling into the sea, sinking, and eventually being swallowed up completely. The series of three long, narrow frames on the next spread, which depicts another man (this time with very crudely drawn features) sinking gradually into the sea, is made much more moving by the text. The words "Tell your mother how much I love her," which are broken up between the frames and descend the page in ever smaller characters, reveal that this drowning man is not anonymous; he is Navratil's father. The frames themselves are a striking combination of engraving and collage. The rather primitive, black-and-white figure of a man whose large hands reach up toward the sky gradually sinks into a sea composed of torn fragments from either the French novel or Homer, on which the wavy lines of the sea have been stamped. In the final frame only the man's large hands are visible above the waves. The narrative is followed by three pages of historical documents that focus on the 1,325 dead and the 711 survivors, one of whom is Navratil. In a kind of epilogue on the inside of the back cover, Navratil reflects on these "unsinkable" memories that never stop resurfacing from the depths of his memory. The devastating effect of experiencing the death of a parent, and that of so many other people, at such a tender age is expressed eloquently by the nonogenarian survivor, whose life ended at the age of four. Since that time he has been adrift on an ocean waiting for the rowboat/cradle that took him to his mother so long ago, and that "this time, will take me to my two parents." Navratil has been a philosopher for eighty-nine years, writes Mollet in the preface to this moving story.

Oscar K. and Dorte Karrebæk approach the subject of death in a very unusual manner in *Børnenes bedemand* (The children's undertaker, 2008), the story of an undertaker by the name of Mr. Jørgensen, who specializes in dead children. The reviewer Steffen Larsen finds it "hard to imagine any new taboo to be broken that is more extreme than *Børnenes bedemand*."[54] Despite the rather unconventional subject matter, it is a very moving and tender story. Instead of the classic literary image of a lugubrious undertaker hovering like a vulture around the dying awaiting their last breath, Jørgensen is a sympathetic, kindly man who dreads the ring of the telephone in his shop because the death of a child makes him so sad. Determined not to let his sorrow affect the dead children and to make their final hours "light and bright, so they don't notice anything," he talks to them about the pear tree and the marigolds, the sky and the angels, and about Miss Ene, who brings him clean overalls twice a week. He also sings them songs from his under-takers' barbershop quartet, bringing little white smiles to the faces of the children in the coffins. As in so many of their books, the Danish husband and wife team focus on society's marginalized and vulnerable members. One day, the police arrive with the body of an unidentified child, who is so dirty that it is only when Jørgensen has tenderly washed her that he discovers it is the body of a girl. The fate of this dead child, to whom he gives his most beautiful casket, is particularly sad, as she has no one to accompany her to the cemetery. The story of the children's undertaker is told with tenderness and a quirky humour that mitigates the darkness of the subject. In addition, the story ends on a happy note, when a stray dog leads Jørgensen and Miss Ene to three homeless young children, the siblings of the dead girl. Thus Dinah is accompanied by her siblings and their dog on her last journey to the cemetery. As Mr. Jørgensen quietly sings a song about Dinah and Miss Ene dances, a smile comes to the lips of the dead girl and they suddenly hear the voice of the angel (the children believe Dinah is now an angel), who, on rare occasions, adds a fifth voice to the barbershop quartet.

Oscar K. and Dorte Karrebæk were not the first to tell the story of an undertaker in a picturebook. In 1999, Eugène and Bertola published the Swiss picturebook *La mort à vivre* (Death to live), which examines a young undertaker's first couple of weeks in the business. Written in the first person, in journal form, the story opens with the words: "Last week, the undertaker died. That would be funny if it wasn't sad. Because the undertaker who died was my father" (8). The author points out that the use of the personal journal offers the opportunity for drawings, which, in turn, offer another opportunity for text.[55] The delicate watercolour illustrations that accompany Eugène's lengthy text sometimes wash up into the text and often contain little notations in cursive by the author. The unusual picturebook has a very interesting genesis because it resulted from an exhibition on death at Geneva's Ethnography Museum in 2000. The curator, Bernard Crettaz, wanted to examine the funeral rites that were once passed down from one generation to the next, traditions which allowed an individual to cope when a loved one died. He recounts how his own mother one day opened a drawer in an old dresser and told him he would find everything he needed there when she and his father passed away. Two books, one of a documentary nature and this picturebook "addressed more particularly to the young," were published to fill this perceived need.[56] In order to bring the story to life, the author met with an undertaker in Lausanne and came up with this format to recount his numerous anecdotes. The young protagonist is confronted with the various real-life situations described by the Lausanne undertaker. The author had never seen a dead person when he wrote the book, which explains the light tone that Crettaz found inappropriate. The brief entry for April 7 ("Triste. Triste. Triste.") is a joke that the author added toward the beginning so that he would not plunge into sadness, but, according to the author, no one realized that it was a reference to the Rolling Stones song "Sad, sad, sad." The tone of the text is announced by the epigraph, which is the threat the French singer-songwriter Georges Brassens once made to a friend: "If you don't come to my funeral, I won't go to yours" (7). Although *La mort à vivre* was published as a children's picturebook by La Joie de lire in Geneva, the author feels it is really "a book for adolescents and adults."[57]

If death is the "ultimate taboo," there are aspects of the subject which are more taboo than others. Although suicide is now being addressed with some frequency in adolescent fiction, it is still a rare topic in picturebooks. In the late 1970s, Christian Bruel hinted at a child's attempted suicide in the dream-like world of *Lison et l'eau dormante*. However, Lison's attempted suicide is depicted metaphorically as a dive into a pond (which brings the protagonist a deep sense of well-being) and it is described so vaguely that other interpretations are also possible. The final page of the picturebook suggests that perhaps Lison was ill and the story is the result of her fevered sleep. The dreamlike atmosphere that distances it from real life and the ambiguity surrounding events lessen the distress for readers. The controversy and censorship that a more direct approach to such a sensitive subject can cause is illustrated by *Petit-Âne* (Little-Donkey), published by Ipomée in 1995. Nicole Maymat's interest in "taboo" subjects that "dérangent" (trouble) is nowhere more evident than in this picturebook, which immediately caused an uproar among librarians, teachers, and critics. Albin Michel, who was bringing out Ipomée's books at the time, hurried to have it removed from bookstore shelves.[58] The text, written by the Russian poet Serge Kozlov in 1964 under the title "Le Dernier conte" (The last tale), begins with the traditional fairy-tale incipit but continues in a highly unexpected manner: "Once upon a time there was a little donkey who wanted to hang himself, but he didn't know how." Some people took the book for a "suicide instruction booklet," an accusation that Maymat denied vehemently in her response to the controversy. Readers had only to look closely at Vitaly Statzynsky's illustrations, she felt, to know that was not the case. According to the publisher, the use of toys creates a certain distance required "to avoid all exhibitionism and violence."[59] The toys depicted in a room on the brown pages of the endpapers come alive at the beginning and fall asleep again on the final endpapers. In her analysis of this picturebook, Kimberley Reynolds points to the "long tradition of using animals and toys as substitute child figures" in children's books: "Anthropomorphising toys and animals (or, as in *Petit-Âne*, a combination of the two) provides a degree of disguise and distance which can be useful when dealing with sensitive or disturbing topics." She suggests that in the case of *Petit-Âne*, the disguise may be "at least as much for the adult, for whom the idea of child suicide is devastating and unspeakable, as for potential child readers."[60]

The atmosphere of *Petit-Âne* is not at all morose or sombre; the colours are bright and cheerful in the decorative style of Russian folk art. However, Statzynsky's highly stylized and symbolic illustrations, as well as his satirical bent, had already caused much controversy in Russia, upsetting the conventions of illustration for children.[61] The events, as depicted by both the author and the illustrator, are not frightening or traumatic. Although the rope is around Petit-Âne's neck in the penultimate doublespread, the final image shows him hanging from his stomach and he is smiling happily. Kozlov describes the suicide in very poetical and entirely imaginary terms: Petit-Âne hangs "between heaven and earth" by a cord that falls "like a refreshing shower" from a nail that shines in the sky "like a star." French critics, unfamiliar with Statzynsky's unconventional style and Kozlov's poetic and philosophical texts, were appalled by the serenity with which such a troubling subject was portrayed, claiming the little donkey's smiling face was a seductive invitation to children to imitate him. As is often the case, the book seemed to trouble adults more than children. The Russian journal *School and Family* asked parents to "have faith in children's ability for compassion" when it published Kozlov's "sad and strange" tale in 1996.[62] Children are often curious about death and enact it in their play. "Children have little experience of death and find the concept strange—sometimes even amusing," writes Reynolds, who adds that they may seek to understand death and "explore their feelings about it through fantasy and play."[63] The illustrator had been guided by children in the first year of elementary school in France. After telling them the story, Statzynsky had listened to the children's

Ni Sapin, ni Hirondelle,
ni ses frères les Petits-Ânes dans l'étable
ne virent Petit-Âne passer
ses oreilles dans la boucle.

Figure 5.7 *Petit-Âne* by Serge Kozlov, illustrated by Vitaly Statzynsky, copyright © 1995 Ipomée, reprinted by permission of Nicole Maymat.

comments ("What if we play being dead?") and studied the images they drew. Maymat, too, suggests that the suicide is perhaps only "play," in which it constitutes "an initiation rite." The publisher wonders if a preface should have been included, but the text on the back cover mitigates the events by framing Petit-Âne's suicide in terms of a longing to journey to a far-away place to escape his melancholy, in the tradition of Saint-Exupéry's classic *The Little Prince*: "What if he simply dreamt of going elsewhere. Not everyone is lucky enough to be the Little Prince. . . ."

Distressed and saddened by the reaction to his story, Kozlov proposed two sequels to Maymat, but, unfortunately, a sequel was never able to be published.[64] In "Le retour de Petit-Âne" (The return of Petit Âne), the protagonist again longs to be elsewhere and his dream of sailing the sky "in the boat-moon" comes true, but he then wonders how to return. The happy ending of this tale is the result of the undying friendship between Petit-Âne and Ourson, the best friend who assists him commit suicide in *Petit-Âne*, and who, in the sequel, ensures his safe return to earth. The blurb on the back cover of the first story had stated: "Fortunately, Ourson is there and he knows which country our Petit-Âne dreams of reaching." In another tale, it is Ourson who wishes to be able "like the summer, to die and to be reborn" because "one is initially sad but so joyous afterwards!"[65] In the sequel, Kozlov expresses within the story itself the possibility that Petit-Âne's adventure is only a dream. Despite the picturebook's hostile critical reception, Maymat remains convinced that *Petit-Âne* was "a story that should have found its public, a poem and images that could have been shared between young and old. . . ."[66] Many readers were of this opinion, notably one woman who thanked them "for having the courage to tackle this question" because her son's father had committed suicide. *Petit-Âne* offers a rare opportunity for young readers who have suicidal thoughts or know someone who has committed suicide to attempt to understand their own and others' emotions and actions.

Suicide is depicted in a much more dramatic and violent manner in Geert De Kockere and Carll Cneut's *Dulle Griet*. Filled with terrifying verbal and visual images of death, decay, and destruction, the challenging picturebook caused quite a stir and, not surprisingly, it has not appeared in English. Human and diabolical creatures try to outdo each other with senseless acts of evil. Humour is used to mitigate the horror and distance the reader. The narrator confides in the reader that the experience would have been so harrowing for him or her and for the reader, that "we" would have screamed, trembled, and our teeth would have chattered. "We would have been so afraid that we would have wet ourselves!" For Meg, however, it is "child's play"; she is amused and feels entirely at home. As she penetrates deeper into the darkness of hell, shouting for the devil, the creatures around her become only dark shadows. Her blue clothes, red basket, and red sword provide the only colour, while her white face contrasts starkly with hell's blackness. When the devil ignores her questions and demands ("Do you want me?"; "Take me."), waiting silently for Meg to give him her soul, she becomes "raving mad" and stabs herself in the heart with her deadly sword. On an empty blood red doublespread, the narrator states: "She was dead. Stone dead. Dead like death." Although Meg is made more human at the beginning of the story by her depiction as a young child, she is quickly transformed into a monstrous character that children are unlikely to identify with, whether or not they realize that she is inspired by a figure in a painting. Her suicide is therefore less likely to disturb young readers.

Oscar K. and Dorte Karrebæk are, to the best of my knowledge, the first picturebook artists to address the question of euthanasia in a children's picturebook. Published in 2009, *Idiot!* caused a certain amount of controversy, but by that time Danish critics certainly knew what to expect from the ground-breaking husband and wife team. Many reviewers nonetheless described *Idiot!* as a picturebook for older children and adults. Readers follow a so-called mentally disabled boy by the name of August (the artist called him "a wonderful monster of a child" during our conversation about the book[67]) and his unmarried mother as they walk through their town, a walk that is transformed into his life journey and his final journey. Once again the husband and wife team turn their attention to marginalized members of society, offering a tender portrait of the "idiot," who charms readers with his ingenuousness and his simple joys. Things are seen through August's eyes: the children who call him names—including the titular "Idiot"—and the mentally challenged children who wave to him. August understands that the children tease him because he is different (he says "they need their noses punched") and he is drawn to the children who resemble him. He is nonetheless happy in his own world with his mother, taking immense pleasure in puddles, kittens, dogs, and angels. Oscar K. tells August's story in a long stream of consciousness, as the boy's wandering mind blends thoughts, bits of information, dialogue, and fragments from songs, nursery rhymes, fairy tales, sayings, and the Bible to form a poetic text that challenges readers of all ages. This flow of thoughts and words is interrupted only when his mother gives him instructions or tries to engage him in conversation. More often, he talks with his companion, "little Monster," a plastic bag on a leash that is, in fact, a kind of double or alter ego (August imagines him wearing the same woolly hat over his ears that he does). Together the two little "Monsters" see things that are invisible to "normal" people.

As the story progresses, the detailed watercolours, in muted, sad colours, make up an ever more important part of the narrative. The atmosphere becomes bleaker and chillier as wintery images pervade the illustrations. Concerned about her son's fate when she is no longer there to look after him, August's poor, unmarried mother gives him an overdose of sleeping pills when she herself is on the point of death. The theme of death is introduced when the mother takes her "little Monster" to the cemetery to visit his grandfather's grave. Readers see the scene through the boy's eyes: the heavenly gates, the angels, the Bogeyman under the ground, and the gravedigger's hole. Some of the references to nursery rhymes and lullabies sprinkled throughout the poetic text announce the impending death. In the English translation by Charlotte Barslund, which the author kindly sent me, the final line from "Ring around the Rosy" ("we all fall down") was

Figure 5.8 Idiot! by Oscar K. and Dorte Karrebæk, copyright © 2009 Oscar K. (text), Dorte Karrebæk (illustrations), and Høst & Søn, reprinted by permission of Dorte Karrebæk and Oscar K.

substituted for a line from a Danish song game in which the one who is last falls "in the black pot." As the mother and son sit on a bench after taking the pills, it gets late and "time to go home." August recites the Danish nursery rhyme "Solen er så rød, mor" (The sun is so red, Mum), which is replaced in the English translation by "Rock a bye baby on the tree top." The Danish nursery rhyme also has death symbolism: "Why does night appear, Mum, / with cold and bitter wind? / . . . Oh, listen, stars are singing now, / they sing me to sleep." August seems to sense what is happening, as he says his final goodbyes not only to his little Monster, but also to himself. Despite the underlying sadness, the ending is depicted in a very positive light, as the dark tunnel the mother and son travel through leads out into the light, where August will be in God's care. Much of the humour lies in August's misunderstandings of the things he has retained and the new meanings that are attributed to them. Even in this moving ending, there is a touch of humour as August misquotes a line from scripture, giving it a touching new meaning: "I will sit on God's right hand and dream the living and the dead." The Danish verb "drømme" (dream) replaces the similar verb "dømme" (judge). Far be it from August to "judge" others, as they have judged him, or, as some readers may be judging his mother. On the last page, Karrebæk depicts August literally sitting "on" God's huge right hand. Most publishers would not touch a story with such a harsh ending, but Høst & Søn bravely took it on and was lauded by some reviewers for its courage. This powerful picturebook is unforgettable for readers of all ages.

Like Dorte Karrebæk and Oscar K., many authors and illustrators "refuse to talk down to children, offering young readers books that deal with the important questions in life." Many children's publishers take the same stand. Interested in "all the big questions of this world," even those that "seem taboo," Nicole Maymat insists that Ipomée's books do not attempt to provide answers but "simply to share the questions that children, like adults, ask at a point of their lives." Cross-generational themes in picturebooks are not always dark and painful, of course; they can also be important philosophical considerations that are often seen to be too complex for children. In the late 1980s, Philippe and Martine Delerm proposed a project titled "Les petites philosophies" (Little philosophies) to Maymat. The unusual book, which is composed of philosophical reflections that Philippe based on Martine's images (rather than the usual reverse scenario), was finally published by Seuil, under the title *Fragiles* (from the French adjective meaning "fragile"), in 2001. The success of the remarkable French picturebook, which sold more than 100,000 copies, amazed even the innovative illustrator Étienne Delessert.[68] The homeland of Descartes and Saint-Exupéry is not the only country publishing philosophical picturebooks for children, however. Publishers in many countries are bringing out picturebooks whose metaphysical subjects are thought-provoking for children and adults alike. It is more widely acknowledged that readers of all ages struggle with metaphysical concerns and ask the big questions about where we come from and where we go. In 2010, Eva Zoller Morf, an expert on philosophy for children in Switzerland, published a book with the subtitle *Grosse Fragen für kleine Philosophen und Philosophinnen* (Big questions for small philosophers), which documents the reactions of children aged three to thirteen to the picturebooks she uses as a starting point for philosophical discussions on "the big questions." Erlbruch's *La grande question* was published by Christian Bruel's publishing house Éditions Être with the assistance of the Conseil Général du Val-de-Marne as the annual gift to children born in that department in 2004. In this "big" book, which won the Bologna Ragazzi Award 2004, twenty-one different characters (human beings, animals, inanimate objects) answer the ultimate existential question concerning the meaning of life from their particular perspective. Young and old readers alike realize that only very personal answers can be given to the question of all questions, which is not even formulated in the book. Erlbruch suggests that we are on this earth precisely to answer that question. The entirely blank doublespread that follows the last answer encourages readers to reflect on their own answer and two pages of lined paper at the end are provided so they can record the answers they find to the "Big Question" as they grow up.

What is or is not appropriate reading material for children is a long-standing debate in the field of children's literature, as Kimberley Reynolds illustrates by pointing to Nicholas Tucker's 1976 study *Suitable for Children?* As she mentions, however, recent years have seen concern shift "from the kind of material that is published to how potentially disturbing material is handled."[69] Oscar K. makes this point in the title of an article published in the *Danish Literary Magazine* in August 2008: "It's not the fact that it is said—in fact it's just the way you say it." Picturebook artists soften the impact of painful and distressing subjects by using a variety of techniques, including fantasy, exaggeration, poetic mode, and, most often, humour. Dorte Karrebæk and Oscar K. deal with the difficulties, challenges, and profundities of existence, but they serve up life's often painful realities with a large dose of both humour and tenderness. Picturebooks such as theirs often make adults feel very uncomfortable and many grown-ups believe they should not be given to children. In an article subtitled "Inappropriate Picturebooks for Young Readers," Carole Scott reminds readers of the role of the adult mediator: "works that may seem shocking or inappropriate for young children can be received through the filter of adult interpretation, the presence of the adult reader/parent providing the young child with a sense of security in dealing with potentially disturbing images and ideas." As she points out, the picturebook artists who so challenge children generally "envisage children who are resilient, curious and well able to cope with the stark facts of life from which some adults may feel they need protection." Scott turns around the conventional view of what is "inappropriate" material: ". . . the authors must view their texts as appropriate, providing an introduction to our world rather than constructing a cocoon for children to shelter from it . . . as artists, they shy away from presenting 'inappropriate' works that are not truthful to the reality they perceive."[70]

Chapter Six
Celebrity Picturebooks

books for children (even grown-up ones)
—Tag line from Madonna's children's books

In *Crossover Fiction*, I discussed the recent trend of bestselling adult writers crossing over from adult books to children's and young adult books in the wake of the unprecedented commercial success of the Harry Potter series that made J. K. Rowling the first international media superstar from the literary world.[1] When famous people such as Michael Chabon, Neil Gaiman, and Isabel Allende invade the field of children's literature, at least they know how to write even if they do not necessarily know how to write children's books. Writing for children has become so trendy over the past fifteen years or so that celebrities from all walks of life have begun moonlighting as children's authors in extraordinary numbers. It seems that everyone who's anyone, from royals to rappers to movie stars to sports superstars, wants to write a children's book. Even mobsters are getting into the game. While in prison, alleged mob boss John Gotti Jr. reportedly wrote a children's book titled "The Children of Shaolin Forest." Although as yet unpublished, the book received a great deal of media attention after the *New York Times* reported that Gotti's lawyer had attempted to have him released on bail on the basis that his client "now prefers writing children's books to extortion and racketeering."[2] The trend is so widespread that when the British children's author Anne Cassidy posted on a blog, in 2010, that Balmoral Press had signed up then Prime Minister Gordon Brown for a series of stories about the heroic adventures of Gordy and gang which were "aimed at children but could warm the hearts of 7 to 70 year olds everywhere," many readers did not realize it was an April Fool's joke. Cassidy, who was shortlisted for the 2004 Whitbread Children's Book Award, laments the fact that writing children's books seems to have become "a fall back career for everyone from sex goddess singers to disgraced royals to yesterday's soap stars."[3]

Unlike the crossover fiction trend in general, the phenomenon of celebrity-authored crossover books is predominantly American, although Britain has seen a significant rise in numbers in recent years. In Australia, the pop singer and actress Kylie Minogue also climbed on the bandwagon in 2006 by publishing *The Showgirl Princess*, in a bid, many felt, to keep up with pop icon Madonna. The craze is largely confined to the English-speaking markets, where celebrity watching is a longstanding favourite pastime. Celebrity children's books are not a new phenomenon, however, and earlier examples are also largely American. The world's greatest child star, Shirley Temple, published a series of children's books in the 1930s. In the 1940s, a fourteen-year-old Elizabeth Taylor wrote and illustrated *Nibbles and Me* (1946), a memoir of the child actress's adventures with her pet chipmunk. The American actress and singer Kay Thompson's most famous song, *Eloise*, was recorded in 1956 after the publication of the first book in her Eloise series, inspired by her own adventures, about a precocious six-year-old girl who wreaks havoc in the New York City Plaza Hotel where she lives. *Eloise*, as well as the three sequels published between 1957 and 1959, were all bestsellers upon release and were adapted for television. *Eloise*, which was subtitled "A Book for Precocious Grown Ups," has sold more than two million copies to date. While most early celebrity books are out of print, the Eloise books are still popular today, and a fifth book, *Eloise Takes a Bawth*, which is based on a manuscript to have been published in 1964, was released in 2002.[4] Thompson is one of the few celebrities whose career as a children's author eclipsed her career in show business. Many readers do not even realize that the author of the Eloise series was a celebrity. Another anomaly in the list of celebrity authors is the American film and stage actress Ally Sheedy, who was actually a published children's author long before she became a celebrity. In fact, her precocious debut as a children's author led to her acting career. At the age of twelve, Sheedy wrote *She Was Nice to Mice*, a look at Queen Elizabeth I through the eyes of an inquisitive mouse that was privy to her deepest secrets, including her baldness. The book was published by McGraw-Hill in 1975, and became an immediate bestseller. Twenty-five years later, one Amazon.com reader (March 31, 2000) states that she was first captivated by the book as a second grader and now keeps it next to *Winnie-the-Pooh* and the Narnia chronicles "as a book [she] will never outgrow." The success of the book led to an appearance on the Mike Douglas Show, where an agent saw Sheedy and signed her up; she would become one of the famous actresses of the 1980s. Despite her early track record as a writer, Sheedy has not jumped on the recent celebrity book bandwagon.

One journalist claims that "the modern era of celebrity children's books" was launched by the British film and stage actress Julie Andrews, who began writing for children more than forty years ago. Her first two novels, *Mandy* and *The Last of the Really Good Whangdoodles*, published in 1971 and 1974 respectively, were very well received by critics and are still in print. However, the American actor Fred Gwynne, best known for his role on the television show *The Munsters*, published his first of ten successful children's books, *The King Who Rained*, the year before *Mandy*, in 1970. According to the same journalist, "most critics credit [Jamie Lee] Curtis with making it fashionable—and profitable—to write for children."[5] Curtis published her first children's book in 1993, but it was actually toward the end of the 1990s, about the same time as publishers began recognizing the lucrative crossover fiction market, that a marked trend began to be noticeable. Just as the phenomenal success of Rowling's Harry Potter opened the floodgate to other aspiring crossover fiction authors, the commercial success of Madonna's *The English Roses* in 2003 encouraged a wave of celebrities to try their hand at writing for children. "Move Over, Harry" was the tag line of an article in *Publishers Weekly* one week after Madonna's first children's book hit the shelves.[6] The *New York Times* list of top ten children's picture books now frequently features at least one title by famous people whose first career is not writing.

The majority of celebrity children's books are picturebooks, no doubt because they require little text or because they are the result of short bedtime stories that celebrities told to their own children, younger siblings, nephews, or nieces. Former president Jimmy Carter invented his story about the encounter between a physically disabled boy and a sea monster for his children more than three decades before the publication of *The Little Baby Snoogle-Fleejer* (1995). The British actor and comedian Lenny Henry turned the bedtime stories he told his daughter into the series that began with *Charlie, Queen of the Desert* (1996), about a tomboy who becomes "queen of the desert" when she digs a deep hole on an English beach and ends up in Australia. Prince Charles based *The Old Man of Lochnagar* (1980) on a story he told his brothers when they were young, about an old man who lives in a cave in the cliffs of Lochnagar, overlooking the royal estate at Balmoral in Scotland. The British comedian Ricky Gervais originally composed his Flanimals stories when he was a teenager in order to make his young nephew laugh.

While a few celebrity picturebooks are well written, the majority of critics share the opinion of Trev Jones, book review editor for *School Library Journal*, who states bluntly that "most of these books are pretty bad." As he rightly points out, the problem with celebrity authors is "there is seemingly no connection between whether they can write and whether they will get published."[7] The publication of celebrity authors has far more to do with their celebrity than with their talent as authors. Whereas debut children's authors usually have to endure countless refusal letters before they finally succeed in getting a manuscript accepted, celebrities can obtain a contract based on their name alone. Ricky Gervais had been trying to get *Flanimals* published for six years, but he could not find a publisher until he won four Baftas for *The Office*. Quentin Blake, Roald Dahl's illustrator, believes that publishers "just want to use the name" of celebrities and don't care what they write.[8] The literary establishment has reservations about using the term "writer" or even "children's author" for the creative or not so creative mega-famous who venture into the world of children's publishing.[9] Certainly no celebrity picturebook has ever won a major literary award. However, they have received more popular awards, such as the Mom's Choice Awards, which, according to their website, honour "excellence in family-friendly media, products, and services." *My Little Girl*, by the American country singer and actor Tim McGraw, and *Say a Little Prayer*, by Dionne Warwick, both won Mom's Choice Awards in 2009. *The Remarkable Farkle McBride* (2000), the first book by the American actor John Lithgow, was a *Time* magazine Best Book of the Year, as well as a *Publishers Weekly* bestseller and an American Booksellers Association Pick of the Lists. The latter two honours, however, reflect sales figures rather than literary quality.

Popular audiences seem more willing to suspend critical judgement when it comes to celebrity books, and especially celebrity children's books. The media covers these books regardless of their literary merit because of the star status of the author. Journalists admit they take as much pleasure from choosing the worst celebrity books as the best books, and blogs ask readers to weigh in on the subject. Madonna's picturebooks overwhelmingly top the worst list (if a specific title is mentioned, it is generally *The English Roses*).[10] Paradoxically, Madonna claims to have started writing children's books because she couldn't find any good books to read to her own children. "I couldn't believe how vapid and vacant and empty all the stories were," she states. "There were like no lessons. . . . There's like no books about anything."[11] Needless to say, her comments provoked a heated reaction on the part of children's authors, who claimed they only demonstrated how little Madonna knew about the subject. Despite scathing critical reviews, Madonna's first children's book instantly became the fastest selling picturebook of all time. The book debuted in the top spot on the *New York Times* children's bestseller list and remained there for eighteen weeks. Many celebrity books are financially successful but fail to win critical approval.

"Celebrity books are one of the great negative features of children's publishing in the 21st century," states Anita Silvey, who oversaw the Children's Division of Houghton Mifflin for several years. "If I were still a publisher, as I used to be [she states], none of these manuscripts would make it past my slush pile."[12] Unfortunately, they do make it past the slush piles of many publishers. The list of celebrities writing children's books grows ever longer and more diverse as publishers seek to fill this lucrative new niche in the children's book market. Celebrity writing has become a formula for bestselling books. Gloria Estefan's first picturebook, *The Magically Mysterious Adventures of Noelle the Bulldog* (2005), was lambasted by critics, but the sequel, *Noelle's Treasure Tale*, about the dog's search for a buried pirate ship in Florida, nonetheless made it to the number three position on the *New York Times* picture book bestseller list in 2006. Even some of the most reputable publishers have embraced the trend of celebrity children's books. Simon &

Schuster, who publish a large number of celebrity children's books, began publishing the American actor Fred Gwynne, best known for his role in the television show *The Munsters*, in the 1970s. Although publishers say that having a celebrity name on the cover is no guarantee of success, it certainly helps. "A first-time book by a celebrity gets more attention than a comparable book by a first-time author, and that helps the book sell into stores," says David Gale, editorial director of Simon & Schuster Books for Young Readers. "However, if it's not a good book, it won't sell to customers."[13] The fact is that many truly bad celebrity books do sell. After the initial buzz, however, many books fizzle out and continue to clutter remainder tables for months after. Jerry Seinfeld's *Halloween* did not live up to expectations, while Jay Leno's *If Roast Beef Could Fly* was a dismal failure.

The widespread trend of publishing series, which became all the rage in crossover fantasy fiction toward the end of the 1990s, is not absent from the celebrity picturebook market. In 1998, the English actress Jane Seymour and her actor husband, James Keach, began publishing their This One 'n That One series about twin kittens. The American actress Julianne Moore had hoped her first children's book, *Freckleface Strawberry* (2007), would be the beginning of a series about the same character and had an option for a second book. It was published under the title *Freckleface Strawberry and the Dodgeball Bully* in 2009, and spent several weeks on the *New York Times* bestseller list. Publishers have even created series for particular types of celebrity books. The music supervisor Karyn Rachtman, who has worked on many major films, created a series of children's books and accompanying CD singles, titled Hip Kid Hop, for Scholastic to promote reading through rap. The series was launched in 2002 with the titles *And the Winner Is . . .*, by the actor and bestselling rapper of all time, James Todd Smith, better known as L. L. Cool J. (Ladies Love Cool James), and *Think Again*, by rap icon Doug E. Fresh. Titles by Shaggy (*Hope*) and Kevi (*Don't Talk to Strangers*) were announced in 2003, as were plans to bring out books by Eve and Common the following year, but these books were never released. The series did not sell as well as expected and Rachtman believes that was due to reluctance on the part of some retailers "to buy books from rap artists." She had hoped to have a major label put them into record stores, where people would be more familiar with the artists. However, most books-and-music retailers place books by recording artists like Madonna and Kylie in their book departments, not in their music departments. Rachtman's plan was to develop a similar book series penned by rock artists.[14] *Little T Learns to Share*, published in 2006 by the American football superstar Terrell Owens, was supposed to be the first in a series titled T. O.'s Time Outs for the independent Dallas publisher, BenBella Books, but it remains his only book to date. One celebrity even has her own eponymous imprint. In 2003, Harper-Collins established The Julie Andrews Collection, a publishing program run by Julie Andrews and her daughter, Emma Walton Hamilton, that is now with Little, Brown Books for Young Readers.

The celebrity children's book business has become extremely profitable and the success of stars turned authors, like Madonna, has encouraged a host of others to take up their pen. Madonna's debut children's book received the widest launch in publication history: *The English Roses* was released simultaneously in one hundred countries and more than thirty languages. According to the U.S. publisher Callaway Arts & Entertainment, it was "the widest simultaneous multi-language release in publishing history." The global bestseller is now available in forty languages and more than 110 countries. Francesca Dow, managing director of Puffin, which publishes Madonna's books in the United Kingdom, as well as those of Kylie and Julie Andrews, says that *The English Roses* "gave birth to a new truism: if you find a celebrity with a story to tell, and get them to commit to publicising it, substantial sales can be guaranteed."[15] The Material Girl has certainly left her material mark on the world of children's books. In 2003, the pop icon signed a deal with publisher Callaway Editions for a series of five illustrated children's books, which would be distributed worldwide by the Penguin Group, but her American publisher declined to reveal how much she was paid. Within a year after the publication of the global bestseller *The English Roses*, Madonna had released two more international bestsellers: *Mr. Peabody's Apples* (2003) debuted at number one on the *New York Times* list and stayed there for ten weeks, while *Yakov and the Seven Thieves* (2004) began at number seven. The last two books in the series, *The Adventures of Abdi* (2004) and *Lotsa de Casha* (2005), are also international bestsellers. To date, Madonna's children's books have sold more than two million copies worldwide. Publishers seem anxious to offer celebrities multi-book deals. Following in Madonna's footsteps, former Spice Girl Geri Halliwell signed a six-book deal with Macmillan Children's Books in 2007 to begin publishing a book a month in May 2008. Despite the fact that the punishing publication schedule was not maintained throughout (the sixth book appeared in June 2009), Halliwell was named the United Kingdom's bestselling children's author in 2008 for the wildly popular series about nine-year-old Ugenia Lavender that introduces Girl Power to a new generation. Whatever their literary merit, celebrity picturebooks are skilfully marketed and they have become very big business.

Publishers defend the publication of celebrity books, insisting that they only select the best, but if that is the case one would hate to see the worst. David Gale, of Simon & Schuster, states: "I don't like to publish a book because it's written by a celebrity. I do like to publish good books, and if they're written by a celebrity, it's all the better because we can get publicity that we could otherwise not get."[16] Much of the publicity department's work is done by the celebrities themselves, who get a great deal of exposure. Unlike even the most famous children's authors, celebrities have many opportunities to promote their books in the media and on major talk shows that reach millions of viewers. Madonna, for example, has done interviews with Oprah, Regis Philbin and Kelly Ripa, David Letterman, and *Dateline NBC*, among others.

Madonna's books have been launched with major international media campaigns, including television appearances and special events. Ricky Gervais and his publisher were guaranteed huge sales to a wide, diverse public when *Flanimals of the Deep* was a Richard and Judy Christmas stocking filler suggestion in 2006. In recognition of its commercial success, *Flanimals of the Deep* was awarded Children's Book of the Year at British Book Awards (called "the Oscars of the Book Trade" and known throughout the trade as the "Nibbies") in March 2007.

Publishers also implement marketing strategies to maximize the publicity that comes with a celebrity author. In the case of the football superstar Terrell Owens's *Little T Learns to Share*, the book's arrival in bookstores in mid-November 2006 was strategically timed at the height of the football season. Borrowing J. K. Rowling's strategy for the Harry Potter books, the plot and the identities of the characters in *The English Roses* were not revealed prior to the book's publication in order to build anticipation. Even the name of the illustrator, different for each book, was not announced until publication day. Not all publicity is necessarily good publicity, however. Madonna's bad press about the adoption of a Malawian child had a very negative impact on sales of the sequel. In the first month, *The English Roses: Too Good to Be True* had sold only about 9,000 copies.[17]

Publicity sometimes comes without any effort on the part of the publisher or the author, as it did in the case of one infamous celebrity. In 1997, the Sub-comandante Marcos, the well-known leader of Mexico's Zapatista Army of National Liberation, published *La historia de los colores* (The story of colours) in Guadalajara, Mexico. When the chairman of the National Endowment for the Arts in the United States revoked funding to the small El Paso, Texas, publisher Cinco Puntos Press for a bilingual edition, *The Story of Colors/La historia de los colores: A Bilingual Storybook from the Jungles of Chiapas*, in 1999, fearing that funds might find their way to the Zapatista guerillas, the story made the front page of the *New York Times* the next day and started a media frenzy that put it in all the major American and Mexican newspapers. In the text, Marcos describes himself lighting up his trademark pipe and sitting down on a jungle pathway to hear a tale from an Indian elder named Antonio. The folk tale, about Mexican gods who fill a grey world with brilliant colours, ends with a message about diversity and tolerance: the colours are pinned on the tail feathers of a macaw that "goes strutting about just in case men and women forget how many colors there are and how many ways of thinking, and that the world will be happy if all the colors and ways of thinking have their place." Although there are no references to the Zapatistas' cause in the story, the original Mexican publisher, Colectivo Callejero, is a press that supports the rebels, and the bilingual edition contains a back cover blurb by Amy Ray, a member of the American folk rock duo the Indigo Girls, who states: "This beautiful book reminds us that the Zapatista movement is one of dignity that emanates from the grassroots of the indigenous people of

Mexico." A Mexican Indian artist, Domitilia Domínguez, created the illustrations for Marcos's story. In addition, the inside flap carries a photo of the rebel leader, who poses in his signature black balaclava with ammunition belts slung across his chest. Thanks to the unexpected publicity, Cinco Puntos, who did not wait for the official publication date, sold out the first printing of 5,000 copies in three days and began selling a larger second printing.[18]

Print runs of celebrity books are significantly higher than those of other children's authors (so, too, are advances and that money has to be recovered). The first print run of Madonna's *The English Roses* was 900,000 in the United States alone. According to Callaway, several countries, including the United Kingdom and France, went back to press based on first-day sales of the book and "Norway sold out in two hours."[19] However, even the more modest print runs of other celebrity authors are higher than those of most children's books. Faber and Faber admitted the initial print run of 100,000 for Ricky Gervais's *Flanimals* was "certainly far greater than a standard children's book,"[20] and that initial print run was extended even before its official release in 2004. The first print run of Terrell Owens's *Little T Learns to Share* was a more modest 10,000 copies, with a $20,000 publicity budget. David Gale admits that celebrities often get higher advances and larger marketing campaigns than non-celebrity children's book authors, but he is quick to point out that this is "charged against the book; it's not stopping something else from getting published or getting publicized."[21] Publishers claim that the revenue generated by celebrity books subsidizes the writing of other children's authors. "That's the attraction of the celebrity book: it allows you to launch new talent on the back of others who are more established," says Francesa Dow of Puffin.[22] Children's authors themselves believe otherwise. The American author Jane Yolen, who has written more than two hundred children's books, maintains that "old adage" no longer holds true: "When even B and C list celebs are now writing their own children's books, there is less and less room for new, untried, but wonderful young talent. And sometimes less room for old valued midlist authors as well."[23] There is widespread concern that the publication of celebrity books prevents other, more talented writers from being published, as there is only so much money to go around.

While it would seem that most celebrities would not need to write children's books to earn a living, the money does seem to be one of the main draws. Sarah Ferguson's books earned quite a lot of money for the debt-ridden Duchess of York. The number of celebrity authors who donate the proceeds of their book sales, or even a portion thereof, to charity is much smaller than one might expect. Prince Charles's *The Old Man of Lochnagar* was published in aid of The Prince's Trust charity, which assists disadvantaged young people. A portion of the proceeds of Alex Rodriguez's *Out of the Ballpark* are donated to the AROD Family Foundation, which supports families in distress. Pop music superstar Sting donates proceeds from *Rock Steady* to the Rainforest Foundation, an organization dedicated to preserving the Amazon rainforests and the cultures that live there, and in which he played an instrumental role. In this case, the charitable goal is highlighted on a sticker on the front cover. Proceeds from John Lithgow's *I'm a Manatee* (2003), about a boy dreaming he is the large, misunderstood animal, help to support the Save the Manatee Club, a nonprofit organization devoted to protecting the endangered species. The back flap of *The English Roses* indicates that the proceeds of Madonna's first book are donated to children's charity, but no specific details are given. According to Madonna's publisher, Callaway, the proceeds go to Madonna, who then allegedly gives them to Philip Berg's Kabbalah organization.[24] The Material Girl is donating all the proceeds from the sequel, dedicated "to orphans everywhere," to Raising Malawi, an orphan-care initiative, and, in support of the charity, her publisher issued a limited edition of the book in Chichewa, an official language of Malawi, which the pop singer distributed to children during a visit in 2006.

Whether or not celebrities are writing children's books for financial gain, that is obviously the reason publishers are taking on their books. Celebrity-authored children's books are first and foremost consumer products. This is clearly demonstrated by the prominence of the celebrity's name on the cover of many books. The author's name may even dwarf the title, as in the case of Jay Leno's *If Roast Beef Could Fly*. The author's name actually becomes an integral part of the title in several cases. Whoopi Goldberg is content to have only her first name appear in the title of *Whoopi's Big Book of Manners*, while Dr. Laura Schlessinger, the controversial self-help author and radio personality who introduces herself on the show as "her kid's mom" and is better known simply as Dr. Laura, includes her surname in *Dr. Laura Schlessinger's But I Waaannt It!* and the subsequent titles. Co-writers generally appear in much smaller type than the celebrity author, if they figure at all. While Terrell Owens's name is splashed across the bottom of the cover of *Little T Learns to Share* in the same type and size as the title, readers are unlikely to notice that the name of the celebrity ghostwriter Courtney Parker appears in small, pale (or appropriately ghostly) letters on a tree in the background. Even country and pop singer LeAnn Rimes's then husband, dancer and choreographer Dean Sheremet, who developed the story of the Jag series, appears in very small type on the cover of the books or is absent entirely. Readers have praised Whoopi Goldberg for not putting her picture on the cover of *Sugar Plum Ballerinas* (2008), but neither did she put the name of her co-author, Deborah Underwood, which seems particularly shocking for a series of lengthy chapter books. Some celebrity books are allegedly written by an uncredited writer who is contractually sworn to secrecy. Francesca Simon, the author of the Horrid Henry series, states: "If a celebrity puts their name to a book without writing it, it's no different from them simply marketing perfume or sheets."[25] Even when the co-author is a minor celebrity in his or her own right, the name is often in smaller print, as in the case of Tim McGraw's co-author and friend, songwriter Tom Douglas. The author of the foreword to *My Little Girl* also gets billing on the cover, in yet smaller type, because she happens to be McGraw's wife, the country singer Faith Hill. Paul McCartney and Geoff Dunbar apparently came up with the idea for *High in the Clouds* (2005), an eighty-eight-page book about a squirrel that sets out on a quest to find the utopic Animalia, when they were working together on a film. On the cover, McCartney's name appears first on a separate line, but he spares us the title "Sir" and the names of both co-authors, Dunbar and Philip Ardagh, are given in the same type size as that of the former Beatle. Julie Andrews has been lauded for writing her first books under her married name, Julie Edwards. With regards to *The Last of the Really Great Whangdoodles*, one reader states: "I didn't know until I was grown that my childhood favourite was actually written by Mary Poppins."[26] The books that she published later in collaboration with her daughter, Emma Walton Hamilton, including the bestselling *Dumpy the Dump Truck* series (2000–2006), are signed Julie Andrews Edwards.[27] As in the case of virtually all family author teams, their names have equal billing on the cover.

The name of the illustrator of a celebrity picturebook may also get very discrete billing, as does Todd Harris on Terrell Owens's book and Julia Denos on Tim McGraw's book, or it may be missing altogether, despite the fact that high quality graphics often seem to be an attempt to compensate for mediocre or bad writing. The artwork of a good illustrator can sometimes turn a second-rate text into an enjoyable book. On Whoopi Goldberg's *Alice*, the pale blue letters of the illustrator's name, John Rocco, appear in such miniscule type below the large vivid orange letters of the author's name that it almost requires a magnifying glass to read them. The name of the renowned fashion artist Jeffrey Fulvimari, whose striking black ink line and watercolour illustrations for *The English Roses* are reminiscent of 1960s sketches of supermodels such as Twiggy, is conspicuously absent from the cover of Madonna's first book. The omission of a picturebook illustrator's name in today's world of children's books seems unthinkable, but that remained the case for Madonna's subsequent titles, even when the illustrators were as renowned in the world of children's' books as Gennady Spirin (*Yakov and the Seven Thieves*) and Olga Dugina and Andrej Dugin (*The Adventures of Abdi*). In contrast, Laura Cornell, who illustrates Jamie Lee Curtis's stories, receives equal billing with the celebrity author. From the beginning, the two have been a team and their books now carry the tag "From the #1 New York Times best-selling team!" Curtis actually approached her publisher, HarperCollins, twenty years ago because she was drawn to Cornell's illustrations and they have been working successfully in tandem ever since. In 2009, however, four of their picturebooks were published together in a volume bearing the title *Jamie Lee Curtis's Books to Grow by Treasury*. No distinction is made between the author and illustrator on the cover of *The Alphabet from A to Y with Bonus Letter Z!*, "by Steve Martin and Roz Chast." The renowned British set and costume designer Tony Walton, whose work on major motion pictures began with *Mary Poppins*, receives equal billing with his ex-wife and daughter, Julie Andrews Edwards and Emma Walton Hamilton, on the books he has illustrated, including the *Dumpy the Dump Truck* series. Sarah Ferguson and her illustrators also appear in the same size type on the cover of her books, but the author's name is followed by her title, The Duchess of York. In the case of Prince Charles's *The Old Man of Lochnagar* (1980), the author's title is given in large type as "H. R. H. The Prince of Wales," while the illustrator's name and title, "Sir Hugh Casson K. C. V. O. [Knight Commander of the Royal Victorian Order]," appear in much smaller type.

In addition to the prominent billing of the author's name on the cover, the majority of celebrity picturebooks have a photograph conspicuously displayed somewhere on the book, often on the back cover, sometimes even on the front cover. Although a small, discrete photograph of a children's author is sometimes found on the back flap or an inside page of the book, this is not the norm in children's book publishing. A very large photo of the celebrity author is often plastered over the entire back cover of the book, as, for example, on Jay Leno's *If Roast Beef Could Fly*, Dionne Warwick's *Say a Little Prayer*, Sting's *Rock Steady*, and Whoopi Goldberg's *Whoopi's Big Book of Manners*. A single photo is not sufficient on *Raymie, Dickie, and the Bean: Why I Love and Hate My Brothers*, which bears a large photo of the star of *Everybody Loves Raymond* on the back cover and a photo of the three Romano brothers as children on the front flap. A more discrete photo of Sarah Ferguson on the back cover of *Little Red* is accompanied by a note to the reader signed simply "Sarah." The image of country singer Tim McGraw in his trademark black cowboy hat appears on the front cover of *My Little Girl*, albeit tucked into the bottom left-hand corner. Even though the author is an important character in the book, the realistic image jars with Denos's delicate pastel artwork. A more subtle approach is taken in Julianne Moore's *Freckleface Strawberry*, where photographs of both the author and illustrator as young girls appear on the back flap. In Jamie Lee Curtis and Laura Cornell's *Tell Me Again About the Night I Was Born*, the author and illustrator are each depicted in photos on the back flap holding their daughter. The photo on the back cover of Lynne Cheney's *America: A Patriotic Primer*, shows her surrounded by children of navy personnel assigned to the U. S. Naval Observatory, the Vice President's residence in Washington. A small photo of Dr. Laura Schlessinger and her son, Deryk, appear on the back cover of *Why Do You Love Me?* The large photo of the Duchess of York with her daughter Princess Beatrice on the back cover of *Budgie the Little Helicopter* was taken by her husband the Duke of York. The child-centred approach to photographs is abandoned in Curtis and Cornell's *It's Hard to Be Five*, where the author and illustrator appear alone on the back flap wearing "Dare to Be 45" and "Dare to Be 45 & Beyond" T-shirts, which echo the "Dare 2 B 5" shirt worn by the protagonist on the cover. These photos are obviously meant to amuse adults buying the picturebooks who are closer to the age of forty-five than five. Celebrity photos in general are intended to catch the eye of adults, as children are often unaware of their identity.

Celebrity-authored children's books indicate clearly how consumerism controls the children's book market and, in this case, picturebooks in particular. They are products marketed skilfully to consumers of all ages, as critics such as Jack Zipes and Henry Giroux have clearly demonstrated. Publishers use a wide variety of gimmicks to grab the attention of consumers. *Out of the Ballpark*, by the American baseball superstar Alex Rodriguez, includes a Special Edition Topps baseball card of the young Alex inside the back cover. Boxed sets and limited editions have become a popular marketing strategy by publishers seeking to increase sales. Ricky Gervais's first four Flanimals books were released, in 2007, in a limited edition boxed set with a distinct title, *Flanimals: A Complete Natural History*. Callaway has published several box sets of Madonna's books. In 2005, her first five children's books were released in a limited edition box set with a two-disc CD collection of the five books narrated by Madonna, a hand signed letter by the author, and a giclée digital print of Madonna signed by the artist Loren Long. Just in time for the Christmas season 2006, Madonna made her television shopping debut on the Home Shopping Network (HSN) to promote a limited edition box set of *The English Roses* and the first sequel, *The English Roses: Too Good to Be True*, which includes an audio CD of Madonna reading the first five books, a signed letter from Madonna, and an exclusive, collectible signed print from illustrator Stacy Peterson. Madonna donated all of the proceeds from her book sales to her Raising Malawi foundation, while HSN gave a portion of the network's proceeds from the broadcast. Bill Brand, Senior Vice President of the Programming at HSN, said: "These books are terrific holiday gifts that give back by supporting a worthwhile cause." For her part, Madonna considered the launching of The English Roses book series and the new title through HSN as "a great chance to reach millions of homes."[28]

The children's books of some celebrity authors have spawned a line of merchandise. Ricky Gervais's Flanimals are available as collectible figures, as well as on apparel, mugs, gift cards, and so forth. Madonna has always been known for her marketing savvy and is a master at cross-promotion. Madonna had an endorsement deal with the Gap for *The English Roses*, the first time the company had ever carried a children's book in its stores. The Gap featured the book jacket in hundreds of Gap Kids windows and created a limited-edition tote bag that was given out with a $75 purchase. In late 2003, she signed a deal with Signatures Network, which licenses for many music artist celebrities, to produce tie-in merchandise, including apparel, collectible dolls, jewellery, and beauty items. "It was a great brand to offer to girls at the high end," stated Matt Hautau, Vice President Licensing and marketing for Signatures Network. "The English Roses" line of girls' apparel, inspired by the illustrations of the five young friends portrayed in the series, was unveiled in the United States in the fall of 2004 and was hailed as "the hippest line of girl's clothing in the US market."[29] It is available at major retailers as well as online at the English Roses Official Store. There is also a "Julie Andrews Collection" online store, which not only sells children's apparel, including Dumpy sweatshirts, caps, and pajamas, but also adult clothing inspired by her children's books, such as a "Mousical" T-shirt.

Some books make absolutely no attempt to hide the commercial intent, on the contrary. The front flap of *Whoopi's Big Book of Manners* bears a very forthright message for potential buyers: "And since you've been standing around SO long reading this book—you should buy it and take it home! It's the mannerly thing to do." Some are deliberately packaged, in style and sensibility, to appeal to adults shopping in large retail stores rather than children's bookstores. Most celebrity children's books are not really books for children, but commercial products designed to appeal to adults. *Jamie Lee Curtis's Books to Grow by Treasury* includes a recipe, "games and activities for the whole family to share together," and other elements designed to catch the eye of adults. Many of the books are explicitly marketed as being suitable for all ages, often in the publisher's blurb on the back cover or the jacket flaps. A tag on the back cover of *The English Roses* bills it as "The first of five books for children (even grown-up ones) by Madonna," and it is repeated on her subsequent picturebooks. On the Puffin website, her U.S. publisher, Nicholas Callaway, dares to compare Madonna's books to Saint-Exupéry's classic *The Little Prince*: "These too are magical stories for all ages—even grown-up ones." According to the front flap blurb, *The Jolly Mon* "will delight Jimmy Buffet fans, young and old," and to ensure that potential buyers know it is intended for a crossover audience, the publisher reiterates that "readers of all ages will treasure" the story and the accompanying CD. Often "the whole family" is encouraged to enjoy the book, as on the front flap of Fred Gwynne's *A Little Pigeon Toad*. The coveted "New York Times Bestselling Author" label, which is guaranteed to sell adult novels, is also featured prominently on the cover of celebrity picturebooks, such as those of the American actor John Lithgow. Authors themselves may also specifically target a crossover audience. The subtitle of John Travolta's *Propeller One-Way Night Coach: A Fable for All Ages* (1997), a nostalgic tale written for his late son Jett just after his birth, about a young boy who makes his first magical airplane trip in 1962, clearly indicates that it is a crossover picturebook intended for young and old alike. The publicity department of Warner Books was careful to point out prior to its release that it was "not a children's book" and that they were "calling it a 'fable for all ages.'"[30] Bill Cosby dedicates his "little fable," *Friends of a Feather*, "to all parents, children, and elders who join to strengthen youngsters." Dionne Warwick assumes that *Say a Little Prayer* will be read by all ages because in the acknowledgments she thanks all of her "little and big readers." The former supermodel Sophie Dahl subtitles her first book, *The Man with the Dancing Eyes* (2003), "A Fairytale for Grownups." However, the lengthy (sixty-four pages), rather old-fashioned love story about a heroine named Pierre has a picturebook format and deals with the "great grand grown-up thing" that she had sensed reading the Song of Solomon in scripture class when she was an eight-year-old.[31] Although they are packaged in picturebook format, *The English Roses* and the sequels are aimed at preteens or tweens; in the second book, *Too Good to Be True*, the five friends plan their first school dance and have their friendship tested when they all fall for a handsome new student, Dominic de la Guardia.

Ricky Gervais's *Flanimals* (2004) was a huge crossover success in the United Kingdom as well as in the United States, where it made the *New York Times* bestseller list. The comedian gained international acclaim that year when *The Office* took two Golden Globe awards. Some Amazon reviewers warn readers that *Flanimals* is an actual children's book and not really written for adult fans of *The Office*, but according to Amazon, most buyers are "fans of alternative comedy and fans of *The Office* and *Little Britain* and *Monty Python*," in other words "fans of Ricky Gervais and his work," rather than "parents buying it for their children." As with so many celebrity books, "it was not the usual children's market" putting in the orders.[32] Gervais's book features thirty-five bizarre imaginary creatures, including the cover Flanimal the Gundit, the Honk, the Puddloflaj, the Flemping Bunthimmler, the Wobboid Mump, the Munge Fuddler, and the Mernimbler, which exists in both an adult and a child version. Like the *Simpsons*, the Flanimals series is not too sophisticated for children, but it has adult undertones, and the clever wordplay is appreciated by all ages. Gervais's sense of humour, like that of Daniel Handler (alias Lemony Snicket), is childlike yet dark, with a level for adults. The first book and the sequels, *More Flanimals*, *Flanimals of the Deep*, and *Flanimals: The Day of the Bletchling*, are all published by Faber and Faber, while *Flanimals: Pop Up* was published in 2009 by Walker Books in the United Kingdom and the following year in the United States by Candlewick Press, which bills itself on its website as a publisher of "outstanding children's books for readers of all ages" and which just happens to be Daniel Handler's publisher. Even with regards to the pop-up version, whose intricate paper engineering gives it a 3-D feel, one Amazon reviewer states: "While suggested for ages 5 and up, my guess it will be most appreciated by those in the 'up' category."[33]

A 2004 *USA Today* article, titled "Comedians Writing Children's Books for a Laugh," stated that "books by comedians are the latest twist in a trend of celebrities moonlighting as children's authors," but, in actual fact, comedians started jumping on the celebrity children's books bandwagon quite early.[34] As we have already seen, Whoopi Goldberg made her debut as an author more than a decade earlier, in 1992, with *Alice*, although she has since made a comeback. In 2004, she signed a multi-book deal with Jump at the Sun, an imprint of Hyperion Books for Children specializing in high quality books that celebrate diversity. Her unique brand of humour marks *Whoopi's Big Book of Manners*, which appeared in 2006. Kids especially seem to like the "rude" side of the book that includes nose picking and opening doors without knocking to find a man with his pants around his ankles sitting on the toilet. Jerry Seinfeld uses material from one of his comedy routines in *Halloween*, published in 2002. In this semi-autobiographical story about the Hallowe'en of the good old days, *Seinfeld* viewers will recognize the "quality" masks with the thin gray rubber bands from one of his stand-up routines. Reviewers generally agree that Seinfeld's book is for all ages, but adults probably appreciate the trademark observational humour and smart-alecky monologue more than children unfamiliar with trick-or-treating in that bygone era. *Tonight Show* host Jay Leno also got into the act, making his children's book debut in 2004 with *If Roast Beef Could Fly*, another autobiographical picturebook about nine-year-old Jay accidentally sabotaging a family dinner party. In 2005, the American comedian and actor Ray Romano published the picturebook *Raymie, Dickie, and the Bean: Why I Love and Hate My Brothers*, based on his childhood relationships with his brothers. The subject of a visit to the amusement park by three siblings should appeal to children, as will the impolite allusions to wedgies and farting that subvert adult decorum, but the tone of the narrative, with its adult perspective and tongue-in-cheek humour, seems aimed largely at the adult fans of Romano's television show. The rambling nature of Bill Cosby's lengthy "little tale" in the fifty-page *Friends of a Feather: One of Life's Little Fables* (2003), about the adventures of birds that perform dangerous acrobatic flying feats, is typical of his signature storytelling style. The comedian and actor Steve Martin has stamped his brand of comedy on an alphabet picturebook, *The Alphabet from A to Y with Bonus Letter Z!* (2007), in which twenty-six zany, alliterative couplets use words that start with a letter of the alphabet, such as Henrietta the hare, whose hairdo hides hunchbacks or Ollie the owl, who owed Owen an oboe. This introduction to the alphabet for young children amuses all ages because, in true Steve Martin style, it combines the sophisticated and the silly.

Many celebrity picturebooks are penned when the authors become parents. Geri Halliwell started writing when she was pregnant with her first child. Jamie Lee Curtis's first children's book, *When I Was Little: A Four-Year Old's Memoir of Her Youth* (1993), was inspired by a comment by her four-year-old daughter and in it, an exuberant four-year-old narrator tells us about when she was a baby. The actress, whose two children are adopted, celebrates adoption in *Tell Me Again about the Night I Was Born*, which is written from an adopted child's point of view. The young protagonist asks her parents to tell her again the beloved family story about her birth and adoption, a story that she knows by heart and proceeds to tell us herself: "Tell me again how the phone rang in the middle of the night and they told you I was born." The picturebook has been lauded by the adoption community and become popular with adoptive parents. Madonna wrote *The English Roses* for her daughter, Lourdes, at a time when the star was just beginning to read to her son. Other books are written when the celebrity becomes a grandparent. In the introduction to *America: A Patriotic Primer* (2002), Lynne Cheney, the wife of former Vice President Richard Cheney, states: "I wrote this book because I want my grandchildren to understand how blessed we are." In a subsequent picturebook, *Our 50*

States: A Family Adventure Across America (2006), the children stay in touch with their grandparents during an extensive road trip.

Celebrity books are often of an autobiographical or a semi-autobiographical nature. They feed the public's intense fascination with, and insatiable curiosity about, the lives of the rich and the famous and their families. Some picturebooks deal with the star's own childhood, while others focus on their children. Julianne Moore's first children's book, *Freckleface Strawberry*, draws its inspiration from the nickname she hated as a seven-year-old, although the actress admits the protagonist is more like her feisty daughter than her. The actress started writing the book when her son became aware of his looks at age seven. The fairy-tale framework is used for a realistic story that begins: "Once upon a time there was a little girl who was just like everybody else," except for her red hair and freckles, and ends with the protagonist's acceptance of the freckles that make her "different like everybody else," so that she "lived happily ever after." The book is dedicated to Moore's "own little, not-so-freckled strawberries," her two children Cal and Liv, who are depicted in the final picture of the grown-up heroine carefully inspecting them for freckles. Although Madonna wrote her first children's book for her daughter, she says the story draws on her own personal experience: "As a child, I experienced jealousy and envy toward other girls for any number of reasons: I was jealous they had mothers, jealous they were prettier and richer."[35]

In many books, the protagonist bears a name that clearly identifies the protagonist as the celebrity in his or her younger years. In *Say a Little Prayer* (2008) by the American singer Dionne Warwick, "Little D" discovers her talent and is encouraged by her grandfather to embrace it. The identity of the protagonist of the picturebook by the American football star Terrell Owens, popularly known as T. O., is revealed in the title *Little T Learns to Share*. In the case of sports star authors, picturebooks are generally about playing their chosen sport in their childhood. The young Owens learns to share his new football with friends because playing football alone is no fun. According to the American baseball superstar Alex Rodriguez, nicknamed A-Rod, *Out of the Ballpark* (2007) is "fictional" but "based on things [he] actually did." The "semi-autobiographical" story about a young Alex who works hard on his skills after performing badly in a playoff game and wins the championship game with a grand slam in the bottom of the final inning appeals mostly to young fans. It would be difficult not to consider the story autobiographical, as it is followed by a three-page scrapbook of photos from Rodriguez's youth. The scrapbook approach exploits the public's curiosity about celebrities and even these photos of the baseball star's youth are more likely to appeal to adult fans than their children. The final acknowledgments and copyright page includes a photo of Rodriguez with his daughter and his wife, who would file for divorce the following year after his alleged affair with Madonna. *Winners Never Quit!* (2004) by the former soccer star Mia Hamm, who remains the world's top goal scorer, is the story of a young Mia who hates losing so badly she quits in the middle of a game, until her soccer-playing siblings teach her a lesson. Hamm's picturebook not only provides photos and facts tracing her rise to fame on the final doublespread, but inside the back cover there is also a removable glossy photo. While many sports stars pen only a single picturebook, the National Football League superstars and twin brothers Tiki and Ronde Barber have collaborated on six children's books since 2004, when they published their first book, *By My Brother's Side*. The titles leave little doubt about the subject of the football players' picturebooks: *Game Day* (2005), *Teammates* (2006), *Kickoff!* (2007), *Go Long!* (2008), and *Wild Card* (2009). In addition, the back covers depict two football cards of the brothers playing for their respective teams and a photo of the young brothers when they played for the same team as numbers 21 and 22.

Politicians' books are also generally autobiographical. In 1992, the former New York City mayor Mario Cuomo published *The Blue Spruce*, which recounts the story of the young Mario and his father saving the beloved tree in their front yard, a lesson in fighting for what you deeply want and love. Writing a kid's book seems to be the thing to do for former New York mayors. In collaboration with his sister, Ed Koch wrote *Eddie: Harold's Little Brother* (2004), based on their childhood memories. This story of sibling rivalry has an unusual twist because the younger brother, who can't compete with Harold's athletic prowess, learns while he enthralls the players after the games with his play-by-play report that he can "talk" and goes on, as we know, to become mayor of New York. The authors manage to avoid the heavy-handed message of so many celebrity books. Koch and his sister continue the family saga in *Eddie's Little Sister Makes a Splash*, published in 2007, in which Eddie rescues his sister while on summer holidays.

Many celebrity picturebooks deal with family relationships between children and parents, children and grandparents, or siblings. The story may be inspired by the author's own childhood or it may be based on that of his or her child or children. According to the back cover blurb of *My Little Girl*, Tim McGraw and Tom Douglas draw "from their own dad and daughter days" to write the story about father–daughter bonding time. McGraw, who has three daughters, dedicates the book "to all [his] girls," while his wife, Faith Hill, writes in the foreword that she hopes this story "provides quality time for fathers and daughters to enjoy each other's company and make memories reading together." The target audience of this picturebook is especially fathers and daughters, but it is parents who will carry away the message that the foreword and the back cover blurb leave with readers. Although less autobiographical than *My Little Girl*, *Trouble Dolls* (1988), the second book that Jimmy Buffet wrote with his young daughter, Savannah Jane Buffet, also deals with father–daughter love. The authors blend myth and reality to tell the story of a young girl who turns to Guatemalan trouble dolls to help find her father, whose plane has been lost in the Everglades. Under her pillow at night, Lizzy discovers an entire village of trouble dolls busily resolving problems, and her four dolls, now come to life, lead her to her father. The bond between Lizzy and her father reflects that shared by Buffet and Savannah, who travelled together extensively. The relationship between a father and a son from birth is the subject of the picturebook *Just the Two of Us* (2001), by the American actor and musician Will Smith. The text consists of the rap lyrics from one of his biggest solo hits, a touching tribute to fatherhood. The original rap of the same title is a remake of the classic love song by American singer-songwriter Bill Withers.

Many celebrity books deal with the relationship between parents and their babies. In 1998, the English actress Jane Seymour and her actor husband, James Keach, began publishing their This One 'n That One series about twin kittens, based on their own twins whom they began calling "This One" and "That One" during prenatal ultrasound imaging. The fourth book in the series, *And Then There Were Three: Introducing the Other One* (2003), deals with the arrival of their new sister. The American filmmaker Spike Lee and his wife, producer Tonya Lewis Lee, dedicate *Please, Baby, Please* (2002) to their two small children, Satchel and Jackson, "for all of [their] curious creative energy." The pleading words of the title, repeated throughout the book, are familiar to all who have brought up a baby. A tiny clock marks the time at the beginning of the lines of text on each doublespread, as the loving and patient parents continually plead with her impish, determined little daughter. Lying on the living room floor with the lively toddler playing on her stomach at 3:01 a.m., the mother implores: "Go back to bed, baby, please, baby, please." The end reserves a charming twist when the tot with the mischievous grin and big dark eyes asks her mother for a kiss: "Mama, Mama, Mama, please." In their next book, *Please, Puppy, Please* (2005), the author-parents turn the tables and put their two young children in their place, as the boy and girl plead with their exuberant, undisciplined new puppy to behave. If they are familiar with the first book, children may be able to appreciate the irony of the situation that makes adult readers smile.

Celebrity grandparents have also gotten into the act. Billy Crystal's first children's book, *I Already Know I Love You* (2004), is the American comedian and actor's "first gift" to his unborn grandchild, whom he addresses on the dedication page. In the book, the grandfather-to-be anticipates the birth of his first grandchild and imagines the future joys and special moments they will share. The book ends with the anxiously-awaited birth of the grandchild whose first years he has already imagined. The sentimental but sincere universal emotion and the intergenerational theme, which is somewhat in the vein of Robert Munsch's *I'll Love You Forever*, should make this a picturebook for young and old alike, but its main appeal is for grandparents-to-be, especially expectant grandfathers, who will want to share it with their grandchildren when they are born. The adult point of view turns Crystal's picturebook into a grandfathers' book rather than a children's book. In 2006, Crystal published a follow-up, *Grandpa's Little*

One, which traces the first year in the life of his granddaughter. Maria Shriver, the television news reporter and ex-wife of former California Governor Arnold Schwarzenegger, adopted a child's perspective to demystify Alzheimer's disease in *What's Happening to Grandpa?* (2004). The book has been widely promoted and endorsed by Nancy Reagan, who hoped that "every child—and every adult" would have the chance to read it.[36] Shriver had previously published *What's Wrong with Timmy?* (2001) about a mentally-disabled child, and *What's Heaven?* (1999), which was inspired by questions asked by her own daughters after the death of their famous great-grandmother, Rose Kennedy. The latter follows the conversations between the young protagonist and her mother about the death and funeral of Kate's great-grandmother.

Publishers consistently tell children's authors not to be moralistic or didactic in their works for young readers. It is the story, not the message, that keeps readers coming back to the same book. Yet celebrity books are message-driven, generally constructed around a message that is often so loud it overpowers the story. Publishers seem to feel that children don't mind being beaten over the head with a moral lesson if it comes from a celebrity. One would think that celebrities, who, for the most part, are entertainers in some form or other, would know better than to preach. "Papa, Don't Preach," pleaded Madonna in her controversial 1986 hit, but she does precisely that in her children's books. Autobiographical books by sports' stars inevitably offer a lesson in how to play the game. The message is clearly stated in the title of several books, including Mia Hamm's *Winners Never Quit!* and Terrell Owens's *Little T Learns to Share*. Some critics have questioned the message offered by the controversial football player renowned for his flamboyant touchdown theatrics because the story centres on Little T and how much he gets thrown the ball. Although Alex Rodriguez's *Out of the Ball Park* is not heavy-handedly moralistic, the message about achieving dreams through hard work is driven home in an author's note at the end of the story, which tells readers they can also use his "recipe for success," a recipe that includes working hard, avoiding drugs, and being respectful. Authorial paratextual elements often underscore the lesson. The message of Dionne Warwick's *Say a Little Prayer* is expressed in the acknowledgments, where the author reminds her fans of all ages: "if you can think it—you can do it!," a mantra that is repeated on the back cover. NBC News' *Today* co-anchor Katie Couric hits both children and parents over the head with the moral in her children's books. She tackles tolerance in *The Brand New Kid* (2000), about a new kid at school who is ostracized by his classmates until Ellie puts herself in his shoes and befriends him. The author's message is hammered home in an introduction that seems to address adults as much as children: "It sometimes takes courage, but I hope this story will inspire all of us to reach out and make someone feel a little less scared and a little less lonely." In the follow-up, *The Blue Ribbon Day* (2004), the author once again explains the moral in a lengthy paratextual note about facing disappointment and discovering one's talent.

Karyn Rachtman created the Hip Kid Hop rapper series in the belief that music can inspire, encourage, and teach children. The lesson is expressed in the catchy refrain that is repeated throughout the story. Doug E. Fresh promotes racial tolerance in *Think Again*, the story of a Black named Zack and a white classmate who discover they have a great deal in common and become best friends. The lesson is expressed in the line that the coach makes the boys write on the blackboard after they fight during basketball tryouts: "Your worst enemy could be your best friend, so think again." In L. L. Cool J.'s *And the Winner Is . . .*, a young basketball player learns the importance of good sportsmanship and of believing in oneself whether one wins or loses. "I never give up, I never give up" is this book's catchphrase. In a Scholastic.com interview, he claims to have done the hip-hop inspired children's book to use the "powerful medium" of hip hop "to educate": "I think that there's room for something positive in hip hop and someone had to have courage and step up and say, 'I care about kids,' and not be afraid to make it sound simple, to slow it down, to clean up and do something that's really going to educate the young kids." The intention is to teach kids a valuable life lesson while promoting reading in this Rap & Read series by Scholastic.

Most celebrity books aim to teach morals and values. Madonna set out deliberately to write morality tales based on the Kabbalah religion. According to the pop star, her Kabbalah teacher of seven years suggested that she write the books, which she originally planned to co-author with her film producer husband Guy Ritchie. It is not surprising, therefore, that all her books have a moralizing tone. *The English Roses* is about not judging by appearances. After a simultaneous dream in which a plump, jolly fairy godmother shows a clique of four fashion-conscious girls that the beautiful, kind Binah they enviously ostracize leads a Cinderella-esque life of chores because her mom is dead, she is welcomed into their group and the five become inseparable. The last installment of Madonna's five-book series is *Lotsa de Casha*, in which one of the world's wealthiest women tells a story based on the old adage "Money doesn't buy happiness." Lotsa de Casha, the richest, and most miserable man (actually a dog) in the world, finds happiness only when he loses all his wealth. Is it a lesson that the Material Girl herself has learned?

Even comedians, who should certainly know better, indulge in moralizing in their children's books. Whoopi Goldberg sets out to teach children manners in *Whoopi's Big Book of Manners*. Bill Cosby's *Friends of a Feather: One of Life's Little Fables* is an adventure story of sorts, but it is also, as the subtitle indicates, a fable that has a moral, albeit more subtle than most, about the importance of friendship and being yourself. Publishers seem to have embraced this moralistic approach in the case of celebrity books. The Julie Andrews Collection publishes books that emphasize virtues and values. Kylie Monogue's editor at Puffin, Jane Richardson, praises the singer's debut book, *The Showgirl Princess*, which "brims with positive messages such as believing in yourself and the importance of friendship and teamwork."[37] Along with self-image, inner beauty, and discovering your talent, these are among the most popular messages in celebrity books. LeAnn Rimes's first picturebook, *Jag* (2003), tells the story of a young jaguar who faces her fears and stands up to her peers by befriending a jaguar ridiculed for his difference. Her second title, *Jag's New Friend* (2004), is an even more didactic tale about keeping the wrong company. Gloria Estafan includes several of these themes in *The Magically Mysterious Adventures of Noelle the Bulldog*, the story of a bulldog puppy who worries about not fitting in when a little girl adopts him. Julianne Moore's message of accepting how you look is wrapped in a more palatable story in *Freckleface Strawberry*. John Lithgow demonstrates how a clear message can be delivered in a delightful story in *Marsupial Sue* (2001). When a discontent kangaroo, whose hopping "rattled her brain" and "gave her migraine," attempts to adopt the lives of other Australian animals, she falls out of the koalas' tree, gets "typhoid, pneumonia, colic, and gout" hanging out by the sea with a platypus, and finally learns to be content with her lot after joining in gaily with a group of bouncing wallabies. Each disaster is punctuated by a refrain about being happy with who you are, so that readers learn the lesson well before Marsupial Sue accepts her kangaroo nature. Lithgow admits that all his books have "an agenda": "They are there to get [kids] thinking about the arts, and education, and the use of language."[38] However, with the exception of *Marsupial Sue*, the message is quite subtle and the emphasis is on entertaining in all his children's books.

A number of celebrity authors offer self-help books for children and their parents. The American broadcast journalist Deborah Norville deals with television's negative influence on a child's dreams in her rhymed pop-up book, *I Don't Want to Sleep Tonight* (1999). She wrote the book after noticing a connection between her seven-year-old son's "weekend TV viewing or Nintendo playing and his inability to sleep soundly." During an interview with Dr. Ronald Goldstein, she described the purpose of her book in the following terms: "In verse form, the book allowed my child—and thousands of others—to discover that when they 'don't watch the TV set' they have quiet dreams. It helped my own children resist the siren song of the television and I've heard from so many other parents who say it has done the same for their children too!"[39] An author's message on the HarperCollins website informs readers that the series of books by the popular talk show host and family therapist Dr. Laura Schlessinger are "designed to suggest subjects worthy of discussion with your children as they mature in their curiosity about important life issues." *Why Do You Love Me?* (1999) was inspired by a question asked by her then six-year-old son, and deals with a mother's unconditional love. The first book was written with the assistance of the seasoned children's author Martha Lambert and became a number one *Publishers Weekly* bestseller, but the subsequent books, which Dr. Laura appears to have written on her own, have a decidedly more didactic tone. These picturebooks, which all feature the young protagonist Sammy, have clear messages about consumerism and greed

(*But I Waaannt It!* 2000), accepting life's responsibilities (*Growing Up Is Hard*, 2001), and being good *Where's God?* (2003). Schlessinger's website says that her show "preaches, teaches, and nags about morals, values and ethics." The same can be said about her children's books.[40]

Even Jamie Lee Curtis's picturebooks, which have been generally well received, are nonetheless seen as "message books that are better written than most."[41] According to the author, *Where Do Balloons Go? An Uplifting Mystery* (2000) is a metaphorical story about the loss of a loved one, while *Is There Really a Human Race?* (2006), which stayed on the *New York Times* bestseller list for several weeks and made it to the number three spot, uses the race metaphor to deal with a child's worries about life's journey. Other topics dealt with in her books include self-control (*It's Hard to Be Five*, 2004) and empowerment (*Big Words for Little People*, 2008).

What makes celebrities experts on manners, behaviour, and child development? While Julie Andrews's Mary Poppins image may be fitting for a children's author, many celebrities' lives are associated in the public mind with extramarital affairs, violence, drugs, and so forth, images that are incongruent with the world of children's books. Madonna's previous foray into the world of literature was the controversial *Sex*, published in 1992. David Hancock begins an article titled "Madonna's Advice for Kids" by reminding us that Madonna herself posed for several of Steven Meisel's erotic photographs in the book.[42] Yet celebrity writers, even those whose own lives are rather messed up, are allowed to tell kids how to live theirs. Publishers seem to give celebrities free reign to write whatever they want because, to quote Roald Dahl once again, they "just want to use [their] name." Not only are they allowed to be moralistic, but they also seem to get away with elements that are generally considered to be inappropriate in children's books, at least in North America. There seems to be a lack of the normal censorship or self-censorship when it comes to this particular variety of picturebook. This would suggest that publishers tend to forget their true target audience when dealing with the lucrative celebrity picturebook market. The rather bawdy humour of Ray Romano's *Raymie, Dickie, and the Bean: Why I Love and Hate My Brothers*, while quite mild in the text, is highlighted in Gary Locke's illustrations of wedgies and farting. This relaxing of the usual rules of appropriateness applies even to ABC books, which address a very young audience. Steve Martin gets away with including a drunk for the letter D in *The Alphabet from A to Y with Bonus Letter Z!* even though the Brothers Grimm version of "Little Red Riding Hood" has been censored in the United States because the heroine carries a bottle of wine to her grandmother. This material would not be considered inappropriate in many European countries. Bobby Byrd, who runs the small Texas publishing company that brought out the bilingual edition of Subcomandante Marcos's *La historia de los colores*, complains about the bowdlerization of children's books in the United States. Both Marcos's text and Domitilia Domínguez's illustrations contain elements that would raise eyebrows in the mainstream American children's book market. The incipit of this tale focuses on human sexuality: "The men and women were sleeping or they were making love, which is a nice way to become tired and then go to sleep." The accompanying illustration depicts a reclining naked woman embracing a figure that appears to be a male god. Byrd comments: "I can imagine how someone would rewrite this story for an Anglo audience. There wouldn't be anybody smoking or making love."[43] It was not, however, the smoking or the sex that caused the flurry of media attention around the controversial book in 1997.

Illustrators of celebrity books, especially those by comedians, seem to be chosen with an eye to adult appeal. In the case of Ed Koch's picturebooks about his childhood, nostalgic watercolours of 1930s American urban life by James Warhola also appeal to adult readers for whom they evoke memories of their own childhood. Bright acrylic paintings by Lambert Davis capture the light and colour of the Caribbean in Buffet's *The Jolly Mon*, which is infiltrated by Buffet's "island escapism" lifestyle and dedicated "to all the people on all the islands of the Caribbean and all the dolphins in the sea below." Buffet's picturebooks are especially popular with his fans, commonly known as Parrot Heads, which probably explains the presence in both of parrots. Readers have a parrot's eye view of the Jolly Mon entertaining the people of Coconut Island on an inside spread of the first book, while the blue parrot that carries the two Guatemalan trouble dolls on its back during their search for Lizzy's missing father in the second is depicted on the back cover of *Trouble Dolls*.

Many illustrators of celebrity books are best known for their illustrations in adult publications. The style, popular in advertising, of exaggerated, cartoon-like drawings that are rendered in a detailed manner usually applied to more realistic images is extremely fashionable. The caricatural figures in these illustrations are often portrayed with a large head on a small body. James Bennett's trademark caricatural figures with large heads from publications such as *Time* and *MAD* magazine find their way into Jerry Seinfeld's *Halloween*. Gary Locke's humorous and expressive oil painting caricature of the rather adult-headed young Ray Romano in *Raymie, Dickie, and the Bean* will be familiar to adult readers from his Coca-Cola and Warner Bros advertisements and his editorial artwork for *Time* and *Sports Illustrated*. S. B. Whitehead, who is best known for his illustrations for *Time* and *Entertainment Weekly*, exaggerates the prominent chin of the large-headed, nine-year-old Jay Leno in *If Roast Beef Could Fly*, evoking caricatures of the *Tonight Show* host in adult publications. The large, adult-looking head of the protagonists in these books resemble the grown-up celebrity rather than the child he or she once was. The same can be said of John Rocco's strident, caricatural illustrations for Whoopi Goldberg's *Alice*, an urban pastiche of Lewis Carroll's classic featuring a "young" African American Alice who looks quite grown-up. Rocco worked for many years as a creative director in the entertainment industry at Walt Disney and Dreamworks, where he was the pre-production art director for *Shrek*. Todd Harris, who illustrated *Little T Learns to Share*, is a commercial illustrator whose work includes film, video games, and comic books. Jib-Jab's computer-aided artwork, which superimposes photos of L. L. Cool J.'s head on cartoon renditions of a basketball player's body, creates some rather jarring images in *And the Winner Is. . . .*

In some celebrity books, the cartoon-style illustrations manage to make a mediocre story and an overbearing message more palatable for young readers, while in others, they are the perfect choice for a humorous, entertaining text. Steve Martin's *The Alphabet from A to Y with Bonus Letter Z* is illustrated by Rosalind (Roz) Chast, a staff cartoonist for *The New Yorker*. Her cartoonish illustrations continue the verbal alliterations with humorous, sometimes subtle comic asides, such as the picture of the beatnik holding balloons hidden behind Bad Baby Bubbleducks. LeUyen Pham's lively illustrations match the energetic style of Julianne Moore's Freckleface Strawberry books, giving them the feel of an animated cartoon. Jack E. Davis's lively, cartoon-like illustrations, in coloured pencil, acrylics, and ink, are a perfect complement to John Lithgow's upbeat, cheery *Marsupial Sue*. Davis's personified, well-dressed down under animals delight readers of all ages: koalas wear caps, wallabies sport headphones, birds wear sunglasses, and Sue is dressed in a straw hat and Birkenstocks. Davis also illustrated the follow-up, *Marsupial Sue Presents "The Runaway Pancake"* (2005), in which the familiar tale is given a new spin when the kangaroo and her friends perform it as a stage play for the neighbourhood. Davis's dynamic pictures of the "play within a story" portray the already fanciful animals dressed in very whimsical costumes. Using a feather duster, a toilet brush, or a branch full of critters for a tail; a scrub brush for a mane; and garden tools for claws, a koala plays a dog, a wallaby a donkey, a sheep a bear, a Tasmanian devil a fox, and so forth. In contrast, the cartoon-style artwork of Daniel McFeeley, who has also worked as a visual effects artist in film and television, clashes with Laura Schlessinger's intensely serious messages.

Two of John Lithgow's bestselling picturebooks are illustrated by C. F. Payne, whose artwork has graced the covers of numerous magazines, including *Time*, *MAD Magazine*, *The Atlantic Monthly*, and *Sports Illustrated*. While Payne is well-known for his portraits of politicians and entertainers, he has also illustrated ten children's picturebooks. His mixed-media illustrations for *The Remarkable Farkle McBride* use the unique blend of realism and caricature that characterize his editorial artwork and his portraits of famous people. Payne also illustrated Lithgow's third book, *Micawber* (2002), the story of an art-loving New York squirrel who leaves his Central Park nest every week to visit the nearby "palace on Fifth Avenue" (the MoMA) and ends up becoming an artist. Humorous details in Igor Oleynikov's illustrations for Lithgow's *Mahalia Mouse Goes to College* have adult appeal. The piece of newspaper that Mahalia wraps up in to go out into the rain looking for scraps for her starving family is part of the front page of the student newspaper *The Harvard Chronicle*, which features a story titled "Harvard to Review Site Access Standards."

Some author–illustrator collaborations are born of a long-time friendship, as in the case of the Flanimals series. Ricky Gervais had done sketches of the absurd creatures that had been developing in his imagination for thirty years, but his friend, Rob Steen, who does "graphic novel-type illustrations," made the Flanimal characters "come to life," according to the author.[44] The heroine of Sophie Dahl's first book was born as she distractedly made a "dreadful" drawing while on the telephone, but a few days later she invited her childhood friend, Annie Morris, to draw Pierre, which she did "magnificently," according to the author.[45]

When celebrity picturebooks are illustrated by genuine children's illustrators, they have a better chance of actually appealing to a young audience. Many books, especially those dealing with family relationships, have soft pastel watercolour illustrations that highlight the sentimental tone of the text. Soft pastels by Sandra Speidel match the delicate tone of the text in Maria Shriver's picturebooks *What's Heaven?*, *What's Wrong with Timmy?*, and *What's Happening to Grandpa?* The artwork of award-winning African American illustrator Kadir Nelson makes a number of celebrity picturebooks more memorable than most. His colourful, richly textured, sentimental paintings for Will Smith's *Just the Two of Us*, published in 2001, portray a father supporting his son's development from newborn to young man by giving him advice, strength, and love. The following year, Nelson illustrated Spike and Tonya Lee's *Please, Baby, Please*, depicting the loving relationship between the members of an African American family in vivid, detailed illustrations. He captures the wilful, lively personality of the toddler with the wide mischievous grin, big dark eyes, and unruly curls. The illustrator of Tim McGraw and Tom Douglas's *My Little Girl*, Julia Denos, brings to life the young protagonist, Katie, who, for her special day with her dad, wears a tiara in case they go to a ball and her jungle boots in case they go to Africa. The French illustrator Christine Davenier's fanciful ink-and-colored-pencil illustrations for *The Very Fairy Princess* (2010) help Julie Andrews and Emma Walton Hamilton capture the magical age when belief in your dreams can transform reality. Despite the denial of everyone around her, the young heroine assures readers that she knows without a doubt that she is a fairy princess and she proves it by taking them through her day, from morning to night, highlighting the many moments that reveal her fairy princess nature. Robin Preiss Glasser illustrated Sarah Ferguson's *Tea for Ruby* (2008), in which a rambunctious, red-headed protagonist by the name of Ruby tries very hard to improve her manners when she receives a card inviting her to have tea with the Queen. The Queen turns out to be her grandmother, who loves her little princess for what she is (the book is dedicated to Ferguson's daughters, Beatrice and Eugenie, two real little princesses). Glasser's illustrations humorously contrast the impetuous behaviour of the exuberant young heroine and her visions of herself as a proper little lady wearing fancy gowns in ornate golden palace settings. Attentive readers will notice that the characters from Ruby's real life appear, dressed in palace finery and in similar poses, in the little girl's visions. Lynne Cheney also teamed up with Glasser to produce the alphabet-format picture-books *America: A Patriotic Primer* and *A Is for Abigail: An Almanac of Amazing American Women*, as well as the road-trip picturebook *Our 50 States: A Family Adventure Across America*. The front flap blurb of the first book informs readers that this "ABC of the principles on which this country was founded" is "a book for children and families to pore over, discuss, and cherish." The pages of these books celebrating America are teeming with interesting facts and playful visual details (even in the decorative borders) to occupy readers of all ages. Cheney's other picturebooks dealing with American history, which are not illustrated by Glasser's exuberant drawings, are less engaging.

Laura Cornell's energetic, cartoon-style watercolour-and-ink illustrations compliment the cheerful, upbeat tone of Jamie Lee Curtis's texts, and together they have become a highly successful team (with numerous bestselling pic-turebooks to their name). In *When I Was Little: A Four-Year Old's Memoir of Her Youth*, a photo of the "mature" four-year-old heroine graces the front cover, while the back cover bears a photo of her as a baby. The accomplish-ments of the four-year-old are contrasted with the behaviour of her baby brother in Cornell's lively, expressive illustrations. "When I was little, I slept in a zoo. Now I sleep in a big bed and get to play monkey," she recounts, as her baby brother, from behind the bars of his crib, watches her swinging from the drapes with her pet monkey. One illustration depicts the little girl in the bath wearing a green face mask and a shower cap, and surrounded by beauty prod-ucts, but with her rubber ducky close at hand and a Band-Aid on her elbow. The illustrations contain many humorous visual asides especially appreciated by older readers. At the beginning of *Tell Me Again About the Night I Was Born*, the heroine and her dog both hold up their baby books as the little girl asks to be told the beloved story, while on the last doublespread they both lie in bed, in matching pink curlers, still holding their baby books. Two of the doublespreads have to be turned sideways and viewed vertically, one to show how "small" the adoptive parents felt when they arrived at the hospital and the other to depict the new baby "actual size," complete with labels such as "future bellybutton" marking the spot covered by Band-Aids. The vertical page layout is used effectively in several of their other picturebooks as well.

A few celebrity books have had the good fortune to be illustrated by world renowned children's illustrators. The talented Russian illustrator Gennady Spirin, who has won both the Golden Apple of the Bratislava International Biennale of children's book illustration and the Premio Grafico at the Bolo-gna Children's Book Fair, has illustrated two celebrity picturebooks. Spirin's masterful artistic skill elevates illustration to the level of fine art and it seems incongruous to combine his exquisite illustrations with a celebrity text. Yet he has illustrated not only *Simeon's Gift* (2003), by Julie Andrews Edwards and Emma Walton Hamilton, but also Madonna's third book, *Yakov and the Seven Thieves* (2004). Spirin was undoubtedly chosen to illustrate Madonna's story because of its eighteenth-century Eastern European setting, while Edwards and Hamilton's story of a minstrel also takes place in the kind of old world European setting for which Spirin is noted. The meticulous detail, rich colour, luminosity, and classical composition of his stunning pencil-and-watercolour illustrations are reminiscent of Renaissance masters. In Madonna's *Yakov and the Seven Thieves* (where his name is mentioned only on the title page), Callaway refers to Spirin's work not as illustration but as "Art by Gennady Spirin." Madonna's next book, *The Adventures of Abdi*, was illustrated by the talented Russian couple, Olga Dugina and Andrej Dugin, in intricately detailed, richly textured illustrations which also evoke great masters of the past. Occasionally, a celebrity author teams up with an artistic family member, as in the case of Jimmy Carter's *The Little Baby Snoogle-Fleejer*, illustrated in pastels by his daughter Amy, and Bill Cosby's *Friends of a Feather: One of Life's Little Fables*, illustrated by his daughter Erika.

In a very few instances, celebrities have both written and illustrated their books. John Travolta did the illustrations for his *One-Way Propeller Night Coach*. Fred Gwynne is a rare example of a celebrity children's author who successfully illustrated numerous books. The actor wrote and illustrated ten children's books in all. His very popular picturebooks about homonyms and figures of speech, *The King Who Rained* (1970), *A Chocolate Moose for Dinner* (1976), *The Sixteen Hand Horse* (1980), and *A Little Pigeon Toad* (1988), have become classics, which, with the exception of the third, are still in print. His hilarious wordplay and zany sense of humour help children to gain an appreciation of the English language, while at the same time amusing adults. Gwynne depicts, in a perceptive and entertaining manner, a child's visual images of everyday phrases from the English language. The bewildered child who narrates shares her misconceptions about the odd things adults—mostly family members—say and gives coherence to the texts. Lively, whimsical full-page illustrations add visual jokes to the verbal gags. The cover of *The King Who Rained* depicts a venerable old king lying horizontal in the air literally raining on the child standing below in a raincoat and carrying an umbrella, while the cover of *A Chocolate Moose for Dinner* portrays the young girl sitting at the table with an enormous chocolate animal wearing a bib. On the cover of *The Sixteen Hand Horse*, a child is mounted on a surreal-looking horse composed of sixteen human hands, and *A Little Pigeon Toad* shows the little girl observing a hybrid creature with a pigeon's body and a toad's head (apparently her father is a little pigeon-toed). Like the French illustrator Jean Claverie, Gwynne often represents himself and other family members in his illustrations. The sentence "Daddy says he has a mole on his nose" in *A Chocolate Moose for Dinner* is accompanied by the picture of a small, brown, furry mammal sitting on the nose of a tall, thin man who is the spitting image of the actor. There is even a surprising resemblance between the author and the dog who takes the little girl's pulse in *A Little Pigeon Toad* (her Daddy says "you can teach dogs to heal"). Adults love these books at least as much as children.

They can appreciate the more dated terms, such as shoe tree, that may be unfamiliar to today's young readers, and the more subtle humour that may go over the heads of less sophisticated readers. At the end of *A Little Pigeon Toad*, the young narrator concludes: "Yarns like these are hard to swallow!" Despite its fitting use as an ending to the book, the little girl has obviously heard the expression without understanding it (exceptionally she does not identify a source), as the accompanying illustration depicts her winding spaghetti-like strands of coloured yarn on her plate around a fork and spoon. Gwynne's books are childhood favourites of the baby boomers who are now reading them to their grandchildren.

Many celebrity books are written in rhyming text, which is often forced and awkward. The picturebooks of Katie Couric, Billy Crystal, and Gloria Estafan, among others, have attracted scathing criticism in this regard. Reviewers are quick to point out that authors who don't know how to write should avoid verse. Critics have been somewhat kinder on Jamie Lee Curtis, who also uses a singsong rhyme in a number of her picturebooks. In *Today I Feel Silly, and Other Moods That Make My Day*, which was listed on the *New York Times* bestseller list for nine weeks in 1998, the little red-headed protagonist discusses, in rhyming couplets, her different mood swings (thirteen in all), ranging from silly to grumpy to lonely to sad, and a mood wheel on the last page allows children to change the little girl's expression (both her eyes and her mouth) to create six different emotions. John Lithgow is perhaps the only celebrity author to receive only praise for his limerick-like verse which amuses readers of all ages. The actor and singer has become a respected author of twelve children's books, several of which are *New York Times* bestsellers, including his first three titles. He debuted with *The Remarkable Farkle McBride*, the story of a musical prodigy who quickly tires of each instrument, until he finally realizes that the entire orchestra is his instrument and he becomes a conductor. Part of the charm of Lithgow's rhymed texts is the fact that he does not talk down to kids or simplify the vocabulary to target a young audience. Nor are the more difficult words simply a nod to the adults reading his books. The author explains: "I don't shy away from words like imprudence. My ideal is for a child to listen to a story read by a parent and to say, 'Mom, what does peregrination mean?' and for the mom to actually not know."[46]

The picturebooks of celebrity authors are often turned into a performance. Numerous celebrities read their story on an accompanying CD, or a cassette in the case of older books, such as the audio version of John Travolta's *Propeller One-Way Night Coach*, published in 1997. The celebrities who most often read their own books on a CD are actors, including Julie Andrews (*Simeon's Gift*) and John Lithgow (*Micawber*), and comedians, for example, Jay Leno and Ray Romano. However, some recording artists also read their stories, the most notable example being Madonna. The pop icon kicked off the release of her second children's book, *Mr. Peabody's Apples*, with a joint promotion on

America Online, Audible.com, and the Apple iTunes Music Store. The promotion included two interviews and a teaser clip of Madonna's narration of the book on AOL; the full narration is available for download from the Apple iTunes Music Store.

Cheech Marin, the American comedian and actor who gained recognition as part of the comedy act Cheech & Chong, is well-known by adults and children alike for his roles in general audience movies such as *The Lion King* and *Spy Kids*. When he published the picturebook *Cheech the School Bus Driver* in 2007, the protagonist was already familiar to a young and not-so-young audience because, in 1992, the comedian had recorded a popular children's album titled *My Name Is Cheech, the School Bus Driver*, about a driver who gets lost on the way to school and the adventures they have while learning math, colours, Spanish, and so forth. The picturebook tells a zany story of Cheech driving kids to the Battle of the Bands, where they are the only mariachi band in a competition that includes great rock and roll bands. John Lithgow had also launched a career as a children's performer prior to publishing his first children's book. In 1999, the actor released his first album of children's music, *Singin' in the Bathtub*, which was followed, in 2002, with *Farkle and Friends*, the musical companion to his first picturebook, published two years earlier. Almost all of John Lithgow's picturebooks have an accompanying CD, on which he reads the text (*Micawber*) and/or performs the song live (*Marsupial Sue*). The musical score of *I'm a Manatee* was written by conductor Bill Elliott especially for children.

When Harvard invited John Lithgow (class of 67) to give the keynote address at commencement, he decided that, as an actor he "better entertain them and finish big," so he wrote *Mahalia Mouse Goes to College* and dedicated it "to the Harvard College class of 2005." It is the tale, in three "chapters," of a poor mouse that lives under Dunster House, an old Harvard dormitory, and one day accidentally finds herself in a classroom and eventually becomes a full-time student. Lithgow's book was, in part, a "cheerful and constructive response" to a controversy raging at Harvard at the time.[47] The former university president questioned a woman's ability to work in the sciences, so Lithgow's female mouse earns a Bachelor of Science degree (her favourite course is human psychology). On the final dedication and copyright page, the tiny Mahalia, in a shirt with the Harvard Veritas shield, stands proudly in front of her Harvard University graduation diploma. *Mahalia Mouse Goes to College*, which was published in 2007, is thus an excerpt from Lithgow's live commencement address, a picturebook born of a performance that was targeted at a crossover audience of graduates and their families. Lithgow now tours the country, performing for children and parents. Although his books have been highly successful, most people seem to prefer seeing him perform his stories rather than reading them themselves.

In the case of recording artists, the accompanying CD generally includes a recording of the celebrity singing a song that either inspired the book or was inspired by the book itself. Many celebrity picturebooks are based on songs. *Say a Little Prayer*, by music legend Dionne Warwick, draws its title from her signature song "I Say a Little Prayer," released in 1967. A sticker on the book informs readers it includes an "Exclusive CD with a New Song by Dionne Warwick!"; on it she sings the well-known children's hymn *Jesus Loves Me*. The original hardcover edition of the first picturebook that the singer and songwriter Jimmy Buffet wrote with his daughter, *The Jolly Mon*, was accompanied by a cassette tape of father and daughter reading the story along with an original score written by Michael Utley. A CD has replaced the cassette in the later edition, which, like Warwick's book, has a sticker on the cover informing potential buyers of the CD. The score and lyrics of Buffet's ballad summarize the rather long story about the adventures, on a Caribbean Island called Bananaland, of a singing fisherman who is rescued from fierce pirates by a dolphin. Readers familiar with the song "Jolly Mon Sing," on which the book is based, will particularly appreciate it. Buffet's books are especially popular with his fans, and Parrot Head parents often give them to their children, who are called Parakeets (the term is also used for his younger fans). Whereas Buffet expands his ballad in *The Jolly Mon*, pop music icon Sting condenses the lyrics of his song *Rock Steady*, from the 1987 recording *Nothing Like the Sun*, in the picturebook *Rock Steady: A Story of Noah's Ark*. In his funky, upbeat retelling of a favourite Bible story, a hip young couple answer an advertisement in the newspaper and sign up with a bearded old man who "heard God's message on the radio," to take a trip "on a big wooden ship" and "commune with Mother Nature." In the book, Sting reminds a new generation that the planet's well-being still rests in our hands.

Often the story is not based on a pre-existing song, but rather an original song is created at the same time as the book. In the Hip Kid Hop series, L. L. Cool J and Doug E. Fresh recorded the accompanying CD single when they wrote the book. With these picturebooks, the reader as well as the author can engage in a performance. On the CD, the performers sing their songs in rap, accompanied by a chorus of youngsters, and on the second track, readers are invited to record their own voice. Not surprisingly, the words work better on the CDs than in the books. Gloria Estafan sings "Noelle's Song (Been Wishin')," about finding a friend, on the CD that accompanies her first book in the Noelle series, and it is certainly more indicative of her talent than the story itself. In some cases, the texts of celebrity picturebooks consist of songs performed by a singer who is not even the original performer or songwriter. Judy Collins is billed as "performer" on the cover of *Over the Rainbow*, a book and audio CD published in 2010 (the CD contains two additional songs recorded by "Grammy Award Winner Judy Collins"). The classic song, sung by Judy Garland in *The Wizard of Oz* and written by the popular Broadway and Hollywood songwriters Harold Arlen and E. Y. Harburg, is rendered in dreamy, magical artwork by Eric Puybaret. The French artist has also illustrated other song picturebooks, including *Puff, the Magic Dragon* (2007), inspired by the

1960s folk song by Peter Yarrow and Lenny Lipton, performed on the CD by Yarrow, his daughter Bethany, and cellist Rufus Cappadocia, and *The Night before Christmas* (2010), performed by Peter, Paul, and Mary.

Composing music to accompany the book has become a common practice with celebrity picturebooks. Julie Andrews's long-time musical director, Ian Fraser, composed and performed music to her narration of *Simeon's Gift* on the accompanying CD. In addition, Andrews and Hamilton created a web-game, Simeon's Music Maker, in which players can take Simeon's journey of musical discovery for themselves by composing their own symphony from the sounds of nature. Several celebrity picturebooks have been adapted as plays, musicals, and films. *Simeon's Gift* was adapted for family theatre as well as a children's musical, which had its world premiere at the Bay Street Theatre in New York in November 2010. Andrews lent her recorded voice as the narrator of the tale of a young wandering minstrel in search of the music within his soul. In 1993, Scottish Television and the Welsh Fourth Channel turned Prince Charles's *The Old Man of Lochnagar* into an animated short family film, *The Legend of Lochnagar*, narrated by the Prince and with Robbie Coltrane providing the voice of the old man. The book was also adapted as a stage play and a ballet that had its première in 2007. In 2001, it was reported that Rob Morrow would direct an IMAX version of *Propeller One-Way Night Coach*, and John Travolta himself would narrate and star in the live-action segments, but the film was never released.[48] ITV, the largest commercial television network in the United Kingdom, was supposed to have begun airing a television series based on the Flanimals series in 2009, but this was abandoned and instead an animated 3D feature film is scheduled for release by Universal's Illumination Entertainment in 2011–2012. Matt Selman, a writer for *The Simpsons*, is the scriptwriter for the Flanimals film. Ricky Gervais himself will provide the voice for the lead role of the Puddloflaj. Madonna also intended that *The English Roses* be turned into an animated film, with the author providing the voice of the fairy godmother.

Writing children's books allows celebrities to find fame and possibly fortune in a new field. While many celebrities write only one children's book, or limit themselves to a single series of books, a significant number go on to write further titles. Some even make a new career of writing. John Lithgow has actually carved out two careers for himself in the world of children's entertainment, one as an author and the other as a performer. Sarah Ferguson published her debut children's book, *Budgie the Little Helicopter*, the first book in a series inspired by her helicopter flying lessons, in 1987. The scandal-prone Fergie even managed to attract negative press as a children's author. *Budgie the Little Helicopter* was alleged to be remarkably similar to a children's book by Arthur W. Baldwin, titled *Hector the Helicopter*, but the Duchess of York denied charges of plagiarism and a claim for copyright infringement was never pursued. In 2003, the flame-haired duchess published the first in a series of picturebooks about *Little Red*. She is one of the few celebrity children's authors to cross over into the field of adult fiction, although she did not abandon writing for children. Her historical novel for adults, *Hartmoor*, published in 2008 with St. Martin's Press, was followed the same year by the picturebook *Tea for Ruby*. Madonna's new status as a children's author may be just another of her many reinventions. However, her publisher Nicholas Callaway believes that "we're going to have a new generation of children who may very well think of Madonna as a children's book author first."[49] That is precisely what happened in the case of Kay Thompson, the author of the Eloise series.

Julie Andrews claims her career as a writer "has taken front and centre,"[50] even though her film career underwent a revival after 2000 with movies such as *The Princess Diairies* and *Shrek*. She now has more than fifteen picturebooks, novels, and early readers to her credit. It was during a lull in her film career in 1993 that the actress Jamie Lee Curtis wrote her first children's book. The status of children's author gave Curtis so much enjoyment that she decided to write her second book, *Tell Me Again About the Night I Was Born*, in 1996, and to date she has published a total of eight picturebooks, each of which has become a bestseller. Although Curtis's books, unlike most celebrity books, have garnered a significant amount of praise on the part of many critics, some still insist that they probably would not be in print if they were not written by a celebrity. Readers may have had higher expectations when the former supermodel Sophie Dahl turned her hand to writing. She is, after all, the granddaughter of Roald Dahl, one of the most popular children's writers of all time, and for many in the world of books, she is known first and foremost for having lent her name to the main character in *The BFG*. Although *The Man with the Dancing Eyes* has received glowing reviews in magazines like *Vogue* and *Tatler*, in general it has been considered merely as a better-than-average first attempt. Only a handful of celebrity books are truly good children's books and win a faithful following among readers and critics alike. Most are eminently forgettable at best. Anita Silvey, a former editor of *The Horn Book Magazine* and author of *100 Best Books for Children*, goes even further, stating categorically: "There's nothing to be gained with reading any of them." She advises parents to buy books "by the real 'celebrities' of children's literature," citing Robert McCloskey and Maurice Sendak.[51]

While it does not seem to bother most celebrities or affect book sales, there is a certain stigma attached to celebrity children's books that does make some celebrity authors squirm. When a journalist asked Julianne Moore how she felt about joining the ever-growing number of celebrity authors of children's books, she replied: "There's something slightly embarrassing about that. But I wanted to be published because I loved books as a kid and I love them now."[52] A few celebrities who have taken up writing for children seriously have been well received by readers and critics alike, overcoming the label of celebrity author. However, the vast majority of celebrity children's books are bought for the author's name and not for the story. Philip Pullman, who was the first children's author to win the prestigious Whitbread Book of the Year Award in

2003 for his novel *The Amber Spyglass*, believes the author should disappear behind the story. That is virtually impossible in celebrity-authored books. The first books published by "Julie Edwards" in the early 1970s are among the few celebrity children's books that have achieved that anonymity. At the beginning of the sequel to her first book, Madonna writes:

> If you haven't heard of the English Roses by now, then you are either:
>
> a. Living under a rock.
> b. Living on the moon.
> c. Away with the fairies.
>
> If you fit the description of a, b, or c, then I am happy to clue you in to what the rest of the world already knows.

A *Guardian* journalist felt these words ranked among "the most self-serving, self-satisfied, and downright smug introductions to any book in recent memory," conceding, however, that unfortunately she is probably right.[53]

By writing children's books, celebrities are perhaps hoping to expand their fan base to an entirely new generation. Stephanie Owens Lurie, president/publisher of Dutton Children's Books, believes that is the case: "Artists who write children's books are trying to build a future fan base," she claimed just prior to the release of LeAnn Rimes's *Jag* in 2003. Some celebrities also have insatiable egos and children's books may be merely another way of gratifying a desire for additional glory. Lurie, whose publishing house brought out Rimes's Jag series, stated, in 2003, that recording artists were starting to realize the importance of the "children's audience," which, she points out, "has a lot of spending money and influence over what their parents buy for them."[54] In general, however, celebrity children's books are not genuine entertainment for children, but consumer products intended to appeal to adults. Joanna Cotler, Jamie Lee Curtis's publisher at HarperCollins for the past fifteen years, says: "Kids aged four or five have no concept of celebrity. They don't care if a book is written by Jamie Lee Curtis or anybody else as long as it's good. That's the beautiful irony."[55] The authors of celebrity-authored children's books come with a built-in audience of fans, few of whom are children. While autographed copies of celebrity books may become prized possessions in the same sense as autographed photographs, they are rarely cherished for their stories. Lured by a celebrity name on the cover, it is adults who are buying these children's books, thereby turning them into crossover picturebooks.

Epilogue
Picturebooks:
The Ultimate Crossover Genre

One is never too young to like texts and images or too old to no longer
need them.

—Sourire qui mord catalogue

Artists' books may have been the "quintessential artform" of the twentieth-
century, but there is no doubt that title belongs to picturebooks, and notably
crossover picturebooks, in the twenty-first-century. At a forum I organized
in 1997 (the year J. K. Rowling launched the landmark Harry Potter series)
for the Modern Language Association on "The State of Children's Books
in this Millennium and the Next," Wendy Lamb, executive editor in the
Books for Young Readers Department at Bantam Doubleday Dell, specu-
lated on the kinds of books children would continue to read in an elec-
tronic age, citing "sophisticated picture books" that would appeal to adults
as well as children. The subsequent years have confirmed her prediction.
Crossover picturebooks and other graphic literatures ensure the survival of
the book in the face of the threatening forces of the new technologies that
the Canadian children's author Tim Wynne-Jones discussed at the same
forum.[1] Picturebooks have embraced the new technologies, interacting with
them, drawing inspiration from them, and, in turn, enriching them. Eliza
Dresang drew attention to picturebooks with interactive qualities reflective
of our digital, multimedia world in *Radical Change: Books for Youth in a
Digital Age*, published in 1999. In her 2007 study titled *Radical Children's
Literature*, Kimberley Reynolds recognizes the importance of this interplay
between picturebooks and the new media: "Picturebooks are responding
to new media and technologies through experiments in form and format
in ways that are significantly affecting the aesthetics of visual narratives."[2]

She illustrates her arguments with two highly acclaimed picturebooks published at the beginning of this century, Sara Fanelli's *Dear Diary* (2000) and Lauren Child's *What Planet Are You from, Clarice Bean?* (2001).

Authors and illustrators have been pushing at the perceived boundaries of picturebooks for many years. "The decade from the late 1980s to the late 1990s has seen an unprecedented trend toward elaborate picture books," wrote Betsy Hearne in 1998, adding that "the audience for these sophisticated books is questionable—definitely older than preschool, perhaps covertly adult." The critic did not, however, see this development in a positive light. In her view, these "elaborate picture books" contained "weak stories . . . overwhelmed by graphic art."[3] Her comments show how greatly perceptions of the picturebook have evolved even over the past decade. Many picturebook artists tell lengthy, powerful narratives entirely through visual images. A case in point is Arnal Ballester's *No tinc paraules*, which was published the year Hearne wrote her article. The increased significance and sophistication of the graphic element of picturebooks reflects the prevalence of visual narratives in the new media and technologies. Some of the most radical experimentation in the arts occurs in picturebooks. Judith Graham recognizes the significant role the genre plays in the development of new technologies in the service of the book: "Perhaps more than most areas of book production, the creation of picturebooks has been closely linked to developments in printing technology, with illustrators and printers working together to push technology to new limits."[4] The fact that almost any medium can now be reproduced in picturebooks has made this art form attractive to an ever increasing number of artists from a diverse range of fields. As Barbara Kiefer points out: "This simplification of process seems to have attracted more and more artists who have discovered the picturebook as a challenging medium for their talents and who seem to be more interested in the possibilities of visual storytelling rather than in providing entertainment to an audience of young children."[5] The picturebook is an extraordinarily rich field of literary and artistic creation, in which authors, illustrators, painters, sculptors, photographers, graphic artists and designers, printers, and book makers are engaged in exciting experimentations with the text–image relationship. The exploration of new formats, techniques, and media that results from this cross-pollination has made the picturebook an exceptionally vibrant and transformative genre. As Kimberley Reynolds has demonstrated, the entire domain of children's literature "is bound up in interactions between formats and media that are beginning to change the nature and delivery of narrative fiction."[6] It is the picturebook genre in particular, however, that is marking radical new directions for future narratives.

Today many artists do not conform to the conventional thirty-two-page format of the children's picturebook, publishing lengthy works that push at generic boundaries. Dorte Karrebæk's bleak, black book *Den sorte bog* extends to seventy-two pages. Eugène and Bertola's *La mort à vivre*, which was published as a children's picturebook even though the author feels it is really "a book for adolescents and adults,"[7] contains seventy-eight pages. Some artists adopt highly innovative formats that completely defy classification. Frédéric Clément's *Muséum*, a "small collection of wings and souls found on the Amazon," according to the subtitle, is presented in a green cardboard box that mimics the wooden box in which the entomologist narrator sends his journal, notes, photographs, and drawings to a friend. The box contains twelve butterflies from his collection, each of which becomes a story. Journal, notes on transparencies, photographs, and drawings, as well as beautiful collage paintings await discovery in the unconventional book in a box. In Clément's aesthetic oeuvre, the picturebook can become a kind of notebook, a poetic inventory, or even a whimsical encyclopedia, as in the case of *Magasin Zinzin: Aux merveilles d'Alys* (English trans., *The Merchant of Marvels and the Peddler of Dreams*), the winner of the Premio Grafico at the Bologna Children's Book Fair in 1996. Innovative formats are created each time for these unique books that defy all boundaries.

Generic boundaries have become increasingly blurred in contemporary literature. It is difficult, if not impossible, to mark the limits of the picturebook. Where does the picturebook end and the comic book, the artists' book, or the graphic novel begin? The picturebook itself is a generic hybrid crossover between text and image, so it is not surprising that it is the source of the greatest generic innovation. As early as 1990, David Lewis stated that the picturebook was beginning "to emerge as a kind of supergenre" able "to absorb and ingest other, more closed and 'finished' forms." He describes the picturebook as "a motley, a ragbag of different genres, types, manners and modes," all of which are "easily accommodated within the flexible category of 'picture book.'"[8] The picturebook has not only been the source of innovative experiments in genre blending, but it has contributed to the creation of new genres and sub-genres. At a conference devoted to the contemporary picturebook and its "new forms and new readers" in Bordeaux in 2007, participants identified a number of hybrid genres, including the "album-poème" (picturebook-poem) and the "album-théâtre" (picturebook-theatre).[9] An excellent example of the latter is Chris Van Allsburg's *The Z Was Zapped: A Play in Twenty-Six Acts*, published in 1987. One of the "picturebook-poems" cited by Régis Lefort was Frédéric Clément's *Le livre épuisé* (the exhausted book), which combines text, photography, painting, and collage to create a poem about a book that gradually wears out with time (ironically, Clément's remarkable book is now also *epuisée* in the sense of out of print). The unusual books in his series Instants Clément, *Minium* and *Méthylène*, dreams of "1 minute 12" and "3 minutes 33" respectively, are a collection of fragmented moments, reminiscent of the haiku, that take the picturebook into the world of poetic silence. The illustrations flow, on a long, wavy banner, through the whimsical, poetic picturebook *Be-Februar*

Figure 7.1 Le livre épuisé by Frédéric Clément, copyright © 1994 Ipomée, reprinted by permission of Nicole Maymat.

Kedai Liknot Pilim (February is a good time for elephant shopping, 1988), by the Hungarian-born Israeli author Yoel Hoffmann. Some picturebooks even integrate a musical element, as in the case of Béatrice Poncelet's intimate and atmospheric *Chut! elle lit* (1995), in which the text floats on the background music of Mozart's *Cosi Fan Tutte*. We have already seen that some of Yvan Pommaux books have been designated "albums-bandes dess-inées" (picturebook-comics) and completely blur the boundaries between the two genres. Raymond Briggs's classic *Fungus the Bogeyman*, published in 1977, has been called a picturebook, a graphic novel, and a cartoon or comic strip book.[10]

The picturebook has been engendering experimental new genres for decades. The first books published by Le Sourire qui mord in 1976, described in their catalogue as "picturebooks . . . in the form of short illustrated nov-els," constitute a very avant-garde hybrid genre in which text and image are intimately linked. The forty-eight-page books of the series, titled À propos d'enfance (About childhood), were intended to appeal to all readers irrespec-tive of age. The pioneering series was launched with the much-acclaimed title *Histoire de Julie qui avait une ombre de garcon* (The story of Julie who had a boy's shadow), which was reprinted many times, translated into at least eleven languages, adapted for the theatre, and reissued by Être in 2009. Christian Bruel has been a pioneer in experimenting with generic hybridity. With the publication of the title *La mémoire des scorpions* (The memory of scorpions) in 1991, he introduced what he called the *photo-roman* (photo-novel), which has subsequently also been referred to as the *roman-photo*. The 120-page detective story, about a young Japanese girl who suffers from amnesia after being the victim of an assault, is staged by the accompanying photographs of Xavier Lambours. The innovative book received the Graphic Prize Special Mention at the Bologna Children's Book Fair in 1992. The following year, Bruel and Lambours collaborated on another experimental book, *Petites musiques de la nuit* (A little night music), a rather surreal pre-sentation of the ritual hour of bedtime. Katy Couprie coloured Lambours's photographs in this story, which is shorter and whimsical rather than dark, explaining perhaps why the publisher chose this time to bill it simply as a "picturebook."

The blurring of the boundaries between the picturebook and the novel are particularly evident in the field of the graphic novel. Shaun Tan's *The Arrival*, which alternates small frames with full-page and double-page spreads in sepia tones, is a blend of picturebook and comic strip. The internationally acclaimed work has been called a graphic novel, a wordless picturebook, and a wordless comic book for all ages. In 2007, *The Arrival* won the Book of the Year for the NSW Premier's Literary Awards over works by literary heavyweights such as Peter Carey, two-time winner of the Booker Prize. The fact that a wordless picturebook claimed the title "Book of the Year" in a major writers' festival attracted some debate as to whether a wordless book is truly literature and should have won a literary prize. A similar controversy was ignited in the lit-erary world when *Jimmy Corrigan: The Smartest Kid on Earth* (2000), by the American comic book artist Chris Ware, won the Guardian First Book Award in 2001. It was the first time a graphic novel had won a major book prize in the United Kingdom.

A number of crossover picturebooks of a biographical or autobiographical nature offer complex and profound graphic memoirs, including the 1994 Caldecott Medal winning *Grandfather's Journey* (1993), by the Japanese American author Allen Say, the 2008 Caldecott Honor Book *The Wall: Growing Up Behind the Iron Curtain* (2007), by the Czech-born author and illustrator Peter Sís, and Chen Jiang Hong's *Mao and Me: The Little Red Guard* (2008). Many information books, often with detailed drawings, are multilayered works that appeal to adults as well as children. David Macaulay's *Cathedral: The Story of Its Construction* (1973), winner of the Deutscher Jugendliteraturpreis for children's non-fiction in 1975, was the first of his many acclaimed crossover picturebooks about architecture and design. Other titles that come immediately to mind are Stephen Biesty's *Incredible Cross-Sections* (1992), Arthur Geisert's *The Etcher's Studio* (1997), and Peter Sís's Caldecott Honor Books *Starry Messenger: Galileo Galilei* (1997) and *Tibet Through the Red Box* (1998). In 2002, Media Vaca received the Bologna Ragazzi Award in both the fiction and non-fiction categories for two crossover books. The non-fiction award went to Lluïsot's *Una temporada en Calcuta* (A season in Calcutta), a collection of disturbing drawings of the old, the sick, the physically impaired, and the abandoned children that the artist did during a three-month stay at Mother Theresa's hospitals and clinics in 1999. The book was published in Media Vaca's series Últimas lecturas, which the publisher's catalogue translates as Late Reading, although it is literally Last Readings. Like the series title, the logo of an old woman dropping her book as she falls back in her chair, presumably dead, suggests that these books are intended for very mature readers. The catalogue states that the series is "aimed especially at non-children and also at non-readers," but the introduction to the collection reminds readers: "A book doesn't ask us how much education we have or if we are experienced readers: readers of three thousand books, let's say. The book doesn't care who we are. . . . "[11]

The picturebook appropriates from other media just as it does from other literary genres. Like comic books, film has had a major influence on the picturebook. David Wiesner's works are inspired by animated cartoons and superhero literature, as well as silent movies. The sparse Japanese text that appears down the right hand side of the pages outside the frame of the bold, vivid illustrations of Koji Suzuki's *Atsusa-no-sei?* (Did all this happen because of the heat?; publisher's translation: A hot day, 1994) is almost like a commentary on an animated film, an effect heightened by large speech balloons. Jean Claverie's *Little Lou* (1990) shifts midway to a dark comic book style that parodies American gangster movies of the mid-twentieth-century, while Yvan Pommaux's John Chatterton series is reminiscent of detective movies of a similar era. Tohby Riddle's *The Great Escape from City Zoo* is referred to as the "silver screen edition," while Wolf Erlbruch's *The Story of the Little Mole* has been called a "'road movie' in picturebook form."[12] This influence

Figure 7.2 Atsusa-no-sei? by Koji Suzuki, copyright © 1994 Koji Suzuki, reprinted by permission of Fukuinkan Shoten.

is not one-sided; the picturebook has also played an important role in the film industry. Jörg Müller and Jörg Steiner's *Aufstand der Tiere oder Die neuen Stadtmusikanten* (The rebellion of the animals or The New Town Musicians, 1989), which borrows heavily from the big and small screen, was released as an animated short film in 1997. A number of crossover picturebooks have inspired feature-length films for a general audience. One of the most notable is William Steig's *Shrek*, on which the blockbuster of the same name was based. Three of Chris Van Allsburg's picturebooks, *The Polar Express*, *Jumanji*, and *Zathura*, have been adapted for the big screen. An animated feature-length film based on Tomi Ungerer's *The Three Robbers* was released in Germany in 2007. Sendak himself was one of the producers when *Where the Wild Things Are* came to the big screen in Spike Jonze's 2009 fantasy drama film. To accompany the Blu-ray edition of the film in 2010, *Higglety Pigglety Pop! or There Must Be More To Life* was released as a live-action/animated short film with Meryl Streep giving voice to Jenny. The screenplay of Jonze's film was novelized by Dave Eggers as *The Wild Things*, published in 2009. Sendak's classic has thus crossed over multiple times, from picturebook to film to novel. In some cases, the film precedes the picturebook. Miki Takahashi's unusual Japanese picturebook series about Kogepan (Burnt Bun), which offers an existential discussion of life seen through the eyes of a burnt red bean bun, appeared in a television anime series before appearing in the first picturebook, *Kogepan: Pan nimo iroiro aru-rashii* (Burnt Bun: It seems there are many kinds of bread) in 2000. The synergy between these media is highlighted in *The Great Paper Caper* (2008), by the Northern Irish picturebook artist Oliver Jeffers, in which a vignette/balloon shows one of the characters watching the animated film version of his second picturebook, *Lost and Found* (2005), on television. The witty allusion seems to be a plug for the film that did not screen until Christmas Eve 2008, several months after the publication of *The Great Paper Caper*.

The distinction between children's books and books for adults is much less rigid in some countries. In Denmark, artists such as Dorte Karrebæk and Lilian Brøgger have altered expectations about picturebooks, which are bought by and for all ages. Fam Ekman, Svein Nyhus, and Iben Sandemose have played a similar role in the Norwegian market. The groundbreaking crossover picturebooks that repeatedly take Norwegian readers by surprise are possible in part thanks to generous government funding that is not, however, available for picturebooks for adults. Arne Marius Samuelsen feels this has led authors and illustrators to create "picture books which in some cases are more for grownups than children" and that "probably would have problems in being published in other countries lacking the financial support from an estate like Kulturrådet."[13] Speaking of the "exceptional, highly sophisticated visual quality" of Norwegian picturebooks in particular, Martin Salisbury, a former Bologna Ragazzi Award judge, writes: "Perhaps we can dare to hope that the postmodern picturebook is leading a revival of illustration in books for adults, with growing awareness of the intellectual demands that narrative pictures can make. Adults are increasingly buying picturebooks for their own consumption."[14] All Fam Ekman's picturebooks are collected by adults, but only one has been released as a picturebook for adults. Although the author-illustrator had wanted to make a picturebook especially for grown-ups for years, she pointed out during our interview in 2001 that such a thing is almost non-existent. Her need to write about "adults and romance" in a way that was not possible in children's books resulted in the "'grown-up' book" *Tilberedning av hjerter* (Making hearts, Cappelen), which met with complete silence when it was published in 1998.

Ekman wonders if "perhaps a picturebook for adults was not such a good idea," but she enjoyed working on it despite the somber tone and she feels that it was "an interesting experiment."[15] The idea of picturebooks for adults has attracted other children's picturebook artists. Much to the chagrin of those working in the field of children's books in France, Olivier Douzou left Rouergue in 2001 in order to explore new territory. His intention was to launch a collection with another publisher based on the idea of images without borders.[16] When the project fell through, he co-founded, in 2002, the publishing house L'ampoule, whose goal, according to the website, is "to develop new dialogues between text and image, photographed, drawn, or textual, in adult literature." Douzou continues to work with authors and illustrators with whom he collaborated at Rouergue, but they now seek to reach a more diverse audience. Other publishers have also moved into the field of graphic narratives for adults. The new genre referred to as "Beaux-Livres-fiction" which Frédéric

FAM EKMAN

TILBEREDNING AV HJERTER

Cappelen

Figure 7.3   Tilberedning av hjerter by Fam Ekman, copyright © 1998,
J. W. Cappelens Forlag a.s, reprinted by permission of Fam Ekman and
Cappelen Damm.

Clément introduced with the publication of *Muséum* with Albin Michel in
1999 has been considered a genre for adults, although it is impossible to divide
the artist's oeuvre into children's books and adult books.

The fact that crossover picturebooks defy traditional categorizations makes
them difficult to market. They tend to be marketed as children's books and
shelved in the children's section, whereas many should appear in the general
section. Crossover picturebooks are not necessarily among the bestselling

picturebooks. Innovative formats and daring subject matter often limit the readership in many markets. Hardcover picturebooks in general are still difficult to sell and publishers rely heavily on co-edition sales. Pioneering experimentation in graphics and content in countries like Norway, Sweden, and Denmark means that co-edition is not necessarily an option. The high quality of many of these books makes them expensive, especially in small language markets. Picturebooks in general have been undervalued because of the format, and the general public is largely unaware of the sophistication and power of a genre that challenges and stimulates culture and society. The media hype and blockbuster sales surrounding children's novels read by adults have not spread to picturebooks. With the exception of a few celebrity picturebooks, they are not supported by extensive publicity and marketing and they do not receive a high profile in the media or in bookstores. It is rare that a picturebook receives the media attention accorded to William Wegman's *Puppies*, which was previewed in the *New York Times Magazine* and secured the author a coveted invitation to appear on *Oprah* in 1997. There is nonetheless a growing confidence in picturebooks and their ability to cross over. *Puppies* falls into the category of what the author's publisher was already referring to at the time as "multipurposed books."[17]

The picturebook is indeed the "supergenre," a vibrant, versatile genre that seems to know no boundaries. The works examined in this study challenge current definitions of the picturebook and certainly defy generic expectations about picturebooks as children's literature only. They explore and develop the potential of the genre as its own unique art form, an art form suitable for all ages. In a graphically-oriented society where culture in general is shifting away from age as a defining category, picturebooks are an increasingly important mode of artistic communication. They not only provide the short, visually stimulating forms of entertainment sought by many contemporary readers, but they promote a graphic literature that renews our reading habits and invites us to see the world differently. As Barbara Kiefer predicts, picturebooks "will continue to delight human audiences of all ages and to attract artists to explore the human condition."[18] Like the artists' book, the picturebook is "a conquest of new territory,"[19] forging new paths and opening up new horizons for narrative and the book.

Notes

Chapter One

1. Kimberley Reynolds, *Radical Children's Literature: Future Visions and Aesthetic Transformations in Juvenile Fiction* (Houndmills: Palgrave Macmillan, 2007), 16–17; David Lewis, "The Constructedness of Texts: Picture Books and the Metafictive," *Signal* 62 (May 1990): 141.

2. Sandra L. Beckett, "Breaking Boundaries with Radical Picture Books" (paper presented at the international conference "Image and Imagery," Brock University, St. Catharines, October 16, 2002). The Swiss authors of a 2000 catalogue on developments in picturebooks also speak of the "radical change" in children's literature that began in the 1960s. See *Schau genau! Variationen im Bilderbuch 1950–2000. Look twice! Variations in picture books 1950–2000*, Katalog zur Ausstellung des Schweizerischen Instituts für Kinder- und Jugendmedien (Zurich: Schweizerischen Institut für Kinder- und Jugendmedien, 2000), 1.

3. Toward the end of a 1993 article devoted to "postmodern tensions" in the picturebook, Clare Bradford raises the fact that "the notion of dual readership" is rarely discussed in relation to the picturebook. She goes on to point out that the genre "offers so many possibilities for ironic interplay and multiple construction of meaning that it inevitably crosses boundaries between younger and older readers, between children's fiction and adult fiction." Clare Bradford, "The Picture Book: Some Postmodern Tensions," *Papers* 4, no. 3 (December 1993): 13, 14. For a detailed study of the postmodern picturebook, see Lawrence R. Sipe and Sylvia Pantaleo, eds., *Postmodern Picturebooks: Play, Parody, and Self-Referentiality* (New York and London: Routledge, 2008).

4. Carole Scott, "A Challenge to Innocence: 'Inappropriate Picturebooks for Young Readers,'" *Bookbird* 43, no. 1 (2005): 12.

5. Jochen Weber, "Pasando los limites: All-Age-Books, Crossover-Literature y otras tendencias actuales de la literatura para jóvenes lectores" (paper presented at the Primer Congreso Nacional de Lectura y Escritura: Escuela y Literatura Infantil, Durango, Mexico, May 16–18), 2004.

6. Lawrence R. Sipe, "First Graders Interpret David Wiesner's *The Three Pigs*: A Case Study," in *Postmodern Picturebooks: Play, Parody, and Self-Referentiality*, 223–237.

7. Barbara Bader, *American Picturebooks: From Noah's Ark to The Beast Within* (New York: Macmillan, 1976), 1; Perry Nodelman, *Words about Pictures: The Narrative Art of Children's Picture Books* (Athens, GA: University of Georgia Press, 1988), vii.

8. "Comments," *Papers* 4, no. 3 (December 1993): 2.

9. Judith Rosen, "Breaking the Age Barrier," *Publishers Weekly*, September 8, 1997, 28.

10. Stian Hole, "Interview with Stian Hole, author and illustrator of *Garmann's Summer* (May 2008)," *Eerdmans Books for Young Readers*, http://www.eerdmans.com/Interviews/holeinterview.htm (accessed June 3, 2010).

11. Maurice Sendak, "Maurice Sendak," in *Pauses: Autobiographical Reflections of 101 Creators of Children's Books*, ed. Lee Bennett Hopkins (New York: HarperCollins, 1995), 142–143.

12. Selma Lanes, *The Art of Maurice Sendak* (New York: Harry N. Abrams, Inc., 1980), 235.

13. Geraldine DeLuca, "Exploring the Levels of Childhood: The Allegorical Sensibility of Maurice Sendak," *Children's Literature* 12 (1984): 4.

14. Jane Doonan, "Into the Dangerous World: *We Are All in the Dumps with Jack and Guy* by Maurice Sendak," *Signal* 75 (1994), 166.

15. Barbara Novak, "Picture Books," *New York Times*, May 24, 1970.

16. Reynolds, *Radical Children's Literature*, 61.

17. "Ruy-Vidal, François," http://www.ricochet-jeunes.org/editeur.asp?name=Ruy-Vidal%2C+Fran%E7ois (accessed October 31, 2007).

18. "François Ruy-Vidal," *Maison des écrivains et de la littérature*, http://www.m-e-l.fr/Fran%C3%A7ois%20Ruy-Vidal,229 (accessed December 11, 2010).

19. Media Vaca catalogue 2005–2006, 6.

20. Ibid., 36.

21. The story was first published in 1966 in a collection of stories, titled *Dichter erzählen Kindern* (Writers tell stories to children), by the important German publisher Gertraud Middelhauve, before appearing, in 1966, in the author's collection *Kindergeschichten* (Children's stories), which won literary prizes in the adult sector. See Sandra L. Beckett, *Crossover Fiction: Global and Historical Perspectives* (New York and London: Routledge 2009), 189.

22. Kota Taniuchi, "Interview," February 2, 2003, *Kota Taniuchi* http://kota.taniuchi.free.fr/pages/interview.html (accessed August 31, 2010); "Shikosha Co., Ltd. since 1949," http://www.ehon-artbook.com/about.html (accessed December 8, 2010).

23. The quotation appears on an Ipomée bookmark created when the series was launched in 1986.

24. Nicole Maymat, "Nicole Maymat, écrivain et intrépide éditrice," interview by Étienne Delessert, 2009, *Ricochet-Jeunes*, http://www.ricochet-jeunes.

org/magazine-propos/article/69-nicole-maymat (accessed January 6, 2010).

25. Jocelyne Béguery, *Une esthétique contemporaine de l'album jeunesse: De grands petits livres* (Paris: L'Harmattan, 2002), 150–151. In an interview with Béguery, Maymat admits also having been accused of producing "books for children of intellectuals," an accusation she also categorically denies.

26. René Turc, "Tête à tête," interview by Elisabeth Lortic, *La Revue des livres pour enfants* 55–56 (Winter 1994): 55.

27. Ibid., 56–57, 52.

28. Oscar K. [Ole Dalgaard], "It's not the fact that it is said—in fact it's just the way you say it," *Danish Literary Magazine* (Autumn 2008): 47.

29. Bernie Goedhart, "Author/illustrator Stian Hole: The Complete Interview," *Montreal Gazette*, May 12, 2010.

30. Rosen, "Breaking the Age Barrier," 28.

31. See Beckett, *Crossover Fiction*, 103–109.

32. Rosen, "Breaking the Age Barrier," 31.

33. Toin Duijx, "Winner of the 2004 Andersen Illustrator Award: Max Velthuijs, The Netherlands," *Bookbird* 42, no. 4 (2004): 11.

34. *Little Crocodile's Big Feet*, which won the Grand Prize in the picturebook category of the first Nissan Children's Storybook and Picture Book Grand Prix in 1984, was published in English in 1996, and was followed by *Little Crocodile's Alarm Clock* in 1997.

35. "All-Time Bestselling Children's Books," *Publishers Weekly* 248, no. 51, December 17, 2001, http://www.publishersweekly.com/article/CA186995.html (accessed December 14, 2010).

36. Rosen, "Breaking the Age Barrier," 29.

37. Jill Lightner, Amazon Review of *Seuss-isms for Success*, by Dr. Seuss, http://www.amazon.com/Seuss-isms-Success-Life-Favors-TM/dp/0679894772 (accessed December 13, 2010).

38. Stian Hole, "Interview with Stian Hole, author and illustrator of *Garmann's Summer* (May 2008)."

Chapter Two

1. Johanna Drucker, *The Century of Artists' Books*, 2nd ed. (New York: Granary Books, 2004), 1.

2. Angela Lorenz, "Artist's Books—For Lack of a Better Name," http://www.angelalorenzartistsbooks.com/whatis.htm (accessed April 21, 2010).

3. See Elisabeth Lortic, "Les livres d'artistes pour enfants," in *Livres d'enfance* (Saint-Yrieix-la-Perche: Pays-Paysage/Centre national du livre d'artiste, 1998), 29–34.

4. I have published two essays on the subject: "Artists' Books for a Cross-audience," in *Studies in Children's Literature 1500–2000*, ed. Celia Keenan

and Mary Shine Thompson (Dublin: Four Courts Press, 2004), 162–169; "Transcending Boundaries with Object-Books," in *L'édition pour la jeunesse: entre héritage et culture de masse*, ed. Ségolène Roy (Eaubonne: IICP, 2005), CD-ROM.

5. Stephen Bury, *Artists' Books: the Book as a Work of Art, 1963–1995* (Aldershot: Scolar Press, 1995), 4, 118–119, 138; Drucker, *The Century of Artists' Books*, 73–74. In 1984, Andy Warhol exhibited a series of paintings for children (mounted at children's eye level) at Gallerie Bruno Bischofberger in Zurich. At the same time, the gallery published *Andy Warhol's Children's Book*, a limited-edition wordless picturebook containing reproductions of twelve different paintings from the exhibition. The book's twelve pages are constructed of heavy cardboard, but the format is quite conventional.

6. Warja Lavater, "Tête à tête: Entretien avec Warja Lavater," interview by Bernadette Gromer, *La Revue des livres pour enfants* 137–138 (Winter 1991): 44.

7. That is not to say that illustrators of other picturebooks do not take an interest in these aspects of the book. An increasing number of picturebook artists routinely use the book's format, paper, typography, and so forth to tell the story.

8. The author herself told me in the same letter that it "was written for all ages, in the spirit of a village storyteller. The children sit in the front row, the grandparents in the back, and the story is for all of them." The youngest listener she is aware of was two and the oldest reader was a woman in her nineties whose eyesight was failing and "she wanted a book of poetry that was printed in big type."

9. El Lissitzky, "Our Book," in *Looking Closer Three: Classic Writings on Graphic Design*, ed. Michael Bierut, Jessica Helfand, Steven Heller, and Rick Poynor (New York: Allworth Press, 1999), 31, 29.

10. Margaret R. Higonnet, "Modernism and Childhood: Violence and Renovation," *The Comparatist* 33 (2009): 98, 97.

11. Sophie Lissitzky-Küppers, *El Lissitzky: Life, Letters, Texts* (Greenwich: New York Graphic Society, 1968), note to plate 91.

12. El Lissitzky, "Our Book," 30; Lissitzky-Küppers, *El Lissitzky: Life, Letters, Texts*, note to plate 91.

13. Kate Steinitz included an English translation of the tale by Robert Haas in her book devoted to Schwitters in 1968, but it was not until 2009 that a complete English-language recreation of *The Scarecrow* was made available by Jack Zipes, with a typographic translation by Barrie Tullet. See Kate Trauman Steinitz, *Kurt Schwitters: A Portrait from Life* (Berkeley: University of California Press, 1968), 127–129; Kurt Schwitters, *Lucky Hans and Other Merz Fairy Tales*, translated and introduced by Jack Zipes, illus. Irvine Peacock (Princeton, NJ: Princeton University Press, 2009). The typographic transcription appears on pp. 72–84, while a running English text appears on pp. 223–225.

14. Steinitz, *Kurt Schwitters*, 40, 41.

15. Ibid., 40.

16. Ibid., 43–44.

17. Ibid., 45.

18. See Higonnet, "Modernism and Childhood," 99; Zipes, "Kurt Schwitters, Politics, and the Merz Fairy Tale," in *Lucky Hans and Other Merz Fairy Tales*, 28.

19. *Éditions MeMo*, http://www.editionsmemo.fr/ (accessed March 4, 2010).

20. It was entitled "alfabetiere" rather than "abecedario" because the letters of the alphabet are not disposed "according to the traditional method: abc," explained Munari in a letter to Nico Orengo on October 6, 1972. Qtd. in Giorgio Maffei, *Munari i libri* (Milan: Edizioni Sylvestre Bonnard, 2002), 27.

21. In 2000, Les Trois Ourses organized an exhibition and published a catalogue, titled "Lire et Jouer avec Enzo Mari" (Read and play with Enzo Mari), to pay homage to the Italian designer's work for children.

22. Katsumi Komagata, "Messages within Picture Books," *Bessatsu Taiyo* "Nihon no Kokoro" 108 (winter 1999): special issue: *Ehon to Asobou: Me to te de tanoshimu ehon-shu* (Let's play with picture books: let's enjoy them with eyes and hands; Tokyo: Heibonsha Inc., 2001), 135.

23. Ibid., 134.

24. Qtd. in Sophie Curtil and Elisabeth Lortic, "1, 2, 3 . . . Komagata," *Visa pour la cité* 33 (1996), 22; Komagata, "Messages within Picture Books," 136.

25. See Laboratorio d'arte, "Dedicated to Munari. 1, 2, 3 . . . Komagata," 2007, 2, english.palazzoesposizioni.it/mediacenter/. . ./StreamAttributoMedia. aspx?. . . (accessed March 24, 2010).

26. See Maffei, *Munari i libri*, 66.

27. Conversation with Marco Meneguzzo, in Marco Meneguzzo, *Bruno Munari* (Bari: Editori Laterza, 1993), 114.

28. Munari had used a similar technique in the second book in the series, *L'uomo del camion* (The man with the truck; English trans., *The Birthday Present*), which contains different-sized pages in a story about a father delivering a birthday present to his son in a variety of vehicles that keep breaking down.

29. *Bloomsbury Auctions*, http://roma.bloomsburyauctions.com/detail/ROMA-28/169.0 (accessed March 6, 2010).

30. Laboratorio d'arte, "Dedicated to Munari. 1, 2, 3 . . . Komagata," 2.

31. "Katsumi Komagata's Gorgeous Baby Books," Daddytypes.com, July 6, 2007, http://daddytypes.com/2007/07/06/katsumi_komagatas_gorgeous_baby_books.php (accessed March 12, 2010).

32. Lavater, "Tête à tête: Entretien avec Warja Lavater," 40.

33. Bruno Munari, *Da cosa nasce cosa* (Rome and and Bari: Editori Laterza, 1981), 218; qtd. in Bruno Munari, Claude Lichtenstein, Alfredo W. Häberli,

K. Salatino, and S. Lindberg, *Making Air Visible/Far vedere l'aria: A Visual Reader on Bruno Munari* (Zurich, Museum für Gestaltung, 1995), 126.

34. Bruno Munari et al., *Making Air Visible/Far vedere l'aria*, 278.

35. Iela Mari, *Il mondo attraverso una lente* (Milano and Bologna: Babalibri, 2010), 26.

36. Valeria Tassinari, "Entretien avec Enzo Mari," in *Quand les artistes créent pour les enfants: des objets livres pour imaginer* (Paris: Le Mook/Autrement, 2008), 64.

37. Carla Poesio, "The Rhythm of Images," *The Lion and the Unicorn* 26 (2002): 225.

38. Warja Lavater, "Perception: When Signs Start to Communicate," in *The Faces of Physiognomy: Interdisciplinary Approaches to Johann Caspar Lavater*, ed. Ellis Shookman (Colombia, SC: Camden House, 1993), 186.

39. Lavater, "Tête-à-tête," 40, 42.

40. The same year that Lavater published her first tale in the series, the Dutch mathematician Dionys Burger published *Sphereland: A Fantasy About Curved Spaces and an Expanding Universe* (1965), which includes a diagram representing the principal characters in the tale of Snow White, as they are described in the version the narrator tells his grandchildren: Snow White is a "lovely, delicate line," the prince is a dodecagon, and the seven dwarfs are triangles, which evoke Lavater's diamond shapes (New York: Apollo Editions, 1969, 66–67).

41. Qtd. in Curtil and Lortic, "1, 2, 3 . . . Komagata," 23.

42. Munari "Un libro illeggibile," in *Da cosa nasce cosa*, 216; qtd. in *Making Air Visible*, 126.

43. Ibid.

44. According to Élisabeth Lortic, a special edition of Enzo and Iela Mari's *L'uovo e la gallina* had wooden pages joined by metal rings that, when turned, imitated the sound of the hen's pecking ("Des livres, de l'art, des enfants . . . ," in *Quand les artistes créent pour les enfants*, 12).

45. "Louise-Marie Cumont," in *Quand les artistes créent pour les enfants*, 51.

46. Bruno Munari, *Design as Art*, trans. Patrick Creagh (Harmondsworth: Penguin Books, 1971), 96.

47. Munari, *Da cosa nasce cosa* (Bari: Laterza, 1981), 225.

48. "I libri scritti da Bruno Munari," *L'arte di Munari*, http://www.munart.org/index.php?p2=1 (accessed March 23, 2010).

49. Munari, *Da cosa nasce cosa*, 219, qtd. in *Far vedere l'aria. Making Air Visible*, 126.

50. Qtd. in Meneguzzo, *Bruno Munari*, 114.

51. Qtd. in Curtil and Lortic, "1, 2, 3 . . . Komagata," 23.

52. Alberto Mondadori, 1950, qtd. in "Munari visto da," *L'arte di Munari*, http://www.munart.org/index.php?p2=2 (accessed March 21, 2010).

53. Milos Cvach, "Le livre comme une œuvre: anatomie d'un livre artistique," in *Quand les artistes créent pour les enfants*, 42.

54. "Milos Cvach," *Les Trois Ourses*, http://troisourses.online.fr/cvach.htm (accessed April 14, 2010).

55. See Komagata, "Messages Within Picture Books," 134.

56. Letter from Warja Lavater to Clive Phillpot, former Chief Librarian at The Museum of Modern Art in New York, August 6, 1986.

57. "Enzo Mari's Playful Simplicity," *Animalarium*, http://theanimalarium. blogspot.com/2009/08/enzo-maris-playful-simplicity.html (accessed February 17, 2011).

58. Warja Lavater, "Tête à tête," 42.

59. Drucker, *The Century of Artists' Books*, 216. I have also mentioned the example of the wild beasts that surround Snow White menacingly when she is abandoned in the forest by the hunter. See Beckett, "Artists' Books for a Cross-Audience," 166.

60. Lavater, "Tête à tête," 42.

61. Letter from Warja Lavater to Clive Phillpot, former Chief Librarian at The Museum of Modern Art in New York, August 6, 1986.

62. Lavater, "Tête à tête," 42.

63. Tassinari, "Entretien avec Enzo Mari," 64. In 1971, Bruno Munari created *L'abitacolo* (Habitat or Dwelling Place or Cockpit), an adaptable, modular structure of welded iron bars designed specifically as a space for children's games and activities, including reading. Produced by the company Robots, it won the Compasso d'oro in 1979. See Munari, *Da cosa nasce cosa*, 196–197.

64. Bruno Munari, "Libro letto," *Domus* 760 (May 1994): 57.

65. Komagata, "Messages within Picture Books," 136.

66. Lavater's *William Tell* was published with an English legend by the Museum of Modern Art in New York and a German legend by the Swiss publisher. The Perrault tales appeared first with a French only legend, but subsequently English, German, and Japanese were added.

67. Lavater, "Tête-à-tête," 42, 44.

68. Komagata, "Messages within Picture Books," 136.

69. See *Corraini*, http://www.corraini.com/chisiamoi.htm (accessed May 1, 2003).

70. In 2002, Les Trois Ourses marketed the "Boîte verte," designed by Bruno Munari and containing twelve green artists' books, in which Munari, Lavater, and Komagata all have a prominent place. At 600€ in 2002, this box of books could only be bought by a rather elite adult audience, but it was nonetheless intended to be shared with children. Munari had previously designed a box for their "Valise Munari," in which Alix Romero organized the space so that fifteen books and a game each have their own spot. Les Trois Ourses has also produced "Livres en valise de Katsumi Komagata."

71. Lavater, "Tête à tête," 43.

72. Lissitzky-Küppers, *El Lissitzky: Life, Letters, Texts*, note to plate 91.

73. See *Ircam*, http://www.ircam.fr/produits/techno/multimedia/imageries-e. html (accessed May 1, 2003).
74. Lortic, "Les livres d'artistes pour enfants," 32.
75. Komagata, "Messages Within Picture Books," 136.
76. Henri Cueco, Interview with Hélène Bernard, *Neuf de Cœur*, no. 2.
77. Paul Cox, "Tête à tête avec Paul Cox," interview with Elisabeth Lortic, *La Revue des livres pour enfants*, 155–156 (Winter 1994): 62.
78. Komagata, "Messages within Picture Books," 136–137.

Chapter Three

1. Jacqueline Danset-Léger, *L'enfant et les images de la littérature enfantine* (Brussels: Pierre Mardaga, 1988), 158.
2. See, for example, Sophie Van der Linden, "Les albums 'sans,'" in *Le livre pour enfants: Regards critiques offerts à Isabelle Nières-Chevrel*, ed. Cécile Boulaire (Rennes: Presses Universitaires de Rennes, 2006), 190.
3. Maria Nikolajeva and Carole Scott, *How Picturebooks Work* (New York: Garland, 2001), 12–13.
4. Marion Durand and Gérard Bertrand, *L'Image dans le livre pour enfants* (Paris: L'École des loisirs, 1975), 134.
5. Van der Linden, "Les albums 'sans,'" 190.
6. Isabelle Nières-Chevrel, "L'Évolution des rapports entre le texte et l'image dans la littérature pour enfants," in *L'Enfance à travers le patrimoine écrit*, Colloque d'Annecy, September 18–19, 2001 (Annecy: ARALD, FCCB, 2002), 70; Isabelle Nières-Chevrel, "The Narrative Power of Pictures: *L'Orage* (The Thunderstorm) by Anne Brouillard," in *New Directions in Picturebook Research*, ed. Teresa Colomer, Bettina Kümmerling-Meibauer, and Cecilia Silva-Díaz (New York and London: Routledge, 2010), 129.
7. "Illustrator Nominee: France: Claude Ponti," *Bookbird* 46, no. 2 (2008): 30.
8. Van der Linden, "Les albums 'sans,'" 191.
9. Isabelle Nières-Chevrel, "Narrateur visuel et narrateur verbal dans l'album pour enfants," *La Revue des livres pour enfants* 214 (December 2003): 74. For a very detailed study of Brouillard's book, see Nières-Chevrel's excellent article "The Narrative Power of Pictures: *L'Orage* (The Thunderstorm) by Anne Brouillard."
10. Brad Holland, "Express Yourself—It's Later than You Think," in *The Education of an Illustrator*, ed. Steven Heller and Marshall Arisman (New York: Alworth Press, 2000), 16.
11. Review from *Parenting* magazine, quoted in the press release for *Flotsam* on the Houghton Mifflin Company website.
12. Carole Scott, "Dual Audience in Picturebooks," in *Transcending Boundaries: Writing for a Dual Audience of Children and Adults*, ed. Sandra L. Beckett (New York: Garland, 1999), 101.

13. Leonard S. Marcus, "The Artist's Other Eye: The Picture Books of Mitsumasa Anno," *The Lion and the Unicorn* 7–8 (1983–1984): 41.

14. Ibid., 42–43.

15. Katy Couprie, "Auteurs et illustrateurs—Entretiens: Katy Couprie," *Livres au Trésor*, September 1992, http://www.livresautresor.net/livres/e57.htm (accessed January 30, 2009). Unless otherwise indicated, all subsequent comments attributed to Couprie are taken from this interview.

16. Conversation with Dorte Karrebæk, May 15, 2009. Unless otherwise indicated, all subsequent comments attributed to Karrebæk are taken from this conversation.

17. Qtd. in Ulla Kofod-Olsen, "In Praise of Childhood," trans. Birgit Stephenson, *Danish Children's Literature* 3 (1992), http://www.danishliterature.info/index.php?id=2092&no_cache=1&tx_lfforfatter_pi3[uid]=202&tx_lfforfatter_pi3[artikel]=315&tx_lfforfatter_pi2[stage]=2&tx_lfforfatter_pi2[lang]=_eng (accessed May 15, 2009).

18. Conversation with Dorte Karrabæk, September 3, 1995.

19. Parsons Illustration Department, "From the Vaults: *Number 24* by Guy Billout (Harlin Quist, 1973)," *Parsons Illustration Newsletter* 1 (Winter 2006).

20. Ibid.

21. See Sandra L. Beckett, *Red Riding Hood for All Ages: A Fairy-Tale in Cross-Cultural Contexts* (Detroit: Wayne State University Press, 2008), 20–21.

22. Catalogue of Le Sourire qui mord, 1995, 9.

23. For a more detailed analysis, see Beckett, *Red Riding Hood for All Ages*, 196–199.

24. Eliza Dresang, *Radical Change: Books for Youth in a Digital Age*, 115, 3.

25. Okiko Miyake and Tomoko Masaki, "A Short History of the Japanese Picture Book," in *Through Eastern Eyes: The Art of the Japanese Picture Book*, catalogue of an exhibition held at the National Centre for Research in Children's Literature and curated by Okiko Miyake and Tomoko Masaki (London: National Centre for Research in Children's Literature, 2001), 19.

26. "Prix Espace Enfants: Lauréats 1987–2004," *Fondation Espace Enfants*, http://www.espace-enfants.org/index.php?option=com_content&task=view&id=17&Itemid=33 (accessed October 3, 2009).

27. Jane Doonan, "A Pictured World through Eastern Eyes," in *Through Eastern Eyes: The Art of the Japanese Picture Book*, 13.

28. E-mail from Arnal Ballester, July 12, 2009.

29. Quentin Blake, "Quentin Blake—The Power of Illustration," *Teachers TV*, 2009, http://www.teachers.tv/videos/quentin-blake-the-power-of-illustration (accessed September 2, 2010).

30. Quentin Blake, "Quentin Blake on . . . ," *Teachers' TV*, http://static.teachers.tv/shared/files/11958.pdf (accessed September 2, 2010). Unless otherwise indicated, all subsequent comments attributed to Blake are taken from these interviews.

31. Lauralyn Persson, Review of *Re-Zoom*, *School Library Journal*.

32. Patricia McCormick, "All Things Reconsidered," *New York Times*, November 12, 1995. A number of other well-known wordless picturebook artists have also had important careers as commercial illustrators. In the case of Guy Billout, it was after publishing *Number 24*, that he went on to become a freelance illustrator and a regular contributor to the *Atlantic Monthly* and *The New Yorker*.

33. Qtd. on Amazon.com, http://www.amazon.com/Re-Zoom-Istvan-Banyai/dp/014055694X (accessed August 25, 2010).

34. See Van der Linden, "Les albums 'sans,'" 197, n. 45.

35. Sara, "L'univers de Sara," http://universdesara.org/article.php3?id_article=67 (accessed October 2, 2009). Unless otherwise stated, all subsequent comments attributed to Sara are taken from this article.

36. The winning entry was created by John Haller, a third-year student in the graduate film program at Columbia University. It was produced by Bobby Miller, with animation by Willy Harland and a voice-over by Sasha Friedenberg.

37. See Gérard Genette, *Seuils* (Paris: Seuils, 1987), 20–37.

38. Tom Feelings, foreword to *The Middle Passage*. Unless otherwise indicated, all subsequent remarks by Feelings are from this foreword.

39. Jennifer Mattson, Review of *The Red Book* by Barbara Lehman, *Booklist*, October 1, 2004: 335.

40. Kirsten Bystrup, "Author Profile: Dorte Karrebæk," trans. Barbara Haveland, *Danish Literature*, http://www.danishliterature.info/index. php?id=2092&n0_cache=1&ltx . . . (accessed May 15, 2009).

41. Maria Nikolajeva, "Play and Playfulness in Postmodern Picturebooks," in *Postmodern Picturebooks: Play, Parody, and Self-Referentiality*, ed. Sipe and Pantaleo, 66.

42. Conversations with Dorte Karrebæk, September 3, 1995, and May 15, 2009.

43. Sara, "Quelques informations sur ma vie privée pour petits et grands curieux," *L'Univers de Sara*, http://universdesara.org/article.php3?id_article=67 (accessed October 23, 2009).

44. Review of *Journey: Travel Diary of a Daydreamer*, by Guy Billout, *Publishers Weekly*, November 15, 1993, 78.

45. The illustrators also contributed the definition they most liked or thought most interesting from the dictionary of their choice.

46. "Visual Journeys" is the title of a project, being led by Evelyn Arizpe from the University of Glasgow, involving the use of two wordless picturebooks, Wiesner's *Flotsam* and Tan's *The Arrival*, with groups of immigrant pupils in the upper years of primary school in Glasgow, Barcelona, Sydney, Arizona, and Texas, to see how they make meaning from the visual text.

47. In an article devoted to David Wiesner's picturebooks, Perry Nodelman makes a similar observation with regard to fantasy sequences, pointing to

the example of Maurice Sendak's *Where the Wild Things Are*. See "Private Places on Public View: David Wiesner's Picture Books," *Mosaic* 34, no. 2 (June 2001): 7.

48. E-mail from Søren Jessen, May 17, 2009.

49. Ibid.

50. Isabelle Nières-Chevrel, "Narrateur visuel et narrateur verbal dans l'album pour enfants," *La Revue des livres pour enfants* 214 (December 2003): 74.

51. Anne Brouillard, extract of an interview granted by Brouillard during the 2009 "Livre comme l'air" in Roubaix. Unless otherwise indicated, all subsequent comments attributed to Brouillard are taken from this interview.

52. Van der Linden, *Lire l'album*, 81.

53. Nières-Chevel, "The Narrative Power of Pictures," 130.

54. Van der Linden, *Lire l'album*, 81.

55. Van der Linden, "Les albums 'sans,'" 195.

56. Nières-Chevel, "The Narrative Power of Pictures," 130.

57. See Sophie Van der Linden, "Interview en images: Anne Brouillard," *Hors Cadre[s]* 1 (October 2007–February 2008): 14–15.

58. Nières-Chevrel, "Narrateur visuel et narrateur verbal dans l'album pour enfants," 75.

59. Ibid.

60. Elizabeth Bird, "Time Taken with Shaun Tan," *School Library Journal*, June 19, 2007, http://schoollibraryjournal.com/blog/1790000379/post/210010821. html (accessed May 22, 2009).

61. Nikolajeva and Scott, *How Picturebooks Work*, 10.

62. Carole Scott, "Dual Audience in Picturebooks," 106.

63. David Wiesner, "Caldecott Acceptance Speech [for *Tuesday*]," *The Horn Book Magazine* 68, no. 4 (August 1992): 420.

64. E-mail from Evelyn Arizpe, March 6, 2009.

65. E-mail from Søren Jessen, May 18, 2009.

66. Van der Linden, "Les Albums 'sans,'" 193.

67. Houghton Mifflin's Press Release for *Flotsam*, http://www.houghtonmif-flinbooks.com/booksellers/press_release/wiesner/ (accessed September 4, 2009).

68. Van der Linden, "Les Albums 'sans,'" 189.

Chapter Four

1. I first explored this subject in "Paintings, Parody, and Pastiche in Picture Books," a paper delivered at the Children's Literature Association Conference on "Children's Literature and the Fine Arts" in Paris in July 1998. A revised version of that paper, "Parodic Play with Paintings in Picture Books," was published in *Children's Literature*, 29 (2001), 175–195. This chapter refers only briefly to the picturebooks examined in the earlier study. The chapter "Artistic Allusions in Picturebooks," published in

New Directions in Picturebook Research, edited by Teresa Colomer, Bettina Kümmerling-Meibauer, and Cecilia Silva-Díaz (London and New York: Routledge, 2010), is based on some of the material in this chapter (see pp. 83–98).

2. E-mail from Sören Jessen, June 15, 2009.

3. Catherine Mah, "Interview with Tohby Riddle," October 12, 2004, http://www.tohby.com/AboutTohbylinnk2.html (accessed September 8, 2005); Julia Eccleshare, "Portrait of the Artist as a Gorilla," *Guardian*, July 29, 2000.

4. Linda Hutcheon, *A Theory of Parody: The Teachings of Twentieth-Century Art Forms* (New York and London: Methuen, 1985), 11. As the term "parody" is commonly used to imply that the purpose of the reference is primarily to ridicule the work evoked, I use the more neutral term of "allusion," reserving the former for references with a comic or satiric intent.

5. John Stephens, "'They Are Always Surprised at What People Throw Away': Glocal Postmodernism in Australian Picturebooks," in *Postmodern Picturebooks: Play, Parody, and Self-Referentiality*, ed. Sipe and Pantaleo, 95.

6. Jean Perrot examines Claverie's works in the context of his study devoted to the influence of baroque art on children's literature, *Art baroque, art d'enfance* (Nancy: Presses de l'Université de Nancy, 1991, 42–53, 184–186).

7. See Perry Nodelman, *Words About Pictures: The Narrative Art of Children's Books* (Athens: University of Georgia Press, 1988), 83; Bader, *American Picturebooks from Noah's Ark to the Beast Within*, 498.

8. Salisbury, "The Artist and the Postmodern Picturebook," in *Postmodern Picturebooks: Play, Parody, and Self-Referentiality*, ed. Sipe and Pantaleo, 26.

9. E-mail from Niamh Sharkey, August 4, 2005.

10. Couprie, "Auteurs et illustrateurs—Entretiens: Katy Couprie."

11. François Ruy-Vidal, "Nous avons rencontré François Ruy-Vidal," *Citrouille, la chronique de Nous Voulons Lire!*, November 22, 2003, http://www.citrouille.net/iblog/B824088992/C497249192?E451790894/ (accessed January 3, 2005).

12. Catherine Ruello, "Chris Van Allsburg Interview," in *Something About the Author*, vol. 53, ed. Anne Commire (Detroit: Gale Research, 1989), 169.

13. For more detailed studies of Chris Van Allsburg and surrealism, see Joseph Stanton, "The Dreaming Picture Books of Chris Van Allsburg," *Children's Literature* 24 (1996): 161–179; Philip Nel, "Just a Dream? Chris Van Allsburg and Surrealism at the End of the Twentieth Century," in *The Avant-Garde and American Postmodernity: Small Incisive Shocks* (Jackson and London: University Press of Mississippi, 2002), 116–135. Stanton mentions a few examples of possible allusions to specific works by René

Magritte and Max Ernst, but they are not obvious references that can be definitely identified.

14. Ruy-Vidal, "Nous avons rencontré François Ruy-Vidal."

15. Bader, *American Picturebooks from Noah's Ark to the Beast Within*, 498.

16. Nodelman, *Words About Pictures*, 86. This is clearly demonstrated in Wim Hofman's disturbing, psychoanalytical retelling of *Snow White*, titled *Zwart als inkt is het verhaal van Sneeuwwitje en de zeven dwergen* (Black as ink is the story of Snow White), whose simple black, white, and red illustrations are strongly influenced by primitivism.

17. TeachingBooks.net, "Anthony Browne: Author Program In-Depth Interview," *TeachingBooks.net* Alberta, Canada, 2004, http://www.teachingbooks.net/content/Browne_qu.pdf (accessed October 11, 2008).

    Erica Hateley accuses Browne of misrepresenting surrealism because children have no need of surrealism, which was intended to allow adults to access "real life" as experienced in childhood. See Hateley, "Magritte and Cultural Capital: The Surreal World of Anthony Browne," *The Lion and the Unicorn* 33, no. 3 (2009): 332–333.

18. Julia Eccleshare. "Portrait of the Artist as a Gorilla," *Guardian*, July 29, 2000.

19. Elaine Williams, "Willy, Magritte and Me," *TES Magazine*, September 15, 2000.

20. Tina L. Hanlon, "The Art and the Dragon: Intertextuality in the Pictorial Narratives of Dragon Feathers," in *Tales, Tellers and Texts*, eds. Gabrielle Cliff Hodges, Mary Jane Drummond, and Morag Styles (London and New York: Cassell, 2000), 92. Hanlon, who has explored the references to several artists in *Dragon Feathers*, points out that Albrecht Dürer's initials are the same as those of Andrej Dugin (80).

21. Nodelman, *Words About Pictures*, 85.

22. For a detailed analysis of this plate, see Beckett, *Recycling Red Riding Hood*, 45–49.

23. Perrot, *Art baroque, art d'enfance*, 39.

24. E-mail from Søren Jessen, November 8, 2009.

25. The painting was also appropriated by Bruno Heitz for the cover illustration he did for the guide of the best children's books reviewed on the popular French radio programme *L'as-tu lu, mon p'tit loup?* (Have you read it, my little wolf?), hosted every Saturday on France Inter by Denis Cheissoux and Patrice Wolf. In a double parody, the wolf, disguised as Little Red Riding Hood's grandmother, sits in granny/Van Gogh's bed reading a book about a wolf and listening to *L'as-tu lu, mon p'tit loup?* on a radio sitting conspicuously on the familiar chair.

26. Carole Scott, "Dual Audience in Picturebooks," 105. She suggests an alternative interpretation of the juxtaposition of Linnaeus and Van Gogh: their very different view of nature.

27. Telephone conversation with Sissel Bjugn, April 28, 2011.

28. Peter Neumeyer, "We Are All in the Dumps with Jack and Guy: Two Nursery Rhymes with Pictures by Maurice Sendak," *Children's Literature in Education* 25, no. 1 (1994): 29–40.

29. W. Nikola-Lisa, "I Spy: A Place for the Arts in Children's Picture-Books," *Journal of Children's Literature* 21, no. 2 (Fall 1995): 53.

30. The title will have a distinctly familiar ring for older readers, as Hugonot borrows the French title of Helme Heine's first picturebook *Elefanteneinmaleins* (Elephant multiplication table), *Un éléphant ça compte énormément*, and simply replaces "compte" (counts) by the rhyming word "trompe" (deceive), which also evokes the word "trompeter" (to trumpet).

31. E-mail from Fam Ekman, October 14, 2005.

32. Erica Hateley, "Magritte and Cultural Capital," 329–330.

33. Perrot, *Art baroque*, 45.

34. "Carll Cneut," International Literature Festival Berlin, http://www.literaturfestival.com/bios1_3_6_745.html (accessed December 17, 2009).

35. Sally Lodge, "All Things Asparagus," *Publishers Weekly*, June 14, 2004, 32.

36. Donald Sassoon, *Mona Lisa: The History of the World's Most Famous Painting* (London: HarperCollins, 2001).

37. Hutcheon, *A Theory of Parody*, 8.

38. See, for example, *Exotic Landscape, Tropical Forest with Monkeys*, and *Tropical Landscape: An American Indian Struggling with an Ape*.

39. Shaun Tan, "Originality and Creativity," http://www.shauntan.net/essay2.html. Subsequent quotations in this paragraph are taken from the same article.

40. Geneviève M. Y. Valleau, "Degas and Seurat and Magritte! Oh My! Classical Art in Picture Books," *The Looking Glass* 10, no. 3 (2006): online, available at http://tlg.ninthwonder.com/rabbit/vl0i3/picture.html (accessed January 30, 2009).

41. René Payant, "Bricolage pictural: l'art à propos de l'art; I—La Question de la citation," *Parachute* 16 (1979): 5.

42. Fam Ekman, Paper presented at the International Research Society for Children's Literature, Kristiansand, Norway, August 9–14, 2003.

43. In light of Browne's familiarity with Magritte's work, it is highly likely that *Piggybook* bears reminiscences of his painting *La bonne fortune*, which depicts a man with a pig's head wearing a suit.

44. Jane Doonan, "Drawing Out Ideas: A Second Decade of the Work of Anthony Browne," *The Lion and the Unicorn* 23 (1999): 46.

45. Hateley, "Magritte and Cultural Capital," 335, 336.

46. David Sylvester, *René Magritte: Catalogue Raisonné*, vol. I: *Oil Paintings: 1916–1930*, ed. David Sylvester and Sarah Whitfield (London: The Menil Foundation/Philip Wilson Publishers, 1992), 168. Browne's reworking is closest to the 1932 version of the *Dream Key*, which is the only vertical one divided into four compartments.

47. See Beckett, "Parodic Play with Paintings in Picture Books," 183.

48. Letter from Yvan Pommaux, February 28, 2001.

49. Richard G. Tansey and Fred S. Kleiner, *Gardner's Art Through the Ages*, 10th ed. (New York: Harcourt Brace, 1996), 390.

50. E-mail from Fam Ekman, January 17, 2001.

51. Tone Birkeland, "At the Crossroad—the Norwegian Picture Book," in *Norwegian Books for Children and Young People* (Lillehammer: Lillehammer Olympic Organizing Committee, 1994), 12. Malevitch himself defines the style as "the supremacy of pure feeling in creative art" (H. H. Arnason, *History of Modern Art*, 3rd ed. [New York: Harry N. Abrams, 1986], 187).

52. Jochen Weber, "Pasando los limites: All-Age-Books, Crossover-Literature y otras tendencias actuales de la literatura para jóvenes lectores," paper presented at the Primer Congreso Nacional de Lectura y Escritura: Escuela y Literatura Infantil, Durango, Mexico, May 16–18, 2004.

53. Pierre Bourdieu, *Distinction: A Social Critique of the Judgement of Taste*, trans. Richard Nice (Cambridge: Polity Press, 1993), 2; Arthur Danto, "The Artworld," in *The Philosophy of the Visual Arts* (New York and Oxford: Oxford University Press, 1992), 431.

54. Erica Hateley questions the cultural value that critics tend to attribute to picturebooks that feature references to canonical art. See "Magritte and Cultural Capital," 331.

55. Bernie Goedhart, "Author/Illustrator Stian Hole: The Complete Interview," *Montreal Gazette*, May 12, 2010.

56. Eccleshare, "Portrait of the Artist as a Gorilla." The previous quotation by Browne is cited in this article.

57. John Stephens, "Children's Literature, Text and Theory: What Are We Interested in Now?" *Papers: Explorations into Children's Literature* 10, no. 2 (2000): 18.

58. "Auteurs et illustrateurs—Entretiens: Katy Couprie."

59. Salisbury, "The Artist and the Postmodern Picturebook," 30.

60. Mitsumasa Anno, "Anno 85–Anno 87," remarks collected by Geneviève Patte and Annie Pissard and by Catherine Germain and Elisabeth Lortic, *Revue des livres pour enfants* 118 (Winter 1987), 56.

61. Lodge, "All Things Asparagus," 32.

62. John Stephens, *Language and Ideology in Children's Fiction* (London: Longman, 1992), 3.

63. E-mail from Sören Jessen, June 15, 2009.

64. TeachingBooks.net, "Anthony Browne."

65. Lodge, "All Things Asparagus," 32.

66. At least one critic wonders whether such allusions are really an homage to the artist whose work is being appropriated or even a desire to make their work accessible to children. Erica Hateley questions whether Browne's goals are truly limited to "encouraging children to look at Magritte paintings," given that the artist's name is never mentioned in

his texts. Hateley feels that the ease with which Browne shifts from surrealism to impressionism indicates that books such as *Willy the Dreamer* are ultimately about "cultural capital" generally rather than any one artist other than Browne himself ("Magritte and Cultural Capital," 337–338).

67. Eccleshare, "Portrait of the Artist as a Gorilla."
68. Ibid.
69. Ibid.
70. Elaine Williams, "Willy, Magritte and Me," *TES Magazine*, September 15, 2000, http://www.tes.co.uk/article.aspx?storycode+338474 (accessed November 6, 2009).
71. Telephone conversation with Kelek, June 25, 2001.
72. See Salisbury, "The Artist and the Postmodern Picturebook," 30; Bernie Goedhart, "Author/Illustrator Stian Hole: The Complete Interview," *Montreal Gazette*, May 12, 2010.
73. E-mail from Sören Jessen, May 18, 2009.
74. Shaun Tan, "Originality and Creativity."
75. Sylvia Marantz and Kenneth Marantz, *Artists of the Page: Interviews with Children's Book Illustrators* (Jefferson, N.C.: McFarland, 1992), 4, 6.
76. Mah, "Interview with Tohby Riddle."

Notes to Chapter 5

1. Oscar K., "It's not the fact that it is said—in fact it's just the way you say it," 46, 47.
2. Ardizzone, "Creation of a Picture Book," 293.
3. Selma Lanes, *The Art of Maurice Sendak*, 206.
4. Maurice Sendak, "Maurice Sendak," in *Pauses: Autobiographical Reflections of 101 Creators of Children's Books*, ed. Lee Bennett Hopkins (New York: HarperCollins, 1995), 142–143.
5. Mark St. John Erickson, "Sendak Show Explores Best-Selling Children's Books for Adults as Well as Kids," *Baltimore Sun*, February 14, 2010; Maurice Sendak, *Caldecott and Co.: Notes on Books and Pictures* (New York: Farrar, Straus and Giroux, 1988), 192–193.
6. Reynolds, *Radical Children's Literature*, 89.
7. Ulla Kofod-Olsen, "In Praise of Childhood," *Danish Children's Literature* 3 (1992).
8. Ibid.
9. Carole Scott, "Frame-making and Frame-breaking in Picturebooks," in *New Directions in Picturebook Research*, 105. See pp. 104–106 for a detailed study of Karrebæk's use of frames in this picturebook.
10. E-mail from Svein Nyhus, July 3, 2010. Unless otherwise indicated, other quotations by Nyhus are taken from this e-mail.

11. Åse Marie Ommundsen, "Girl Stuck in the Wall: Narrative Changes in Norwegian Children's Literature Exemplified by the Picture Book *Snill*," *Bookbird* 42, no. 1 (February 2004): 25.

12. "Svein Nyhus: Illustrator, Norway," *Bookbird* 42, no. 4 (2004): 50.

13. Ommundsen, "Girl Stuck in the Wall," 25.

14. Nikolajeva, "Play and Playfulness in Postmodern Picturebooks," 56.

15. Konrad Heidkamp, "How Simple Stories Become Great Books," trans. Sally-Ann Spencer, http://www.new-books-in-german.com/featur42.htm (accessed May 29, 2010).

16. For an analysis of this picturebook, see Beckett, *Crossover Fiction*, 48.

17. Qtd. in Guitta Pessis Pasternak, "Tournier le sensuel," *Le Monde*, August 13, 1984.

18. Letter from Anne Bertier, July 31, 2003; e-mail from Anne Bertier, September 21, 2003.

19. For a detailed study of this book, see Beckett, *Red Riding Hood for All Ages*, 76–81.

20. Van der Linden, *Lire l'album*, 50.

21. Jens Thiele, "Sie tanzen Hula-Hula," *Die Zeit* 49 (November 2004).

22. Madeleine Brettingham, "New Storm Brews Over Gay Books," *Times Educational Supplement*, October 20, 2006, 6.

23. E-mail from Anne de Vries, May 26, 2010.

24. Joke Linders, *Ik bof dat ik een kikker ben: Leven en werk van Max Velthuijs* (Amsterdam: Leopold; 's-Gravenhage: Letterkundig Museum, 2003).

25. Gégène, "Cependant . . . Paul Cox," *Citrouille* 38 (June 2004): 21.

26. Yvan Pommaux, "Le discours de Caracas ou Yvan au bord de la rivière," *Griffon* 171 (March & April 2000): 6.

27. John Cech, *Angels and Wild Things: The Archetypal Poetics of Maurice Sendak* (University Park: Pennsylvania State University Press, 1995), 211.

28. Elke Schmitter and Franziska Bossy, "Mikropenis erregt US-Verlag," *Der Spiegel Online*, July 11, 2007, http://www.spiegel.de/kultur/literatur/0,1518,493297,00.html (accessed May 21, 2010). The comment by Berner is cited in this article.

29. Pasternak, "Tournier le sensuel."

30. Tournier, "Les Enfants dans la bibliothèque," 57.

31. Gilles Lapouge, "Michel Tournier s'explique," *Lire* 64 (December 1980): 45.

32. Oscar K., "It's not the fact that it is said—in fact it's just the way you say it," 47.

33. Stanton, "The Dreaming Picture Books of Chris Van Allsburg," 164–165.

34. Ruy-Vidal, "Nous avons rencontré François Ruy-Vidal. "

35. Bart Moeyaert translated *L'ogresse en pleurs* in 1996 as *Ik ruik kindervlees* (I smell children's flesh), which won the Silver Pencil award in 1997.

36. Horst Künneman. "How Much Cruelty Can a Children's Picturebook Stand? The Case of Wolf Erlbruch's *Die Menschenfresserin*," *Bookbird* 43, no. 1 (2005): 17, 16.

37. Ibid., 18.

38. Reynolds, *Radical Children's Literature*, 88. She examines the French edition of *Juul* briefly before turning to a detailed discussion of the subject in juvenile novels (see pp. 96–97).

39. Ibid., 97.

40. Agnes-Margrethe Bjorvand, "Do Sons Inherit the Sins of their Fathers? An Analysis of the Picturebook Angry Man," in *New Directions in Picturebook Research*, 217.

41. Ibid., 225.

42. The discussion in the media concerned both the problem of domestic violence and what is appropriate for children.

43. Meg Rosoff, "*Duck, Death and the Tulip* by Wolf Erlbruch," *Guardian*, December 19, 2009.

44. Nikolajeva and Scott, *How Picturebooks Work*, 229.

45. Salisbury, "The Artist and the Postmodern Picturebook," 26.

46. Ibid., 29.

47. English translations are taken from Nikolajeva and Scott's *How Picturebooks Work*, which offers a detailed analysis of this picturebook (pp. 203–208).

48. Nikolajeva and Scott, *How Picturebooks Work*, 204.

49. Birgitta Fransson, "Anna-Clara Tidholm's Previous Books," Anna-Clara Tidholm Nominated for the 2010 H. C. Andersen Prize by the Swedish Section of IBBY, 16, http://ibby.se/wp-content/uploads/2009/09/anna-tidholmibby.pdf (accessed May 29, 2010).

50. See Jean Perrot, "L'esthétisme et/ou la mort: les exigences d'Ipomée," *La Revue des livres pour enfants* 128 (Summer 1989): 39–42.

51. David Larsen, "Children's Books of the Year Feature," *Listener*, December 20, 2008.

52. Dina Rabinovitch, "Author of the Month: Michael Rosen," *Guardian*, November 24, 2004.

53. Reynolds, *Radical Children's Literature*, 99.

54. Oscar K., "It's not the fact that it is said—in fact it's just the way you say it," 47. When Larsen asks if Dorte Karrebæk and Oscar K. will be able to find a more extreme taboo to break, he suggests: "There is always the Holocaust!" The author and illustrator took up his challenge, publishing the much-acclaimed picturebook *Lejren* (The camp) in 2011.

55. Eugène, "Eugène: La mort à vivre," interview by Ardian, *Zwook*, http://zwookedu.ch/eugene/zwook/espaces-livres/lamortavivre (accessed June 19, 2010).

56. The other book is *Petit Manuel des rites mortuaires*, intended to pass on "to new generations a little manual" which would assist them in creating their own "ritual drawer." The author told me that during the preparations for the

exhibition in 1999, the curator's wife, anthropologist Yvonne Preiswerk, died suddenly, and Crettaz now organizes café encounters, titled "Café mortel," on the theme of death (e-mail from Eugène, June 20, 2010).

57. E-mail from Eugène, June 20, 2010.
58. See Maymat, *Images images*, 38.
59. Odile Belkeddar, "Un Petit Âne dérangeant," *La Revue des livres pour enfants* 171 (September 1996): 144.
60. Reynolds, *Radical Children's Literature*, 95.
61. Extract from *L'Illustration soviétique pour enfants* (Moscow: Iskustvo, 1980).
62. Belkeddar, "Un Petit Âne dérangeant," 144.
63. Reynolds, *Radical Children's Literature*, 95–96.
64. The sequel did appear at the end of an article by André Delobel in the first issue of *Les Cahiers du CRILJ* (November 2009), which was titled "Peut-on tout dire (et tout montrer) dans les livres pour enfants?"
65. Belkeddar, "Un Petit Âne dérangeant," 146.
66. Béguery, *Une esthétique contemporaine de l'album jeunesse*, 152.
67. Telephone conversation with Dorte Karrebæk, May 2009.
68. Nicole Maymat, "Nicole Maymat, écrivain et intrépide éditrice," interview with Étienne Delessert, 2009, *Ricochet-Jeunes*, http://www.ricochet-jeunes.org/magazine-propos/article/69-nicole-maymat (accessed January 13, 2010).
69. Reynolds, *Radical Children's Books*, 88–89.
70. Carole Scott, "A Challenge to Innocence: 'Inappropriate Picturebooks for Young Readers,'" *Bookbird* 43, no. 1 (2005): 12.

Chapter Six

1. Beckett, *Crossover Fiction*, 163–171.
2. Julia Preston, "Junior Gotti Is Denied Bail in Shooting of Radio Host," *New York Times*, October 6, 2004.
3. Anne Cassidy, "Celebrity Authors," *Jacketflap*, March 31, 2010, http://www.jacketflap.com/megablog/index.asp?tagid=128458&tag=Gordon+Brown+++Celebrity+Authors (accessed April 23, 2010).
4. Thompson removed the Eloise sequels from print in the mid-1960s and pulled from publication the nearly completed manuscript of *Eloise Takes a Bawth*. This situation ended with her death in 1998.
5. Karen MacPherson, "Critics, Authors Chafe as More Celebrities Join Ranks of Children's Authors," *Pittsburgh Post-Gazette*, November 3, 2004.
6. Diane Roback, "*The English Roses* Off to Fast Start," *Publishers Weekly*, September 22, 2003: 20.
7. Ibid.
8. "Madonna Brought to Book by Roald Dahl's Illustrator," *Telegraph. co.uk*, September 23, 2008, http://www.telegraph.co.uk/news/newstopics/

mandrake/3069597/Madonna-brought-to-book-by-Roald-Dahls-illustrator. html (accessed May 13, 2010).

9. Although it is less pronounced since the recent crossover fiction phenomenon, a distinction has often been made between "children's authors" and "writers" who write solely or primarily for adults, a distinction that reflects the lower status of children's literature. See Beckett, *Crossover Fiction*, 12.

10. "One Not-So Impossible Favor before Breakfast," *Seven Impossible Things before Breakfast*, a blog about books, April 25–30, 2010, http://blaine.org/ sevenimpossiblethings/?p=1927 (accessed May 6, 2010).

11. "Madonna Plans 'Morality Tale,'" *BBC News*, April 17, 2003, http://news. bbc.co.uk/2/hi/entertainment/2955837.stm (accessed May 6, 2010).

12. Ed Pilkington, "Once Upon a Time," *Guardian*, November 3, 2006.

13. MacPherson, "Critics, Authors Chafe as More Celebrities Join Ranks of Children's Authors."

14. Carla Hay, "Artists Add New Voice to Children's Books," *Billboard*, August 16, 2003: 68.

15. Pilkington, "Once Upon a Time."

16. MacPherson, "Critics, Authors Chafe as More Celebrities Join Ranks of Children's Authors."

17. Roger Friedman, "Madonna's Adoption Kills Book Sales," *Fox News*, November 17, 2006, http://www.foxnews.com/story/0,2933,230158,00. html (accessed May 10, 2010).

18. Bobby Byrd, "The Story behind *The Story of Colors*," http://www.cinco-puntos.com/storyofcolors.sstg (accessed May 5, 2010).

19. Roback, "*The English Roses* Off to Fast Start," 20.

20. "Gervais Story Book Is Adult Hit," *BBC News*, October 6, 2004, http:// newsvote.bbc.co.uk/mpapps/pagetools/print/news.bbc.co.uk/2/hi/ entertainment/3719684.stm (accessed May 2, 2010).

21. MacPherson, "Critics, Authors Chafe as More Celebrities Join Ranks of Children's Authors."

22. Pilkington, "Once Upon a Time."

23. Elizabeth Kennedy, "Jane Yolen on 'Celebrity' Authors and Favorite Authors," *About.com: Children's Books*, http://childrensbooks.about.com/ od/authorsillustrato/a/janeyolen_2.htm (accessed May 6, 2010).

24. Friedman, "Madonna's Adoption Kills Book Sales."

25. "Madonna Brought to Book by Roald Dahl's Illustrator."

26. Genevieve, "One Not-So Impossible Favor before Breakfast," *Seven Impossible Things before Breakfast*, April 26, 2010.

27. On the HarperCollins website, the authors claim that *Simeon's Gift*, published in 2003, is actually the first book on which they collaborated as a mother-daughter writing team because they wrote the initial draft when Emma was six years old. Thirty years later, they revisited the simple fable about a penniless minstrel and developed it into a more substantial tale.

Celebrity writing has also spawned a number of father-daughter teams, including Jimmy and Savannah Buffet, Jimmy and Amy Carter, and Bill and Erika Cosby.

28. Hall, "Madonna: Like a Pitchwoman."

29. Karen Raugust, "English Roses Blossom," *Publishers Weekly*, February 7, 2005: 23; "Madonna's Best Selling Children's Books Inspire Children's, Young Girls and 'Tweens Apparel Line," *PR Newswire*, January 30, 2007, http://www.prnewswire.co.uk/cgi/news/release?id=189127 (accessed May 17, 2010).

30. Beth Landman Keil and Deborah Mitchell, "Intelligencer," *New York Magazine*, May 26, 1997: 10.

31. Sophie Dahl, "Notes from the Author," *The Man with the Dancing Eyes*, http://www.dancingeyes.net/notes.htm (accessed May 14, 2010).

32. "Gervais Story Book Is Adult Hit."

33. Gail Cooke, "You Have to See It to Believe It," *Amazon.com*, March 9, 2010, http://www.amazon.com/Flanimals-Pop-Up-Ricky-Gervais/dp/0763647810 (accessed May 2, 2010).

34. César G. Soriano, "Comedians Writing Children's Books for a Laugh," *USA Today*, March 17, 2004.

35. David Hancock, "Madonna's Advice for Kids," *CBSNews.com*, September 15, 2003, http://www.cbsnews.com/ stories/2003/09/30/print/main575841.shtml (accessed May 18, 2010).

36. "A Poignant Story About Alzheimer's Disease by Maria Shriver," *PR Newswire*, June 4, 2008.

37. "Kylie to Publish Children's Book," *BBC News,* March 8, 2006, http://news.bbc.co.uk/2/hi/entertainment/4785786.stm (accessed May 17, 2010).

38. Caitlin A. Johnson, "John Lithgow Pens 7th Children's Book," *CBSNews.com*, March 27, 2007, http://www.cbsnews.com/stories/2007/03/27/earlyshow/leisure/books/main2611660.shtml (accessed May 17, 2010).

39. Dr. Ronald Goldstein, "Beauty and the Media: A Special Interview with Deborah Norville," *Season Magazine* (Spring 2005), http://www.seasonmagazine.com/profiles/norville.htm (accessed May 9, 2010).

40. "About the Show: Frequently Asked Questions," *DrLaura.com*, http://www.drlaura.com/radio/about_show.html (accessed November 24, 2009).

41. Liz B., "One Not-So Impossible Favor before Breakfast," *Seven Impossible Things before Breakfast,* April 26, 2010.

42. Hancock, "Madonna's Advice for Kids."

43. Julia Preston, "U.S. Cancels Grant for Children's Book Written by Mexican Guerrilla," *New York Times*, March 10, 1999. This article was retitled "N.E.A. Couldn't Tell a Mexican Rebel's Book by Its Cover" in late editions.

44. Sally Lodge, "Q & A with Ricky Gervais," *Publishers Weekly*, February 25, 2010.

45. Dahl, "Notes from the Author."

46. Johnson, "John Lithgow Pens 7th Children's Book."

47. Ibid.

48. Rebecca Ascher-Walsh, "Air Time," *Entertainment Weekly*, November 21, 2001.

49. Hay, "Artists Add New Voice to Children's Books," 5.

50. Holly G. Miller, "At Home with Julie Andrews," *Saturday Evening Post* 280, no. 5 (September–October 2008): 49.

51. MacPherson, "Critics, Authors Chafe as More Celebrities Join Ranks of Children's Authors."

52. Bob Minzesheimer, "What's Freckled and Read All Over? Moore's New Book," *USA Today*, October 16, 2007, http://www.usatoday.com/life/books/news/2007–10–16-freckleface-moore_N.htm (accessed April 23, 2010).

53. Pilkington, "Once Upon a Time."

54. Hay, "Artists Add New Voice to Children's Books," 5.

55. Pilkington, "Once Upon a Time."

Epilogue

1. Wendy Lamb, "Strange Business: The Publishing Point of View," *Signal* 87 (September 1998): 171–172; Tim Wynne-Jones, "The Survival of the Book," *Signal* 87 (September 1998): 160–166.

2. Reynolds, *Radical Children's Literature*, 38.

3. Betsy Hearne, "Perennial Picture Books Seeded by the Oral Tradition," *Journal of Youth Services* 12, no. 1 (Fall 1998): 27.

4. Judith Graham, "Reading Contemporary Picturebooks," in *Modern Children's Literature: An Introduction*, ed. Kimberley Reynolds, 209.

5. Barbara Kiefer, "What is a Picturebook, Anyway? The Evolution of Form and Substance through the Postmodern Era and Beyond," in *Postmodern Picturebooks: Play, Parody, and Self-Referentiality*, ed. Sipe and Pantaleo, 19.

6. Reynolds, *Radical Children's Literature*, 17.

7. E-mail from Eugène, June 20, 2010.

8. Lewis, "The Constructedness of Texts: Picture Books and the Metafictive," 142.

9. Lefort, Régis. "L'album-poème," in *L'album contemporain pour la jeunesse: nouvelles formes, nouveaux lecteurs?* 29–38; Bernanoce, Marie. "L'album-théâtre': typologie et questions posées à sa lecture," in *L'album contemporain pour la jeunesse: nouvelles formes, nouveaux lecteurs?* 39–52.

10. Without using the designation "album-bande dessinée," Nicolas Rouvière devoted his paper at the Bordeaux conference to the comic book's influence on the picturebook. ("L'influence de la bande dessinée sur les albums pour enfants : histoire, esthétique et thématiques," in *L'album contemporain pour la jeunesse: nouvelles formes, nouveaux lecteurs?* 17–28).

11. Media Vaca catalogue, 2005–2006, 2, 64.
12. Künneman, "How Much Cruelty Can a Children's Picturebook Stand?," 16.
13. Arne Marius Samuelsen, "Nyere norske billedbøker," *Nordisk Blad* (1998): 17.
14. Martin Salisbury, "The Artist and the Postmodern Picturebook," 32.
15. Interview with Fam Ekman, April 25, 2001; Fam Ekman, "Fam Ekman and Her Children's Books," paper presented at the International Research Society of Children's Literature Congress, Agder University College, Kristiansand, August 9–14, 2003.
16. See Ricochet, "Entretien avec Olivier Douzou," *Ricochet-Jeunes*, September 2003, http://www.ricochet-jeunes.org/entretiens/entretien/59-olivier-douzou (accessed October 3, 2009).
17. Rosen, "Breaking the Age Barrier," 28. Lisa Holton, publisher of Hyperion Books for Children and Disney Press, is careful to claim, however, that quality rather than potential adult audience is the determining factor and that Wegman is an artist for whom kids come first and the adult audience is secondary.
18. Barbara Kiefer, "What is a Picturebook, Anyway? The Evolution of Form and Substance through the Postmodern Era and Beyond," in *Postmodern Picturebooks: Play, Parody, and Self-Referentiality*, 20.
19. Henri Cueco, Interview with Hélène Bernard.

Bibliography

Primary Works

Ache, Jean. *Des carrés et des ronds: Fables et contes*. Paris: Balland, 1974.
———. *Le monde des ronds et des carrés*. Adapted and translated by Christine Huet. Tokyo: Librairie Ça et Là, 1975.
Albisola, Tullio d'. *L'anguria lirica*. Illus. Bruno Munari. Rome: Edizioni Futuriste di Poesia, 1934.
Anno, Mitsumasa. *Topsy-Turvies: Pictures to Stretch the Imagination*. New York: Walker/Weatherhill, 1970. Original Japanese edition published Tokyo: Fukuinkan Shoten, 1968.
———. *Upside-Downers: More Pictures to Stretch the Imagination*. New York: Walker/Weatherhill, 1971. Original Japanese edition published Tokyo: Fukuinkan Shoten, 1969.
———. *Tabi no ehon*. Tokyo: Fukuinkan Shoten, 1977. Translated under the title *Anno's Journey*. London: Bodley Head, 1978.
———. *Mori no ehon*. Tokyo: Fukuinkan Shoten, 1977. Translated under the title *Anno's Animals*. London: Bodley Head, 1979.
———. *Tabi no ehon II*. Tokyo: Fukuinkan Shoten, 1978. Translated under the title *Anno's Italy*. London: Bodley Head, 1979.
———. *Anno's Medieval World*. Text adapted by Ursula Synge. London: Bodley Head, 1980.
———. *Tabi no ehon III*. Tokyo: Fukuinkan Shoten, 1981. Translated under the title *Anno's Britain*. London: Bodley Head, 1982.
———. *Tabi no ehon IV*. Tokyo: Fukuinkan Shoten, 1983. Translated under the title *Anno's U.S.A.* New York: Philomel Books, 1983.
———. *Kageboshi*. Tokyo: Fuzanbo, 1976. Translated under the title *In Shadowland*. New York: Orchard Books, 1988.
———. *Anno's Magic Seeds*. New York: Putnam, 1994.
———. *Tabi no ehon V*. Tokyo: Fukuinkan Shoten, 2003. Translated under the title *Anno's Spain*. New York: Philomel, 2004.
———. *Tabi no ehon VI*. Tokyo: Fukuinkan Shoten, 2004.
Anonymous. *East o' the Sun and West o' the Moon*. Illus. PJ Lynch. Trans. Caroline Peachey. London: Andersen Press, 1991.
Arai, Ryoji. *Basu ni note*. Tokyo: Kaisei-sha, 1992.
———. *Mori no ehon*. Tokyo: Kodansha, 1999. Translated in a bilingual Japanese-English edition by Peter Milward under the title *A Forest Picture-Book*. Tokyo: Kodansha, 2001.
Arbat, Carlos. *El sueño de Dalí*. Valencia: Brosquil, 2003.
Artell, Mike. *Petite Rouge: A Cajun Red Riding Hood*. Illus. Jim Harris. New York: Dial Books for Young Readers, 2001.
Aulnoy, Madame d'. *La Belle et la bête*. Illus. Étienne Delessert. Mankato, MN: Creative Company, 1983.
Bachelet, Gilles. *Mon chat le plus bête du monde*. Paris: Seuil, 2004. Translated under the title *My Cat, the Silliest Cat in the World*. New York: Abrams Books for Young Readers, 2006.
Ballester, Arnal. *No tinc paraules*. Valencia: Media Vaca, 1998.
Banyai, Istvan. *Zoom*. New York: Viking, 1995.
———. *Re-Zoom*. New York: Viking, 1995.

————. *REM: Rapid Eye Movement*. New York: Viking, 1997.

————. *Minus Equals Plus*. New York: Harry N. Abrams, 2001.

————. *The Other Side*. San Francisco: Chronicle Books, 2005.

Barber, Tiki, and Ronde Barber, with Robert Burleigh. *By My Brother's Side*. Illus. Barry Root. New York: Simon & Schuster Books for Young Readers, 2004.

————. *Game Day*. Illus. Barry Root. New York: Simon & Schuster Books for Young Readers, 2005.

————. *Teammates*. Illus. Barry Root. New York: Simon & Schuster Books for Young Readers, 2006.

Barber, Tiki, and Ronde Barber, with Paul Mantell. *Kickoff!* Illus. Barry Root. New York: Simon & Schuster Books for Young Readers, 2007.

————. *Go Long!* Illus. Barry Root. New York: Simon & Schuster Books for Young Readers, 2008.

————. *Wild Card*. Illus. Barry Root. New York: Simon & Schuster Books for Young Readers, 2009.

Bernard, Fred. *La Comédie des ogres*. Illus. François Roca. Paris: Albin Michel, 2002.

Bertier, Anne. *Mon Loup*. Orange: Grandir, 1995.

————. *Un amour de triangle*. Orange: Grandir, 2001.

Bichsel, Peter. *Kindergeschichten*. Neuwied: Luchterhand, 1969.

————. *Ein Tisch ist ein Tisch*. Illus. Angela von Roehl. Frankfurt am Main: Suhrkamp, 1995.

Biesty, Stephen. *Stephen Biesty's Incredible Cross-Sections*. London: Dorling Kindersley, 1992.

Billout, Guy. *Number 24*. New York: Harlin Quist, 1973.

————. *Journey: Travel Diary of a Daydreamer*. Mankato, MN: Creative Education, 1993.

————. *Il y a quelque chose qui cloche*. Paris: Harlin Quist, 1998. Translated under the title *Something's Not Quite Right*. Boston: David R. Godine, 2002.

Björk, Christina. *Linnea in Monet's Garden*. Illus. Lena Anderson. Stockholm: Rabén & Sjögren, 1985.

Bjugn, Sissel. *Jente i bitar*. Illus. Fam Ekman. Oslo: Det Norske Samlaget, 1992.

Blake, Quentin. *Clown*. London: Jonathan Cape, 1995.

————. *Zagazoo*. London: Jonathan Cape, 1998.

Braud, François. *À quoi sert le zizi des garçons?* Illus. Maud Lenglet. Rodez: Rouergue, 2002.

Briggs, Raymond. *Fungus the Bogeyman*. London: Hamish Hamilton, 1977.

————. *The Snowman*. London: Hamish Hamilton, 1978.

Brouillard, Anne. *Trois chats*. Paris: Éditions du Sorbier, 1990.

————. *Le sourire du loup*. Paris: Epigones, 1992.

————. *Il va neiger*. Paris: Syros Jeunesse, 1994.

————. *Promenade au bord de l'eau*. Paris: Éditions du Sorbier, 1996.

————. *L'orage*. Orange: Grandir, 1998.

————. *Le bain de la cantatrice*. Paris: Éditions du Sorbier, 1999. Translated under the title *The Bathtub Prima Donna*. New York: Harry N. Abrams, 1999.

————. *La famille foulque*. Paris: Seuil, 2007.

————. *La vieille dame et les souris*. Paris: Seuil, 2007.

Brown, Margaret Wise. *Goodnight Moon*. Illus. Clement Hurd. New York: Harper, 1947.

Browne, Anthony. *Through the Magic Mirror*. London: Hamilton, 1976.

————. *Look What I've Got!* London: Julia MacRae Books, 1980.

————. *Gorilla*. London: Julia MacRae Books, 1983.

————. *Piggybook*. London: Julia MacRae Books, 1986.

————. *The Tunnel*. New York: Knopf, 1989.

————. *Changes*. London: Walker Books, 1990.

————. *Zoo*. London: Julia MacRae Books, 1992.

————. *The Big Baby: A Little Joke*. London: Julia MacRae Books, 1993.

————. *Willy the Dreamer*. London: Walker Books, 1997.

————. *Voices in the Park*. London: Walker Books, 1998.

————. *Willy's Pictures*. London: Walker Books, 2000.

————. *The Shape Game*. London: Random House, 2003.

Bruel, Christian. *Jérémie du bord de mer*. Illus. Anne Bozellec. Paris: Le Sourire qui mord, 1984.

————. *Vous oubliez votre cheval*. Illus. Pierre Wachs. Paris: Le Sourire qui mord, 1986.

————. *Premières nouvelles*. Illus. Pef. Paris: Le Sourire qui mord, 1988.

————. *La mémoire des scorpions*. Photographs by Xavier Lambours. Paris: Le Sourire qui mord, 1991.

————. *Petites musiques de la nuit.* Photographs by Xavier Lambours. Coloured by Katy Couprie. Paris: Le Sourire qui mord, 1992.

————. *Rien n'est trop beau pour les amies de Zorro.* Illus. Zaven Paré. Paris: Le Sourire qui mord, 1995.

————. *Petits Chaperons Loups.* Illus. Nicole Claveloux. Paris: Éditions Être, 1997.

————. *L'heure des parents.* Illus. Nicole Claveloux. Paris: Éditions Être, 1999.

Bruel, Christian, and Anne Galland. *Histoire de Julie qui avait une ombre de garçon.* Illus. Anne Bozellec. Paris: Le Sourire qui mord, 1976.

————. *Lison et l'eau dormante.* Illus. Anne Bozellec. Paris: Le Sourire qui mord, 1978.

————. *Mon grand album de bébé.* Illus. Anne Bozellec and Nicole Claveloux. Paris: Le Sourire qui mord, 1989.

Bruel, Christian, and Didier Jouault. *Rouge, bien rouge.* Illus. Nicole Claveloux. Paris: Le Sourire qui mord, 1986.

Brunhoff, Jean de. *Histoire de Babar, le petit éléphant.* Paris: Éditions du Jardin des Modes, 1931. Translated under the title *The Story of Babar the Little Elephant.* New York: Harrison Smith and Robert Haas, 1933.

Buffet, Jimmy, and Savannah Jane Buffet. *The Jolly Mon.* Illus. Lambert Davis. Orlando: Harcourt, 1988.

————. *Trouble Dolls.* New York: Harcourt Children's Books, 1991.

Cadot, Édith. *Le songe.* Paris: Autrement Jeunesse, 2009.

Carroll, Lewis. *Alice's Adventures in Wonderland.* Illus. Anthony Browne. London: Julia MacRae Books, 1988.

Carter, Jimmy. *The Little Baby Snoogle-Fleejer.* Illus. Amy Carter. New York: Times Books, 1995.

Cave, Kathryn. *Something Else.* Illus. Chris Riddell. London: Viking, 1994.

Chen, Jiang Hong. *The Magic Horse of Han Gan.* Translated from Chinese by Claudia Zoe Bedrick. New York: Enchanted Lion Books, 2006.

————. *Mao and Me: The Little Red Guard.* New York: Enchanted Lion Books, 2008.

Cheney, Lynne. *America: A Patriotic Primer.* Illus. Robin Preiss Glasser. New York: Simon & Schuster Books for Young Readers, 2002.

————. *A Is for Abigail: An Almanac of Amazing American Women.* New York: Simon & Schuster Books for Young Readers, 2003.

————. *Our 50 States: A Family Adventure Across America.* New York: Simon & Schuster Books for Young Readers, 2006.

Child, Lauren. *What Planet Are You from, Clarice Bean?* London: Orchard Books, 2001.

Claveloux, Nicole. *479 Espèces de poux.* Paris: Le Sourire qui mord, 1985.

————. *Quel genre de bisous?* Paris: Le Sourire qui mord, 1990.

————. *Vaguement.* Paris: Le Sourire qui mord, 1990.

————. *Dedans les gens.* Paris: Le Sourire qui mord, 1993.

Claverie, Jean. *Little Lou.* Paris: Gallimard, 1990.

Clément, Frédéric. *Le collier.* Paris: Ipomée-Albin Michel, 1992.

————. *Magasin Zinzin, ou, Aux merveilles d'Alys.* Paris: Ipomée-Albin Michel, 1995. Translated under the title *The Merchant of Marvels and the Peddler of Dreams.* San Francisco: Chronicle Books, 2001.

————. *Songes de la Belle au bois dormant.* Paris: Casterman, 1996.

————. *Muséum*: petite collection d'ailes et d'âmes trouvées sur l'Amazone. Paris: Ipomée-Albin Michel, 1999.

————. *Minium: rêve rare d'1 minute 12.* Paris: Albin Michel, 2000.

————. *Méthylène: rêve ronde de 3 minutes 33.* Paris: Albin Michel, 2000.

————. *Mille et une nuits: Histoire du portefaix avec les jeunes filles.* Paris: Albin Michel, 2002.

Collodi, Carlo. *Pinocchio.* Trans. Emma Rose. Illus. Sara Fanelli. London: Walker Books, 2003.

Cool J, L. L. [James Todd Smith]. *And the Winner Is. . . .* Illus. JibJab Media. Hip Kid Hop. New York: Scholastic, 2002.

Cosby, Bill. *Friends of a Feather: One of Life's Little Fables.* Illus. Erika Cosby. New York: HarperCollins, 2003.

Couprie, Katy. *Anima.* Paris: Le Sourire qui mord, 1991.

————. *Robert Pinou.* Paris: Le Sourire qui mord, 1991.

Couratin, Patrick. *Shhh!* New York: Harlin Quist, 1974.

Couric, Katie. *The Brand New Kid.* Illus. Marjorie Priceman New York: Doubleday, 2000.

————. *The Blue Ribbon Day.* Illus. Marjorie Priceman. New York : Doubleday, 2004.

Cox, Paul. *Mon amour*. Paris: Le Sourire qui mord, 1992. Reissued Paris: Seuil, 2003.

———. *Cependant . . .* Paris: Seuil, 2002.

———. *Le livre le plus long du monde* (quadrichonie). Paris: Les Trois Ourses, 2002.

Crowther, Kitty. *Va faire un tour*. Paris: Pastel/L'École des Loisirs, 1995.

———. *Moi et Rien*. Paris: Pastel/L'École des Loisirs, 2000.

———. *La visite de Petite Mort*. Paris: Pastel/L'École des Loisirs, 2004.

Crystal, Billy. *I Already Know I Love You*. Illus. Elizabeth Sayles. New York: HarperCollins, 2004.

———. *Grandpa's Little One*. Illus. Guy Porfiro. New York: HarperCollins, 2006.

Cullum, Albert. *The Geranium on the Windowsill Just Died but Teacher You Went Right On*. New York: Harlin Quist, 1971.

———. *You Think Just Because You're Big You're Right*. New York: Harlin Quist, 1976.

Cuomo, Mario. *The Blue Spruce*. Ann Arbor, MI: Sleeping Bear Press, 1999.

Curtis, Jamie Lee. *When I Was Little: A Four-Year Old's Memoir of Her Youth*. Illus. Laura Cornell. New York: HarperCollins, 1993.

———. *Tell Me Again About the Night I Was Born*. Illus. Laura Cornell. New York: Joanna Cotler Books, 1996.

———. *Today I Feel Silly, & Other Moods That Make My Day*. Illus. Laura Cornell. New York: Joanna Cotler Books, 1998.

———. *Where Do Balloons Go? An Uplifting Mystery*. Illus. Laura Cornell. HarperCollins, 2000.

———. *It's Hard to Be Five: Learning How to Work My Control Panel*. Illus. Laura Cornell. New York: Joanna Cotler Books, 2004.

———. *Big Words for Little People*. Illus. Laura Cornell. New York: Joanna Cotler Books, 2008.

———. *Jamie Lee Curtis's Books to Grow by Treasury*. Illus. Laura Cornell. HarperCollins, 2009.

Cvach, Milos. *Dans tous les sens*. Paris: Les Trois Ourses, 2007.

Dahl, Sophie. *The Man with the Dancing Eyes*. Illus. Annie Morris. London: Bloomsbury, 2003.

Dahle, Gro, and Svein Nyhus. *Bak Mumme bor Moni*. Oslo: Cappelen, 2000.

———. *Snill*. Oslo: Cappelen, 2002.

———. *Sinna Mann*. Oslo: Cappelen, 2003.

Daly, Niki, and Nola Turkington. *The Dancer*. Illus. Niki Daly. Cape Town: Human & Rousseau, 1996.

Dayre, Valérie. *L'Ogresse en pleurs*. Illus. Wolf Erlbruch. Toulouse: Milan, 1996.

Deharme, Lise [Anne-Marie Hirtz]. *Le Cœur de pic*. Illus. Claude Cahun [Lucy Schwob]. Paris: José Corti, 1937. Reissued, Nantes: MeMo, 2004.

De Kockere, Geert. *Dulle Griet*. Illus. Carll Cneut. Wielsbeke: De Eenhoorn, 2005.

———. *Voorspel van een gebroken liefde*. Illus. Isabelle Vandenabeele. Wielsbeke: De Eenhoorn, 2007.

Delerm, Martine. *Origami*. Paris: Ipomée-Albin Michel, 1990.

———. *Fragiles*. Paris: Seuil, 2001.

DePaola, Tomie. *Sing, Pierrot, Sing: A Picture Book in Mime*. New York: Harcourt Brace Jovanovich, 1983.

———. *Bonjour, Mr. Satie*. New York: G. P. Putnam's Sons, 1991.

———. *Jingle, the Christmas Clown*. New York: G. P. Putnam's Sons, 1992.

Die Drachenfedern. Retold by Arnica Esterl. Illus. Andrej Dugin and Olga Dugina. Esslingen: Verlag J. F. Schreiber, 1993. Translated under the title *Dragon Feathers*. Charlottesville, VA: Thomasson-Grant, 1993.

Die drei Raüber. Dir. Hayo Freitag. Berlin: Animation X. Gesellschaft zur Produktion von Animationsfilmen, 2007.

Die Nibelungen. Interpreted by Franz Keim and illustrated by Carl Otto Czeschka. Gerlachs Jugendbücherei, vol. 22. Vienna and Leipzig: Verlag Gerlach und Wiedling, 1909.

Di Rosa, Hervé. *Jungle*. Paris: Albin Michel, 1991.

Douzou, Olivier. *Jojo La Mache*. Rodez: Rouergue, 1993.

———. *Esquimau*. Rodez: Rouergue, 1996.

———. *Navratil*. Illus. Charlotte Mollet. Rodez: Rouergue, 1996.

Dubelaar, Thea, and Ruud Bruijn. *Op zoek naar Vincent*. Amsterdam: Uitgeverij Polegsma, 1990. Translated under the title *Looking for Vincent*. New York: Checkerboard, 1992.

Dubois, Bertrand. *Sens interdit*. Rodez: Rouergue, 1998.

Dumas, Philippe. *Ce changement-là*. Paris: L'École des loisirs, 1981.

Duras, Marguerite. *Ah! Ernesto!* Illus. Bernhard Bonhomme. Paris: Harlin Quist and François Ruy-Vidal, 1971.

Edwards, Julie. *Mandy*. Illus. Judith Gwyn Brown. New York: Harper & Row, 1971.
———. *The Last of the Really Great Whangdoodles*. New York: Harper & Row, 1974.
Edwards, Julie Andrews, and Emma Walton Hamilton. *Dumpy the Dump Truck*. Illus. Tony Walton. New York: Hyperion Books for Children, 2000.
———. *Simeon's Gift*. Illus. Gennady Spirin. New York: HarperCollins, 2003.
———. *The Very Fairy Princess*. Illus. Christine Davenier. New York: Little, Brown Books for Young Readers, 2010.
Eggers, Dave. *The Wild Things*. San Francisco: McSweeneys, 2009.
Ekman, Fam. *Hva skal vi gjøre med Lille Jill?* Oslo: Cappelen, 1976.
———. *Rødhatten og Ulven*. Oslo: Cappelen, 1985.
———. *Frøken Mosekvist og det flyvende teppe*. Oslo: Cappelen, 1986.
———. *En sky over Pine-Stine*. Oslo: Cappelen, 1987.
———. *Den nye vesken*. Oslo: Cappelen, 1988.
———. *Sonate for en fiolin*. Oslo: Cappelen, 1989.
———. *Kattens Skrekk*. Oslo: Cappelen, 1992.
———. *Dagbok Forsvunnet*. Oslo: Cappelen, 1995.
———. *Kaffeebønneslekten*. Oslo: Cappelen, 1996.
———. *Tilberedning av hjerter*. Oslo: Cappelen: 1998.
———. *Skoen*. Oslo: Cappelen, 2001.
———. *Da solen gikk ned*. Oslo: Cappelen, 2002.
———. *Fredag den trettende*. Oslo: Cappelen, 2004.
Erlbruch, Wolf. *Die fürchterlichen Fünf*. Wuppertal: Hammer, 1990. Translated under the title *The Fearsome Five*. Wellington, NZ: Gecko Press, 2009.
———. *Frau Meier, die Amsel*. Wuppertal: Peter Hammer Verlag, 1995. Translated under the title *Mrs. Meyer the Bird*. New York: Orchard, 1997.
———. *'s Nachts*. Amsterdam: Stichting CPNB, 1999. Published in German under the title *Nachts*. Wuppertal: Hammer, 2002.
———. *La grande question*. Paris: Éditions Être, 2003. Translated under the title *The Big Question*. New York: Europa, 2005.
———. *Ente, Tod und Tulpe*. Munich: Verlag Antje Kunstmann, 2007. Translated under the title *Duck, Death and the Tulip*. Wellington, NZ: Gecko Press, 2008.
Escala, Jaume, and Carmen Solé Vendrell. *Los niños del mar*. Madrid: Siruela, 1991.
Estefan, Gloria. *The Magically Mysterious Adventures of Noelle the Bulldog*. New York: HarperCollins, 2005.
———. *Noelle's Treasure Tale*. Illus. Michael Garland. New York: HarperCollins, 2006.
Eugène, and [Pierre Alain] Bertola. *La mort à vivre*. Geneva: La joie de lire, 1999.
Fagerli, Elise. *Ulvehunger*. Oslo: Cappelen, 1995.
Fanelli, Sara. *Button*. London: ABC, 1994.
———. *Wolf!* London: William Heinemann, 1997.
———. *Dear Diary*. London: Walker Books, 2000.
Feelings, Tom. *Soul Looks Back in Wonder*. New York: Dial Books, 1993.
———. *The Middle Passage: White Ships/Black Cargo*. Introduction by John Henrik Clarke. New York: Dial Books, 1995.
Ferguson, Sarah. *Budgie the Little Helicopter*. London: Simon & Schuster, 1989.
———. *Little Red*. Illus. Sam Williams. London: Simon & Schuster, 2003.
———. *Tea for Ruby*. Illus. Robin Preiss Glasser. New York: Simon & Schuster/Paula Wiseman Books, 2008.
Fernández-Pacheco, Miguel Ángel. *La verdadera historia del perro Salomón*. Madrid: SM, 2000.
Ferrar, Vicente, ed. *Mis primeras 80.000 palabras*. Valencia: Media Vaca, 2000.
Fitzpatrick, Marie-Louise. *You, Me and the Big Blue Sea*. London: Gullane Children's Books, 2002.
———. *I Am I*. New Milford, CT: Roaring Brook Press, 2006.
Fresh, Doug E. *Think Again*. Illus. Joseph Buckingham Jr. Hip Kid Hop. New York: Scholastic, 2002.
Fromental, Jean-Luc, and Miles Hyman. *Le Cochon à l'oreille coupée*. Paris: Seuil Jeunesse, 1994.
Galli, Letitzia. *Connais-tu Igor?* Zurich: Palazzo, 1998.
Garland, Michael. *Dinner at Magritte's*. New York: Dutton, 1995.
Geisert, Arthur. *Pa's Balloon and Other Pig Tales*. Boston: Houghton Mifflin, 1984.
———. *Oink*. Boston: Houghton Mifflin, 1991.
———. *Oink Oink*. Boston: Houghton Mifflin, 1993.
———. *The Etcher's Studio*. Boston: Houghton Mifflin, 1997.

———. *Lights Out*. Boston: Houghton Mifflin, 2005.

———. *Eau glacée*. Paris: Autrement Jeunesse, 2009.

Gervais, Ricky. *Flanimals*. Illus. Rob Steen. London: Faber and Faber, 2004.

———. *More Flanimals*. Illus. Rob Steen. London: Faber and Faber, 2005.

———. *Flanimals of the Deep*. Illus. Rob Steen. London: Faber and Faber, 2006.

———. *Flanimals: A Complete Natural History*. Illus. Rob Steen. London: Faber and Faber, 2007.

———. *Flanimals: The Day of the Bletchling*. Illus. Rob Steen. London: Faber and Faber, 2007.

———. *Flanimals Pop-Up*. Illus. Rob Steen. Paper Engineering by Richard Ferguson. London: Walker Books, 2009.

Gilman, Charlotte Perkins. *The Yellow Wallpaper*. Boston: Small & Maynard, 1899.

Gilman, Phoebe. *The Balloon Tree*. Markham, ON: Scholastic: 1984.

Godon, Ingrid. *Wachten op Matroos*. With words by André Sollie. Amsterdam: Querido, 2000. Translated under the title *Hello, Sailor*. London: Macmillan, 2003.

Goldberg, Whoopi. *Alice*. Illus. John Rocco. New York: Bantam Books, 1992.

———. *Whoopi's Big Book of Manners*. Illus. Olo. New York: Hyperion Books for Children, 2006.

———. *Sugar Plum Ballerinas: Plum Fantastic*. With help from Deborah Underwood. Illus. Maryn Roos. New York: Hyperion, 2008.

Gomi, Taro. *Gaikotsu-san*. Tokyo: Bunka-Shuppan Kyoku, 1982.

Greder, Armin. *Die Insel*. Aarau; Frankfurt am Main: Sauerländer, 2002. Translated under the title *The Island*. Crow's Nest, N. S. W.: Allen & Unwin, 2007.

Grimm, Wilhelm and Jacob. *El señor Korbes y otros cuentos de Grimm*. Illus. Oliveiro Dumas. Valencia: Media Vaca, 2001.

Gwynne, Fred. *The King Who Rained*. New York: Windmill Books, 1970.

———. *A Chocolate Moose for Dinner*. New York: Windmill Books, 1976.

———. *The Sixteen Hand Horse*. New York: Windmill/Wanderer Books, 1980.

———. *A Little Pigeon Toad*. New York: Simon & Schuster Books for Young Readers, 1988.

Haller, Bent. *Ispigen*. Illus. Dorte Karrebæk. Copenhagen: Høst & Søn, 2001.

Halliwell, Geri. *Ugenia Lavender*. London: Macmillan Children's Books, 2008.

———. *Ugenia Lavender and the Burning Pants*. London: Macmillan Children's Books, 2008.

———. *Ugenia Lavender and the Temple of Gloom*. London: Macmillan Children's Books, 2008.

———. *Ugenia Lavender Home Alone*. London: Macmillan Children's Books, 2008.

———. *Ugenia Lavender and the Terrible Tiger*. London: Macmillan Children's Books, 2009.

———. *Ugenia Lavender, The One and Only*. London: Macmillan Children's Books, 2009.

Hamm, Mia. *Winners Never Quit!* Illus. Carol Thompson. New York: HarperCollins, 2004.

Harburg, E. Y. *Over the Rainbow*. Illus. Eric Puybaret. Performer: Judy Collins. Composer: Harold Arlen. Peter Yarrow Books, 2010.

Heidelbach, Nikolaus. *Papa, Maman*. Paris: Le Sourire qui mord, 1994.

———. *Tout-petits déjà*. Paris: Le Sourire qui mord, 1994.

———. *Ein Buch für Bruno*. Weinheim: Beltz & Gelberg, 1997.

Heine, Helme. *Elefanteneinmaleins*. Cologne: Middelhauve, 1976.

Heitz, Bruno. *Renaud le corbeau*. Paris: Seuil, 1995.

Hellsing, Lennart. *Ägget*. Illus. Fibben Hald. Stockholm: Raben & Sjögren, 1978.

Henry, Lenny. *Charlie, Queen of the Desert*. Illus. Chris Burke. London: Gollancz, 1996.

Herbauts, Anne. *L'Heure Vide*. Brussels: Casterman, 2000.

Hest, Amy. *When Jessie Came Across the Sea*. Illus. P. J. Lynch. London: Walker Books, 1997.

Hiratsuka, Takeji. *Tamamushi no zushi no monogatari*. Illus. Daihachi Ohta. Tokyo: Doshinsha, 1980.

Hobby, Hollie. *Toot and Puddle*. Boston, MA: Little, Brown Books for Young Readers, 1997.

Hoestlandt, Jo. *L'amour qu'on porte*. Illus. Carmen Segovia. Toulouse: Milan Jeunesse, 2007.

Hoffman, Heinrich. *Lustige Geschichte und drollige Bilder*. Frankfurt am Main: Literarische Anstalt (J. Rütten), [1845].

Hoffmann, Yoel. *Be-Februar Kedai Liknot Pilim*. Moshav Ben Shemen: Modan, 1988.

Hofman, Wim. *Zwart als inkt is het verhaal van Sneeuwwitje en de zeven dwergen*. Amsterdam: Querido, 1998.

Hole, Stian. *Garmanns Sommer*. Oslo: Cappelen, 2006. Translated by Don Bartlett under the title *Garmann's Summer*. Grand Rapids, MI: Eerdmans Books for Young Readers, 2008.

Holzwarth, Werner. *Vom kleinen Maulwurf, der wissen wollte, wer ihm auf den Kopf gemacht hat*. Illus. Wolf Erlbruch. Wuppertal: Peter Hammer Verlag, 1989. Translated under the titles

The Story of the Little Mole Who Knew It Was None of His Business. St. Albans: David Bennett Books, 1994 (Pop-up edition. London: Pavilion, 2007); *The Story of the Little Mole Who Went in Search of Whodunit.* New York: Stewart, Tabori & Chang; Distributed in the U.S. by Workman Pub., 1993.

Hugonot, Marie-Christine. *Un éléphant, ça trompe énormément.* Illus. Maïté Laboudigue. Paris: Épigones, 1993.

Iino, Kazuyoshi. *Negi-bouzu no Asatarou.* Tokyo: Fukuinkan Shoten, 1999.

Innocenti, Roberto. *Rose Blanche.* Text by Christophe Gallaz. Mankato, MN: Creative Education, 1985. Later edition with Ian McEwan. London: Jonathan Cape, 1995.

Ionesco, Eugene. *Conte numéro 1, pour enfants de moins de trois ans.* Illus. Étienne Delessert. Paris: Harlin Quist and François Ruy-Vidal, 1968. Translated under the title *Story Number 1, for Children Under Three Years of Age.* Illus. Étienne Delessert. New York: Harlin Quist; distributed by Crown Publishers, 1968.

———. *Présent passé, passé présent.* Paris: Mercure de France, 1968. Translated by Helen R. Lane under the title *Present Past, Past Present: A Personal Memoir.* New York: Grove Press, 1971.

———. *Conte numéro 2.* Illus. Étienne Delessert. Paris: Harlin Quist and François Ruy-Vidal, 1970. Translated under the title *Story Number 2.* Illus. Gerard Failly. New York: Harlin Quist, 1978.

———. *Conte numéro 3.* Illus. Philippe Corentin. Paris: Harlin Quist and François Ruy-Vidal, 1971. Translated under the title *Story Number 3; for Children Over Three Years of Age.* Illus. Philippe Corentin. New York: Harlin Quist, 1971.

———. *Conte numéro 4.* Illus. Nicole Claveloux. Paris: J.-P. Delarge, 1976. Translated under the title *Story Number 4 for Children of Any Age.* Illus. Jean-Michel Nicollet. New York: Harlin Quist/Delacorte, 1973.

———. *Contes 1, 2, 3, 4.* Illus. Étienne Delessert. Paris: Gallimard Jeunesse, 2009.

Jandl, Ernst. *Ottos Mops.* Illus. Norman Junge. Weinheim and Basel: Beltz & Gelberg, 2001.

Jansson, Tove. *Det osynliga barnet.* Helsingfors: H. Schildts, 1963.

Jeffers, Oliver. *Lost and Found.* London: HarperCollins Children's Books, 2005.

———. *The Great Paper Caper.* London: HarperCollins Children's Books, 2008.

Jessen, Søren. *En fuldmånenat.* Copenhagen: Apostrof, 1995.

———. *Faldt du?* Copenhagen: Apostrof, 1999.

———. *Gaven.* Copenhagen: Gyldendal, 2007.

Jolin, Dominique. *Qu'est-ce que vous faites là?* Saint Hubert, QC: Éditions du Raton Laveur, 1993.

Jonas, Ann. *Round Trip.* New York: Greenwillow Books, 1983.

———. *Reflections.* New York: Greenwillow Books, 1987.

K., Oscar [Ole Dalgaard]. *Min familie.* Dorte Karrebæk. Copenhagen: Alma, 2004.

———. *Børnenes bedemand.* Illus. Dorte Karrebæk. Copenhagen: Gyldendal, 2008.

———. *Idiot!* Illus. Dorte Karrebæk. Copenhagen: Høst & Søn, 2009.

———. *Lejren.* Illus. Dorte Karrebæk. Copenhagen: Høst & Søn/Rosinante & Co., 2011.

Kafka, Franz. *Le Pont.* Illus. Henri Galeron. Paris: Gallimard, 1981.

Kalman, Maira. *Ooh-la-la (Max in Love).* New York: Viking, 1991.

———. *Roarr: Calder's Circus.* Photographs by Donatella Brun. New York: Delacorte/Whitney Museum of Art, 1991.

Kamm, Katja. *Unsichtbar.* Zürich: Bajazzo, 2002. Translated under the title *Invisible.* New York; London: North-South, 2006.

———. *Das runde Rot.* Zürich: Bajazzo, 2003.

Karrebæk, Dorte. *Der er et hul i himlen: en hyldest til dagdrømmeren!* Copenhagen: Munksgaard, 1989.

———. *Pigen der var go' til mange ting.* Copenhagen: Forum, 1996.

———. *Hvad mon der sker?* Copenhagen: Gyldendal, 1997.

———. *Mesterjaegeren: en bog om arv og miljø; dedikeret til jer der hele tiden overtager verden.* Copenhagen: Forum, 1999.

———. *Den nye leger.* Copenhagen: Gyldendal, 2001.

———. *Den sorte bog: om de syv dødssynder.* Hillerød: Alma, 2007.

Karrebæk, Dorte, and Sussi Karrebæk. *Stamtræet.* Copenhagen: Mallings, 1997.

Kemmler, Melanie. *Der hölzerne Mann.* Berlin: Aufbau-Verlag, 2003.

Khalsa, Dayal Kaur. *I Want a Dog.* Montreal: Tundra Books, 1987.

———. *Green Cat.* Toronto: Tundra Books, 2002.

Kharms, Daniil et al., and Nikolai Radlov. *Picture Stories.* Moscow: Raduga, 1987 (*Rasskazy v kartinkakh,* 1958).

Kidd, Richard. *Almost Famous Daisy.* London: Frances Lincoln, 1996.

Kindl, Patrice. *The Woman in the Wall*. Boston: Houghton Mifflin, 1997.

King-Smith, Dick. *Triffic Pig Book*. London: Victor Gollancz, 1991.

Kitamura, Satoshi. *Me and My Cat?* London: Andersen Press, 1999.

Koch, Ed, and Pat Koch Thaler. *Eddie: Harold's Little Brother*. Illus. James Warhola. New York: G. P. Putnam's Sons, 2004.

———. *Eddie's Little Sister Makes a Splash*. Illus. James Warhola. New York: G. P. Putnam's Sons, 2007.

Komagata, Katsumi. *First Look*. Little Eyes 1. Tokyo: Kaiseisha, 1990.

———. *Meet Colours*. Little Eyes 2. Tokyo: Kaiseisha, 1990.

———. *Play with Colors*. Little Eyes 3. Tokyo: Kaiseisha, 1990.

———. *One for Many*. Little Eyes 4. Tokyo: Kaiseisha, 1991.

———. *1 to 10*. Little Eyes 5. Tokyo: Kaiseisha, 1991.

———. *What Color?* Little Eyes 6. Tokyo: Kaiseisha, 1991.

———. *The Animals*. Little Eyes 7. Tokyo: Kaiseisha, 1992.

———. *Friends in Nature*. Little Eyes 8. Tokyo: Kaiseisha, 1992.

———. *Walk and Look*. Little Eyes 9. Tokyo: Kaiseisha, 1992.

———. *Go Around*. Little Eyes 10. Tokyo: Kaiseisha, 1992.

———. *Mori ni nohara ni*. Tokyo: Kaiseisha, 1993.

———. *Tsuchi no naka ni wa*. Tokyo: Kaiseisha, 1993.

———. *Umi no bōken*. Tokyo: Kaiseisha, 1993.

———. *Blue to Blue*. Tokyo: One Stroke, 1994.

———. *Green to Green*. Tokyo: One Stroke, 1994.

———. *Yellow to Red*. Tokyo: One Stroke, 1994.

———. *Boku, Umareru-yo!* Tokyo: One Stroke, 1995.

———. *Snake*. Tokyo: One Stroke, 1995.

———. *Soraga Aoito Umimo Aoi*. Tokyo: One Stroke, 1995.

———. *Motion*. Tokyo: One Stroke, 1996.

———. *Scene*. Tokyo: One Stroke, 1996.

———. *Pata Pata*. Tokyo: One Stroke, 1997.

———. *Workbooks: Red Series* [and] *Green-Yellow Series*. Tokyo: One Stroke, 1997.

———. *Namida*. Tokyo: One Stroke, 2000.

———. *Found It!* Tokyo: One Stroke, 2002.

———. *Plis et plans*. Tokyo: One Stroke; Paris: Les Trois Ourses; Talant: Les Doigts qui rêvent, 2003.

———. *Leaves*. Tokyo: One Stroke; Paris: Les Trois Ourses; Éditions du Centre Pompidou; Talant: Les Doigts qui rêvent, 2004.

———. *A Place Where Stars Rest*. Tokyo: One Stroke, 2004.

———. *Sound Carried by the Wind*. Tokyo: One Stroke, 2004.

———. *Little Tree*. Tokyo: One Stroke, 2008.

Kozlov, Serge. *Petit-Âne*. Illus. Vitaly Statzynsky. Trans. Pavlik de Bennigsen. Paris: Ipomée-Albin Michel, 1995.

Laâbi, Abdellatif. *L'orange bleue*. Illus. Laura Rosano. Trans. from Arabic by Jean Elias. Les livres-fresques du Seuil. Paris: Seuil Jeunesse, 1995.

Lago, Angela. *Cena de rua*. Belo Horizonte, Brazil: RHJ Livros Ltda., 1994.

Lascault, Gilbert. *5 + 1 histoires en forme de trèfle*. Illus. Denis Pouppeville. Paris: Éditions des Lires, 2003.

Lavater, Warja. *Die Party*. Folded Story 4. Basel: Basilius Presse, 1962.

———. *La promenade en ville*. Folded Story 5. Basel: Basilius Presse, 1962.

———. *William Tell*. New York: Junior Council, Museum of Modern Art, 1962.

———. *Leidenschaft und Vernunft*. Basel: Basilius Presse, 1963. Reissued as *Passion et raison*. Paris: Adrien Maeght, 1985.

———. *Walk, Dont Walk, Walk, Attendez, Gehe, Dont Walk, Passez, Warte, Walk, Dont*. Folded Story 11. Basel: Basilius Presse, 1965.

———. *Re . . . Re . . . Revolution Re. . . .* Folded Story 12. Basel: Basilius Presse, 1965.

———. *Homo Sapiens ?* Folded Story 13. Basel: Basilius Presse, 1965.

———. *Hans im Glück*. Folded Story 14. Basel: Basilius Presse, 1965.

———. *Das hässliche junge Entlein*. Folded Story 15. Basel: Basilius Presse, 1965.

———. *Le Petit Chaperon rouge: une imagerie d'après un conte de Perrault*. Paris: Adrien Maeght, 1965.

———. *Conform . . . . ismus . . . . isme*. Folded Story 17. Basel: Basilius Presse, 1966.

———. *Ramalalup*. Folded Story 18. Basel: Basilius Presse, 1967.

———. *Das Feuer und seine Höhlen*. Folded Story 19. Basel: Basilius Presse, 1967.

———. *La fable du hasard: une imagerie d'après un conte de Perrault.* Paris: Adrien Maeght, 1968.

———. *La mélodie de Turdidi.* Paris: Adrien Maeght, 1971. Translated under the title *The Melody of Turdidi.* New York: Juliette Halioua, 1971.

———. *Moon Ballad.* New York: Juliette Halioua, 1973.

———. *Blanche-Neige: une imagerie d'après le conte.* Paris: Adrien Maeght, 1974.

———. *Cendrillon: une imagerie d'après un conte de Perrault.* Paris: Adrien Maeght, 1976.

———. *Die Rose und der Laubfrosch: eine Fabel.* Zurich: Edition Schlegl, 1978.

———. *Le Petit Poucet: une imagerie d'après un conte de Perrault.* Paris: Adrien Maeght, 1979.

———. *La Belle au bois dormant: une imagerie d'après un conte de Perrault.* Paris: Adrien Maeght, 1982.

———. *Le miracle des roses, une imagerie d'après la légende française.* Paris: Adrien Maeght, 1986.

———. *Ergo, un pictogram sur les conséquences de "Je pense donc je suis."* Paris: Adrien Maeght, 1988.

———. *Spectacle.* Paris: Adrien Maeght, 1990.

———. *Ourasima.* Paris: Adrien Maeght, 1991.

———. *Tanabata.* Paris: Adrien Maeght, 1994.

———. *Kaguyahime.* Paris: Maeght, 1997.

Lee, Spike, and Tonya Lewis Lee. *Please, Baby, Please.* Illus. Kadir Nelson. New York: Simon & Schuster Books for Young Readers, 2002.

———. *Please, Puppy, Please.* Illus. Kadir Nelson. New York: Simon & Schuster Books for Young Readers, 2005.

Leer-Salvesen, Paul. *Fy Fabian.* Illus. Hilde Gamman. Kristiansand: Barnas Forlag, 2001.

Legrand, Édy. *Macao et Cosmage ou L'expérience du bonheur.* Paris: Éditions de la Nouvelle Revue Française, 1919. Reissued, Paris: Circonflexe, 2000.

Lehman, Barbara. *The Red Book.* Boston: Houghton Mifflin, 2004.

———. *Rainstorm.* Boston: Houghton Mifflin, 2007.

———. *Trainstop.* Boston: Houghton Mifflin, 2008.

Leip, Hans. *Das Zauberschiff: Ein Bilderbuch nicht nur für Kinder.* Hamburg: Hammerich & Lesser, 1947.

Leno, Jay. *If Roast Beef Could Fly.* Illus. S. B. Whitehead. New York: Simon & Schuster Books for Young Readers, 2004.

Lindgren, Barbro. *Titta Max grav!* Illus. Eva Eriksson. Stockholm: Eriksson & Lindgren, 1991.

Lionni, Leo. *What? Pictures to Talk About.* New York: Pantheon Books, 1983.

———. *When? Pictures to Talk About.* New York: Pantheon Books, 1983.

———. *Where? Pictures to Talk About.* New York: Pantheon Books, 1983.

———. *Who? Pictures to Talk About.* New York: Pantheon Books, 1983.

Lissitzky, El (Eliezer Markovich). *Suprematicheskii skaz pro dva kvadrata v shesti postroikakh.* Berlin: Scythian, 1922. Translated by Christiana van Manen under the title *About Two Squares: A Suprematist Tale.* Facsimile reprint. Forest Row: Artists Bookworks, 1990. Rpt., Cambridge: Massachusetts Institute of Technology, 1991.

Lithgow, John. *The Remarkable Farkle McBride.* Illus. C. F. Payne. New York: Simon & Schuster Children's Publishing, 2000.

———. *Marsupial Sue.* Illus. Jack E. Davis. New York: Simon & Schuster Children's Publishing, 2001.

———. *Micawber.* Illus. C. F. Payne. New York: Simon & Schuster Children's Publishing, 2002.

———. *I'm a Manatee.* Illus. Ard Hoyt. New York: Simon & Schuster Children's Publishing, 2003.

———. *Marsupial Sue Presents "The Runaway Pancake."* Illus. Jack E. Davis. New York: Simon & Schuster Children's Publishing, 2005.

———. *Mahalia Mouse Goes to College.* Illus. Igor Oleynikov. New York: Simon & Schuster Children's Publishing, 2007.

Lluïsot. *Una temporada en Calcuta.* Valencia: Media Vaca, 2001.

Louchard, Antonin. *La belle étoile.* Paris: Gallimard Jeunesse-Giboulées, 2001. Translated under the title *Little Star.* New York: Hyperion Books for Children, 2003.

Lowell, Susan. *The Three Javelinas.* Illus. Jim Harris. Flagstaff: Rising Moon, 1992.

Macaulay, David. *Cathedral: The Story of Its Construction.* Boston: Houghton Mifflin, 1973.

———. *Black and White.* Boston: Houghton Mifflin, 1990.

———. *Rome Antics.* Boston: Houghton Mifflin, 1997.

Maeyer, Gregie de, and Koen Vanmechelen. *Juul.* Averbode: Altiora, 1996. Translated into French by Christian Merveille under the title *Jules.* France: Mango, 1996.

Marcos, Subcomandante. *La historia de los colores.* Illus. Domitilia Domínguez. Guadalajara: Colectivo Callejero, 1997.

Mari, Enzo. *L'altalena.* Milan: Danese, 1961. Reissued, Mantova: Corraini, 2001.

———. *Il posto dei giochi.* Milan: Danese, 1967.

———. *Il gioco delle favole.* Mantova: Corraini, 2004.

Mari, Enzo, and Iela Mari. *La mela e la farfalla.* Milan: Bompiani, 1960. Translated under the titles *The Apple and the Moth.* New York: Pantheon, 1970; *The Apple and the Butterfly.* London: A & C Black, 1970.

———. *L'uovo e la gallina.* Milan: Emme Edizioni, 1969. Translated under the title *The Chicken and the Egg.* New York: Pantheon, 1970.

Mari, Iela. *Il palloncino rosso.* Milan: Emme Edizioni, 1967. Translated under the title *The Magic Balloon.* New York: S. G. Phillips; London: Angus and Robertson, 1969. Published subsequently as *The Red Balloon.* London: A & C Black, 1975; *The Little Red Balloon.* Woodbury, NY: Barrons, 1979.

———. *L'albero.* Milan: Emme Edizioni, 1972. Translated under the titles *The Tree.* London: Dent, 1977; *The Tree and the Seasons.* Woodbury, NY: Barrons, 1979.

———. *Mangia che ti mangio.* Milan: Emme Edizioni, 1980. Translated under the title *Eat and Be Eaten.* Woodbury, NY: Barrons, 1980.

Mari, Iela, and Silvana Di Lernia. *Il paesaggio infinito.* Torino: Emme Edizioni; Petrini junior, 1988.

Marin, Richard Anthony "Cheech." *My Name Is Cheech the School Bus Driver.* Album. Sony, 1992.

———. *Cheech the School Bus Driver.* Illus. Orlando L. Ramírez. New York: HarperCollins, 2007.

Marsden, John. *The Rabbits.* Illus. Shaun Tan. Port Melbourne, Vic.: Lothian Books, 1998.

Martin, Bill Jr., and John Archambault. *Chicka Chicka Boom Boom.* Illus. Lois Ehlert. New York: Simon & Schuster Books for Young Readers, 1989.

Martin, Steve, and Roz Chast. *The Alphabet from A to Y with Bonus Letter Z!* New York: Flying Dolphin Press, 2007.

Maruki, Toshi. *Hiroshima no pika.* Komine Shoten, 1980. Translated under the title *Hiroshima no pika.* New York: Lothrop, Lee & Shepard Books, 1980.

Mativat, Marie-André Boucher. *Le sourire de La Joconde.* Illus. Élisabeth Eudes-Pascal. Saint-Laurent, QC: Éditions Pierre Tisseyre, 1999.

Matute, Ana María. *Los niños tontos.* Illus. Javier Olivares. Valencia: Media Vaca, 2000.

Mayhew, James. *Katie's Picture Show.* London: Orchard, 1989.

Maymat, Nicole. *L'histoire d'Héliacynthe.* Illus. Frédéric Clément. Moulins: Ipomée, 1979.

McAfee, Annalena, and Anthony Browne. *The Visitors Who Came to Stay.* London: Hamish Hamilton, 1984.

McCartney, Paul, Geoff Dunbar, and Philip Ardagh. *High in the Clouds.* London: Faber and Faber, 2005.

McGraw, Tim, and Tom Douglas. *My Little Girl.* Illus. Julia Denos. Foreword by Faith Hill. Nashville: Thomas Nelson, 2008.

Meunier, Henri. *Ronde de nuit.* Rodez: Rouergue, 2002.

Middelhauve, Gertraud. *Dichter erzählen Kindern.* Cologne: Middelhauve, 1966.

Minogue, Kylie. *The Showgirl Princess.* Illus. Swan Park. London: Puffin, 2006.

Miyazaki, Hirokazu. *Wani-kun no e-nikki.* Osaka: BL Publishing House, 1991.

———. *Wani-kun no mukashi-banashi.* Osaka: BL Publishing House, 1994.

———. *Little Crocodile's Big Feet.* Translated from Japanese by H. Rebecca Teele. Tokyo: Book Loan Publishing, 1996.

———. *Little Crocodile's Alarm Clock.* Translated from Japanese by H. Rebecca Teele. Tokyo: Book Loan Publishing, 1997.

Moeyaert, Bart, and Wolf Erlbruch. *De schepping.* Amsterdam: Querido; Wuppertal: Hammer Verlag, 2003.

Moore, Clement C. *The Night before Christmas.* Illus. Eric Puybaret. Performer Peter, Paul, and Mary. Bournemouth: Imagine, 2010.

Moore, Julianne. *Freckleface Strawberry.* Illus. LeUyen Pham. New York: Bloomsbury U.S.A. Children's Books, 2007.

Morgenstern, Susie. *Musée Blues.* Illus. Jean Claverie. Folio Cadet. Paris: Gallimard, 1986.

Muller, Gerda. *Histoires en 4 images.* Albums du Père Castor. Paris: Flammarion, 1967.

Müller, Jörg. *Alle Jahre wieder saust der Preßlufthammer nieder oder Die Veränderung der Landschaft*. Aarau: Sauerländer, 1973. Translated under the title *The Changing Countryside*. New York: Atheneum, 1977.

Munari, Bruno. *Mai contenti*, I libri Munari n. 1. Verona (Milan): Mondadori, 1945. Translated under the titles *What I'd Like to Be*. London: Harvill, 1953; *The Elephant's Wish*. New York: World Publishing Company, 1959.

———. *L'uomo del camion*. I libri Munari n. 2. Verona (Milan): Mondadori, 1945. Translated under the titles *Lorry Driver*. London: Harvill, 1953; *The Birthday Present*. New York: World Publishing Co., 1959.

———. *Toc Toc: Chi è? Apri la porta*, I libri Munari n. 3, Verona (Milan): Mondadori, 1945. Translated by Maria Cimino as *Who's There? Open the Door*. New York: World Publishing Company, 1957.

———. *Il prestigiatore verde*. I libri Munari n. 4. Verona (Milan): Mondadori, 1945.

———. *Storie di tre uccellini*, I libri Munari n. 5. Verona (Milan): Casa Editrice A. Mondadori, 1945. Translated by Maria Cimino under the title *Tic, Tac and Toc*. New York: World Publishing Company, 1957.

———. *Il venditore di animali*, I libri Munari n. 6, Verona (Milan): Arnoldo Mondadori Editore, 1945. Translated by Maria Cimino under the title *Animals for Sale*. New York: World Publishing Company, 1957.

———. *Gigi cerca il suo berretto: Dove mai l'avrà cacciato?* I libri Munari n. 7. Verona (Milan): Arnoldo Mondadori Editore, 1945. Translated under the title *Georgie Has Lost His Cap*. London: Harvill, 1953; *Jimmy Has Lost His Cap*. New York: World Publishing Company, 1959.

———. *Nella notte buia*. Milan: Muggiani, 1956. Translated under the title *In the Darkness of the Night*. Mantova: Corraini, 2000.

———. *ABC*. Cleveland and New York: World Publishing Company, 1960. Published in Italian as *L'alfabetiere*. Torino: Einaudi, 1960.

———. *Libro illeggibile N.Y. 1*. New York: The Museum of Modern Art, 1967.

———. *Nella nebbia di Milano*. Milan, Emme Edizioni, 1968. Reissued, Mantova: Corraini, 1996. Translated under the title *The Circus in the Mist*. New York: World Publishing Company, 1969.

———. *I prelibri*. Milan: Danese Edizioni per Bambini, 1980.

———. *Libro illeggibile MN 1*. Mantova: Corraini, 1984.

———. *Il merlo ha perso il becco*. Milan: Danese Edizioni per Bambini, 1987.

———. *Libro letto*. Milan: Produzione Interflex, 1993.

———. *La favola delle favole*. Mantova: Corraini, 1994.

———. *Il prestigiatore giallo*. Mantova: Corraini, 1997. Translated under the title *The Yellow Conjurer*. Mantova: Corraini, 2003.

———. *Buona notte a tutti*. Mantova: Corraini, 1997. Translated under the title *Goodnight Everyone*. Mantova: Corraini, 2003.

Munsch, Robert. *Love You Forever*. Illus. Sheila McGraw. Scarborough, ON: Firefly Books, 1986.

Nathan, Fernand [pseud. Jean Perrot], and Fernand Fau. *Trente histoires en images sans paroles à raconter par les petits*. Paris: F. Nathan, 1902.

Nikly, Michelle. *L'Art du Pot*. Illus. Jean Claverie. Paris: Albin Michel, 1990.

———. *L'Art des bises*. Illus. Jean Claverie. Paris: Albin Michel, 1993.

Nishimura, Shigeo. *Gatagoto Gatagoto*. Tokyo: Doshinsha, 1999.

Nordqvist, Sven. *Pannkakstårtan*. Translated under the title *Pancake Pie*. New York: Morrow, 1985.

Nygren, Tord. *Den röda tråden*. Stockholm: Raben & Sjögren, 1987. Translated under the title *The Red Thread*. Stockholm: R & S Books, 1988.

Obiols, Miquel. *El cuadro más bonito del monde*. Illus. Roger Olmos. Pontevedra: Kalandraka, 2001.

Ohta, Daihachi. *Kasa*. Osaka: Bunken Shuppan, 1975.

Osada, Hiroshi. *Mori no ehon*. Illus. Ryôji Arai. Translated by Peter Milward under the title *A Forest Picture-Book*. Japan: Angel Foundation, 1999.

Owens, Terrell "T.O." (with Courtney Parker). *Little T Learns to Share*. Illus. Todd Harris. Dallas: BenBella Books, 2006.

Perrault, Charles. *Le chat botté*. Illus. Gérard Franquin. Albums du Père Castor. Paris: Flammarion, 1979.

———. *Riquet à la houppe*. Illus. Jean Claverie. Paris: Albin Michel, 1988.

Pilkey, Dav. *When Cats Dream*. New York: Orchard, 1992.

Piquemal, Michel. *Le cheval de Léonard de Vinci*. Illus. Daniel Maja. Paris: Épigones, 1997.

Pommaux, Yvan. *La pie voleuse*. Paris: L'École des loisirs, 1984.

———. *Le théâtre de Corbelle and Corbillo*. Colors: Nicole Pommaux. Paris: L'École des loisirs, 1986.

———. *Disputes et chapeaux*. Paris: L'École des loisirs, 1991.

———. *John Chatterton détective*. Paris: L'École des loisirs, 1993.

———. *Une nuit, un chat. . . .* Paris: L'École des loisirs, 1994.

———. *Libérez Lili*. Paris: L'École des loisirs, 1999.

Poncelet, Beatrice. *J'aurais tombé*. Paris: Syros Alternatives, 1989.

———. *Chut! elle lit!* Paris: Seuil Jeunesse, 1995.

———. *Chez elle ou chez elle*. Paris: Seuil Jeunesse, 1997.

———. *Chaise et café*. Paris: Seuil Jeunesse, 2000.

———. *. . . Et la gelée, framboise ou cassis?* Paris: Seuil Jeunesse, 2001.

Ponti, Claude. *L'Album d'Adèle*. Paris: Gallimard, 1986.

———. *Okilélé*. Paris: L'École des loisirs, 2002.

Poulter, Jim. *Le secret du rêve*. Illus. Claire Forgeot. Trans. Syvie Caffarel. Les livres-fresques du Seuil. Paris: Seuil Jeunesse, 1995.

Prince of Wales, Charles. *The Old Man of Lochnagar*. Illus. Sir Hugh Casson. London: Hamish Hamilton, 1980.

Pullman, Philip. *The Amber Spyglass*. London: Scholastic, 2000.

Quesemand, Anne. *Le colporteur d'images*. Illus. Laurent Berman. Paris: Syros, 1986.

———. *La Mort-Marraine*. Illus. Laurent Berman. Moulins: Ipomée-Albin Michel, 1987.

Radunsky, Vladimir. *The Mighty Asparagus*. New York: Harcourt/Silver Whistle, 2004.

Rego, Paula. *Nursery Rhymes*. London: South Bank Centre, 1990.

Renberg, Tore. *Hando Kjendo: Søndag*. Illus. Kim Hiorthøy. Oslo: Gyldendal, 1999.

———. *Hando Kjendo: Torsdag*, Oslo: Gyldendal, 2000.

Rey, Hans Augusto, and Margret Rey. *Curious George*. Boston: Houghton Mifflin, 1941.

Ribas, Teresa, Pilar Casademunt, and Roser Capdevila (Illus.). *La Campagne*. Brussels: Casterman, 1985.

———. *La Maison*. Brussels: Casterman, 1985.

———. *La Ville*. Brussels: Casterman, 1985.

———. *Les Alentours*. Brussels: Casterman, 1988.

———. *Les Magasins*. Brussels: Casterman, 1988.

———. *Les Vacances*. Brussels: Casterman, 1992.

Richelson, Geraldine. *What Is a Baby?* Illus. John E. Johnson. New York: Harlin Quist distributed by Crown Publishers, 1966.

———. *What Is a Child?* Illus. John E. Johnson. New York: Harlin Quist distributed by Crown Publishers, 1966. Translated into French by François Ruy-Vidal under the title *Qu'est qu'un enfant?* Paris: Harlin Quist, 1968.

———. *What Is a Grown-up?* Illus. John E. Johnson. New York: Harlin Quist distributed by Crown Publishers, 1967.

———. *Qu'est-ce qu'un enfant?* Illus. Nicole Claveloux. Paris: Harlin Quist, 1998.

Riddle, Tohby. *The Great Escape from City Zoo*. Sydney: HarperCollins, 1997.

Riff, Hélène. *Le jour où papa a tué sa vieille tante*. Paris: Albin Michel Jeunesse, 2000.

———. *Papa se met en quatre*. Paris: Albin Michel Jeunesse, 2004.

Rigo [Martín Martínez Navarro], and Ricardo Alcántara. *El caballo acróbata: una fantasía con Marc Chagall*. Barcelona: Ediciones B., 1991.

Rimes, LeAnn. *Jag*. Story developed by Dean Sheremet. Illus. Richard Bernal. New York: Dutton Children's Books, 2003.

———. *Jag's New Friend*. Story developed by Dean Sheremet. Illus. Richard Bernal. New York: Dutton Children's Books, 2004.

Ritchie, Madonna. *The English Roses*. Illus. Jeffrey Fulvimari. New York: Callaway, 2003.

———. *Mr. Peabody's Apples*. Illus. Loren Long. New York: Callaway, 2003.

———. *The Adventures of Abdi*. Illus. Olga Dugina and Andrej Dugin. New York: Callaway, 2004.

———. *Yakov and the Seven Thieves*. Illus. Gennady Spirin. New York: Callaway, 2004.

———. *Lotsa de Casha*. Illus. Rui Paes. New York: Callaway, 2005.

———. *The English Roses: Too Good to Be True*. Illus. Stacy Peterson. New York: Callaway, 2006.

Rodari, Gianni. *La guerra delle campane*. Illus. Pef. Illus. coloured by Geneviève Ferrier. Rome: Riuniti, 1982. Translated into French by Roger Salomon under the title *Scoop!* Voisins-Le-Bretonneux: Rue du monde, 1999.

Rodrigez, Alex. *Out of the Ballpark*. Illus. Frank Morrison. New York: HarperCollins, 2007.

Romano, Ray, with brothers, Richard and Robert. *Raymie, Dickie, and the Bean: Why I Love and Hate My Brothers*. Illus. Gary Locke. New York: Simon & Schuster Books for Young Readers, 2005.

Rosen, Michael. *Michael Rosen's Sad Book*. Illus. Quentin Blake. London: Walker Books, 2004.

Ross, Tony. *Little Red Riding Hood*. London: Andersen Press, 1978.

Rossof, Meg. *How I Live Now*. London: Penguin, 2004.

Roth, Dieter. *Bilderbuch*. Reykjavik: D. Rot, 1956.

———. *Kinderbuch*. Reykjavik: forlag ed., 1957.

———. *Gesammelte Werke*, Bd. 1: 2 Bilderbücher. Stuttgart: Edition Hansjörg Mayer, 1976.

Ruy-Vidal, François. *Le Bistouri de Mlle Dard*. Illus. Jacques Lerouge. Paris: Éditions de l'Amitié, 1979.

———, ed. *Les Papillons de Pimpanicaille, comptines et formulettes d'ici, de là-bas et d'ailleurs*, réunies et présentées par F. Ruy-Vidal. Illus. Alain Gauthier. Éditions de l'Amitié, 1981.

Sadat, Mandana. *De l'autre côté de l'arbre*. Orange: Grandir, 1997.

———. *Mon lion*. Paris: Autrement, 2005.

Sainsbury, Geoffrey. *Patavant et patarrière*. Illus. John Willett. Nantes: Éditions MeMo, 2001.

Sara. *Dans la gueule du loup*. Paris: Epigones, 1990.

———. *Révolution*. Paris: Seuil, 2003.

———. *À quai*. Paris: Seuil Jeunesse, 2005.

Sasaki, Maki. *Yappari Okami*. Tokyo: Fukuinkan Shoten, 1973.

Say, Allen. *Grandfather's Journey*. Boston: Houghton Mifflin, 1993.

Schlessinger, Laura, and Martha Lambert. *Why Do You Love Me?* Illus. Daniel McFeeley. New York: HarperCollins, 1999.

———. *Dr. Laura Schlessinger's But I Waaannt It!* Illus. Daniel McFeeley. New York: HarperCollins, 2000.

———. *Dr. Laura Schlessinger's Growing Up Is Hard*. Illus. Daniel McFeeley. New York: HarperCollins, 2001.

———. *Dr. Laura Schlessinger's Where's God?* Illus. Daniel McFeeley. New York: HarperCollins, 2003.

Schnack, Asger. *Bløde punkter*. Illus. Dorte Karrebæk. Copenhagen: Høst, 2000.

Schnurre, Wolfdietrich. "Die Prinzessin." In *Das Los unserer Stadt*. Olten: Walter, 1959. 73.

———. *Die Prinzessin kommt um vier*. Illus. Rotraut Susanne Berner. Berlin: Aufbau-Verlag, 2000.

Schössow, Peter. *Meehr!!* Hamburg: Carlsen, 1999.

Schwitters, Kurt. *Lucky Hans and Other Merz Fairy Tales*. Translated and introduced by Jack Zipes. Illus. Irvine Peacock. Princeton, NJ: Princeton University Press, 2009.

Schwitters, Kurt, and Kate Steinitz. *Die Märchen vom Paradies*. Hannover: Apossverlag, 1924.

———. *Hahnepeter*. Hannover: Merz Publishing Co., 1924.

Schwitters, Kurt, Kate Steinitz, and Theo van Doesburg. *Die Scheuche: Märchen*. Hannover: Apossverlag, 1925.

Scieszka, Jon, and Lane Smith. *The Stinky Cheese Man and Other Fairly Stupid Tales*. New York: Viking, 1992.

Seinfeld, Jerry. *Halloween*. Illus. James Bennett. New York: Little, Brown, and Company, 2002.

Sendak, Maurice. *Where the Wild Things Are*. New York: Harper & Row, 1963.

———. *Higglety Pigglety Pop! or, There Must Be More to Life*. New York: Harper & Row, 1967.

———. *In the Night Kitchen*. New York: Harper & Row, 1970.

———. *Outside Over There*. New York: HarperCollins, 1981.

———. *We Are All in the Dumps with Jack and Guy*. New York: HarperCollins, 1993.

Seuss, Dr. [Theodor Seuss Geisel]. *Oh, the Places You'll Go!* New York: Random House, 1990.

———. *Seuss-isms: Wise and Witty Prescriptions for Living from the Good Doctor*. New York: Random House, 1997.

———. *Seuss-isms for Success: Insider Tips on Economic Health from the Good Doctor*. New York: Random House, 1999.

Seymour, Jane, and James Keach. *Yum! A Tale of Two Cookies*. This One 'n That One. Illus. Geoffrey Planer. New York: Putnam Juvenile, 1998.

———. *And Then There Were Three: Introducing the Other One*. Illus. Geoffrey Planer. Los Angeles: Angel Gate, 2003.

Shalev, Meir. *Aunt Michal* [in Israeli]. Tel Aviv: Am Oved, 2000.

———. *A Lion in the Night* [in Israeli]. Tel Aviv: Am Oved, 2004.

———. *The Underplate* [in Israeli]. Tel Aviv: Am Oved, 2008.

Sharp, Margery, and Roy McKie. *Mélisande*. London: Collins, 1960.

Sheedy, Alexandra Elizabeth (Ally). *She Was Nice to Mice*. New York: McGraw-Hill, 1975.

Shriver, Maria. *What's Heaven?* Illus. Sandra Speidel. New York: Golden Books, 1999.

———. *What's Wrong with Timmy?* Boston: Little, Brown Books for Young Readers, 2001.

———. *What's Happening to Grandpa?* Illus. Sandra Speidel. Boston: Little, Brown Books for Young Readers, 2004.

Simmonds, Posy. *Lulu and the Flying Babies*. New York: Knopf, 1989.

Sís, Peter. *Starry Messenger:* A book depicting the life of a famous scientist, mathematician, astronomer, philosopher, physicist, Galileo Galilei. New York: Farrar, Straus and Giroux, 1996.

———. *Tibet Through the Red Box*. New York: Farrar, Straus and Giroux, 1998.

———. *The Wall: Growing Up Behind the Iron Curtain*. New York: Farrar, Straus and Giroux, 2007.

Smith, Will. *Just the Two of Us*. Illus. Kadir Nelson. New York: Scholastic, 2001.

Sollie, André, and Ingrid Godon. *Wachten op matroos*. Amsterdam: Querido, 2000. Translated under the title *Hello, Sailor*. London: Macmillan Children's Books, 2002.

———. *De bus naar Hawaii*. Amsterdam: Querido, 2003.

Solotareff, Grégoire. *Toi grand et moi petit*. Paris: L'École des loisirs, 1996.

———. *Mathieu*. Paris: L'École des loisirs, 1998.

———. *La Chambre de Vincent*. Paris: L'École des loisirs, 1999.

Sortland, Bjørn, and Lars Elling. *Raudt, blått og litt gult*. Oslo: Det Norske Samlaget, 1993. Translated by James Anderson under the title *Anna's Art Adventure*. Minneapolis: Carolrhoda/Lerner Books, 1999.

Steig, William. *Sylvester and the Magic Pebble*. New York: Windmill Books, 1969.

———. *Doctor De Soto*. New York: Farrar, Straus and Giroux, 1982.

———. *Shrek*. New York: Farrar, Straus and Giroux, 1990.

Steiner, Jörg. *Der Bär, der ein Bär bleiben wollte*. Illus. Jörg Müller. Aarau: Sauerländer, 1976. Translated under the title *The Bear Who Wanted to Be a Bear*. New York: Atheneum, 2007.

———. *Die Kanincheninsel*. Aarau, Frankfurt am Main: Sauerländer, 1977. Translated into English by Ann Conrad Lammers under the title *Rabbit Island*. New York: Harcourt Brace, 1978.

———. *Aufstand der Tiere oder Die neuen Stadtmusikanten*. Aarau, Frankfurt am Main; Salzburg: Sauerländer, 1989.

Sting. *Rock Steady: A Story of Noah's Ark*. Illus. Hugh Whyte. New York: HarperCollins, 2001.

Suzuki, Koji. *Atsusa-no-sei?* Tokyo: Fukuinkan Shoten, 1994.

Takahashi, Miki. *Kogepan: Pan nimo iroiro aru-rashii*. Tokyo: Sony Magazines, 2000.

Tan, Shaun. *The Lost Thing*. South Melbourne: Lothian Books, 2000.

———. *The Red Tree*. South Melbourne: Lothian Books, 2001.

———. *The Arrival*. South Melbourne: Lothian Books, 2006.

Taniuchi, Kota. *Natsu no asa*. Tokyo: Shiko-sha, 1970. Translated under the titles *Boy on a Hilltop*. London: A & C Black, 1970; *Up on a Hilltop*. New York: F. Watts, 1971.

———. *Nichiyobi*. Tokyo: Shiko-sha, 1997.

Taylor, Elizabeth. *Nibbles and Me*. New York: Duell, Sloan and Pearce, 1946.

Tejima, Keizaburo. *Oohakuchou no sora*. Tokyo: Hukutake Shoten, 1983. Translated under the title *Swan Sky*. New York: Philomel Books, 1988.

Thompson, Colin. *Looking for Atlantis*. London: Julia MacRae Books, 1993.

Thompson, Kay. *Eloise: A Book for Precocious Grown Ups*. Illus. Hillary Knight. New York: Simon & Schuster, 1955.

———. *Eloise in Paris*. Illus. Hillary Knight. New York: Simon & Schuster, 1957.

———. *Eloise at Christmastime*. Illus. Hillary Knight. New York: Random House, 1958.

———. *Eloise in Moscow*. Illus. Hillary Knight. New York: Simon & Schuster, 1959.

———. *Eloise Takes a Bawth*. Illus. Hilary Knight and additional plumbing by Mart Crowley. New York: Simon & Schuster Books for Young Readers, 2002.

Tidholm, Thomas, and Anna-Clara Tidholm. *Resan till Ugri-La-Brek*. Stockholm: Alfabeta, 1987.

———. *Snälla Barn*. Stockholm: Alfabeta, 2007.

Tournier, Michel. *Le coq de bruyère*. Paris: Gallimard, 1978. Translated by Barbara Wright under the title *The Fetishist*. New York: Doubleday, 1984.

———. *Pierrot ou les secrets de la nuit*. Enfantimages. Paris: Gallimard, 1979.

Travolta, John. *Propeller One-Way Night Coach: A Fable for All Ages*. New York: Warner Books, 1997.

Uchida, Rintaro. *Gatagoto Gatagoto*. Illus. Shigeo Nishimura. Tokyo: Doshinsha, 1999.

Ungerer, Tomi. *Snail, Where Are You?* New York: Harper and Row, 1962.
———. *The Three Robbers*. New York: Atheneum, 1962.
———. *The Beast of Monsieur Racine*. New York: Farrar, Straus and Giroux, 1971.
———. *Flix*. Zurich: Diogenes, 1998. Translated under the title *Flix*. Boulder, CO: Roberts Rinehart Publishers, 1998.
Uziel, Rachel. *La maison des mots*. Illus. Angela Lago. Les livres-fresques du Seuil. Paris: Seuil Jeunesse, 1995.
Van Allsburg, Chris. *Jumanji*. Boston: Houghton Mifflin, 1981.
———. *Ben's Dream*. Boston: Houghton Mifflin, 1982.
———. *The Mysteries of Harris Burdick*. Boston: Houghton Mifflin, 1984.
———. *The Polar Express*. Boston: Houghton Mifflin, 1985.
———. *The Z Was Zapped: A Play in Twenty-Six Acts*. Boston: Houghton Mifflin, 1987.
———. *Just a Dream*. Boston: Houghton Mifflin, 1990.
———. *The Wretched Stone*. Boston: Houghton Mifflin: 1991.
———. *The Sweetest Fig*. Boston: Houghton Mifflin, 1993.
———. *Zathura*. Boston: Houghton Mifflin, 2002.
Velthuijs, Max. *Kikker is verliefd*. Amsterdam: Leopold, 1989. Translated by Anthea Bell under the title *Frog in Love*. London: Andersen Press, 1989.
———. *Kikker en het vogeltje*. Amsterdam: Leopold, 1991. Translated under the title *Frog and the Birdsong*. London: Andersen, 1991.
Ventura, Piero, and Marco. *Anna dei porci*. Milan: Mondadori, 1987.
Vilela, Fernando. *Le chemin*. Paris: Autrement Jeunesse, 2007.
Vincent, Gabrielle. *Ernest et Célestine au musée*. Paris: Duculot, 1985.
Vos, Philip de. *Carnival of the Animals*. Illus. Piet Grobler. Cape Town: Human & Rousseau, 1998.
Walker, Richard. *Jack and the Beanstalk*. Illus. Niamh Sharkey. Bristol: Barefoot Books, 1999.
Walton, Ann. *Hier is ek*. Illus. Piet Grobler. Cape Town: Juta, 1996. Translated by Emma Booyens under the title *Here I Am*. Cape Town: Juta, 1998.
Ware, Chris. *Jimmy Corrigan: The Smartest Kid on Earth*. New York: Pantheon Books, 2000.
Warhol, Andy. *Andy Warhol's Children's Book*. Zurich: Bruno Bischofberger, 1983.
Warwick, Dionne, David Freeman Wooley, and Tonya Bolden. *Say a Little Prayer*. Illus. Soud. Philadelphia: Running Press, 2008.
Wegman, William. *Puppies*. New York: Hyperion Books for Children, 1997.
Wehrli, Ursus. *Kunst aufräumen*. Zurich: Klein & Aber AG, 2002. Translated under the title *Tidying Up Art*. New York: Prestel, 2003.
Weitzman, Jacqueline Preiss. *You Can't Take a Balloon into the Metropolitan Museum*. Illus. Robin Preiss Glasser. New York: Dial, 1998.
Wiesner, David. *Free Fall*. New York: Lothrop, Lee & Shepard Books, 1988.
———. *Tuesday*. New York: Clarion Books, 1991.
———. *Sector 7*. New York: Clarion Books, 1999.
———. *The Three Pigs*. New York: Clarion Books, 2001.
———. *Flotsam*. New York: Clarion Books, 2006.
Willard, Nancy. *A Visit to William Blake's Inn: Poems for Innocent and Experienced Travelers*. Illus. Alice and Martin Provensen. New York: Harcourt Brace & Company, 1981.
———. *Pish, Posh, Said Hieronymus Bosch*. Illus. Leo and Diane Dillon with Lee Dillon. San Diego: Harcourt Brace Jovanovich, 1991.
Willhoite, Michael. *The Entertainer: A Story in Pictures*. Boston: Alyson Publications, 1992.
Wojciechowski, Susan. *The Christmas Miracle of Jonathan Toomey*. Illus. P. J. Lynch. London: Walker Books, 1995.
Yarrow, Peter, and Lenny Lipton. *Puff, the Magic Dragon*. Paintings by Eric Puybaret. New York: Sterling Pub., 2007.
Yoguchi, Takao. *Active ukiyoe—Classical Japanese Pictures Revisited*. English text by Arthur Binard. Tokyo: Fukuinkan Shoten, 2005.
Zelinsky, P. O. *Rapunzel*. New York: Dutton, 1997.

Secondary Works

Andersen, Carsten. "We Laugh the Weirdness Backwards Out of the Book." Trans. Thomas E. Kennedy. *Danish Literary Magazine* (Autumn 2008): 23–24.

"A Poignant Story About Alzheimer's Disease by Maria Shriver." *PR Newswire*, June 4, 2008.

Ardizzone, Edward. "Creation of a Picture Book." In *Only Connect: Readings on Children's Literature*. Ed. Sheila Egoff, G. T. Stubbs, and L. F. Ashley. 2nd ed. New York: Oxford University Press, 1980: 289–298.

———. "Anno 85–Anno 87." Interview by Geneviève Patte and Annie Pissard; Catherine Germain and Elisabeth Lortic. *La Revue des livres pour enfants* 118 (Winter 1987): 53–57.

Arnason, H. H. *History of Modern Art*. 3rd ed. New York: Harry N. Abrams, 1986.

Ascher-Walsh, Rebecca. "Air Time." *Entertainment Weekly*, November 21, 2001.

Atzmon, Leslie. "The Scarecrow Fairytale: A Collaboration of Theo Van Doesburg and Kurt Schwitters." *Design Issues* 12, no. 3 (Autumn 1996): 14–34.

Avery, Gillian, and Kimberley Reynolds, eds. *Representations of Childhood Death*. Basingstoke: Macmillan, 2000.

Bader, Barbara. *American Picturebooks from Noah's Ark to the Beast Within*. New York: Macmillan, 1976.

Bal, Mieke, and Norman Bryson. "Semiotics and Art History." *Art Bulletin* 73, no. 2 (1991): 174–208.

Beckett, Sandra L. "Parodic Play with Paintings in Picture Books." *Children's Literature* 29 (2001): 175–195.

———. "Breaking Boundaries with Radical Picture Books." Paper presented at the international conference "Image and Imagery," Brock University, St. Catharines, ON, October 16, 2002.

———. *Recycling Red Riding Hood*. New York and London: Routledge, 2002.

———. "Artists' Books for a Cross-audience." In *Studies in Children's Literature 1500–2000*. Ed. Celia Keenan and Mary Shine Thompson. Dublin: Four Courts Press, 2004: 162–169.

———. "Transcending Boundaries with Object-Books." In *L'édition pour la jeunesse: entre héritage et culture de masse*. Ed. Ségolène Roy. Eaubonne: IICP, 2005. CD-ROM.

———. "Épilogue: 'Crossover Picturebooks' ou les albums pour tous." In *L'album contemporain pour la jeunesse: nouvelles formes, nouveaux lecteurs?* Ed. Connan-Pintado, Christiane, Florence Gaiotti, and Bernadette Poulou. Modernités 28. Bordeaux: Presses Universitaires de Bordeaux, 2008: 305–314.

———. *Red Riding Hood for All Ages: Fairy-Tale Icon in Cross-Cultural Contexts*. Detroit: Wayne State University Press, 2008.

———. *Crossover Fiction: Global and Historical Perspectives*. New York and London: Routledge, 2009.

———. "Artistic Allusions in Picturebooks." In *New Directions in Picturebook Research*. Ed. Teresa Colomer, Bettina Kümmerling-Meibauer, and Cecilia Silva-Díaz. New York and London: Routledge, 2010: 83–98.

———. "Picturebooks That Transcend Boundaries." *Irish Children's Literature and Culture: New Perspectives on Contemporary Writing*. Ed. Valerie Coghlan and Keith O'Sullivan. New York and London: Routledge, 2010: 169–182.

———, ed. *Reflections of Changes: Children's Literature Since 1945*. Westport: Greenwood, 1997.

———. *Transcending Boundaries: Writing for a Dual Audience of Children and Adults*. New York: Garland, 1999.

Béguery, Jocelyne. *Une esthétique contemporaine de l'album jeunesse: De grands petits livres*. Paris: L'Harmattan, 2002.

Belkeddar, Odile. "Un Petit Âne dérangeant." *La Revue des livres pour enfants* 171 (September 1996): 143–146.

Bernanoce, Marie. "L'album-théâtre? Un genre en cours de constitution." In *Les Cahiers de Lire Écrire à l'école, Texte et images dans l'album et la bande dessinée pour enfants*. CRDP de Grenoble, 2007: 121–135.

———. "'L'album-théâtre': typologie et questions posées à sa lecture." In *L'album contemporain pour la jeunesse: nouvelles formes, nouveaux lecteurs?* Ed. Christiane Connan-Pintado, Florence Gaiotti, and Bernadette Poulou. Modernités 28. Bordeaux: Presses Universitaires de Bordeaux, 2008. 39–52.

Beronä, David A. *Wordless Books: The Original Graphic Novels*. New York: Abrams, 2008.

Bird, Elizabeth. "Time Taken with Shaun Tan." *School Library Journal*, June 19, 2007. http://schoollibraryjournal.com/blog/1790000379/post/210010821.html (accessed May 22, 2009).

Birkeland, Tone. "At the Crossroad—the Norwegian Picture Book." In *Norwegian Books for Children and Young People*. Lillehammer: Lillehammer Olympic Organizing Committee, 1994. 10–13.

Birkeland, Tone, Gunvor Risa, and Karin Beate Vold. *Norsk barnelitteraturhistorie*. Oslo: Samlaget, 1997.

Bjorvand, Agnes-Margrethe. "Do Sons Inherit the Sins of their Fathers? An Analysis of the Picture-book *Angry Man*." In *New Directions in Picturebook Research*. Ed. Teresa Colomer, Bettina Küm-merling-Meibauer, and Cecilia Silva-Díaz. New York and London: Routledge, 2010. 217–231.

Blake, Quentin Blake. "Quentin Blake on. . . ." *Teachers' TV.* http://static.teachers.tv/shared/files/11958.pdf (accessed September 2, 2010).

———. *Quentin Blake—The Power of Illustration*, Teachers TV, 2009, http://www.teachers.tv/videos/quentin-blake-the-power-of-illustration (accessed September 2, 2010).

Boyer, Perrine. "Álbumes españoles (1990–2003)." *CLIJ* 172 (2004): 44–52.

Bradford, Clare. "The Picture Book: Some Postmodern Tensions," *Papers* 4, no. 3 (December 1993): 14.

Brettingham, Madeleine. "New Storm Brews over Gay Books." *Times Educational Supplement*, October 20, 2006: 6.

Brouillard, Anne. "Interview en images: Anne Brouillard." Interview by Sophie van der Linden. *Hors Cadre[s]* 1 (October 2007–February 2008): 14–15.

Bruel, Christian. "Des albums comme autant de points de vue sur le monde." Interview with A. C. December 18, 1997. <http://www.humanite.fr/1997–12–18_Articles_-Des-albums-comme-autant-de-points-de-vue-sur-le-monde> (accessed September 4, 2009).

———. *Anthony Browne*. Paris: Éditions Être, 2001.

———. "À propos de Wolf Erlbruch. . . ." *AEIOU* 6 (December 2004): 24–28.

Burger, Dionys. 1965. Translated by Cornelie J. Rheinboldt under the title *Sphereland: A Fantasy About Curved Spaces and an Expanding Universe*. New York: Apollo Editions, 1969.

Bury, Stephen. *Artists' Books: The Book as a Work of Art, 1963–1995*. Aldershot: Scolar Press, 1995.

Bystrup, Kirsten. "Author Profile: Dorte Karrebæk." Trans. Barbara Haveland. *Danish Literature.* http://www.danishliterature.info/index.php?id=2092&n0_cache=1&ltx (accessed May 15, 2009).

Cech, John. *Angels and Wild Things: The Archetypal Poetics of Maurice Sendak*. University Park: Pennsylvania State University Press, 1995.

Chabrol-Gagne, Nelly. "Écriture de la disparition chez Anne Herbauts." In *L'album contemporain pour la jeunesse: nouvelles formes, nouveaux lecteurs?* Ed. Christiane Connan-Pintado, Florence Gaiotti, and Bernadette Poulou. Modernités 28. Bordeaux: Presses Universitaires de Bordeaux, 2008. 161–172.

Christensen, Nina. "How to Make Sense: Reflections on the Influence of Eighteenth Century Picturebooks on Picturebooks of Today." In *New Directions in Picturebook Research*. Ed. Teresa Colomer, Bettina Kümmerling-Meibauer, and Cecilia Silva-Díaz. New York and London: Routledge, 2010. 55–67.

Coghlan, Valerie. "P. J. Lynch." In *Irish Children's Writers and Illustrators 1986–2006*. Ed. Valerie Coghlan and Siobhan Parkinson. Dublin: Children's Books Ireland and Church of Ireland College of Education Publications, 2007. 54–69.

Colomer, Teresa, Bettina Kümmerling-Meibauer, and Cecilia Silva-Díaz, eds. *New Directions in Picturebook Research*. New York and London: Routledge, 2010.

"Comments." *Papers* 4, no. 3 (December 1993): 2.

Connan-Pintado, Christiane. "Des lectures pour tous: les 'bouquins' de Béatrice Poncelet." In *L'album contemporain pour la jeunesse: nouvelles formes, nouveaux lecteurs?* Ed. Christiane Connan-Pintado, Florence Gaiotti, and Bernadette Poulou. Modernités 28. Bordeaux: Presses Universitaires de Bordeaux, 2008. 173–186.

Connan-Pintado, Christiane, Florence Gaiotti, and Bernadette Poulou, eds. *L'album contemporain pour la jeunesse: nouvelles formes, nouveaux lecteurs?* Modernités 28. Bordeaux: Presses Universitaires de Bordeaux, 2008.

Couprie, Katy. "Auteurs et illustrateurs—Entretiens: Katy Couprie." *Livres au Trésor*, September 1992. http://www.livresautresor.net/livres/e57.htm (accessed January 30, 2009).

Cox, Paul. "Tête à tête avec Paul Cox." Interview by Elisabeth Lortic. *La Revue des livres pour enfants* 155–156 (Winter 1994): 58–62.

Curtil, Sophie, and Elisabeth Lortic. "1, 2, 3 . . . Komagata." *Visa pour la cité* 33 (1996): 22–23.

Dahl, Sophie. "Notes from the Author." *The Man with the Dancing Eyes*. http://www.dancing-eyes.net/notes.htm (accessed May 14, 2010).

Danset-Léger, Jacqueline. *L'enfant et les images de la littérature enfantine*. Brussels: Pierre Mardaga, 1988.

Danto, Arthur. "The Artworld." In *The Philosophy of the Visual Arts*. New York and Oxford: Oxford University Press, 1992. 426–433.

Debattista, Marina. "Eugene Ionesco's Writing for Children." *Bookbird* 43, no. 4 (2005): 15–21.

Delobel, André. "L'Affaire Petit-Âne." *Les Cahiers du CRILJ* 1 (November 2009).

DeLuca, Geraldine. "Exploring the Levels of Childhood: The Allegorical Sensibility of Maurice Sendak." *Children's Literature* 12 (1984): 3–24.

Derrien, Marie. "Radical Trends in French Picturebooks." *The Lion and the Unicorn* 19, no. 2 (April 2005): 170–189.

Doonan, Jane. "Into the Dangerous World: *We Are All in the Dumps with Jack and Guy* by Maurice Sendak." *Signal* 75 (1994): 155–171.

———. "Drawing Out Ideas: A Second Decade of the Work of Anthony Browne." *The Lion and the Unicorn* 23 (1999): 30–56.

———. "Quentin Blake, The Children's Laureate: Selected Picture Books." *Children's Literature in Education* 31, no. 2 (June 2000): 53–71.

———. "A Pictured World Through Eastern Eyes." In *Through Eastern Eyes: The Art of the Japanese Picture Book*. Catalogue of an exhibition held at the National Centre for Research in Children's Literature and curated by Okiko Miyake and Tomoko Masaki. London: National Centre for Research in Children's Literature, 2001. 6–15.

Dresang, Eliza T. *Radical Change: Books for Youth in a Digital Age*. New York: The H. W. Wilson Company, 1999.

———. "Radical Change Theory, Postmodernism, and Contemporary Picturebooks." In *Postmodern Picturebooks: Play, Parody, and Self-Referentiality*. Ed. Lawrence R. Sipe and Sylvia Pantaleo. New York and London: Routledge, 2008. 41–54.

Drucker, Johanna. *The Century of Artists' Books*. 2nd ed. New York: Granary Books, 2004.

Dubois-Marcoin, Danielle. "Entrer dans l'album comme dans un magasin de curiosités, l'éloge de la discontinuité." In *L'album contemporain pour la jeunesse: nouvelles formes, nouveaux lecteurs?* Ed. Christiane Connan-Pintado, Florence Gaiotti, and Bernadette Poulou. Modernités 28. Bordeaux: Presses Universitaires de Bordeaux, 2008. 53–63.

Ducor, Jérôme, Bernard Crettaz, Dhristian Delécraz, and Christophe Gallaz. *Petit Manuel des rites mortuaires*. Geneva: La Joie de Lire, 1999.

Duijx, Toin. "Winner of the 2004 Andersen Illustrator Award: Max Velthuijs, The Netherlands." *Bookbird* 42, no. 4 (2004): 11–15.

Durand, Marion, and Gérard Bertrand. *L'Image dans le livre pour enfants*. Paris: L'Écoles des loisirs, 1975.

Eccleshare, Julia. "Portrait of the Artist as a Gorilla: Anthony Browne Explains His Surrealist Children's Style to Julia Eccleshare." *Guardian*, July 29, 2000.

Ekman, Fam. "Fam Ekman and Her Children's Books." Paper presented at the International Research Society of Children's Literature Congress, Agder University College, Kristiansand, August 9–14, 2003.

Erickson, Mark St. John. "Sendak Show Explores Best-Selling Children's Books for Adults as Well as Kids." *Baltimore Sun*, February 14, 2010.

Eubanks, Paula. "Understanding Picture Books as an Art Medium." *Art Education* 52, no. 6 (November 1999): 38–44.

Eugène. "Eugène: La mort à vivre." Interview by Ardian. *Zwook*, http://zwookedu.ch/eugene/zwook/espaces-livres/lamortavivre (accessed June 19, 2010).

Fransson, Birgitta. "Anna-Clara Tidholm's Previous Books." Anna-Clara Tidholm Nominated for the 2010 H. C. Andersen Prize by the Swedish Section of IBBY, 15–23. http://ibby.se/wp-content/uploads/2009/09/anna-tidholmibby.pdf (accessed May 29, 2010).

Friedman, Roger. "Madonna's Adoption Kills Book Sales." *Fox News*, November 17, 2006. http://www.foxnews.com/story/0,2933,230158,00.html (accessed May 10, 2010).

Gégène. "Cependant . . . Paul Cox," *Citrouille* 38 (June 2004): 21–22.

Genette, Gérard. *Palimpsestes: La littérature au second degré*. Paris: Seuil, 1982.

———. *Seuils*. Paris: Seuil, 1987.

"Gervais Story Book Is Adult Hit." *BBC News*, October 6, 2004. http://newsvote.bbc.co.uk/mpapps/pagetools/print/news.bbc.co.uk/2/hi/entertainment/3719684.stm (accessed May 2, 2010).

Giroux, Henry A. "Animating Youth: The Disneyfication of Children's Culture." *Socialist Review* 24, no. 3 (1995): 23–55.

Goedhart, Bernie. "Author/Illustrator Stian Hole: The Complete Interview." *Montreal Gazette*, May 12, 2010.

Goldstein, Ronald, Dr. "Beauty and the Media: A Special Interview with Deborah Norville." *Season* Magazine, Spring 2005. http://www.seasonmagazine.com/profiles/norville.htm (accessed May 9, 2010).

Gollapudi, Aparna. "Picture Book as Personal Journey: A Kristevan Reading of Peter Sís's *Tibet: Through the Red Box*." *Jeunesse: Young People, Texts, Cultures* 2, no. 1 (Summer 2010): 10–44.

Graham, Judith. "Reading Contemporary Picturebooks." In *Modern Children's Literature: An Introduction*. Ed. Kimberley Reynolds. Houndmills, Basingstoke: Palgrave Macmillan, 2005. 209–226.

Hall, Sarah. "Madonna: Like a Pitchwoman." *Eonline*, November 22, 2006. http://ca.eonline. com/uberblog/b53816_madonna_like_pitchwoman.html (accessed May 10, 2010).

Hancock, David. "Madonna's Advice or Kids." *CBSNews.com*, September 15, 2003. http://www. cbsnews.com/stories/2003/09/30/print/main575841.shtml (accessed May 18, 2010).

Hanlon, Tina L. "The Art and the Dragon: Intertextuality in the Pictorial Narratives of *Dragon Feathers*." In *Tales, Tellers and Texts*. Ed. Gabrielle Cliff Hodges, Mary Jane Drummond, and Morag Styles. London and New York: Cassell, 2000. 79–94.

Hateley, Erica. "Magritte and Cultural Capital: The Surreal World of Anthony Browne." *The Lion and the Unicorn* 33, no. 3 (2009): 324–348.

Hay, Carla. "Artists Add New Voice to Children's Books." *Billboard* 115, no. 33, August 16, 2003, 5, 68.

"HCA Award Illustrator Winner 2010." *Bookbird* 2 (2010).

Hearne, Betsy. "Perennial Picture Books Seeded by the Oral Tradition." *Journal of Youth Services* 12, no. 1 (Fall 1998): 26–33.

Heidkamp, Konrad. "How Simple Stories Become Great Books." Trans. Sally-Ann Spencer. http://www.new-books-in-german.com/featur42.htm (accessed May 29, 2010).

Hidalgo Rodriguez, María Carmen. "La ilustración infantil española actual. " *CLIJ* 144 (2001): 51–60.

Higonnet, Margaret R. "Modernism and Childhood: Violence and Renovation." *The Comparatist* 33 (2009): 86–108.

Hodges, Gabrielle Cliff, Mary Jane Drummond, and Morag Styles, eds. *Tales, Tellers and Texts*. London and New York: Cassell, 2000.

Hole, Stian. "Interview with Stian Hole, Author and Illustrator of *Garmann's Summer* (May 2008)." *Eerdmans Books for Young Readers*. http://www.eerdmans.com/Interviews/holeinterview.htm (accessed June 3, 2010).

Holland, Brad. "Express Yourself—It's Later than You Think." In *The Education of an Illustrator*. Ed. Steven Heller and Marshall Arisman. New York: Allworth Press, 2000.

Hollindale, Peter. *Signs of Childness in Children's Books*. Stroud: Thimble Press, 1997.

Hunt, Peter. *Criticism, Theory and Children's Literature*. Oxford: Basil Blackwell, 1991.

———. *An Introduction to Children's Literature*. Oxford: Oxford University Press, 1994.

———, ed. *Children's Literature: The Development of Criticism*. London: Routledge, 1990.

———. *International Companion Encyclopedia of Children's Literature*. 2 vols. London: Routledge, 2004.

Hutcheon, Linda. *A Theory of Parody: The Teachings of Twentieth-Century Art Forms*. New York and London: Methuen, 1985.

"Illustrator Nominee: France: Claude Ponti." *Bookbird* 46, no. 2 (2008): 30.

"Illustrator Nominee: USA." *Bookbird* 46, no. 2 (2008): 66.

Johnson, Caitlin A. "John Lithgow Pens 7th Children's Book." *CBSNews.com*, March 27, 2007. http://www.cbsnews.com/stories/2007/03/27/earlyshow/leisure/books/main2611660. shtml (accessed May 17, 2010).

Joosen, Vanessa. "True Love or Just Friends? Flemish Picture Books in English Translation." *Children's Literature in Education* 41, no. 2 (June 2010): 105–117.

K., Oscar [Ole Dalgaard]. "It's not the fact that it is said—in fact it's just the way you say it." *Danish Literary Magazine* (Autumn 2008): 46–48.

Keil, Beth Landman, and Deborah Mitchell. "Intelligencer." *New York Magazine*, May 26, 1997: 9–10.

Kennedy, Elizabeth. "Jane Yolen on 'Celebrity' Authors and Favorite Authors." *About.com: Children's Books*. http://childrensbooks.about.com/od/authorsillustrato/a/janeyolen_2.htm (accessed May 6, 2010).

Kiefer, Barbara. "What Is a Picturebook, Anyway? The Evolution of Form and Substance through the Postmodern Era and Beyond." In *Postmodern Picturebooks: Play, Parody, and Self-Referentiality*. Ed. Lawrence R. Sipe and Sylvia Pantaleo. New York and London: Routledge, 2008. 9–21.

Kofod-Olsen, Ulla. "In Praise of Childhood." Trans. Birgit Stephenson. *Danish Children's Literature* 3 (1992).

Komagata, Katsumi. "Messages Within Picture Books." *Bessatsu Taiyo "Nihon no Kokoro"* no. 108 (Winter 1999): Special issue: *Ehon to Asobou: Me to te de tanoshimu ehon-shu* (Let's play with the picture books: let's enjoy them with eyes and hands). Tokyo: Heibonsha Inc., 2001: 134–137.

Künneman, Horst. "How Much Cruelty Can a Children's Picturebook Stand? The Case of Wolf Erlbruch's *Die Menschenfresserin.*" *Bookbird* 43, no. 1 (2005): 14–19.

"Kylie To Publish Children's Book," *BBC News*, March 8, 2006, http://news.bbc.co.uk/2/hi/entertainment/4785786.stm (accessed May 17, 2010).

Laboratorio d'arte. "Dedicated to Munari. 1, 2, 3 . . . Komagata." 2007: 1–9. english.palazzoesposizioni.it/mediacenter/. . ./StreamAttributoMedia.aspx?. . . (accessed March 24, 2010).

Lamb, Wendy. "Strange Business: The Publishing Point of View." *Signal* 87 (September 1998): 167–173.

Lanes, Selma. *The Art of Maurice Sendak.* New York: Harry N. Abrams, Inc., 1980.

Lapeyre-Desmaison, Chantal. "De l'illisibilité dans l'album contemporain (Sur Frédéric Clément)." In *L'album contemporain pour la jeunesse: nouvelles formes, nouveaux lecteurs?* Ed. Christiane Connan-Pintado, Florence Gaiotti, and Bernadette Poulou. Modernités 28. Bordeaux: Presses Universitaires de Bordeaux, 2008. 197–208.

Lapouge, Gilles. "Michel Tournier s'explique." *Lire* 64 (December 1980): 28–46.

Larsen, David. "Children's Books of the Year Feature." *Listener*, December 20, 2008.

Lavater, Warja. Letter to Clive Phillpot, former Chief Librarian of the Museum of Modern Art. Artist's File on Warja Honnegger-Lavater, Library of the Museum of Modern Art, 1986.

———. "Tête à tête: Entretien avec Warja Lavater." Interview by Bernadette Gromer. *La Revue des livres pour enfants* 137–138 (Winter 1991): 40–49.

———. "Perception: When Signs Start to Communicate." In *The Faces of Physiognomy: Interdisciplinary Approaches to Johann Caspar Lavater.* Ed. Ellis Shookman. Columbia, SC: Camden House, 1993. 182–187.

Lechner, J. "Picture Books as Portable Art Galleries." *Art Education* 46, no. 2 (1993): 34–40.

Lefort, Régis. "L'album-poème." In *L'album contemporain pour la jeunesse: nouvelles formes, nouveaux lecteurs?* Ed. Christiane Connan-Pintado, Florence Gaiotti, and Bernadette Poulou. Modernités 28. Bordeaux: Presses Universitaires de Bordeaux, 2008. 29–38.

Lesnik-Oberstein, Karin, ed. *Children in Culture: Approaches to Childhood.* Basingstoke: Macmillan, 1998.

Lewis, David. "The Constructedness of Texts: Picture Books and the Metafictive." *Signal* 62 (May 1990): 131–146.

———. "Going Along with Mr. Gumpy: Polysystemy & Play in the Modern Picture Book." *Signal* 80 (May 1996): 105–119.

L'Illustration soviétique pour enfants. Moscow: Iskustvo, 1980.

Linders, Joke. *Ik bof dat ik een kikker ben: Leven en werk van Max Velthuijs.* Amsterdam: Leopold; 's-Gravenhage: Letterkundig Museum, 2003.

Lissitzky, El (Eliezer Markovitch). "Our Book." In *Looking Closer 3, Classic Writings on Graphic Design.* Ed. Michael Bierut, Jessica Helfand, Steven Heller, and Rick Poynor. New York: Allworth Press, 1999. 27–31.

———. "Typographie der Typographie." *Merz* 4 (1923): 47.

Lissitzky-Küppers, Sophie. *El Lissitzky: Life, Letters, Texts.* Greenwich: New York Graphic Society, 1968.

Lodge, Sally. "All Things Asparagus." *Publishers Weekly*, June 14, 2004, 32.

———. "Q & A with Ricky Gervais." *Publishers Weekly*, February 25, 2010.

Lortic, Elisabeth. "Les livres d'artistes pour enfants." In *Livres d'enfance.* Saint-Yrieix-la-Perche: Pays-Paysage/Centre national du livre d'artiste, 1998.

"Madonna Brought to Book by Roald Dahl's Illustrator." *Telegraph.co.uk.*, September 23, 2008. http://www.telegraph.co.uk/news/newstopics/mandrake/3069597/Madonna-brought-to-book-by-Roald-Dahls-illustrator.html (accessed May 13, 2010).

"Madonna's Best Selling Children's Books Inspire Children's, Young Girls and 'Tweens Apparel Line." *PR Newswire*, January 30, 2007. http://www.prnewswire.co.uk/cgi/news/release?id=189127 (accessed May 17, 2010).

Maffei, Giorgio. *Munari i libri.* Milan: Edizioni Sylvestre Bonnard, 2002.

Mallan, Kerry, and Sharyn Pearce. *Youth Cultures: Texts, Images, Identities.* Westport, CT: Praeger, 2003.

Marantz, Kenneth. "The Picture Book as Art Object: A Call for Balanced Reviewing." *Wilson Library Bulletin* 52, no. 2 (1977): 148–151.

———. *The Picturebook: Source and Resource for Art Education.* Reston, VA: National Art Education Association, 1994.

Marcus, Leonard S. "The Artist's Other Eye: The Picture Books of Mitsumasa Anno." *The Lion and the Unicorn* 7–8 (1983–1984): 34–46.

Mari, Enzo. *Funzione della ricera estetica.* Milan: Edizioni di Comunita, 1970.

Mari, Iela. *Il mondo attraverso una lente*. Milan and Bologna: Babalibri, 2010.

Mattson, Jennifer. Review of *The Red Book* by Barbara Lehman. *Booklist*, October 1, 2004, 335.

Maymat, Nicole. *Images Images*. Paris: L'Art à la page, 2008.

———. "Nicole Maymat, écrivain et intrépide éditrice." Interview by Étienne Delessert, 2009. *Ricochet-Jeunes*. http://www.ricochet-jeunes.org/magazine-propos/article/69-nicole-maymat (accessed January 6, 2010).

McCloud, Scott. *Understanding Comics: The Invisible Art*. Northampton MA: Tundra, 1993.

McCormick, Patricia. "All Things Reconsidered." *New York Times*, November 12, 1995.

McGillis, Roderick. "Ages All': Readers, Texts, and Intertexts in *The Stinky Cheese Man and Other Fairly Stupid Tales*." In *Transcending Boundaries: Writing for a Dual Audience of Children and Adults*. Ed. Sandra L. Beckett. New York: Garland, 1999. 111–126.

Meneguzzo, Marco. *Bruno Munari*. Bari: Editori Laterza, 1993.

Miller, Holly G. "At Home with Julie Andrews." *Saturday Evening Post* 280, no. 5 (September–October 2008): 49–50.

Minzesheimer, Bob. "What's Freckled and Read All Over? Moore's New Book." *USA Today*, October 16, 2007. http://www.usatoday.com/life/books/news/2007-10-16-freckleface-moore_N.htm (accessed April 23, 2010).

Mirabel, Annie Pissard Mirabel. "'À quoi sert un livre?': La réponse de Bruno Munari." In *Livres d'enfance*. Saint-Yrieix-la-Perche: Pays-Paysage/Centre National du Livre d'artiste, 1998. 35–42.

Miyake, Okiko, and Tomoko Masaki. "A Short History of the Japanese Picture Book." In *Through Eastern Eyes: The Art of the Japanese Picture Book*. Catalogue of an exhibition held at the National Centre for Research in Children's Literature and curated by Okiko Miyake and Tomoko Masaki. London: National Centre for Research in Children's Literature, 2001: 16–19.

Moebius, William. "Introduction to Picturebook Codes." *Word & Image* 2, no. 2 (1986): 141–158.

Morf, Eva Zoller. *Selber denken macht schlau: Grosse Fragen für kleine Philosophen und Philosophinnen*. Zurich: Zytglogge Verlag, 2010.

Munari, Bruno. *Arte come mestiere*. Bari: Editori Laterza, 1966. Translated by Patrick Creagh under the title *Design as Art*. Harmondsworth: Penguin Books, 1971.

———. *Da cosa nasce cosa*. Rome and Bari: Editori Laterza, 1981.

———. "Libro letto," *Domus* 760 (May 1994): 57–59.

Munari, Bruno, Claude Lichtenstein, Alfredo W. Häberli, K. Salatino, and S. Lindberg. *Making Air Visible/Far vedere l'aria: A Visual Reader on Bruno Munari*. Zurich: Museum für Gestaltung, 1995.

Nel, Philip. *The Avant-Garde and American Postmodernity: Small Incisive Shocks*. Jackson and London: University Press of Mississippi, 2002.

———. "Just a Dream? Chris Van Allsburg and Surrealism at the End of the Twentieth Century." In *The Avant-Garde and American Postmodernity: Small Incisive Shocks*. Jackson and London: University Press of Mississippi, 2002. 116–135.

Neumeyer, Peter. "We Are All in the Dumps with Jack and Guy: Two Nursery Rhymes with Pictures by Maurice Sendak." *Children's Literature in Education* 25, no. 1 (1994): 29–40.

Nières-Chevrel, Isabelle. "L'Évolution des rapports entre le texte et l'image dans la littérature pour enfants." In *L'Enfance à travers le patrimoine écrit*. Colloque d'Annecy, September 18–19, 2001. Annecy: ARALD, FCCB, 2002. 55–69.

———. "Narrateur visual et narrateur verbal dans l'album pour enfants." *La Revue des livres pour enfants* 214 (December 2003): 69–81.

———. "The Narrative Power of Pictures: *L'Orage* (The Thunderstorm) by Anne Brouillard." In *New Directions in Picturebook Research*. Ed. Teresa Colomer, Bettina Kümmerling-Meibauer, and Cecilia Silva-Díaz. New York and London: Routledge, 2010. 129–138.

———, ed. *Littérature de jeunesse, incertaines frontières*. Actes du colloque de Cerisy-la-Salle, 4–11 June 2004. Rennes: Presses universitaires de Rennes, 2005.

Nikola-Lisa, W. "I Spy: A Place for the Arts in Children's Picture-Books." *Journal of Children's Literature* 21, no. 2 (Fall 1995): 52–56.

Nikolajeva, Maria. *Children's Literature Comes of Age: Toward a New Esthetic*. New York and London: Garland, 1996.

———. "Exit Children's Literature?" *The Lion and the Unicorn* 22 (1998): 221–236.

———. "Play and Playfulness in Postmodern Picturebooks." In *Postmodern Picturebooks: Play, Parody, and Self-Referentiality*. Ed. Lawrence R. Sipe and Sylvia Pantaleo. New York and London: Routledge, 2008. 55–74.

Nikolajeva, Maria, and Carole Scott. *How Picturebooks Work*. New York: Garland, 2001.

Nodelman, Perry. *Words about Pictures: The Narrative Art of Children's Picture Books*. Athens, GA: The University of Georgia Press, 1988.

———. "Private Places on Public View: David Wiesner's Picture Books." *Mosaic* 34, no. 2 (June 2001): 1–16.

Novak, Barbara. "Picture Books." *New York Times*, May 24, 1970.

Ommundsen, Åse Marie. "Girl Stuck in the Wall: Narrative Changes in Norwegian Children's Literature Exemplified by the Picture Book *Snill*." *Bookbird* 42, no. 1 (February 2004): 24–26.

———. Litterære grenseoverskridelser: Når grensene mellom barne- og voksenlitteraturen viskes ut [Literary boundary crossings: erasing the borders between literature for children and adults]. Ph.D. diss., Universitetet i Oslo, 2010.

———. "Bildeboka for voksne [The picture book for adults]." *Norsk Litterær Årbok* 201. Oslo: Samlaget, 2010. 178–210.

"One Not-So Impossible Favor before Breakfast." *Seven Impossible Things before Breakfast*, a blog about books, April 25–30, 2010. http://blaine.org/sevenimpossiblethings/?p=1927 (accessed May 6, 2010).

O'Sullivan, Emer. *Comparative Children's Literature*. Trans. Anthea Bell. London and New York: Routledge, 2005.

Paley, Nicholas. "Why the Books of Harlin Quist Disappeared—Or Did They?" *Children's Literature Association Quarterly* 14, no. 3 (Fall 1989): 111–114.

———. "Experiments in Picture Book Design: Modern Artists Who Made Books for Children 1900–1985." *Children's Literature Association Quarterly* 16 (1991): 264–269.

Parmegiani, Claude-Anne. "Castor des années trente." *La Revue des livres pour enfants* (May–June 1980): 21–25.

Parsons Illustration Department. "From the Vaults: *Number 24* by Guy Billout (Harlin Quist, 1973)." *Parsons Illustration Newsletter* 1 (Winter 2006). http://www.parsons.newschool.edu/applications/PIN1.pdf (accessed May 22, 2009).

Pasternak, Guitta Pessis. "Tournier le sensual." *Le Monde*, August 13, 1984.

Paterson, Tony. "Author's Nude Drawings Too Hot for US Publisher." *Independent*, July 13, 2007.

Paul, Lissa. "Sex and the Children's Book." *The Lion and the Unicorn* 29, no. 2 (April 2005): 222–235.

Payant, René. "Bricolage pictural: l'art à propos de l'art; I—La Question de la citation." *Parachute* 16 (1979): 5–8.

Perrin, Raymond. *Littérature de jeunesse et presse des jeunes au début du XXIe siècle*. Paris: L'Harmattan, 2007.

Perrot, Jean. *Du jeu, des enfants, des livres*. Paris: Éditions du Cercle de la Librarie, 1987.

———. "L'esthétisme et/ou la mort: les exigences d'Ipomée." *La Revue des livres pour enfants* 128 (Summer 1989): 39–42.

———. *Art baroque, art d'enfance*. Nancy: Presses Universitaires de Nancy, 1991.

———. *Tomi Ungerer, Prix Hans Christian Andersen/Tomi Ungerer's Toys and Tales*. Paris: In Press, 1998.

———. *Carnets d'illustrateurs*. Paris: Les Éditions du cercle de la Librairie, 2000.

Pilkington, ed. "Once Upon a Time." *Guardian*, November 3, 2006.

Poesio, Carla. "The Rhythm of Images." *The Lion and the Unicorn* 26 (2002): 223–235.

Pommaux, Yvan. "Le discours de Caracas ou Yvan au bord de la rivière." *Griffon* 171 (March & April 2000): 3–9.

Preston, Julia. "Junior Gotti Is Denied Bail in Shooting of Radio Host." *New York Times*, October 6, 2004.

Punter, Jennie. "Sendak's Higglety Pigglety Pop! Bursts onto the Screen." *Globe and Mail*. http://www.theglobeandmail.com/news/arts/sendaks-higglety-pigglety-pop-bursts-onto-the-screen/article1493749/ (accessed July 4, 2010).

Quand les artistes créent pour les enfants: des objets livres pour imaginer. Paris: Le Mook/Autrement, 2008.

Rabinovitch, Dina. "Author of the Month: Michael Rosen." *Guardian*, November 24, 2004.

Raugust, Karen. "English Roses Blossom." *Publishers Weekly*, February 7, 2005: 23.

Read, D., and H. Smith. "Teaching Visual Literacy Through Wordless Picture Books." *Reading Teacher* 35, no. 8 (1982): 928–933.

Reynolds, Kimberley. *Radical Children's Literature: Future Visions and Aesthetic Transformations in Juvenile Fiction*. Houndmills: Palgrave Macmillan, 2007.

Reynolds, Kimberley, ed. *Modern Children's Literature: An Introduction*. Houndmills: Palgrave Macmillan, 2005.

Rhedin, Ulla. "A Children's Perspective as a Constant Point of Departure: Anna-Clara Tidholm and the Road to a Completely New Picture Book." Anna-Clara Tidholm Nominated for the 2010 H. C. Andersen Prize by the Swedish Section of IBBY. http://ibby.se/wp-content/uploads/2009/09/anna-tidholmibby.pdf (accessed May 29, 2010).

Rijke, Victoria de, and Howard Hollands. "Leap of Faith: An Interview with Max Velthuijs." *Children's Literature in Education*, 37, no. 2 (June 2006): 185–197.

Roback, Diane. "*The English Roses* Off to Fast Start." *Publishers Weekly*, September 22, 2003, 20.

Ronnen, Meir. "Frida Kahlo's Father Wasn't Jewish After All." *Jerusalem Post*, April 20, 2006.

Rose, Jacqueline. *The Case of Peter Pan, or, The Impossibility of Children's Fiction*. Basingstoke and London: Macmillan, 1984.

Rosen, Judith. "Breaking the Age Barrier," *Publishers Weekly*, September 8, 1997, 28–31.

Rosoff, Meg. "*Duck, Death and the Tulip* by Wolf Erlbruch." *Guardian*, December 19, 2009.

Rouvière, Nicolas. "L'influence de la bande dessinée sur les albums pour enfants: histoire, esthétique et thématiques." In *L'album contemporain pour la jeunesse: nouvelles formes, nouveaux lecteurs?* Ed. Christiane Connan-Pintado, Florence Gaiotti, and Bernadette Poulou. Modernités 28. Bordeaux: Presses Universitaires de Bordeaux, 2008. 17–28.

Ruello, Catherine. "Chris Van Allsburg Interview." In *Something About the Author*, vol. 53. Ed. Anne Commire. Detroit: Gale Research, 1989. 160–172.

Salisbury, Martin. *Play Pen: New Children's Book Illustration*. London: Laurence King, 2007.

———. "The Artist and the Postmodern Picturebook." In *Postmodern Picturebooks: Play, Parody, and Self-Referentiality*. Ed. Lawrence R. Sipe and Sylvia Pantaleo. 22–40.

Samuelsen, Arne Marius. *Billedboken: en glede og utfordring også for voksne*. Oslo: Pedagogisk Forum, 1995.

———. "Nyere norske billedbøker." *Nordisk Blad* (1998): 12–17.

Sassoon, Donald. *Mona Lisa: The History of the World's Most Famous Painting*. London: Harpercollins, 2001.

Schau genau! Variationen im Bilderbuch 1950–2000. Look Twice! Variations in Picture Books 1950–2000. Katalog zur Ausstellung des Schweizerischen Instituts für Kinder- und Jugendmedien. Zurich: Schweizerischen Institut für Kinder- und Jugendmedien, 2000.

Schmitter, Elke, and Franziska Bossy. "Mikropenis erregt US-Verlag." *Der Spiegel Online*, July 11, 2007. http://www.spiegel.de/kultur/literatur/0,1518,493297,00.html (accessed May 21, 2010).

Scott, Carole. "Dual Audience in Picturebooks." In *Transcending Boundaries: Writing for a Dual Audience of Children and Adults*. Ed. Sandra L. Beckett. New York: Garland, 1999. 99–110.

———. "A Challenge to Innocence: 'Inappropriate Picturebooks for Young Readers.'" *Bookbird* 43, no. 1 (2005): 5–13.

———. "Frame-making and Frame-breaking in Picturebooks." In *New Directions in Picturebook Research*. Ed. Teresa Colomer, Bettina Kümmerling-Meibauer, and Cecilia Silva-Díaz. New York and London: Routledge, 2010. 101–112.

Sendak, Maurice. *Caldecott and Co.: Notes on Books and Pictures*. New York: Farrar, Straus and Giroux, 1988.

———. "Maurice Sendak." In *Pauses: Autobiographical Reflections of 101 Creators of Children's Books*. Ed. Lee Bennett Hopkins. New York: HarperCollins, 1995. 141–143.

Shavit, Zohar. *Poetics of Children's Literature*. Athens: University of Georgia Press, 1996.

Sipe, Lawrence R. "First Graders Interpret David Wiesner's *The Three Pigs*: A Case Study." In *Postmodern Picturebooks: Play, Parody, and Self-Referentiality*. Ed. Lawrence R. Sipe and Sylvia Pantaleo. New York and London: Routledge, 2008. 223–237.

Sipe, Lawrence R., and Sylvia Pantaleo, eds. *Postmodern Picturebooks: Play, Parody, and Self-Referentiality*. New York and London: Routledge, 2008.

Søndergaard, Karen Lise. "Always Believe Your Own Eyes." Trans. John Mason. *Danish Literary Magazine* (Autumn 2008). http://www.danishliterarymagazine.dk/index.php?id=2185 (accessed May 17, 2009).

Sonheim, Amy. *Maurice Sendak*. New York: Twayne, 1991.

Stanton, Joseph. "The Dreaming Picture Books of Chris Van Allsburg." *Children's Literature* 24 (1996): 161–179.

———. "Maurice Sendak's Urban Landscapes." *Children's Literature* 28 (2000): 132–146.

Steinitz, Kate Traumen. *Kurt Schwitters: A Portrait from Life*. Berkeley: University of California Press, 1968.

Stephens, John. *Language and Ideology in Children's Fiction*. London: Longman, 1992.

———. "Children's Literature, Text and Theory: What Are We Interested in Now?" *Papers: Explorations Into Children's Literature* 10, no. 2 (2000): 12–21.

———. "'They Are Always Surprised at What People Throw Away': Glocal Postmodernism in Australian Picturebooks." In *Postmodern Picturebooks: Play, Parody, and Self-Referentiality.* Ed. Lawrence R. Sipe and Sylvia Pantaleo. New York and London: Routledge, 2008. 89–102.

Styles, Morag, and Eve Bearne, eds. *Art, Narrative and Childhood.* Stoke on Trent: Trentham Books, 2003.

"Svein Nyhus: Illustrator, Norway." *Bookbird* 42, no. 4 (2004): 50.

Sylvester, David. *René Magritte: Catalogue Raisonné.* Vol. I: *Oil Paintings: 1916–1930.* Ed. David Sylvester and Sarah Whitfield. London: The Menil Foundation/Philip Wilson Publishers, 1992.

Tan, Shaun. "Originality and Creativity." http:llwww.shaun.tan.net/essay2.html (accessed May 29, 2010).

Tanchis, Aldo. *Bruno Munari: Design as Art.* Cambridge, MA: The MIT Press, 1987.

Tansey, Richard G., and Fred S. Kleiner. *Gardner's Art Through the Ages.* 10th ed. New York: Harcourt Brace, 1996.

Thiele, Jens. "Sie tanzen Hula-Hula." *Die Zeit* 49, November 2004.

Tournier, Michel. "Les enfants dans la bibliothèque." Interview with Jean-François Josselin. *Le Nouvel Observateur,* December 6, 1971, 56–57.

Turc, René. "Tête à tête." Interview by Elisabeth Lortic. *La Revue des livres pour enfants* 155–156 (Winter 1994): 52–57.

"Un *Petit Âne* dérangeant." *La Revue des livres pour enfants* 171 (September 1996): 143–146.

Valleau, Geneviève M. Y. "Degas and Seurat and Magritte! Oh My! Classical Art in Picture Books." *The Looking Glass* 10, no. 3 (2006): Online. Available at: http://tlg.ninthwonder.com/rabbit/vl0i3/picture.html (accessed January 30, 2009).

Van der Linden, Sophie. *Claude Ponti.* Paris: Éditions Être, 2000.

———. "Ces albums que l'on dit sans texte." *AEIOU* 4 (December 2003): 4–9.

———. "Les albums 'sans.'" In *Le livre pour enfants: Regards critiques offerts à Isabelle Nières-Chevrel.* Ed. Cécile Boulaire. Rennes: Presses Universitaires de Rennes, 2006. 189–197.

———. *Lire l'album.* Puy-en-Velay: L'Atelier du Poisson Soluble, 2006.

Wall, Barbara. *The Narrator's Voice: The Dilemma of Children's Fiction.* London: Macmillan, 1992.

Walter, Virginia A., and Susan F. March. "Juvenile Picture Books about the Holocaust: Extending the Definitions of Children's Literature." *Publishing Research Quarterly* 9, no. 3 (1993): 36–51.

Warner, Marina. *Monsters of Our Own Making: The Peculiar Pleasures of Fear.* Lexington, KY: University Press of Kentucky, 2007.

Weber, Jochen. "Pasando los limites: All-Age-Books, Crossover-Literatura y otras tendencias actuales de la literatura para jóvenes lectores." Paper presented at the Primer Congreso Nacional de Lectura y Escritura "Escuela y Literatura Infantil," Durango, Mexico, May 16–18, 2004.

Wiesner, David. "Caldecott Acceptance Speech [For *Tuesday*]." *Horn Book Magazine* 68, no. 4 (August 1992): 416–423.

Williams, Elaine. "Willy, Magritte and Me." *TES Magazine,* September 15, 2000. http://www.tes.co.uk/article.aspx?storycode+338474 (accessed November 6, 2009).

Wynne-Jones, Tim. "The Survival of the Book." *Signal* 87 (September 1998): 160–166.

Index

An environmentally friendly book printed and bound in England by www.printondemand-worldwide.com

PEFC Certified

This product is
from sustainably
managed forests
and controlled
sources

www.pefc.org

This book is made entirely of sustainable materials; FSC paper for the cover and PEFC paper for the text pages.

#0173 - 091015 - C0 - 229/152/22 - PB - 9780415730372